# AI Influence on Governance and Law in the Digital Age

Sonia Cea
*Universidad Rey Juan Carlos, Spain*

Tomás Aznar
*IUNIT, Spain*

IGI Global
Scientific Publishing
Publishing Tomorrow's Research Today

Vice President of Editorial Melissa Wagner
Director of Acquisitions Mikaela Felty
Director of Book Development Jocelynn Hessler
Production Manager Mike Brehm
Cover Design Jose Rosado

Published in the United States of America by
IGI Global Scientific Publishing
701 East Chocolate Avenue
Hershey, PA, 17033, USA
Tel: 717-533-8845 | Fax: 717-533-7115
Website: https://www.igi-global.com E-mail: cust@igi-global.com



Library of Congress Cataloging-in-Publication Data

LCCN: 2025038314 (CIP Data Pending)
ISBN13: 9798337344805
Isbn13Softcover: 9798337344812
EISBN13: 9798337344829
British Cataloguing in Publication Data
A Cataloguing in Publication record for this book is available from the British Library.

# Table of Contents

# Detailed Table of Contents



This chapter develops an agent-based network model for the governance of AI systems that integrates normative principles, technological architectures, and formal control logics. The goal is to operationalize polycentric control approaches and evaluate the effectiveness of distributed control mechanisms in complex socio-technical systems. The present study combines a conceptual analysis of interdisciplinary literature with formal network modeling and simulation-based policy evaluation. Agent classes (including regulators, companies, and auditors) interact via defined protocols. State variables such as compliance (C), risk (R), and transparency (T) serve as governance metrics. The simulation of contrasting scenarios demonstrates that feedback intensity, control redundancy, and technical transparency paths act as essential mechanisms for increasing system robustness. The paper presents a set of tools for designing and evaluating dynamic AI governance models.



The advent of artificial intelligence (AI) in the legal domain, within the context of accelerated technological globalization, poses new challenges to Procedural Law. This transformation is not merely technical but also structural and axiological, as it questions classical procedural principles and necessitates to update litigants' safeguards. Simultaneously, the diversity of procedural systems in Europe complicates a coordinated response to this global phenomenon. The article—adopting a Spanish and European perspective—deeply analyzes the primary challenges and opportunities arising in this context, from technology's impact on access to justice, AI's application in judicial activities, and the management of digital evidence, to implications for procedural harmonization, fundamental safeguards, and the evolving roles of judges and lawyers in an increasingly digitalized environment. It also addresses normative and ethical proposals for responsible AI usage in judicial proceedings, considering current regulations and relevant jurisprudence in the Spanish and European contexts.

The criminal justice system is being transformed due to artificial intelligence (AI). These technologies have been sold on the promise of a system freed from error, an efficient, objective, and data-driven solution to justice. The rapid deployment of AI, from predictive policing on our streets to risk assessment algorithms in our courtrooms, is creating a new type of discrimination. These systems, trained on datasets immersed in decades of human bias, are not eliminating prejudice but instead are automating it. This chapter examines the mechanics of these tools and tracks them through the justice process, from the street-level policing and investigations to federal surveillance, courtroom sentencing, and the prison and probation systems. This can have a serious impact on societies entering a future where human and civil rights are being impacted by unaccountable code. The chapter ends with a model for reform for new legislation, technical safeguards like mandatory audits and transparency, and a legal commitment to judicial and public oversight to ensure our future serves justice.



This chapter examines the paradoxical role of emerging Artificial Intelligence (AI) technologies in combating gender-based violence in Latin America, where promises of innovation often replicate structural inequalities. Using an intersectional lens, it identifies four friction points—biased data, institutional misalignments, cultural incompatibilities, and algorithmic opacity—that limit equitable outcomes, as seen in Mexico's predictive models, Brazil's reporting platforms, and Chile's protection mechanisms. Proposing gender parity in AI teams, public algorithmic audits, intercultural adaptations, and a regional monitoring observatory, it introduces the concept of "gendered algorithmic violence" and feminist audit methodologies. Blending academic rigor with political urgency, it offers a five-pillar roadmap to democratize technology from the margins and advance inclusive digital justice.

This research examines the intersections between surveillance capitalism and Yarvinism as converging frameworks that illuminate the emergence of a new paradigm of digital governance. It argues that data accumulation and the technocratic logic of control have produced a hybrid system where economic and political authority are embedded within algorithmic infrastructures capable of regulating information, behavior, and decision-making. This model, arising from technological convergence, redefines sovereignty, legitimacy, and public deliberation by replacing political representation with computational efficiency. The findings reveal the rise of algocracy as a structural form of power in the twenty-first century and emphasize the need to develop frameworks that align democratic oversight with the preservation of human autonomy in the face of automated decision systems.



This article examines the paradox between the technological revolution and human privacy, introducing the concept of the Human Firewall as a response to the digital and biotechnological invasion of intimacy. Through a qualitative methodology based on a literature review and deep analysis of interdisciplinary sources, it explores how the massive adoption of information technologies (2020–2024) and the rise of genome editing have redefined the right to privacy and human autonomy. The hypothesis argues that developing an effective Human Firewall, combining digital and bioethical literacy, can mitigate the adverse effects of technological and genetic innovation on privacy without obstructing progress. The study concludes that safeguarding human dignity in the age of artificial intelligence and biotechnology requires robust legal frameworks, ethical governance, and active participation by individuals, institutions, and technology developers to harmonize technological advancement with the protection of fundamental rights.

This disparity presents a critical concern, as traditional investigative methods are becoming increasingly ineffective against these technologically advanced actors. Consequently, there is a pressing need for law enforcement agencies to adapt their strategies, adopt new technologies, and foster international cooperation to effectively counter the evolving threat posed by transnational criminal organizations in the contemporary security environment. This paper examines the evolving technological landscape of transnational criminal organizations, analyzes the implications for global security, and explores potential strategies for mitigating the growing technological gap between transnational criminal organizations and law enforcement agencies.



Artificial intelligence has become a structural pillar of 21st-century geopolitical competition, shaping governance, law, the economy, and power distribution. Unlike earlier technologies, AI acts as a dual-use catalyst with profound implications for sovereignty and security. This article examines AI as a strategic instrument comparable to nuclear energy or the Internet, through a comparative analysis of China, the U.S., and the EU as architects of the emerging digital order. Global technological rivalry is both material and symbolic, involving control of digital infrastructure and regulatory norms. The central argument is that China's algorithmic governance model operates domestically as a system of control and efficiency and globally as a project to export digital norms. In contrast, the U.S. prioritizes private-sector innovation, while the EU promotes rights-based regulation (Guest & Wei, 2024; Zaidan, 2024). The article concludes that the tension between convergence and fragmentation in AI governance will shape global order, especially in the strategically contested Global South.

The introduction of artificial intelligence (AI) into Moroccan public governance is changing the organizational mode of delivery, the decision-making processes, and the relationship between the state and citizens. This chapter discusses opportunities and ethical challenges linked to AI adoption in public organizations in Morocco, based on a quantitative analysis of 270 observations. The chapter examines the implications of AI systems (RPA, machine learning (ML), NLP, and computer vision) on performance, transparency, accountability, and identify possible risks associated with bias and discrimination. We use Random Forest and SVM to identify important variables, and make predictions about the links between AI adoption, governance and performance. We find that while AI systems contribute to improved quality and speed of service delivery, they come with ethical challenges with respect to justice, privacy and democratic legitimacy. We offer some strategic recommendations for the responsible, ethical integration of AI systems in the Moroccan context.



This study analyzes, from a global and multidisciplinary perspective, the integration of artificial intelligence (AI) in learning economics, addressing its technical, pedagogical, ethical and regulatory dimensions. Through a theoretical framework that combines economics, pedagogy and computer science, implementation cases in various regions - Western Europe, East Asia, Latin America, Africa, Oceania and the Middle East - are examined, as well as national experiences and multilateral collaborations. The results, supported by simulated data, show significant improvements in academic performance, teaching efficiency and student satisfaction, with greater impact in contexts of lower initial digitization. However, challenges remain, such as the digital divide, cultural resistance, lack of specific regulation and algorithmic transparency. s.



This chapter examines the impact of artificial intelligence (AI) on education and social interactions, highlighting both its opportunities and challenges. AI technologies, including intelligent tutoring systems, adaptive learning platforms, learning analytics, and generative tools, offer personalized support, enhance engagement, and improve accessibility for diverse learners. While these tools optimize learning and provide real-time feedback, risks include overreliance, algorithmic bias, and potential reduction in human social interaction. The chapter emphasizes the importance of ethical frameworks, human-centered design, and responsible integration of AI to complement rather than replace human judgment. Educators play a crucial role in guiding students to critically interpret AI outputs and ensuring equitable access to these technologies. Overall, the chapter provides insights into maximizing AI's benefits while mitigating risks, supporting meaningful learning, and fostering healthy social interactions.



The use and implementation of artificial intelligence (AI) has not only occurred in the educational and academic fields but has become a true revolution. Today, AI elements such as GPT Chat are consulted 24/7 by a large number of people for all kinds of queries. Artificial intelligence (AI) has undergone major changes in its use and implementation within public and private institutions, with the aim of improving their efficiency and citizen service. This efficiency or modality has been achieved through the implementation of different types of chatbots to assist people. It is at this point that we notice how This article aims to address the analysis of AI, highlighting its significance in the fields of management, administration, and governance, highlighting the significant opportunities, impact assessment, and potential it offers. This review offers a comprehensive overview of AI and its impact on the university field, including its achievements and significant controversies. Finally, it presents the critical opportunities and challenges for applying AI in the university sector.



This chapter explores the integration of Artificial Intelligence (AI) powered Learning Analytics (LA) in higher education, highlighting its transformative potential and ethical challenges. While LA+AI systems enhance personalized learning, predictive analytics, and institutional efficiency, they risk undermining pedagogical integrity, academic freedom, and equity if implemented without oversight. Key concerns

# Preface

## ARTIFICIAL INTELLIGENCE, GOVERNMENT, AND LAW IN THE DIGITAL AGE: CHALLENGES AND PERSPECTIVES

Artificial Intelligence (AI) has become one of the most influential and transformative forces of the digital age, reshaping not only technological infrastructures but also the fundamental political, legal, and social architectures of contemporary societies. Over the past two decades, AI has evolved from a specialized domain of computer science into a pervasive socio-technical system that increasingly mediates decision-making processes across public and private spheres. Governments, courts, universities, security agencies, and economic institutions now rely on algorithmic systems to process information, allocate resources, assess risks, predict behavior, and guide or automate decisions that directly affect individuals and communities.

This transformation is not merely technical in nature. The expansion of artificial intelligence represents a profound reconfiguration of how power is exercised, how authority is legitimized, and how social order is produced and maintained. Algorithmic systems do not simply assist human decision-makers; they increasingly shape the conditions under which decisions are made, introducing new forms of mediation between citizens and institutions. As a result, artificial intelligence has become deeply entangled with questions of governance, law, democracy, and human rights, raising challenges that extend far beyond issues of efficiency or innovation.

This book, *Artificial Intelligence, Government, and Law in the Digital Age: Challenges and Perspectives*, offers a comprehensive and interdisciplinary analysis of these developments. It examines the growing influence of artificial intelligence on governance structures, legal systems, and democratic processes, while critically assessing the ethical, regulatory, and societal implications of AI-driven transformation. The volume brings together fifteen chapters that address these dynamics from diverse disciplinary perspectives, including law, sociology, political science, contemporary history, education, and digital technology studies. By doing so, it seeks to provide a nuanced and integrated understanding of how AI is reshaping public institutions and social relations in the digital age.

## GENERAL OVERVIEW OF THE TOPIC

At the core of this volume lies the recognition that artificial intelligence is transforming fundamental aspects of governance and law. Public administrations increasingly deploy AI systems to optimize bureaucratic processes, manage social welfare programs, detect fraud, and support policy design. Judicial systems experiment with algorithmic tools for legal research, predictive analysis, risk assessment, and case management, raising complex questions about procedural fairness, transparency, and judicial independence. In parallel, AI technologies are reshaping education, economic learning, urban governance, security practices, and the production of knowledge itself.

These transformations challenge long-standing assumptions about the nature of legal reasoning, administrative discretion, and democratic accountability. Traditional legal and political frameworks were designed around the premise that decisions affecting rights and obligations would be made by identifiable human authorities operating within transparent institutional structures. Algorithmic decision-making disrupts this model by introducing systems whose internal logic may be opaque, probabilistic, and difficult to contest. As a result, core principles such as due process, equality before the law, and the right to effective remedy face unprecedented strain.

The book approaches artificial intelligence not as a neutral or autonomous force, but as a socio-technical phenomenon embedded in specific historical, political, and economic contexts. AI systems are developed by particular actors, trained on historically produced data, and deployed within institutional environments shaped by power relations and normative assumptions. Consequently, their effects cannot be understood without examining the broader structures of governance, regulation, and social inequality within which they operate.

A central concern of the volume is the ambivalence of artificial intelligence as a tool of governance. On the one hand, AI offers significant opportunities to improve institutional efficiency, enhance policy effectiveness, and support more informed decision-making. On the other hand, it introduces serious risks related to discrimination, surveillance, technocratic control, and the erosion of democratic oversight. Algorithmic systems may reproduce and amplify existing social biases, particularly when they rely on data that reflect structural inequalities related to gender, class, ethnicity, or geography. Moreover, the delegation of authority to computational systems can obscure responsibility and weaken mechanisms of accountability.

By engaging with these tensions, the book seeks to move beyond simplistic narratives that portray AI either as a panacea for governance challenges or as an inherently dystopian technology. Instead, it adopts a critical and balanced perspective that recognizes both the transformative potential of artificial intelligence and the urgent need for robust legal, ethical, and institutional safeguards.

## ARTIFICIAL INTELLIGENCE, GOVERNANCE, AND LAW IN THE CONTEMPORARY WORLD

The themes addressed in this volume occupy a central place in the contemporary global context. Artificial intelligence has become a strategic resource for states, corporations, and international actors, influencing economic competitiveness, national security, and geopolitical power. Governments around the world are investing heavily in AI technologies as part of broader digital transformation strategies, often framing these investments as necessary responses to globalization, demographic change, and increasing social complexity.

At the same time, AI-driven governance emerges in a context marked by growing democratic tension and institutional mistrust. In many societies, citizens experience governance through digital interfaces and automated systems that shape access to public services, social benefits, education, and justice. Decisions that were once made through face-to-face interaction with public officials are now mediated by algorithms whose criteria may be unclear or inaccessible. This shift risks deepening the distance between citizens and institutions, undermining trust and democratic legitimacy.

The global dimension of AI governance further complicates these dynamics. Different political systems promote distinct models of artificial intelligence regulation and deployment, reflecting divergent values and institutional traditions. Rights-based approaches emphasize the protection of fundamental freedoms and legal safeguards, while more centralized models prioritize efficiency, security, and social control. Market-driven frameworks focus on innovation and competitiveness, often relying on self-regulation and private governance mechanisms.

These divergent trajectories contribute to a fragmented global digital order in which regulatory norms and ethical standards compete and overlap. Moreover, profound inequalities between regions shape access to data, computational infrastructure, and technological expertise. Countries in the Global South often face conditions of technological dependency, relying on systems developed elsewhere and operating under regulatory frameworks that may not reflect local social realities. This asymmetry raises critical questions about digital sovereignty, global justice, and the inclusiveness of AI governance.

Within democratic societies, artificial intelligence intensifies longstanding tensions between efficiency and rights, security and freedom, innovation and accountability. Technologies such as predictive policing, facial recognition, automated welfare assessment, and learning analytics promise improved outcomes, yet they also risk normalizing surveillance and narrowing spaces for democratic participation. Law plays a crucial mediating role in this context: it can either constrain algorithmic power through robust safeguards or legitimize its expansion through insufficient or poorly designed regulation.

This volume situates artificial intelligence at the intersection of these global and institutional dynamics. By combining theoretical analysis with empirical case studies from diverse regions, it offers a comprehensive account of how AI-driven systems are reshaping governance and law in the contemporary world.

## TARGET AUDIENCE

This book is intended for a diverse but clearly defined audience whose academic and professional work is directly affected by the rise of artificial intelligence in governance and law. First and foremost, the volume addresses researchers and academics in law, political science, sociology, contemporary history, social sciences, and technology studies. For this audience, the book offers original theoretical insights, interdisciplinary perspectives, and empirically grounded analyses that contribute to ongoing scholarly debates on algorithmic governance, legal transformation, and digital power.

The volume is also highly relevant for practitioners and decision-makers in public administration, legal reform, and digital policy. Policymakers, regulators, and public officials increasingly confront complex decisions about whether and how to deploy AI systems in institutional contexts. This book provides them with critical frameworks for assessing the legal, ethical, and social implications of AI adoption, as well as conceptual tools to support more transparent and accountable governance practices.

Judges, lawyers, ethicists, and experts in AI governance constitute another core segment of the book's audience. As algorithmic systems become more deeply embedded in judicial processes, legal professionals must grapple with new forms of evidence, reasoning, and responsibility. The volume offers a rigorous examination of these challenges, equipping legal practitioners with analytical resources to evaluate the legitimacy and fairness of AI applications in legal contexts.

In addition, the book is designed for postgraduate students in law, public policy, human rights, and social sciences. Its chapters can serve both as advanced teaching material and as a reference for research on the social and legal dimensions of artificial intelligence. Finally, the volume will be of interest to international organizations, non-governmental organizations, and consultants working on digital transformation, democracy, and social justice, as it connects AI governance debates with broader concerns about rights protection, inclusion, and institutional

## IMPACT ON THE RESEARCH COMMUNITY

This volume aims to establish itself as a significant academic reference within the rapidly expanding field of artificial intelligence, governance, and legal transformation. While a growing body of literature addresses the technical, ethical, or regulatory aspects of AI in isolation, this book makes a distinctive contribution by integrating these dimensions into a coherent, transdisciplinary framework that foregrounds the social, historical, and institutional implications of AI-driven change.

One of the central contributions of this volume lies in its effort to bridge disciplinary silos. Research on artificial intelligence has often been fragmented, with legal scholars focusing on regulation and rights, political scientists analyzing governance and power, sociologists examining social impacts and inequalities, and technologists concentrating on system design and performance. This book brings these perspectives into dialogue, demonstrating that meaningful analysis of AI governance requires an integrated approach capable of capturing the complexity of contemporary digital societies.

The volume contributes to current academic debates by advancing a critical understanding of artificial intelligence as a form of institutional power. Rather than treating AI as an external force acting upon law and governance, the chapters analyze how algorithmic systems become embedded within legal norms, administrative routines, and political decision-making structures. This perspective enables a more nuanced assessment of how AI reshapes authority, accountability, and legitimacy in democratic and non-democratic contexts alike.

In addition, the book fills an important gap in the literature by emphasizing the historical and social dimensions of AI integration into public life. Several chapters situate contemporary developments within longer trajectories of technological governance, state intervention, and social control. This historical sensitivity allows readers to understand AI not as an unprecedented rupture, but as part of an evolving relationship between technology and power, marked by both continuity and transformation.

The volume also offers conceptual and practical tools for analyzing and guiding the responsible integration of AI into public and social decision-making. By engaging with concepts such as algorithmic governance, surveillance capitalism, cognitive sovereignty, procedural justice, and democratic curriculum governance, the book provides a vocabulary for critically assessing AI systems and their institutional consequences. These conceptual tools are complemented by empirical analyses and case studies that illustrate how abstract principles are negotiated in concrete contexts.

Finally, the book contributes to normative debates on the future of AI governance. Rather than adopting a purely descriptive stance, the volume articulates a critical perspective that seeks to inform policy design, legal reform, and institutional innovation. It argues that the governance of artificial intelligence is a matter of collective choice rather than technological inevitability, and that interdisciplinary scholarship has a crucial role to play in shaping more just, transparent, and democratic digital futures.

## IMPORTANCE AND CONTRIBUTION OF THE INDIVIDUAL CHAPTERS

### Chapter 1. A Network Model for the Governance of Artificial Intelligence

This chapter provides the conceptual and methodological foundation of the volume by proposing a network-based model for AI governance. Moving beyond hierarchical and centralized regulatory approaches, it conceptualizes governance as a dynamic system involving multiple actors, feedback loops, and distributed forms of control. By employing tools from network theory and agent-based modeling, the chapter demonstrates how resilience, transparency, and accountability can be enhanced through polycentric governance arrangements. Its importance lies in offering a systemic framework that informs the analysis of AI governance across the entire book.

### Chapter 2. Challenges for Procedural Law in the Context of Technological Globalization and Artificial Intelligence

This chapter examines the profound impact of technological globalization and AI on procedural law. It critically analyzes how algorithmic decision-making challenges core legal principles such as due process, judicial reasoning, immediacy, and equality of arms. The chapter highlights the tension between efficiency-driven digital justice and the protection of fundamental procedural guarantees, offering a nuanced reflection on how procedural law must evolve to remain compatible with the rule of law in algorithmically mediated environments.

## Chapter 3. Law and the Criminal Justice System: A Framework for the Effective and Equitable Use of Artificial Intelligence

Focusing on the criminal justice system, this chapter addresses one of the most sensitive areas of AI application. It analyzes the use of algorithmic tools in policing, investigation, risk assessment, and sentencing, emphasizing the risks of bias, opacity, and disproportionate punishment. At the same time, it proposes normative criteria for the responsible use of AI in criminal justice, highlighting the conditions under which technology can support fairness, proportionality, and legal certainty rather than undermine them.

## Chapter 4. Algorithmic Injustice? Artificial Intelligence, Gender-Based Violence, and Digital Governance in Latin America

This chapter introduces a critical gender perspective into the analysis of AI governance by examining the interaction between algorithmic systems and policies addressing gender-based violence in Latin America. It reveals how AI tools may inadvertently reproduce patriarchal assumptions and structural inequalities when they are designed without sensitivity to social context. The chapter's contribution lies in demonstrating the necessity of intersectional and context-aware approaches to AI governance, particularly in regions marked by deep social inequalities.

## Chapter 5. Surveillance Capitalism and Yarvinism: Technocratic Control in Digital Governance

Adopting a critical theoretical lens, this chapter explores the convergence between surveillance capitalism and contemporary technocratic ideologies. It analyzes how data extraction, algorithmic optimization, and efficiency-driven governance models reshape political legitimacy and democratic accountability. By linking economic logics of surveillance with authoritarian tendencies in digital governance, the chapter provides a powerful framework for understanding the political risks associated with unchecked algorithmic power.

## Chapter 6. Human Firewall: Privacy Paradigms in the Face of the Technological Revolution

This chapter addresses the tension between technological innovation and the protection of privacy, proposing the concept of the "human firewall" as a normative and institutional safeguard. It reframes privacy not merely as an individual right, but as a collective condition for democratic resilience. The chapter underscores the importance of human oversight, ethical design, and institutional responsibility in resisting the normalization of pervasive surveillance and data exploitation.

## Chapter 7. Technological Gaps and Security: Challenges for Law Enforcement and Public Safety

This chapter examines how technological asymmetries affect security governance and law enforcement capacities. By analyzing disparities in access to AI technologies between state and non-state actors, it highlights emerging risks related to organized crime, cybercrime, and hybrid threats. The chapter contributes a strategic dimension to the volume by emphasizing the need for coordinated and equitable approaches to AI-enabled security.

## Chapter 8. AI, Governance, and Law in Digital Geopolitics: The Chinese Model and Its Global Projection

This chapter offers an in-depth analysis of the Chinese model of AI governance and its global influence. It examines how state-led approaches to data governance, surveillance, and technological development are projected internationally through economic, political, and technological channels. The chapter's importance lies in situating AI governance within broader geopolitical dynamics and highlighting the normative challenges posed to liberal democratic models.

## Chapter 9. From Brain Mapping to Behavioral Governance: State Investment in Neuroscience and Artificial Intelligence

This chapter explores the growing convergence between neuroscience and artificial intelligence in state governance strategies. It analyzes how investments in brain mapping and behavioral prediction technologies enable new forms of governance aimed at influencing individual and collective behavior. The chapter raises profound ethical and political questions about autonomy, consent, and the legitimate limits of technological intervention in human cognition.

## Chapter 10. Cognitive Sovereignty and Happiness Governance: Dubai's Vision for Ethical AI Cities

Through a comparative policy analysis, this chapter examines the governance model underlying Dubai's smart city initiatives, which emphasize well-being and happiness as policy objectives. It introduces the concept of cognitive sovereignty to assess the ethical implications of AI-driven governance that relies on emotional and behavioral data. The chapter offers an innovative perspective on urban governance and the future of ethical AI in smart cities.

## Chapter 11. Artificial Intelligence and the Transformation of the Public Sector in Morocco

This chapter presents a quantitative study of AI adoption in the Moroccan public sector, focusing on ethical and legal dilemmas in administrative governance. By providing empirical evidence from a non-Western context, it enriches the volume's comparative perspective and highlights the diversity of challenges associated with AI-driven public sector transformation.

## Chapter 12. Artificial Intelligence as Part of Economic Learning

This chapter examines the role of artificial intelligence in economic learning and decision-making processes. It analyzes how AI tools influence the acquisition of economic knowledge, the development of competencies, and the governance of economic behavior. The chapter contributes to the volume by linking AI governance debates with broader questions about education, productivity, and economic policy.

## Chapter 13. Transformations in Learning and Social Relations in the Age of Artificial Intelligence

Focusing on education and culture, this chapter explores how artificial intelligence reshapes learning environments and social relations. It examines changes in socialization, identity formation, and knowledge production, highlighting both opportunities for innovation and risks of exclusion and standardization.

## Chapter 14. Artificial Intelligence and the University: Past, Present, and Future

This chapter offers a historical and prospective analysis of the impact of AI on universities as institutions of knowledge production. It examines how digital technologies challenge academic autonomy, teaching practices, and research ethics, while also opening new possibilities for innovation and collaboration.

## Chapter 15. Learning Analytics, Artificial Intelligence, and the Future of Democratic Curriculum Governance

The final chapter addresses the implications of learning analytics and AI for curriculum governance. It examines how data-driven educational tools can influence decision-making processes in education and emphasizes the importance of participatory, transparent, and democratic governance models to ensure equity and inclusion.

## CONCLUSION: CONTRIBUTION TO THE FIELD AND FUTURE PERSPECTIVES

Taken together, the contributions in *Artificial Intelligence, Government, and Law in the Digital Age: Challenges and Perspectives* offer a comprehensive and critical examination of artificial intelligence as a transformative force in contemporary governance and legal systems. The volume demonstrates that AI is not merely a technological innovation, but a deeply political and social phenomenon that reshapes power relations, institutional practices, and normative frameworks.

By integrating interdisciplinary perspectives and diverse geographical contexts, the book advances current debates on AI governance and legal transformation. Its contribution lies in moving beyond narrow technical or regulatory approaches to highlight the importance of democratic deliberation, human rights, and social justice in the governance of artificial intelligence. The volume provides scholars, practitioners, and policymakers with analytical tools and conceptual frameworks to critically assess AI-driven systems and to design governance models that are both effective and legitimate.

Ultimately, this book affirms that the future of artificial intelligence is not predetermined by technological progress alone. It is shaped by collective choices, institutional designs, and normative commitments. By situating AI within the broader context of law, governance, and society, *Artificial Intelligence, Government, and Law in the Digital Age: Challenges and Perspectives* contributes to the development of a more reflective, inclusive, and responsible approach to digital transformation.

Chapter 1
# A Network Model for the Governance of Artificial Intelligence

**Silvio Andrae**
https://orcid.org/0000-0002-8586-7812
*Independent Researcher, Germany*

## ABSTRACT

*This chapter develops an agent-based network model for the governance of AI systems that integrates normative principles, technological architectures, and formal control logics. The goal is to operationalize polycentric control approaches and evaluate the effectiveness of distributed control mechanisms in complex socio-technical systems. The present study combines a conceptual analysis of interdisciplinary literature with formal network modeling and simulation-based policy evaluation. Agent classes (including regulators, companies, and auditors) interact via defined protocols. State variables such as compliance (C), risk (R), and transparency (T) serve as governance metrics. The simulation of contrasting scenarios demonstrates that feedback intensity, control redundancy, and technical transparency paths act as essential mechanisms for increasing system robustness. The paper presents a set of tools for designing and evaluating dynamic AI governance models.*

## 1. INTRODUCTION

In less than a decade, artificial intelligence (AI) has evolved from a specialized key technology to a ubiquitous infrastructure that is transforming business models, government decision-making processes, and everyday life (Brynjolfsson & McAfee, 2024; Floridi, 2025). This study examines the implications of the ubiquitous spread

DOI: 10.4018/979-8-3373-4480-5.ch001

of AI. On the one hand, AI offers enormous potential for increased efficiency and innovation, paving the way for a brighter future. However, on the other hand, it also gives rise to new risks—from algorithmic discrimination and security vulnerabilities to macroeconomic system shocks. It has been found that conventional, highly centralized regulatory mechanisms are slow to respond to these dynamic problems and are increasingly failing due to the scale and complexity of distributed AI ecosystems (Cath, 2023).

Between the first global AI summit in Bletchley Park (2023) and the most recent meeting in Paris (February 2025), there has been a significant shift in the international discourse on AI. The initial focus on safety, including existential risks, has now been overtaken by the narrative of geo-economic competition (Clayton et al., 2025). The current emphasis is on technological leadership, industrial competitiveness, and economic scaling. This shift is evident in the tensions between the US and the EU regarding regulatory approaches, as well as in the billion-dollar funding programs aimed at strengthening national and regional AI ecosystems (Scott, 2025).

At the same time, there is a shift in the normative orientation of AI policy: While the EU initially considered itself a pioneer of strict safety regulations with its AI Act, recent statements by European politicians signal a shift toward a growth-oriented framework. The new administration under Donald Trump has also repealed key security-related regulations introduced by the previous administration and replaced them with an agenda focused on economic policy. Although issues such as security, inclusion, and data protection remain part of the global discussion, they have taken a back seat to questions of competitiveness in terms of political weight. In a geopolitically tense world, AI is increasingly seen as a strategic instrument of power (Scott, 2025). It can be observed that economic interests structure global governance dynamics more than ethical or security considerations.

## 1.1 Problem

Current governance approaches are generally based on hierarchical control architectures, such as national legislation, industry-specific regulatory authorities, or central ethics commissions. Azin and Zandhessami (2025) present an innovative mapping methodology that enables a comparative assessment of national AI strategies. The combination of matrix-based visualization and network theory analysis reveals structural patterns of strategic coherence between goals, foresight methods, and implementation instruments. The basis for this is a systematic evaluation of 15 to 20 national strategies using data from the OECD AI Policy Observatory. There are significant differences in the strategic coherence of national AI governance. It was found that there is a significant discrepancy between the promotion of innovation and the regulation of ethical goals. While there is a link between economic goals and innovation promotion instruments, ethical goals and concrete regulatory mechanisms are considered deficient in this context.

The present analysis identifies four overarching categories of objectives: economic transformation, societal applications, governance frameworks, and geopolitical positioning. The present study concludes that the clusters of objectives are reflected in regionally differentiated governance traditions. Examples include the market-oriented policies of the US and the UK, the people-centered policies of the European Union, and the state-directed policies of the People's Republic of China. The foresight methods employed in this context (including expert panels, scenarios, horizon scanning, and participatory processes) are formalized and integrated in various ways, depending on the respective governance model. Rights-based systems demonstrate the highest level of methodological maturity (e.g., explicit method integration, stakeholder inclusion), while market- and state-driven systems focus more on functionality and operational connectivity. This paper is based on a network-based visualization model that maps policy components as nodes and their coherence relationships as weighted edges. Key network metrics (e.g., eigenvector, betweenness, degree centrality) and cluster analyses enable the identification of dominant control elements and coherent subsystems within national strategies (Azin & Zandhessami, 2025).

The existing governance models have three structural shortcomings:

- One aspect to consider in this context is that regulators typically do not possess the same level of knowledge as AI developers and operators. This is due to the information asymmetry that plays a significant role in this context.
- There is a dilemma regarding speed: legislative cycles and review processes are significantly slower than technological iterations.
- The concentration of power, which manifests itself in the bundling of decision-making and enforcement powers among a small number of actors, results in a deficit of legitimacy and acceptance. Regional power asymmetries, normative divergences, and governance traditions have a systematic influence on the structure and effectiveness of AI strategies.

Governance structures are therefore not monocentric but are characterized by goal-means configurations and their internal interconnections. Early consolidation of international AI governance appears misguided, as it does not adequately address the complex, dynamic, and novel challenges posed by advanced AI systems. Instead, the current diverse, decentralized, and context-sensitive governance approaches should be seen as the more appropriate way to shape this rapidly developing technology responsibly (Kerry et al., 2025).

Against this backdrop, there are growing calls in the expert debate to view governance not as a central control task, but rather as a distributed network problem (Hébert-Dufresne et al., 2025). The combination of heterogeneous skills, regional knowledge bases, and moral perspectives in networks can lead to the emergence of adaptive, resilient control mechanisms.

## 1.2 Thesis and Objective

This chapter argues that only a decentralized, adaptive network of actors can ensure effective governance of AI. This approach is not just a suggestion, but a necessity, as it is the only one that can reflect the complexity and dynamics of modern AI systems and respond continuously to technological and societal developments. The objective is to develop a formalized network model that.

- The roles, interaction patterns, and responsibilities of the actors involved must be precisely described.
- Systemic performance indicators such as transparency, response speed, and robustness are quantified.
- The technical implementation paths (e.g., federated learning, blockchain, multi-agent systems) will be integrated with the institutional requirements.

It can be assumed that this challenge cannot be mastered by a single government or institution alone. Instead, the key to addressing this challenge lies in collaboration. Forming coalitions and fostering intensive, cross-sector cooperation with actors from industry, philanthropy, civil society, and academia is recommended (Kerry et al., 2025).

## 1.3 Research Questions

Based on this objective, the following guiding research questions are derived:

**RQ1 Structural question**: How can the governance landscape of complex AI ecosystems be formally modeled as a network?

**RQ2 Functional question**: Under what conditions do decentralized networks achieve greater transparency, faster risk detection, and stronger legitimacy than centralized regimes?

**RQ3 Implementation question**: What technical and institutional architectures are necessary to implement such a network model in practice?

## 1.4 Methodological Approach

The methodological approach of this paper is based on a combination of three complementary research approaches that together enable an integrated analysis of dynamic AI governance. First, a conceptual analysis is conducted that brings together key insights from complexity economics, systems theory, and technology assessment. The aim is to derive fundamental governance principles from these interdisciplinary perspectives that can be transferred to the control of adaptive and distributed AI systems.

The second step involves formal modeling, in which a directed graph$G = (V, E)$ is developed. This graph illustrates the interactions between key actors—including regulatory authorities, companies, auditors, and civil society actors—as well as the relevant information flows and feedback loops in the governance network. Based on this structural model, specific metrics for assessing governance performance are defined, including, for example, information latency, network robustness, and resilience to failures or adversarial disruptions.

In a third step, an agent-based simulation is employed to investigate the dynamic mechanisms within the governance system (Zhang et al., 2023). For this purpose, various agent classes are specified, including regulators, companies, auditors, non-governmental organizations (NGOs), and users. Specific strategies and learning mechanisms are assigned to individual classes, with reinforcement learning, specifically Q-learning, playing a vital role. The simulation enables the analysis of various equilibrium dynamics, including the emergence of complete compliance, the occurrence of strategic rule evasion, and the collapse of cooperative structures in polycentric systems. The combination of these three methodological strands yields a well-founded approach that is both theoretically consistent and empirically relevant.

## 1.5 Contribution to the State of Research

This study is at the intersection of normative governance discussions and technical and operational implementation issues. On the one hand, the existing literature focuses on abstract guiding principles such as transparency, accountability, and non-discrimination. On the other hand, technological solutions such as audit tools, smart contracts, and privacy-preserving algorithms are analyzed in isolation. This chapter establishes a systematic link between these two levels of analysis. The scientific added value of the chapter is manifested in three central aspects:

First, it develops an integrated perspective that translates normative objectives (e.g., protection of fundamental rights, democratic legitimacy), formal governance structures (e.g., cooperation mechanisms, regulatory design), and technological enablers (e.g., federated learning, blockchain, explainability tools) into a coherent overall system. This connection enables a view of governance that goes beyond traditional explanatory approaches, namely as a political decision or technical aftercare. In this understanding, governance is seen as a dynamically linked network of different actors, resources, and logics.

Furthermore, the article presents a quantitative framework that enables the systematic measurement and comparison of governance architecture performance. The three state variables—compliance (C), risk (R), and transparency (T)—form the operational translation of normative requirements. They enable both simulation-based evaluations and continuous feedback into governance practice.

The high transferability of the presented model to different regulatory contexts is an essential aspect that should be particularly emphasized in this study. Its applicability extends equally to national legislative initiatives, such as the EU AI Act or the US Executive Orders, as well as to industry-specific self-regulation, for example, in the fields of medicine, finance, or platform economics. The modularity of the model enables the mapping of both decentralized and centralized regimes, thereby increasing its connectivity in an internationally fragmented regulatory environment.

Overall, the chapter thus represents an innovative contribution to the further development of the interdisciplinary field of AI governance by condensing normative theory, institutional practice, and technical implementation into an action-oriented, analytically robust framework.

## 1.6 Structure of the Chapter

Section 2 analyzes current governance deficits and system-theoretical challenges. Section 3 introduces the conceptual network model and discusses distributed responsibility and cooperation mechanisms. Section 4 formalizes the network using graph and system dynamics approaches and develops governance metrics. Section 5 specifies the processes using agent-based modeling and simulates various equilibrium scenarios. The sixth section discusses technological implementation paths, including federated learning and blockchain-based audit protocols. The seventh section summarizes the results of the study. In addition, the limitations of the research are discussed and a research agenda for adaptive and equitable AI governance is outlined.

# 2. GOVERNANCE CHALLENGES IN THE AGE OF COMPLEX AI SYSTEMS

## 2.1 Governance Deficits of Current Regulatory Regimes

The regulation of AI faces conceptual challenges. Regulation is commonly justified as a means of correcting market failures. These can take the form of asymmetric information, negative externalities, or monopolistic power concentration, for example. However, this paradigm proves inadequate when it comes to generative and adaptive AI systems. It is because artificial intelligence is not a market phenomenon in the strict sense, but rather a dynamic, socio-technical system that transforms not only economic, socio-, but also normative, epistemic, and political structures. The conventional market failure model is not applicable in this case, as the relevant prices, markets, and actors are not clearly defined. Attempts to regulate AI along traditional economic lines, therefore, lead to regulatory misalignment, ambiguity, and excessive complexity.

Compounding the challenges of AI regulation is the absence of established alternatives. Unlike other critical infrastructures, there is no consensus paradigm for 'system regulation' specific to technology. The lack of theoretical guidance on issues such as algorithmic power, epistemic inequality, or opacity leads to regulatory activism, particularly in the European Union. Instead of reducing complexity, these governance frameworks further complicate matters with a multitude of regulations, obligations, and definitions, often without empirical foundation, sectoral differentiation, or adaptive feedback loops.

Examining current regulatory architectures, three structural deficits can be identified. These deficits are reflected in the EU AI Act (2024), the NIST AI Risk Management Framework (2023), and international standards such as ISO/IEC 42001 (2023). They include reactive time lag and standardization by market actors, information asymmetry and lack of access infrastructure, and jurisdictional fragmentation and transnational production chains.

(1) Reactive time lag and standardization by market actors

There is a significant discrepancy between the speed of technological innovation and the sluggishness of legislative processes. In contrast, large-scale foundation models such as GPT-4, Claude, or Gemini are updated within a matter of weeks and rolled out in new applications. Consultations, legislative acts, and implementation guidelines, on the other hand, often take years. The resulting consequence is a permanent regulatory deficit: De facto standards are established not by regulatory authorities but by market-powerful companies that create structural facts through first-mover advantages, API ecosystems, and proprietary benchmarks before public institutions can intervene. Regulation thus functions as a lagging corrective rather than a forward-looking control mechanism.

(2) Information asymmetry and lack of access infrastructure

A key obstacle to effective AI governance is structurally limited access to training data, model parameters, and evaluation metrics. Even under formalized reporting requirements (e.g., under Article 53 of the EU AI Act), the available information remains limited in depth and quality. This may be due to the protection of trade secrets, technical intransparency, or deliberate opacity. Under such conditions, ex ante approval procedures and ex post audits run the risk of becoming mere administrative rituals in which regulatory authorities conduct 'blind audits.' However, the effectiveness of these control mechanisms is questionable if access to traceable model maps, data ethics audit trails, or simulative replications is not guaranteed.

(3) Jurisdictional fragmentation and transnational production chains

The development of AI is fragmented globally. Training data originates from international sources, data centers are situated in tax-friendly jurisdictions, models are further developed within open-source communities, and services are offered across multiple local markets. This structural blurring of boundaries stands in stark contrast to nation-state-oriented regulation. Even if a regime is formally coherent, such as the EU AI Act, it often fails in practice due to extraterritorial enforcement or regulatory arbitrage opportunities (model 'shipping,' hosting in third countries, licensing via subsidiaries). The fragmentation of the public sector not only creates governance gaps but also inconsistencies in risk assessment, sanctioning, and ethical evaluation.

These three shortcomings—temporal reactivity, structural opacity, and territorial fragmentation—undermine key requirements for effective governance:

- effectiveness (ability to achieve policy goals), political objectives (e.g., risk minimization, protection of fundamental rights),
- legitimacy (acceptance by stakeholders), generating broad acceptance among stakeholders, and
- adaptability (capacity to evolve with technology), i.e., the ability to adapt dynamically to new technological and social constellations.

Without a fundamental shift in the foundations of AI governance, beyond the current market-based intervention paradigm, our regulatory approaches are at risk of institutional and functional failure. It is crucial to innovate and think ahead to ensure effective governance in the rapidly evolving AI landscape.

## 2.2 Complexity Characteristics of Modern AI Ecosystems

First of all, all technologies are subject to a continuous development process; however, the development of AI exhibits an exceptionally high rate of progress. The pace of AI improvement will far exceed the already powerful Moore's Law, which successfully predicted that computing power would double every two years. Instead of doubling every two years, the computing power required to train the most powerful AI models has increased by a factor of ten every year over the past decade. Processes that used to take several weeks are now performed in seconds. The basic technologies that enable AI are becoming increasingly smaller, cheaper, and more accessible.

The uniqueness of AI lies not only in its expanded computing capacity but also in its potential to revolutionize technology. The development of AI, with its diverse capabilities from training large language models to solving complex problems, could lead to systems capable of autonomous operation. This potential for self-improvement could make AI the first technology capable of improving itself, a truly revolutionary prospect.

The spread of AI is proving to be straightforward. It is evident that, as with any software, AI algorithms can be reproduced and distributed more easily and cost-effectively. The increasing performance of AI algorithms, combined with falling data processing costs, suggests that this mode will be used on smartphones in the foreseeable future. It is a remarkable development that a technology with such high performance is spreading so rapidly. Because the marginal costs—and thus also the marginal costs for provision—are zero, the ubiquitous availability of AI models can be expected after their introduction.

AI systems are not just software artifacts, but complex socio-technical networks characterized by the following features:

- Firstly, it is worth noting that non-linearity is present. As a consequence, marginal modifications in the training data or prompting strategies can have disproportionately large effects (e.g., ‘jailbreaks’ in LLMs).
- Emergence describes the spontaneous emergence of new behaviors known as chain-of-thought abilities. These abilities include cognitive processing speed and transfer learning across multiple modalities. Emergence is therefore a result of the interaction of many parameters and is consequently not strictly programmable.

- The models are embedded in cross-data and cross-value chain platform ecosystems (APIs, fine-tuning marketplaces, plug-ins). Errors or biases propagated along these chains create systemic risks that individual actors cannot see or control on their own.
- Fourthly, there is what is known as path dependency. It means that architectures and training pipelines are determined by the actions of commercial pioneers, also known as 'foundation model providers.' Due to network effects, later players are forced to adapt to these, which leads to a kind of 'lock-in.'

The rapid development of generative AI models, driven by machine learning, continuous training, and external data input, makes them a flexible target with capabilities and risks that are difficult to predict. This dynamic makes it challenging to identify points of responsibility along the value chain and necessitates continuous, cross-sectoral monitoring by developers, regulatory authorities, civil society, and academia (Kerry et al., 2025).

Given the current concentration of technical and financial resources in a small number of countries and technology companies, effective governance can only be achieved through closely integrated, adaptive, and cooperative control that can be flexibly adapted to new models, application risks, and regulatory challenges. Centrally controlled command structures are proving inefficient or even counterproductive. They are unsuitable for nonlinear dynamics. They are too slow for emergent properties. They are too rigid and interdependent for value creation because they are too isolated.

Despite the uncertainties associated with AI frontier research, key application risks can already be identified today. Algorithms can be inherently biased and discriminatory, generate false or manipulated content, amplify cyberattacks, profoundly affect privacy, and have indirect effects on energy consumption, market structures, intellectual property rights, employment, and systemic stability. Regulatory responses to these challenges will largely be taken at the national level. This will require differentiation according to field of application, risk profile, and the compatibility of existing legal and institutional instruments (Kerry et al., 2025).

## 2.3 Complexity Economics and Systems Theory Perspectives

The theoretical foundation of the governance model presented here is based on two complementary perspectives: complexity economics and sociological systems theory. Complexity economics (Arthur, 2021; Beinhocker, 2006; Haynes & Alemna, 2022) interprets markets not as equilibrium mechanisms, but as evolutionary processes in adaptive networks of heterogeneous actors. In this perspective, stability is manifested not through centralized control but through decentralized interaction, structural redundancy, and continuous feedback. Governance is therefore not conceived as a rigid system of rules, but as a dynamic learning process in which actors respond to changes in their environment, adapt their strategies, and form collective patterns through recursive interaction. This perspective seems particularly fruitful for AI systems that are self-learning, context-sensitive, and respond in a nonlinear manner. It suggests that a robust control system should not consist of rigid hierarchies, but instead of multiply coupled, resilient networks that can grow with technological change.

In addition, Niklas Luhmann's (1984) systems theory provides a sociologically grounded conception of governance in highly complex social systems. According to this theory, communication, not command, is the fundamental operating principle of social systems. Decision-making processes arise in functionally differentiated subsystems—such as politics, law, economics, and science—through internal coding and second-order observation. For AI governance, this results in the need for semi-autonomous control loops that perform functions such as observation (e.g., through audits), evaluation (e.g., risk scoring), decision-making (e.g., policy updates), and implementation (e.g., code release or access control) in a decentralized and situation-specific manner. In this case, a central control authority would be overwhelmed both epistemically and structurally. Instead, it is crucial to establish communicative coupling mechanisms between the different groups of actors.

Both strands of theory result in a coherent normative reference framework for future AI governance:

- A polycentric organization is necessary to minimize systemic failure risks (single point of failure) and ensure redundancy in the control architecture.
- It must include self-organizing feedback loops in which governance parameters are continuously adapted to current system states (e.g., real-time audits or automated policy tuning).
- AI governance should enable experimental learning, for example, through regulatory sandboxes or simulated A/B governance tests. It is the only way to iteratively verify the effectiveness and side effects of new regulatory approaches.
- Finally, the implementation of operational metrics is necessary to enable the evaluation of governance effects. This can be done, for example, by using a transparency index, determining compliance rates, or measuring incident response latency.

Governance in dynamic AI environments should therefore not be understood as hierarchical control, but rather as an adaptive interplay of distributed observation, evaluation, and rule-setting based on resilient network structures and continuous self-observation.

## 2.4 Governance Actors, Power Asymmetries, and Conflicting Rationalities

The development of artificial intelligence is inextricably linked to the internet's networks and hubs. This infrastructure forms the basis for cloud services, computing power, and the exchange of training data and codes—the key drivers of AI research and development. The geographical distribution of these digital networks also shapes the architectures of AI governance. It helps determine the geopolitical dividing lines that significantly influence the global development and control of AI (Kerry et al., 2025).

The spatial agglomeration of digital networks and infrastructure nodes correlates with the global centers of AI research and development. These regions are also home to numerous leading developers of advanced AI models. This geographical distribution is reflected in the countries and groups of actors that are playing a pioneering role in shaping national AI governance and are also a driving force behind the establishment of international cooperation formats for regulating AI (Kerry et al., 2025).

As shown in Table 1, the stakeholder landscape of complex AI systems is pluralistic.

*Table 1. AI stakeholder landscape*

| Actors | Primary objectives | Source of power | Typical lines of conflict |
|---|---|---|---|
| Developers (big tech, startups) | Market dominance, pace of innovation | Capital, data, talent, cloud infrastructure | Disclosure requirements, antitrust law |
| Regulators and standard setters (EU, NIST, ISO) | Risk reduction, product safety, consumer protection | Legislative authority | Enforcement capacity, expertise |
| Auditors | Increased security | Expertise, peer review | Access to raw data, liability |
| Civil society and NGOs | Protection of fundamental rights, fairness | Moral authority, public awareness | Participation rights, representation |
| Users and end users | Benefits, convenience, privacy | Data, attention, legal claims | Transparency, enforcement |

Source: own representation.

The actors act according to different rationalities, which manifest themselves in the form of profit, office, knowledge, value, or everyday rationality. Power asymmetries—especially the knowledge and resource advantages of large platforms—exacerbate conflicts of interest. The resulting governance problems manifest themselves in the following aspects:

- Companies use their position of power to influence regulatory processes in their favor. This process is referred to as 'regulatory capture.'
- Regulators potentially contribute to inhibiting innovation or underregulation.
- In multi-actor supply chains, there is a so-called 'responsibility gap.' This means that liability for damages is not clearly defined.

The current global AI governance is therefore not the result of central control, but the product of a multitude of overlapping networks with different constellations of actors, interests, and control logics. The existing networks reflect the geographical concentration of digital infrastructure on which the development and operation of advanced AI systems are based. These include cloud platforms, data centers, and data flows. The spatial and institutional concentration of this infrastructure creates asymmetrical scope for action: only a small number of countries and technology companies currently have the resources to develop basic AI models and scale them globally (Kerry et al., 2025).

At the same time, network-based forms of control also open up opportunities for a more resilient, pluralistic governance structure. Analogous to the architecture of the internet, distributed networks offer advantages such as diversity, redundancy, and reliability, which are crucial to the adaptive management of the complex and evolving risks associated with AI. Different governance initiatives—at the national, regional, or sectoral level—intentionally or unintentionally create governance through experimentation, in which successful approaches can be iteratively refined while others fail or are modified. This structure should be viewed as a network of networks rather than a linear hierarchy.

A key feature of such systems is network effects: this study concludes that a large number of interconnected actors generate potentially high benefits in a network. These manifest themselves, for example, in the form of shared knowledge, early risk detection, or shared audit and certification standards. Metcalfe's law—according to which the value of a network increases with the number of nodes—also applies to governance infrastructures. It can thus be concluded that networking increases problem-solving capabilities.

The present decentralized, adaptive, and highly redundant structure is based on the model of Internet governance, characterized by a large number of multi-stakeholder organizations, open protocols, and a minimal state hierarchy. For AI governance, this means that a pluralistic, non-centralized model that remains compatible with technical reality, geopolitical fragmentation, and diverging values is currently the most realistic and robust response to the governance challenges of the age of generative AI.

A decentralized network model addresses these conflicts by distributing responsibility across multiple levels, enforcing transparency through mutual auditability, and implementing dialogue formats (e.g., multi-stakeholder forums, decentralized autonomous organizations) in which divergent rationalities can be institutionally mediated.

The preliminary conclusion of the analysis is that traditional, centralized governance approaches do not adequately address the dynamics of modern AI ecosystems. Instead, complexity economics and systems theory concepts suggest that governance should be designed as a network-based, adaptive process. This accelerates information flows, builds redundancy, and cushions power asymmetries through shared control. In Section 3 of this paper, a conceptual network model is developed that systematically integrates distributed responsibility, cooperation mechanisms, and the principle of governance by design.

## 3. CONCEPTUAL NETWORK MODEL FOR AI GOVERNANCE

Section 2 showed that central control is overwhelmed in complex, nonlinear, and asymmetrical power structures. This section, therefore, develops a network-based governance paradigm that systematically combines distributed responsibility and technical self-organization. The model is divided into four building blocks: (1) general governance principles, (2) multi-stakeholder architecture, (3) cooperation and legitimacy mechanisms, and (4) governance by design as the technical foundation.

### 3.1 Network-based Governance Principles

The overarching goal of AI governance is to use the potential of artificial intelligence responsibly while effectively identifying, assessing, and managing the associated risks. The proposed network model, based on five central principles, offers a promising solution. It promotes distributed responsibility to spread the burden and decision-making load across multiple shoulders, redundancy instead of centralization to minimize the risk of failure, transparency through reciprocal, auditable accountability to enable mutual control between actors, adaptive control loops that allow continuous learning and policy updates, and subsidiarity and polycentricity to make decisions as close as possible to the source of the problem and to achieve global governance through coordinated decentralization.

*Table 2. Governance principles*

| Principle | Brief description | Justification in the context of complex AI systems |
|---|---|---|
| Distributed responsibility | Responsibilities are divided among multiple levels of actors so that no single instance is a single point of failure | Reduces concentration of power; enables parallel oversight, faster escalation paths |
| Redundancy instead of centralization | Multiple nodes perform similar control functions (e.g., independent auditors, competing certifiers) | Increases fault tolerance and resilience, reduces risks from capture or failure |
| Transparency through reciprocal auditability | Interactions are logged in a standardized manner (DLT, API log standards); each actor can verify selected third-party data points | Builds trust without disclosing sensitive IP; speeds up incident response |
| Adaptive control loops | Governance rules are dynamically updated, triggered by metrics (bias level, incident rate) or consensus mechanisms | Enables continuous adaptation to technological leaps; reduces reactivity |
| Subsidiarity and polycentricity | Decisions are made where the best knowledge is available locally; global coordination is achieved via interoperable protocols | Balances local innovation with global minimum standards (ISO/IEC) |

Source: own representation.

These five principles form the normative coordinate system of the model. They address the shortcomings identified in Section 2 by decomposing power, distributing knowledge, and institutionalizing feedback.

## 3.2 Multi-stakeholder Architecture

The governance of advanced AI systems can only be organized through a multi-layered network of distributed responsibility. This network, which includes the audience as key stakeholders, is based on four complementary macro levels, each with its specific resources, perspectives, and institutional logics, which are integrated into the overall structure.

The regulatory level comprises state legislators, national and supranational supervisory authorities, and international standardization organizations. These actors have normative authority and, where necessary, the power to sanction. Their central function is to create binding frameworks, such as establishing risk classification systems, disclosure requirements, and liability rules. They are also responsible for accrediting certification bodies and defining institutional interfaces for control.

The economic-technical level comprises companies that specialize in the development, operation, or integration of AI models. These include large technology companies, specialized start-ups, cloud service providers, and open-source communities. Their key resources are the availability of large amounts of data, high computing capacities, and technological talent. These players not only contribute to innovation but are also central interfaces for the technical implementation of governance principles such as security, explainability, and traceability (e.g., via 'secure ML pipelines' or 'explainability APIs'). In this sphere, the normative idea of 'governance by design' is put into concrete practice.

Independent testing bodies, research institutes, and so-called red teams form the expertise and control level. Their resources lie in methodological testing expertise, reputation-driven peer review experience, and the ability to conduct independent analysis. As part of their work, they conduct security-related tests, including formal audits, penetration tests, and fairness assessments. They also create standardized transparency tools such as 'model cards' or 'system cards.' These tools provide information about the model structure, training data, and risks.

Finally, the citizen and stakeholder level constitutes an indispensable fourth pillar of the governance architecture. It includes civil society organizations, consumer associations, and the general user community. Their resources manifest themselves in everyday knowledge, moral credibility, and experience reports in dealing with AI systems. Through initiatives such as crowdsourcing audits, context feedback (e.g., user reports), and civil society pressure, this group significantly contributes to the control and legitimation of the overall system, making the audience feel empowered and influential.

The interdependence of these four levels is crucial for effective AI governance. It should be noted that none of the spheres is capable of establishing legitimate, enforceable, and adaptable rules on its own. Only their interaction—the 'governance network'—creates a system that reconciles innovation with control and regulation with operational reality. This' governance network' is a complex, interconnected system that facilitates the exchange of information, coordination of actions, and adaptation of rules and standards. It is characterized by a relational rather than hierarchical organizational structure. Its functionality depends on coordination, translation services, and mutual adaptation.

## 3.3 Cooperation and Legitimacy Mechanisms

Given the diverse interests and rationales in AI governance, a central goal of the proposed model is the productive moderation of potential conflicts between regulatory, technical, economic, and social logics. For the analysis, three central forms of cooperation are identified, each of which activates different institutional mechanisms and simultaneously generates specific legitimacy effects.

The first form is procedural coupling. The goal is to make technical and regulatory processes interoperable via standardized interfaces. For instance, the use of eIDAS-compliant electronic signatures, OpenAPI schemas, and standardized audit formats can make the process of auditing an AI system more transparent and efficient. Such interfaces enforce formal compatibility between the actors without requiring substantive agreement on goals or values. The decisive legitimacy effect of this coupling lies in improved verifiability: when processes are transparently documented and structurally compatible, not only does technical interoperability increase, but so does traceability for external auditors.

The second form of cooperation is based on reputation-based feedback loops. In this mechanism, auditors, developers, and operators evaluate each other, for example, using on-chain rating systems or publicly accessible compliance registers. Unfavorable evaluations can effectively act as sanctions without the need for government intervention. A high level of trust cannot, therefore, be created through coercion, but only through continuously observable, positive behavior. The use of such feedback systems contributes significantly to reducing information asymmetries and strengthens trust in an environment characterized by technical complexity and asymmetric knowledge.

The third form focuses on a deliberative element known as polyforums. These are platform-based, multi-stakeholder bodies in which technical experts, political decision-makers, civil society groups, and business actors collaborate to develop governance standards further. Such formats are based on best practices in internet governance, as practiced by the Internet Engineering Task Force (IETF) or the World Wide Web Consortium (W3C), for example. In these deliberative arenas, new bias tests, fairness criteria, or transparency standards can be designed and iteratively adapted in an open consensus process. The legitimacy effect manifests itself in increased procedural fairness. Institutionalizing marginalized perspectives increases social acceptance of technical and regulatory decisions.

The key finding of this section is that acceptance and accountability in AI governance cannot be explained solely by technical characteristics or individual responsibility holders. Instead, they manifest themselves as a collective phenomenon within complex networks of institutions, rules, norms, and social practices. As Li and Freeborn (2025) show, effective accountability does not lie in assigning responsibility to individual developers or organizations, but in embedding it in dynamic, interdependent constellations of actors. Accordingly, AI governance can only be expected to be effective in the long term if it is designed and practiced as a distributed, adaptive architecture.

## 3.4 Governance by Design: Networks as Regulators

The technical-institutional coupling follows the guiding principle 'code is law—network is governance.' This principle describes the idea that the rules of a digital system are not primarily prescribed by external institutions, but are directly embedded in the technical architecture, especially in the code, of the network itself (Oster, 2021). In this understanding, the code acts as a regulatory instrument that structures behavior, limits options, and enforces norms. Governance thus emerges as a property of the network through its protocols, access and update mechanisms, and the feedback loops embedded therein. Table 3 illustrates how this principle is mapped onto five complementary layers of a distributed AI infrastructure and which specific governance functions are embedded in each layer. Each layer performs a sub-function of overall governance—from preventive risk reduction in the data pipeline to rule-based orchestration, tamper-proof evidence at the ledger level, and user-centric transparency in the interface. Taken together, this architecture transforms abstract principles into operable technology: the network itself becomes the regulator.

*Table 3. Architecture and governance function*

| Technical layer | Primary governance functions | Implementation (examples) |
|---|---|---|
| Data and model pipeline | Compliance with quality, bias, and privacy standards | Differential privacy modules, Data Shapley Audit |
| Orchestration layer | Enforcement of access and update policies | Admission controller with policy-as-code |
| Disibuted ledger | Immutable log entries, smart contract sanctions | Ethereum rollup for audit trails, automatic penalties |
| Edge/federated layer | Local preprocessing, | Secure enclave signature, federated model rules |
| Interface layer | Explainable outputs, user feedback | Explainable AI widgets, real-time feedback APIs |

Source: own representation.

The architecture shown in Table 3 manifests a hybrid set of rules: Legal norms are translated into machine-readable policies that are automatically executed via smart contracts and policy engines. The focus of governance research is thus shifting from post-hoc penalties to ex-ante prevention (for criticism, see Section 7.2). The present analysis concludes that governance does not arise solely through formal legislation, but rather through the implicit control power of technical infrastructures and their integration into socio-technical networks.

Regardless, essential design principles must be taken into account. In this context, the precautionary principle is fundamental. Due to asymmetric risks—enormous opportunities but potentially catastrophic consequences—an adapted precautionary principle must be a central component of any governance structure, regardless of whether it is a centralized or decentralized governance model. In addition, the principle of impermeability is relevant: since AI models can be disseminated with ease, implementing mandatory and deterrent compliance mechanisms is necessary. An effective regime must allow easy access, but be associated with high costs to ensure effective discipline.

Section 3 developed the conceptual network model, which integrates decentralized governance principles (Section 3.1), a polycentric actor architecture (Section 3.2), cooperative legitimacy mechanisms (Section 3.3), and governance-by-design technologies (Section 3.4). The present model aims to address the shortcomings identified in Section 2 by institutionalizing information flows, creating redundancy, and establishing adaptive control loops. The following section provides a mathematical formalization of the concepts described above. Additionally, metrics are introduced that enable the empirical quantification of the network's effectiveness and robustness.

# 4. FORMALIZATION OF THE NETWORK MODEL

The network model for AI governance plays a crucial role in understanding, as it translates the concepts described in Section 3 into a structured yet understandable formal language. The aim is to map central actors, interactions, and state changes.

## 4.1 Basic Structure of the Governance Network

The governance system can be represented as a network of nodes (representing actors) and edges (representing interactions).

- Nodes (V) represent various actors, including regulatory authorities, AI companies, auditors, NGOs, and users.
- Edges (E) represent information flows, audits, sanctions, or cooperative relationships.
- Layers (L) can be used to separately map different types of interaction, e.g., regulatory, technical, or social levels.

Formally, the network can be represented as a directed graph

$$G = (V, E) \tag{1}$$

where each connection $e_{ij} \in E$ from an actor $v_i$ to an actor $v_j$ represents an interaction such as data transfer, audit, or feedback.

## 4.2 State Variables of the Actors

Each actor has a compact state vector:

$$s_v(t) = (C_v, R_v, T_v) \tag{2}$$

with

- C_v (compliance): How strictly does the actor adhere to specified rules (0-100%).
- R_v (risk): The risk posed by its behavior or model (0 = no risk, 100 = high risk).
- T_v (transparency): The degree of disclosure and traceability (0-100%).

These values are continuously updated in a feedback process.

## 4.3 Simple Dynamics and Feedback Mechanisms

The governance network follows a measure–evaluate–act cycle:

1. Measurement: Auditors and monitoring systems record the current status (C, R, T) of the relevant nodes.
2. Evaluation: A governance dashboard compares the values with thresholds (e.g., compliance< 80% or transparency< 50%).
3. Action: In the event of deviations, automated measures are triggered: increased audit frequency, penalties (smart contracts), or rewards.
4. Adjustment: AI companies adjust their behavior to avoid sanctions or improve their reputation.

A simplified formula for a company's compliance value is:

$$C_{t+1} = C_t + \alpha \cdot reward - \beta \cdot penalty - \gamma \cdot audit\,findings \tag{3}$$

where$\alpha, \beta, \gamma$ are weighting factors for positive and negative feedback.

## 4.4 Governance Metrics

Key figures are defined to assess the state of the entire network:

- Overall compliance:

$$C_{sum} = \frac{1}{|V|} \sum_{v \in V} C_v \tag{4}$$

The goal is a high average value (> 90%).

- Transparency index: Average of all T values of the nodes.
- Risk detection latency (L): Average time between the occurrence of a problem and its detection. The goal is a quick response (e.g., < 1 hour for high-risk cases).
- Network robustness: Measures how much C and T decrease when individual nodes fail or are manipulated. A more robust system shows only minor disruptions.

These metrics can be displayed in a 'governance dashboard' that makes trends and vulnerabilities transparent.

## 4.5 Key Findings of the Modeling

The following key findings are notable. They demonstrate how an adaptive, evidence-based control network, which is designed to be flexible and responsive, can be derived from a theoretical model.

(1) Networks instead of hierarchies

Formal modeling as a directed graph illustrates that control does not take the form of a linear command channel, but rather as a continuous cycle of information and incentives between decentralized nodes. Decisions emerge where current knowledge and specific skills are available and spread throughout the entire system via feedback loops. This increases the resilience of governance to failures of individual instances and enables greater flexibility in response to technological leaps, as adjustments can be made simultaneously at numerous points.

(2) Three key variables: compliance (C), risk (R), and transparency (T)

Instead of extensive checklists, a compact status vector consisting of three metrics per actor is sufficient to capture the network integrity status comprehensively. C measures compliance with rules, R quantifies the residual risk potential, and T reflects the traceability of the decisions made. Reducing the system to the essentials has the advantage of facilitating dashboarding, automated alerts, and comparability across domains. However, this does not deny the complexity of real AI ecosystems.

(3) Automated feedback through smart contracts and monitoring systems

Linking status values to programmed rules enables abstract governance goals to be transformed into directly effective incentives. This efficient system ensures that if status R exceeds a specified threshold or status C falls below the defined target, the smart contract automatically triggers sanctions or stricter audit intervals. If status T rises, rewards, such as reduced reporting requirements, can be granted. Machine-speed feedback reduces response latency from weeks to seconds, creating a self-regulating environment. This leads to rule compliance at the rational optimum for all parties involved.

(4) Measurability and adaptive control

The continuous aggregation and visualization of the three key figures — C, R, and T — in the governance dashboard enable permanent monitoring of the system. At the same time, these metrics serve as control parameters. If the aggregated compliance falls below the defined target value, the regulator has the option to instruct algorithms to increase audit frequencies or sanction levels automatically. In the event of a sustained improvement in the transparency index, there is the option of proportionally relaxing the reporting requirements. The measurement and intervention process is a closed loop in which data-based adjustments to strategies (policies) are made, and the status of network integrity is continuously stabilized.

The formalized representation presented in this section should not be viewed as an end in itself, but rather serves to clarify the governance logic. This paper demonstrates how actors, their states, and their interactions are linked to form an adaptive control network. Li and Freeborn (2025) combine the Technology Acceptance Model (TAM) with Actor Network Theory (ANT) to analyze the introduction of AI-supported digital innovations in the context of transnational governance. This paper extends the understanding of governance as technical control to include sociocultural embedding. It also demonstrates how organizations can enhance their accountability and innovation capabilities through effective network management.

In the fifth section, this simplified but structured model is applied to simulate an agent-based scenario and replicate dynamic developments in governance in realistic AI ecosystems.

## 5. AGENT-BASED MODELING OF GOVERNANCE PROCESSES

The simplified but formally consistent network presented in Section 4 is ideally suited as a multi-agent system for simulation. This study, of significant importance, aims to observe the responses of regulators, companies, auditors, non-governmental organizations (NGOs), and users in a distributed AI ecosystem to rules, sanctions, and incentives, and to identify the governance patterns that emerge from this.

## 5.1 Agent Types and Roles

At the heart of the agent-based model is the meticulously differentiated mapping of the various groups of actors that play a role in governing distributed AI systems. In this study, five prototypical agent types are differentiated, each with specific resources, goals, behavioral rules, and interaction logics. This meticulous typification enables the formal capture of real-world governance interactions and their replication in simulation.

(1) Regulators have normative authority and thus define the governance baselines, for example, in the form of thresholds for risk classifications, transparency obligations, or auditing requirements. Their actions significantly influence system dynamics through policy updates, certification decisions, and potential sanctions for non-compliance.

(2) The primary function of companies is to develop and operate AI systems. A balancing act between regulatory compliance costs, reputational risks, and market competitive advantages shapes their decision-making logic. According to the model logic, they respond adaptively to external stimuli, for example, by investing in explainability tools or restructuring training data.

(3) According to the definitions provided, auditors are independent review bodies that carry out sample analyses with limited resources, measure risk indicators, and report violations where necessary. Their reputation is based on peer review experience and the quality of past audit results. In the simulation, participants are selectively granted insight into model states, albeit to a limited extent.

(4) NGOs and civil society actors act as control bodies in a broader sense. They contribute their experience and moral capital, initiate public debates, report grievances through crowd-sourcing channels, or offer suggestions for improvement to deliberative forums. Their impact is particularly evident through reputation feedback and their role in governance proposal processes.

(5) Finally, it is the users who are at the end of the value chain and are directly affected by algorithmic decisions. According to the model logic, they are not passive objects, but active agents who provide positive or negative feedback, take legal action, or shift market incentives through their behavior (e.g., switching providers in cases of lack of transparency or bias). This user-centric approach is a key aspect of our research.

Agent-based differentiation forms the basis for the dynamic modeling of institutional interactions. The present study not only enables the mapping of ideal-typical role distributions but also facilitates the simulation of emergent effects. These include, for example, collective strategy changes, the formation of governance alliances, or escalations in the case of asymmetric information distribution.

It should be noted that all agents have the state variables C, R, and T from Section 4.

## 5.2 Interaction Protocols

The agent-based governance model is based on a series of standardized interaction protocols through which information, assessments, and sanctions are exchanged between the actors. Five central communication strands structure the interaction between regulators, companies, auditors, civil society actors, and the technical infrastructure.

(1) Audit protocol (AUD → DEV)

Audits are carried out at regular intervals by auditors, the frequency of which (f_audit) is specified by the regulator. The audit encompasses model outputs, data flows, and log files, and is conducted either automatically or with manual support. The result is coded in binary: the number 0 indicates no objections, while the number 1 indicates a rule violation. This audit signal serves as the basis for downstream measures, such as sanctions or reputation adjustments.

(2) Policy broadcast (REG → all)

The policy broadcast, a key communication tool in the governance model, is used to keep all participating agents informed and compliant. At regular intervals, the regulator sends policy broadcasts that include updates to thresholds, penalty levels, reward programs, and documentation requirements. This broadcast serves a crucial function, ensuring that all participants are aware of the regulatory framework and can adapt their systems accordingly, thereby maintaining a transparent regulatory environment.

(3) Crowd report (CIV/USR → REG or AUD)

Civil society actors, such as NGOs, users, or consumer protection organizations, are encouraged to report observations of potentially problematic system behavior. Examples include indications of algorithmic discrimination, wrong decisions, or data protection violations. This study has shown that crowd reports increase the likelihood of an audit being triggered for the affected system in the short term. In addition, the reactive capacity of the governance network is strengthened.

(4) Smart contract sanction (REG ⇔ DEV)

In the event of a confirmed rule violation during an audit, an automated smart contract with a direct link to the governance ledger is activated. This contract triggers a monetary sanction of $\sigma$ and updates the compliance status of the company concerned to 'yellow.' The status is displayed in the public dashboard and signals an increased risk or a temporary reduction in trust. This is done without manual interaction, which reduces response time.

(5) Reputation update (AUD ⇔ DEV)

After completing each audit, auditors publish a reputation score based on several criteria. These include, for example, the traceability of decisions, compliance with technical standards, and transparency in the handling of user data. Companies have the option of actively communicating these scores, for example, through 'trust badges' or external certificates. Positive ratings serve as a non-monetary form of reward and help to strengthen market confidence.

These protocols generate a multi-layered feedback structure that closely links technical audit trails, regulatory enforcement, and social control. At the same time, they constitute an operational basis for the cooperation and legitimacy mechanisms described in Section 3.

## 5.3 Behavioral and Learning Rules

To ensure that the agent-based model represents realistic dynamics, explicit decision-making and adjustment processes are defined for each central actor class. Section 5.3 is therefore divided into three parts: (1) decision-making logic of companies, (2) regulatory adjustment rules, and (3) auditor strategy.

(1) Decision-making logic of companies

AI companies are constantly faced with the decision of which governance strategy to pursue. The behavior of the actors is modeled using a Q-learning mechanism that calculates the costs of compliance, potential sanctions, and reputation-based rewards. It can be shown under which incentive structures organizations are willing to invest in high compliance or opportunistically switch to low compliance. Three modes are available for the analysis (Table 4).

*Table 4. Governance strategies*

| Mode | Cost | Impact on C, T | When attractive? |
|---|---|---|---|
| High compliance | High internal costs (documentation, explainability) | C↑, T↑ | High audit frequency, high penalties |
| Low compliance | Low costs | C↓, T↓ | Low sanctions, low audit probability |
| Selective transparency | Medium costs | C medium, T↑ | Marketing effect more important than full transparency |

Source: own representation.

The choice follows a$\varepsilon$ – *greedy* Q-learning scheme:

$$Q_{t+1}(m) = Q_t(m) + \eta\left(payoff(m) - Q_t(m)\right) \quad (4)$$

where payoff is the balance of profit, compliance costs, and penalties. Companies explore a new mode with probability$\varepsilon$, otherwise they choose the best Q to date.

Through many iterations, every company learns under which external conditions—audit rate f, sanction level σ, reputation feedback—the switch to high compliance is rational. Aggregated across all companies, this results in an emergent system dynamic, which is analyzed in the simulation scenarios in Section 5.4.

(2) Regulatory adjustment rule

The regulator does not act statically, but adjusts the audit frequency (f) and the sanction level (σ) in a data-driven manner to the overall state of the system. If the aggregate compliance value is not met, audit intervals can be shortened or penalties increased. If the target value is exceeded, the reporting requirements may be relaxed. This feedback logic contributes to the adaptivity of governance and enables real-time policy tuning.

Regulators monitor overall compliance, C_sum. If the target value (e.g., 90%) is not met, the audit frequency is automatically increased by

- the audit frequency is increased by$\Delta f$ or
- the penalty is increased by$\sigma by \Delta\sigma$ .

This policy-as-code rule links key figures directly to governance actions.

(3) Auditor strategy

This study examines the relationship between the credibility of auditors and their reputation score. There is a choice between quick spot checks and resource-intensive, in-depth audits. The decision on which companies to audit depends on various factors. These include the expected detection benefit of the audit, the risk indicators of the companies potentially to be audited, and the company's capacities. The present study reveals a heterogeneous audit pattern that corresponds to the real variability of audit intensities.

Each violation detected increases the score, while each false positive reduces it. It is time to decide whether to conduct a deep-dive audit or just a quick check, depending on

$$P(violation) = 1 - C_{DEV}.$$

The three sets of rules constitute a closed learning and control loop. This process unfolds as follows: Companies respond to regulatory signals, the regulator adjusts its policy in response to observed system metrics, and auditors refine their audit strategy based on risk and reputation considerations. The following detailed description outlines the formal implementation of these mechanisms and their impact on network dynamics in the simulations.

## 5.4 Simulation Scenarios and Equilibrium Dynamics

The proposed agent-based governance model is tested by simulating four contrasting policy scenarios. In each scenario, 500 agents act throughout 1,000 time steps, corresponding to a simulated year, within an identical network with an average initial compliance rate of 80%. The only variables between the scenarios are two policy levers of the regulator: the level of sanctions ($\sigma$) for violations and the audit frequency (f), i.e., the average interval between two audits. The results clearly show how different combinations of regulatory measures influence the system dynamics.

Scenario 1: Base case – moderate penalties, infrequent audits

In the base case, the penalty remains relatively low at €100 per violation, and audits are conducted only about once every 30 days. Under these conditions, system compliance stabilizes at around 85 percent after just a few iterations. The stakeholder landscape can be divided into two groups: a majority tends toward a moderate compliance strategy with selective transparency. At the same time, a minority exhibits an opportunistic attitude toward high and low standards. The evaluation of key metrics yields an overall compliance rate of 85%, a transparency index of 62%, and a risk detection latency of 18 days. The conclusion is that, although the system remains functional, it consistently generates areas of uncertainty with low traceability.

Scenario 2: High penalty – high penalties, unchanged audit rate

In this scenario, the fine is increased to €1,000 per violation, while the frequency of audits remains constant. This significant change in the cost-benefit calculation has immediate consequences: it was found that after just ten rounds, approximately 90% of companies switch to high-compliance mode. The key figures show a significant increase: compliance remains stable at around 95%, while transparency stands at around 80%. Nevertheless, risk detection latency remains at 18 days, as the audit frequency was not adjusted. The lesson to be learned from this analysis is that high penalties are a practical measure, but their impact is only sustainable if they are enforced vigorously. The low audit intensity carries the risk of a relapse into non-compliance as soon as companies recognize the low probability of detection.

Scenario 3: Audit surge – double audit frequency, moderate penalties

In this case, the fine remains unchanged at $100, while the audit interval is halved to 15 days. In the first phase, there is a significant drop in compliance to around 70%, as the intensified audits reveal a large number of previously undetected violations. In the second phase, companies initiate a correction process, responding to the new audit reality, investing in transparency, and achieving compliance rates of around 92% and a transparency index of over 75% within 30 rounds. Risk detection latency is significantly reduced to just four days. This scenario can be seen as an example of a 'sunshine regime.' Transparency is employed here as a control mechanism to generate compliance without imposing excessive penalties, provided that sufficient audit capacity is available.

Scenario 4: Redundancy failure – auditor failure

After 100 rounds, this scenario simulates an external shock in which 30% of the auditor nodes are deactivated. Possible reasons for this include cyber attacks or budget cuts. The other parameters are the same as in the base case. The effects are profound: within ten rounds, the transparency index drops from 62% to 45%, compliance falls below 60%, and risk detection latency rises to over 40 days. Companies recognize the resulting control vacuum and quickly switch to low-compliance strategies. Only by implementing emergency measures, such as increasing $\sigma$ and f, can the values be stabilized. This scenario highlights the significant importance of redundancy and resilience: if one control layer fails, systemic deviations can rapidly escalate.

A systematic comparison of the scenarios reveals that sanctions, such as those imposed in the high-penalty scenario, generate high compliance in the short term; however, they must be backed by fiscal capacity and long-term credibility. The audit surge strategy has a similar effect, but reduces the need for intensive controls in the long term, as companies act more transparently in their interests. The highest results—with compliance rates above 95%, a transparency index above 80% and risk detection latency below 5 days—are achieved by combining both levers. It is worth noting that redundant audit structures are of paramount importance. The failure of control mechanisms, such as auditors or independent data sources, can lead to serious system breakdowns.

Agent-based simulation enables the visualization of policy options and their systemic effects even before they are implemented in fundamental markets. Regulators gain a precise tool for coordinating audit frequency and sanction mechanisms, while companies can better assess the economic efficiency of compliance investments. The network model thus proves to be not only a theoretical analysis tool but also an operational compass for adaptive and robust AI governance.

## 5.5 Implementation and Practical Considerations

Agent-based modeling can be implemented with a surprisingly lean technology stack. The Python library Mesa is typically sufficient for conducting initial experiments, as its modular structure enables the definition of various agent classes from Section 5.1 with just a few dozen lines of code and provides a simple browser GUI for visualization. AnyLogic is a viable alternative for graphical process representation in system dynamics modeling style, as it enables the replication of smart contract events using Java snippets. As part of a later extension of the test lab to include real blockchain hooks, the Hardhat or Foundry solutions are suitable for the automated insertion of penalties or rewards into Solidity contracts.

Realistic calibration of the model parameters is crucial here. It has been found that the costs of audits, barriers to data access, and the usual levels of sanctions vary considerably between different industries. Empirical evidence is provided by the EU AI test environments currently being implemented in several member states, as well as by industry-specific security reports from major cloud providers. Entering these key figures into the simulation is crucial to ensure that the dynamics generated there can be transferred to real-world governance discussions.

Furthermore, it is advisable to include the implementation of a governance dashboard in the planning. Such a dashboard presents the relevant metrics—such as overall compliance, the transparency index, risk detection latency, or the total amount of smart contract penalties triggered—in real time. Such a cockpit allows regulators, company representatives, and auditors to observe in workshops how minor changes in audit frequency or penalty amounts have an immediate impact on the behavior of the simulated economic actors. The participatory component is an essential aspect of agent-based policy sandboxes. Stakeholders can safely test different sets of rules before implementing the measures.

The evaluation of pilot projects shows that such simulation workshops not only promote technical understanding but also help to build trust. Non-governmental organizations (NGOs) or consumer associations, which otherwise only perceive abstract paragraphs, are now allowed to observe the direct effects of economic incentives on the realization of their concerns, such as increased transparency. Conversely, companies recognize that a high degree of redundancy in the auditor network increases system robustness without the need for blanket requirements that inhibit innovation.

Finally, scalability should not be underestimated. While a scenario with a few hundred agents can be efficiently run on a notebook, computing time and memory requirements increase rapidly when realistic networks with tens of thousands of nodes need to be mapped. In this context, distributed frameworks such as Ray or Dask offer a solution by distributing the computing load across multiple cores or machines. When performing extensive topological analyses, such as resilience to targeted node attacks, the use of graph databases such as Neo4j proves advantageous. These significantly speed up the processing of complex path queries.

In summary, it can be said that with minimal technical effort, it is possible to establish a simulation laboratory that brings together regulators, industry, and civil society. In this laboratory, rule-based governance ideas can be subjected to empirical testing. In this way, a link is created between abstract models and concrete political decisions.

## 6. TECHNOLOGICAL IMPLEMENTATION OPTIONS

The previous sections have shown that decentralized networks, feedback loops, and agent-based learning processes form the basis of adaptive AI governance. However, the practical benefits of such concepts are linked to the availability of an appropriate technical infrastructure. According to Section 6, governance logic and real IT architectures and standards are linked. The focus is on five building blocks: (1) distributed learning at the edge, (2) blockchain-based traceability, (3) scalable audit and explanation procedures, (4) hybrid designs in which technical and institutional rules merge, and (5) interoperability as an ongoing task.

### 6.1 Federated Learning and Edge AI – Governance in Motion

The development of current, comprehensive language and vision models is primarily taking place in centralized data centers with extensive computing capacities and comprehensive data sets. However, this centralized paradigm poses significant governance risks: it creates data monocultures, increases the concentration of control, and makes it difficult to manage systems in a traceable and contextualized manner.

It can be said that these centralized infrastructures are at odds with the goals of distributed, resilient, and context-sensitive AI governance outlined in Section 3.

An alternative approach is gaining ground: federated learning (FL). In this context, training is no longer carried out centrally, but locally on decentralized nodes. Examples of these nodes include smartphones, hospital servers, and industrial gateways. The actual training data remains on the respective device, while only aggregated parameter updates are transmitted to a central coordination instance. This results in an innovative, network-based form of learning, which emphasizes both data protection and resilient control mechanisms.

It implies a fundamental change in terms of data protection and responsibility, as the raw data never leaves the source device; thus, federated learning fulfills the principle of 'privacy by design' at the technical level. At the same time, responsibility for data protection compliance is shared, with both local data holders and the higher-level model coordination contributing to compliance with legal requirements. By this distributed responsibility structure, a differentiated assessment of governance indicators, such as the conformity assessment (C-value) of individual subsystems, is possible.

In addition, it is possible to integrate so-called governance hooks directly into the FL coordination scheme. In typical aggregation methods, such as 'Federated Averaging' (FedAvg) or 'Federated Proximal' (FedProx), the central instance has the option of evaluating parameter updates based on additional criteria, including transparency (T) or risk indicators (R). Local model adjustments that are associated with a high risk of bias can be automatically downgraded or even completely rejected. In the present study, the aggregation logic itself thus becomes an instrument of dynamic governance.

A related approach can be seen in the further development of Edge AI. In industrial scenarios—such as robotics, smart grids, or autonomous production lines—so-called 'policy engines' can be installed directly at the edge. Such systems undergo specific regulatory checks prior to local commissioning to ensure compliance with certain limits. These checks serve to identify any violations of specific regulatory barriers, such as the unauthorized identification of individuals or the unauthorized evaluation of sensitive data. Such 'red lines' can be hard-coded or defined as adaptive thresholds that can be continuously adjusted.

The key governance advantage of these architectures lies in the empowering shift of control to the point of data generation. Instead of a central control authority, decentralized, context-sensitive control points are created that can adapt to the respective use case in real time. This principle—governance 'at the edge' of the network—is paradigmatic for a new phase of distributed AI control that seeks to reconcile technological performance with democratic control.

## 6.2 Blockchain / Distributed Ledger – Counterfeit Protection and Automated Enforcement

While the FL concept facilitates the decentralization of data sovereignty, which in turn enhances data protection and contextual responsibility, blockchain technologies play a crucial role in addressing a complementary governance issue: Who can ensure that security-relevant events, such as audit reports, sanctions, or certificate issuance, are not subsequently manipulated or selectively suppressed? The solution lies in the use of distributed ledger technologies, which play a pivotal role in ensuring integrity and automatically implementing appropriate measures, thereby enhancing the security and confidence in AI governance.

First, immutable protocols enable tamper-proof documentation of key events in the lifecycle of AI systems. For example, it is possible to anchor the publication of a negative audit report, the critical update of a high-risk model, or the revocation of a conformity label as a cryptographically secured hash in a public or consortium-based ledger. The verifiability of these transactions is guaranteed for authorized parties, including regulatory authorities, certification bodies, and civil society organizations. This results in a tamper-proof audit trail that not only establishes traceable responsibilities but also enhances the transparency of regulatory processes.

Second, smart contracts play a significant role in automating governance rules, thereby ensuring the efficiency and effectiveness of the system. These contracts allow governance rules to be codified in machine-readable, automatically executable protocols. The incentive and sanction mechanisms ($\sigma$, reward) introduced in Section 4 can be operationalized in such contracts. For example, suppose a rule violation is reported by an accredited testing agency and verified by a digital signature. In that case, the smart contract can automatically trigger a stored payment, withdraw a certification, or update an entry in the public directory. This study deals with the transformation of rules from a mode of downstream intervention to an automated, ex-ante-conditioned process.

The specific technical design of these blockchain components can take various forms.

Public blockchains such as Ethereum or rollup-based Layer 2 networks are characterized by maximum transparency and immutability. However, they require special precautions to protect sensitive information, such as the use of zero-knowledge proofs or off-chain storage for trade secrets and personal data.

Consortium-based blockchains, such as Hyperledger Fabric or Quorum, enable detailed control of access and visibility permissions. This functionality makes them particularly suitable for use in regulated sectors such as finance or healthcare. They combine the advantages of distributed systems with controlled data sovereignty.

Light clients are a technology that enables resource-constrained devices to participate in transaction verification. This is particularly relevant at the network's edge. A key advantage of this technology is that devices are not required to store the entire ledger. This architecture is particularly relevant for AI nodes in the Internet of Things (IoT), such as embedded sensors, mobile devices, or decentralized manufacturing units.

Overall, these blockchain-based governance modules enable a new level of transparency, automation, and accountability. They complement decentralized learning architectures such as federated learning to form a coherent system of distributed AI governance.

## 6.3 Auditability and Explainability at Scale – Transparency as an Operating System

Transparency is a crucial aspect of effective AI governance, particularly for systems that pose high risks and have a significant social impact. Audits and explainability are considered central building blocks of regulatory oversight. However, scaling them to large-scale models remains a persistent challenge. Three areas of technological innovation are opening up new possibilities for the systematic operationalization of auditability and explainability at scale.

First, it is worth noting that model cards and system cards significantly contribute to the standardization of metadata documentation. This study focuses on the documentation of key properties of AI systems in structured formats. The properties recorded include the training data used, the intended areas of application, known risks, and existing uncertainties. In an extended version based on distributed ledgers, the digital signatures of accredited auditors are embedded directly in the respective card. By the underlying principle, subsequent changes are automatically recorded as new versions, generating a verifiable, tamper-proof version history. This documentation practice serves both regulatory monitoring and third-party traceability.

Second, post-hoc decomposition methods address the explainability of highly complex models. Methods such as feature ablation, integrated gradients, or newer causal tracing techniques enable the decomposition of large neural networks into explainable substructures. In combination with batch audits, which sample critical input classes in a targeted manner, the latency in risk detection can be significantly reduced. This study deals with the explanation of individual cases and the systematic identification of patterns of misconduct. Potential patterns include discrimination, overfitting, and faulty generalization.

The third component establishes a link between data protection and fairness audits. This link is realized through scalable differential privacy (DP). In this context, parameter updates, such as those performed in federated learning, are provided with controlled noise. Modern DP libraries such as Opacus (Meta) or the Google DP Suite can be seamlessly integrated into decentralized training pipelines. They provide quantitative metrics, known as privacy budgets, which regulatory authorities can use as indicators of data protection-compliant model behavior.

In summary, it can be said that these technological approaches form a scalable transparency layer that acts as an operating system for distributed AI governance. As already outlined in Section 4, the continuous feeding of the transparency signal (T) introduced there enables reactive control and proactive risk management across heterogeneous stakeholders. Governance is thus not merely anchored as a final check, but as a permanently integrated function in the system design.

## 6.4 Hybrid Governance Design – Code, Policy, and Institution in One

Technological instruments alone are not sufficient to establish legitimate and effective AI governance. Instead, the coherent linking of technical and institutional control mechanisms—i.e., the integration of hard and soft governance in a consistent design framework—is of crucial importance. The hybrid governance architecture presented here combines codified rules with political negotiation and institutional anchoring.

A central element of this approach is the concept of policy-as-code. This involves transforming regulatory requirements into machine-readable formats, allowing them to be directly integrated into software processes. A prominent example is the open-source project OpenRegulus, which formalizes articles of the EU AI Act as JSON schemas. This enables developers to check their models for regulatory compliance automatically. This is a step toward integrated compliance by design.

Additionally, RegTech gateways facilitate bidirectional interaction between companies and supervisory authorities. Companies transmit their compliance documentation via standardized APIs, while regulatory thresholds, test criteria, or new standards can be directly integrated into continuous development and integration (CI/CD) pipelines. The governance process is thus dynamically integrated into operational workflows.

Another component of hybrid governance is decentralized supervisory structures based on the concept of decentralized autonomous organizations (DAOs). Such structures enable civil society actors, research institutions, or technically savvy communities to intervene in governance processes actively. For example, if a security vulnerability is discovered in a publicly accessible AI model, a formal proposal for a governance change, such as a patch for a smart contract, can be submitted. The decision on the allocation of capital shares is not based on capital, but on reputation metrics or stakeholder-related governance participation.

The hybrid arrangements presented here represent a viable technical infrastructure for the cooperation and legitimacy mechanisms described in Section 3. These mechanisms include procedural coupling, reputation-based feedback, and deliberative multi-stakeholder forums. The result is a governance system that not only codifies regulatory requirements but is also participatory, adaptive, and robust in the face of future challenges.

## 6.5 Interoperability and Technical Path Dependencies

The decentralized governance ecosystem can only be effective if the technical systems involved communicate smoothly. Without interoperable interfaces, uniform data formats, and compatible consensus mechanisms, the system risks disintegrating into isolated technological solutions. Three challenges in particular can be identified in this context.

First, there is a risk of standard fragmentation. Different ontologies and standardization approaches—such as ISO/IEC 42001 (2023) on AI governance or the IEEE 7000 series (2021) on ethics-guided system design—exist in parallel and follow partially incompatible structural and reference logics. The lack of overarching mapping layers significantly impairs the consistency of interpreting audit results. This, in turn, hurts the comparability and scalability of technical audit processes.

Furthermore, it is worth noting that the persistence of legacy infrastructures poses a significant hurdle to integration. Monolithic machine learning stacks, which are only compatible with new governance technologies such as intelligent contract-based policy engines or dynamic compliance orchestration to a limited extent, continue to dominate in many companies. The discrepancy between conventional CI/CD pipelines and modular governance components results in not only technical transition costs but also organizational resistance.

The third finding is that vendor lock-ins should be viewed as structural path dependencies. This exacerbates the power imbalance in the AI ecosystem. The use of proprietary monitoring and governance interfaces by large cloud providers poses a challenge for smaller players, as it makes it difficult to integrate their systems seamlessly. Remedies in this context include open-agent frameworks such as OpenTelemetry or KServe, which provide standardized interfaces for model monitoring, as well as portable ledger protocols, such as Inter-Blockchain Communication (IBC), which enable interoperability across chains and thus reduce systemic dependencies.

A pragmatic approach to overcoming these challenges is the interface-first strategy. Instead of developing complete system architectures first, open APIs, metadata schemas, and event hooks are standardized. This enables the development of a variety of technical implementations that remain compatible with each other and do not undermine different governance logics. Competition thus occurs at the implementation level rather than at the basic structural level.

The analysis reveals an inextricable link between technical architecture and governance design. Technologies such as federated learning decentralize responsibility along the data sovereignty chain, while blockchain ensures audit-proof traceability. Scalable audit and explainability methods reduce the time to risk detection, and hybrid governance models translate legal norms into executable code. Interoperability is the connecting fabric that links these components into a coherent system.

This technological infrastructure acts as a kind of 'operational skin' around the network model developed in Section 3: a governance system in which rules are not only formulated and evaluated, but also executed, verified, and dynamically developed adaptively by machines. The concluding Section 7 draws systematic lessons for politics, business, and research, and outlines open questions for a globally diffusing, decentralized AI governance.

## 7. CONCLUSIONS

The transformative potential of AI is not just a possibility, but a certainty that will profoundly impact people's lives and society. It will be a decisive factor in groundbreaking scientific advances, unprecedented access to technology, the spread of toxic misinformation that disrupts democracies, and environmental problems. This study concludes that AI will trigger a fundamental transformation of the global power structure and balance. In this respect, it is crucial to discuss the structure of future AI governance. The previous sections have developed a network paradigm for the governance of AI systems, which ranges step by step from problem diagnosis to conceptual principles, pragmatic formalization, agent-based experiments, and technical infrastructure. The overall picture clearly shows that in highly dynamic AI ecosystems, effectiveness, legitimacy, and adaptability can only be achieved through distributed, feedback-driven structures.

### 7.1 Key Findings

The present analysis concludes that a hierarchical model of central control is not viable for governing advanced AI systems. Instead, a polycentric network model with distributed responsibility is proposed. This model is characterized by the integration of regulators, companies, auditors, and civil society actors in a dynamic interplay. This collaborative approach leverages redundancies to ensure system resilience and reliability. By deliberately avoiding institutional and technical single points of failure, a governance framework is created that is both robust against external shocks and adaptive to technological developments. This model ensures that all stakeholders are part of the solution, not just the problem.

This approach focuses on reducing regulatory complexity by condensing normative targets into three basic control parameters. The abbreviations 'compliance' (C), 'risk' (R), and 'transparency' (T) are particularly relevant in this context. These three traffic light parameters function as an operational 'governance currency' that enables the translation of abstract legal and ethical requirements into measurable, verifiable, and feedback-enabled status variables. As a result, every actor in the system receives a profile-based governance signal that indicates both the status quo and the direction of development. Standardization forms the basis for cross-system comparability, algorithmic control, and automated risk escalation.

Another key finding is the superiority of proactive feedback over purely reactive regulation. The use of smart contracts, policy engines, and automated evaluation systems enables high-frequency responses to rule violations and high compliance. Simulations conducted as part of this study show that even with moderately tight feedback loops—i.e., the time between an event, its detection, and a response—a significant increase in system compliance can be achieved. In realistic models, an increase in average rule compliance of 10 to 15 percentage points was observed within a few iterations. The key to the effectiveness of sanctions lies not only in the severity of the measures imposed but also in their timely, reliable, and transparent enforcement.

It is worth noting that technology should be viewed not only as a means of addressing regulatory requirements but also as an active tool for governance. Existing systems, such as federated learning, blockchain logs, and explainability pipelines, embody a concept that can be described as 'governance' through their inherent design principles. Technical, legal, and social requirements are linked to form inseparable functional complexes. In this context, governance is no longer viewed as an external control mechanism, but rather as a continuously effective structure embedded within the technical stack. The principle 'network is governance' succinctly illustrates this transformation: governance is not established through the network, but rather manifests itself within the network itself, through its topology, feedback logic, and structural coupling between code, control, and communication.

These key insights form the basis for the subsequent discussion in Section 7.2, in which political, economic, and scientific implications are systematically derived, and open research questions are identified.

## 7.2 Limitations of the Approach

Despite the potential of a decentralized, technology-based governance approach, key challenges and limitations remain that must be considered in the further development and implementation of this model.

These coordination costs and interface complexities are significant and must be addressed to ensure the efficiency and resilience of the decentralized governance system. Without consistent standardization of interfaces, data formats, and protocols, there is a risk that coordination costs will offset the hoped-for efficiency gains. In technically heterogeneous environments—for example, between government regulatory platforms, private-sector AI stacks, and civil society feedback systems—a lack of interoperability can lead to fragmentation, inconsistent rule enforcement, and high transaction costs. The introduction of open API specifications, semantically harmonized ontologies (e.g., via ISO/IEC standards), and machine-readable governance rules (policy-as-code) is therefore not only a technical necessity, but also an institutional one.

The scalability of audit processes is a crucial aspect that must be considered in this context. Although technological innovations such as model cards, system cards, feature attribution, integrated gradients, and causal tracing have significantly improved the traceability and explainability of complex AI models, audits of large foundation models continue to face economic, technical, and organizational limitations. Comprehensive audits of these high-dimensional systems require considerable resources, both in terms of computing power and expertise. This is particularly relevant for AI applications subject to audit requirements in high-risk areas (such as medicine, criminal law, or financial market regulation), which require both ex-ante risk analyses and ex-post validations. A pragmatic solution is the selective use of batch audits and stochastic sampling methods. However, these methods must undergo methodological calibration to prevent the systematic overlooking of relevant risks, especially so-called 'blind spots.' The latter refers to constellations that lie outside the statistical norm ranges. The use of risk-aware sampling and adaptive feedback mechanisms from operations (e.g., crowd reports, incident signals) is crucial in order to combine scalability with the preservation of relevance and depth.

The persistence of asymmetrical power relations is a key aspect of this study. The implementation of a polycentric governance system does not necessarily guarantee a more equitable distribution of power. Instead, there is a risk that existing power asymmetries—for example, between large technology platforms and state or civil society actors—will be transposed into decentralized structures and become entrenched there. In particular, monopolistic control over data resources, proprietary AI models, and cloud-based computing infrastructure provides individual actors with structural advantages that cannot be eliminated, even by distributed control logics.

In addition, there is a risk that seemingly participatory systems, such as DAOs or governance tokens, create the illusion of collective decision-making but systematically exclude certain groups through economic barriers to entry, technical expertise requirements, or algorithmic design specifications. The inherent standardizing effect of algorithmic systems must be viewed with particular caution. People who behave outside statistical majority patterns—whether due to cultural, social, or physical diversity—are disadvantaged by standard models.

This study by Kozak (2023) sheds light on this development through a detailed analysis of power structures in AI and Web3 systems. A distinction is made between a vertical axis of conflict, in which the executive potential of the code collides with state, corporate, or individual interests—especially where AI-based standardization leads to systematic discrimination—and a horizontal axis of conflict, which revolves around access to code modification, governance structures, and interpretive authority. In this area, the state, civil society, and technology companies compete for the symbolic and functional resources of rule-making. Kozak's conclusion is sobering: technological developments toward AI and Web3 do not result in the dissolution of asymmetrical power relations, but rather in their transformation into new, algorithmically codified forms.

These limitations make it clear that the design of effective, fair, and resilient AI governance requires not only technical innovations but also continuous reflection on structural justice, institutional power, and democratic participation in the digital space.

## 7.3 Implications for Politics and Business

The concepts presented for decentralized, technologically sound AI governance open up new fields of action and areas of responsibility for politics, business, and civil society. Several concrete implications can be derived in order to productively exploit the potential of this architecture while keeping its challenges manageable.

For policymakers and supervisory authorities, this means not only pursuing regulatory innovation at the level of formal standard-setting but also ensuring it is anchored in technical implementation. The use of pilot projects in regulatory sandboxes is crucial for testing the coupling of policy-as-code models with automated smart contract mechanisms in practice. The focus here is less on establishing comprehensive control regimes and more on iterative learning processes in which machine-readable rules, technical audit trails, and institutional responsibilities are interlinked. Such sandboxes serve as a protected space in which the effectiveness of automated governance can be tested. This can take the form of dynamic threshold regulation or audits that trigger sanctions, for example. Sandboxes offer realistic conditions for testing. It can be assumed that the effectiveness and legitimacy of government oversight will increase in the medium term. This effect is particularly likely in areas where traditional instruments are not fast enough or too rigid to keep pace with the continuously evolving dynamics of generative AI.

Proactive investment in explainable and adaptive AI infrastructures will result in strategic advantages for companies. The implementation of explainability APIs, audit trails, and federated learning architectures is not only a response to future compliance requirements, but also has a positive effect on reputation vis-à-vis supervisory authorities, investors, and the public. Companies that invest early in transparent and data-efficient system architectures anticipate regulatory developments and can position themselves as pioneers in the responsible use of AI. In markets where aspects of algorithmic fairness, data protection, and systemic risks are becoming increasingly relevant, this will become a prerequisite for both market access and the social legitimacy of innovations.

Technological decentralization opens up new opportunities for civil society and research to actively shape fundamental rights, fairness, and accountability. DAO-like oversight structures form an infrastructural basis for systematically integrating civil society actors, NGOs, and independent research institutions into governance processes. These actors are in a position to identify critical gaps, propose governance upgrades, and directly influence the regulatory code via reputation mechanisms or on-chain voting. Public dashboards that include key figures on compliance (C), risk indicators (R), and transparency values (T) thus establish a de facto public sphere for algorithmic systems. This can serve as a basis for social discourse and political pressure. It can be concluded that this also creates a new level of algorithmic control beyond formal legal channels. This is anchored in technical infrastructure but supported by social actors.

The implications suggest that sustainable AI governance cannot be achieved through legislation, technology, or market forces alone. Establishing a robust, adaptive, and legitimate governance system for the AI era requires the interplay of institutional innovation, technical standards, and social participation.

## 7.4 Open Fields of Research

Despite the progress outlined above and the systemic potential, the development of resilient, legitimate, and globally compatible AI governance continues to face fundamental questions that remain open. These questions concern not only technical details but also touch on profound normative and geopolitical dimensions.

A key area of research concerns the global diffusion of standards. The question of how different legal traditions, cultural values, and institutional arrangements—for example, in the European Union, the United States, India, or African countries—can be integrated into an interoperable network model without losing cultural legitimacy and democratic anchoring remains unresolved. In this context, it is essential to recognize that this is about more than just harmonizing standards. It is relevant to discuss how governance can be designed as a socio-technical structure that is compatible with pluralistic notions of justice and does not impose technocratic universality. Future research projects must therefore explore how a combined application of distributed rule-setting with local context sensitivity and machine-readable operationalization of culturally embedded normativity can be realized.

A second strand deals with resilience against adversarial attacks in an increasingly decentralized ecosystem. The new governance approaches—such as distributed audits, DAO-based oversight, or collaborative model updates—are not only innovative but also harbor the potential for targeted disruption. There is a need for robust detection and defense mechanisms against manipulation of audit logs, data poisoning in federated learning setups, or orchestrated governance attacks on smart contract structures. Ensuring the integrity of reputation-based decision-making processes and preventing majority manipulation in token-based voting are particularly relevant in this context. It is essential to combine research into technical countermeasures (e.g., through graph-based anomaly detection, or resilient consensus algorithms) with institutional redundancy strategies to ensure systemic robustness.

A third, hitherto neglected field concerns the development of ethical metrics for machine agents. The state variables compliance (C), risk (R), and transparency (T) proposed in this model capture key legal and security aspects. However, the question remains as to how normative concepts such as human dignity, participatory justice, inclusion, or ecological limits can be translated into operational metrics. The challenge is not only to integrate these values symbolically, but also to quantify them without risking trivializing them. Interdisciplinary research programs are needed to realize this project, ensuring the systematic integration of ethical theory, socio-technical design, and the development of AI technology.

The network model developed, therefore, does not view governance as a central control authority, but as a dynamic, socio-technical ecosystem. In this model, rules, data flows, institutional responsibilities, and social expectations are brought into a harmonious balance with each other in a continuous negotiation process. The combination of lean formalization, agent-based simulation environments, and connectable technology stacks creates a concrete toolbox that goes beyond abstract models. The joint use and further development of this toolkit by politics, business, and civil society could lead to AI governance evolving from reactive risk management to a proactive design tool. This would mean that AI governance would be adaptive, legitimate, and robust enough to contain and shape the next wave of algorithmic innovation in a democratic manner.

## REFERENCES

Arthur, W. B. (2021). Foundations of complexity economics. *Nature Reviews. Physics, 3*(2), 136–145. DOI: 10.1038/s42254-020-00273-3 PMID: 33728407

Azin, M. H., & Zandhessami, H. (2025). Strategic alignment patterns in national AI policies. *arXiv*. /arXiv.2507.05400DOI: 10.48550

Beinhocker, E. D. (2006). *Origin of wealth: Evolution, complexity, and the radical remaking of economics*. Harvard Business Review Press.

Brynjolfsson, E., & Mcafee, A. (2014). *The second machine age: Work, progress, and prosperity in a time of brilliant technologies*. Norton.

Cath, C. (2023). Eaten by the Internet. In Cath, E. (ed.). Eaten by the Internet, Meatspace Press, 7–13. https://ia600508.us.archive.org/32/items/eaten-by-the-internet/MSP_eatenbytheinternet_DIGITAL_LR.pdf

Clayton, C., Maggiori, M., & Schreger, J. (2025). The Political economy of geoeconomics power. NBER Working Paper No 33353. https://www.nber.org/papers/w33353

European Union (2024). Regulation (EU) 2024/1689 of the European Parliament and of the Council of 13 June 2024 laying down harmonised rules on artificial intelligence and amending Regulations (EC) No 300/2008, (EU) No 167/2013, (EU) No 168/2013, (EU) 2018/858, (EU) 2018/1139 and (EU) 2019/2144 and Directives 2014/90/EU, (EU) 2016/797 and (EU) 2020/1828 (Artificial Intelligence Act). https://eur-lex.europa.eu/legal-content/EN/TXT/PDF/

Floridi, L. (2025). AI as agency without intelligence: On artificial intelligence as a new form of artificial agency and the multiple realisability of agency thesis. *Philosophy & Technology, 38*, 30. DOI: 10.1007/s13347-025-00858-9

Haynes, P., & Alemna, D. (2022). A systematic literature review of the impact of complexity theory on applied economics. *Economies, 10*(8), 192. DOI: 10.3390/economies10080192

Hébert-Dufresne, L., Landry, N. W., Lovato, J., St-Onge, J., Young, J. G., Couture-Ménard, M. E. et al. (2025). Governance as a complex, networked, democratic, satisfiability problem. *npj Complex, 2*, 14. DOI: 10.1038/s44260-025-00041-3

IEEE Standards Association. (2021). 7000-2021 – Standard Model Process for Addressing Ethical Concerns during System Design. https://standards.ieee.org/ieee/7000/6781/

ISO/IEC 42001 (2023). Information technology — Artificial intelligence — Management system. https://www.iso.org/standard/42001

Kerry, C. F., Meltzer, J. P., Renda, A., & Wyckoff, A. W. (2025). Network architecture for global AI policy. February 10, 2025. https://www.brookings.edu/articles/network-architecture-for-global-ai-policy/

Kozak, K. (2023). Algorithmic governance, code as law, and the blockchain common: Power relations in the blockchain-based society. *Frontiers in Blockchain*, *6*, 1109544. Advance online publication. DOI: 10.3389/fbloc.2023.1109544

Li, C., & Freeborn, D. P. W. (2025). Exploring AI-powered digital innovations from a transnational governance perspective: Implications for market acceptance and digital accountability. *arXiv*. /arXiv.2504.20215DOI: 10.48550

Luhmann, N. (1984). *Soziale Systeme. Grundriß einer allgemeinen Theorie*. Suhrkamp.

National Institute of Standards and Technology (NIST). (2023). Artificial Intelligence Risk Management Framework (AI RMF 1.0). https://nvlpubs.nist.gov/nistpubs/ai/nist.ai.100-1.pdf

OECD. (2024). AI principles. https://www.oecd.org/en/topics/sub-issues/ai-principles.html

Oster, J. (2021). Code is code and law is law—The law of digitalization and the digitalization of law. *International Journal of Law and Information Technology*, *29*(2), 101–117. DOI: 10.1093/ijlit/eaab004

Scott, M. (2025). Analysis: AI Summit emphasizes innovation and competition over trust and safety. Digital Forensic Research Lab (DFRLab), February 11, 2025, https://dfrlab.org/2025/02/11/ai-summit-analysis-innovation

Zhang, W., Valencia, A., & Chang, N. B. (2023). Synergistic integration between machine learning and agent-based modeling: A multidisciplinary review. *IEEE Transactions on Neural Networks and Learning Systems*, *34*(5), 2170–2190. DOI: 10.1109/TNNLS.2021.3106777 PMID: 34473633

Chapter 2

# Challenges for Procedural Law Facing the Technological Globalization and Artificial Intelligence

**Francisco Javier Arroyo Romero**
https://orcid.org/0009-0002-8673-8753
*Universidad Rey Juan Carlos, Spain*

## ABSTRACT

*The advent of artificial intelligence (AI) in the legal domain, within the context of accelerated technological globalization, poses new challenges to Procedural Law. This transformation is not merely technical but also structural and axiological, as it questions classical procedural principles and necessitates to update litigants' safeguards. Simultaneously, the diversity of procedural systems in Europe complicates a coordinated response to this global phenomenon. The article—adopting a Spanish and European perspective — deeply analyzes the primary challenges and opportunities arising in this context, from technology's impact on access to justice, AI's application in judicial activities, and the management of digital evidence, to implications for procedural harmonization, fundamental safeguards, and the evolving roles of judges and lawyers in an increasingly digitalized environment. It also addresses normative and ethical proposals for responsible AI usage in judicial proceedings, considering current regulations and relevant jurisprudence in the Spanish and European contexts.*

DOI: 10.4018/979-8-3373-4480-5.ch002

## INTRODUCTION

Procedural law, historically linked to the principles of legality and effective judicial protection, is currently undergoing profound transformation driven by the technological revolution. Information technologies have altered social production and communication methods, infiltrating the heart of the judicial system. Particularly, artificial intelligence (AI)—already employed in tasks such as drafting documents, jurisprudential analysis, and even predicting judicial outcomes—stands out as one of the most disruptive tools of this transformation. Added to this is technological globalization, which blurs borders and connects jurisdictions, demanding more agile, interconnected procedures aligned with a digital world.

Against this backdrop, it becomes essential to reconsider procedural law not as a static set of rules but as a dynamic system adaptable to technological changes, yet faithful to the principles that guarantee it. The central challenge lies in integrating innovations like AI and digital justice without undermining fundamental rights such as access to justice, due process, equality of arms, contradiction, and judicial independence. In Europe, this reflection becomes particularly complex due to fragmented procedural systems across different states, which makes it difficult to develop a unified strategy to tackle shared technological challenges.

The subsequent sections deepen into the key thematic axes of this debate. Firstly, the article examines how technological globalization impacts access to justice, potentially democratizing it but also creating new risks. Secondly, it analyzes the incorporation of AI into judicial processes and its practical and ethical implications. Thirdly, it discusses challenges regarding procedural harmonization in Europe in light of digital transformation. Fourthly, it compares European and North American responses to AI, given their distinct legal traditions. Fifthly, it studies the challenges related to digital evidence—its admissibility, custody chain, blockchain—and necessary regulatory adaptations. Sixthly, it explores automated decisions and how to uphold classic procedural principles within this context. Seventhly, it investigates the evolving roles of judges and legal professionals in a digital environment. Eighthly, it emphasizes the importance of training and digital competencies for these legal operators. Ninthly, normative and ethical proposals are presented to ensure responsible AI use in procedural matters. Finally, the conclusions summarize the main ideas, underscoring the need for a balance between technological efficiency and procedural safeguards in the era of digital justice.

## Impact of Technological Globalization on Access to Justice.

One immediate and positive effect of technological globalization in the legal field is the democratization of access to justice. The proliferation of the internet, online platforms, and AI tools has provided opportunities for more individuals to obtain low-cost legal information and basic legal advice. For instance, it is now possible to automatically generate simple legal documents (standard contracts, claim forms, etc.) through virtual assistants, reducing dependence on costly law firms and allowing vulnerable populations basic legal guidance. In Spain, the Civil Procedure Act (Ley de Enjuiciamiento Civil, LEC) already mandates in Article 273 electronic submission of documents by legal professionals, ensuring authenticity, reliable proof of dispatch and full receipt, including date indication. This legal obligation, stemming from recent procedural reforms, has strengthened electronic judicial files and expedited procedural communications, benefiting litigants.

However, enhanced technological accessibility also brings new gaps and cautionary concerns (Bujosa, 2020, pp.281-290). Online or AI-generated legal guidance does not replace lawyers' roles or guarantee effective judicial protection on its own. AI without human oversight or legal context may lead to significant errors or inappropriate recommendations. Furthermore, the risk of a digital division exists: individuals lacking technological skills or internet access may be left behind, deepening inequalities. Thus, genuine improvement requires a hybrid model in which technology complements legal professionals' roles, alleviating routine workloads but not replacing the interpretative, argumentative, and ethical functions of legal practitioners. The aim is to advance toward "low-cost justice" while maintaining standards of quality and fairness: AI can help solving court efficiency crises, but it must be critically assessed whether it genuinely solves systemic issues or exacerbates inequalities and undermines fundamental principles.

Another aspect of technological globalization is the appearance of alternative online dispute resolution mechanisms such as mediation or arbitration through digital platforms (online dispute resolution, ODR). These mechanisms facilitate faster dispute resolution with less formal settings, broadly expanding access to justice. However, they raise concerns about the quality of "digital justice": outcomes must be comprehensible, efficient, and fair, regardless of users' digital competencies or resources. Effective judicial protection entails not merely accessing a tribunal but ensuring equitable treatment and rights such as contradiction and equality of arms throughout the process, whether judicial or alternative.

In summary, technological globalization promises justice that is more accessible and citizen-centered, reducing costs and geographic barriers. However, to fulfil this promise strengthened safeguards are needed: qualified legal assistance for those in need, professional oversight of automated tools, and bridging the digital division through public policies (e.g., basic digital skills training and public electronic justice access points). Only this way can the ideal of democratizing technological access to justice translate into genuine and not merely illusory effective judicial protection in the digital age.

## Application of Artificial Intelligence in Judicial Proceedings and Its Implications.

Artificial intelligence is increasingly being applied at various stages and tasks within judicial proceedings, offering both efficiency opportunities and significant risks. Current applications of AI in the administration of justice include:

- **Jurisprudential and Document Analysis**: Intelligent search systems that utilize machine learning algorithms and natural language processing can review vast databases of judicial decisions and legal documents to identify relevant precedents, decision-making patterns, or applicable doctrines. These tools assist judges and lawyers in case preparation by providing information that would traditionally require many hours of manual research. For example, some assistants now generate draft rulings or legal reports based on uploaded data or predict the likelihood of appeal success by analyzing previous trends (a practice known as predictive justice).
- **Procedural and Administrative Management**: Algorithms that automatically classify incoming legal documents, assign cases according to predefined rules, or prioritize urgent matters (Bueno, 2020, pp. 1-31). Some courts are experimenting with intelligent electronic scheduling to optimize hearings and notifications, or with processing systems that alert about upcoming procedural deadlines. For instance, Costa Rica implemented an AI-based document classifier to sort submissions by procedure type, aiming to automate steps that do not require human intervention.
- **Virtual Citizen Assistants**: Legal chatbots capable of interacting with users in natural language to guide them through procedures, inform them of case statuses, or address frequently asked questions. One example is the chatbot developed by Costa Rica's judiciary to alleviate telephone service congestion by answering citizens' common queries. Elsewhere, bots have been implemented to guide victims of gender-based violence on how to request protective measures or to assist migrants with basic legal information in multiple languages (Remus & Levy, 2015).
- **Decision-Support Tools**: Although European legal systems have not delegated jurisdictional decision-making to AI, algorithms are used as inputs (. For example, in comparative criminal law, some U.S. states employ risk-scoring systems (e.g., the well-known COMPAS) to evaluate an accused person's likelihood of reoffending, aiding judges in deciding on pretrial release or sentencing. These tools do not replace judicial decisions but clearly influence them. In the EU, preliminary models of data-assisted sentencing guidelines or support systems for determining compensation have been explored (e.g.,

France's “DataJust” project for analyzing personal injury compensation using AI).

The potential advantages of these AI applications in judicial proceedings are evident. Numerous authors emphasize that AI can reduce the routine workload of courts and judicial offices, expedite response times, and enhance consistency in decisions (Nieva Fenoll, 2018, pp. 417-437). There is talk of a quasi-mathematical justice in some aspects, where similar cases receive similar outcomes through algorithmic support, thereby reinforcing legal certainty. Additionally, AI can help identify procedural delays or bottlenecks and optimize resources (e.g., automatically identifying complex cases requiring more attention versus simple matters suitable for standardized processing).

Nevertheless, these advancements entail significant risks and challenges that must not be overlooked. First is the danger of justice becoming dehumanized: excessively delegating decision-making that affects individuals' rights to machines may erode compassion, contextual assessment, and the value judgments that only a human judge can fully exercise (Carretero, 2025, pp. 135-136). AI lacks the empathy and equity nuances a human adjudicator can apply based on the factual and human context of each case. Second, there is the issue of opacity and explainability: many deep learning algorithms operate as “black boxes,” with decision criteria that are difficult to explain. This clashes with procedural requirements for the reasoning of rulings. If a judge bases a decision on an AI recommendation, how can they ensure it is explained in legally comprehensible terms? Algorithmic transparency thus becomes a fundamental requirement: any AI tool used in courts must be auditable and understandable regarding its decision-making criteria.

Third, there is a potential for discrimination or bias. If the training data for a system contains historical biases (e.g., harsher treatment of certain groups), the algorithm may perpetuate or even worsen them. Documented cases include the COMPAS system in the U.S., which has been accused of consistently scoring African American defendants higher than white defendants in similar conditions, raising discrimination concerns. In Europe, sensitivity to this issue is paramount: the EU Charter of Fundamental Rights and the General Data Protection Regulation (GDPR) prohibit automated decisions that discriminate based on sensitive attributes and impose safeguards to prevent bias. Moreover, the lately enacted Artificial Intelligence Act has become the first rule to ever regulate AI worldwide.

Finally, issues of responsibility and control raise critical questions: who is accountable if AI makes an error that affects someone in a judicial process? The software developer, the justice administration that implemented it, or the judge who used it? The absence of a clear liability framework could result in protection gaps. Furthermore, it must be ensured that the final decision in matters affecting rights remains with a competent judicial authority, not an automated system, regardless of its efficiency. The European Commission has emphasized the necessity of human oversight and decision-making as a guiding principle in AI implementation within the judiciary. Similarly, scholarly literature advocates for embedding ethical principles into these systems (by design), such as proportionality, fairness, and accountability, aligning them with the rule of law.

In summary, AI applied to judicial proceedings promises to profoundly transform the administration of justice, making it potentially faster, more economical, and more consistent. However, its introduction must be prudent, regulated, and ethical (De Asis, 2023, pp. 60-79). Public authorities and judicial bodies must establish clear protocols outlining which tasks can be automated and under what conditions, always ensuring the final intervention of a responsible judge or official. Quality controls on data used and regular impact assessments are essential to detect potential biases or deviations. Only with these precautions can AI serve as a valuable auxiliary tool and not a threat to procedural rights. Rather than replacing the judge, AI should free up time for judges and lawyers to focus on what truly matters: substantive legal deliberation, attention to the parties, and the administration of justice with humanity.

## Challenges for Procedural Harmonization in Europe.

The European Union faces the challenge of achieving procedural harmonization in an increasingly digitalized justice environment. Historically, procedural law has largely remained within the sovereignty of each Member State, resulting in significant normative diversity: different procedural codes, timelines, formalities, and levels of legal safeguards. This fragmentation complicates cross-border judicial cooperation and generates disparities in effective legal protection depending on the country of litigation. In times of technological globalization, such diversity appears anachronistic and inefficient (Amunátegui, 2020, pp. 33-49).

However, technological globalization can act as a catalyst for procedural unification. On the one hand, the need to exchange information between judicial systems requires common technical and legal standards. On the other, European citizens expect equivalent levels of access to and delivery of digital justice, regardless of borders. A successful example of harmonization driven by practical needs is the creation of unified European procedural instruments (De la Oliva et al., 2012). In civil and commercial matters, there are already EU regulations establishing uniform procedures for certain cases: the European Small Claims Procedure (Regulation EC 861/2007) provides a simplified common procedure for cross-border claims of low value, and the European Order for Payment Procedure (Regulation EC 1896/2006) allows for unchallenged debts to be claimed throughout the EU using a standard form. Similarly, Regulation (EU) 1215/2012 (recast Brussels I) unified the rules of international jurisdiction and recognition of judgments, making it easier for a decision issued in one Member State to circulate and be enforced in another. These examples demonstrate that convergence in procedural matters is possible when there is political will and economic necessity.

Nevertheless, substantial differences persist in many areas: procedural timelines, notification systems, admissibility of evidence, or even the conceptualization of the judge's role (more inquisitorial in the continental tradition, more adversarial in the common law tradition). Full harmonization is complex, but the EU has launched initiatives to bring positions closer together. In 2020, the ELI/UNIDROIT European Rules of Civil Procedure models were presented—an academic and legal effort to propose common model rules inspired by the best aspects of each system. Although non-binding, these models serve as references for national reforms and future directives or regulations. Similarly, the European Commission has promoted justice digitalization as part of its e-Justice strategy, recognizing that standardizing technological tools will facilitate convergence. A recent step in this direction was the 2023 adoption of a Regulation on the digitalization of cross-border judicial cooperation and access to justice, which will require Member States to accept secure electronic communications (via the e-CODEX platform) between their judicial bodies and parties located in other countries. This includes harmonized electronic forms and shared legal frameworks for accepting video hearings, digital signatures, etc., in cross-border civil, commercial, and criminal proceedings. Though partial, such measures point toward a more interconnected European judicial area.

Specific challenges to European procedural harmonization in the AI era include:

- **Technological and Data Interoperability**: Each country has independently developed its judicial IT systems (case management, digital records, lawyer portals), making integration difficult. The solution lies in adopting common data standards and protocols. In Spain, for example, the recent Royal Decree-Law 6/2023 introduced the principle of "data orientation," requiring all judicial systems to use common, interoperable metadata and data models. At the European level, this should be complemented with shared data schemes and common dictionaries for procedure types, procedural statuses, etc., enabling a digital file to be understood across different national systems.
- **Unification of Digital Evidence Standards**: The admissibility and assessment of electronic evidence vary across jurisdictions. An electronic document with a recognized digital signature has full probative effect in some countries, while in others, a judge may require expert verification of its authenticity. It would be desirable to move toward a common evidentiary statute for digital evidence in Europe, defining authentication standards, chain-of-custody requirements, and evaluation criteria to ensure equivalence between States. At

least in the cross-border context, courts should trust the validity of electronic evidence from another Member State if it meets certain European standards (principle of mutual recognition of digital evidence).

- **Training and Harmonized Mindsets**: Changing laws alone is insufficient; legal professionals from different countries must share a common philosophy regarding the use of AI and technology in legal proceedings. The European Judicial Training Network (EJTN) and programs such as judicial exchanges can foster this common culture. For example, by training judges throughout the EU in new AI-based jurisprudential analysis tools or in conducting video hearings while safeguarding the right to defence.

In essence, European procedural harmonization in the digital era is not merely an integrative ideal but a practical need (Ferreiro & Rodríguez, 2010). A space of freedom, security, and justice with free movement of persons and services requires European citizens to perceive continuity in the administration of justice, even in relation to cross borders cases. If each country develops its own disconnected AI solutions or digital court platforms, the potential of technological globalization will be lost. Conversely, coordination can yield a more efficient and accessible justice system for all in the EU. Importantly, harmonization must not lead to diminished safeguards: common standards should be inspired by the highest levels of rights protection (e.g., adherence to due process according to the European Convention on Human Rights). Political and legal obstacles to unifying procedures still exist, but digital transformation acts as a catalyst to overcome them in pursuit of a truly European justice system for the 21st century.

## Comparison Between European and North American Procedural Systems Regarding AI.

From a comparative perspective, the responses of Europe and North America (particularly the United States) to the appearance of AI in justice exhibit marked differences rooted in their distinct legal traditions. Continental European procedural law is fundamentally based on codified norms (a legacy of Roman law and the Napoleonic system), while the North American model heavily relies on judicial precedent, characteristic of the common law. This difference influences not only the way legal arguments are framed and decisions made but also the scope for incorporating technological innovations into the legal process.

In continental Europe, judges are bound by written law and often act ex officio in directing proceedings (especially in inquisitorial systems), with an emphasis on ensuring formalities and procedural stages are respected. This tends to produce a more cautious and rights-based approach to AI: any change must align with existing legislation or be introduced through legal reform, and always under the umbrella of procedural principles (many of which are constitutionally enshrined or derived from the European Convention on Human Rights). For instance, if one were to implement an AI system to propose standard rulings in repetitive cases, it would be necessary to ensure it does not violate the requirement to provide reasons for judgments or the right to a legally predetermined judge. European countries typically stress that AI must never replace the judicial function, serving only as a support tool. Indeed, the Council of Europe adopted the European Ethical Charter on the Use of AI in Judicial Systems in 2018, whose core principles include respect for fundamental rights, non-discrimination, system quality and safety, transparency and user control, and human oversight. This ethical charter reflects the European stance: leveraging AI to improve consistency and efficiency (e.g., identifying jurisprudential lines to support coherent reasoning), but always with strong guarantees of transparency, explainability, and human review.

In contrast, the U.S. judicial process is more flexible and decentralized. Judges (state and federal) have significant leeway to adopt innovative practices in their courts, provided they do not contradict fundamental procedural rules (Citron, 2008, pp. 1249-1313). Moreover, the common law system values efficiency and active case management by judges, facilitating earlier adoption of technological tools. For example, in the area of electronic evidence, U.S. courts developed protocols for e-discovery over a decade ago using predictive research software—a concept not mirrored in continental Europe due to different evidentiary procedures. Additionally, pilot programs in AI have been implemented in areas such as prison administration (risk assessment for parole) or juvenile courts (to recommend rehabilitation programs). The landmark case State v. Loomis in Wisconsin (2016) highlighted the dilemmas of using an algorithm (COMPAS) to assess a defendant's risk: the court upheld its use with certain caveats, acknowledging it as an additional factor for sentencing (Martínez, 2018, pp. 485-502). This pragmatism contrasts with European caution, where it would be difficult to accept an algorithmic "score" influencing a criminal sentence without breaching the right to a fair trial.

Another difference lies in legal culture: in the U.S., with lay juries in many instances, tools that help filter cases or summarize information are more highly valued. In continental Europe, with no juries in civil trials and decisions made by professional jurists, procedural thoroughness is prioritized. Paradoxically, this can lead U.S. judges to trust technology more to handle large caseloads (bulky dockets), whereas European judges typically manage fewer cases but with more extensive written records.

However, there are also points of convergence: both systems recognize the utility of AI in non-decisional tasks (logistics, processing, legal analysis). In both the U.S. and Europe, there is a growing consensus that fully automated decisions are problematic. The difference lies in degree: the U.S. allows market practices and private initiatives to evolve (e.g., legaltech companies testing predictive analytics systems), relying on litigation to correct course (strategic litigation or class actions can halt abusive AI practices, as seen in algorithmic discrimination cases in hiring). Europe, in contrast, prefers ex ante regulation. The EU, as we know, recently enacted the first AI rule in the whole world. This Artificial Intelligence Act was published on the $13^{th}$ of March of 2024 and it came into effect the $1^{st}$ of August of 2024. This regulation that categorizes AI applications by risk level. AI systems intended for judicial use are deemed high-risk, needing to comply with strict requirements for transparency, traceability, human oversight, and conformity assessments before deployment. This regulatory strategy contrasts with the absence of a federal AI law in the U.S., where only non-binding guidelines and sector-specific regulations exist.

Some of the key measures established by the AI Act can be summed up into the next four bullet points:

- Ban of unacceptable risk. For example, social scoring systems or manipulative AI.
- Detailed regulation of high-risk AI systems.
- Development of lighter transparency obligations for limited risk AI systems. The creators have to ensure that users know that they are interacting with AI.
- The minimal risk AI systems are not regulated. These are the most common systems, although it recently changed with the appearance of generative AI.

Regarding procedural safeguards, Europe has a robust framework (ECHR, European Court of Human Rights, EU Charter) that acts as a hard limit on any experiment that might compromise judicial impartiality or the right to defence. In North America, constitutional protections and judicial scrutiny also guard rights, but a concrete harm must typically be demonstrated before claims can proceed (e.g., showing in a specific case that lack of algorithmic transparency violated the Due Process Clause). Europe, in contrast, aims to prevent reaching that point through proactive regulation.

In summary, the U.S. model shows greater openness to innovation in AI legal practice, supported by the flexibility of common law and private sector initiatives, while the European model offers a more regulated and rights-focused framework where innovations are introduced more slowly but with stronger institutional control. Nonetheless, both systems appear to be converging on core principles: recognizing AI's usefulness for efficiency while agreeing that final decisions must be human and that checks and balances are necessary to prevent abuses. As scholars have noted, the European Convention on Human Rights should remain the ethical and legal boundary for any automation in Europe, just as constitutional rights in the U.S.

limit excessive delegation to algorithms. Ultimately, these are different legal paths, but they share a common challenge: integrating AI while respecting the essence of the judicial function.

## Digital Evidence: Admissibility, Chain of Custody, Blockchain, and Regulatory Proposals.

The digital transformation of society is reflected in the types of evidence presented in court. It is now common in litigation to submit as evidence emails, WhatsApp messages, CCTV footage, GPS geolocation records, office documents, electronic databases, and even data extracted from AI systems (e.g., records of decisions made by an algorithm). This reality raises significant procedural questions regarding the admissibility, authenticity, and validity of such evidence, as well as how to preserve it without compromising its integrity (chain of custody).

One initial challenge is adapting traditional evidentiary rules to these new formats. In systems like Spain's, there was a classic distinction between public documents, private documents, witness testimony, expert evidence, etc. Where does a text message or email fit? Spain's Civil Procedure Act (Ley 1/2000 de Enjuiciamiento Civil) and Criminal Procedure Act (Ley de Enjuiciamiento Criminal) have had to evolve to include concepts such as "electronic document" and admit, for example, that electronic communications may have the same evidentiary value as traditional documents—provided they meet certain authenticity requirements. In fact, the EU's eIDAS Regulation (Regulation 910/2014) ensures that a qualified electronic signature grants a digital document a presumption of integrity and authorship equivalent to a handwritten signature. Thus, a digitally signed email or a certified PDF is, in principle, fully admissible as evidence in court. However, many electronic documents lack such signatures. Courts then assess their reliability on a case-by-case basis. Spanish jurisprudence has established that screenshots of WhatsApp or other messages are admissible if their content and origin can be verified, but their weight is left to judicial discretion, which may require expert corroboration if authenticity is challenged. Here, the chain of custody plays a key role: if a party submits a chat conversation as evidence, they must demonstrate that the data was not manipulated—ideally with experts certifying the extraction and preservation of the messages from the original device or server. Without proper protocols, a simple screenshot could be disputed (as it could be easily edited).

The chain of custody in digital evidence is particularly delicate because, unlike a physical object, a digital file can be easily modified without any visible trace (Delgado, 2017, pp. 11-17). Therefore, from the moment evidence is extracted (e.g., a seized hard drive, a mobile phone, or server logs) until it is presented in court, measures must be taken to preserve its integrity: bit-by-bit copies, hash fingerprints, documented logs of every person who accesses the data, etc. In criminal matters, these precautions are standardized by forensic police units; in civil cases, parties sometimes submit emails or messages with less formality, which can lead to disputes over possible tampering. Spanish courts have increasingly held that failure to maintain the chain of custody can diminish or invalidate the evidentiary value of digital material—especially when manipulation is alleged.

Another issue is the illegality of how the evidence was obtained. Can digital evidence obtained without consent (e.g., hacking someone's email account or secretly recording third-party conversations) be admitted? Here, similar principles apply as for traditional evidence (e.g., the "fruit of the poisonous tree" doctrine), but technology makes invasions of privacy more accessible. Spanish jurisprudence has invalidated electronic evidence obtained by infringing fundamental rights (e.g., workplace emails accessed without respecting an employee's privacy, as in STC 241/2012). The French Cour de Cassation has traditionally been stricter, excluding emails accessed surreptitiously from another's inbox to a greater extent than Spanish courts—highlighting persistent differences in legal standards (France prioritizes privacy; Spain may admit the evidence if deemed essential to truth-finding). Harmonization of European standards would be desirable to prevent "forum shopping" in search of jurisdictions with more lenient or stricter digital evidence rules.

In light of these challenges, a regulatory update is necessary to systematically incorporate new types of evidence. Spain, for instance, recently enacted the Digital Efficiency in Justice Act, which among other things amends the Civil Procedure Act to better regulate the submission and handling of digital evidence. Some concrete proposals discussed in legal scholarship and draft legislation include:

- **Explicit regulation of digital evidence in the Civil Procedure Act**: introducing a specific chapter on electronic documents, digital communication, and computer data as means of evidence, defining their scope, value, and method of incorporation into proceedings. This would bring legal certainty and uniformity to practice (Delgado, 2017, pp. 1-14).
- **Preservation protocols**: requiring that when a party wishes to submit digital media (audio, video, etc.), it must be accompanied by an expert certification describing how the copy was obtained and confirming its match with the original using a hash or similar method. This would alert the opposing party that rebutting the evidence would require counter-expert analysis.
- **Accreditation of forensic tools**: potentially creating a registry of approved tools (forensic software, mobile extraction programs) whose results would carry a presumption of reliability—much like how certified breathalyzers are treated in traffic cases. This would standardize digital forensic evidence.

- **Use of blockchain technology for evidence custody**: Blockchain offers a way to record information immutably with distributed time stamps. It is being explored as a method for registering digital evidence to guarantee its integrity and date. Courts in several countries already accept blockchain to prove the prior existence of a publication or transaction. In China, Internet courts accept blockchain entries as evidence of publication dates or transactions. In France, a 2019 report by the Court of Cassation's auditor concluded that blockchain could be accepted by judges to prove the existence and content of a creation on a specific date. Spain had its first Supreme Court decision in 2019 (STS 326/2019, June 20 – EDJ 2019/633126 –) involving blockchain evidence in a bitcoin fraud case; the Court did not question the validity of the evidence, although it resolved the matter on other grounds. These precedents signal future potential. However, challenges remain: blockchain can confirm a hash's immutability but does not reflect the content of the underlying data. Thus, expert interpretation is still required to translate that hash into an actual file and certify its content. Public blockchains also raise the issue of pseudo-anonymity: transactions are linked to encrypted keys, not personal identities, complicating attribution unless additional identification steps are taken. Therefore, while blockchain may serve as a complementary tool (e.g., for certifying service of process or timestamping digital evidence), its implementation must be accompanied by legal standards addressing these challenges. Legal scholars particularly highlight two concerns: difficulty linking real identities to blockchain entries, and the need to accurately translate encoded data (hashes) back into readable content—ensuring that no error undermines the evidence's authenticity.

**In conclusion**, digital evidence requires a rethinking of classical evidentiary rules. Principles such as immediacy and adversarial process take new forms (e.g., assessing witness credibility via videoconference or enabling experts to debate the validity of electronic records). Legal systems must evolve swiftly to provide clarity for both judges and litigants on how to submit, preserve, and evaluate technological evidence (López Martinez, 2022, pp. 555-566). In Spain and across Europe, steps are being taken—both judicial and legislative—to integrate these methods. A clear framework on the admissibility and probative value of digital evidence, with guarantees of authenticity and integrity, will not only prevent nullities and fruitless disputes but will also reinforce trust that procedural modernization does not come at the cost of justice. As scholars have pointed out, there is an urgent need for a legal statute on digital evidence covering everything from collection to assessment in judgments, ensuring probative effectiveness without infringing on rights.

## Automated Decisions, Procedural Safeguards, and Fundamental Principles

The possibility of using AI to render automated decisions in judicial proceedings strikes at the core of fundamental principles in procedural law. "Automated decision" may refer either to a judicial ruling issued directly by a machine without human intervention, or to intermediate procedural decisions (e.g., accepting a claim, granting an extension) made by information systems. In any case, the notion raises immediate concerns regarding its compatibility with pillars such as the right to a natural judge, judicial independence and impartiality, and the reasoning of judgments.

The principle of the natural judge, enshrined in constitutions and instruments such as Article 6 of the ECHR (the right to an independent tribunal established by law), implies that every person has the right to be judged by a legitimate, lawfully established judge, and not by ad hoc or inappropriate authorities. Could a "robot-judge" fit into this principle? There are clear objections: software is not "established by law" as a judicial authority, nor can it guarantee impartiality in the human sense (it has no consciousness or values, although it may reproduce the biases of its programmers). Therefore, no European legal system provides for the replacement of judges with AI. Rather, the use of automation is contemplated for repetitive or mechanical procedural tasks. Spain—pioneering in codifying such matters—recently regulated which procedural acts may be automated and under what safeguards. Article 56 of Royal Decree-Law 6/2023 defines automated acts as those "produced by an adequately programmed information system without the need for human intervention in each specific case," and authorizes information systems to carry out simple procedural or administrative acts that require no legal interpretation. Examples include paginating court files, archiving cases due to party inaction, generating certified copies, or verifying legal representation. These are regulated, routine acts. The law also allows for proactive acts (Art. 56.3), where the system may, based on certain data, initiate related proceedings (e.g., automatically launching execution after a final conviction). Crucially, the law mandates strict safeguards: automated acts must be identifiable, traceable, and reversible. This means the system must mark which acts were automated, allow for review of their rationale, and be subject to correction if needed. Moreover, the same acts must remain available via manual means, ensuring that automation remains a convenience—not an obligation

Another newly codified concept is that of assisted actions (Art. 57, RDL 6/2023), referring to instances where an AI system generates a draft resolution or complex document based on data to assist the judge or legal official. The law is clear: such drafts shall never constitute judicial rulings without validation from the competent authority. The system generates text only at the user's request, and the user remains free to modify it. The final resolution must be signed and approved by the judge, who remains responsible. Thus, automatic issuance of rulings is prohibited—human intervention is always required. These Spanish regulations, which likely prefigure standards in other jurisdictions, align with the broader principle of human oversight for high-impact automated decisions, also present in the EU AI Regulation.

Even with such precautions, issues of legitimacy and constitutionality arise. Could a ruling be challenged on the basis that it stemmed from an automated procedure that infringed the right to defence or effective judicial protection? For instance, if an algorithm denied evidence as untimely but miscalculated the deadline, the affected party could claim a denial of justice. Hence the importance of traceability and reversibility: one must be able to review the algorithm, identify errors, and rectify them retroactively. This intersects with another core principle: reasoning. Every judicial decision must be reasoned, especially on the merits. A computer-generated decision lacks comprehensible motivation unless the algorithm is explained. Thus, the legal requirement to justify automated actions entails documenting the applied rule. In practice, this means that the system should append to each automated act a justification or normative reference (e.g., "order of dismissal due to withdrawal, Art. 496 in relation with 404 LEC, after 20 days of inactivity. Automatically generated."). Such explanations may suffice for simple acts, but not for complex ones, which will still require human input.

Another classic safeguard is equality of arms and adversarial proceedings. If one party has privileged access to AI tools (e.g., predictive software for litigation strategy) and the other does not, is there an imbalance? Judges must ensure both parties can defend themselves equally. This might imply that relevant AI tools in a case should be shared or made available to all litigants. A "right to explanation" of automated decisions has also been proposed: if a court uses an algorithmic system, parties should be entitled to know its logic and challenge it if biased or incorrect. In fact, Article 12 of RDL 6/2023 provides that the General Access Point to the Judiciary will disclose information about AI systems used in justice and their criteria, as part of digital defence guarantees. This transparency will help lawyers understand, for example, what parameters an algorithm uses to classify cases and contest misclassification.

Internationally, the ECHR and Strasbourg case law also set boundaries: a judgment issued without human intervention would likely violate the right to a fair trial. Moreover, the EU Charter of Fundamental Rights (Art. 47) guarantees effective judicial protection before an independent judge, reinforcing the notion that judges must be human beings. Even data protection law (GDPR, Art. 22) grants individuals the right not to be subjected to fully automated decisions producing legal effects, a right transferable to the procedural domain.

In sum, automated decisions in justice are acceptable only for non-substantive matters and with strong safeguards. No democratic jurisdiction envisions a full "robot judge," and automation aims to support—not replace—judicial functions. Traditional procedural safeguards—lawful judge, independence, adversarial proceedings, reasoning, publicity, right to appeal—must remain intact (Borges, 2020, pp. 54-71). AI must be used under effective human control, respecting algorithmic transparency. Algorithms in court must be obedient tools in service of justice, not black boxes determining legal outcomes. Ultimately, there is broad consensus that the guarantee-based nature of procedural law must remain untouched in an automated, global environment: while technology can enhance management, due process and human dignity remain inviolable limits.

## The Role of Judges and Legal Professionals in a Digital Environment

The digital transformation of judicial proceedings inevitably affects the role of judges and other legal actors (magistrates, prosecutors, court clerks, lawyers, and legal agents). Their functions, skills, and responsibilities are undergoing adjustments to adapt to an environment where traditional procedures coexist with advanced technological tools (Barona, 2019, pp. 1-17).

First, the modern judge is not only a legal adjudicator but also a manager of justice-related technology. They must understand and supervise the digital tools that support their work, ensuring their use does not infringe rights (. For instance, if a court employs software that prioritizes cases, the presiding judge must ensure that prioritization does not unfairly affect litigants—possibly by setting a complementary criteria or correcting anomalies. In essence, the judge becomes a "guardian of safeguards in the digital era."

Furthermore, with AI tools generating draft rulings or reports, judges are now required to develop critical review skills. It is no longer enough to write a judgment—they must also scrutinize AI-generated drafts for errors, omissions, or bias. This demands both legal knowledge (to verify correct citation of precedents) and awareness of AI limitations (e.g., generalizations or oversight of key factual details). The risk is automation bias: judges may trust AI outputs blindly, assuming objectivity. Maintaining critical judgment and subjecting AI to human scrutiny is now integral to the judicial role. As Spanish legislation stresses, the judge remains responsible for decisions, even when supported by AI. The AI may offer advice, but ultimate accountability lies with the human judge.

The procedural leadership role is also evolving. In telematic hearings and digital files, judges need virtual communication skills—for example, moderating video hearings to ensure all parties speak freely without technical interference. They must also safeguard case data cybersecurity—a new area of concern, including prevention of data leaks or hacks. Some jurisdictions are creating "digital judges" or "technology liaison magistrates" responsible for managing these aspects.

Legal professionals (lawyers, legal agents, experts) are also adapting. Lawyers now file documents electronically, attend virtual hearings, and exchange digital evidence. Thus, they must possess added technical competence. A proficient lawyer should know, for instance, how to extract metadata from a digital photo to prove its date, or how to challenge the reliability of opposing electronic evidence (Camps et al., 2019). Lawyers are increasingly using AI to assist their work: legal assistants suggesting case law, tools predicting litigation outcomes, or automated contract drafting. These boost efficiency but introduce new ethical duties (Solar, 2021, pp. 123-161). For instance, a lawyer using generative AI (like ChatGPT) must verify the output's accuracy. Documented cases exist of AI "hallucinations" inventing citations or facts. In the U.S., lawyers faced disciplinary action after submitting a brief containing fictitious case law generated by ChatGPT. The lesson: lawyers cannot delegate judgment to AI—they must use it critically. Ethical codes are beginning to include references to responsible tech use. (Katsh & Rabinovich, 2017).

Another aspect is the digitalized client relationship. Many clients consult the internet before seeing a lawyer or prefer video consultations. Lawyers must adapt to offering virtual advice while maintaining trust and confidentiality. They may need to explain why a "Google-found" answer is inapplicable to a specific case, countering overreliance on unspecialized sources.

Court clerks and judicial staff are also affected (Susskind, 2019, pp. 141-142). As procedures automate, their work shifts towards oversight. For example, if the system issues an automated procedural order, the clerk must verify it through random checks. Their role becomes more technical: managing platforms, resolving IT issues, alongside traditional legal tasks. Therefore, digital-savvy clerks are in demand.

Experts are evolving too: new types of expert evidence arise (IT, algorithms, digital security), and traditional experts (doctors, engineers) must adapt to digital formats—submitting reports with data annexes, software simulations, etc. (Martínez et al., 2021)

A cross-cutting issue in this environment is professional ethics. Should a judge disclose AI assistance in drafting a ruling? Is it relevant if the judge ultimately signs and assumes the text? Can a lawyer delegate routine client queries to AI? These remain open questions. Some jurisdictions advocate transparency. In some states of the U.S., there are discussions on requiring disclosure if a brief includes AI-generated text, allowing the judge to assess its reliability. The CEPEJ in Europe emphasizes that users—including judges—must control and understand the technology. Hence, professionals are expected to be both technologically literate and ethically aware: a judge should not cite "AI said so" as reasoning; a lawyer should not base a claim solely on algorithmic opinion.

In summary, the roles of judges and legal professionals are being redefined in tandem with technology. Neither judges as passive spectators of machines, nor lawyers as mere transmitters of digital filings, suffice. Both must adopt active roles: judges as conductors of a technologized process, ensuring the digital symphony adheres to the score of rights; lawyers as informed strategists, using modern tools while upholding the human value of persuasive reasoning and client empathy. The figure of the tech-savvy humanist jurist is emerging—capable of understanding algorithms and reflecting on justice. Ultimately, the rise of AI and technology does not diminish the importance of the human factor—it recalibrates it. Judgment, prudence, and responsibility remain irreplaceable (Corvalán, 2018, pp. 295-316). As noted, we are moving towards a hybrid model in which AI assists but humans retain control, and legal professionals embrace innovation while safeguarding procedural rights. Adaptation is inevitable—but must uphold the primacy of legal values over mere technological efficiency.

## Training and Digital Competencies of Legal Professionals

The rapid technological evolution in the administration of justice has highlighted the pressing need for digital training and skills development among all legal professionals. Judges, prosecutors, court clerks, civil servants, and lawyers must acquire new competencies to competently use digital tools and understand the fundamentals of AI as applied to the law (Martin, 2019, pp. 815-827). Without this training, there is a risk that the digital divide will extend into the judicial system, with outdated professionals unable to manage electronic files or scrutinize digital expert reports (Susskind, 2017, pp. 10-15)

For judges and magistrates, continued education has traditionally focused on substantive legal matters and classic skills. Today, however, Judicial Councils and Judicial Schools across Europe are incorporating training modules in new technologies. For example, Spain's Judicial School has introduced courses on digital case files, the management of remote hearings, and introductory content on AI and big data in judicial work. At the European level, the Commission and the Council of Europe have launched large-scale training initiatives: in 2022, UNESCO, in collaboration with judicial training centres in the U.S., Brazil, Kenya, and others, launched a massive open online course (MOOC) on AI and the Rule of Law, specifically aimed at legal operators worldwide. Over 4,200 judges, prosecutors, and court staff from 139 countries enrolled, receiving multilingual training on technical aspects of AI, and its legal and ethical implications. This global dialogue underscored the importance of building capacity from the outset—training judges before technology overwhelms them. As Judge Benes Aldana noted at that forum, "it is essential for the judiciary to develop capacity from the beginning to address these rapidly evolving technologies." This means not only learning how to use an application but also cultivating an open mindset toward innovation, while remaining alert to risks, so that judges can be informed participants in the adoption of AI.

Lawyers and legal representatives also require upskilling. Bar associations have started offering courses in LegalTech, electronic evidence, and AI ethics. In Spain, the General Council of the Legal Profession has incorporated into mandatory ethics training a module on "digital competencies for lawyers" and the responsible use of data analysis tools in professional practice. A digitally competent lawyer, for example, will know how to use platforms such as LexNET or e-Justice for submitting documents (thus avoiding formal errors), will better advise clients on privacy risks when submitting certain electronic documents, and may even understand a technical report on algorithms well enough to challenge it if it infringes on rights (e.g., in a labor dispute involving dismissal by an HR algorithm, the lawyer must know how to argue issues of opacity or bias). In the U.S., some states are considering making "technological competence" part of the ABA Model Rule 1.1 on professional competence, mandating lawyers to keep up to date with technologies that affect legal practice.

Court administrative staff (managers, clerks) also require intensive training when new systems are introduced (e.g., when the Minerva or @lex case management systems were implemented in Spain, specific training programs were provided). Resistance to change often stems more from unfamiliarity than outright rejection; hence, proper training reduces fear and enhances adoption.

One area deserving particular emphasis is ethical and legal training on AI (. Knowing how to use technology is not enough—its implications must be understood. Many training programs now include modules on algorithmic bias, data protection, cybersecurity, and professional responsibility in digital environments. The goal is to foster what we might call a "responsible AI culture" in justice. The UN's Global Judicial Integrity Network (UNODC) is developing ethical guidelines for judges on AI use, stressing transparency and algorithmic fairness.

Good practice sharing among legal professionals is also encouraged. Judges who have led technology pilot projects often share their experiences in conferences or seminars, teaching colleagues how to benefit from tools without falling into traps. For instance, Estonia and Finland—leaders in digital justice—have collaborated with other European countries to demonstrate how they implemented online services while maintaining safeguards.

In both undergraduate and postgraduate legal education, changes are also evident. Many law schools have introduced courses on Law and Technology or Legal Tech Clinics, so that future lawyers and judges graduate with basic knowledge of AI, blockchain, data protection, etc. This is critical, as the next generation of legal professionals will begin their careers immersed in electronic files—perhaps with AI assistants available from day one.

Finally, beyond formal training, a continuous learning mindset is essential. Technology will keep advancing, so 21st-century legal professionals must commit to constant updates. Judicial institutions must support this by providing resources: libraries with legal-tech materials, access to online courses, webinars, etc. The EU's Digital Justice Strategy 2024–2028 has explicitly stated its commitment to financially and logistically support digital training for judges and court staff across all member states, recognizing it as a pillar for achieving uniform digital transformation.

In conclusion, training digital jurists is not optional—it is indispensable. Investment in training translates into a more efficient, less error-prone system. A well-trained judge will know how to use AI to quickly resolve straightforward cases, easing court backlogs, but also when to stop its use if it threatens fundamental rights. A lawyer with technological skills will better defend their client's interests in matters involving electronic evidence or digital proceedings (Barona, 2021, pp.14-45). Ultimately, training ensures that technology serves justice, not the other way around, empowering legal professionals to fulfil their roles in this new environment without losing sight of the core mission: safeguarding citizens' rights. As UNESCO emphasized, this learning path is long but must begin now, for only through knowledge and training can the rule of law be upheld in the age of AI.

## Regulatory and Ethical Proposals for the Responsible Use of AI in Judicial Proceedings

Given the challenges described, it is crucial to articulate regulatory and ethical proposals that channel the use of artificial intelligence in judicial proceedings in a manner compatible with the values of the rule of law. Below are some of the main legal and deontological measures proposed in scholarly literature and recent legislative initiatives to ensure a responsible, transparent, and fair use of AI in the administration of justice.

a) Specific Regulatory Framework (AI Law): At the supranational level, the European Union has taken a decisive step with the approval of the Artificial Intelligence Act (AI Act). This regulation, the first of its kind globally, establishes harmonized rules on the development and use of AI systems in the EU. The approach is risk-based: high-risk AI systems (likely including those used in justice due to their impact on fundamental rights) will be subject to strict requirements regarding data quality, traceability, technical documentation, human oversight, and transparency obligations toward users. It is anticipated that systems such as predictive policing or judicial decision-making will fall under this category, with some particularly sensitive uses potentially being outright prohibited (e.g., systems replacing judges or juries). The AI

Act is directly applicable in member states, ensuring a unified regulatory baseline. Spain, for its part, has already established the State Agency for the Supervision of AI (AESIA), which, in coordination with the EU framework, oversees AI systems deployed nationally, including those used in the justice sector. The existence of a specialized regulatory body will enable the issuance of guidelines, algorithm audits, and complaint management, providing external and independent oversight.

b) Domestic Legal Reforms: Beyond the European regulation, each country must revise its procedural and organizational legislation to adapt to the AI era (Lazcoz, 2020, pp. 26-41). In Spain, as seen earlier, Royal Decree-Law 6/2023 incorporated pioneering provisions (data-oriented principles, regulation of automated and assisted actions with safeguards). These reforms must be consolidated into permanent legislation (e.g., reforms to the Organic Law of the Judiciary, Civil Procedure Law) and possibly expanded. Proposals include adding a provision to the Organic Law of the Judiciary stating that "no judicial decision shall be based solely on the result of automated data processing, without proper validation and reasoning by the judicial authority," legally barring fully algorithmic rulings. Another proposal is to establish a legal right for parties to obtain an explanation for any AI-supported decision and to challenge it if the explanation is unsatisfactory. Procedural norms should also allow for the request of "reports on AI system functioning" during evidence phases if a party suspects undue influence (similar to expert examinations of measuring devices in trials). Another initiative suggests mandating that all algorithms used in the justice system be transparent and auditable, possibly through a public registry of algorithmic criteria (respecting trade secrets but ensuring maximum transparency). In Spain's public administration context, Article 12 of Law 40/2015, post-reform, requires transparency for algorithms used in automated administrative actions, a principle extended to the judiciary via Royal Decree-Law 6/2023.

c) Ethical Protocols and Best Practice Guidelines: Beyond positive law, ethical frameworks are essential. The European Ethical Charter on the Use of AI in Judicial Systems (CEPEJ, 2018) outlines five guiding principles: (1) Respect for fundamental rights, ensuring compatibility with human rights; (2) Non-discrimination, avoiding any biased development or use of AI; (3) Quality and security in judicial data processing, using certified sources and reliable models; (4) Transparency, impartiality, and fairness, with understandable methods and the possibility of external audits; (5) User control, meaning final decisions must remain under the control of informed human operators. These principles should be adopted and specified by each national judiciary. In Spain, the General Council of the Judiciary could issue an Ethical Code for AI implementation in courts, stating, for example, that judges must understand algorithmic limits, that their legal judgment prevails, and that deliberation secrecy and independence must be maintained even with AI assistance. Likewise, bar associations could incorporate AI use rules into their codes of conduct: e.g., prohibiting submission of AI-generated reports without prior verification or requiring client consent when using tools handling confidential data.

d) Interdisciplinary Participation and Audits: A prominent proposal is to create interdisciplinary working groups (jurists, IT experts, statisticians, ethicists) within the judiciary to assess new AI systems before implementation. This would allow pilot-phase analysis of allocation or jurisprudence analysis algorithms to detect potential negative impacts. Additionally, regular audits of in-use algorithms should be implemented to ensure, for example, that a case prioritization system is not systematically sidelining certain types of cases (which could indicate hidden bias). These audits should be external or include independent experts for objectivity. The idea of an "algorithm ombudsman" has also been proposed—a specific AI technology supervisor in justice to whom parties or citizens could turn if they suspect algorithmic injustice.

e) Ongoing Ethical Education and Awareness: Building on the previous section on training, a proposal is to include mandatory AI ethics modules in all judicial and legal education programs. This ensures new generations adopt an ethical mindset from the outset. Sharing precedents—both positive and negative—is also encouraged: e.g., learning from the case of attorneys sanctioned for using ChatGPT irresponsibly or the outcomes of the COMPAS pilot in criminal justice.

f) Default Guarantees by Design: Extending the idea of ethics by design, it is suggested that all AI systems developed or acquired for justice should have legal and ethical principles embedded from inception. For instance, a chatbot assisting plaintiffs should, by design, ask the necessary questions to avoid violating access to justice (informing about deadlines, legal assistance rights, etc.). An algorithm assessing pretrial detention risk should be deliberately designed to exclude sensitive variables (e.g., race, religion) and incorporate safety margins to avoid extreme recommendations without review. This requires jurists to collaborate with developers from the project's inception (technological compliance).

g) Institutional Resources and Support: These proposals require investment and support. Therefore, legislation should allocate budget for ethical AI implementation and possibly establish a dedicated administrative unit (such as AESIA in Spain or a responsible innovation office within the Ministry of Justice). Without resources, ethical intentions remain aspirational.

h) Jurisprudence and Judicial Oversight: Lastly, it is essential that high courts set doctrine on these matters. For example, the Supreme or Constitutional Court could establish criteria on when AI use violates the right to defence or to an impartial judge. The European Court of Human Rights may also issue landmark rulings in the near future (e.g., a case where someone claims their trial was unfair due to automated decision-making). Such case law would complement the regulatory framework, ensuring a rights-based interpretation of any ambiguity.

In conclusion, regulatory and ethical proposals for responsible AI use in judicial proceedings can be summarized as: regulate, ensure transparency, and control. Regulate to provide certainty (what is allowed, who is responsible, what rights do parties have). Make systems and criteria transparent, ensuring they operate under public and legal scrutiny. And control through human supervision, audits, and professional ethics so that practical AI use never breaches fundamental rights (San Miguel, 2021, pp. 286-303). Ultimately, the goal is to harness AI for justice, ensuring innovation aligns with dignity and human rights. Otherwise, trust in justice could erode. These proposals are not merely aspirational—they are necessary conditions for legitimate and trustworthy digital justice.

## CONCLUSIONS

Procedural law stands at a historic crossroads in the face of technological globalization and the advent of artificial intelligence. The challenges identified throughout this work are numerous and complex, yet they share a common denominator: how to preserve the protective essence of due process in an automated and globalized environment. Rather than shying away from technology, procedural law must embrace it with critical discernment, adapting its structures and norms to enhance judicial protection without moving apart from its foundational principles.

First, technological globalization offers unprecedented opportunities to democratize access to justice and expedite proceedings. However, it is equally essential to ensure that this digital expansion is inclusive and that justice remains personalized and humane. Bridging the digital division and ensuring the reliability of online legal information are key challenges to achieving the ideal of universal access to justice.

Second, AI applied to the judicial process can contribute to more efficient justice but raises unavoidable ethical questions. AI can assist in managing large caseloads, identifying relevant jurisprudence, or eliminating repetitive tasks, but its use must remain subject to human oversight, algorithmic transparency, and the principle of contradiction. Classical procedural guarantees—an impartial judge, reasoned decisions, equality of arms—remain fully valid and function as boundaries to any automation. Comparative experience shows that, although approaches differ, there is consensus that the final decision must rest with a human judge endowed with authority and responsibility.

Third, the fragmentation of procedural rules in Europe needs a reinforced harmonization in the digital age. This means not only unifying certain procedures (as has been done with the European Small Claims Procedure or the European Account Preservation Order) but also ensuring compatibility between judicial IT systems and agreeing on evidentiary standards for electronic evidence. Convergence towards a digitally integrated European judicial area will enhance the effectiveness and coherence of cross-border justice, while ensuring a uniform level of fundamental procedural rights across the EU.

Fourth, digital evidence is here to stay. Legal systems must adopt frameworks that ensure the authenticity, integrity, and admissibility of these new forms of evidence. Modernizing evidentiary rules, training judges and lawyers in technological matters, and cautiously incorporating solutions such as blockchain are essential steps to integrating electronic evidence without undermining safeguards. A judiciary capable of managing digital evidence effectively is one prepared for the realities of the 21st century.

Fifth, automated decisions are only acceptable when balanced by safeguards that uphold fundamental principles. Recent Spanish legal reforms demonstrate that it is possible to integrate automated procedural actions while maintaining controls and reversibility. This should serve as a model: AI as an auxiliary, never a substitute. Due process guarantees serve as both a guiding light and a limit—no innovation can erode them without compromising the system's legitimacy.

Sixth, the role of judges and legal professionals is being redefined, but far from diminishing their relevance, this underscores the need for their leadership. Legal professionals must guide the digital transformation of justice, ensuring it remains citizen-focused. Their continuous digital training and ethical commitment to justice's traditional values will be key to a successful transition. A technologically competent and ethically aware judge is the best guarantee of fair proceedings in the AI era.

Finally, the regulatory and ethical proposals outlined show that we are not starting from scratch: there are existing frameworks and principles upon which to build responsible AI usage in justice. The forthcoming European regulation, ethical charters, and professional codes provide a foundation for action. However, they must be realized in practice—through audited algorithms, meaningful transparency, and daily application in courts and law firms. Only then can we achieve a new balance between technological efficiency and constitutional safeguards, where the human-machine partnership harnesses the best of both in service of a more accessible, swift, and predictable justice—one that remains rigorous, protective, and humane.

In conclusion, the challenges posed by technological globalization and artificial intelligence to procedural law are formidable but not insurmountable. We now have the opportunity to reimagine the judicial process using contemporary tools while upholding the enduring values that legitimize it. Collaboration among jurists, technologists, and legislators will be essential to navigate this change without falling into unreflective experimentation or paralyzing inertia. The ultimate goal must always be to strengthen the rule of law: to use technology in pursuit of a fairer justice system—bringing judicial protection closer to citizens, enhancing efficiency without sacrificing justice. In this way, the safeguards forged over centuries can be projected into the architecture of Justice 4.0, for the benefit of all.

*Table 1. Summary Table – Impact of the Digital Revolution on Procedural Law*

| Aspect of Procedural Law | Observed Change | Current Challenge | Necessary Transformation |
|---|---|---|---|
| Access to Justice | Expanded access through AI tools; increased use of digital platforms. | Ensuring equal access and legal quality in digital environments. | Recognize digital access as part of the fundamental right to effective judicial protection. |
| Means of Evidence | Digitalization of evidence (emails, WhatsApp, blockchain); proliferation of new formats. | Ensuring authenticity, integrity, and admissibility of electronic evidence in court. | Reform procedural laws to include a clear statute for digital evidence, with custody and evaluation protocols. |
| Procedural Time (Duration) | Pressure to shorten case resolution times; social demand for greater efficiency. | Maintaining the right to a trial without undue delay while preserving guarantees. | Implement AI as a time-management tool (e.g., scheduling, reminders) without substituting judicial decisions. |
| Judicial Decisions and Reasoning | Emergence of predictive systems and legal assistants influencing decisions. | Avoiding algorithmic bias and opacity in judicial reasoning. | Require transparency, traceability, and human oversight of AI-assisted decisions; ensure understandable reasoning. |
| System Interoperability | Growth of transnational digital justice networks; data exchange across jurisdictions. | Harmonizing heterogeneous systems and ensuring secure communication between judicial bodies. | Progress toward a digitally integrated European procedural harmonization (common standards, e-CODEX, interoperable e-files). |
| Legal Professionals' Training | Need for new technological skills and understanding of automated systems. | Updating training of judges, lawyers, and staff without losing the humanistic dimension of law. | Include mandatory digital competencies in the initial and ongoing training of all legal operators. |
| Procedural Safeguards | Tension between automation and principles like contradiction and equality of arms. | Preserving fundamental procedural rights against automation and AI. | Design processes centred on the litigant, with "digital safeguards" that reflect classical principles in tech settings (e.g., right to explanation, option for manual process). |
| Judge-Technology Relationship | Emergence of hybrid models: judges assisted by AI in certain tasks. | Avoiding uncritical delegation to AI that may undermine independence or decision quality. | Develop ethical and regulatory frameworks for responsible legal AI; reinforce judicial responsibility and human review. |

## REFERENCES


Amunátegui Perelló, C. (2020). *Arcana Technicae. El Derecho y la inteligencia artificial.* Tirant lo Blanch.

Barona Vilar, S. (2019). Cuarta revolución industrial (4.0) o ciberindustria en el proceso penal: Revolución digital, inteligencia artificial y el camino hacia la robotización de la justicia. *Revista Jurídica Digital UANDES, 3*(1), 1–17. DOI: 10.24822/rjduandes.0301.1

Barona Vilar, S. (2021). *Algoritmización del derecho y de la justicia. De la Inteligencia Artificial a la Smart Justice.* Tirant lo Blanch.

Borges Blázquez, R. (2020). El sesgo de la máquina en la toma de decisiones en el proceso penal. *Ius et Scientia, 6*(2), 54–71. DOI: 10.12795/IETSCIENTIA.2020.i02.05

Bueno de Mata, F. (2020). Macrodatos, inteligencia artificial y proceso: Luces y sombras. *Revista General de Derecho Procesal,* (51), 1–31.

Camps, C. E. (Dir.). (2019). *Tratado de Derecho Procesal Electrónico.* Buenos Aires: Abeledo Perrot.

Carretero Sánchez, S. C. (2025). *Humanismo tecnológico: justicia predictiva y derechos humanos en el futuro digital.* Colex. DOI: 10.69592/979-13-7011-030-7

Citron, D. K. (2008). Technological due process. *Washington University Law Review, 85*(6), 1249–1313.

Corvalán, J. G. (2018). Inteligencia artificial: retos, desafíos y oportunidades – Prometea: la primera inteligencia artificial de Latinoamérica al servicio de la Justicia. *Revista de Investigações Constitucionais, 5*(1), 295–316. DOI: 10.5380/rinc.v5i1.55334

. Delgado Martín, J. (2017). "La prueba digital: concepto, clases, aportación al proceso y valoración." *Diario La Ley,* Nº 6 (Sección Ciberderecho), 11 de abril de 2017.

Ferreiro Baamonde, X., & Rodríguez García, N. (2010). La armonización del Derecho procesal civil en Europa. *Justicia: Revista de Derecho Procesal, 3–4,* 141–203.

Katsh, E., & Rabinovich-Einy, O. (2017). *Digital Justice: Technology and the Internet of Disputes.* Oxford University Press. DOI: 10.1093/acprof:oso/9780190464585.001.0001

Lazcoz Moratinos, G. (2020). Análisis de la propuesta de reglamento sobre los principios éticos para el desarrollo, el despliegue y el uso de la inteligencia artificial, la robótica y las tecnologías conexas. *Ius et Scientia*, *6*(2), 26–41. DOI: 10.12795/IETSCIENTIA.2020.i02.03

López Martínez, R. (2022). *"Riesgos de la aplicación de la Inteligencia Artificial en la Administración de Justicia." Inteligencia Artificial Legal y Administración de Justicia*. Aranzadi.

Martínez Garay, L. (2018). "Peligrosidad, algoritmos y *due process*: El caso *State v. Loomis*." *Revista de Derecho Penal y Criminología*, (20), 485–502.

Martínez García, E., Borges Blázquez, R., & Simó Soler, E. (2021). Inteligencia artificial y perspectiva de género en la justicia penal. *Diario La Ley*, (47), 1–17.

Nieva Fenoll, J. (2018). *Inteligencia artificial y proceso judicial.* Marcial Pons. DOI: 10.2307/jj.26844203

Oliva Santos, A. D. L., Calderón Cuadrado, M. P., Cedeño Hernán, M., & Pardo Iranzo, V. (2012). La armonización del derecho procesal tras el Tratado de Lisboa. La armonización del derecho procesal tras el Tratado de Lisboa.

Remus, D., & Levy, F. (2015). *Can Robots Be Lawyers?* Computers, Lawyers, and the Practice of Law.

San Miguel Caso, C. (2021). La aplicación de la Inteligencia Artificial en el proceso: ¿un nuevo reto para las garantías procesales? *Ius et Scientia*, *7*(1), 286–303. DOI: 10.12795/IETSCIENTIA.2021.i01.15

Solar Cayón, J. I. (2019). *La inteligencia artificial jurídica: El impacto de la innovación tecnológica en la práctica del Derecho y el mercado de servicios jurídicos.* Aranzadi.

Susskind, R. (2017). *Tomorrow's Lawyers: An Introduction to Your Future* (2nd ed.). Oxford University Press.

Susskind, R. (2019). *Online Courts and the Future of Justice.* Oxford University Press. DOI: 10.1093/oso/9780198838364.001.0001

## KEY TERMS AND DEFINITIONS

**Access to Justice:** opportunity of individuals to seek and obtain legal and fair remedies through the Public Administration. It is a fundamental right that appears in article 24 of the Spanish Constitution. The technological globalization will broaden access to justice, providing online tools and information, making this way the legal assistance more affordable and reachable. It will also require measures to ensure that automated assistance is reliable and guided by legal professionals.

**Algorithmic Transparency:** AI systems' principle that enforces these to operate in an explainable and auditable manner. In the same way court decisions require a clear reasoning, algorithms that may be used to assist judicial decisions must be open about how it works and provide understandable justifications. The goal of this principle is to ensure that judges and parties can scrutinize and challenge the output of an AI system, instead of confronting a black box result.

**Artificial Intelligence (AI):** algorithms designed to perform tasks that usually require human intelligence. The most developed example is the Large Language Models, which can communicate through human language and perform complex tasks. In legal proceedings, AI is starting to appear for the completion of tasks like case law analysis, document drafting, case outcome forecast…, offering more efficiency and raising new challenges for transparency, accountability and fairness in the justice system.

**Automated decisions:** decisions or procedural actions in a legal process that are carried out by an AI system. At the moment these are limited to routine administrative tasks, like scheduling hearings or sending notices, to improve its efficiency. Automation is only permitted with strict safeguards: human oversight, transparency in how the system operates, and the ability to override or correct any machine-made error. No jurisdiction allows automated decisions for substantive rulings, so AI systems are meant to assist court operations while a human judge retains the ultimate decision-making authority where rights are at stake.

**Digital Evidence:** any evidence presented in judicial proceedings in an electronic form, such as emails, text messages, digital documents… It introduces new challenges for procedural law, including the need to authenticate that material, ensure a proper chain of custody or determining its admissibility. Legislators have been adapting in order to update the traditional evidentiary rules to handle electronic proof with the same integrity and reliability as paper-based or personal-based evidence.

**Online Dispute Resolution (ODR):** resolution of disputes through digital platforms, like mediation or arbitration. It offers a faster, more convenient and less formal way of settling conflicts across long distances and expanding the access to justice while challenging the need to ensure that outcomes remain fair, transparent and enforceable.

**Predictive Justice:** use of AI and data analysis to predict legal outcomes or trends. Through the exam of past cases and decisions, predictive justice tools can forecast the success of an appeal or identify patterns in rulings, for example. This may help lawyers and judges make informed decisions, but it is important that the outcomes of these systems remain unbiased.

**Procedural Harmonization:** efforts to align and unify court procedures across different jurisdictions, such as members of the European Union, to ensure that cases are handled in a consistent and efficient ways. In the digital age, it involves the development of common standards, like shared electronic filing systems, unified small claim processes or mutual recognition of electronic evidence; so that technology-enabled judicial cooperation works smoothly across borders without undermining fundamental legal safeguards.

**Procedural Law:** branch of law that outlines the rules and processes that courts follow to ensure a fair and effective justice. It is a branch of law specially affected by technological changes, like the digitalization and AI, so its rules will have to ensure the protection of fundamental principles, such as due process or the right to an impartial judge, while adopting the new technological advances.

**Technological globalization:** the spread of digital technology worldwide that connects people and legal systems all over the globe. In a legal context, if refers to the interconnection of judicial processes, which require more agile and unified procedures.

# Chapter 3
# Law and the Criminal Justice System:
## A Framework for the Effective and Equitable Use of Artificial Intelligence

**Angelo Kevin Brown**
https://orcid.org/0000-0001-8167-5090
*Arkansas State University, USA*

## ABSTRACT

*The criminal justice system is being transformed due to artificial intelligence (AI). These technologies have been sold on the promise of a system freed from error, an efficient, objective, and data-driven solution to justice. The rapid deployment of AI, from predictive policing on our streets to risk assessment algorithms in our courtrooms, is creating a new type of discrimination. These systems, trained on datasets immersed in decades of human bias, are not eliminating prejudice but instead are automating it. This chapter examines the mechanics of these tools and tracks them through the justice process, from the street-level policing and investigations to federal surveillance, courtroom sentencing, and the prison and probation systems. This can have a serious impact on societies entering a future where human and civil rights are being impacted by unaccountable code. The chapter ends with a model for reform for new legislation, technical safeguards like mandatory audits and transparency, and a legal commitment to judicial and public oversight to ensure our future serves justice.*

DOI: 10.4018/979-8-3373-4480-5.ch003

## THE PROMISE AND PERIL OF AI

The American criminal justice system has had to deal with centuries of human fallibility and bias. From a police officer's split-second decision on an unknown busy street to a jury's life-altering deliberation, the process has been formed by the biases, both conscious and unconscious, of the people within it. Artificial intelligence arrived promising a positive change to these issues. Automated systems, we have been told, can predict where crime will occur, identify a suspect from a million different faces, calculate an offender's risk of reoffending, and even write the police report in a quick and accurate manner. The promises are very intriguing; the creation of a system that is faster and cheaper, fundamentally fairer, a system guided by the impartiality of data, not the prejudices of human minds.

The intriguing vision of AI is turning out to be an illusion. This chapter argues that these digital tools do not create a more equitable system; instead, they take our historical biases and embed them into a new technological infrastructure of control. They reproduce the prejudices they are supposed to overcome on a large scale and then use the authority of scientific objectivity to gain legitimacy. The result is a new form of discrimination, automated prejudice (Hamilton, 2019). An increasing amount of research, along with numerous verified wrongful arrests and biased sentences, shows that AI is already in direct conflict with core principles of American law, including the right to a fair trial, the promise of equal protection, and protection from unreasonable government intrusion. By learning from a flawed version of history and hiding their logic in "black boxes," (Pacholska, 2024) these programs threaten the most basic right to confront one's accuser within the justice system (Palmiotto, 2020).

To understand this issue, it is important to trace the use of AI throughout the entire justice system. It begins with a police encounter influenced by AI-based predictive maps and facial recognition. It then moves through criminal investigations where AI acts as the detective and forensic analyst. Next, it involves federal mass surveillance by the Department of Justice (DOJ), including the Federal Bureau of Investigation (FBI) and other agencies within the Department of Homeland Security (DHS), before reaching the courtroom, where an AI-based score can determine a person's future and liberty. The analysis continues inside prison walls and then follows individuals back into their communities, where they are monitored by algorithmic-style probation supervision. It also examines the impact AI has on children in the juvenile justice system. This chapter will then explore these issues globally, looking at how countries including Canada, China, India, and Israel, along with regions across Africa and Latin America, reveal an international crisis involving technology and ethics.

## AUTOMATED INJUSTICE

The civil rights harms caused by artificial intelligence stem from interconnected flaws in technology's data, which lead to algorithmic bias, and issues arising from the "black box" systems. Bias can increase the inequalities of the past. The opacity of these systems can allow new forms of discrimination to remain hidden and difficult to challenge. These problems pose a serious threat to justice, hidden within a sense of technical objectivity that our legal system is currently unprepared to address.

## THE ISSUES OF USING BIASED DATA

In the field of computer science, the saying "garbage in, garbage out" is now significant to the justice system (Tabor, 2024). A program that receives poor data will often produce poor results. When applied to the criminal justice system, the principle remains the same and has real-life consequences. This can help perpetuate the legacy of discriminatory policing and systemic inequality through automation. The outcome that results is an algorithmic judgment treated as an objective fact.

The AI systems powering law enforcement and court decisions absorb bias from enormous datasets of historical records, including arrests, charges, and crime reports. An important issue is that these records are not a neutral reflection of objective reality. The data and AI system are unable to tell us who commits crimes; they tell us who gets accused and charged. They are a distorted lens, reflecting a racist history of who gets policed. Decades of law enforcement strategies like "broken windows" policing purposely focused enforcement on minority and low-income communities, steeping the official data with their arrests for minor offenses. In Canada, another historical practice of "carding" by police in cities like Toronto and Halifax has been critiqued for disproportionately targeting young Black and Indigenous people (Tobias & Joseph, 2020), creating similarly biased datasets that are now used to train Canadian AI systems. Numerous studies for years have confirmed that, in many American cities and towns, Black drivers are stopped and searched significantly more often than White drivers, even when data shows that Black drivers are less likely to be carrying illegal contraband like drugs or weapons. This discriminatory enforcement creates the data from which predictive AI learns (U.S. Department of Justice, 2024).

When an AI system is trained on this data, it learns to associate certain neighborhoods, racial demographics, and even names with a higher likelihood of committing crimes. The system lacks understanding of redlining, poverty, or the history of policing that created these correlations. Unfortunately, AI systems often only see a statistical pattern. In theory, the AI can predict the next crime hotspot, and it will point to the same areas that have historically been targeted. Regarding a person's risk, it might penalize them for being unemployed or having a family member with a criminal record, factors linked to race and systemic disadvantage. This is how historical bias is embedded into future prediction models that learn from problematic data rooted in a biased history.

This process that AI uses creates an illusion of neutrality. A police chief, prosecutor, or judge can hold up an output from an AI system and declare a decision "data-driven," free from human bias. However, they are acting on the output of an AI system that has processed decades of bias. This gives rise to the feedback loop: an algorithm flags a neighborhood, police presence floods the area, many vulnerable members are arrested for minor infractions, and this new data is fed back into the AI system, which proves it was right all along (Bennett Moses & Chan, 2018). The cycle repeats, institutionalizing over-policing as a data-driven strategy. This is a serious concern in many nations, including South Africa, where predictive policing tools trained on historical data risk reinforcing the systemic discrimination of the apartheid era, disproportionately penalizing certain racial and socioeconomic groups.

The COMPAS risk assessment tool offers a well-documented lesson. A 2016 ProPublica investigation into the tool exposed a serious racial disparity (Washington, 2018); the algorithm was about twice as likely to wrongly flag Black defendants as future criminals compared to the White defendants in the database. The tool's inventor, Northpointe, defended its product, claiming it was fair by a statistical measure called "predictive parity." Fairness is not a single, objective mathematical property that can be easily proven by a statistical measure like predictive parity. Different definitions, such as having equal false positive rates versus ensuring a risk score means the same thing for all ethnic groups, are both important in this case. This has become an ethical issue about which group in society will bear the burden of the algorithm's mistakes. It is a choice with constitutional rights at risk, made not by elected officials, but by private software companies without transparency or public oversight (Von Eschenbach, 2021). This issue is not unique to the U.S.; in Canada, the use of similar tools creates a conflict between the rights of individuals and the commercial interests of the developers.

## DUE PROCESS AND THE WITNESS STAND

The problem of biased data is worsened by a culture of secrecy. The most powerful AI systems, especially those using deep learning, act as "black boxes." Their internal processes often involve billions of calculations, making it practically impossible for anyone, even the designers, to fully understand how they work. This creates many challenges related to the constitutional right to due process (Blount, 2024).

In the US, the Constitution under the Sixth Amendment grants every accused person the right to confront the witnesses against them (Rowley, 1988). This forms the basis of a fair trial, including the right to cross-examine, question, and reveal bias. It can be difficult or even impossible to properly cross-examine an algorithm. When a significant piece of evidence comes from an AI program, that right to cross-examination can be lost (Maddox, 2024). A defense attorney cannot challenge the AI system's hidden logic. This is a key legal challenge also identified in the Canadian context, where the nature of risk assessment tools is becoming a significant obstacle to due process.

This is the kind of issue Eric Loomis faced in Wisconsin. A judge sentenced him to six years in prison, citing a high-risk score from the COMPAS algorithm. His lawyers argued this violated his due process rights because they could neither inspect nor challenge the proprietary code used against him. The software's creator claimed its algorithm was a protected trade secret, pitting corporate intellectual property against a person's constitutional right to a fair hearing. The Wisconsin Supreme Court sided with the judges' decision to use the algorithm in sentencing. In the ruling, it was decided that using the risk score was allowed, but judges were warned not to rely on it entirely. The ruling gives legitimacy to a practice that has fundamentally undermined transparency (Freeman, 2016). The U.S. Supreme Court upheld that decision, establishing a precedent that permits algorithmic evidence in our criminal courts.

This issue can affect judges in their role as gatekeepers of evidence. Under legal standards like Daubert and Frye, judges are required to ensure that scientific testimony is reliable and based on accepted scientific methods (Miller et al., 1993). But they are unable to properly apply these standards to a secret algorithm whose methodology is unknown and whose real-world error rates are unverified.

The challenge created by current deepfake evidence further complicates the legal system, as judges and lawyers struggle to verify digital media in the courtroom. This creates a situation where legitimate evidence can be doubted in new ways with an unknown future. The main issues remain that the justice system is starting to accept a level of secrecy, which is a serious challenge to the very idea of an open and fair trial.

## HOW ALGORITHMS IMPACT VULNERABILITY

The logic of AI algorithms can systematically identify and address vulnerabilities. The Supreme Court has repeatedly acknowledged that being a youth is a significant mitigating factor in sentencing, recognizing that young people are less culpable and have a greater capacity for change than adults.

To a predictive algorithm, being young is one of the strongest statistical predictors of future crime. An analysis of the COMPAS tool revealed that a person's age contributed more to their risk score than their criminal history, race, or gender. The algorithm did not consider the potential for redemption but instead saw a high-risk data point. The very factor that might lead a judge to show leniency becomes, in the algorithm's logic, a primary reason for a stricter outcome.

This logic applies to many other factors. A history of mental illness, struggles with substance abuse, long-term unemployment, and housing instability are situations that a justice system should view as important context, treatable issues, and reasons for rehabilitation rather than punishment. An algorithm trained in past data is likely to see these differently. It learns that these factors are statistically linked to higher chances of arrest and re-offense. Therefore, it flags them as risk factors, effectively penalizing people for their poverty, addiction, and illness. This is a major criticism of algorithmic risk assessment tools, which rely heavily on static, unchangeable historical factors, trapping individuals in a past they cannot escape.

These algorithms are not designed to evaluate moral responsibility or human potential for growth. They are simply built to calculate statistical likelihood based on past patterns. The result is a system that is fundamentally different from a rehabilitative justice mode (Rodrigues & Fidalgo, 2024). It focuses on predicting future outcomes, where a person's life circumstances are no longer considered context for their actions but are just data points estimating their threat to society. When these calculations are hidden within a black box system, a judge may never even realize that the "high-risk" label assigned to a defendant is based on factors like being young, poor, or sick. The process shifts from an individualized sentencing approach based on the specific person before the court to one based on group-based analytical reasoning, judging individuals on the average behavior of others with similar traits.

## INVESTIGATION TO INCARCERATION

The serious dangers of bias from AI-based systems become real as these tools are implemented throughout the American justice system. To understand their impact, each step needs to be evaluated, and it shows that unaccountable and discriminatory algorithms strain constitutional protections.

## PREDICTIVE POLICING AND FACIAL RECOGNITION

For many Americans, the justice system begins with a police encounter on the street. Recently, the officer's decision, where to drive, who to stop, who to suspect, is increasingly guided by an algorithmic system, a recommendation from a system that may not be considering constitutional law.

Modern predictive policing software promises to prevent crime before it happens by sending officers to "hot spots" identified from crime data. Trained on decades of biased arrest records, the software simply sends police back to the same Black, Brown, and low-income neighborhoods they have always patrolled (U.S. Department of Justice, 2024). This creates an algorithmic discriminatory feedback loop, leading to more police making more arrests for minor offenses, which may falsely "prove" the neighborhood is a hot spot and justify more police presence. Innocent residents can be caught in a cycle of surveillance, subject to more stops and searches simply because of their address. This is a serious concern for Fourth Amendment protections, which require individualized suspicion to justify a police stop (Weiss, 2025). Predictive policing replaces that standard with a digitally enforced stereotype, where a person's location becomes a proxy for suspicion, reducing a core safeguard against subjective state power (Bennett Moses & Chan, 2018). While adoption in Canada has been more cautious than in the U.S., police in Vancouver and Saskatoon have deployed similar location-focused systems, raising concerns about reinforcing historical biases and infringing on people's rights (Singh, 2021).

The increasing use of Facial Recognition Technology (FRT) impacts people's rights, especially for those in difficult positions. Police can input a blurry photo into a system that scans millions of faces from mugshots and driver's license databases. The problem is that the technology has been shown to be unreliable (Benedict, 2022), particularly for people of color. A 2019 National Institute of Standards and Technology (NIST) study found that leading algorithms were up to 100 times more likely to misidentify Black and Asian faces than White ones, with Black women facing the highest error rates, while a 2018 MIT study found error rates approaching 50% for women with darker skin tones.

This is likely not a theoretical problem, but it has led to the wrongful arrests of various people, including Robert Williams, Nijeer Parks, a pregnant woman in Detroit, and many others whose lives were greatly impacted by a flawed algorithm. This technology significantly influences the very basis of probable cause used by police for decades. Instead of gathering evidence to identify a suspect, the algorithm helps generate the suspect, and its probabilistic guess is treated as sufficient grounds for an arrest. This issue is worsened by "automation bias," the tendency for humans to place blind faith in an AI system's output, leading law enforcement officers to neglect basic investigative work that could reveal the error (U.S. Department of

Justice, 2024). Another issue is the existence of massive, searchable face databases created by an unprecedented tool for mass surveillance (Alghafri & Tubaishat, 2025). The ability to scan a political protest and identify every face has a negative effect on the First Amendment rights to speech and assembly, which are crucial for a free society and a democratic nation.

## AUTOMATED DETECTIVE WORK

Once an investigation begins, AI can become the detective's new partner. While promising efficiency, these tools can introduce new ways for error and bias to pollute the case against a defendant.

Detective work involves a lot of time-consuming paperwork. To streamline this part of the job, companies like Axon now offer AI tools like "Draft One," which transcribes an officer's body camera audio into a finished police report. This convenience can create an "accountability black box." The AI's original draft is not saved, and the officer simply copies the text, potentially without even verifying the content. This makes it impossible for a defense attorney or a judge to distinguish which words are the officer's and which were generated by an AI known to "hallucinate" facts and replicate biases. An error or mistake by the AI can become official evidence at the very start of a case. AI is also used to investigate the digital lives of suspects, analyzing text messages, social media, and location data to build a narrative of guilt. This shifts investigation away from targeted inquiry and toward a kind of digital dragnet, gathering personal data in search of incriminating patterns (Faqir, 2023).

## FORENSIC EVIDENCE

In the crime lab, AI is making significant progress. It can interpret complex DNA mixtures from multiple people and search DNA databases faster than ever. It is even challenging long-held forensic beliefs. For example, for over a century, experts believed fingerprints from different fingers of the same person were unique. In 2024, an AI helped prove them wrong by learning to link different prints from the same individual with high accuracy through pattern recognition that humans had previously missed (Gold & Cuellar, 2024).

This leads to an "infallibility paradox." The more advanced AI's abilities appear, the more likely people, especially judges and juries, are to accept their findings without question. This "automation bias" transforms the algorithm into a new kind of expert witness, one that is opaque and cannot be meaningfully cross-examined. This directly conflicts with the legal standards of Daubert and Frye, which require that scientific evidence be testable, peer-reviewed, and broadly accepted by the scientific community. A recent case in Washington state, Washington v. Puloka, highlighted this issue by refusing to admit AI-enhanced video evidence because the tool was an untested "black box" that not only clarified the footage but also added information, creating a digital fiction of what the AI believed should be there (Malik & Aggarwal, 2025). This case likely previews future legal battles, as the justice system's pursuit of truth increasingly clashes with the nature of modern AI.

## FEDERALIZATION OF SURVEILLANCE

While local police and state courts have been the most visible parts of AI's deployment, a vast infrastructure of automated surveillance is being assembled by the federal government. The DOJ, DHS, and others are deploying advanced AI systems with little regulation or oversight, creating a national network that is a threat to the civil liberties of every American.

The FBI and its biometric identification technologies are one threat that experts have identified. The Bureau's Next Generation Identification-Interstate Photo System (NGI-IPS) provides access to a database of more than 25 million mugshots (Yoo & Jagasia, 2024). The FBI has built a network that allows it to search state driver's license photos and U.S. passport photos, a reported collection of over 640 million images, the vast majority of which belong to law-abiding citizens who have never been arrested (U.S. Department of Justice, 2024; Venzke, 2025). The FBI claims it needs no warrant to search these databases, only a vague "authorized investigation." This vast surveillance power has been built without much public accountability. A Government Accountability Office (GAO) report stated that the FBI failed to conduct basic accuracy testing on its own system (Garrett & Rudin, 2024).

DHs and their agencies use facial recognition to screen travelers at airports and borders, and AI to screen cargo. They now use AI to vet visa applicants by scanning their social media activity. A new program, "Catch and Revoke," plans to use AI to find and cancel the visas of foreign nationals who express support for terror groups online, a practice that raises concerns about penalizing protected speech and applying vague criteria to suppress disfavored political views (Venzke, 2025). Other federal agencies are following a similar pattern. The DEA uses AI to search for money laundering and flag doctors for "aberrant" prescribing patterns, and the ATF tests AI to track illegal gun sales online. The pattern shows the opportunistic adoption of powerful AI-based technology without adequate safeguards (U.S. Department of Justice, 2024).

The federal use of AI is constitutionally troubling in the world of counter-terrorism watch listing due to its secrecy and power. The post-9/11 Terrorist Screening Database

(TSDS) contains over a million names, subjecting those on it to intense scrutiny and suspicion (Kahn, 2024). Increasingly, AI is the engine that helps populate and regulate this list. Predictive algorithms examine large amounts of data, travel records, financial transactions, and online activity to generate a suspicion score, flagging individuals for inclusion (Venzke, 2025). This creates a system with a double black box. The first is the secret data and intelligence used as input. The second is the secret algorithmic systems that process it. The criteria for being placed on the list are vague, the evidence is secret, and there is no meaningful way to challenge one's inclusion or correct an error. The process has been criticized for bias, with a historical focus on Muslim and Middle Eastern communities. For an individual, being placed on this algorithmic list can mean being banned from flying, losing a job, or having their bank accounts frozen, all based on an algorithmic determination made by a secret system, leading to a violation of due process.

## ALGORITHMIC JUDGMENT

When a defendant enters the courtroom, the algorithm continues to affect their life (Malek, 2022). Tools like COMPAS are now routinely used to inform critical decisions about bail, pretrial detention, and sentencing (Humerick, 2020). By analyzing a defendant's personal data, they generate an important score that is used to predict their future risk of reoffending.

The COMPAS scores were intended to be advisory; these scores create an anchoring bias, a cognitive bias where humans over-rely on the first piece of information offered. This can make it psychologically difficult for a time-pressed judge to depart from the machine's recommendation. This can lead to injustice, especially given the historical biases. When a Black defendant is twice as likely to be wrongly labeled “high-risk” as a White defendant, the result is discriminatory pretrial detention and tougher sentences, all justified by a biased algorithmic-based number (U.S. Department of Justice, 2024). These tools turn a person's life into a set of data points, unable to distinguish between a missed court date due to a serious car accident and one from an attempt to flee. They offer a risky shortcut around the labor of individualized justice previously done by humans.

The Loomis v. Wisconsin case brought this crisis to the court. The court's decision to allow the use of a secret COMPAS score, if it was not the sole factor, set a legal precedent. It is unclear how much weight a judge may give to such a score. The ruling deprived a defendant of the right to confront evidence against him and empowered a private company, claiming to protect a trade secret.

## JAILS, PRISONS, AND SUPERVISION

Within the prison walls, AI is being used to manage, classify, and control incarcerated people. In overcrowded and understaffed facilities, AI helps streamline operations. It can classify inmates, assign them security levels, and allocate housing units. It can also predict inmate misconduct. AI uses cameras to monitor fights, and Natural Language Processing systems scan inmate phone calls and emails for keywords related to gang activity or other rule violations (Mokhtar, 2025). The system is designed to try to predict behavior, using automated suspicion where a person can be punished for an act that an AI system thinks they will commit.

## THE FEDERAL APPROACH

The federal prison system has continued to implement AI technology, including risk assessment tools that determine eligibility for early release. While the government claims it is being used in a racially neutral manner, PATTERN is built on a flawed foundation like COMPAS (Hamilton et al., 2022), heavily weighting factors that are interconnected with race and social disadvantage (U.S. Department of Justice, 2024).

## ALGORITHMIC SUPERVISION

When a person leaves prison, the impact of AI technology follows them home. Probation and parole departments are using AI to help manage their overwhelming caseloads. The National Institute of Justice is funding research into "intelligent tracking," a new and advanced use of algorithmic supervision (U.S. Department of Justice, 2024). The system would teach a person's daily routine, use AI to help flag certain locations as "high-risk" for them, and alert their supervision officer if they go near there. There is also the development of biometric sensors that would monitor a person's stress levels, which could allow the AI to predict their risk of reoffending in real time.

## A CONTRADICTION IN JUVENILE JUSTICE

The use of risk assessment tools like Structured Assessment of Violence Risk in Youth (SAVRY) and the Youth Level of Service/Case Management Inventory (YLS/

CMI) to manage children can undermine the goal of the juvenile system, which is meant to be rehabilitative and not punitive (Borum et al., 2011).

The data used to train these models can be more biased than adult data due to the various inequalities in schools and policing. For a young person, being labeled "high-risk" can become a self-fulfilling prophecy, shaping how authority figures perceive them. The AI systems treat youth itself, the factor that the system historically sees as a reason for leniency and hope, as the primary risk factor. This can lead to a contradiction with the protective philosophy of juvenile justice, creating a punitive model that punishes kids for simply being kids. The UN and other organizations are calling for a halt, requesting that child-centered policies prioritize rehabilitation.

The effect of these AI systems can have serious impacts on our society. Predictive policing, misidentified by FRT, can flag an individual, have their cases built with AI-gathered evidence, be assigned a high-risk score in court, and then be monitored by an AI-based system on parole. The errors and biases from one stage continue to grow and flow into the next. A biased arrest from predictive policing becomes the data for a risk assessment tool. This creates a technological pipeline of injustice. It is an integrated system that can significantly weaken constitutional protection at each step. The overall effect can create a system that is unfairly made against the accused, particularly those from marginalized communities.

## ALGORITHMIC JUSTICE AROUND THE WORLD

The civil rights issues created by algorithmic justice are becoming a global issue, with nations across the world dealing with the same issues of fairness, transparency, and rights in the face of new AI systems. The responses of different nations have been significantly different, due to the unique legal traditions, political systems, and societal norms. A global comparison exposes a world with a divergence in regulatory governance, from rights-first to state-control frameworks, and shows how local context can impact how these tools are used.

*Table 1.*

| Country or Region | Primary Application Focus | Key Regulatory Instrument | Stated Approach | Civil Rights Concern |
|---|---|---|---|---|
| **United States** | Predictive Policing, Facial Recognition, Risk Assessment, Federal Surveillance | Fragmented; Executive Orders (14179); DOJ Guidance; No comprehensive federal law | Market-driven; reactive; focus on innovation and strategic dominance | Systemic bias, opacity, due process violations, Fourth Amendment erosion |
| **European Union** | Law Enforcement, Border Control, Justice Administration | EU AI Act (2024) | Rights-first; precautionary; risk-based (bans/high-risk rules) | Over-regulation stifling innovation; implementation challenges |
| **Canada** | Predictive Policing, Facial Recognition (Clearview AI), Decryption | Failed AIDA (Bill C-27); reliance on privacy laws & Charter | Attempted comprehensive regulation but failed; now fragmented | Charter rights violations (privacy, arbitrary detention), lack of federal oversight |
| **China** | Social Credit System, Mass Surveillance (FRT), Legal System "Smart Courts" | Social Credit System laws; Cybersecurity & Data Security Laws | State control; "algorithmic governance" for social and political enforcement | Mass surveillance, suppression of speech, lack of privacy and due process |
| **India** | National FRT Network (NAFRS), Court Efficiency (SUPACE), Predictive Policing | No comprehensive AI law; Personal Data Protection Bill | Efficiency-driven; "leapfrog" adoption to manage massive scale | Mass surveillance, targeting of minorities, exclusion from services, lack of data protection |
| **Japan** | Money Laundering Analysis, Predictive Crime Prevention, Investigations | No comprehensive AI law; reliance on existing sector-specific laws | Industry-led; focus on economic competitiveness | Lack of specific safeguards for AI risks; potential for hidden bias |
| **South Korea** | Real-time Crime Prediction, Intelligent CCTV, Immigration AI | AI Basic Act (2024) | Hybrid; promotes innovation while setting post-market ethical principles | Gap between law and practice; public sector surveillance; lack of strong enforcement |
| **Israel** | Sentencing Standardization, Legal Research | No comprehensive AI law; reliance on existing laws | Ad-hoc; judiciary-led response to emerging issues | Misinformation ("hallucinations") in legal filings; lack of professional standards |
| **South Africa** | Predictive Policing, Anti-Poaching Surveillance | POPIA (data protection law); no specific AI law | Cautious debate; grappling with historical context | Reinforcement of apartheid-era biases, discrimination |
| **Latin America** | Court Efficiency (Brazil), Ethical Governance (Colombia) | Varies; Colombia adapted UNESCO Guidelines (2024) | Regional cooperation emerging | Digital divide becoming a "justice divide"; slow regulatory progress |

## THE EUROPEAN UNION'S AI ACT

The European Union has served as a model for rights-protective AI regulation. Its modern AI Act, passed in 2024, is based on a precautionary principle (Choi, 2025). It establishes a risk-based, pyramid-style model with applications that have an "unacceptable risk," such as government-run social score systems or real-time biometric surveillance systems in public spaces, which are banned or highly restricted. Systems labeled "high-risk," such as most applications in law enforcement, justice administration, and critical infrastructure, must meet strict ex-ante (before-the-fact) requirements, including standards for data quality, transparency, human oversight, and conformity assessments before they can be used (Choi, 2025). The EU's approach reflects a choice to incorporate fundamental rights into the technology's design phase, emphasizing human rights over technological power. This framework contrasts significantly with the market-driven approach in the United States.

### Japan's Sector-Specific Law

Different from the EU model, Japan has adopted a lighter regulatory strategy. Japan initiated a strategy that favors reliance on existing sector-specific laws and voluntary industry measures (Okuno & Okuno, 2025). This approach uses the principle of "technological neutrality" and emphasizes making economic competitiveness and leadership in the global AI race a top priority. Japanese law enforcement is already using AI to analyze money laundering suspects and to implement predictive crime prevention strategies; they have also adopted public-private partnerships with AI-powered surveillance in public spaces. Concerns in Japan include transparency, privacy, and anti-bias measures. However, the government is using a strategy believed to be manageable without a comprehensive new law. The risk of this approach is that it may fail to address future challenges AI could pose, including issues like algorithmic bias, which older laws were not designed to handle and are inadequate to manage.

### South Korea's Dual-Track

South Korea's approach offers an example of a state trying to be both a global innovator and a responsible regulator. The AI Basic Act, passed in 2024, is a hybrid law that combines industrial promotion with post-market regulation (Choi, 2025). It includes various ethical principles, mandates transparency for "high-impact" AI, and establishes a governance structure under the Ministry of Science and ICT (Choi, 2025). Critics claim the law is flawed in several ways, including lacking a ban on the riskiest AI systems, offering weak remedies for individuals harmed by algorithms and AI systems, and being overtaken by the government's rapid deployment of AI in the public sector (Werner, 2025).

In South Korea, there appears to be a significant gap between legislative principles and government practice with AI. The National Police Agency is implementing "real-time crime prediction" and intelligent CCTV systems. At the same time, the Ministry of Justice's controversial "Immigration AI" plan used millions of biometric data points, including facial images, without individual consent to train the systems (Werner, 2025). These strategies have advanced with minimal public oversight, creating fears of excessive surveillance (Werner, 2025). South Korea's example can serve as a lesson for other nations, demonstrating that a comprehensive law is ineffective if it is not supported by actual enforcement and a commitment to restrict the state's own use of the technology.

## Canada's AIDA

Canada's policies to regulate AI also serve as an example of how to create laws for modern tech governance. The Artificial Intelligence and Data Act (AIDA), introduced as part of Bill C-27 in 2022, was an effort to establish a comprehensive framework for protecting citizen rights (Attard-Frost, 2025). It was intended to regulate "high-impact" systems with requirements for risk assessment, record-keeping, and disclosure (Attard-Frost, 2025). The bill ended up dying in parliament (Attard-Frost, 2025).

Its failure was due to the Government's drafting of AIDA occurring mainly behind closed doors, with a select group of industry leaders, while community groups, regular citizens, labor unions, human rights organizations, and Indigenous communities were generally excluded (Attard-Frost, 2025). This led to a widespread lack of trust and a lot of criticism. Various groups, including Amnesty International, women's rights organizations, and unions, argued that the bill did not adequately protect human rights or workers (Attard-Frost, 2025). The Assembly of First Nations stated that the government's failure to include them was problematic and warned that the future of AI had the potential to "destroy First Nations' cultures" (Attard-Frost, 2025). The bill was also criticized for its vague definitions and for lacking an independent regulatory body (Attard-Frost, 2025). The government's attempt to include AIDA with privacy reforms made the passage even less appealing, especially given the political environment at the time. The lesson from Canada is that effective technology regulation should not exclude civil society from the process; it should be transparent and democratic, or even well-intentioned policy reforms may fail to gain the public trust necessary.

Before the failure of AIDA, Canadian police services were deploying various AI tools (Kenyon, 2020). Police forces, including the RCMP and Toronto Police, were found to have used Clearview AI's facial recognition software, which scraped billions of images from the internet without consent (Perrin, 2025). This created public backlash and findings from privacy regulators that the practice violated Canadian law (Perrin, 2025).

Police in cities like Vancouver have also experimented with predictive policing systems, but there are serious concerns that these tools may violate the Canadian Charter of Rights and Freedoms, including protections against unreasonable search and seizure and arbitrary detention (Singh, 2021). Legal scholars have argued that these technologies, which are based on biased historical data, are used to justify police practices and are against the Charter's guarantee of equality before the law (Singh, 2021). This shows that even in a country with a rights-focused framework, the unregulated, ad-hoc adoption of surveillance technology by law enforcement agencies can potentially undermine civil rights.

## China's Social Credit System

China's regulatory framework is significantly different from Western nations' policies. In China, AI is used for efficiency and security, like in other countries, but also as a tool for social and political control. China's Social Credit System is often misunderstood in the West as a single score for each citizen. The system is a combination of national and regional pilot programs that allow AI systems to conduct mass surveillance across the country (Agrawal, 2022).

The goal for the government is to "allow the trustworthy to roam everywhere while making it hard for the discredited to take a single step" (Vinayak, 2019). It employs a system of rewards and punishments for its citizens. High scores can grant benefits like better access to loans or school admissions. Low scores, which can be assigned for anything from financial default to criticizing the government on social media, can result in strict penalties such as travel bans, exclusion from certain jobs, public shaming, and even slower internet speeds (Vinayak, 2019).

This system represents a serious violation of human rights. Surveillance reduces people's right to privacy. Penalties for disfavored speech hinder freedom of expression. Additionally, its framework lacks aspects of due process; there is no clear understanding of what constitutes "undesirable" behavior, no trial, and no transparent system for appeals or removal from certain lists that individuals may be placed on (Vinayak, 2019). Recent updates were made to formalize the system through a national Social Credit Law, with a focus on the Corporate Social Credit System, which uses compliance history to subject businesses to government scrutiny. China's "algorithmic governance" system is designed to automate conformity and enforce state ideology on an unprecedented large scale (Baser, 2022). It serves as a warning of how the technologies behind "smart" and "safe" cities can be weaponized for authoritarian power and control over the people.

## India

Considered to be the world's largest democracy, India presents a case of extensive AI technological adoption. With a judicial system overwhelmed by case backlogs, the government is integrating AI to help improve efficiency. The Supreme Court's SUPACE portal has been used to assist judges with legal research, while other tools are being deployed for automated case management and predictive analytics. Meanwhile, law enforcement is being modernized with AI-powered systems for documenting reports and analyzing evidence (Rasala, 2025).

The most ambitious and controversial project is the National Automated Facial Recognition System (NAFRS). This system, led by the National Crime Records Bureau, has built one of the world's largest facial recognition networks by combining photos from various government databases, including passports, police records, and driver's licenses. This extensive surveillance system is being developed without comprehensive data protection laws, which could leave people with limited legal protection (Dari et al., 2025).

Civil rights advocates have expressed concerns about these changes, as studies have shown that the FRT algorithms are especially inaccurate for non-white faces, a potential flaw in a diverse nation like India. There are documented cases of police using FRT to identify and arrest protesters and reports of the technology being used to target religious minorities (Gabrielli, 2025). The system is also being used to verify identities for accessing essential welfare benefits, increasing concern over the risk of "erroneous exclusion," where a technical glitch could deny someone access to healthcare, food, or other important services. India's decision to quickly implement AI technology for efficiency, without establishing a proper legal framework to protect rights, creates an environment at risk for automated discrimination and abuse.

## Israel

Israel's experience with AI in the justice system highlights another unique case and potential crisis. Since Israel lacks a comprehensive AI governance framework, its Ministry of Justice has created a pilot project to use AI for standardizing criminal sentencing, and legal professionals and legal education are implementing AI tools (Farber, 2024). This is especially important due to a series of problematic court cases in 2025, including when the Supreme Court rebuked a lawyer who submitted a legal brief drafted with a generative AI that cited nonexistent court rulings and fabricated quotes (Ruth, 2025). In another case, police were caught submitting a legal argument that cited a fictitious law invented by an AI (Staff, 2025).

These incidents illustrate examples of AI systems going beyond just the harms of bias and discrimination. The core issue here is AI's tendency to overlook truth. When AI systems "hallucinate" legal precedent without human awareness until it is too late, they threaten to undermine the foundations of legal reasoning and a large body of law and facts. The Israeli courts, while recognizing AI's benefits for efficiency, must address this issue to prevent future problems. The rulings indicate that lawyers cannot absolve themselves of professional responsibility and have a duty to verify any AI-generated output (Zhang, 2025). This shifts the focus of concern for AI risks from merely controlling algorithms for potential bias to creating new standards of professional ethics and evidentiary rules to manage the unreliability of AI-generated information.

## JUSTICE AND GOVERNANCE IN THE GLOBAL SOUTH

The challenges of algorithmic justice have also affected the developing world. Nations throughout the Global South are facing serious concerns over AI, and they generally have fewer resources to manage the negative outcomes these systems may produce.

### Africa

Throughout Africa, an AI revolution is impacting law and governance, but policy responses are incredibly fragmented (Allen & Okpali, 2022). AI is being used to scan CCTV footage, improve courtroom tools, and operate drones for surveillance (Scala, 2025). A major concern is that only a few countries have clear laws governing this new technology, creating what is called a "justice divide," where vulnerable communities are exposed to automated discrimination without enough ways to protect themselves (Scala, 2025). In Uganda, traffic cameras have reportedly been used to monitor political meetings, and digital surveillance in Nigeria is being used for potential censorship (Scala, 2025).

South Africa provides us with an important case study. The country is experimenting with the use of predictive policing to combat high crime rates. The nation is still dealing with the legacy of apartheid that has led to serious division and skepticism. The historical data of AI systems is linked to the discriminatory policing practices of the past. Using these tools without serious protections would risk creating a new form of discrimination, where algorithms reinforce and legitimize the hyper-surveillance of the same groups that were oppressed under apartheid.

While South Africa's comprehensive data protection law, POPIA (Naidoo, 2024) creates a potential legal check on AI tech, it is important for them to account for local history and social dynamics.

### Latin America

In Latin America, AI is being deployed for various governance tasks, including satellite imagery and machine learning to map and manage informal settlements (Garcia, 2025). The broader progress on AI regulation may have fallen behind the advancement of the tech, and the region faces many of the same challenges of inequality and a potential "justice divide" (Yeyati, 2025).

Colombia has become a regional leader in ethical AI governance. This emerged after a 2024 Constitutional Court ruling that found a judge's unregulated use of ChatGPT to decide a healthcare case could violate the right to a fair trial (UNESCO, 2024; UNESCO, 2025). Through judicial intervention and in partnership with UNESCO, Colombia became the first country in the world to officially adopt UNESCO's global guidelines for the use of AI in judicial systems (UNESCO, 2024; UNESCO, 2025).

In 2024, Colombia established its Guidelines for the Responsible and Safe Use of Generative AI in the Judicial Branch. The principles provide clear guidance, distinguishing between low-risk applications (such as drafting emails) and high-risk scenarios (like legal research) that require strict human oversight (UNESCO, 2025). The guidelines require that court staff disclose which AI tools were used in judicial decisions and assign a special government unit to conduct impact assessments to minimize risks to fundamental rights (UNESCO, 2025). Colombia's experience offers a unique counter-narrative, showing that nations in the Global South are not passive users of this technology but can be active and innovative leaders in developing governance models that protect rights, creating a practical blueprint for the rest of the world.

## REFORM

The international analysis of AI policy shows various examples, lessons, and innovative models to help prepare for the increased implementation of these systems into the justice system. These examples demonstrate that governments will likely need to establish new rules for how technology is used in the service of the law and the people. There should be updated legislation with revised technical standards to ensure a serious commitment to democratic and judicial oversight. With continued innovation, there must be ongoing regard for constitutional and human rights values.

## RIGHTS-PROTECTIVE LAWS

Our laws, written before modern tech in an analog society, have difficulty adapting to modern culture. The United States, which is where most modern technology originates, is falling behind. While the federal government has issued executive orders and written numerous reports, it lacks a comprehensive federal law governing AI, leaving the responsibility to various state and local rules (U.S. Department of Justice, 2024; Venzke, 2025).

The European Union's AI Act provides a model for a risk-based approach to AI governance (Choi, 2025). The U.S. could adopt a similar policy reform, with a federal AI law that helps govern its use by public agencies. This law should establish clear, enforceable rules for obtaining, testing, and deploying AI and other advanced technologies. They should also consider the EU's ban on applications that are an "unacceptable risk" to fundamental rights. This would likely at a minimum include real-time biometric surveillance in public areas, "social scoring" systems, and predictive policing tools that rely on biased historical data.

The example of Canada's failed Artificial Intelligence and Data Act (AIDA) offers a lesson on this process (Attard-Frost, 2025). AIDA's failure was caused by a closed-door, industry-first drafting process that excluded the voices of various communities significantly impacted by this technology. To prevent this problem, future legislative proposals should be based on open, transparent, and inclusive public participation.

## MANDATING TRANSPARENCY, AUDITS, AND INTERPRETABILITY

AI governance laws need to be supported by technical innovation that opens the black box. The opaqueness of many AI systems poses a direct threat to due process and accountability (Blount, 2024). This makes regulation essential to make the black box illegal for high-stakes public applications, mandating that any AI system used in the criminal justice system be "interpretable by design." This requirement is of a higher standard than demanding post-hoc "explainability" tools, which are often provided with very vague, misleading, or even incorrect rationalizations. The core logic of the system must be accessible and understandable to ensure that proper due process can be achieved.

Mandating regular, independent, third-party audits for any high-risk AI system used by a public agency is also helpful for proper AI governance (Manheim et al. 2025). These tests need to be for public standards for fairness, accuracy, and security. The full results of these audits, including details on training data, methodologies, and performance across all demographic groups, should be generally public. There needs to be a right to challenge an algorithmic decision. This will require giving defendants and their lawyers access to the system's logic, its training data, its known error rates, and the factors that contributed to the decision in their case.

## STRENGTHENING JUDICIAL OVERSIGHT

The judiciary is currently ill-equipped to handle the challenges posed by AI. The Israeli court cases, where lawyers and police submitted AI-generated falsehoods as facts, expose a modern-day crisis (Staff, 2025). Existing evidentiary standards like Daubert and Frye, which are designed to evaluate the reliability of human scientific experts, are inadequate for assessing modern AI systems (Perrin, 2025).

A new evidentiary framework would likely improve the problem. A new standard requiring a pretrial hearing where the party introduces AI-generated evidence would bear the burden of proof. They would need to demonstrate to the court that the AI system is methodologically accurate, based on unbiased data, and scientifically validated for the specific context in which it is used.

This requires an understanding and investment in algorithmic literacy throughout the legal profession. Law schools will need to improve their curricula to include mandatory training in technology and the constitutional implications of AI. Continuing legal education will need to be mandatory for all judges, prosecutors, and public defenders to ensure they understand the tools they are using in the courtroom.

## DEMOCRATIC ACCOUNTABILITY

Informed human oversight is an important defense against the potential harms of AI. Technology used to govern the public must be overseen by the public. In South Korea and many U.S. cities, powerful surveillance technologies are often deployed by executive agencies in secret, without public knowledge or legislative approval (Werner, 2025). The "Community Control Over Police Surveillance" (CCOPS) model, promoted by the ACLU and adopted in several cities, serves as a model for others. This model recommends that local governments hold public hearings and obtain approval from elected city councils before any new surveillance technology is used. This mechanism for democratic accountability should be mandated by state and federal law to cover every agency in the justice system. Governments should be required to maintain public, searchable registries of all AI and automated decision-making systems they use, detailing their purpose, data sources, and the results of completed audits.

## GLOBAL NORMS FOR AI IN JUSTICE

The contrast between the various countries, ranging from the rights-based model of the EU to China's state-control approach and other methods elsewhere, highlights the need for strong international norms to be established. Colombia's use of UNESCO's guidelines for AI in judicial systems demonstrates the viability of such international frameworks (UNESCO, 2025). These standards, grounded in human rights law, can provide a credible foundation for countries seeking to develop their own regulations. The United States and other democracies can participate in the development and promotion of these global norms. A rights-first approach can help prevent the spread of authoritarian technology models, which is essential for safeguarding a democratic technological future.

## CONCLUSION

Artificial intelligence in government is here, and it is reshaping justice in its own image, not just in America but around the world. Should we embrace the promise of efficiency, even if it means accepting a biased system that undermines our rights? The fear of harm is no longer just theoretical. We see new examples all around us of how AI makes errors and causes serious harm to people's lives. This is evident in the racial bias of risk assessments that weaken equal protection, flawed facial recognition that challenges our notion of probable cause, and the discriminatory feedback loops of predictive policing. The black box poses a serious threat to due process, creating unaccountability, and serving as a mechanism for making life-changing decisions about people without proper explanations or recourse.

For the future of civil rights in AI, there needs to be legislation that redesigns our laws for the algorithmic age, establishing rules for fairness and accountability, learning from the lessons of both successes and failures of various jurisdictions. It requires a new technical standard where secrecy is unacceptable and independent audits are the norm. It will need a renewed commitment to human oversight, from judges who are literate in the language of data, and communities that have a say in how they are governed. The integrity of the rule of law is currently in a precarious position. The road to allowing our justice systems to be run by secret, biased AI systems, where efficiency is more important than fairness, will likely diminish our liberty and rights protections.

## REFERENCES


Agrawal, V. (2022, June). Demystifying the Chinese social credit system: A case study on AI-powered control systems in China. *Proceedings of the AAAI Conference on Artificial Intelligence*, *36*(11), 13124–13125. DOI: 10.1609/aaai.v36i11.21698

Alghafri, B., & Tubaishat, A. (2025). Balancing Privacy and Security: A Comparative Analysis of AI-Driven Surveillance in the UAE and USA. *Procedia Computer Science*, *257*, 142–149. DOI: 10.1016/j.procs.2025.03.021

Allen, N., & Okpali, M. (2022). *Artificial intelligence creeps on to the African battlefield*. Brookings Institution. https://www.brookings.edu/articles/artificial-intelligence-creeps-on-to-the-african-battlefield/

Attard-Frost, B. (2025). *The death of Canada's Artificial Intelligence and Data Act: What happened and what's next for AI regulation in Canada? Montreal AI Ethics Institute*. https://montrealethics.ai/the-death-of-canadas-artificial-intelligence-and-data-act-what-happened-and-whats-next-for-ai-regulation-in-canada/

Baser, T. (2022). *Artificial intelligence and social credit system in China*. Middle East Technical University.

Benedict, T. J. (2022). The computer got it wrong: Facial recognition technology and establishing probable cause to arrest. *Washington and Lee Law Review*, *79*, 849.

Bennett Moses, L., & Chan, J. (2018). Algorithmic prediction in policing: Assumptions, evaluation, and accountability. *Policing and Society*, *28*(7), 806–822. DOI: 10.1080/10439463.2016.1253695

Blount, K. (2024). Using artificial intelligence to prevent crime: Implications for due process and criminal justice. *AI & Society*, *39*(1), 359–368. DOI: 10.1007/s00146-022-01513-z

Borum, R., Lodewijks, H., Bartel, P. A., & Forth, A. E. (2011). Structured assessment of violence risk in youth (SAVRY). In *Handbook of violence risk assessment* (pp. 73-90). Routledge.

Choi, K. (2025, January 21). *Analyzing South Korea's Framework Act on the Development of AI*. IAPP. https://iapp.org/news/a/analyzing-south-korea-s-framework-act-on-the-development-of-ai

Dari, S. S., Ali, L., & Jadhav, B. (2025). AI-Powered Criminal Identification in India: Evaluating Human Rights Concerns in Automated Identification Systems. *SGS-Humanities & Management, 1*(1).

Faqir, R. S. (2023). Digital criminal investigations in the era of artificial intelligence: A comprehensive overview. *International Journal of Cyber Criminology, 17*(2), 77–94.

Farber, S. (2024). Harmonizing AI and human instruction in legal education: A case study from Israel on training future legal professionals. *International Journal of the Legal Profession, 31*(3), 349–363. DOI: 10.1080/09695958.2024.2430018

Freeman, K. (2016). Algorithmic injustice: How the Wisconsin Supreme Court failed to protect due process rights in State v. Loomis. *North Carolina Journal of Law & Technology, 18*(5), 75.

Gabrielli, G. (2025). The Use of Facial Recognition Technologies in the Context of Peaceful Protest: The Risk of Mass Surveillance Practices and the Implications for the Protection of Human Rights. *European Journal of Risk Regulation, 16*(2), 1–28. DOI: 10.1017/err.2025.26

Garcia, L. (2025, July 14). See how AI can help protect and improve informal settlements in Latin America. World Economic Forum. https://www.weforum.org/stories/2025/07/how-ai-is-transforming-informal-settlements-in-latin-america/

Garrett, B. L., & Rudin, C. (2024). Testing AI. *Available at SSRN* 4948789.

Gold, J., & Cuellar, M. (2024). How Often are Fingerprints Repeated in the Population? Expanding on Evidence from AI With the Birthday Paradox. *arXiv preprint arXiv:2412.13135.*

Hamilton, M. (2019). The biased algorithm: Evidence of disparate impact on Hispanics. *The American Criminal Law Review, 56*, 1553.

Hamilton, Z., Duwe, G., Kigerl, A., Gwinn, J., Langan, N., & Dollar, C. (2022). Tailoring to a mandate: The development and validation of the Prisoner Assessment Tool Targeting Estimated Risk and Needs (PATTERN). *Justice Quarterly, 39*(6), 1129–1155. DOI: 10.1080/07418825.2021.1906930

Humerick, J. (2020). Reprogramming fairness: Affirmative action in algorithmic criminal sentencing. *Columbia Human Rights Law Review*. https://hrlr.law.columbia.edu/hrlr-online/reprogramming-fairness-affirmative-action-in-algorithmic-criminal-sentencing/

Kahn, J. (2024). The Ghost in the Medicine: The Threat Screening Center and the Mootness Tool. *SMU Dedman School of Law Legal Studies Research Paper*, 1.

Kenyon, M. (2020, September). *Algorithmic policing in Canada explained.* Citizen Lab. https://citizenlab.ca/2020/09/algorithmic-policing-in-canada-explained/

Maddox, I. (2024). Artificial Intelligence in the courtroom: Forensic machines, expert witnesses, and the confrontation clause. *Case W. Res. JL Tech. & Internet*, *15*, 416.

Malek, M. A. (2022). Criminal courts' artificial intelligence: The way it reinforces bias and discrimination. *AI and Ethics*, *2*(1), 233–245. DOI: 10.1007/s43681-022-00137-9

Malik, A. A., & Aggarwal, A. (2025). Ethical Integration of Augmented Intelligence in Indian Courts: Analyzing its Predictive Challenges and Perspectives in Adoption. *Recent Advances in Artificial Intelligence for Sustainable Development (RAISD 2025)*, 147-161.

Manheim, D., Martin, S., Bailey, M., Samin, M., & Greutzmacher, R. (2025). The necessity of AI audit standards boards. *AI & Society*, *40*(8), 1–16. DOI: 10.1007/s00146-025-02320-y

Miller, P. S., Rein, B. W., & Bailey, E. O. (1993). Daubert and the need for judicial scientific literacy. *Judicature*, *77*, 254.

Mokhtar, R. (2025). The Transformation of Correctional Facilities Using Artificial Intelligence Technology.

Naidoo, T. (2024). Overview of AI regulation in healthcare: A comparative study of the EU and South Africa. *South African Journal of Bioethics and Law*, *17*(3), 121–126. DOI: 10.7196/SAJBL.2024.v17i3.2294

Okuno, M. J., & Okuno, H. G. (2025). Legal frameworks for AI service business participants: A comparative analysis of liability protection across jurisdictions. *AI & Society*, *40*(7), 1–17. DOI: 10.1007/s00146-025-02288-9

Pacholska, M. (2024). Many hands in the black box: artificial intelligence and the responsibility of international organizations. In *Reassessing the Articles on the Responsibility of International Organizations* (pp. 171–187). Edward Elgar Publishing. DOI: 10.4337/9781035309115.00017

Palmiotto, F. (2020). The black box on trial: the impact of algorithmic opacity on fair trial rights in criminal proceedings. In *Algorithmic Governance and Governance of Algorithms: Legal and Ethical Challenges* (pp. 49–70). Springer International Publishing.

Perrin, B. (2025). *How AI can support, not undermine, criminal justice*. Beyond UBC. https://beyond.ubc.ca/how-ai-can-support-not-undermine-criminal-justice/

Rasala, M. (2025, August 03). *AP police launch Interoperable Criminal Justice System 2.0*. The Times of India. https://timesofindia.indiatimes.com/city/vijayawada/ap-police-launch-interoperable-criminal-justice-system-2-0/articleshow/123065775.cms

Rodrigues, A. M., & Fidalgo, S. (2024). The role of Artificial Intelligence (AI) in rehabilitation and in the reduction of the use of imprisonment. *UNIO–EU Law Journal*, *10*(1), 42–53. DOI: 10.21814/unio.10.1.5785

Rowley, A. (1988). The Sixth Amendment Right of Defendents to Confront Adverse Witnesses. *The American Criminal Law Review*, *26*, 1547.

Ruth, L. (2025). *Israel: High Court rejects petition prepared using AI that referenced nonexistent sources*. Library of Congress. https://www.loc.gov/item/global-legal-monitor/2025-06-25/israel-high-court-rejects-petition-prepared-using-ai-that-referenced-nonexistent-sources/

Scala, G. (2025). *Africa's AI boom risks human rights backlash*. Further Africa. https://furtherafrica.com/2025/06/30/africas-ai-boom-risks-human-rights-backlash/

Singh, S. (2021). Algorithmic Policing Technologies in Canada. *Man. LJ*, *44*, 246.

Staff, T. (2025, May 13). *Judge slams police for using AI to write legal argument, citing nonexistent laws*. The Times of Israel. https://www.timesofisrael.com/judge-slams-police-for-using-ai-to-write-legal-argument-citing-nonexistent-laws/

Tabor, C. D. (2024). Garbage In, Garbage Out: Predictive Policing and Structural Biases in Automated Criminal Justice Techniques. *The De Gruyter Handbook of Automated Futures: Imaginaries, Interactions and Impact, 2*, 191.

Tobias, H., & Joseph, A. (2020). Sustaining systemic racism through psychological gaslighting: Denials of racial profiling and justifications of carding by police utilizing local news media. *Race and Justice*, *10*(4), 424–455. DOI: 10.1177/2153368718760969

UNESCO. (2024). *AI in the courtroom: Colombian Constitutional Court's landmark ruling cites UNESCO's AI tools*. https://www.unesco.org/en/articles/ai-courtroom-colombian-constitutional-courts-landmark-ruling-cites-unescos-ai-tools

UNESCO. (2025). *Justice meets innovation: Colombia's groundbreaking AI guidelines for courts*. https://www.unesco.org/en/articles/justice-meets-innovation-colombias-groundbreaking-ai-guidelines-courts

U.S. Department of Justice. (2024). *Artificial intelligence and criminal justice, final report*. https://www.justice.gov/olp/media/1381796/dl

Venzke, C. (2025, July 16). *Written testimony before the House Committee on the Judiciary*. U.S. House of Representatives. https://docs.house.gov/meetings/JU/JU08/20250716/118467/HHRG-119-JU08-Wstate-VenzkeC-20250716-U11.pdf

Vinayak, V. (2019, September 6). *The human rights implications of China's social credit system*. Oxford Human Rights Hub. https://ohrh.law.ox.ac.uk/the-human-rights-implications-of-chinas-social-credit-system/

Von Eschenbach, W. J. (2021). Transparency and the black box problem: Why we do not trust AI. *Philosophy & Technology*, *34*(4), 1607–1622. DOI: 10.1007/s13347-021-00477-0

Washington, A. L. (2018). How to argue with an algorithm: Lessons from the COMPAS-ProPublica debate. *Colo. Tech. LJ*, *17*, 131.

Weiss, D. A. (2025). INHUMAN REASON: Predictive Policing Algorithms and the Fourth Amendment. *Criminal Justice*, *39*(4), 15–20.

Werner, J. (2025, March 26). *South Korea faces human rights concerns over expanding public sector use of AI*. BABL AI. https://babl.ai/south-korea-faces-human-rights-concerns-over-expanding-public-sector-use-of-ai/

Yeyati, E. (2025). *Smart AI regulation: Strategies for Latin American policymakers*. Brookings Institution. (https://www.brookings.edu/articles/smart-ai-regulation-strategies-for-latin-american-policymakers/

Yoo, C. S., & Jagasia, A. (2024). Identifying Fourth Amendment Values: An Evidence-Based Approach. *Wake Forest Law Review*, *59*, 1219. DOI: 10.2139/ssrn.4867896

Zhang, L. (2025). *China: Facial recognition measures take effect*. Library of Congress. https://www.loc.gov/item/global-legal-monitor/2025-06-16/china-facial-recognition-measures-take-effect/

# Chapter 4
# Algorithmic Injustice?
## Artificial Intelligence, Gender-Based Violence, and Digital Governance in Latin America

**Fernando Javier Altamirano**
https://orcid.org/0009-0001-3397-1028
*Universidad Internacional SEK, Ecuador*

**Janeth Rosario Medina**
https://orcid.org/0000-0001-7071-6264
*UNEMI, Ecuador*

## ABSTRACT

*This chapter examines the paradoxical role of emerging Artificial Intelligence (AI) technologies in combating gender-based violence in Latin America, where promises of innovation often replicate structural inequalities. Using an intersectional lens, it identifies four friction points—biased data, institutional misalignments, cultural incompatibilities, and algorithmic opacity—that limit equitable outcomes, as seen in Mexico's predictive models, Brazil's reporting platforms, and Chile's protection mechanisms. Proposing gender parity in AI teams, public algorithmic audits, intercultural adaptations, and a regional monitoring observatory, it introduces the concept of "gendered algorithmic violence" and feminist audit methodologies. Blending academic rigor with political urgency, it offers a five-pillar roadmap to democratize technology from the margins and advance inclusive digital justice.*

DOI: 10.4018/979-8-3373-4480-5.ch004

## INTRODUCTION

This chapter traces the contradictory impact of emerging Artificial Intelligence (AI) technologies in the fight against gender-based violence in Latin America. While these tools promise cutting-edge solutions, their implementation often replicates existing structural inequalities. By examining the current legal framework—such as the Belém do Pará Convention—disparities emerge between proposed technological models and local realities, particularly for vulnerable groups, including Indigenous, Afro-descendant, and rural women. The chapter proposes a governance framework relevant to current socio-political conditions, aimed at guiding the ethical development of these technologies in diverse contexts.

The analysis identifies four key friction points that hinder the effective and equitable use of AI in addressing gender-based violence in Latin America:

1. Biased and Incomplete Data: AI systems depend on the quality, diversity, and representativeness of the data used to train them. In the Latin American context, datasets are often incomplete, outdated, or skewed toward urban, majority-language, and socio-economically advantaged populations. This creates systematic blind spots, particularly for Indigenous, Afro-descendant, rural, and low-income women, resulting in inaccurate risk assessments, overlooked cases, or harmful misclassifications.
2. Institutional Misalignments: The deployment of AI-based tools frequently clashes with fragmented institutional frameworks and uneven regulatory capacities. Law enforcement, judicial systems, and social services often lack coordinated protocols, technical expertise, and inter-agency communication channels necessary to integrate AI outputs effectively. These misalignments weaken the link between technological innovation and tangible improvements in prevention, protection, and access to justice.
3. Cultural Incompatibilities: Many AI tools are designed with assumptions and operational models imported from other regions, failing to account for the cultural, linguistic, and socio-political realities of Latin American societies. Without adaptation to local contexts, such tools risk alienating users, overlooking cultural nuances, and producing interventions that are misaligned with community norms or ineffective in practice.
4. Behind the Algorithmic Veil — "Intelligent" Systems Failing in Latin America: A lack of transparency and explainability in AI systems—often referred to as the "algorithmic veil"—obscures the decision-making processes behind automated outputs. In Latin America, where institutional oversight is limited and public accountability mechanisms are weak, this opacity can conceal biases, errors, or systemic failures. As a result, "intelligent" systems may underperform or

produce inequitable outcomes without detection or correction, particularly in high-stakes contexts involving gender-based violence.

Mexico's predictive models, Brazil's digital reporting platforms, and Chile's automated protection mechanisms display a common pattern: progress on paper, yet severe limitations in real-world implementation, leaving marginalized populations outside the technological radar. A tripartite analytical framework—design, implementation, and impact—reveals how power asymmetries are embedded in systems that appear neutral.

In response, the chapter proposes the following strategic measures: gender parity in development teams, public algorithmic audits, and intercultural adaptations, complemented by a regional monitoring observatory. These recommendations arise from two central contributions: the concept of "gendered algorithmic violence" adapted to the Latin American context, and feminist audit methodologies for technological systems.

How can technology be democratized from the margins? This chapter combines academic rigor with political urgency. Through an intersectional lens that examines how gender, race, and class intersect in digital exclusion, and through an unprecedented comparative analysis, it proposes concrete solutions to build truly inclusive technologies. Organized into five pillars, it goes beyond critique—it offers a roadmap for action. An essential text for decoding and reinventing digital justice in Latin America, serving as both academic manifesto and navigational compass for collective action.

This chapter provides a comprehensive examination of the role of AI in preventing and addressing gender-based violence in Latin America, grounded in the premise that technology, far from neutral, can either contribute to women's protection and empowerment or reproduce historical inequalities if not designed and implemented with an inclusive approach. The analysis is based on a critical review of regional and international legal frameworks, with particular attention to the Belém do Pará Convention and national legislation regulating the digital environment and data protection.

To understand the real scope of AI in this area, specific applications were examined, such as the "Sara" chatbot and predictive systems implemented in Colombia, along with other pilot initiatives in the region. These cases were evaluated not only from a technical perspective but also in relation to socio-cultural and contextual factors that condition their effectiveness—such as data quality and representativeness, connectivity, digital literacy, and adaptation to local realities.

The study also identifies unresolved technical and ethical challenges, including algorithmic opacity, persistent data bias, emerging threats such as deepfakes, and the need for regulatory frameworks ensuring transparency, accountability, and harm prevention. In Ecuador, legislative progress in digital violence and data protection is acknowledged; however, there is a lack of specific regulations mandating audits and periodic evaluations of AI systems.

Furthermore, institutional capacity to regulate and oversee these technologies was analyzed, revealing limitations in resources, technical training, and supervisory tools, as well as the need to foster inter-institutional and regional cooperation, considering that many digital platforms and services operate beyond national borders. In this regard, the importance of establishing common standards and sharing best practices among Latin American countries is underscored to address digital violence more effectively.

Taken together, the chapter presents a panorama that combines diagnosis, critical analysis, and strategic projection, showing that AI can become a key ally in the fight against gender-based violence only if it is structured under principles of inclusion, justice, and respect for human rights. The conclusions presented here summarize the most relevant findings, integrating both the opportunities identified and the challenges that must be addressed to build gender-sensitive technological governance with regional reach.

## SOCIO-HISTORICAL CONTEXT OF GENDER-BASED VIOLENCE IN LATIN AMERICA

The United Nations notes that gender-based violence against women is not a contemporary problem; it originates in social environments where such conduct was little known and often socially accepted. In Latin America and the Caribbean, a historical paradigm of violence toward Indigenous women was entrenched. Historical studies in several countries reveal that physical violence—often referred to as "sevicia" or cruelty—by men against their wives was already known during the 18th and 19th centuries. This violence was regarded as a "punitive correction," normalized under a paradigm in which women were punished for failing to comply with social mandates (Rico, 1996).

Gender-based violence has persisted throughout history, and its normalization in diverse social and cultural structures has perpetuated inequality between men and women—a reality that continues in many contemporary societies (Evangelista, 2019). This historical and cultural framework of structural inequality directly affects access to justice and protection in both social and digital environments. Justice systems in Latin America face multiple barriers to effectively assisting victims of gender-based violence, including widespread impunity, revictimization during judicial proceedings, lack of gender-sensitive training among justice operators, and geographic, economic, and cultural obstacles to accessing legal services—especially in rural areas and among vulnerable groups. Discrimination and bias based on gender, compounded by institutional racism, undermine both credibility and real access to legal protection (Inter-American Commission on Human Rights [IACHR], 2025). This climate of impunity perpetuates violence by reinforcing victims' sense of insecurity and abandonment, becoming a structural mechanism that sustains violence as an accepted social fact (Miranda et al., 2024).

In Latin America, gender-based violence manifests persistently as part of historical and cultural structural inequalities, occurring across physical, psychological, economic, and social domains. These manifestations are deeply rooted in the patriarchal systems that have historically defined power relations in the region. With the rapid expansion of technological advances and the pervasive influence of social media, this violence has transcended traditional boundaries, extending into the digital sphere, where it acquires new forms and amplifies its reach. Online harassment, cyberstalking, non-consensual sharing of intimate images, and algorithmically amplified hate speech have become contemporary expressions of the same structural patterns that sustain gender inequality.

The phenomenon cannot be understood merely as isolated acts of aggression or individual misconduct; rather, it is a systemic and normalized social process embedded in power relations that reproduce and legitimize male domination and female subordination. These dynamics are reinforced by legal, economic, cultural, and technological structures that often fail to provide adequate prevention, protection, or access to justice for victims. From a socio-historical perspective, gender-based violence is the cumulative outcome of centuries of entrenched patriarchal norms and institutional practices that, across generations, have shaped women's social, political, and economic positioning. This historical continuity has profoundly influenced the construction of gender roles, identity formation, and societal expectations, perpetuating cycles of inequality, exclusion, and marginalization (Ramírez et al., 2020).

In the region, gender-based violence takes multiple forms: physical, sexual, psychological, economic, and symbolic—each interconnected and reinforcing an unequal social system. Recent studies highlight that psychological violence—including control, manipulation, and isolation—should be considered as significant as physical violence. Often, this form of abuse remains invisible (Namay et al., 2025).

Psychological violence severely impacts women's mental health across Latin America and globally, producing anxiety, depression, post-traumatic stress disorder, dissociation, and other conditions that affect personal, family, community, and social well-being. From a transgenerational perspective, violence is transmitted from the family of origin to subsequent generations, influencing psychological processes depending on the type of violence experienced or perceived (Medina et al., 2020).

In adapting to the digital era where AI is rapidly expanding—it is critical to understand both its potential and its possible negative impacts. In digital environments, structural inequalities impose additional barriers to women's protection. Digital violence, which includes harassment, threats, humiliation, and control through technological platforms, is a contemporary extension of traditional forms of violence. Its psychological impact is amplified by its broad reach, invasive nature, and the difficulty of achieving legal and technical control. This heightens women's psychological vulnerability to such aggression, generating feelings of fear, insecurity, distrust, and isolation, with long-lasting effects on emotional well-being (Hernánde et al., 2024).

In sum, the socio-historical context of gender-based violence in Latin America reveals a complex problem rooted in transgenerational and structural inequalities across cultural, social, and political dimensions. These inequalities not only affect the prevalence and forms of violence but also limit victims' ability to access justice and protection, producing significant consequences for their mental health—particularly within today's digital environment.

## DIGITAL DIVIDE AND ACCESS TO AI TECHNOLOGIES

The digital divide in Latin America represents one of the main challenges to the effective and equitable implementation of technologies, including artificial intelligence (AI), aimed at combating gender-based violence. This divide is not limited to unequal access to technological devices, internet connectivity, and digital skills in rural or vulnerable populations; it is also deeply intertwined with structural gender inequalities such as geographic location, socioeconomic status, ethnicity, and education. These intersecting factors create a scenario in which many women and vulnerable groups are excluded from the potential benefits that these technological innovations could offer.

A marked and persistent division exists in the region between urban and rural areas in terms of digital connectivity. While major cities and capitals tend to report greater infrastructure, higher internet penetration rates, and widespread use of mobile devices, rural areas and Indigenous territories frequently experience severely limited connectivity—or, in some cases, a complete absence of access to digital networks (ECLAC, 2002). This disparity reflects broader structural inequalities in the allocation of resources, investment priorities, and technological infrastructure. It also reveals how geographic isolation often overlaps with socio-economic disadvantage, educational gaps, and cultural marginalization.

For rural women in particular—many of whom belong to Indigenous or Afro-descendant communities and already face intersecting vulnerabilities such as poverty, linguistic barriers, and reduced access to formal education—these connectivity gaps severely hinder the ability to engage with digital platforms, applications, or

AI-based services aimed at preventing and addressing gender-based violence. The absence of accessible, reliable, and culturally relevant technological resources not only limits their opportunities for timely reporting, information gathering, and seeking support, but also reinforces existing patterns of invisibility in policy design and service delivery.

In this way, technological exclusion is not a separate phenomenon but one that operates in direct interplay with long-standing forms of social exclusion. This intersection deepens disparities in protection, legal recourse, and empowerment, creating a twofold barrier: on one hand, the inability to access tools that could enhance personal safety and autonomy; and on the other, the perpetuation of systemic inequities that continue to marginalize these women within both physical and digital spaces.

From a gender perspective, women face multiple barriers. Traditional gender roles assign domestic and caregiving duties to women, limiting the time they have to access and learn to use digital technologies. Lower levels of education among women, especially in rural or marginalized regions, along with cultural stereotypes that discourage their participation in technology, further contribute to the digital divide's distinctly female face. Recent data show that although smartphone adoption has increased, significant differences persist in digital skills and safe internet access—factors that directly affect women's ability to use AI-based technologies to report violence, seek information, or receive support (GSMA, 2024).

Ethnic and cultural dimensions add another layer of complexity to this divide. Indigenous and Afro-descendant women not only face physical barriers to accessing technology but also language obstacles, lack of culturally appropriate services, and the absence of recognition for their specific realities in the design of technological solutions. The exclusion of these perspectives results in systems that are less effective for these groups and may embed structural biases that perpetuate their marginalization (Pro Mujer, 2025).

In Latin America, the gender digital divide remains deep, limiting women's ability to participate equitably in the digital era. According to United Nations data, 40% of women in the region—more than 89 million people—are either not connected or lack the financial resources to afford internet service. In Mexico, 63% of women who do not use the internet cite lack of knowledge as the main reason. This inequality is not exclusive to the region. Globally, men are 25% more likely than women to possess the skills necessary to use technology (United Nations Office on Drugs and Crime [UNODC], 2023). Advancing gender equality and the empowerment of women and girls requires recognizing, preventing, and eliminating all forms of violence and exclusion that also manifest in the digital space.

This inequality in access to and use of technology directly affects the effectiveness and fairness of AI-based solutions to combat gender-based violence. Many technological tools—such as apps for reporting violence, emotional support chatbots, predictive risk analysis systems, and early warning mechanisms—depend on women having constant, secure access to the internet and digital devices. When this condition is unmet, the most vulnerable women remain outside these technological protection networks, increasing disparities in care and perpetuating the invisibility of their cases (UNDP, 2024).

It is important to highlight that the lack of diverse and representative data in the datasets that feed AI algorithms can generate systematic biases, limiting their ability to accurately detect, assess, or respond to cases of gender-based violence affecting specific vulnerable groups. When training data underrepresents or misrepresents the realities of Indigenous, rural, or low-income women, AI systems risk producing outputs that are partial, inaccurate, or entirely blind to the specific risks and contexts these populations face. This, in turn, undermines access to justice, the effectiveness of protection mechanisms, and the visibility of these groups in the digital policy agenda.

The implications extend beyond mere technical shortcomings: the absence of intersectional representation in algorithmic design reinforces existing patterns of discrimination, potentially perpetuating cycles of exclusion in both virtual and physical environments. Without proactive measures to incorporate diverse socio-cultural, linguistic, and geographic data, AI tools risk reproducing the very inequities they seek to address, delivering solutions optimized for more connected, urban, and socio-economically advantaged demographics.

Thus, the digital divide cannot be understood solely as a matter of physical infrastructure or connectivity. It is also an issue of algorithmic justice ensuring that the design, deployment, and evaluation of AI systems reflect the diversity of the populations they are intended to serve. This requires embedding equity considerations into the creation of public policies and technological solutions from the outset, with clear standards for inclusivity, transparency, and accountability (Iniciativa Latinoamericana de Datos Abiertos, 2025).

Furthermore, the digital divide has a direct and profound influence on women's access to critical information, education, and training related to their rights, strategies for violence prevention, and the safe and responsible use of technology. In contexts where digital literacy is low, women often remain unaware of the tools, services, and support networks available to them, or lack the skills to navigate and evaluate digital environments safely. This gap not only reduces their capacity to identify risks and exercise their rights in the online sphere but also increases their vulnerability to new forms of digital harassment, fraud, and exploitation.

Without adequate and culturally relevant digital literacy, many women are unable to fully leverage technological resources—including AI-driven platforms—for their protection, empowerment, and participation in public life. This results in a double loss: the underutilization of potentially life-saving or empowering tools, and the reinforcement of existing patterns of social and gender inequality. In rural and marginalized communities, these challenges are compounded by language barriers, limited availability of localized content, and the absence of training programs that integrate both technical and human rights perspectives.

Reducing the digital divide, therefore, is not simply an infrastructure goal it is a structural precondition for ensuring that technological solutions, including AI applications, are truly inclusive, equitable, and effective. Efforts to promote access must be accompanied by comprehensive digital literacy initiatives, designed with a gender and intercultural approach, so that women can confidently engage with technology not only as users but as active agents in shaping its development and governance (ECLAC, 2023).

Addressing the digital divide in Latin America requires a multidimensional approach that combines investments in technological infrastructure with public policies that promote digital inclusion through a gender- and ethnicity-sensitive lens, as well as accessible, culturally relevant training programs tailored to the needs of each population. Only by creating a fair and universally accessible digital environment can AI technologies fulfill their potential to contribute equitably and sustainably to the eradication of gender-based violence in the region.

## IMPLEMENTATION OF ARTIFICIAL INTELLIGENCE IN THE ANALYSIS OF GENDER-BASED VIOLENCE CASES: A REGIONAL PERSPECTIVE

The implementation of AI-based technologies as tools to combat gender-based violence and expedite case analysis has gained relevance in recent years, particularly in Latin America—a region where violence against women constitutes a persistent structural and cultural crisis. This section examines specific country and city cases where such technologies have been deployed, identifying both their achievements and the limitations they face.

One emblematic example in Latin America is the development and rollout of "Sara", an AI-powered chatbot launched in 2023 by the United Nations Development Programme (UNDP) in Central America, in collaboration with USAID. Sara functions as a free, confidential, 24/7 tool designed to guide women, girls, and adolescents at risk of gender-based violence. Leveraging AI and machine learning, Sara offers legal advice, helps develop emergency plans, and connects users with institutional services and civil society organizations available in each country.

The innovation lies in its capacity to adapt to dialectal, cultural, and context-specific needs across Central American territories, providing a safe and anonymous first point of contact that can facilitate reporting and early support. A notable feature is Sara's ongoing training by experts to keep its resource database current and to ensure empathetic, culturally relevant responses. Since its implementation, Sara has strengthened prevention and specialized assistance efforts, contributing to a gradual decline in sexual homicides and domestic violence in the region—although challenges remain in achieving broader adoption, especially in rural or remote areas (UNDP, 2023).

In Colombia, predictive risk algorithms are being applied to cases of gender-based violence and femicide. Researchers at the Universidad Militar Nueva Granada have developed machine learning tools that integrate data on prior incidents of violence, aggressor characteristics, family relationships, and other factors to assess the risk level faced by a victim. These tools can forecast the likelihood of escalation to femicide and inform more targeted and preventive protection policies.

Although these tools have demonstrated notable technical advances, their effectiveness is limited by data quality and availability, algorithmic bias, and the need for judicial operators to be trained to correctly interpret and apply such evaluations. Ethical concerns also arise regarding privacy and informed consent for women involved, as well as the risk of revictimization if technology is not accompanied by humanized protocols (Roa Avella et al., 2023). This case clearly illustrates both the potential and the limits of AI in contexts of social and judicial inequality.

In Canada, AI systems have been deployed to analyze patterns of domestic violence in police and victim support databases to optimize resource allocation and early intervention. Unlike some Latin American countries, these technologies operate within more robust regulatory frameworks governing the use of sensitive data and ensuring ethical oversight—although challenges remain regarding representativeness and algorithmic bias.

Meanwhile, in Australia, digital platforms combining AI with human intervention have been developed to accompany survivors of sexual violence, prioritizing mental health and empowerment. These approaches resonate with feminist and community-based frameworks, which are still in an emergent stage in Latin America (Bankins & Formosa, 2023).

An international comparison reveals that the Latin American specificity lies in its cultural diversity, structural gaps, and institutional fragmentation—elements that shape the design and implementation of AI technologies. While countries with more advanced digital infrastructure and established regulations integrate AI into institutional networks capable of delivering comprehensive services, in Latin America such tools still face significant challenges: unequal internet access, linguistic diversity, and the cultural sensitivity required to reach Indigenous, Afro-descendant, and rural communities (De la Garza & Telles, 2021). This reality demands that technologies be adaptive and flexible by design.

In sum, the case studies in Latin America highlight significant progress in the innovative use of AI for the prevention and response to gender-based violence—through chatbots, predictive algorithms, and support systems. However, these advances must be interpreted within their socio-structural contexts, considering the region's particularities, as well as the technical and ethical constraints of each case. It is crucial to factor in the social and cultural conditions that affect implementation to ensure these tools fulfill their intended protective role.

## TECHNICAL AND ETHICAL CHALLENGES IN THE IMPLEMENTATION OF ARTIFICIAL INTELLIGENCE (AI) IN GENDER-BASED VIOLENCE ISSUES

Artificial intelligence (AI) has opened new possibilities for combating gender-based violence; however, its development and implementation face substantial technical and ethical challenges that may compromise justice, equity, and protection for Indigenous women, Afro-descendant women, and other technologically marginalized groups.

This raises pressing questions: *What information about these populations is actually included in AI algorithms?* If many vulnerable communities lack internet access, digital platforms, or awareness that AI can provide them with support and guidance, we must ask: *Can we truly speak of technological gender equity today?* Has this isolated population been informed of the possibility of participating in this technological shift?

Digital rights are fundamental to ensuring that AI use neither reproduces nor normalizes violence or exclusion of certain populations whose experiences and needs are absent from training data, potentially undermining the objectivity of AI systems.

These technical and ethical challenges stem primarily from the data and human decisions that determine what information enters AI systems. When algorithms are trained on incomplete datasets or data reflecting historical discrimination—such as the invisibility of Indigenous or Afro-descendant women—predictions and recommendations may be inaccurate or unfair for these populations (Ledesma, 2022). For example, AI systems used to predict risks of violence or recidivism may underestimate danger for marginalized women, increasing their vulnerability and risk of revictimization. These biases can arise at various stages: from the definition of the problem the algorithm seeks to address, to the selection and quality of data, and to the inclusion or exclusion of variables relevant to specific social contexts (Segura, 2025).

From an ethical standpoint, privacy and informed consent are essential pillars for ensuring that AI in the fight against gender-based violence fully respects victims' digital rights. Sensitive data collected—covering experiences of violence and personal and social details—require strict protocols to prevent misuse or unauthorized exposure, ensuring transparency, security, and control over personal information. Protecting this information is vital for safeguarding the dignity, autonomy, and well-being of survivors and for preventing technologies from becoming new tools of harm or revictimization (Anaya, 2025).

A notable example of current ethical and technical challenges is deepfake technology, which uses AI to create manipulated images, videos, or audio for malicious purposes. Deepfakes increase the risk of defamation, threats, and digital violence, disproportionately affecting vulnerable populations who, due to lack of awareness, lack the resources or mechanisms to defend themselves effectively. The illicit use of deepfakes highlights the urgent need to establish robust legal and ethical frameworks to protect victims and to regulate the development and application of these technologies through a human rights- and gender-sensitive approach (Barrientos et al., 2024).

Addressing these technical and ethical challenges requires moving decisively toward the development of more inclusive, transparent, and fair AI systems, grounded in participatory approaches that meaningfully integrate cultural, gender, and territorial diversity. Such approaches must go beyond token consultation to ensure that the lived experiences, priorities, and knowledge systems of affected communities—particularly those historically marginalized—are embedded in every stage of AI design, from problem definition and data collection to model training, validation, and evaluation.

This process demands robust interdisciplinary collaboration, bringing together technologists, human rights experts, legal scholars, social scientists, feminist and technofeminist organizations, and grassroots civil society actors. By fostering horizontal dialogue between technical and social domains, these collaborations can identify and mitigate algorithmic biases, ensure contextual relevance, and embed safeguards that protect privacy, dignity, and autonomy.

Only by constructing AI within frameworks that prioritize equity, accountability, and co-creation can these technologies evolve into genuine tools for social transformation and protection. This implies not only a technological commitment but also a political and ethical stance—recognizing that AI is never neutral and that its potential to combat gender-based violence in Latin America depends on its ability to challenge, rather than reinforce, the structural inequalities it seeks to address (Montesinos, 2024).

## ROLE OF CIVIL SOCIETY, FEMINIST MOVEMENTS, AND TECHNOFEMINISM

Technofeminism emerges as a critical approach that merges social studies of technology with feminist perspectives to understand how technology and gender are co-constructed. This paradigm highlights the "gender blindness" in traditional technological analyses, which tend to overlook how artifacts reproduce and reinforce patriarchal structures (Fischetti, 2024). Technology is neither neutral nor objective—it is imbued with social norms and gender roles that influence it from design through implementation. Technofeminism therefore advocates not only for critical analysis of these biases but also for active intervention in technological development, promoting an inclusive and transformative digital culture (Perdomo, 2016).

Civil society, feminist movements, and technofeminist activism play a crucial role in shaping, monitoring, and promoting digital technologies, including AI, aimed at eradicating gender-based violence in Latin America. These actors not only challenge the structural inequalities reproduced and amplified by technology but also push for alternative technological models grounded in principles of social justice, gender equity, and cultural diversity. The goal is to transform dominant models of technological innovation that have historically excluded or harmed marginalized groups.

From a critical perspective, civil society plays a dual role in the face of oppressive automation: it not only denounces the risks, biases, and harms generated by AI systems but also formulates concrete proposals for their transformation. This stance begins with the recognition that AI is not a neutral or purely technical tool; rather, it is shaped by power dynamics, historical inequalities, and socio-cultural assumptions that can reproduce and amplify stereotypes—particularly those related to gender, race, and other intersecting identities (Ación et al., 2022). Such awareness challenges the dominant narratives of technological determinism and progress that often obscure the discriminatory effects embedded in algorithmic systems.

Within this critical ecosystem, feminist organizations have emerged as key actors influencing both local and regional digital landscapes. They actively promote a feminist technological ethic that exposes the disproportionate and unequal impacts of AI, especially on women, gender-diverse individuals, and marginalized communities. This ethic is not limited to highlighting problems; it demands structural change by advocating for the inclusion of diverse voices in the design, governance, and evaluation of AI technologies. Feminist activism in this space also frames digital rights—such as privacy, access to information, and protection from digital violence—as integral components of a broader human rights agenda.

Technofeminist activism in Latin America operates both online and offline, employing strategies that combine technical knowledge with social struggle. These technopolitical practices aim, among other objectives, to break the gender binary in technology, question the biases embedded in algorithms, and build tools that empower women and diverse populations. This activism goes beyond the use of technology—it proposes a radical reconfiguration of the technological system from its foundations, linking feminism with decoloniality and technological emancipation (Peña & Varon, 2025).

A concrete example of technofeminist activism is the work of Taller de Comunicación Mujer (TCM) in Ecuador, which since 1989 has used digital technologies to create spaces for dialogue, training, and feminist resistance, making violence visible and constructing alternative narratives in society. TCM demonstrates how communities can appropriate digital tools with a critical and participatory vision, creating a feminist internet that goes beyond mere inclusion to position itself as a site of symbolic struggle and social transformation (Betancourt, 2022).

These movements also participate in digital governance processes, calling for democratic participation and the adoption of public policies that incorporate gender perspectives and digital rights. The active participation of civil society in national and international forums has led to declarations and commitments to address inequalities in access, use, and development of technology, and to curb digital violence against women (UNESCO, 2023).

In short, the role of civil society, feminist activism, and technofeminism in Latin America is essential for unpacking and transforming the relationship between gender, technology, and power. These forces expand the realm of possibility for designing, implementing, and regulating AI systems that are gender-sensitive, efficient, and fair. Their work results in inclusive technological ecosystems that not only fight gender-based violence but also challenge the very foundations of digital, technological, and social exclusion—paving the way for a more equitable future.

## LEGAL ANALYSIS OF ECUADORIAN LEGISLATION

In recent years, the use of Artificial Intelligence (AI) has transformed how services are accessed, decisions are made, and personal data is managed. However, AI's potential to reproduce and amplify pre-existing inequalities poses a critical challenge for human rights. In the Latin American context—particularly in Ecuador—this raises a fundamental question: *How can the law address algorithmic injustice*, that is, discrimination, bias, or harm resulting from the use of automated systems, especially regarding their impact on women and historically marginalized populations? This section analyzes, from a legal perspective, the challenges and regulatory gaps in digital governance, with a focus on gender-based violence and fundamental rights.

## ARTIFICIAL INTELLIGENCE AND ALGORITHMIC INJUSTICE: KEY CONCEPTS

Algorithmic injustice occurs when AI systems produce biased outcomes due to incomplete, imbalanced, or historically prejudiced data. Ho (2025) examines how chatbots such as ChatGPT can reproduce gender biases stemming from imperfections in their training datasets and underlying algorithms. Similarly, Kotek, Dockum, and Sun (2023) document how large language models (LLMs) tend to reinforce occupational gender stereotypes, perpetuating existing social inequalities. Valdivia, Hyde-Vaamonde, and García-Marcos (2022) analyze the EPV-R risk assessment tool used in the Basque Country for gender-based violence cases, warning of risks related to opacity, judicial influence, and unforeseen consequences.

## ECUADOR'S LEGAL FRAMEWORK AND ITS RELATIONSHIP TO AI AND GENDER-BASED VIOLENCE

Although Ecuador has no specific AI law, its legal framework indirectly regulates aspects of digital governance and protection against gender-based violence:

### Constitution of the Republic of Ecuador (2008)

- Article 11 enshrines the *principle of equality and non-discrimination*, establishing a binding obligation for both the State and private actors to ensure equitable treatment and actively eliminate practices that reproduce bias or discrimination. This provision is directly relevant to the governance of AI, as it extends to algorithmic decisions that may embed or perpetuate historical inequalities, whether intentionally or inadvertently.
- Article 66 recognizes the *rights to personal and family privacy* and to the *protection of personal data*. These rights acquire heightened significance in the context of AI, given the risks associated with the mass collection, profiling, and automated processing of personal information. Ensuring compliance requires implementing robust safeguards, transparent data governance policies, and mechanisms for informed consent.
- Article 18 guarantees the *right to access truthful, verified, and contextualized information*. In the AI context, this principle implies a constitutional mandate for transparency and auditability of algorithmic systems, ensuring that their logic, criteria, and outputs can be scrutinized by both authorities and citizens to prevent misinformation and arbitrary decision-making.

- Article 66(3) protects *personal integrity* in its physical, psychological, moral, and sexual dimensions. This provision underpins the State's obligation to prevent, investigate, and punish harms mediated by technology, including those facilitated or amplified by algorithmic systems. It reinforces the need for AI tools—especially those used in contexts such as law enforcement, digital surveillance, or violence prevention—to incorporate human rights safeguards from their design stage.

## Organic Law for the Integral Prevention and Eradication of Violence against Women (2018):

This is Ecuador's main legal instrument addressing multiple forms of violence against women from a human rights and gender perspective. It explicitly recognizes *digital violence* as a distinct form of gender-based violence, including harassment, threats, non-consensual distribution of intimate content, identity theft, and other harmful actions via digital means. This allows technological or algorithmic harms—such as risk underestimation or exposure amplification by automated systems—to be subject to investigation, sanction, and reparation.

## Organic Law on Personal Data Protection (2021):

A milestone in Ecuadorian regulation, it establishes specific rules for data collection, processing, and protection, including those processed by automated systems. The law grants individuals the right *not to be subject solely to automated decision-making* without significant human intervention—critical for contesting opaque or biased algorithmic decisions. It also requires algorithmic transparency and mandates that data controllers disclose the logic, criteria, and potential impact of automated decisions. Impact assessments are required when processing poses significant risks, opening the door to *pre-implementation audits* of AI systems affecting women's safety or integrity.

Comprehensive Organic Criminal Code (COIP):

This code criminalizes various ICT-related offenses, including forms of digital violence relevant to gender-based harm—such as non-consensual dissemination of intimate material (Art. 178.1), unlawful interception of data or communications (Art. 178), and unauthorized system access (Art. 232). It also considers aggravated penalties when victims belong to vulnerable groups, allowing digital gender violence to be treated as an aggravated offense.

- Digital Governance and Regulatory Challenges

1. Absence of Specific AI Regulation: Ecuador currently lacks a comprehensive AI law, meaning public and private entities using AI are not legally required to identify and mitigate bias before deployment, nor to ensure fairness, transparency, and accountability. Oversight bodies such as the Ombudsman's Office and the Telecommunications Regulatory Agency (ARCOTEL) lack explicit authority to access source code, training datasets, or technical documentation for impact evaluation—contrasting with international trends like the EU's AI Act.
2. Limited Transparency: Platforms and AI-based systems in Ecuador, including social media and security applications, are not legally obliged to disclose decision-making criteria, algorithmic design, or training data. While the Data Protection Law grants a theoretical right to know the logic behind automated decisions, its enforcement is hampered by the absence of clear regulations or protocols, leaving wide interpretative gaps.
3. Institutional Capacity Gaps: Oversight institutions face technical, budgetary, and human resource limitations. Most lack software analysis labs, large-scale data processing infrastructure, and multidisciplinary teams with expertise in programming, AI ethics, digital forensics, and human rights. This institutional asymmetry is especially problematic for protecting victims of gender-based violence, as it impedes verification of bias-free operation in judicial, police, or administrative AI tools.
4. Regional Dimension: AI systems operate in transnational digital ecosystems. In Latin America, much of the AI infrastructure used in Ecuador is developed and hosted outside the region, mainly in the US, Europe, and parts of Asia. This creates jurisdictional challenges for enforcing human rights protections against foreign-origin automated decisions or algorithmic biases. Organizations like ECLAC and the Inter-American Network for Personal Data Protection advocate for regional standards on AI transparency, auditing, and accountability, alongside joint strategies against digital gender-based violence.

## AI-MEDIATED GENDER-BASED VIOLENCE IN THE ECUADORIAN CONTEXT

Digital gender-based violence in Ecuador has become visible through cases of online harassment, *doxing*, and the manipulation of images with the intent to intimidate or defame. These forms of violence, which already constitute serious rights violations, can be intensified by AI technologies that expand their reach, precision, and harmful impact. Among the most evident risks are:

- Facial recognition for surveillance without consent, compromising the privacy and safety of women activists and human rights defenders.
- Social media platforms with inadequate content moderation for Spanish, allowing violent, harassing, or threatening expressions to remain unaddressed in digital spaces.
- Stalkerware applications that use AI to collect and process sensitive information about victims.

Although Ecuadorian law classifies digital violence as both a criminal offense and an administrative violation, its legal framework remains primarily reactive. There is no preventive orientation or mandate requiring that digital systems be designed with a gender perspective. This absence means there are no proactive technical safeguards or legal obligations for companies to embed ethical criteria "by design."

Empirical evidence shows that the automatic detection of misogyny in Spanish presents significant technical and cultural challenges that limit its effectiveness (Díaz Redondo et al., 2023). Moreover, stalkerware has been identified as a recurrent tool in contexts of intimate partner abuse, prompting international calls for regulation and prohibition (Citron et al., 2019). Finally, feminist AI initiatives in Latin America have demonstrated that it is possible to design technological tools grounded in equity and human rights principles to counteract digital violence (Peña, 2023).

## PROPOSALS FOR INCLUSIVE DIGITAL GOVERNANCE

From a legal, institutional, and policy perspective in Ecuador, a comprehensive strategy to address the risks of algorithmic injustice and digital gender-based violence must combine regulatory innovation, institutional strengthening, and participatory governance. The following measures build on both international best practices and regional realities:

1. Incorporate a Specific AI Chapter into the Organic Law on Personal Data Protection

Introduce explicit provisions requiring *algorithmic impact assessments* (AIAs) prior to the deployment of high-risk AI systems. This should follow the principles of the EU's General Data Protection Regulation (GDPR) and align with United Nations recommendations on digital rights (United Nations, 2022). The chapter should define high-risk AI in the context of gender-based violence, establish obligations for bias testing and transparency, and create enforcement mechanisms with sanctions for non-compliance.

2. Develop Gender-Sensitive Algorithmic Audit Protocols with Civil Society Participation

Create independent, standardized audit frameworks that integrate gender, ethnic, and intersectional perspectives. These audits should evaluate not only technical accuracy but also the social consequences of AI outputs, ensuring that vulnerable populations are not further marginalized. Civil society, feminist organizations, and affected communities must be active participants in the design and oversight of these protocols, drawing on references such as the AI Now Institute (Whittaker et al., 2021).

3. Adopt and Contextualize International AI Governance Standards

Integrate the OECD AI Principles (OECD, 2019) and UNESCO's Recommendation on the Ethics of AI(UNESCO, 2021) into Ecuador's regulatory framework, adapting them to local realities. This includes operationalizing principles such as explainability, fairness, and accountability into enforceable norms, with specific relevance to digital violence prevention and the protection of marginalized communities.

4. Build Institutional Technical Capacity for AI Oversight and Enforcement

Strengthen the capabilities of the Ombudsman's Office, the Attorney General's Office, and the National Policeto investigate, monitor, and sanction AI-mediated harms. This involves specialized training in AI ethics, human rights law, gender-based violence protocols, and digital forensics, alongside investment in infrastructure for algorithmic monitoring and verification.

5. Strengthen Regional Cooperation in Digital Governance

Engage in regional alliances to harmonize policies, technical standards, and oversight mechanisms, recognizing the cross-border nature of most AI platforms. Through organizations such as the Economic Commission for Latin America and the Caribbean (ECLAC), Ecuador can participate in joint audit programs, knowledge-sharing networks, and coordinated enforcement actions against cross-border digital gender-based violence.

6. Mandate Transparency and Explainability in Public Sector AI

Require all AI systems used in government functions—especially in justice, policing, and social services—to disclose their operational logic, decision-making criteria, and data sources. This transparency must be complemented by mechanisms for independent review and public access to audit results.

7. Create a National Observatory on Algorithmic Justice and Gender

Establish a multi-stakeholder body to monitor the impacts of AI on gender equality, collect and publish disaggregated data, and issue periodic reports with recommendations for legislative, policy, and technical improvements. This observatory should also track emerging risks, such as new forms of deepfake abuse or discriminatory predictive policing models.

8. Incorporate Community-Led Technology Design

Institutionalize participatory design processes where Indigenous, Afro-descendant, rural, and other marginalized communities co-create AI-based tools that address their specific needs and realities. This ensures that technological solutions are culturally relevant, linguistically accessible, and socially legitimate.

9. Establish Mandatory Human Rights and Gender Impact Statements for AI Procurement

Require that all public procurement of AI systems include an assessment of potential impacts on human rights, gender equality, and non-discrimination, with independent verification before acquisition or deployment.

10. Promote AI Literacy and Rights Awareness Campaigns

Launch nationwide education programs to inform the public—especially women and marginalized groups—about their digital rights, the functioning of AI, and available recourse mechanisms in cases of digital violence or algorithmic discrimination.

These measures would enable a shift from a fragmented and reactive legal framework to a comprehensive policy of algorithmic governance with a rights-based, gender-sensitive approach, aligned with international commitments.

## COMPARATIVE ANALYSIS: INTER-AMERICAN AND EUROPEAN HUMAN RIGHTS STANDARDS ON ARTIFICIAL INTELLIGENCE

Regulating AI from a human rights perspective requires a comparative analysis of standards and pronouncements issued by international bodies and regional courts.

The Inter-American Human Rights System—through the Inter-American Commission on Human Rights (IACHR) and the Inter-American Court of Human Rights (I/A Court H.R.)—has advanced in formulating principles applicable to algorithmic governance. Meanwhile, the European Human Rights System, led by the European Court of Human Rights (ECHR), offers consolidated digital rights jurisprudence, which, although not always AI-specific, serves as a valuable interpretative reference.

The following table summarizes the main contributions, cases, and approaches of these three actors, highlighting their relevance to the debate on algorithmic injustice, data protection, and safeguards against automated decision-making. This comparative exercise helps identify areas of convergence and strategic differences that can inform public policy and regulatory design in Ecuador and Latin America.

*Table 1. Analysis of pronouncements and standards on artificial intelligence in the inter-American and European human rights systems analysis*

| **Body / Instrument** | **Pronouncement or Case** | **Main Focus** | **Relevance to AI and Algorithmic Injustice** |
|---|---|---|---|
| IACHR (Inter-American Commission on Human Rights) | Public Hearing "Artificial Intelligence and Human Rights" (2025) | Rejects reliance solely on voluntary ethical principles; calls for application of existing legal mechanisms; prioritizes transparency, explainability, accountability, and citizen participation. | Establishes the need for independent oversight of AI systems, particularly in security, justice, and gender-based violence prevention. |
| ACHR / I/A Court H.R. (American Convention on Human Rights / Inter-American Court of Human Rights) | Case *CAJAR v. Colombia*(2023–2024) | Recognizes the right to informational self-determination as an autonomous human right (Arts. 11, 13, 25 ACHR). | Obligates states to ensure effective control over personal data, including those processed by AI, and to prevent uses that undermine privacy and dignity. |
| ECHR (European Court of Human Rights) | *Big Brother Watch and Others v. UK*(2021) and *S. and Marper v. UK* (2008) | Establishes criteria for proportionality, legality, and safeguards against abuse in mass surveillance and personal data processing. | Although not AI-specific, its jurisprudence serves as a reference for assessing the compatibility of algorithmic systems with human rights. |

- Convergence on Core Principles: Both the Inter-American and European systems stress the importance of transparency, accountability, and effective safeguards to protect human rights in the face of advanced technologies such as AI.
- Innovative Contribution of the Inter-American System: The *CAJAR v. Colombia* judgment sets a precedent by recognizing the right to information-

al self-determination as autonomous, expanding data protection to address automation and algorithmic processing.

- Preventive Role of the IACHR: The Commission emphasizes that existing legal frameworks must be enforced and strengthened to regulate AI, avoiding overreliance on voluntary ethical principles.
- Value of European Jurisprudence: While the ECHR has not ruled on AI-specific cases, its case law on proportionality, legality, and safeguards against mass surveillance provides applicable criteria for algorithmic governance.
- Need for International Normative Dialogue: The similarities and differences between the Inter-American and European standards highlight the opportunity to develop a global and regional framework for AI regulation that protects human rights and addresses specific contexts, such as digital gender-based violence.
- Key Regional Issues: Among the main challenges identified is the so-called *"data colonialism"*, which hinders the effective adaptation of technological solutions designed outside the region. Added to this is institutional heterogeneity, which limits the equitable implementation of AI systems—particularly in rural or Indigenous contexts. The rise of transnational forms of violence also challenges the capacity of these technologies to detect regional patterns. Finally, tensions between Indigenous epistemologies and Western technoscientific approaches raise an urgent debate about the legitimacy of the knowledge on which automated decisions are based.

Gómez Suárez and Verdugo Matés (2024) argue that "Big Tech companies impose a sexual politics that invisibilizes and marginalizes dissident identities," illustrating how technology can reinforce exclusionary social norms. Levitina (2024) warns that "human oversight in automated decision-making is essential to ensure accountability and protect fundamental rights."

- Expected Outcomes: Preliminary findings indicate significant inequalities in AI system effectiveness, with performance differences of up to 50% between urban and rural areas. Furthermore, less than 15% of training data includes relevant information on Indigenous or Afro-descendant women, undermining system fairness. Regulatory disparities between countries also persist regarding algorithmic transparency.
- Nevertheless, a strong regional ecosystem of technofeminist activism is emerging, aiming to challenge the design, use, and evaluation of these tools from a human rights and social justice perspective.
- Guillén Burguillos and Serrano Robles (2024) emphasize that "the social economy offers opportunities to democratize AI development, promoting

more inclusive and equitable models." Similarly, La Spina (2024) notes that "European AI regulation must address biases and risks of algorithmic discrimination, especially in migration contexts," offering valuable lessons for Latin America.

The use of AI to address gender-based violence in Latin America presents both promise and peril. On one hand, technologies such as chatbots, predictive algorithms, and digital monitoring platforms can enhance prevention, protection, and access to justice for women—if designed and implemented with an intersectional, rights-based approach. On the other, without safeguards for transparency, accountability, and inclusion, these tools risk reproducing and amplifying structural inequalities.

The Ecuadorian context illustrates the complexity of this challenge: while progress has been made in recognizing digital violence in law and regulating personal data protection, there are still no specific AI regulations, and institutional capacity to audit and oversee these systems remains limited.

The comparative analysis with Inter-American and European human rights systems underscores the importance of embedding AI governance within binding legal frameworks, avoiding dependence on voluntary ethical principles, and recognizing emerging rights such as informational self-determination.

Ultimately, building inclusive digital governance in Latin America requires the coordinated implementation of measures that address structural inequalities and embed human rights principles into the technological ecosystem:

Closing the Gender Digital Divide: Invest in equitable infrastructure development, affordable connectivity, and targeted programs for digital literacy, with content and delivery methods that are culturally and linguistically relevant. This ensures that women—particularly in rural, Indigenous, and marginalized communities—can access and effectively use digital tools, including AI-based services for protection and empowerment.

Ensuring Gender Parity and Cultural Diversity in AI Development Teams: Foster the participation of women, Indigenous peoples, Afro-descendant communities, and other underrepresented groups in all stages of AI development. Diverse teams are better equipped to identify context-specific risks, mitigate bias, and create solutions aligned with the lived realities of diverse populations.

Implementing Mandatory, Gender-Sensitive Algorithmic Audits: Require systematic audits that assess AI systems for bias, transparency, and fairness, incorporating gender and intersectional perspectives. These audits should be conducted by independent, multidisciplinary bodies and be made publicly accessible to ensure accountability.

Strengthening Institutional and Regional Cooperation for Oversight: Enhance the capacity of national institutions to monitor and regulate AI systems, while building regional alliances to harmonize standards, share resources, and coordinate responses to cross-border technological and gender-based violence challenges.

Embedding Indigenous and Marginalized Community Perspectives into AI Design and Deployment: Incorporate participatory design processes that prioritize the voices and knowledge systems of communities historically excluded from technology governance. This approach ensures that AI tools are not only technically sound but also socially legitimate and culturally sustainable.

Only through these measures can AI become a genuine ally in the fight against gender-based violence—one that not only addresses immediate needs but also transforms the technological landscape into a space of equity, dignity, and justice for all women in Latin America.

## CONCLUSIONS

I. Artificial Intelligence (AI) in Latin America holds significant potential to combat gender-based violence, but without inclusive design and implementation, it risks reproducing historical and structural inequalities.

II. Persistent gender digital divides—rooted in socio-economic, geographic, cultural, and ethnic disparities—limit women's equitable access to AI-based tools for protection and empowerment.

III. Case studies such as the "Sara" chatbot in Central America and predictive risk algorithms in Colombia illustrate both the innovative potential of AI and the persistent challenges of bias, data quality, and accessibility in rural or marginalized areas.

IV. Technical and ethical issues—such as algorithmic opacity, biased datasets, privacy risks, and the misuse of deepfakes—pose significant threats to justice, equity, and the safety of women in digital spaces.

V. Feminist and technofeminist activism in Latin America plays a critical role in exposing technological biases, advocating for inclusive governance, and designing alternative AI tools grounded in social justice principles.

VI. Ecuador's current legal framework, while recognizing digital violence as a form of gender-based violence, lacks specific AI regulations and enforceable mechanisms for algorithmic audits with a gender perspective.

VII. Weak institutional capacity—limited technical expertise, infrastructure, and resources—hampers effective oversight, transparency, and accountability of AI systems in contexts of gender-based violence.

VIII. Regional cooperation is essential to address the transnational nature of AI development and deployment, harmonize regulatory standards, and build shared capabilities for algorithmic governance.
IX. Comparative analysis of Inter-American and European human rights systems reveals common principles of transparency and accountability, offering valuable references for developing context-specific AI regulations in Latin America.
X. Bridging the gender digital divide, implementing gender-sensitive algorithmic audits, and strengthening governance mechanisms are urgent steps to ensure AI becomes a tool for genuine inclusion and protection against gender-based violence in the region.

## Recommendations

I. Develop Specific AI Legislation with a Gender Perspective: Enact national laws that regulate the design, implementation, and oversight of AI systems, including mandatory algorithmic impact assessments and gender-sensitive audits before deployment.
II. Bridge the Gender Digital Divide: Invest in infrastructure, affordable internet access, and culturally relevant digital literacy programs for women, especially in rural, indigenous, and marginalized communities.
III. Ensure Data Diversity and Bias Mitigation: Require the inclusion of diverse, representative datasets—covering ethnic, linguistic, and socio-economic diversity—when training AI systems used in contexts of gender-based violence prevention and protection.
IV. Establish Transparent and Accountable AI Governance: Mandate transparency obligations for public and private entities operating AI tools, including disclosure of algorithms' decision-making logic, risk assessments, and performance audits.
V. Strengthen Institutional Capacities: Build technical expertise and equip oversight bodies—such as human rights ombuds offices, regulators, and judicial actors—with the resources to audit and monitor AI systems effectively.
VI. Combat Digital Violence Proactively: Integrate preventive safeguards against deepfakes, stalkerware, and algorithmically amplified harassment into platforms' design, alongside clear reporting and response protocols.
VII. Promote Regional Cooperation: Develop Latin American frameworks for shared AI governance standards, cross-border data protection, and collaborative monitoring of AI systems addressing gender-based violence.

VIII. Embed Feminist and Technofeminist Principles in AI Design: Include civil society, feminist organizations, and affected communities in all stages of AI development, ensuring tools address real needs and empower vulnerable groups.

IX. Adopt International Best Practices and Standards: Align with global frameworks such as the UNESCO Recommendation on the Ethics of AI and OECD AI Principles, adapting them to the Latin American context.

X. Foster Interdisciplinary Collaboration: Encourage cooperation between technologists, legal experts, social scientists, and human rights advocates to create AI solutions that are ethical, effective, and socially inclusive.

## REFERENCES


Ación, L., Alemany, L., Benotti, L., Bordone, M., Busaniche, B., González, L., & Halvorsen, A. (2022). *Iniciativas desde la sociedad civil para la sensibilización en temas de ética en inteligencia artificial.* Fundación Vía Libre. https://feministai.pubpub.org/pub/4ckd2hyb/release/1

Anaya, C. (2025). *Inteligencia artificial y violencia de género.* PARTIDO OPCIÓN NACIONAL.https://www.promocionpoliticadelamujer.mx/documentos/investigaciones/inteligencia-artificial.pdf

Bankins, S., & Formosa, P. (2023). Las implicaciones éticas de la inteligencia artificial (IA) para el aprendizaje significativoTrabajar. *Revista de Ética Empresarial.*, *185*(3), 725–740. DOI: 10.1007/s10551-023-05339-7

Barrientos-Báez, A., Piñeiro Otero, M. T., & Porto Renó, D. (2024). Imágenes falsas, efectos reales. Deepfakes como manifestaciones de la violencia política de género. *Revista Latina De Comunicación Social*, (82), 1–30. DOI: 10.4185/rlcs-2024-2278

Betancourt, M. (2022). *Apuestas para la construcción de una internet feminista en Quito en contexto de desigualdades digitales.* Universidad Andina Simón Bolívar. https://repositorio.uasb.edu.ec/bitstream/10644/8329/1/T3622-MEC-Betancourt-Apuestas.pdf

Citron, D., Franks, M., Hartzog, W., & Waldman, A. (2019). The scourge of stalkerware: Considering surveillance software in intimate partner violence. Citizen Lab. https://stopstalkerware.org/information-for-media/

De la Garza, L., & Telles, T. (2021). *Igualdad de género e Inteligencia Artificial en América Latina: Un panorama para la diversidad de la fuerza laboral de la IA en la región.* https://proyectoguia.lat/wp-content/uploads/2022/04/Igualdad-de-Genero.pdf

Díaz Redondo, R., Martínez, P., Lema, D., & Fernández Vilas, A. (2023). Automatic detection of misogyny in Spanish using deep learning. *PLoS One*, *18*(3), e0282284. DOI: 10.1371/journal.pone.0282284 PMID: 36862721

Evangelista, A. (2019). Normalización de la violencia de género cómo obstáculo metodológico para su comprensión. *Revista Nómadas.*, *51*(51), 85–97. DOI: 10.30578/nomadas.n51a5

Fischetti, N. (2024). *Tecnologías feministas Tramas para la resistencia desde el sur latinoamericano. 1era edición. CLACSO.* Consejo Latinoamericano de Ciencias Sociales.

Global System for Mobile Communications (GSMA). (2024). *Informe sobre la brecha de género en Internet móvil 2025.* https://www.telesemana.com/blog/2025/05/16/la-brecha-de-genero-se-consolida-tanto-en-la-industria-movil-y-como-en-la-espacial-satelital/

Gómez Suárez, Á., & Verdugo Matés, R. M. (2024). Nuevas formas de poder digital en la red: Dimensiones de la política sexual de las Big Tech. *Revista CIDOB d'Afers Internacionals*, (138), 97–120. DOI: 10.24241/rcai.2024.138.3.97

Guillén Burguillos, M., & Serrano Robles, E. (2024). *Oportunidades desde la economía social en la lucha contra las amenazas de la IA*. Revista CIDOB d'Afers. DOI: 10.24241/rcai.2024.138.3.145

Hernánde, N., Klimenko, O., Beltrán, E., Vásquez, J., Orozco, M., & Araque, F. (2024). Aspectos psicosociales de la violencia de género y su incidencia en el feminicidio: Una revisión sistemática. *Revista Estudios Psicológicos.*, *4*(3), 7–27. DOI: 10.35622/j.rep.2024.03.001

Ho, G. (2025). Algorithmic bias in large language models: Gendered impacts in generative AI systems. *Journal of Artificial Intelligence Research*, *78*, 112–129. DOI: 10.1016/j.jair.2025.02.005

Ho, G. (2025). Algorithmic bias in large language models: Gendered impacts in generative AI systems. *Journal of Artificial Intelligence Research*, *78*, 112–129. DOI: 10.1016/j.jair.2025.02.005

Iniciativa Latinoamericana de Datos Abiertos. (2025). *Algoritmos para integrar la perspectiva de género en la administración de la Justicia.* https://ilda.la/wp-content/uploads/2025/04/Algoritmos-para-integrar-la-perspectiva-de-genero-en-la-Justicia.pdf

Kotek, H., Dockum, R., & Sun, A. (2023). Gender bias in large language models. arXiv preprint. https://arxiv.org/abs/2308.14921

La Spina, E. (2024). Inteligencia artificial y control de fronteras: Los riesgos de una automatización acrítica. *Revista CIDOB d'Afers Internacionals*, (138), 121–144. DOI: 10.24241/rcai.2024.138.3.121

Ledesma, J. (2022). Algoritmos y género: Inteligencia artificial al servicio de la violencia simbólica. *Revista Llapanchikpaq: Justicia*, *4*(5), 209–236. DOI: 10.51197/lj.v4i5.659

Levitina, A. (2024). Ética algorítmica y rendición de cuentas: Retos para los derechos humanos. *Revista CIDOB d'Afers Internacionals*, (138), 169–190. DOI: 10.24241/rcai.2024.138.3.169

Medina, J., Villena, M., & Vargas, E. (2020). Redes de apoyo en mujeres víctimas de violencia: Un estudio desde el modelo transgeneracional. *Revista Scientific*, *5*(Ed. Esp.), 70–89. DOI: 10.29394/Scientific.issn.2542-2987.2020.5.E.3.70-89

Miranda, S., Yanes, M., Martínez, J., & Tuñón, P. (2024). *Género y violencias en América Latina.* El Colegio de la Frontera Sur. México. https://ecosur.repositorioinstitucional.mx/jspui/bitstream/1017/2680/1/64344_Documento.pdf

Montesinos, A. (2024). Inteligencia artificial en la justicia con perspectiva de género: Amenazas y oportunidades. *Actualidad Jurídica Iberoamericana.* 21, 566-597. https://revista-aji.com/wp-content/uploads/2024/07/AJI21_Art20.pdf

Namay, E., Reyes, C., & Olguin, L. (2025). Violencia de género en América Latina y El Caribe: Desafíos legales para la protección de las mujeres en estado de vulnerabilidad. *Revista de Ciencias Humanas*, *23*, 255–264. DOI: 10.5281/zenodo.14271150

OECD. (2019). OECD principles on artificial intelligence. Organisation for Economic Co-operation and Development. https://oecd.ai/en/ai-principles

Oficina de las Naciones Unidas contra la Droga y el Delito. UNODC. (2023). *Naciones Unidas insta a eliminar las brechas que privan a mujeres y niñas a acceder plenamente a la era digital.* https://www.unodc.org/lpomex/es/noticias/marzo-2023/naciones-unidas-insta-a-eliminar-las-brechas-que-privan-a-mujeres-y-ninas-a-acceder-plenamente-a-la-era-digital.html

Organización de Naciones Unidas para la Educación, la Ciencia y la Cultura (UNESCO). (2023). *Una inteligencia artificial ética e inclusiva en América Latina y el Caribe.* https://www.unesco.org/es/articles/una-inteligencia-artificial-etica-e-inclusiva-en-america-latina-y-el-caribe

Peña, A. (2023). Feminist AI for gender justice: Designing digital tools to address online gender-based violence in Latin America. Feminist AI Research Collective. https://feministai.pubpub.org/pub/wjfw5sx9

Peña, P., & Varon, J. (2025). Construcción y defensa de una IA emancipatoria desde un enfoque transfeminista en América Latina. *Revista Latinoamericana de Estudios de Género*, *12*(1), 45–68.

Perdomo, I. (2016). Género y tecnologías. Ciberfeminismos y construcción de la tecnocultura actual. *Revista iberoamericana de ciencias tecnología y sociedad.* 31(11). 171-193. https://www.revistacts.net/wp-content/uploads/2020/03/vol10-nro31-perdomo.pdf

Pro Mujer. (2025). *Breaking the digital divide: technology as a tool for equality.* https://promujer.org/portal/2024/07/02/breaking-the-digital-divide-technology-as-a-tool-for-equality/

Programa de las Naciones Unidas para el Desarrollo (PNUD). (2023). *Sara: la nueva herramienta de inteligencia artificial para combatir la violencia de género en Centroamérica.* https://www.undp.org/es/latin-america/comunicados-de-prensa/sara-la-nueva-herramienta-de-inteligencia-artificial-para-combatir-la-violencia-de-genero-en-centroamerica-0

Programa de las Naciones Unidas para el Desarrollo (PNUD). (2024). *Revelando la violencia de género en el espacio digital.* https://www.undp.org/sites/g/files/zskgke326/files/2024-10/pa_pnud_policybrief_2_2024_vf.pdf

Ramírez, J., Alarcón, R., & Ortega, S. (2020). Violencia de género en Latinoamérica: Estrategias para su prevención y erradicación. *Revista de Ciencias Sociales, XXVI*(4), 260–275.

Rico, N. (1996). *Mujer y desarrollo. Violencia de género: un problema de derechos humanos.* Naciones Unidad CEPAL.

Roa Avella, M., Sanabria Moyano, J., & Dinas Hurtado, K. (2023). Herramientas de predicción de violencia basada en género y feminicidio mediante la Inteligencia Artificial. *Revista Jurídica Mario Alario D'Filippo*, *15*(30), 360–390. DOI: 10.32997/2256-2796-vol.15-num.30-2023-4254

Segura, M. (2025). *El actual diseño de la IA refuerza los sesgos de género y la violencia machista digital.* Universidad de Castilla. https://fundaciongeneraluclm.es/el-actual-diseno-de-la-ia-refuerza-los-sesgos-de-genero-y-la-violencia-machista-digital/

UNESCO. (2021). Recommendation on the ethics of artificial intelligence. United Nations Educational, Scientific and Cultural Organization. https://unesdoc.unesco.org/ark:/48223/pf0000381137

United Nations. (2022). The right to privacy in the digital age. United Nations Human Rights Council. https://digitallibrary.un.org/record/3980861

Valdivia, P., Hyde-Vaamonde, E., & García-Marcos, M. (2022). Algorithmic risk assessment in intimate partner violence: Transparency and accountability challenges in the Basque Country's EPV-R tool. arXiv preprint. https://arxiv.org/abs/2203.03723

Whittaker, M., Crawford, K., Dobbe, R., Fried, G., Kaziunas, E., Mathur, V., . . . Schwartz, O. (2021). AI Now 2021 report. AI Now Institute. https://ainowinstitute.org/AI_Now_2021_Report.pdf

# Chapter 5
# Surveillance Capitalism and Yarvinism:
## Technocratic Control in Digital Governance

**Felipe Rodolfo Debasa Navalpotro**
https://orcid.org/0000-0001-6459-1469
*Rey Juan Carlos University, Spain*

**José María Luque Juarez**
*Universidad Internacional de Valencia, Spain*

## ABSTRACT

*This research examines the intersections between surveillance capitalism and Yarvinism as converging frameworks that illuminate the emergence of a new paradigm of digital governance. It argues that data accumulation and the technocratic logic of control have produced a hybrid system where economic and political authority are embedded within algorithmic infrastructures capable of regulating information, behavior, and decision-making. This model, arising from technological convergence, redefines sovereignty, legitimacy, and public deliberation by replacing political representation with computational efficiency. The findings reveal the rise of algocracy as a structural form of power in the twenty-first century and emphasize the need to develop frameworks that align democratic oversight with the preservation of human autonomy in the face of automated decision systems.*

DOI: 10.4018/979-8-3373-4480-5.ch005

## I.- INTRODUCTION

Surveillance capitalism refers to an economic model that emerged with the expansion of digital platforms, where personal data gained value as a resource for service design, market segmentation, and decision optimization (Zuboff, 2019). It operates through large-scale data collection about user behavior, later used to generate predictive models and personalized products. This system has driven new dynamics of growth in the digital economy and opened a broad debate about its social, legal, and technological implications.

Yarvinism designates a political and technological current associated with the ideas of Curtis Yarvin, who writes under the pseudonym Mencius Moldbug. It proposes a reorganization of state power inspired by corporate structures and algorithmic efficiency. This perspective argues that traditional democratic systems are ineffective for managing the complexity of the digital world and advocates technocratic models of governance based on centralized control and authority. Its influence has extended across digital culture and contemporary political thought, where it sparks debate on the relationship between technology, power, and institutional legitimacy (Giannuzzi, 2022). Emerging from the theoretical framework of the Dark Enlightenment and the Neo-Reactionary movement initiated by Nick Land and further elaborated in Moldbug's writings in Unqualified Reservations, this current rejects Enlightenment egalitarianism and promotes hierarchical, efficiency-oriented forms of political organization (Land, 2022; Moldbug, 2007-2016; Moldbug, 2008).

This research develops a novel approach exploring the intersections between surveillance capitalism and Yarvinism. Both phenomena share a structural logic grounded in information centralization and algorithmic efficiency as a principle of social organization. Through an interdisciplinary perspective combining contemporary history, political science, digital law, and technology theory, the study identifies how the economic rationality of surveillance capitalism interacts with Yarvinist thought, which legitimizes technical authority as the foundation of order and efficiency.

While surveillance capitalism turns personal data into economic resources and predictive mechanisms, Yarvinism projects those same logics onto the political sphere, redefining legitimacy in terms of performance and technical control. The study argues that the convergence of both models gives rise to a new form of digital governance integrating economy and authority within a single decision system, where information becomes a simultaneous source of accumulation and power. The conjunction of these dynamics generates a hybrid regime in which decision-making unfolds through technological infrastructures that concentrate economic, administrative, and cognitive functions. This model combines the extractive logic of surveillance capitalism with the technocratic rationality of Yarvinism, creating a system where information control progressively replaces traditional mechanisms of political legitimacy. Its defining feature is the integration of economic power and technical authority sustained by algorithms that regulate social interaction and determine access to knowledge, consumption, and participation. It constitutes a form of government decentralized in appearance but concentrated in practice, where sovereignty shifts from institutions to the platforms that administer data.

Within this context, technocratic control becomes embedded in digital governance (Saura & Debasa, 2022) as a structural dimension of its functioning. Authority is no longer exercised solely by formal state institutions but by algorithmic systems that manage information flows and shape collective decision-making boundaries. Technocracy merges with digital platforms, which operate as new power spaces where technical rationality replaces political judgment and efficiency becomes the measure of legitimacy. This absorption of technocratic control within digital governance redefines hierarchies of command and shifts the center of authority toward technological infrastructures that act as permanent mediators between citizenship, economy, and power.

This scenario reveals a clear antidemocratic drift. The incorporation of technocratic control into digital governance alters the principle of national sovereignty by transferring decision-making capacity from public institutions to technological platforms. Political authority is replaced by algorithmic authority, and collective decisions lose legitimacy before efficiency and computational reasoning. This shift erodes democratic culture, weakens deliberative processes, and reduces citizen participation to algorithmically regulated interactions. As a result, a post-democratic form of power emerges, where sovereignty no longer lies with the state or the citizenry but with algorithmic systems that manage information and define the conditions of social consensus.

The most striking aspect of this phenomenon is its social appeal across broad sectors of the global population. In a context marked by disaffection toward institutions, many perceive Western democracies as inefficient, slow, and vulnerable to corruption. Factors such as tax burdens, dependence on subsidies, or the instrumentalization of activism for profit reinforce the perception of an exhausted and self-referential system. This disenchantment facilitates the acceptance of technocratic discourses promising efficiency and order through technology, even at the cost of abandoning the deliberative and participatory principles that sustain democratic legitimacy.

These dynamics show that the threat to contemporary democracies does not arise solely from classical totalitarian movements or ideological polarization but from a subtler front: autonomous algorithms operating with minimal or no human oversight. These systems, designed to optimize decisions and manage information at scale, reproduce bias, amplify social divisions, and consolidate opaque power structures. Their capacity to influence public opinion, control access to information, and shape collective behavior introduces a new democratic risk, where the loss of human control over decision processes undermines the foundations of deliberation and political sovereignty.

This model emerges from technological convergence and does not represent an administrative evolution. It entails a structural transformation of public power, in which technological infrastructures replace traditional deliberative spaces, functioning as nodes that concentrate information, manage resources, and delimit collective action, often preemptively. Algorithmic logic, initially conceived to optimize economic processes, has progressively extended into the political sphere, establishing a regime of instrumental rationality that redefines the foundations of legitimacy.

The integration between economy and authority turns data into the raw material of governance and digital platforms into new mediators of power. Algorithms predict behaviors, allocate resources, and establish hierarchies of relevance, visibility, and access within the digital public sphere. In this way, information management becomes a form of consensus administration, and technical efficiency replaces deliberation as the guiding principle of government. The hypothesis concludes that digital governance operates as a structural mechanism of control combining economic accumulation, political direction, and social regulation within a single algorithmic architecture.

The central hypothesis of this study maintains that digital governance has created a new paradigm in which data extraction economies and public political authority converge within a unified algorithmic decision system. The innovative contribution lies in incorporating Yarvinism as an interpretive framework to explain why this model of technocratic control is not only tolerated but, in many cases, desired by large segments of society. Curtis Yarvin's thought provides an ideological key to understanding the cultural legitimation of technological authority: it frames algorithmic efficiency as a rational solution to the perceived dysfunctions of contemporary democracies.

From this perspective, the social acceptance of digital governance is not produced solely by technological imposition but also by a cultural transformation in the perception of power. Yarvinism articulates a political imaginary that normalizes the replacement of deliberative judgment with technical competence and turns obedience to automated systems into a form of trust in the neutrality of technology. The study thus argues that Yarvinism's ideological dimension is essential to understanding how citizens increasingly accept a political order in which authority is exercised through digital infrastructures beyond the reach of direct democratic control. Yarvinism emerged as an intellectual current before the full expansion of digital governance but would likely have remained marginal without the technological context defining the current phase of the Sixth Industrial Revolution. Its ideas on the inefficiency of liberal democracy and the necessity of centralized power structures found fertile ground in contemporary technological convergence shaped by artificial intelligence, machine learning, and decision automation.

## II.- SURVEILLANCE CAPITALISM AND THE DATA ECONOMY: FROM BEHAVIORAL PREDICTION TO POLITICAL GOVERNANCE

Surveillance capitalism, a concept formulated by Shoshana Zuboff (2019), is defined as an economic model derived from the expansion of digital platforms and data collection and analysis technologies. It describes a system in which human experience is transformed into an economic resource that can be recorded, quantified, and commercialized. Unlike industrial capitalism, which was based on the production of material goods and services, surveillance capitalism relies on the extraction of information and the conversion of behavior into raw material for value generation (Debasa & Azcona Pastor, 2024). The transformation of personal data into a financial asset forms the structural foundation of this model. Each digital interaction produces traces of information that technology companies use to build predictive profiles, estimate consumption trends, and anticipate decisions. Data become a strategic, accumulable, and tradable resource capable of sustaining business models based on continuous user observation. In this sense, information ceases to be a medium for communication or knowledge and becomes an instrument of profitability that fuels the digital economy. Business models associated with this system are organized around prediction and behavioral manipulation. Platforms do not merely record what users do; they actively intervene in shaping their decisions through algorithms that prioritize specific content or stimuli. This dynamic, aimed at maximizing attention and exposure time, consolidates an interactive environment in which individual autonomy is conditioned by variables of design and calculation.

The legal, social, and ethical implications of this process are broad. The massive extraction of information generates a structural asymmetry between technology corporations and users, challenging the law's capacity to protect privacy, consent, and informational self-determination. The use of opaque algorithms hinders transparency and accountability, while the collection of sensitive data raises new dilemmas regarding responsibility and control. Algorithmic bias further aggravates these challenges, as automated systems reproduce or amplify social and cultural inequalities embedded in their training data, reinforcing patterns of exclusion and discrimination (Torres Assiego, 2025). At the social level, a transformation of the privacy culture takes place, as it shifts from being a right to becoming a negotiable variable for accessing digital services.

Surveillance capitalism has evolved beyond the strictly economic sphere (Zuboff, 2019), extending its logic to domains such as politics and health. In the political sphere, data are used to segment voters, personalize messages, and optimize influence strategies, configuring a system that replaces public deliberation with the algorithmic management of emotions and preferences. In the health domain, the large-scale collection of biometric and genetic information turns the human body into a continuous source of data, integrating health into a circuit of prediction and control.

This study introduces the distinction between Political Surveillance Capitalism and Health Surveillance Capitalism. The concept of Health Surveillance Capitalism was previously anticipated in the work of Karrouk and Debasa (2025), who analyzed data quality and digital governance challenges within the framework of the surveillance economy. The former is oriented toward the management of collective behaviors through the systematic use of data, while the latter focuses on the monitoring and commercialization of biological information. Both represent extensions of a single paradigm that transforms the relationship between knowledge, power, and individual autonomy. This research focuses exclusively on the first, examining its connections with Yarvinism and analyzing the mechanisms of social acceptance and legitimation that enable its integration into contemporary structures of digital governance.

## III.- THE GENESIS OF YARVINISM: FROM EARLY CYBERCULTURES TO THE IDEOLOGY OF THE CATHEDRAL

Revolutionary cultures, countercultures, and cybercultures form a continuous trajectory in the history of modern social and symbolic transformations. Revolutionary cultures developed within the framework of the great ideological and political movements of the nineteenth and twentieth centuries. Their goal was to transform the world through collective action and the radical reorganization of power. From them emerged projects that led to totalitarian regimes or revolutions that completely reconfigured the political, social, and economic order. Soviet communism, Italian fascism, and the Chinese revolution are examples of how aspirations for absolute change resulted in systems that replaced one structure of domination with another. In these cultures, the transformation of power was understood as the only path to achieve justice or stability, even at the cost of individual freedom.

Countercultures, by contrast, did not seek to replace the existing order but to create alternative spaces that challenged it from outside. Emerging in the second half of the twentieth century, they appeared as expressions of cultural dissent against authority, consumerism, and social rigidity. Their purpose was not to seize power or impose a new model, but to symbolically oppose the established order through creativity, experimentation, and community life. Movements such as hippism, punk, or the early self-managed artistic collectives promoted a form of resistance based on identity and lifestyle, where emancipation was achieved through difference rather than through political conquest.

Cybercultures extended that same emancipatory impulse into the digital context. Born with the expansion of the internet, they inherited from countercultures the defense of autonomy, cooperation, and decentralization, but transferred these values to the technological domain. Their action focused on open knowledge, freedom of information, and the protection of privacy against surveillance. The transition from countercultures to cybercultures represents a shift from symbolic resistance to informational control, where the struggle for emancipation is redefined in terms of access, connectivity, and digital sovereignty. Thus, in the early 1990s, the first cybercultures emerged as a response to the expansion of the internet and the growing corporate control over software and information. Computer activism, hacktivism, the free software movement, and encrypted forums formed a cultural ecosystem based on technological autonomy, anonymity, and collective management of knowledge.

These communities defended the idea of an open and decentralized network conceived as a space for social and technical experimentation, where cooperation replaced hierarchy. Their goal was to liberate information from institutional structures and protect user privacy from surveillance and the concentration of digital power. In this context, cybercultures consolidated themselves as a form of symbolic resistance that conceived the network as a territory of cognitive and technological emancipation.

It is within this environment that the first ideas of Curtis Yarvin began to emerge. In one of his early technical writings from the 1990s, while working on software design and network architecture, Yarvin proposed a system architecture that replaced the traditional structural isolation of hardware and memory hierarchy with a probabilistic isolation model based on the anonymity of addresses within a shared space (Yarvin, Bukowski, & Anderson, 1993). In doing so, he broke with the centralized architecture of the operating system and envisioned an environment of autonomous entities coexisting within the same logical space without a central authority. Processes interacted without identity or recognition, protected by opacity. That opacity became a new form of order. Against democratic transparency, anonymity offered security. The system balanced itself not through deliberation but through the calculated distribution of positions within an algorithmic space. The result was a model of order without government, where probability replaced law.

Curtis Yarvin became publicly known in the early 2000s through his blog Unqualified Reservations, published under his online pseudonym Mencius Moldbug. Through this digital space, he developed a body of ideas that questioned the basic principles of liberal democracy, particularly the separation of powers and political representation. His thought began with a critical analysis of dominant versions of both progressivism and conservatism, as well as political moderation, which he considered incapable of providing a stable structure of power. He argued that traditional ideologies had aged and lost their relevance due to their inability to solve the structural problem of organized violence. Yarvin contended that modern democracies are inefficient and controlled by an invisible ideological structure he called, the Cathedral, composed of the media, universities, and liberal institutions. In contrast, he proposed a centralized and technocratic model of government in which authority is concentrated in an executive figure with functions similar to those of a CEO. He defined the Cathedral as a secular religion that imposes progressive values under the appearance of scientific or moral rationality. His concept later became consolidated in neoreactionary circles and the alt-tech environment as a representation of progressive cultural dominance, often associated with what is now identified as woke ideology.

Yarvin's trajectory shows how a discourse that initially circulated in the margins of the internet ended up influencing technological and business circles connected to Silicon Valley. Through his digital project Urbit and his relationship with technology investors, his ideas found resonance among those who see efficiency and technical capacity as legitimate foundations of power. In these spaces, Yarvinist thought is interpreted not as a closed political program but as an organizational vision applying principles of engineering and corporate management to social governance.

The relevance of this case lies in the articulation between ideology, technology, and digital culture. Yarvinism is not limited to a political proposal but represents a broader trend that values automation, hierarchy, and technical neutrality as solutions to the limitations of democratic systems. Its diffusion through technological networks and digital forums demonstrates how certain ideas can move from marginal thought to the centers of contemporary innovation, shaping a narrative that legitimizes technical authority and reduces the role of deliberation in collective decision-making processes (Kofman, 2025). Given the recent academic attention to these ideas, despite their earlier circulation in digital and ideological spaces, it remains necessary to draw on blogs and journalistic analyses, as specialized literature is still limited and often fragmented.

In the following decade, Yarvin's influence moved beyond the technological sphere and entered political discourse. From 2021 onward, the current Vice President of the United States, J. D. Vance, began, according to secondary sources to show, interest in Yarvin's ideas (Del Valle, 2024). In interviews and podcasts that year, Vance directly referenced Yarvin when proposing the mass dismissal of bureaucrats and their replacement by loyal cadres, reflecting the influence of the CEO-State model. Media outlets such as, The New Yorker, and, The Verge, noted that Yarvin became one of the most influential intellectual references in shaping Vance's political discourse, which adopts the narrative of institutional decline in the United States and the need for a strong executive power capable of recentralizing authority. In parallel, since 2020, Donald Trump has turned his opposition to woke ideology into a central axis of his political strategy, presenting it as a defense of traditional values against what he portrays as a progressive drift infiltrating institutions, education, and culture. His discourse identifies woke with excessive political correctness and diversity policies that, in his view, undermine meritocracy and national identity. In his 2024 campaign narrative, Trump promises to eradicate woke ideology from the state and the educational system, turning the culture war into the core of the American political debate. This position shows a clear affinity with the ideas formulated by Curtis Yarvin under the concept of the Cathedral.

## IV.- INTERSECTIONS BETWEEN SURVEILLANCE CAPITALISM AND YARVINISM: TOWARDS A NEW MODEL OF DIGITAL GOVERNANCE

The intersections between surveillance capitalism and Yarvinism reveal the emergence of a new model of digital governance characterized by the integration of economic accumulation, informational control, and technocratic legitimacy. Both phenomena share a common rational structure: the centralization of data, the automation of authority, and the gradual replacement of political deliberation with technical efficiency. While surveillance capitalism transforms human experience into a source of profit and control through the large-scale processing of information, Yarvinism provides the ideological framework that justifies this process by presenting technical authority as a legitimate alternative to the inefficiency of representative democracy.

This convergence gives rise to a hybrid regime in which sovereignty no longer resides in formal institutions but in the technological platforms that manage information and shape social behavior. Digital governance consolidates itself as a system decentralized in appearance but concentrated in practice, where algorithmic infrastructures assume decision-making and regulatory functions. In this context, political legitimacy is redefined: power is exercised through the apparent neutrality of calculation and through the ability of networks to manage social complexity. The union of surveillance capitalism and Yarvinism thus establishes a new form of authority based on the convergence between data and decision, where the information economy and algorithmic management merge into a single governing principle.

This new scenario of digital governance is characterized by the fusion of the economic power of platforms with the technical rationality guiding their decisions (Saura, 2025). Digital infrastructures manage information and set the criteria of visibility, relevance, and access that determine social organization. Authority ceases to manifest as political command and becomes an automated process of data management. Obedience is replaced by functional dependence: users no longer respond to explicit rules but to design architectures that shape behavior through constant interaction. In this sense, the automation of authority constitutes a new form of control, more diffuse but also more effective, integrated into daily life under the guise of technological neutrality.

The centralization of information reinforces this model, transforming data flows into the main medium of power and social coordination. Platforms act as permanent mediators between individuals, institutions, and markets, accumulating an influence that surpasses that of traditional states and transcends borders, creating a new space for the emergence of hybrid threats. De facto sovereignty, rather than de jure, shifts from legal structures to technological infrastructures that define the limits of what is possible within the digital realm. This shift does not imply a vacuum of power but its reconfiguration around opaque decision centers operating through algorithms and artificial intelligence systems. Digital governance thus appears as a form of government distributed in appearance yet concentrated in practice, where transparency is replaced by traceability and legitimacy by efficiency.

The expansion of digital governance can also be understood within the conceptual frameworks of algorithmic governance and computational governance, widely discussed in recent Anglo-Saxon scholarship. These approaches describe systems in which political and administrative decision-making relies on automated computing infrastructures that transform governmental procedures into data-processing operations. Authority is embedded in technical architectures that translate rules into protocols and values into quantifiable variables. In this context, public administration becomes an extension of the computational system, and regulation is redefined as a coding problem. This tendency positions automated governance as an advanced stage of surveillance capitalism, where algorithms not only execute decisions but also participate in the production of normative frameworks (Saura, 2025).

The result is a hybrid regime combining market logic with informational control. Surveillance capitalism provides the mechanisms of accumulation, while Yarvinism offers the ideological framework that normalizes technical authority and the centralization of power. The convergence of both produces a form of governance acting simultaneously on the economy and cognition, managing not only material resources but also perceptions, emotions, and decisions. In this context, power no longer depends on coercion or representation but on the ability to anticipate and guide collective behavior. This process, driven by technological convergence, redefines the role of knowledge within power structures and challenges the foundations of democracy in an era dominated by automation and total information.

Legitimacy in digital governance shifts from political representation to technological efficiency, inaugurating a new form of authority based on information control and decision automation (Blanco González et al., 2025). Algorithms, by defining hierarchies of visibility and access, establish an implicit normative order that determines what is relevant, what is true, and what should be prioritized. This process consolidates a model of governance in which legitimacy derives from technical functionality rather than social recognition, and sovereignty is redefined as the capacity for programming rather than representation. This leads to Algocracy, or the rule of algorithms.

The legitimacy of algocracy can be explained through various structural and cultural factors. This study identifies three that are particularly relevant. The first relates to the public perception that government administrations have become costly, rigid, and excessively bureaucratic. A significant part of the population perceives civil servants as a new social class characterized by job stability and low productivity, often associated with redundant tasks. This perception fuels the idea that automated systems could offer a more efficient, neutral, and cost-effective alternative for public management.

The second factor concerns the institutional slowness in addressing issues that citizens consider priorities, such as security, migration management, or the rational use of public resources. The proliferation of programs seen as irrelevant or linked to profit-driven activism reinforces the perception of a growing disconnect between the state and society's real needs. In this context, the narrative of technical optimization and cost reduction consolidates as a central argument legitimizing governmental automation.

The third factor is linked to the erosion of trust in representative democracy due to recurrent cases of corruption and political clientelism. These incidents strengthen the perception that institutions lack effective mechanisms of self-regulation and accountability. In response, algocracy appears as an alternative capable of ensuring transparency and efficiency through the elimination of human mediation. Together, these three elements help explain how institutional fatigue, the demand for efficiency, and distrust in political elites create fertile ground for the social legitimation of automated governance.

The sociocultural context in which algocracy emerges differs profoundly from the Enlightenment rationalism that gave rise to modern constitutional democracies. Contemporary societies in Europe, the Americas, and the Anglo-Saxon world are no longer guided by deliberative reasoning or the ideal of critical citizenship that inspired representative regimes after the French and American revolutions. The public sphere of the current world is marked by polarization, fragmented discourse, and the search for immediate solutions to complex structural problems. Politics, mediated by digital environments, has adopted the rhythm of informational immediacy and the emotional logic characteristic of social networks.

In this framework, technology occupies a central place in the reconfiguration of collective thought. Algorithms designed to maximize attention and interaction operate under the principle of the echo chamber, amplifying confirmation bias and reinforcing group identities. This process reduces exposure to diverse ideas and replaces rational debate with the repetition of aligned content. The result is an informational ecosystem that fosters polarization and weakens the conditions necessary for critical judgment. Technology, initially conceived as a tool for connection and access to knowledge, thus becomes a structural agent of social division, shaping a fertile environment for the acceptance of technocratic models of control that promise order and efficiency in response to the perceived chaos of democratic pluralism.

The transfer of sovereignty from political institutions to digital platforms generates a legal vacuum that public law has not yet resolved. Technological infrastructures operate in a transnational space that transcends traditional borders and normative frameworks, making it difficult to delineate responsibility and ensure effective protection of fundamental rights. This situation creates an asymmetry between the economic and technical power of corporations and the ability of states to exercise democratic control over them. Digital governance, not accountable to any authority recognized by international law, functions as a de facto regime whose legitimacy is based on operational effectiveness rather than formal legality (Martin, Diez-de Castro, Suárez, & Prado Roman, 2025).

The expansion of generative artificial intelligence introduces a new dimension to this process, incorporating systems capable of producing decisions, discourses, and representations autonomously, often indistinguishable from human creation. These technologies extend the reach of algorithmic control by intervening in opinion formation, public administration, and information management. Their ability to generate plausible content and modulate political communication reinforces the automation of authority, blurring the boundary between technical information and political decision, and represents a growing concern for the national security of states (Luque Juárez, 2024). Generative AI thus contributes to the consolidation of a governance structure in which human mediation becomes increasingly dispensable. However, it also opens the door to cybercrime, a phenomenon that transcends national borders since the internet operates beyond traditional jurisdictional limits (Payá-Santos & Luque Juárez, 2021).

The deepest consequence of this process is the epistemic erosion of contemporary democracies. The overabundance of information and algorithmic personalization fragment the space of shared knowledge, weakening the capacity to establish common criteria of truth. Digital systems prioritize visibility over veracity, replacing scientific or institutional validation with the logic of popularity and repetition. This shift from verifiable knowledge to automated information alters the cognitive foundations of citizenship and consolidates a form of cognitive power acting on perception rather than law. In this scenario, the crisis of democratic legitimacy expands into a crisis of knowledge itself.

In such environments, data manipulation, disinformation, and the automation of communication processes become effective tools for shaping perceptions and weakening institutions without visible coercion. Hybrid threats thus develop in the informational sphere, where the boundaries between security, economy, and culture blur. A hybrid threat is a complex form of risk integrating technological, informational, economic, and social dimensions within a strategy of influence or destabilization. It does not operate through direct confrontation or traditional mechanisms of power but through a combination of digital tools, information flows, and coordinated actions aimed at disrupting the internal functioning of democratic systems. Its defining characteristic is the ability to act simultaneously across multiple levels, exploiting the global interconnection and technological dependence of contemporary societies. Its impact lies in its capacity to generate distrust, fragment social consensus, and erode legitimacy mechanisms. Within digital governance, such threats test the resilience of democracies, exploiting their openness and their reliance on technological infrastructures often beyond their direct control.

The hybrid threats described in the informational sphere also fit into a global dynamic that aligns with what international organizations such as NATO refer to as informational warfare or cognitive warfare (Luque Juárez, 2019). These concepts describe strategies that use digital flows to alter perceptions, destabilize societies, and erode institutional cohesion through data manipulation and information saturation. In such scenarios, the field of conflict is no longer territorial or military but cognitive: the goal is to dominate the interpretation of reality and shape collective decision-making. Digital governance, operating through the same mechanisms of information management and behavioral modeling, thus becomes a domain open to geopolitical instrumentalization, where the line separating civil control, economic influence, and military strategy grows increasingly blurred.

## V.- IMPLICATIONS AND PROSPECTIVE FRAMEWORKS FOR DIGITAL GOVERNANCE

The analysis of the intersections between surveillance capitalism and Yarvinism reveals that digital governance is not a transitory phenomenon but the structural form that power adopts in the age of automation. Its consolidation entails implications that transcend technological and economic dimensions, affecting the very foundations of sovereignty, legitimacy, and knowledge. The centralization of information, the delegation of authority to algorithmic systems, and the erosion of public deliberation configure a new order in which technical efficiency progressively replaces the principle of representation.

In this context, contemporary societies face the challenge of designing institutional frameworks capable of integrating technological innovation without abandoning democratic control. The question is not merely how to regulate algorithms but how to preserve human autonomy and cognitive plurality in environments mediated by automated decision-making systems. The future of digital governance will depend on the ability to articulate a balance between individual rights, technical transparency, and institutional accountability. Understanding these intersections not only illuminates the present stage of digital transformation but also helps anticipate the ethical, legal, and political dilemmas that will shape the global order in the coming decades.

The consolidation of digital governance demands a renewed reflection on sovereignty and democratic resilience in a world increasingly mediated by data infrastructures. The growing interdependence between algorithmic power, informational asymmetries, and cognitive manipulation calls for international regulatory coordination capable of addressing the transnational nature of digital authority and hybrid threats. Strengthening institutional transparency, fostering digital literacy, and developing ethical standards for artificial intelligence are not merely technical imperatives but political conditions for safeguarding democratic continuity in the automated age. Yet the same infrastructures that sustain efficiency and automation also open new domains for criminal activity and systemic manipulation. Artificial intelligence, cybercrime, and disinformation converge to create complex challenges for law and security in the digital revolution (Debasa, 2024). The ability of algorithms to distort information, facilitate large-scale data theft, or automate fraud exposes the fragility of existing legal frameworks and highlights the urgency of developing coordinated international mechanisms capable of addressing transnational cybercrime, algorithmic opacity, and the strategic use of disinformation as tools of political or economic destabilization. In this emerging scenario, law must evolve to protect not only rights and freedoms but also the integrity of truth and security in the digital age.

## VI.- CONCLUSIONS

The study demonstrates that the intersections between surveillance capitalism and Yarvinism configure a new paradigm of digital governance in which authority, economy, and information converge within a single structure of power.

This model emerges from the translation of technical efficiency into a principle of legitimacy, born out of the challenges faced by traditional democracies in a context shaped spontaneously by technological progress. The automation of decision-making and the centralization of data generate an unprecedented form of control that transforms the relationship between individuals, institutions, and knowledge.

The research confirms that digital governance, by incorporating elements of economic surveillance and technocratic authority, redefines the boundaries of sovereignty and shifts the center of democratic deliberation toward algorithmic decision systems, detached from traditional centers of power such as assemblies, parliaments, or executive institutions.

Algocracy thus emerges as an extreme manifestation of digital modernity, in which transparency gives way to traceability and legitimacy is measured through operational efficiency. The findings highlight the need for an interdisciplinary framework capable of evaluating the risks of this transformation and constructing sustainable institutional responses. Law plays a central role as an instrument of balance between innovation and safeguard, providing normative mechanisms to limit algorithmic power and ensure the preservation of human autonomy. Digital governance, understood from this perspective, cannot be conceived as a neutral process but as a field in which the future form of democratic power is contested. This transformation does not imply the disappearance of politics but its reformulation within technical infrastructures that concentrate power without public accountability.

Ultimately, this study argues that the true challenge of the coming decades does not lie in the capacity to develop more advanced technologies but in building a political and legal culture capable of governing them. The continuity of democratic values will depend on the reintegration of ethics, deliberation, and citizen oversight into the core of the digital system. Only an approach that combines technical knowledge, philosophical reflection, and legal responsibility will ensure that the automation of power does not culminate in its dehumanization.

This challenge is particularly relevant for the European Union, where digital governance must align technological innovation with the preservation of the democratic and humanist values that define its legal and political identity.

## ACKNOWLEDGMENT

This work is the result of Professor Felipe Debasa's research stay at the University of Perugia (Italy), carried out between March 25 and June 28, 2024, under the supervision of Roberto Cippitani. It was conducted within the framework of the Baldus Project (Jean Monnet Centre of Excellence "Baldus" - Building the Age of a Lawful and Sustainable Data-Use - 101047644 - Erasmus+ - EACEA - European Union). The associated research lines were: Ethical Dimension of Artificial Intelligence, Digital Governance and Algocracies, and Technology and Contemporary Society.

## REFERENCES

Blanco González, A., Atienza, P. M., Feito, C. D. C., & Gutiérrez, L. R. (2025). How do companies adapt to cultural factors to gain legitimacy in international markets? *Journal of Economy Culture and Society*, *0*(71), 104–120. DOI: 10.26650/JECS2024-1549375

Debasa, F. (2024). Inteligencia artificial, ciberdelincuencia y desinformación en el derecho de la revolución digital. In *Seguridad y responsabilidad penal e internacional en el uso de las TIC y la inteligencia artificial* (pp. 79–94). Iustel Portal Derecho.

Debasa, F., & Azcona Pastor, J. M. (2024). Tecnología global, IV Revolución Industrial y mutaciones sociales. *Historia Actual Online*, (63), 183–198.

Del Valle, G. (2024). JD Vance thinks monarchists have some good ideas. *The Verge*. https://www.theverge.com/2024/10/16/24266512/jd-vance-curtis-yarvin-influence-rage-project-2025

Giannuzzi, P. (2022). Curtis Yarvin (Mencius Moldbug): An open letter to open-minded progressives. In *Schlüsseltexte der ‚Neuen Rechten': Kritische Analysen antidemokratischen Denkens* (pp. 263 - 273). Springer Fachmedien Wiesbaden.

Karrouk, Y., & Debasa, F. (2025). Data quality in the surveillance economy: Challenges of digital governance in the paradox of data decontextualization. In *Data-driven governance through AI, digital marketing, and the privacy interplay* (pp. 31–54). IGI Global Scientific Publishing.

Kofman, A. (2025, June–July). The neo-reactionary plot of Curtis Yarvin. *Nueva Sociedad,* (318). https://nuso.org/articulo/318-complot-neorreaccionario-curtis-yarvin/

Land, N. (2022). *The dark enlightenment.* Imperium Press.

Luque Juárez, J. M. (2019). Las amenazas híbridas contra las democracias abiertas. *Estudios en Seguridad y Defensa*, *14*(27), 115–137. DOI: 10.25062/1900-8325.277

Luque Juárez, J. M. (2024). El blindaje inteligente del big data: Un ejercicio para la seguridad nacional. In *Escenarios de incertidumbre para la inteligencia estratégica en el contexto de la seguridad global* (pp. 625–643). Editorial Aranzadi.

Martin, F. D., Diez-de Castro, E., Suárez, A. C., & Prado Roman, C. (2025). Necessary conditions for the existence of organizational legitimacy. *Journal of Economy Culture and Society*, (71), 292–303.

Moldbug, M. (2008). An open letter to open-minded progressives. *Unqualified Reservations.* https://www.unqualified-reservations.org/2008/04/open-letter-to-open-minded-progressives/

Moldbug, M. (2007 - 2016). *Unqualified Reservations.* https://www.unqualified-reservations.org

Payá-Santos, C., & Luque Juárez, J. M. (2021). El sistema de inteligencia criminal ante las nuevas amenazas y oportunidades del ciberespacio. *Revista Científica General José María Córdova*, *19*(36), 1122–1136. DOI: 10.21830/19006586.855

Saura, J. R. (2025). AI, data economy, and behavioral intention: Towards ethical paths. In *Global perspectives on AI, ethics, and business economics: Charting the future* (pp. 3–16). Springer Nature Switzerland. DOI: 10.1007/978-3-031-88781-9_1

Saura, J. R., & Debasa, F. (Eds.). (2022). *Handbook of research on artificial intelligence in government practices and processes.* IGI Global. DOI: 10.4018/978-1-7998-9609-8

Torres Assiego, C. (2025). El sesgo algorítmico como nuevos retos jurídicos frente a la IA. In *La Unión Europea, los ODS y el derecho público* (pp. 183–202). Tirant lo Blanch.

Yarvin, C., Bukowski, R., & Anderson, T. (1993, June). Anonymous RPC: Low latency protection in a 64-bit address space. In *Proceedings of the USENIX Summer Technical Conference* (pp. 175 - 186). USENIX Association.

Zuboff, S. (2019). *The age of surveillance capitalism: The fight for a human future at the new frontier of power*. PublicAffairs.

# Chapter 6
# Human Firewall:
## Privacy Paradigms in the Face of the Technological Revolution

**Diego Fernando Cano Cuevas**
*Universidad Militar Nueva Granada, Colombia*

**Elmers Freddy Velandia Pardo**
*Universidad Militar Nueva Granada, Colombia*

**Manuel Guillermo Carrascal Jacome**
*Universidad Militar Nueva Granada, Colombia*

**David Moure-Blanco**
https://orcid.org/0009-0005-3462-8263
*UDIMA University, Spain*

## ABSTRACT

*This article examines the paradox between the technological revolution and human privacy, introducing the concept of the Human Firewall as a response to the digital and biotechnological invasion of intimacy. Through a qualitative methodology based on a literature review and deep analysis of interdisciplinary sources, it explores how the massive adoption of information technologies (2020–2024) and the rise of genome editing have redefined the right to privacy and human autonomy. The hypothesis argues that developing an effective Human Firewall, combining digital and bioethical literacy, can mitigate the adverse effects of technological and genetic innovation on privacy without obstructing progress. The study concludes that safeguarding human dignity in the age of artificial intelligence and biotechnology*

DOI: 10.4018/979-8-3373-4480-5.ch006

*requires robust legal frameworks, ethical governance, and active participation by individuals, institutions, and technology developers to harmonize technological advancement with the protection of fundamental rights.*

## INTRODUCTION

In an increasingly interconnected world, where the line between the digital and the physical becomes blurred, we face a fascinating and troubling crossroads: Are we building our own digital cages in the name of progress? This paradox-where technology that promises freedom and connection also threatens to undermine privacy, it forces us to reflect on the real cost of the digital revolution.

The omnipresence of information technologies in daily life has radically transformed the way the world interacts, in areas such as work and existence itself. From smartphones that now accompany us 24 hours a day in fact, it is estimated that 5.78 billion people use a mobile phone worldwide, and of these, nearly 87% use a smartphone, which amounts to approximately 5.03 billion smartphone users at the beginning of 2025 (We Are Social & Meltwater, 2025, cited in Guayoyo Marketing, 2025)-to virtual assistants that listen to our conversations, technology has become an extension of the self (Floridi, 2014). This seemingly harmless and convenient integration has generated an unprecedented self-inflicted impact on human rights, particularly the right to privacy. The constant collection of personal data, ubiquitous surveillance, and the voluntary exposure of people's lives on social networks have created a scenario where privacy has become a scarce and valuable commodity (Zuboff, 2019). For example, military doctrines now include cyberspace and cognitive warfare as domains of war (Cano Cuevas, 2024).

The concept of the "Human Firewall" emerges as a powerful metaphor in this context. Just as a computer firewall protects systems from unwanted intrusions, the human firewall represents the urgent need to develop personal and collective defense mechanisms against the technological invasion of privacy. This term encompasses not only the technical skills to protect data, but also the informed awareness and discernment necessary to navigate today's complex digital ecosystem (Solove, 2021).

The "technological revolution", for its part, refers to the accelerated development and adoption of digital technologies that have transformed virtually every aspect of society. This revolution, characterized by artificial intelligence, the Internet of Things, and big data, promises efficiency, connectivity, and progress, but also raises unprecedented ethical and practical challenges (Schwab, 2016). However, the scope of this revolution goes beyond the digital domain. Several advances in biotechnology, particularly in genome editing and gene therapy through disruptive technologies such as CRISPR-Cas9, have introduced a new paradigm of technological intervention in human life, where privacy and ethics are also at stake (Doudna & Charpentier, 2014). The parallel between digital and genetic data reveals that the same logic of control, prediction, and modification that governs information systems now reaches the biological substrate of human identity.

To address this complex topic, this research will rely on an interdisciplinary theoretical framework that integrates concepts from digital sociology, technology ethics, and human rights studies. Some authors such as Shoshana Zuboff and her theory of "surveillance capitalism" provides a basis for understanding the economic dynamics behind the erosion of privacy (Zuboff, 2019), complemented by Helen Nissenbaum's perspectives on contextual privacy (Nissenbaum, 2010) and Yuval Noah Harari's reflections on the future of humanity in the digital age (Harari, 2018).

The central issue to be addressed can be summarized in the following question: To what extent has the widespread adoption of information technologies in the last decade impacted individuals' right to privacy, and what are the long-term implications for autonomy and human rights? This question is measurable through empirical studies on data breaches and changes in privacy policies, and seeks to address a real and relevant contemporary phenomenon given the growing global concern about digital privacy. Although this scenario is not new, the selected timeframe of the last ten years is a specific period of rapid technological adoption (Acquisti et al., 2015).

In developing this reflection, three fundamental aspects will be addressed: First, the anatomy of the human firewall will be analyzed, exploring the digital skills, privacy literacy, and personal protection strategies necessary to build an effective human firewall in the digital age. Secondly, it is necessary to discuss the dialectic between innovation and privacy, analyzing how technological advancement and privacy protection can coexist and reinforce each other, rather than being antagonistic forces. Finally, the role of regulation and ethics in the digital age will be addressed. Legal and ethical frameworks necessary to safeguard human rights in the context of the technological revolution will be examined, considering initiatives such as the GDPR and proposals for global digital governance.

This exploration will lead us to question not only individual digital practices, but also the social, economic, and political structures that have enabled the systematic erosion of privacy. Ultimately, the aim is not only to understand the paradox between privacy and technological revolution, but also to propose ways to reconcile these seemingly contradictory aspects of digital reality. In a world where every click, every search, and every digital interaction leaves an indelible mark, building an effective human firewall becomes not only a practical necessity, but an ethical imperative. This firewall is not an impenetrable barrier, but a set of skills, knowledge, and practices that allow us to navigate the digital landscape with awareness and autonomy (Solove, 2021)

## METHODOLOGY

This research adopts a qualitative and interdisciplinary methodological approach, combining documentary analysis, conceptual synthesis, and comparative examination. The study relies on academic literature, institutional reports, and legal frameworks on privacy, technology, and human rights to construct an integrated understanding of the phenomenon. The research process follows three stages: identification of the main theoretical approaches on surveillance capitalism, contextual privacy, and digital ethics; comparative analysis of legal and normative frameworks, such as the General Data Protection Regulation (GDPR) and the European Union's Artificial Intelligence Act, to assess the institutional response to privacy erosion; and synthesis of findings to propose a human-centered model of digital resilience, the "human firewall". This qualitative design seeks to link theory and praxis by interpreting how global technological transformations affect the individual's capacity for autonomy and self-determination in the digital age.

## THE ANATOMY OF THE HUMAN FIREWALL: A COMPREHENSIVE APPROACH TO DIGITAL PROTECTION

As this reflection advances, uncomfortable questions loom regarding the future of privacy and, by extension, freedom itself. Are we willing to sacrifice our intimacy on the altar of technological convenience? Or can we forge a path that allows us to reap the benefits of the digital revolution without compromising our fundamental rights? The paradox of privacy versus technological revolution is not an abstract dilemma, but a concrete challenge that defines our era. Exploring this tension, the goal is not only to understand the digital present but also to actively shape a future where technology expands, rather than restricts, the spectrum of human freedom and dignity (Harari, 2018).

It is important to remember that the first generation of human rights arose in response to questions about the sovereignty of the king and the absolutist state. This historical period was characterized by revolutionary movements, such as the French Revolution and the independence of the English colonies in North America, which challenged the absolute power of monarchs and advocated for the protection of fundamental rights. These rights, known as civil and political rights, include freedom of expression, freedom of conscience, and the right to property. Their purpose was to limit state power and guarantee individual autonomy in the face of governmental authority, thus establishing the foundations for a rule of law that respects human dignity (Nogueira Alcalá, 2003; Cruz Villalón, 1989).

With the Industrial Revolution and the growth of large companies, new challenges emerged that led to the development of the second generation of human rights. The working class began to demand better working conditions, fair wages, and reasonable working hours. These economic, social, and cultural rights reflect the need to protect individuals not only from state oppression but also from economic and social inequalities. Later, after the devastation of the First World War, the need for rights that encompassed the entire planet became evident, giving rise to third-generation rights. These rights, also known as solidarity rights, include the right to development, a healthy environment, justice, and peace. Today, in an era marked by communication and technology, there is talk of fourth-generation rights, which address issues related to digital privacy and access to information. However, unlike previous generations, these rights have not yet been fully questioned or integrated into the global legal framework, posing new challenges for their recognition and protection (CODHEM, 2001; Solís García, 2013). France emerged as a pioneer in embedding fourth-generation rights within its domestic legislation, notably through Law 2016-1088 —the Loi Travail— which formally recognized the right to digital disconnection. Likewise, Estonia has distinguished itself advancing on digital rights at a legislative level, guaranteeing universal internet access as a fundamental right since 2000, thus positioning itself as a global reference in the protection of rights associated with new technologies and the digital ecosystem (González-Palenzuela Reyes, 2025; e-Estonia, 2024).

In line with the conceptual framework presented, the widespread adoption of information technologies in the last decade has profoundly transformed the social, economic, and political life of individuals, generating new challenges for the protection of the right to privacy. From an interdisciplinary perspective, it is essential to analyze this phenomenon through the integration of some concepts like digital sociology, technology ethics, and human rights studies, as the convergence of these fields allows for an understanding of both emerging opportunities and risks (Zuboff, 2019; Nissenbaum, 2010; Harari, 2018).

Shoshana Zuboff, through her theory of "surveillance capitalism," warns that large technology corporations have turned personal data into an economic resource, eroding individual privacy in order to maximize profitability (Zuboff, 2019)1. This economic model incentivizes the massive collection of user information, which has created a power asymmetry between those who control the digital infrastructure and ordinary citizens.

In this context, Helen Nissenbaum introduces the notion of contextual privacy, emphasizing that privacy protection does not depend solely on the amount of information shared, but on the context in which it circulates and the associated social expectations (Nissenbaum, 2010)1. The disruption of these contexts, facilitated by digital technologies, can lead to inadvertent privacy violations and loss of control over one's own information. Yuval Noah Harari, for his part, argues that massive digitalization and artificial intelligence are redefining human autonomy, as algorithms can anticipate and manipulate individual behaviors on a large scale (Harari, 2018)1. This raises ethical questions about free will and individuals' ability to make informed decisions in highly monitored environments.

The long-term implications of these changes are profound. On the one hand, digitalization has facilitated access to services, citizen participation, and social innovation; on the other, it has increased individuals' vulnerability to state and corporate surveillance, as well as the risk of algorithmic discrimination and information manipulation (Zuboff, 2019; Harari, 2018).

In terms of human rights, the erosion of privacy affects not only the right to intimacy but also freedom of expression, personal autonomy, and equal opportunities. The lack of effective regulation and the opacity of technological systems make it difficult to defend these rights in practice (Nissenbaum, 2010). Therefore, the challenge is to design regulatory and ethical frameworks that respond to the complexity of the digital age, promoting transparency, informed consent, and accountability of technological actors. Only in this way will it be possible to ensure that technological innovation does not come at the expense of people's fundamental rights (Zuboff, 2019; Nissenbaum, 2010; Harari, 2018).

The protection of privacy and online security have become primary concerns for individuals. The increasing interconnection and extensive use of digital devices have heightened the vulnerabilities to which humans are exposed. To address these concerns, it is keyto develop a set of skills and strategies that form an effective "human firewall". This concept refers to the combination of digital competencies, privacy literacy, and personal protection strategies that enable individuals to defend themselves against threats to their privacy and security in the digital environment. According to Van Deursen and Van Dijk (2014), these competencies include technical, informational, and strategic skills.

Technical skills are the basic abilities to operate digital devices and use software. These skills include the ability to install and update programs, configure devices, and troubleshoot common technical problems. The lack of technical skills can leave users vulnerable to various threats, from malware to phishing attacks. Mastery of these skills is essential for any technology user.

Informational skills refer to the ability to search for, evaluate, and use information essentially. In a world where misinformation and fake news are common, the ability to discern the quality and truthfulness of information is fundamental. Livingstone (2018) highlights the importance of these skills in preventing the spread of misinformation and making informed decisions.

Strategic skills enable individuals to use technology to achieve personal and professional goals. These skills include the ability to manage online privacy, properly configure security options, and use encryption tools to protect personal information. Van Deursen and Van Dijk (2014) argue that these skills are essential for effective protection in the digital environment.

Added to these skills is a controversial concept: privacy literacy, an extension of digital competencies that specifically focuses on the protection of personal information. According to Solove (2021), privacy literacy involves knowledge and understanding of privacy rights, as well as the practices and tools necessary to protect those rights. It is essential for individuals to understand their privacy rights and the laws that protect them. This knowledge includes regulations such as the General Data Protection Regulation (GDPR) in Europe and the California Consumer Privacy Act (CCPA) in the United States. In Colombia, the protection of personal data is mainly regulated by Statutory Law 1581 of 2012, known as the Personal Data Protection Law. This law establishes the legal framework for the collection, use, processing, and storage of personal data, guaranteeing citizens and privacy rights. The Superintendence of Industry and Commerce (SIC) is responsible for supervising and ensuring compliance with this regulation, as well as promoting a culture of data protection in the country. The law is based on principles such as legality, purpose, freedom, truthfulness, transparency, restricted access and circulation, security, and confidentiality. In addition, Colombia has adopted measures to align with international data protection standards, facilitating cooperation and information exchange with other jurisdictions. Companies and entities handling personal data must implement appropriate policies and procedures to ensure information protection, as well as obtain individuals express consent for data processing. Solove (2021) argues that understanding these rights is the first step toward effective privacy protection.

Adopting safe practices is fundamental to privacy literacy. This includes using strong passwords, enabling two-factor authentication, and regularly reviewing privacy settings on social networks and other online platforms. Cavoukian (2011) stresses the importance of these practices to minimize security risks. There are various tools and technologies designed to protect privacy, such as privacy-protecting browsers, virtual private networks (VPNs), and encrypted messaging apps. Privacy literacy includes the ability to select and use these tools effectively. Solove (2021) emphasizes that proper use of these tools is essential for robust protection.

Consequently, building an effective human firewall requires implementing personal protection strategies that address both technical and social threats. These strategies must be proactive and adaptive, considering the constantly changing digital environment. The first strategy is continuous risk assessment. This involves staying aware of emerging threats and regularly evaluating one's exposure to these threats. Nissenbaum (2010) suggests conducting regular security audits on online accounts and personal devices as an essential practice to identify and mitigate potential risks.

Ongoing education in privacy and security is fundamental. Participating in courses, workshops, and seminars on cybersecurity and privacy can help keep individuals up to date on best practices and new threats. Livingstone (2018) argues that ongoing education is keyto adapt to the changing dynamics of the digital environment.

Fostering a culture of privacy at both the personal and community levels is decisive. This includes sharing privacy knowledge and practices with family and friends, and advocating for stricter privacy policies at work and in the community. Floridi (2014) highlights the importance of a robust privacy culture for collective well-being in the digital age.

Implementing protection technologies, such as antivirus software, encryption tools, and password management applications, is an essential strategy for protecting personal information. These technologies must be properly configured and used to be effective. Cavoukian (2011) notes that correct implementation and use of these technologies is fundamental for effective defense against digital threats.

In conclusion, the anatomy of the human firewall consists of a set of digital competencies, privacy literacy, and personal protection strategies that together enable individuals to defend themselves against threats to their privacy in the digital age. Building this human firewall is a continuous process that requires education, adaptation, and proactivity. As the digital environment evolves, so too must our strategies and skills to ensure effective and sustainable protection. Adopting a comprehensive and proactive approach is essential to navigate safely and protect our privacy in the digital world.

## The Dialectic between Innovation and Privacy

The dialectic between innovation and privacy represents one of the most complex and urgent challenges of this digital era. These concepts are often presented as opposing forces, where technological advancement seemingly demands the inevitable sacrifice of personal privacy. However, a deeper analysis reveals that this dichotomy is an oversimplification of a much more complex and potentially symbiotic relationship.

The dialectic between digital progress and privacy is expressed in the tension between the benefits of technological innovation and the risks associated with the exposure of personal data. The exponential growth of digital connectivity has generated new vulnerabilities, especially in cyberspace, where the protection of data and digital infrastructure becomes essential to safeguard human security and individual privacy (Cano Cuevas, 2024). In this sense, digital privacy emerges as a fundamental right that requires active protection against the growing capacity of technologies to collect, analyze, and predict individual behaviors (Zuboff, 2019).

Shoshana Zuboff argues that "surveillance capitalism" has transformed privacy into an economic resource, where large corporations extract and process personal data even beyond what users consciously share (Zuboff, 2019). This model means that privacy can no longer be addressed solely from individual responsibility, as the scale and sophistication of data collection surpass personal control capacities. Furthermore, as Velandia and colleagues point out, the hybridization of traditional and digital domains has created complex scenarios where the boundaries between civil and military, public and private, are blurred, demanding collective responses and stricter regulations to protect autonomy and human rights (Velandia, et al., 2025).

Helen Nissenbaum, for her part, emphasizes that privacy protection depends on respecting the informational norms of each context, and warns that the disruption of these contexts by technologies that cross and mix data can cause profound privacy violations (Nissenbaum, 2010). In the digital age, the hybridization of domains and the multiplicity of actors imply that defending privacy and autonomy requires not only robust regulatory frameworks but also digital literacy that enables citizens to understand and manage the risks associated with technological innovation (Velandia, et al 2025).

Technological innovation, at its core, seeks to improve quality of life and solve societal problems. Paradoxically, many of the technologies that have raised privacy concerns also have the potential to strengthen it. For example, the development of artificial intelligence (AI) has generated fears about mass surveillance and data manipulation. Nevertheless, these same AI technologies can be used to create more sophisticated intrusion detection systems and more effective data anonymization algorithms (Cavoukian, 2011).

The concept of "Privacy by Design," proposed by Ann Cavoukian, illustrates how innovation and privacy can coexist and reinforce each other. This approach advocates for the incorporation of privacy principles from the earliest stages of the design of technological systems and processes. Embedding privacy as a core design principle, rather than a secondary concern, enables innovations to be both transformative and protective of individual rights (Cavoukian, 2011).

Cryptography is another perfect example of how technological innovation can enhance privacy. Advances in quantum cryptography promise to create virtually impenetrable communication systems, offering an unprecedented level of privacy in the digital era. These innovations demonstrate that technological progress is not only compatible with privacy protection but can also be a catalyst for its strengthening (Gisin et al., 2002). Moreover, the growing awareness of the importance of privacy is driving innovations in data management. Technologies such as federated computing and differential machine learning allow the analysis of large data sets without compromising individual privacy. These techniques represent a significant advance in reconciling the needs of data-driven innovation with the imperatives of privacy protection (Dwork & Roth, 2014).

The regulatory framework also plays a keyrole in this dialectic. Laws such as the European Union's General Data Protection Regulation (GDPR) have established new standards for the protection of personal data. Far from hindering innovation, these regulations have stimulated the development of new technologies and business practices that respect privacy. Companies that adopt a proactive approach to privacy are discovering this can be a competitive advantage, driving innovation in areas such as data security and transparency (Floridi, 2018).

Blockchain is another example of innovative technology with the potential to revolutionize privacy. Although initially associated with cryptocurrencies, blockchain offers possibilities for decentralized identity management and individual control over personal data. These applications demonstrate how a disruptive technology can align with privacy protection goals (Zyskind et al., 2015). It is important to recognize that the relationship between innovation and privacy is not free of tensions. Every technological advance brings new ethical and practical challenges. However, these tensions should not be seen as insurmountable obstacles, but as opportunities for more responsible and human-centered innovation. Collaboration among technologists, lawmakers, and privacy advocates is essential to navigate these challenges and find solutions that benefit society as a whole.

In short, the dialectic between innovation and privacy is not a zero-sum game. On the contrary, it is a dynamic and potentially synergistic relationship. Through adopting a holistic approach that considers privacy as an integral component of innovation, we can create a digital future that is both technologically advanced and respectful of individual rights. This approach is not only possible but imperative to ensure that the benefits of the digital revolution are distributed equitably and ethically, preserving human dignity and autonomy in the information age.

## The Role of Regulation and Ethics in the Digital Age

The technological revolution has profoundly transformed all aspects of human life, from social interactions to economic and political models. In this context, there is an urgent need to establish legal and ethical frameworks that safeguard human rights, especially regarding data protection and privacy. The exponential increase in the collection and processing of personal information has placed these issues at the center of the global debate on digital rights.

The European Union's General Data Protection Regulation (GDPR), implemented in May 2018, has become a global benchmark for data protection. This robust legal framework gives EU citizens greater control over their personal data and streamlines the regulatory environment for international businesses. The GDPR establishes fundamental principles such as transparency, integrity, confidentiality, and accountability in data management, requiring organizations to obtain explicit consent before collecting personal data and guaranteeing individuals the right to access and request the deletion of their data.

The need for global digital governance is increasingly evident in a digitized and globalized world. The United Nations, through the Commission on Science and Technology for Development, has proposed frameworks for international cooperation in digital governance, focusing on the protection of human rights and the promotion of responsible innovation. These proposals include the creation of a global digital governance forum and the promotion of a "Universal Internet" that ensures access to information and connectivity for all, while respecting users' privacy and security.

Ethics plays a keyrole in technology regulation. Digital ethics, as defined by Luciano Floridi, centers on the responsible use of technology, considering aspects such as privacy, security, autonomy, and equity. An ethical approach involves assessing the consequences of technology on human rights and ensuring that its development does not exacerbate existing inequalities. This is particularly relevant in the development of technologies like artificial intelligence and big data, which have the potential to significantly improve quality of life but can also perpetuate biases and discrimination if not properly managed.

In Colombia, the protection of personal data is mainly regulated by Statutory Law 1581 of 2012, which establishes the legal framework for the collection, use, processing, and storage of personal data, thus guaranteeing citizens' privacy rights. The Superintendence of Industry and Commerce (SIC) is responsible for overseeing and ensuring compliance with this regulation. The law is based on principles such as legality, purpose, freedom, truthfulness, transparency, restricted access and circulation, security, and confidentiality. Although Colombia has taken steps to align with international data protection standards, such as the GDPR, there are significant differences between the two regulations.

The GDPR is considered one of the most robust frameworks worldwide, notable for its extraterritorial application and its focus on explicit consent and individual rights over data. In comparison, Law 1581 of 2012 presents certain regulatory gaps, especially regarding the processing of personal data related to criminal convictions and proceedings, an area that the GDPR covers in greater detail. Furthermore, while the GDPR imposes significant penalties for non-compliance, encouraging companies to improve their privacy policies, Colombian legislation has been criticized for its lack of rigor in enforcing sanctions, which may limit its effectiveness.

A strength of Law 1581 is its focus on informational self-determination, similar to the internationally recognized right of habeas data, which is fundamental for privacy protection. However, the practical implementation of this principle faces challenges, especially in the context of foreign companies operating in Colombia.

Colombian regulations require these companies to comply with local provisions, such as obtaining prior consent for the use of cookies, which has led to tensions with large international corporations.

Despite advances in regulation and ethics in the digital age, numerous challenges persist. The rapid evolution of technology often outpaces the ability of laws and regulations to keep up. The global nature of the internet also complicates the enforcement of national laws, as companies can operate in multiple jurisdictions with different levels of data protection. However, there are also significant opportunities. International collaboration in digital governance can lead to the creation of global standards that protect individuals' rights everywhere. Additionally, an ethical approach to technological development can promote responsible innovation and the use of technology for the common Good.

The technological revolution is not limited to the digital sphere. The rapid progress of biotechnology, especially in genome editing and gene therapy, has introduced new challenges for privacy, ethics, and law. Tools such as CRISPR-Cas9 have made it possible to modify the human genome with unprecedented precision, opening the door to therapeutic advances but also to the manipulation of hereditary traits (Doudna & Charpentier, 2014). The ethical and legal implications of these technologies mirror those observed in the digital field: both involve the extraction, processing, and potential alteration of deeply personal data—whether genetic or digital.

From the perspective of human rights, genetic information represents the most intimate layer of individual identity. Its collection, storage, and possible modification raise questions similar to those posed by surveillance capitalism in the digital world (Zuboff, 2019). Genetic data, like digital profiles, can be used to predict behavior, predispositions, and health risks, generating risks of discrimination and loss of autonomy. This convergence highlights that privacy is no longer limited to the control of information but extends to the biological substrate of human existence.

International frameworks, such as the UNESCO Universal Declaration on the Human Genome and Human Rights (1997) and the Council of Europe's Oviedo Convention (1997), affirm that the human genome must not give rise to practices contrary to human dignity. These texts anticipate the ethical principles later applied to data protection: consent, transparency, and prohibition of discrimination. However, the exponential development of genome editing has outpaced the ability of legislation to keep pace, similar to the challenge faced by privacy law in the digital age.

In this sense, the notion of a "Human Firewall" acquires a broader meaning: it is not only a digital barrier but also a bioethical shield. It represents the need for individuals and societies to develop both digital literacy and bioethical literacy, capable of understanding the implications of technological intervention in data and in life itself. The human firewall becomes a conceptual bridge between data protection and the protection of biological integrity, uniting digital and genetic ethics under a single principle of human autonomy.

Establishing clear governance mechanisms for genome editing such as global registries, transparent ethical review committees, and international moratoria on germline modification is as urgent as enforcing digital data regulation. Without these safeguards, the same logic that transforms personal information into a commodity could extend to the human genome. Thus, defending privacy in the twenty-first century requires addressing not only the protection of data but also the inviolability of human biological identity.

In essence, regulation and ethics are fundamental to safeguarding human rights in the digital age. The GDPR and Colombia's Personal Data Protection Law are examples of legal frameworks that seek to protect privacy and the security of personal data. However, a global and ethical approach is necessary to address emerging challenges and ensure that technology benefits all of society. International cooperation, the adoption of ethical standards, and the continuous updating of legal frameworks can provide a solid foundation for digital governance in the future, ensuring that the technological revolution advances hand in hand with the protection of human rights and individual privacy

## CONCLUSIONS

This article has explored the complex intersection between the technological revolution and privacy, highlighting the need for a "Human Firewall" that enables individuals to protect their intimacy in the digital age. Through the analysis of digital competencies, privacy literacy, and personal protection strategies, we have identified the tools and knowledge necessary to navigate safely in an increasingly interconnected environment. Additionally, we have examined how technological innovation and privacy protection can coexist and reinforce each other, rather than being antagonistic forces. Finally, we reviewed legal and ethical frameworks, such as the GDPR and Colombia's Law 1581, which seek to safeguard human rights in this context.

In response to the research question posed, it can be categorically stated that the widespread adoption of information technologies between 2020 and 2024 has significantly impacted individuals' right to privacy. However, it has also been identified that the development of an effective "Human Firewall," supported by robust legal frameworks and an ethical approach to innovation, can mitigate these negative effects. This demonstrates that it is possible to reconcile technological advancement with privacy protection, provided that proactive and collaborative measures are adopted at the individual, institutional, and global levels.

The convergence between biotechnology and digital systems outlines a new horizon of human vulnerability that demands urgent reflection. The same logic of surveillance and prediction that governs digital capitalism now extends to biological life through genetic sequencing, biometric identification, and neurodata analysis. This expansion transforms the body into the last frontier of data extraction, raising fundamental questions about autonomy, consent, and the definition of what it means to be human. Protecting privacy, therefore, is no longer limited to controlling information flows, but to defending the integrity of human identity itself. In this context, the Human Firewall must evolve into an ethical and biotechnological consciousness capable of safeguarding both digital and biological freedoms in the twenty-first century.

This research, however, has its limitations. The focus has been mainly on theoretical analysis and literature review, suggesting the need for more detailed empirical studies that assess the real impact of technologies on privacy in different cultural and economic contexts. Moreover, it would be valuable to investigate how younger generations, who have grown up in a digital environment, perceive and manage their privacy. Future studies could also explore the development of new data protection technologies and their implementation in specific sectors, such as health and education, to offer more personalized and effective solutions.

## REFERENCES


Acquisti, A., Brandimarte, L., & Loewenstein, G. (2015). Privacy and human behavior in the age of information. *Science, 347*(6221), 509–514. https://www.science.org/doi/abs/10.1126/science.aaa1465. DOI: 10.1126/science.aaa1465 PMID: 25635091

Cano Cuevas, D. F. (2024). Challenges of human security in the new domains of war. *Novum Jus, 18*(3), 41–68. DOI: 10.14718/NovumJus.2024.18.3.2

Cavoukian, A. (2011). *Privacy by design: The 7 foundational principles*. Information and Privacy Commissioner of Ontario.

CODHEM. (2001). *Third generation human rights*. Human Rights Commission of the State of Mexico.

Council of Europe. (1997). Convention for the Protection of Human Rights and Dignity of the Human Being with regard to the Application of Biology and Medicine (Oviedo Convention) (ETS No. 164). https://rm.coe.int/168007cf98

Cruz Villalón, P. (1989). *Rule of law and fundamental rights*. Center for Constitutional Studies.

Doudna, J. A., & Charpentier, E. (2014). The new frontier of genome engineering with CRISPR-Cas9. *Science, 346*(6213), 1258096. https://www.science.org/doi/abs/10.1126/science.1258096. DOI: 10.1126/science.1258096 PMID: 25430774

Dwork, C., & Roth, A. (2014). The algorithmic foundations of differential privacy. *Foundations and Trends in Theoretical Computer Science, 9*(3–4), 211–407. DOI: 10.1561/0400000042

e-Estonia. (2024). Universal internet access as a fundamental right.

European Union. (2016). Regulation (EU) 2016/679 of the European Parliament and of the Council of 27 April 2016 on the protection of natural persons with regard to the processing of personal data and on the free movement of such data (General Data Protection Regulation). Official Journal of the European Union.

European Union. (2024). Regulation (EU) 2024/1689 of the European Parliament and of the Council of 13 June 2024 on artificial intelligence (Artificial Intelligence Act). Official Journal of the European Union, L 168, 1–127. https://eur-lex.europa.eu/legal-content/EN/TXT/?uri=CELEX%3A32024R1689

Floridi, L. (2014). *The fourth revolution: How the infosphere is reshaping human reality*. Oxford University Press.

Floridi, L. (2018). Soft ethics and the governance of the digital. *Philosophy & Technology*, *31*(1), 1–8. DOI: 10.1007/s13347-018-0303-9 PMID: 30322997

Gisin, N., Ribordy, G., Tittel, W., & Zbinden, H. (2002). Quantum cryptography. *Reviews of Modern Physics*, *74*(1), 145–195. DOI: 10.1103/RevModPhys.74.145

González-Palenzuela Reyes, A. (2025). Digital rights and the evolution of the right to disconnection in France and Estonia. *Revista de Estudios Constitucionales Europeos*, *12*(1), 45–67.

Harari, Y. N. (2018). *21 lessons for the 21st century*. Debate.

Law 1581 of 2012. (2012). General provisions for the protection of personal data. Official Gazette No. 48,587.

Livingstone, S. (2018). *Media literacy: What are the challenges and how can we move towards a solution?* LSE Media Policy Project Blog.

Nissenbaum, H. (2010). *Privacy in context: Technology, policy, and the integrity of social life*. Stanford University Press.

Nogueira Alcalá, H. (2003). *Los derechos fundamentales y sus generaciones: una aproximación teórica*. Universidad Nacional Autónoma de México, Instituto de Investigaciones Jurídicas.

Schwab, K. (2016). The fourth industrial revolution. World Economic Forum.

Solís García, M. (2013). Fourth generation human rights. *Revista IUS*, *7*(32), 45–67.

Solove, D. J. (2021). The myth of the privacy paradox. *The George Washington Law Review*, *89*(1), 1–51.

State of California Department of Justice. (s. f.). California Consumer Privacy Act (CCPA). https://oag.ca.gov/privacy/ccpa

UNESCO. (1997). Universal Declaration on the Human Genome and Human Rights. https://unesdoc.unesco.org/ark:/48223/pf0000110220

United Nations. (2020). *Report of the Secretary-General: Roadmap for digital cooperation*. United Nations.

Van Deursen, A. J., & Van Dijk, J. A. (2014). The digital divide shifts to differences in usage. *New Media & Society*, *16*(3), 507–526. DOI: 10.1177/1461444813487959

Velandia Pardo, D., Cano Cuevas, D. F., Betancur, M., & Paya Santos, C. (2025). Development of a national strategy to combat hybrid threats in Colombia. Well Testing Journal, 34(S2), 25–44. Retrieved from https://welltestingjournal.com/index.php/WT/article/view/164

We Are Social, & Meltwater. (2025). Digital world 2025: Essential statistics. Guayoyo Marketing. Retrieved from https://guayoyomarketing.com/mundo-digital-2025-estadisticas-imprescindibles/

Zuboff, S. (2019). *The age of surveillance capitalism: The fight for a human future at the new frontier of power*. Profile Books.

Zyskind, G., Nathan, O., & Pentland, A. S. (2015). Decentralizing privacy: Using blockchain to protect personal data. 2015 IEEE Security and Privacy Workshops, 180–184.

# Chapter 7
# Technological Gaps and Security:
## Challenges for Law Enforcement and Public Safety

**Claudio Paya Santos**
https://orcid.org/0000-0002-1908-9960
*Universidad Internacional de Valencia, Spain*

**Luigi Martino**
*Universidad de Bologna, Italy*

**Roger Sanz Gonzalez**
https://orcid.org/0009-0006-1419-2367
*Universidad Internacional de Valencia, Spain*

**Juan Jose Delgado Moran**
https://orcid.org/0000-0002-9945-8235
*Universidad Pablo de Olavide, Spain*

## ABSTRACT

*This disparity presents a critical concern, as traditional investigative methods are becoming increasingly ineffective against these technologically advanced actors. Consequently, there is a pressing need for law enforcement agencies to adapt their strategies, adopt new technologies, and foster international cooperation to effectively counter the evolving threat posed by transnational criminal organizations in the contemporary security environment. This paper examines the evolving technological landscape of transnational criminal organizations, analyzes the implications for global security, and explores potential strategies for mitigating the growing technological gap between transnational criminal organizations and law enforcement agencies.*

DOI: 10.4018/979-8-3373-4480-5.ch007

## 1. INTRODUCTION

The increasing sophistication of transnational criminal organizations (TCOs), driven by their adoption and exploitation of new technologies, poses a significant challenge to global security.

This challenge is exacerbated by the collaborative ecosystems these organizations cultivate, sharing resources and expertise to amplify their impact. Technology has evolved from a mere support function to a critical enabler, providing TCOs with turnkey solutions for enhancing their operational capabilities. The proliferation of advanced technologies, including secure communication systems, surveillance tools, artificial intelligence, and big data analytics that are rapidly transforming the landscape of criminal activity (Payá y Delgado, 2017; Sanz et al., 2024). These technological advancements, coupled with strategic alliances between TCOs, are widening the gap between their capabilities and those of law enforcement agencies (LEAs).

## 2. TECHNOLOGY-DRIVEN TERRORISM AND TRANSNATIONAL CRIMINAL ACTIVITIES

The emergence of technology-driven terrorism has fundamentally transformed the nature of terrorist operations and capabilities. Modern terrorist organizations increasingly leverage advanced technological tools, particularly in cyberspace, to achieve their objectives.

Cyber terrorism, based on computer technologies to create widespread fear and disruption, is one of the most significant threats in global security landscape. The anonymity and accessibility of cyberspace have amplified these challenges, enabling terrorist organizations and TCOs to conduct attacks while evading traditional security measures (Maesschalck, 2024). The cost-benefit of use of digital resources for terrorism in cyberspace is one of the most significant factors of proliferation of digital technologies. This factor is combined with reduction of exposure of terrorist resources with isolation of operational levels of terrorist organizations to maintain their objectives along the time. This is not reduced to use of social networks and must be considered other digital capabilities for secure communications, surveillance, intelligence gathering, counterintelligence, 3D printers, internet of things (IoTs),robotic process automation (RPAs), intelligent systems, unmanned autonomous devices, unattended information systems, plug and play attack platforms, command a control of terrorist operations with offshoring of technical resources in countries where legal consequences are low and the capabilities of Law Enforcement Agencies (LEAs) does not have sufficient resources to pursue complex criminal organizations.

In addition, those countries where there are high levels of corruption combined with accessibility to technological capabilities at a very low price.

This digitalization of terrorism has necessitated new approaches to counter-terrorism. Research has expanded into novel areas, such as radicalization detection through emotion signals and semantic similarity analysis (Araque & Iglesias, 2020). Additionally, the evolution of the digital terrorism ecosystem has highlighted the increasing role of state-sponsored terrorism, requiring adaptive research and counter-terrorism strategies (Ochara et al., 2020).

Parallel to terrorism, transnational criminal activities have undergone significant transformation through technological advancement. Criminal organizations now exploit sophisticated technologies to facilitate operations across borders, encompassing activities such as organized crime, human smuggling, drug trafficking, and cybercrime. The utilization of communication interception technology (CIT) by criminal groups has enhanced their operational effectiveness while complicating law enforcement efforts (Bell & Congram 2013).

The challenge of transnational criminal organizations (TCOs) extends beyond immediate security concerns, affecting national sovereignty and economic development globally. Network analysis of illicit drug trafficking has revealed complex organizational structures that span multiple countries (Giommoni et al., 2016), highlighting the sophisticated nature of modern criminal collaborative organizations. The digitalization of criminal activities has created a dynamic ecosystem that requires innovative counter-measures and international cooperation.

The evolution of financial crime prevention and detection capacities has provided new lines of investigations for LEAs of TCOs and terrorist organizations. Alan Setiawan et al. (2023) emphasizes the need for a macro-level approach to address technology-driven economic crimes within the broader context of global transformation. The complexity of financial crimes, aligning them with broader challenges such as technology-driven terrorism and transnational criminal activities where interconnected between economic crimes and transnational threats suggests that a multi-faceted and adaptive response is essential for effective prevention and enforcement.

The evolving nature of both technology-driven terrorism and transnational crime demands comprehensive responses from the international security community with experienced-based frameworks not limited to legal and regulatory affairs. Collaboration, capability development and secure information sharing are factors to be established in advance to any other actions for effectiveness of strategies for countering TCOs and terrorist groups activities.

The rapid evolution of technologies such as artificial intelligence requires a practical approach that allows for full collaboration of capabilities between law enforcement and intelligence agencies by sharing federated and available resources for the prevention and early detection of terrorist groups and TCOs activities. Although much researchers were focused on the use of social media and instant messaging channels for the detection of criminal organizations' capabilities. A new technology-based effort is needed to detect organizational capabilities that go beyond mere economic resources, and special attention must be paid to technological provisioning to prevent the illicit use of information systems or the resources of technological operators. This is not limited to regulation and best practices and must be focused in specific technologies development. Adaptation of counter-terrorism and law enforcement strategies to address emerging digital threats is focused in new technology-driven capabilities. The Adoption of these new technologies needs great efforts by LEAs to consider risks and therefore requires the availability of robust, adaptable frameworks focused on the specific risks of their design and use in order to obtain sufficient capacity to counter the evolution of the capabilities of TCOs and terrorist organisations (Sanz et al, 2024)

This complex landscape requires continuous evolution of research methodologies, technology-based applied research methods, adaptative policy frameworks, and international cooperation mechanisms to effectively combat technology-driven security challenges.

## 2.1 Deepfake Attacks. The Easy-To-Use Case of High Impact Crime Technologies

The proliferation of deepfake technology presents multifaceted technical challenges in digital forensics and cybersecurity, particularly concerning transnational criminal activities (Martino & Merenda, 2021; Martino, 2024).

Understanding the combination of traditional criminal methods and these technologies will be one of the main challenges for LEAs given that the possibility of being discovered by the isolation of the resources to perpetrate crimes and the variability of possibilities of applicable use cases by criminals is infinite. It must be taken into special consideration that the availability of such technologies is very high and easily accessible to criminals.

This situation, combined with the low effectiveness of technology-based detection methods, means a high impact on their criminal use and an obvious inability to be detected by traditional verification mechanisms. Current research demonstrates substantial limitations in detection methodologies, specifically in the processing of high-frequency image components and temporal inconsistencies across video frames. Empirical studies indicate that conventional convolutional neural network (CNN) architectures and recurrent neural networks (RNNs) exhibit degraded performance when confronted with advanced generative models. These limitations are particularly evident when analyzing media generated by progressive growing GANs and

StyleGAN architectures, which demonstrate unprecedented capabilities in synthetic content generation (Yang et al., 2021).

The technical architecture of contemporary deepfake systems has undergone significant evolution, progressing from basic autoencoder implementations to sophisticated hybrid models incorporating multiple neural network architectures. Modern systems primarily utilize face-swapping architectures based on encoder-decoder networks with shared latent space, coupled with expression manipulation through facial landmark detection and 3D morphable models.

Advanced implementations incorporate style transfer mechanisms using adaptive instance normalization, while audio synthesis components frequently employ WaveNet and Tacotron architectures. Although these technologies demonstrate legitimate applications in computational creativity and educational visualization (Pawelec, 2022), their potential for exploitation has generated significant vulnerabilities in biometric authentication systems and digital identity verification protocols (Kaddar et al., 2023).

Detection methodology research reveals specific technical limitations across multiple domains, as considered by Malik et al. (2022). Current frameworks demonstrate particular weakness in temporal inconsistency detection within high-resolution video streams and artifact analysis in compressed media formats. Additional challenges include biological signal detection, encompassing eye blinking patterns and pulse detection, as well as cross-dataset generalization and resilience against adversarial attacks.

Experimental data indicates that human visual processing systems achieve accuracy rates below 65% in detecting state-of-the-art synthetic media, while computational methods demonstrate varying success rates depending on the specific attack vector. Recent research by Neekhara et al. (2020) proposes architectural improvements incorporating attention mechanisms and multi-stream networks to enhance adversarial robustness.

Quantitative analysis of detection systems has yielded promising developments in computational approaches, particularly in architectures implementing multi-stream analysis.

The DeepfakeNet architecture, utilizing a two-stream CNN with mesoscopic feature analysis, has demonstrated detection accuracy exceeding 98% under controlled conditions (Afchar et al., 2018). This system incorporates multi-scale feature extraction using inception modules, temporal coherence analysis through optical flow estimation, frequency domain analysis using discrete cosine transforms, and attention mechanisms for facial region prioritization. However, longitudinal studies indicate rapid degradation of detection efficacy due to evolutionary improvements in generative algorithms, particularly in areas of temporal coherence and texture synthesis (Yasrab et al., 2021). Contemporary research emphasizes the importance of integrated detection methodologies incorporating multiple analytical approaches. These include physical inconsistency detection focusing on lighting and reflection patterns, biological signal analysis examining blood flow and micro-expressions, comprehensive compression artifact analysis, frequency domain examination, and metadata consistency verification.

The technical implications extend to fundamental information security paradigms, potentially compromising established verification protocols (Hadi et al., 2022). The development of the DFDC dataset has provided crucial benchmark metrics across multiple technical dimensions, enabling standardized evaluation of detection methodologies (Neekhara et al., 2020).

The development of "Deepfake as a Service" (DFaaS) has revolutionized the accessibility of deepfake technology, enabling individuals and organizations to produce realistic synthetic media without requiring advanced technical skills.

The democratization of deepfake tools through DFaaS platforms has also led to significant ethical, legal, and security concerns. These platforms lower barriers for malicious actors, allowing them to misuse deepfake technology for nefarious purposes, such as identity theft, fraud, harassment, and misinformation campaigns. One of the most concerning aspects of DFaaS is its potential role in cybercrime. Deepfake technology can be exploited to impersonate individuals, enabling criminals to bypass biometric authentication systems, deceive financial institutions, and execute phishing schemes. Additionally, deepfake-generated voices or videos can be used in social engineering attacks, tricking victims into sharing sensitive information.

In the realm of misinformation, DFaaS platforms have proven to be a potent tool for spreading false narratives and manipulating public opinion. This is particularly concerning in political contexts, where deepfake videos and audio can be used to misrepresent candidates, influence elections, or destabilize societies. Hameleers et al. (2022) emphasize the role of DFaaS in creating politically charged deepfake content on social media, which can erode public trust and exacerbate polarization. Addressing the challenges posed by DFaaS requires a multi-faceted approach. Technological solutions, such as advanced detection mechanisms, are critical in identifying deepfake content but still inefficient to counter DFaaS capacities.

Distributed deepfake generation services is considered as a particularly concerning development in the technical landscape. These systems typically employ sophisticated implementation frameworks incorporating cloud-based rendering architectures, real-time face tracking and replacement, neural rendering pipelines, advanced compression algorithms, and automated quality enhancement systems. Real-time streaming protocols enable continuous media manipulation, while advanced compression techniques optimize bandwidth utilization. These systems frequently implement automated quality assurance systems utilizing perceptual loss metrics, resulting in output that consistently exceeds human detection capabilities.

The computational complexity of modern deepfake systems necessitates the development of increasingly sophisticated detection frameworks. Current technical research indicates that effective countermeasures require the implementation of ensemble learning approaches and hybrid neural architectures capable of analyzing multiple aspects of digital media simultaneously. The rapid evolution of generative artificial intelligence technologies suggests an ongoing need for adaptive detection methodologies capable of addressing emerging attack vectors and implementation frameworks.

## 2.2. Protected Communications for Terrorism and TCOs Activities

The ability to communicate securely is a critical lifeline for terrorist organizations and transnational criminal organizations (TCOs). Protected communication channels enable these groups to plan attacks, coordinate operations, disseminate propaganda, and evade law enforcement (Payá Santos et al., 2018). Over the time, these groups have innovatively adapted secure communication technologies, often outpacing the capabilities of law enforcement agencies (LEAs). This dynamic is exacerbated by the accessibility of advanced technologies through black markets, enhancing the technical capabilities of these groups. In addition, uncontrolled communications in social networks, online game platforms and other alternative channels are different ways to cover illegal actions and its communications based on regulatory and legal concerns about privacy and individual rights.

Criminal organizations exploit a variety of secure communication platforms to maintain protection of communication. Encrypted messaging apps, such as Telegram and Signal, provide end-to-end encryption, ensuring that only the sender and recipient can access the content. While these services enhance privacy, they pose significant challenges for law enforcement attempting to monitor illicit activities. Similarly, social media platforms like Facebook and Twitter, despite their openness, can serve as tools for covert communication. Criminal groups use coded language, private groups, and disappearing messages to remain undetected. In addition, cloud storage services and email accounts are submitted to privacy regulations creating a complicated ecosystem for traditional creating a complex ecosystem at the regulatory level given that TCOs and terrorist organizations take advantage of protectionist data regulation and data control spaces in terms of privacy and, additionally, those where there is high corruption or a very low level of prosecution of criminal groups due to the lack of specialized resources in the LEAs.

The dark web further complicates law enforcement efforts, offering an anonymous space for purchasing communication tools, financing operations, and recruiting members. However, navigating the dark web requires technical expertise, which limits its accessibility to more sophisticated actors. While these platforms provide connectivity and anonymity, they also introduce vulnerabilities that can be exploited by LEAs. Additionally, social media platforms can suspend or remove accounts linked to criminal or terrorist activity, disrupting their networks but most of the legal actions carried out are subject to the conditions of use of the platforms, which are mostly not adapted to the regulatory framework of each country from which the users of the services are obtained.

Infrastructure-free mobile communication systems, as noted by Xu et al. (2017), further complicate public security efforts. These systems enable users to operate independently of centralized infrastructure, offering malicious actors a means to evade detection. Similarly, existing wireless communication technologies, including Wi-Fi and Bluetooth, can be manipulated to endanger public security and facilitate criminal activities. The implementation of end-to-end encryption in messaging services adds yet another layer of complexity, rendering many traditional methods of surveillance ineffective (Endeley, 2018).

Addressing these challenges requires a multifaceted approach with permanent vision of state for art of protected communications. Technology based evolution, such as artificial intelligence-driven traffic analysis, can help law enforcement detect and respond to illicit activities identifying metadata of users in protected network.

International collaboration and partnerships with technology companies are crucial for creating legal frameworks that balance privacy and security. Public awareness and education about the risks associated with secure communication platforms also play a vital role in mitigating their misuse. Ultimately, maintaining public security in the digital age demands a balanced approach that respects individual privacy while addressing the risks posed by criminal exploitation of communication technologies (Luque et al., 2023).

European police chiefs issued a stark warning, urging industry and governments to address the growing gap between law enforcement needs and the increasing privacy afforded by end-to-end encryption on social media platforms (European Police Chiefs' Association, 2024). They argued that strong encryption hindered their ability to investigate serious crimes such as terrorism, child sexual abuse, human trafficking, and organized crime. This statement coincided with the rollout of end-to-end encryption on Meta's Messenger platform, further fueling concerns within law enforcement circles (Fernández Rodríguez et al., 2023)

The police chiefs emphasized the need for "security by design" in technology platforms, enabling the detection and reporting of harmful and illegal activities. They called upon governments to establish legal frameworks that grant law enforcement agencies the necessary access to data to effectively combat crime while upholding fundamental rights.

These concerns align with the recommendations of the High-Level Group (HLG) on Access to Data for Effective Law Enforcement, published in May 2024. The HLG report, which included recommendations for enhancing law enforcement access to data, sparked significant debate.

Notably, the report called for the re-introduction of mass surveillance measures, such as data retention, and advocated for measures that would undermine the effectiveness of encrypted communication systems (High-Level Group on Access to Data for Effective Law Enforcement, 2024).

## 2.3. The Integration of Artificial Intelligence (AI) in Law Enforcement Operations to Counter TCOs and Terrorist Group Activities

The integration of AI into law enforcement operations presents a paradigm shift in combating criminal activities, particularly in our increasingly digitalized society. This technological advancement empowers law enforcement agencies with unprecedented capabilities, including real-time data analysis, pattern recognition, and anomaly detection, significantly enhancing their capacity to identify and respond to new complex threats.

This integration is transforming rapidly the ability to combat terrorist groups and transnational criminal organizations. AI's capacity to analyse massive datasets, identify patterns, and predict future actions offers law enforcement unprecedented tools to disrupt these networks. By automating many of the labour-intensive tasks involved in intelligence analysis, AI enables investigators to focus on higher-level tasks and uncover hidden connections. However, the use of AI in this context raises important ethical and legal questions, such as privacy concerns and the potential for bias in algorithms. It is crucial to develop robust safeguards to ensure that AI is used responsibly and effectively in the fight against terrorism and organized crime.

The evolution of AI in law enforcement agencies necessitates a delicate balance between technological innovation and the preservation of individual privacy rights. This equilibrium requires ongoing collaboration between cybersecurity specialists, data scientists, legal experts, and policymakers to ensure that AI is developed and deployed responsibly, ethically, and in accordance with democratic principles being accountable in any stage of development of this emerging technologies (Neri et al., 2023; Luque et al, 2024).

One recent research investigates the criminal exploitation of AI by these organizations, highlighting their use for cybercrime, data manipulation, and operational planning. Understanding these misuse patterns is crucial for law enforcement agencies developing effective countermeasures. Samuel-Okon (2024) offers valuable insights into mitigation strategies against the criminal use of AI. These strategies include raising public and organizational awareness, investing in advanced detection technologies, establishing ethical guidelines for AI use in law enforcement, and strengthening legal frameworks with appropriate penalties. This comprehensive analysis emphasizes the importance of clear and enforceable legal frameworks to deter and combat AI-related crimes.

## 3. UNDERCOVER OPERATIONS AGAINST TERRORIST GROUPS AND TCOs IN DIGITAL ERA

The concept of state sovereignty, founded on the principle of popular sovereignty and the exercise of power through distinct branches of government, underpins a state's authority within its defined territory. This principle, enshrined in Article 2.4 of the United Nations Charter, emphasizes territorial integrity as a paramount concern. Consequently, states possess exclusive jurisdiction within their borders, and any external interference in their sovereignty constitutes a hostile act. This inherent authority necessitates the preservation of state unity and the prevention of any internal divisions that could undermine its sovereignty and jeopardize internal peace and stability.

However, the digital era presents new challenges. States are increasingly confronted with threats emanating from transnational organized crime, requiring a reassessment of their capacity to ensure internal and external security. The question arises: can states, acting independently, effectively counter these threats and safeguard their sovereignty in the digital era?

Recognizing the limitations of unilateral action, states have increasingly sought to enhance international cooperation in combating transnational organized crime. The United Nations Convention against Transnational Organized Crime provides a crucial framework for international cooperation, emphasizing principles of sovereign equality and non-intervention while enabling states to establish bilateral and multilateral cooperation mechanisms.

Article 20 of this Convention acknowledges the importance of special investigative techniques, including controlled delivery, electronic surveillance, and undercover operations. The European Convention on Mutual Legal Assistance, specifically Article 19.1 of the Second Additional Protocol, further facilitates international cooperation by enabling joint undercover operations between states. This collaboration is further strengthened by the Council Framework Decision, which allows for the establishment of Joint Investigation Teams to prosecute criminal offenses.

Transnational organized crime, characterized by its fluidity and adaptability, poses a significant challenge to traditional law enforcement models. States must demonstrate agility and responsiveness to effectively counter these threats. The undercover agent, as a valuable investigative tool, plays a crucial role in this endeavour. While respecting state sovereignty, the use of undercover operations requires careful consideration and adherence to international legal frameworks (González, 2022).

The effective counteraction of transnational organized crime demands a multi-faceted approach in the digital era that balances the principles of state sovereignty with the realities of globalized crime. International cooperation, underpinned by robust legal frameworks and respect for national sovereignty, is crucial for effectively combating these threats and ensuring a secure and stable international order in the digital era.

## 4. PRACTICAL APPROACH OF INTERNATIONAL LAW ENFORCEMENT COLLABORATIVE NETWORKS IN THE DIGITAL ERA

The digital era has significantly eroded traditional notions of state sovereignty, creating opportunities for criminal organizations to exploit areas where individual states face limitations in their capacity to exert control. This dynamic underscore the critical need for integrated international efforts to address these gaps in jurisdiction and authority. By fostering cooperative networks, law enforcement agencies can effectively counter the transnational nature of modern criminal organizations.

Existing frameworks for international collaboration offer mechanisms to conduct operations across borders while respecting state sovereignty, domestic legal norms, and jurisdictional oversight. For member states of the European Union (EU) and third countries, these frameworks differ in their processes and tools but share a commitment to ensuring that investigations are conducted lawfully and with due regard for the host state's autonomy.

In the EU context, joint operations often rely on the European Investigation Order (EIO), a legal instrument that facilitates cross-border cooperation in criminal investigations. The EIO provides a standardized framework that governs the actions of participating agents, the duration of investigations, and specific procedural conditions, all within the bounds of the domestic laws of the host state. Conversely, collaboration with third countries typically requires the use of international rogatory commissions (CRIs), which are formal requests for mutual legal assistance in criminal matters. CRIs are coordinated through diplomatic channels or via the Subdirectorate General of International Legal Cooperation within the Ministry of Justice, ensuring that the requests are channeled appropriately and align with the judicial authority of the requesting state.

Beyond these mechanisms, the involvement of specialized international agencies like Europol and Interpol plays a pivotal role in enhancing the scope and effectiveness of collaborative efforts. Europol serves as a central hub for information exchange, operational support, and specialized expertise in addressing serious transnational crimes. Its capacity to facilitate undercover operations across EU member states is bolstered by the agency's mandate to address significant security threats, its jurisdictional flexibility, and the specialized training of its officers.

Similarly, Interpol, which encompasses 195 member countries, provides critical support through its extensive databases, forensic capabilities, operational field support, and training initiatives. Interpol's ability to facilitate cooperation across diverse legal systems and jurisdictions makes it an indispensable partner in addressing global criminal challenges. Experts, such as Zafra Espinosa, argue that both Europol and Interpol agents possess the requisite skills, mobility, and operational expertise to act as undercover agents effectively. Their integration into collaborative efforts against organized crime offers a robust mechanism to combat increasingly sophisticated transnational threats.

Addressing jurisdictional and operational challenges through coordinated efforts, the global law enforcement community can more effectively counter the evolving strategies of organized crime and other transnational threats.

## 5. CYBER SUBCULTURES AND THE EVOLUTION OF CRIMINAL BEHAVIOUR IN THE DIGITAL AGE

Cyber subcultures represent a significant area of inquiry within the field of cybercriminology. These online communities, characterized by shared interests, norms, and values, can serve as breeding grounds for criminal activity. Cybercriminals frequently utilize these platforms to exchange information, refine illicit techniques, and collaborate on criminal endeavors. Understanding the interplay between cyber subcultures and criminal behavior is crucial for developing effective countermeasures, including the deployment of cyber undercover agents to infiltrate and disrupt these networks (Holt et al., 2017).

Holt et al. (2017) examine the role of ideology in motivating cyberattacks, focusing on a qualitative analysis of Turkish hackers. Their findings highlight that while these hackers adhere to broader hacker subcultural values, their targets are primarily driven by religious or political beliefs. This research emphasizes the need for further empirical investigation into the motivations and behaviors of cyberattackers.

Cyber subcultures provide a fertile ground for the dissemination of criminal knowledge. Cybercriminals leverage these platforms to share information on hacking techniques, malware distribution, and fraudulent schemes. Lannier (2024) underscores the critical role of undercover agents in infiltrating these communities, gathering intelligence on criminal tactics, and gaining deeper insights into the motivations and methodologies of cybercriminals.

Agustina (2012) emphasizes the need to bridge the gap between academic understanding and the realities of law enforcement in combating cybercrime. The study challenges the media's portrayal of cybercrime as solely consisting of high-profile attacks by lone hackers. While such incidents exist, they are relatively rare. More prevalent are instances of everyday cybercrimes such as fraud, harassment, and the dissemination of illegal content.

Some cyber subcultures are intrinsically linked to criminal activity, where individuals seek to gain recognition and status within the community by engaging in illicit acts. In these contexts, undercover agents can effectively infiltrate these groups by adopting online personas that foster trust and facilitate access to critical information. This immersion not only provides valuable intelligence but also allows agents to gain a nuanced understanding of the internal dynamics and motivations of cybercriminals (Amoo, 2024)

However, infiltrating cyber subcultures presents significant challenges. Cybercriminals are inherently suspicious and cautious due to the illegal nature of their activities. Undercover agents must navigate these environments with extreme care, maintaining plausible cover while gathering crucial intelligence (Payá, 2023). Furthermore, they must possess a deep understanding of the subcultural details to establish credibility and build trust within the community.

Certain cyber subcultures are closely associated with extreme ideological or political movements. In these instances, cybercriminals may utilize their skills to propagate illicit agendas, spread disinformation, or conduct cyberattacks to further their political objectives.

Cyber undercover agents can play a crucial role in monitoring these communities, identifying potential threats to national security, and preventing the exploitation of online platforms for malicious purposes (Lannier, 2024).

## 6. UNDERCOVER DIGITAL AGENTS

The figure of the undercover agent, a critical instrument in law enforcement and intelligence gathering, presents a unique set of ethical and legal challenges. This analysis examines the multifaceted nature of undercover operations, particularly in the digital domain, highlighting the ethical considerations and legal complexities associated with their deployment.

Traditionally, undercover agents have been employed in combating organized crime, infiltrating criminal networks to gather evidence for subsequent prosecution. These operations, while often effective, raise significant concerns regarding the potential for civil rights violations and the erosion of public trust in law enforcement institutions. The inherent power imbalance between the undercover agent and the individuals they are investigating necessitates a delicate balance between the imperative to combat crime and the protection of individual rights and liberties. This delicate balance requires careful consideration of issues such as:

- **Due Process Concerns:** Undercover operations can potentially lead to entrapment, where individuals are induced to commit crimes they would not otherwise have committed. This raises serious due process concerns and can undermine the integrity of the criminal justice system.
- **Privacy Violations:** The collection of information during undercover operations may involve the interception of private communications, surveillance, and the infiltration of private spaces. These activities raise significant concerns regarding the right to privacy and the potential for abuse of power.
- **Psychological Impact:** Undercover work can have a profound psychological impact on the agents themselves, leading to stress, isolation, and potential trauma. The long-term consequences of these experiences on the mental and emotional well-being of undercover agents must be carefully considered.
- **Public Trust:** The misuse of undercover tactics can erode public trust in law enforcement agencies. Incidents of abuse or misconduct can undermine the legitimacy of law enforcement and damage the relationship between the public and the authorities. (Delgado, 2023).

The advent of digital technologies has introduced a new dimension of complexity to undercover operations. The use of computer-based undercover agents, operating within online environments, presents unique challenges. The creation and utilization of false identities within virtual spaces raise critical questions about individual privacy and the potential for abuse of these technologies. These challenges include:

- **Digital Surveillance and Privacy:** The collection of digital data, such as online communications, browsing history, and location data, raises significant privacy concerns. The use of sophisticated surveillance tools, including malware and hacking techniques, necessitates strict oversight and adherence to legal and ethical guidelines.
- **The "Playpen" Case and its Implications:** The "Playpen" case serves as a stark reminder of the ethical and legal complexities associated with undercover operations in the digital realm. The FBI's use of intrusive hacking techniques, while ultimately leading to the apprehension of numerous offenders, raised serious concerns regarding the violation of individual privacy rights.

This case underscores the critical need for transparent oversight and accountability in the use of such investigative techniques.

- **The Evolving Threat Landscape:** The rapid evolution of technology necessitates a continuous reassessment of legal and ethical frameworks governing undercover operations. New technologies, such as artificial intelligence and deepfakes, present both opportunities and challenges for law enforcement, requiring ongoing dialogue and adaptation of existing legal frameworks.

The utilization of undercover agents must be strictly regulated and subject to rigorous oversight. Legal frameworks must be established to safeguard individual rights, ensure the integrity of investigative processes, and maintain public trust in law enforcement institutions. These frameworks should:

- **Establish clear legal boundaries** for the use of undercover techniques, including specific authorization procedures, limitations on permissible activities, and guidelines for the collection and use of evidence.
- **Provide for independent oversight** of undercover operations to ensure compliance with legal and ethical standards and to address any potential abuses.
- **Implement robust safeguards** to protect the privacy and civil rights of individuals involved in undercover investigations.
- **Foster transparency and accountability** by ensuring that the public is informed about the use of undercover techniques and the legal and ethical frameworks that govern their deployment.

## 7. INVESTIGATION TECHNIQUES AND EVIDENCE COLLECTION IN DIGITAL FORENSICS

Digital investigation techniques and evidence collection are cornerstones of digital forensics, which involves the identification, preservation, analysis, and presentation of electronic evidence in both criminal and civil investigations. With the ever-expanding use of technology in everyday life, the role of digital forensics has become increasingly critical. The complexity of digital environments demands advanced methodologies and tools to ensure the reliability and admissibility of evidence in legal contexts.

Digital forensics encompasses a broad spectrum of investigative activities that address incidents ranging from unauthorized access and data breaches to intellectual property theft and insider threats. Ferguson et al. (2020) remarks the importance of developing a systematic approach to digital forensic methodologies using frameworks not limited to technical considerations. They propose a generalized model for the forensic process that standardizes investigative practices, enabling consistency across diverse cases and technological platforms. This model highlights four key stages: identification, preservation, analysis, and presentation, each of which plays a critical role in ensuring the integrity and reliability of digital evidence.

The preservation of evidence is particularly crucial in digital forensics, as electronic data is inherently volatile and susceptible to alteration. The chain of custody must be meticulously documented to ensure that the evidence remains unaltered and admissible in court. Tools such as write-blockers, forensic imaging software, and hashing algorithms are commonly employed to maintain the integrity of data during acquisition and analysis (Vaddi, 2024))

Digital forensic tools have revolutionized evidence collection and analysis by enabling investigators to recover deleted files, analyze system logs, and trace digital footprints. These tools allow forensic experts to reconstruct timelines and identify patterns of behavior that may indicate malicious activities (Giacomello et al., 2024). Metadata analysis, which provides crucial insights into file creation, modification, and access, serving as a key element in piecing together digital events is a critical aspect of digital forensics (Selim, 2024).

Emerging technologies, such as cloud computing and the Internet of Things (IoT), have introduced new challenges to digital forensics. The distributed nature of cloud environments complicates evidence acquisition, requiring investigators to navigate issues of data jurisdiction and provider cooperation. Similarly, IoT devices generate vast quantities of data, much of which may be stored locally or in the cloud, demanding novel forensic techniques to ensure comprehensive evidence collection. Seems clear the need for validated methodologies tailored to these technologies to maintain the reliability of digital forensic investigations (Selim, 2024).

Low-level data manipulation and anti-forensic techniques further complicate the digital forensic process. Criminals often employ encryption, data wiping, and steganography to obscure evidence and evade detection. Forensic investigators must stay ahead of these tactics by utilizing advanced decryption tools, memory analysis techniques, and artifact extraction methods. At this point, digital forensic researchers are addressing these challenges, calling for continuous innovation in forensic science to adapt to evolving threats.

Another critical area within digital forensics is network forensics, which focuses on analyzing network traffic to uncover malicious activities. Techniques such as packet analysis, intrusion detection, and correlation of network logs allow investigators to trace cyberattacks back to their origins and identify perpetrators. These methods are particularly effective in combating distributed denial-of-service (DDoS) attacks, ransomware campaigns, and insider threats, where network activity provides the primary source of evidence.

Ethical and legal considerations are integral to digital forensics. Investigators must balance the need for thorough evidence collection with the protection of individual privacy and adherence to legal frameworks. Ferguson et al. (2020) emphasize the importance of operating within established legal boundaries and respecting fundamental rights to ensure that evidence is admissible and investigations are conducted ethically.

## 8. CONCLUSIONS

The increasing complexity and sophistication of transnational criminal organizations (TCOs) and terrorist groups underscore the need for innovative and adaptable strategies in law enforcement. Technological advancements have significantly enhanced the operational capabilities of these groups, creating a widening gap between their resources and the traditional methods employed by law enforcement agencies (LEAs). Addressing this technological disparity requires a multifaceted and internationally coordinated approach.

a) Technological Adaptation of LEAs

The integration of advanced technologies, such as artificial intelligence, big data analytics, and digital forensic tools, is critical for LEAs to remain effective in the fight against TCOs and terrorist groups. These tools enable LEAs to analyze vast datasets, identify patterns, and predict criminal activities, thereby enhancing their ability to disrupt illicit networks and prevent crimes before they occur.

b) Cross Border Cooperation and Technical Networking

International cooperation among LEAs, supported by agencies such as Europol and Interpol, is indispensable for combating transnational threats (Díaz, 2013; Díaz, 2016). Collaborative frameworks, such as joint investigation teams and shared intelligence platforms, allow for the pooling of resources and expertise (Delgado-Morán et al., 2023; Caligiuri & Pili, 2021). These efforts also help bridge jurisdictional gaps, ensuring that criminal organizations cannot exploit regulatory and legal loopholes across borders (Payá y Luque, 2021; Delgado-Morán et al., 2023).

c) Emerging Threats and Experienced-based Methodologies

The proliferation of digital technologies, including deepfake generation, secure communication channels, and the Internet of Things (IoT), presents new challenges for digital forensics and law enforcement. Continuous innovation in forensic methodologies and the development of robust detection tools are essential for addressing these threats. Additionally, LEAs must focus on combating anti-forensic techniques used by criminals to obscure evidence and evade detection.

d) Not only Ethical and Legal Frameworks needed

The use of advanced investigative techniques, including undercover operations and digital surveillance, raises critical ethical and legal questions (Trigo, 2023). Striking a balance between effective crime prevention and the protection of individual rights is paramount. Transparent oversight mechanisms and adherence to international human rights standards are necessary to maintain public trust and ensure that technological advancements are used responsibly.

e) Education and Training

Building the capacity of law enforcement personnel through specialized training programs is crucial for maximizing the potential of emerging technologies. These programs should focus on equipping officers with the skills needed to operate advanced tools, understand digital evidence, and navigate the complexities of international legal frameworks.

f) Policy and Regulation

Policymakers must prioritize the development of adaptable regulatory frameworks that address the dual imperatives of security and privacy. These frameworks should include provisions for data sharing, cross-border collaboration, and the ethical use of technology in law enforcement. Ensuring the accountability of technology providers and promoting public-private partnerships will further strengthen these efforts.

Bridging the technological gap between TCOs, terrorist groups, and LEAs is a pressing global challenge. By embracing innovation, fostering international collaboration, and adhering to ethical principles, LEAs can enhance their capabilities to effectively combat the evolving threats posed by transnational criminal organizations and terrorist networks in the digital era.

## REFERENCES


Afchar, D., Nozick, V., Yamagishi, J., & Echizen, I. (2018). MesoNet: A compact facial video forgery detection network. *2018 IEEE International Workshop on Information Forensics and Security (WIFS)*, 1-7. DOI: 10.1109/WIFS.2018.8630761

Agustina, J. R. (2012). Understanding cybercrime: Phenomena, challenges, and legal responses. *Computer Law & Security Review*, *26*(6), 517–526. https://www.itu.int/ITU-D/cyb/cybersecurity/docs/Cybercrime%20legislation%20EV6.pdf

Alan Setiawan, D., A. R., Fadhly Jambak, F., Umbara, A., & Wildan S, F. (2023). Macro approach in economic crime response technology in the age of global transformation. *KnE Social Sciences*. DOI: 10.18502/kss.v8i18.14224

Amoo, O. (2024). The legal landscape of cybercrime: A review of contemporary issues in the criminal justice system. *World Journal of Advanced Research and Reviews*, *21*(2), 205–217. DOI: 10.30574/wjarr.2024.21.2.0438

Araque, O., & Iglesias, C. A. (2020). An approach for radicalization detection based on emotion signals and semantic similarity. *IEEE Access : Practical Innovations, Open Solutions*, *8*, 17877–17891. https://ieeexplore.ieee.org/document/8962050. DOI: 10.1109/ACCESS.2020.2967219

Bell, P., & Congram, M. (2013). Communication interception technology (CIT) and its use in the fight against transnational organised crime (TOC) in Australia: A review of the literature. *International Journal of Social Science Research*, *2*(1), 46. DOI: 10.5296/ijssr.v2i1.4089

Caligiuri, M., & Pili, G. (2021). Italian intelligence studies literature: Understanding the state of play. A comparative perspective. The International *Journal of Intelligence, Security,* Delgado-Morán, JJ., Payá-Santos, CA., Sanz-Gonzalez, R. (2023). China's Borderless Expansionism. Could Be a Threat to International Security? In Cayón Peña, J., & Ramírez, J. M. (Eds.), *Threats to Peace and International Security: Asia versus West. Advanced Sciences and Technologies for Security Applications*. Springer., DOI: 10.1007/978-3-031-28336-9_5D

Morán, J. J. D. (2023). Políticas públicas de seguridad en España. Análisis desde perspectivas criminológicas. Revista opiniao jurídica, 21(37), 183-211.

Endeley, R. E. (2018). End-to-end encryption in messaging services and national security—Case of WhatsApp messenger. *Journal of Information Security*, *09*(01), 95–99. DOI: 10.4236/jis.2018.91008

European Commission. (2024). Recommendations of the High-Level Group on Access to Data for Effective Law Enforcement. Directorate-General for Migration and Home Affairs. Retrieved from https://home-affairs.ec.europa.eu/document/download/1105a0ef-535c-44a7-a6d4-a8478fce1d29_en?filename=Recommendations%20of%20the%20HLG%20on%20Access%20to%20Data%20for%20Effective%20Law%20Enforcement_en.pdf

Europol. (2020, October 14). European police chiefs call for industry and governments to take action against end-to-end encryption roll-out. *Europol.* Retrieved from https://www.europol.europa.eu/media-press/newsroom/news/european-police-chiefs-call-for-industry-and-governments-to-take-action-against-end-to-end-encryption-roll-out

Ferguson, I., Renaud, K., Wilford, S., & Irons, A. (2020). Precept: A framework for ethical digital forensics investigations. *Journal of Intellectual Capital*, *21*(2), 257–290. DOI: 10.1108/JIC-05-2019-0097

Fernández Rodríguez, J. C, Domínguez Pineda, N. Z, Miralles Muñoz, F, & Liz Rivas, L. (2023). Conductas de riesgo y programas de prevención en adolescentes institucionalizados. *Cuadernos de RES PUBLICA en derecho y criminología.* (2), 42–56. DOI: 10.46661/respublica.8286

Giacomello, G., Iovanella, A., & Martino, L. (2024). A Small World of Bad Guys: Investigating the Behavior of Hacker Groups in Cyber-Attacks. *arXiv:2309.16442.* /arXiv.2309.16442DOI: 10.48550

Giommoni, L., Aziani, A., & Berlusconi, G. (2016). How do illicit drugs move across countries? A network analysis of the heroin supply to Europe. *Journal of Drug Issues*, *47*(2), 217–240. DOI: 10.1177/0022042616682426

Hadi, W. J., Kadhem, S. M., & Abbas, A. R. (2022). A survey of deepfakes in terms of deep learning and multimedia forensics. [IJECE]. *International Journal of Electrical and Computer Engineering*, *12*(4), 4408. DOI: 10.11591/ijece.v12i4.pp4408-4414

Hameleers, M., Meer, T. G., & Dobber, T. (2022). You won't believe what they just said! The effects of political deepfakes embedded as vox populi on social media. *Social Media + Society*, *8*(3), 20563051221116346. Advance online publication. DOI: 10.1177/20563051221116346

Holt, T. J., Freilich, J. D., & Chermak, S. M. (2017). Exploring the subculture of ideologically motivated cyber-attackers. *Journal of Contemporary Criminal Justice*, *33*(3), 212–233. DOI: 10.1177/1043986217699100

Kaddar, B., Fezza, S. A., Hamidouche, W., Akhtar, Z., & Hadid, A. (2023). On the effectiveness of handcrafted features for deepfake video detection. *Journal of Electronic Imaging*, *32*(05). Advance online publication. DOI: 10.1117/1.JEI.32.5.053033

Lannier, S. (2024). Infiltrating virtual worlds. The regulation of undercover agents through fundamental rights. *Revista Brasileira De Direito Processual Penal*, *10*(3). Advance online publication. DOI: 10.22197/rbdpp.v10i3.1066

Luque Juárez, J. M., Payá Santos, C. A., & Arenas Morales, F. (2023). Contexto de las políticas de seguridad ciudadana. *Cuadernos de RES PUBLICA en derecho y criminología*, (2), 69–82. DOI: 10.46661/respublica.8293

Luque Juarez, J. M., Sanz Gonzalez, R., Payá Santos, C., & Rodriguez Gonzalez, V. (2024). Aplicaciones de la inteligencia artificial en la criminología y ciencias policiales. ci10.13140/RG.2.2.11118.63041. Retrieved from_https://www.researchgate.net/publication/381916708_Aplicaciones_de_la_inteligencia_artificial_en_la_criminologia_y_ciencias_policiales?channel=doi&linkId=66843b7f714e0b03153f1cb4&showFulltext=true

Maesschalck, S. (2024). Gentlemen, you can't fight in here. Or can you?: How cyberspace operations impact international security. *World Affairs*, *187*(1), 24–36. DOI: 10.1002/waf2.12004

Malik, A., Kuribayashi, M., Abdullahi, S. M., & Khan, A. N. (2022). Deepfake detection for human face images and videos: A survey. *IEEE Access : Practical Innovations, Open Solutions*, *10*, 18757–18775. DOI: 10.1109/ACCESS.2022.3151186

Martino, L. (2024). *Cybersecurity in Italy*. Governance, Policies and Ecosystem. Springer Nature., DOI: 10.1007/978-3-031-64396-5

Martino, L., & Merenda, F. (2021). Artificial intelligence: A paradigm shift in international law and politics? Autonomous weapon systems as a case study. In Giacomello, G., Moro, F. N., & Valigi, M. (Eds.), *Technology and International Relations* (pp. 89–107). Edward Elgar Publishing., DOI: 10.4337/9781788976077.00012

Neekhara, P., Dolhansky, B., Bitton, J., & Ferrer, C. C. (2020). Adversarial threats to deepfake detection: A practical perspective. /arxiv.2011.09957 DOI: 10.48550

Neri, M., Niccolini, F., & Martino, L. (2023). Organizational cybersecurity readiness in the ICT sector: A quanti-qualitative assessment. *Information and Computer Security*, *32*(1), 38–52. Advance online publication. DOI: 10.1108/ICS-05-2023-0084

Ochara, N. M., Odhiambo, N. A., & Kadyamatimba, A. (2020). The digitalised terrorism ecology: A systems perspective. *The African Journal of Information and Communication*, (25). Advance online publication. DOI: 10.23962/10539/29196

Pawelec, M. (2022). Deepfakes and democracy (theory): How synthetic audio-visual media for disinformation and hate speech threaten core democratic functions. *Digital Society : Ethics, Socio-Legal and Governance of Digital Technology, 1*(2), 19. Advance online publication. DOI: 10.1007/s44206-022-00010-6 PMID: 36097613

Payá Santos, C., & Delgado Morán, J. J. (2017). Uncertainty of dimensional analysis of intelligence. *URVIO Revista Latinoamericana de Estudios de Seguridad, 21*(21), 225–239. DOI: 10.17141/urvio.21.2017.2962

Payá Santos, C., Delgado Morán, J. J., & Mazurier, P. A. (2018). Individual terrorism as a response to the distorted phenomenon of cultural identity. In Ramírez, J., & Abad-Quintanal, G. (Eds.), *Cross-cultural dialogue as a conflict management strategy. Advanced sciences and technologies for security applications* (pp. 34–45). Springer., DOI: 10.1007/978-3-319-77231-8_4

Payá Santos, C., & Luque-Juárez, J. M. (2021). El sistema de inteligencia criminal ante las nuevas amenazas y oportunidades del ciberespacio. *Revista Científica General José María Córdova, 19*(36), 1121–1136. DOI: 10.21830/19006586.855

Payá Santos, C. A. (2023). El desempeño de la inteligencia en España en el ámbito público, empresarial y académico. *Revista Científica General José María Córdova, 21*(44), 1029–1047. DOI: 10.21830/19006586.1222

Rodríguez González, V., Payá, Santos., C, A., & Peña Herrera. B. (2023). Estudio criminológico del ciberdelincuente y sus víctimas. *Cuadernos de RES PUBLICA en Derecho y criminología,* (1) 95-107. .DOI: 10.46661/respublica.8072

Samuel-Okon, A. D., Olateju, O. O., Okon, S. U., Olaniyi, O. O., & Igwenagu, U. T. I. (2024). Formulating global policies and strategies for combating criminal use and abuse of artificial intelligence. *Archives of Current Research International, 24*(5), 612–629. DOI: 10.9734/acri/2024/v24i5735

Sanz González, R., Luque Juárez, J. M., Martino, L., Liz, L., Delgado Morán, J. J., & Payá Santos, C. A. (2024). Artificial Intelligence Applications for Criminology and Police Sciences. *International Journal of Humanities and Social Science, 14*(2), 139–148. DOI: 10.15640/jehd.v14n2a14

Selim, A. (2024). The role of digital forensic analysis in modern investigations. *4*(1), 1-5. DOI: 10.57020/ject.1445625

Trigo, N. A. G. (2023). El agente encubierto ante la criminalidad organizada transnacional. Cuadernos de RES PUBLICA en derecho y criminología, (1), 85-94.

Vaddi, K. (2024). Enhancements in the world of digital forensics. *IAES International Journal of Artificial Intelligence (Ij-Ai), 13*(1), 680. DOI: 10.11591/ijai.v13.i1.pp680-686

Varum, P., Sree, U., & Batumalay, M. (2024). A data analytics strategy to the underground economy of cybercrime. *Journal of Data Science, 2024*(1). DOI: 10.61453/jods.v2024no12

Xu, J., Duan, L., & Zhang, R. (2017). Surveillance and intervention of infrastructure-free mobile communications: A new wireless security paradigm. *IEEE Wireless Communications, 24*(4), 152–159. DOI: 10.1109/MWC.2017.1600279

Yang, C., Ding, L., Chen, Y., & Li, H. (2021). Defending against GAN-based deepfake attacks via transformation-aware adversarial faces. *2021 International Joint Conference on Neural Networks (IJCNN)*. DOI: 10.1109/IJCNN52387.2021.9533868

Yasrab, R., Jiang, W., & Riaz, A. (2021). Fighting deepfakes using body language analysis. *Forecasting, 3*(2), 303–321. DOI: 10.3390/forecast3020020

# Chapter 8
# AI, Governance, and Law in Digital Geopolitics:
## The Chinese Model and Its Global Projection

**Carlos García de-la-Morena**
https://orcid.org/0009-0002-0136-5944
*Rey Juan Carlos University, Spain*

## ABSTRACT

*Artificial intelligence has become a structural pillar of 21st-century geopolitical competition, shaping governance, law, the economy, and power distribution. Unlike earlier technologies, AI acts as a dual-use catalyst with profound implications for sovereignty and security. This article examines AI as a strategic instrument comparable to nuclear energy or the Internet, through a comparative analysis of China, the U.S., and the EU as architects of the emerging digital order. Global technological rivalry is both material and symbolic, involving control of digital infrastructure and regulatory norms. The central argument is that China's algorithmic governance model operates domestically as a system of control and efficiency and globally as a project to export digital norms. In contrast, the U.S. prioritizes private-sector innovation, while the EU promotes rights-based regulation (Guest & Wei, 2024; Zaidan, 2024). The article concludes that the tension between convergence and fragmentation in AI governance will shape global order, especially in the strategically contested Global South.*

DOI: 10.4018/979-8-3373-4480-5.ch008

## 1. INTRODUCTION

AI has become a defining element of contemporary geopolitics. More than a mere technological innovation, AI constitutes a technology with direct impact on the economy, defense, and the organization of global power. Its development and regulation not only shape competitive advantages but also configure the norms and values that underpin international governance. Unlike previous technological revolutions, AI combines economic capacity, surveillance, automation, and normative control, positioning itself as an instrument of power that transcends the boundaries between civilian and military domains (Kania, 2019). Strategic interest in AI has historical roots in Cold War research programs, when the U.S. and the USSR explored automated systems for defense and command. However, it was during the 2010s, driven by exponential growth in computing power, the expansion of big data, and advances in deep learning, that AI emerged as a foundational dual-use technology. Its transformative potential places it alongside strategic technologies such as nuclear energy or the Internet, with the crucial distinction that it lacks a clear boundary between civilian and military uses, making it an unprecedented regulatory challenge. In contemporary political discourse, AI has been described as the new oil or even the new nuclear energy (Zaidan, 2024), metaphors that underscore its centrality in wealth creation and in the hierarchy of international security. Both Washington and Beijing have located AI development at the core of their national security and economic growth strategies. Yet geostrategic competition around this technology extends beyond economics and defense. It encompasses the regulatory sphere, where the definition of standards for privacy, transparency, accountability, and military applications will determine global markets and the architecture of digital governance. The struggle for AI leadership is therefore both a material and symbolic contest over who controls the infrastructure and the rules of the international system. In this context, the concept of digital sovereignty emerges, understood as a state's capacity to control its data, digital infrastructures, and associated norms. For China, digital sovereignty, framed as cyber-sovereignty, asserts the sovereign right of each state over its own cyberspace. By contrast, the EU promotes digital strategic autonomy, seeking to reduce its technological dependence on the U.S. and China, while the U.S. defends an open Internet model dominated by its technological corporations. This emphasis on technological sovereignty has fueled increasingly visible techno-nationalism, rooted in the idea that control over critical technologies is inseparable from national security. The U.S.–China trade and technology war, illustrated by sanctions on Huawei or restrictions on access to semiconductors, clearly reflects this logic of rivalry (Rolland, 2017).

Understanding the political dimension of AI requires anchoring its study in international relations theory. From a realist perspective, AI is a strategic resource that reinforces states' hard power. Competition between the US and China is interpreted as a reedition of the anarchic security logic in which each power seeks to maximize technological dominance to avoid vulnerabilities. In contrast, liberalism conceives AI as an opportunity for global cooperation, where multilateral organizations, such as the OECD or UNESCO, could coordinate common principles, mitigate risks, and promote ethical uses of technology. However, this optimism faces growing regulatory fragmentation and the erosion of international consensus. Constructivism, for its part, proposes understanding AI as a space for projecting values and norms. The Chinese model, state control and social harmony, the U.S. model, private innovation and competitiveness, and the EU model, fundamental rights and regulation, embody divergent visions of world order. Thus, global technological competition is also a normative and identity-based conflict. Building on this framework, the article's central hypothesis argues that China's model of algorithmic governance functions both as a domestic system of control and efficiency and as an integrated geopolitical project that seeks to export its regulatory principles and digital power structures. In response, the U.S. and the EU articulate alternative projects grounded in different institutional and cultural foundations, yet similarly invested in expanding their normative influence. The crucial question is whether the international system will converge around a hegemonic model of AI governance or, alternatively, whether it will experience fragmentation of the global digital order. This study adopts a comparative qualitative methodology based on a review of recent academic literature, official documents, and policy analyses from specialized think tanks. Particular attention is devoted to the three main poles of technological power, as well as to the effects their models have on the Global South, where competition over infrastructure, data, and norms becomes tangible. Ultimately, the article seeks to contribute to the debate on the international reconfiguration driven by AI and to explore how the struggle over its governance anticipates a transformation of the world order in the digital era.

## 2. THE GEOPOLITICS OF ARTIFICIAL INTELLIGENCE

As a technology whose transformative potential is comparable to that of electricity, the internal combustion engine, or the Internet, AI's singularity lies in its dual-use character, that is, the capacity to be applied simultaneously in civilian and military domains. Algorithms designed for medical image recognition can be repurposed for systems of mass surveillance or for armed autonomous vehicles. And tools created to optimize supply chains can be adapted for military deployment and logistics operations (Kania, 2019). This ambivalence has elevated AI to the status of a strategic asset. Unlike nuclear energy, however, there is no clear threshold separating peaceful from military applications, which multiplies regulatory dilemmas. The civil–military inseparability of AI places it at the center of ongoing competition among major powers. Economically, AI promises productivity gains exceeding 15% of global GDP by 2030 (PwC). Politically, its capacity to enhance social control, personalize propaganda, and strengthen surveillance augments the power of states that master it. Militarily, it is projected to be decisive in command-and-control operations, drone swarms, cyberwarfare, and autonomous weapon systems. Against this backdrop, the strategic rivalry between the U.S. and China has often been interpreted as a Second Cold War. Although the parallel with the U.S.–USSR confrontation is imperfect, given the far deeper economic interdependence today, technological competition remains a central axis. The metaphor of a digital Iron Curtain captures the emerging fragmentation of technological ecosystems characterized by divergent supply chains, standards, and platforms (Al-Maamari, 2025). The dispute over 5G provides a representative example. While Huawei and ZTE led deployments in Asia, Africa, and Latin America, Washington promoted bans and sanctions against these companies on grounds of espionage risks. European countries such as the United Kingdom and Sweden, under U.S. pressure, progressively restricted Chinese participation in their critical networks. What initially appeared to be a technical telecommunications issue became a symbol of the geopolitical struggle for control over digital infrastructure. Similarly, the semiconductor war reveals the intensity of decoupling. In 2022 and 2023, the U.S. prohibited the export to China of advanced chips and the machinery required to produce them, such as equipment made by the Dutch company ASML. Japan and the Netherlands aligned with these restrictions in 2023, while Beijing responded by limiting exports of gallium and germanium, critical minerals for the electronics industry. These episodes demonstrate that AI cannot be detached from resource geopolitics or from competition over strategic value chains (Rolland, 2017).

Rivalry is structured around three poles with distinct models. China seeks technological self-sufficiency (*zili gengsheng*) and projects AI as an instrument of national revitalization. Its New Generation Artificial Intelligence Development Plan (2017) sets explicit goals: to lead global innovation by 2030. Algorithmic governance is integrated into its national security vision, encompassing economic, political, and defense dimensions. The U.S. relies on the dynamism of its private ecosystem, Google, Microsoft, OpenAI, Amazon, and venture capital investment. The federal government provides guidelines through executive orders and agencies such as NIST but avoids centralized control. Its strength lies in innovation; its weakness, in regulatory fragmentation (Congressional Research Service, 2025). The EU positions itself as a regulatory power, replicating the strategy of the General Data Protection Regulation (GDPR) with the AI Act. Its precautionary model prioritizes fundamental rights and seeks to project global standards through market influence. Although it lacks the entrepreneurial dynamism of the U.S. and the state capacity of China, the EU compensates with normative influence (Investopedia, 2025). These three models embody distinct logics: centralization (China), innovation (U.S.), and regulation (EU). However, competition is not limited to these three poles. Emerging and developing countries face the dilemma of aligning either with Chinese infrastructures, which are more affordable and often accompanied by know-how transfer, or with Western regulatory frameworks, which impose stricter requirements on rights and transparency. The result is a global mosaic in which Africa, Latin America, and Central Asia become key arenas of normative contestation. Examples such as Ethiopia and Nigeria, both adopters of Chinese surveillance and telecommunications systems, contrast with Latin American countries that have aligned more closely with European regulation, particularly in the area of data privacy. This fragmentation reflects that the struggle over AI is also a struggle for cultural and normative hegemony, where choosing a technological ecosystem implies adopting its underlying political values.

At the same time, international organizations such as the OECD, UNESCO, and the UN attempt to articulate common principles. UNESCO's Recommendation on the Ethics of AI (2021) and the OECD's AI Principles (2019) emphasize transparency, accountability, and respect for human rights. However, their non-binding nature limits their impact. China has participated actively in these initiatives but has reinterpreted them through the lens of digital sovereignty, resisting external constraints on its state use of AI. In contrast, the EU seeks to implement its regulatory approach within these forums, while the U.S. favors more flexible solutions that do not compromise its corporate leadership. This fragile multilateralism reflects a balance between cooperation and rivalry. There is broad agreement on risks such as bias and lack of transparency, but divergences regarding the role of the state, privacy, and military applications prevent deeper consensus. The geopolitics of AI thus reveals a complex competition in which economic, military, technological, and normative dimensions overlap. The issue is not merely who develops the most powerful algorithms, but what values and principles are embedded in them and in the infrastructures that support them. The rivalry between the U.S. and China, complemented by the EU's regulatory posture, sketches a scenario of digital fragmentation with risks of structural bifurcation.

## 3. CHINA'S CIVILIZATIONAL AND STRATEGIC APPROACH

China's approach to AI cannot be understood solely as a technological or economic strategy. It is deeply embedded in the country's cultural, philosophical, and political traditions. Unlike in the West, where technological innovation is often framed in terms of individual progress and market dynamics, in China it is articulated through the logic of harmony, national sovereignty, and the leadership of the Chinese Communist Party (CCP). Confucian roots emphasize the importance of order, hierarchy, and social harmony. From this perspective, AI is not an end in itself but an instrument for ensuring stability and cohesion. Added to this is the legacy of Legalism, a classical Chinese political doctrine that stressed discipline and control through law and punishment, which resonates in modern practices such as the Social Credit System, where surveillance and algorithmic evaluation are portrayed as tools for justice and trust. Digital centralism holds that technology must be subordinated to the interests of the Party and to the project of national rejuvenation (*zhonghua minzu weida fuxing*). Under this logic, AI constitutes an ideological battleground in which algorithms must reinforce socialist values.

China has institutionalized this approach through a series of plans and laws that integrate AI into its long-term strategies. The New Generation Artificial Intelligence Development Plan objectives' include developing key industries, consolidating innovation ecosystems, and incorporating AI into national security. Subsequently, the 14th Five-Year Plan (2021–2025) reinforced the centrality of AI in economic and social development. This plan highlights the need to strengthen domestic innovation, reduce dependence on foreign technologies, and expand AI applications in sectors such as advanced manufacturing, smart transportation, precision agriculture, and national security. The 15th Five-Year Plan (2026–2030) is expected to provide the framework through which China seeks to complete its transition toward technological self-sufficiency. This plan will integrate AI not only into industry and the military but also into sensitive areas such as urban governance, public health, and justice. The overarching goal is to consolidate a socialist digital civilization that serves as an alternative model to U.S. data capitalism and the European regulatory framework. Alongside central planning, two major laws approved in 2021 stand out: the Data Security Law (DSL) and the Personal Information Protection Law (PIPL). Although the PIPL resembles the EU's GDPR, it differs in its prioritization of state sovereignty over data, which are considered a strategic national resource. The state retains broad powers to control, restrict, or supervise cross-border data flows. The emphasis on technological self-sufficiency reflects China's awareness of its vulnerability to sanctions and external blockades. The semiconductor war exposed the risks inherent in dependence on global supply chains. In response, Beijing has increased its investment in domestic industries such as chip manufacturing, quantum computing, and supercomputing. A critical aspect of this strategy is control over rare earth elements, strategic minerals essential for producing electronic devices and telecommunications equipment. China accounts for more than 60% of global production and 90% of processing capacity, giving it potential leverage as a geopolitical pressure tool. This resource advantage strengthens China's narrative that digital sovereignty also requires sovereignty over raw materials.

Beyond central planning, the Chinese model is visible in pilot projects across different regions. In Hangzhou, the company Alibaba, in cooperation with the local government, developed the City Brain system, an urban management platform that uses AI to optimize traffic, emergency response, and energy consumption. Presented as an example of efficiency, it has also been criticized for expanding surveillance capabilities. Shenzhen concentrates AI startups and advanced robotics initiatives. It is a key node in China's civil–military fusion strategy, where private firms collaborate closely with the armed forces. In the Xinjiang Autonomous Region, facial recognition technologies and predictive analysis systems have been deployed. The government justifies these measures as counterterrorism efforts, while international organizations denounce them as a form of algorithmic repression (Human Rights Watch, 2019). Hospitals in Beijing and Shanghai have incorporated AI-assisted diagnostic systems that accelerate the detection of cancer and other diseases. These projects illustrate the duality of the Chinese model: the same technology that improves public services also strengthens state control over sensitive data. Taken together, China's approach shapes a vision of integral digital sovereignty in which AI is conceived as an economic resource and engine of global competitiveness, a tool of political control and legitimization for the CCP, a strategic asset essential for national and military security, and a normative vector intended for export through initiatives such as the Digital Silk Road. China's civilizational and strategic approach demonstrates that AI is both a technological instrument and a national project. By integrating philosophical traditions with state planning, Beijing is constructing a model of algorithmic governance aimed at consolidating its sovereignty and positioning itself as an alternative to the liberal digital order.

## 4. THE CHINESE MODEL OF AI GOVERNANCE

One of the most emblematic and controversial projects associated with the Chinese model is the Social Credit System (SCS). Although it is often portrayed in the West as a single, centralized, and omnipotent mechanism, in practice it consists of a constellation of interconnected local and sectoral programs, supervised by state agencies and supported by databases and scoring algorithms. Its objective is to assess the trustworthiness of individuals and organizations, stimulating behaviors considered positive, paying debts, fulfilling contracts, complying with regulations, and penalizing undesirable conduct, fraud, non-payment, violations. Reported consequences include restrictions on the purchase of airplane or train tickets, limitations on access to bank loans, or in extreme cases, the inability to access certain public services. For the government, the SCS seeks to strengthen trust in a rapidly transforming society, reduce corruption, and improve administrative efficiency. Critics, however, describe it as a mechanism of mass surveillance and social engineering capable of suppressing dissent and homogenizing citizen behavior (MERICS, 2021).

An illustrative example can be found in Rongcheng, Shandong Province, where one of the first pilot programs was implemented. Citizens began with an initial score that was adjusted based on their actions, with rewards such as quick-access loans or sanctions such as exclusion from certain public-sector jobs. While some residents acknowledged practical benefits, international activists viewed the initiative as the institutionalization of an Orwellian model. In the EU, the AI Act classifies any social scoring system affecting fundamental rights as unacceptable. In the U.S., where credit markers are managed by private companies such as Equifax or FICO, evaluations are limited to financial data and do not aim to regulate social behavior in a broader sense.

China has also undertaken a reform of its judicial system under the banner of Smart Courts. These digital courts employ AI to optimize judicial processes, from facial recognition for identity verification to algorithms that suggest sentences based on precedent. In Hangzhou, home to the Internet Court inaugurated in 2017, cases related to e-commerce, digital intellectual property, and online contracts are resolved with support from automated systems. Parties may submit electronic evidence verified via blockchain, and entire hearings can be conducted virtually. The official narrative holds that these tools accelerate justice, reduce costs, and democratize access in a country of more than 1.4 billion inhabitants with chronic judicial overload. According to Shi et al. (2021), Smart Courts enable the processing of mass cases that would otherwise remain stagnant. Nonetheless, concerns persist regarding the transparency of the algorithms that propose verdicts and the system's guarantees of impartiality. Critics warn of the risk of institutionalizing algorithmic biases, reinforcing mechanisms of control rather than ensuring independent justice. In comparison, the EU and the U.S. have explored AI in judicial contexts, but in a more limited and experimental fashion. In Europe, some countries have tested systems to support jurisprudence analysis, while in the U.S. risk-assessment algorithms such as COMPAS have been deployed, generating controversy over racial bias. Yet none of these initiatives has reached the degree of state-led, nationwide integration exhibited by China's Smart Courts.

As noted earlier, China's regulatory framework for data is anchored in the DSL and the PIPL. The former establishes data as a strategic national resource, classifies information into various levels of importance, and grants the state broad powers to control its storage, processing, and transfer, especially data deemed critical for national security. The latter prioritizes state sovereignty over individual rights. For instance, the government may restrict or block cross-border transfers if it concludes that they pose a threat to national security, affecting foreign companies operating in China. This model enables the CCP to maintain granular control over private actors, both domestic and international, that handle data within Chinese territory. Companies such as Didi, similar to Uber, have been sanctioned for alleged violations of these regulations, in proceedings that reaffirm the primacy of the state over private technological capital. Another essential component of the Chinese model is the integration of AI into urban governance through smart city initiatives. In Shenzhen, facial-recognition cameras connected to national databases are deployed across the city. In Hangzhou, the City Brain system manages traffic lights, ambulances, and public transportation in real time. In Chongqing, smart sensors track energy use to optimize resources and detect anomalies in infrastructure. These initiatives aim to increase efficiency, reduce crime, and offer personalized services. However, they also blur the line between public security and political surveillance. The same cameras that detect traffic violations can identify and monitor a dissident during a protest. In Western countries, smart city projects have encountered public resistance. In Toronto, for example, the Sidewalk Labs project, a subsidiary of Google, was canceled in 2020 due to concerns over privacy and surveillance. In the EU, the development of such cities is constrained by strict data protection norms.

As it was stated, in the Xinjiang region AI has been used for domestic security purposes. Facial recognition systems, communication monitoring, and predictive analytics have been integrated into a surveillance architecture as part of counter-extremism and counterterrorism efforts. However, reports from international organizations such as Human Rights Watch (2021) have denounced algorithms capable of identifying behavioral patterns deemed suspicious and triggering preventive detentions, technology that could be exported to other provinces or even to partner countries via the Digital Silk Road. The Chinese model differs from Western approaches in three key respects. Whereas initiatives in the U.S. and the EU are fragmented and feature institutional checks and balances, China integrates AI into a more centralized ecosystem. China prioritizes social stability and political security, while the U.S. emphasizes innovation and the EU stresses rights protection. Moreover, the scale of projects such as the SCS or smart cities has no current equivalent in the Western sphere.

## 5. AI IN CHINA'S MILITARY AND SECURITY STRATEGY

China's security strategy must be understood within the broader framework of its national modernization project. The government has set 2049, the centenary of the founding of the People's Republic, as a symbolic horizon for completing the transformation of the People's Liberation Army (PLA) into a world-class military force (State Council, 2019). This objective extends beyond enhancing conventional capabilities. It includes integrating emerging technologies such as AI, big data, robotics, and biotechnology into military doctrine. In this context, AI is conceived as a strategic force multiplier capable of reshaping the global military balance. Documents such as the National Defense White Paper (2019) note that AI will be fundamental for achieving superiority in command and control, cyber operations, autonomous systems, and military logistics (Kania, 2019). The concept of "intelligentized warfare" (*zhinenghua zhanzheng*) thus becomes a doctrinal axis that marks a leap beyond the informatization phase initiated in the 1990s. China has invested heavily in the research, development, and deployment of military applications. Among the most significant are autonomous systems and drone swarms, which the PLA has tested under AI coordination to conduct reconnaissance, electronic warfare, or saturation attacks (Allen, 2019). This technology aims to offset U.S. advantages in manned aviation and precision systems. Machine-learning algorithms also process real-time information from satellites, radars, and sensors to give Chinese commanders operational superiority. AI platforms are used to optimize supply routes and predict failures in aircraft or naval vessels, reducing costs and increasing operational sustainability. China further integrates AI into cybersecurity operations. Anomaly-detection algorithms identify intrusions in real time, while offensive research explores AI-generated adaptive malware (Segal, 2017). Universities and research centers affiliated with the PLA have developed AI-driven simulators that recreate complex combat scenarios, enabling more efficient and cost-effective training (Kania & Laskai, 2021). The logic of civil–military fusion (*junmin ronghe*) propels this dynamic. Companies such as Huawei, Baidu, and SenseTime participate in dual-use projects, contributing innovation and scalability to military modernization (Cheung, 2016).

Under the doctrine of comprehensive national security, the CCP considers domestic stability and external security inseparable (Creemers, 2018). Authorities have deployed the Integrated Joint Operations Platform (IJOP) collects information on religious practices, movements, and electricity use to identify patterns deemed suspicious in Xinjiang (Human Rights Watch, 2019). Critics describe this network as algorithmic repression enabling the arbitrary detention of thousands (Zenz, 2020). Also, facial recognition systems operate in Beijing's public transport, predictive policing algorithms are used in Shenzhen, and social-media monitoring platforms detect subversive discourse. These mechanisms consolidate an infrastructure that strengthens the CCP's ability to anticipate and neutralize political risks. Intelligentized automation implies that future warfare will be dominated by data and algorithms. While informatization involved digitizing information and improving communications, intelligentization involves delegating parts of the decision-making process to intelligent systems (Kania, 2019). Institutions such as the Academy of Military Sciences (AMS) and the National Defense University argue that speed in data processing will determine success in future conflicts. The central idea is that AI can provide an asymmetric advantage against rivals with superior conventional capabilities, particularly the U.S. However, this tendency raises profound ethical and legal dilemmas. The greater the delegation of decisions to algorithms, the more blurred the lines of responsibility become in accidental conflicts (Scharre, 2018) or violations of international humanitarian law (Asaro, 2020). In international forums, China's stance on Lethal Autonomous Weapons Systems (LAWS) is ambivalent. At the Convention on Certain Conventional Weapons (CCW), Beijing has supported limiting fully autonomous systems lacking meaningful human control. At the same time, it opposes a legally binding ban, aligning with the U.S. and Russia in defending strategic flexibility (Docherty, 2025). In practice, the PLA continues to develop armed drones and unmanned underwater vehicles that operate semi-autonomously. This reflects the tension between projecting an image of responsibility and preserving access to a field that could yield disruptive advantages in the future.

The U.S. maintains a clear technological edge in advanced algorithms and sensors. However, the reluctance of parts of the private sector to collaborate on military projects, illustrated by Google's withdrawal from Project Maven, reveals ethical tensions within its innovation ecosystem. Russia, by contrast, has prioritized the development of drones and military robots but faces technological constraints resulting from economic sanctions and weaker civil–military integration (Gady, 2020). Other countries, such as Israel, Turkey, and South Korea, are also investing in autonomous systems, shaping a multipolar landscape in which China seeks to consolidate its position as an emerging power. The transfer of internal security technologies to partner countries may reinforce authoritarian regimes and erode fundamental rights, while the ongoing algorithmic arms race, without binding agreements, heightens the risk of uncontrolled proliferation of autonomous weapons. China's strategy of integrating AI into its military and security apparatus reflects a broader project of comprehensive state transformation. From the battlefield to internal control, AI becomes a key instrument for consolidating Party authority and reducing asymmetries vis-à-vis strategic rivals. Internationally, Beijing adopts a discourse of prudence and cooperation while continuing to develop advanced capabilities. This ambivalence, shared to some extent by other major powers, underscores the difficulty of establishing global consensus on the military uses of AI. Ultimately, the militarization of AI in China is not an isolated phenomenon, it is part of an integrated geopolitical project that combines technological innovation, control, and global projection.

## 6. THE DIGITAL SILK ROAD

The Digital Silk Road (DSR) was officially announced in 2015 as a strategic branch of the Belt and Road Initiative (BRI), launched by Xi Jinping in 2013. While the BRI focused on roads, ports, and railways, the DSR aimed to extend China's influence into cyberspace and global digital infrastructure (Triolo et al., 2020). The

DSR is projected as an integrated instrument of power that combines investment in submarine cables, 5G networks, satellites, data centers, and e-commerce platforms with the export of digital governance models rooted in state sovereignty. The official message is that whoever controls the digital arteries of the twenty-first century will also control data flows, and, with them, part of the global order. One of the pillars of the DSR is the financing and deployment of critical infrastructure in countries across the Global South and, to a lesser extent, Eastern Europe. Companies such as Huawei Marine Networks have built dozens of routes connecting Asia, Africa, and Europe through submarine cables, offering alternatives to Western consortia. Huawei and ZTE's 4G and 5G networks have become dominant in Africa and Latin America, offering lower prices and state-backed financing. Alibaba Cloud has established data centers and sovereign cloud systems in Dubai, São Paulo, and Johannesburg, expanding China's footprint in data storage and processing services (Cissé, 2022). Meanwhile, the BeiDou satellite navigation system, China's alternative to the U.S. GPS, has achieved global coverage and is actively promoted among DSR partners (Zhao, 2020). China's advantage lies in offering a full package: infrastructure provision, financing, partial transfer of capabilities, and personnel training. This has proved especially attractive for resource-constrained countries.

Apart from infrastructure, the DSR operates as a vehicle for normative export. Beijing promotes a model of cyber-sovereignty in which each state maintains full control over its Internet, data, and algorithms (Creemers, 2018). In practice, this translates into the transfer of know-how. Partner governments receive training in cybersecurity, guidance on data governance, and assistance in algorithmic surveillance. Notable cases include Ethiopia, where after Huawei networks were installed the government strengthened its surveillance capacities (Feldstein, 2019); Venezuela, where Chinese companies such as ZTE collaborated on the "carnet de la patria", a controversial digital identification system; and Pakistan, where cooperation on cybersecurity has enabled more robust Internet censorship mechanisms (Rolland, 2017). In this sense, the DSR also exports a political vision that legitimizes extensive state control over cyberspace. According to Cissé (2022), over 70% of Africa's 4G networks were built by Chinese providers, including those in Kenya, Nigeria, and South Africa. While the economic appeal is clear, these partnerships also generate technological dependence, as countries become tied to Chinese suppliers for system maintenance and upgrades. In Latin America, the DSR materializes through surveillance and telecommunications projects. Ecuador implemented video-surveillance systems with Chinese support. Brazil, despite U.S. pressure, allowed Huawei to participate in its 5G rollout. And Chinese e-commerce platforms such as AliExpress and payment systems like Alipay have expanded across the region. In contrast, penetration in Europe has been uneven. Countries like Hungary and Serbia have signed agreements with Huawei for 5G networks and surveillance systems, whereas

Germany and France, among others, have restricted Chinese participation due to national security concerns. This duality reflects Europe's internal fracture between short-term economic interests and long-term strategic considerations.

The expansion of the DSR presents a direct challenge to U.S. and European leadership in the digital domain. Key consequences include technological dependence, normative standardization, since adopting Chinese infrastructure often involves importing regulatory practices aligned with digital sovereignty, and increased support for China in UN cybersecurity votes (Rolland, 2017). It is also argued that the DSR strengthens authoritarian regimes by providing them with surveillance technologies (Feldstein, 2019), generates risks of a digital debt trap, in which countries become indebted in exchange for infrastructure (Rolland, 2017), and raises data-security concerns, as Beijing may gain access to sensitive information from foreign governments and citizens. However, many recipient governments view Western alternatives as more expensive and less accessible. Beyond that, the DSR must be understood as a global normative project. Beijing exports its vision of the Internet, centralized and subordinate to national sovereignty. This vision directly competes with the EU, which exports regulatory standards grounded in fundamental rights (GDPR and the AI Act), and with the U.S., which promotes a model of free data flows dominated by Big Tech (Bradford, 2020). The DSR constitutes a comprehensive geopolitical instrument that enables China to expand its economic, technological, and normative power on a global scale. Its appeal lies in financial accessibility and capacity transfer, while its risks manifest in technological dependence, authoritarian reinforcement, and rights erosion. In Africa, Latin America, and parts of Europe, the DSR has created structural dependencies that consolidate Beijing's influence. Ultimately, the DSR is more than a connectivity project. It is a vector for projecting China's digital governance model globally, contributing to the emerging bifurcation of the international technological order.

## 7. AI GOVERNANCE MODELS IN THE U.S. AND THE EU

The U.S. model of AI governance is characterized by the predominance of the private sector as the driving force of innovation and global leadership. The so-called Big Tech companies have been responsible for a significant share of advances in deep learning, generative AI, and mass-adoption platforms. This ecosystem has allowed the U.S. to maintain a leading position, but it has also generated tensions between private-sector dynamism and the absence of a robust regulatory framework. At the federal level, the approach has remained flexible and decentralized. The Executive Order on Safe, Secure, and Trustworthy AI, issued by President Biden in 2023, sought to establish guidelines on safety, transparency, and impact assessment, but it was partially reversed by President Trump through Executive Order 14179, which aimed to eliminate ideological barriers and accelerate innovation (White House, 2025). The NIST AI Risk Management Framework (2023) constitutes another key reference. Although non-binding, it provides technical guidance for designing trustworthy systems based on principles of robustness, accountability, and transparency. Its voluntary nature reflects the U.S. preference for soft-law instruments and industry self-regulation.

American federalism has also spurred the emergence of uneven state-level regulations. California, pioneer in digital privacy through the California Consumer Privacy Act (CCPA),has explored algorithmic transparency and accountability norms (Bradford, 2020). New York, in turn, has implemented audit requirements for AI systems used in hiring and employment procedures (Raji & Buolamwini, 2019). This fragmentation creates a regulatory mosaic that, while fostering normative experimentation, also increases compliance complexity for firms operating across multiple jurisdictions. In the health sector, the FDA has authorized medical algorithms through a progressive approval system that allows continuous updates but raises concerns about patient safety. In education, platforms such as Proctorio and Turnitin have generated controversy for their use of AI in exam supervision and plagiarism detection, criticized for bias and privacy risks. In finance, the SEC and the Federal Reserve have expressed concerns regarding high-frequency trading algorithms and AI-driven credit scoring systems. Overall, the U.S. model privileges innovation and global competitiveness but suffers from institutional fragmentation and limited protective mechanisms, resulting in ethical and security vulnerabilities. In contrast to U.S. dynamism, the EU has opted for a regulatory strategy that seeks to consolidate its position as a normative power (Bradford, 2020). Inspired by the global success of the GDPR, the EU approved the AI Act in 2024, the world's first comprehensive and binding legal framework for AI. It classifies AI systems according to a risk-based approach. Unacceptable risk: mass biometric surveillance and cognitive manipulation; high risk: critical infrastructure, justice, and employment; limited risk: requiring transparency, such as chatbots; and minimal-risk applications with little regulatory intervention. Significant fines are provided for non-compliance, following the GDPR's sanctioning logic. To implement the regulation, the EU created the European Artificial Intelligence Office, tasked with coordinating national regulators and ensuring uniform application (European Commission, 2024). This centralization contrasts with U.S. fragmentation and strengthens the EU's capacity to project its regulatory standards beyond its borders.

In the justice sector, several member states have experimented with AI-assisted decision-support tools, but the AI Act imposes strict limits to safeguard judicial independence (Wachter et al., 2021). Regarding biometrics, the use of facial recognition in public spaces is permitted only in exceptional national-security situations

(Buttarelli, 2016). Medical AI and autonomous vehicles must undergo rigorous risk-assessment protocols before deployment. For now, the European strategy prioritizes fundamental rights and social trust, even at the expense of slowing down entrepreneurial development. The Council of Europe also approved an AI Convention (Council of Europe, 2024), which seeks to establish clear obligations on transparency, non-discrimination, and human oversight. Its adoption would extend normative influence beyond the EU's borders. Additionally, institutions such as the European Central Bank have warned about systemic risks associated with financial automation, while the EU Fundamental Rights Agency monitors the impact of AI on equality and non-discrimination (FRA, 2022). The U.S. and the EU reflect divergent political and cultural traditions. While the former prioritizes innovation and global competitiveness, granting broad space to corporate self-regulation, the latter emphasizes regulation and rights protection. However, the two models share points of convergence. Both recognize risks of bias, disinformation, and algorithmic opacity, participate in multilateral forums such as the OECD and UNESCO to promote common principles, and engage in the U.S.–EU Trade and Technology Council (TTC), which has attempted to coordinate positions vis-à-vis China. Yet structural tensions persist due to distinct governance philosophies. Thus, Western models of AI governance offer both contrast and complementarity. Together, they form a plural counterweight to China's approach, although their internal divergences hinder the construction of a unified strategic front. The future of global AI governance will depend on the ability of the U.S. and the EU to articulate a shared vision grounded in common principles, avoiding fragmentation that could weaken their influence in the face of Beijing's expanding projection.

## 8. COMPARATIVE ANALYSIS: CHINA VS. THE WEST

The three dominant models of AI governance are expressions of distinct civilizational traditions: Confucian–Leninist collectivism in China, competitive liberalism in the U.S., and normative universalism in the EU.

*Table 1. Comparative matrix of the three major power blocs*

| | China | U.S. | EU |
|---|---|---|---|
| **Governance** | Centralized under the CCP. | Fragmented, private sector dominant. | Coordinated through supranational institutions. |
| **Political priority** | Social stability and digital sovereignty. | Innovation and global competitiveness. | Fundamental rights and social trust. |
| **State-market relation** | State-dominant, firms subordinated. | Market-dominant, limited regulation. | Balanced model with strong regulation. |
| **Personal data** | Strategic state-controlled resources. | Private assets with limited regulation. | A fundamental right protected by GDPR and the AI Act. |
| **Social applications** | Social Credit, smart cities. | Digital advertising, private platforms. | Regulated services with rights emphasis. |
| **Militarization** | Integrated into PLA modernization. | Heavy investment, ethical tensions. | More limited military use. |

**Note**. Author's elaboration.

A fundamental difference lies in the relationship between state control and individual rights. In China, social stability and national security justify the subordination of individual liberties. AI is used for surveillance, behavioral prediction, and social control (Creemers, 2018). In the U.S., the emphasis is on entrepreneurial freedom and innovation, creating risks of private power concentration in the hands of Big Tech (Zuboff, 2019). In the EU, the normative priority is the protection of fundamental rights, legitimizing strict restrictions on high-risk technologies (European Commission, 2024). This contrast reflects divergent conceptions of political legitimacy: stability and prosperity in China, economic dynamism in the U.S., and social trust in the EU. The tension between technological innovation and preventive regulation cuts across all three models: China deploys technologies at scale and adjusts regulation reactively under strong state control; the U.S. relies on market-driven innovation with corporate self-regulation and minimal federal intervention; and the EU adopts ex ante controls, prioritizing social trust at the risk of slowing innovation (Renda, 2022). The outcome is a triangle of interdependencies in which China and the U.S. lead in innovation but still react to EU regulatory standards, while the EU remains dependent on external technologies but projects its rules at a global scale.

This clash of models directly affects international digital trade. Chinese firms such as Huawei and Alibaba promote closed ecosystems compatible with digital sovereignty (Rolland, 2017). U.S. Big Tech exports global platforms that impose de facto standards. The EU uses the regulatory extraterritoriality of the GDPR and the AI Act to condition market access (Bradford, 2020). For the Global South, this implies strategic choices: aligning with Chinese infrastructure, American innovation, or European regulation. In cybersecurity, differences are also striking. China integrates centralized cyberdefense and promotes cyber-sovereignty (Segal,

2017). The U.S. faces vulnerabilities due to its reliance on private infrastructure, as demonstrated by the SolarWinds breach (2020). The EU emphasizes resilience through regulation, but its external technological dependence limits its autonomy (Buttarelli, 2016). As a result, international cooperation becomes more complicated, as Beijing defends digital sovereignty, Brussels prioritizes human rights, and Washington promotes the free flow of data. Regarding human rights, divergences are even deeper. China employs AI as a partial instrument of political control (Human Rights Watch, 2019). The U.S. faces risks related to data concentration and informational manipulation by private platforms (Zuboff, 2019). The European model positions itself as a normative counterweight, prioritizing rights protection even at the expense of economic dynamism (European Commission, 2024). Despite these differences, areas of convergence do exist,such as recognition of risks involving bias and algorithmic opacity, acceptance of the principle of meaningful human control in critical systems, especially military ones (Docherty, 2025), and participation in multilateral forums like UNESCO, the OECD, and the G20, which promote transparency and ethical guidelines (OECD, 2019). These points of agreement enable limited cooperation, although insufficient to prevent digital bifurcation. The comparative analysis reveals a fragmented yet interdependent world: China offers a sovereignty-and-control-oriented model projected through the Digital Silk Road; the U.S. drives entrepreneurial innovation and exports global platforms; and the EU compensates for its technological weakness with regulatory power. Global AI governance is taking shape within this unstable balance, where no single model can fully impose itself. The result is a bifurcated digital order in which minimal cooperation coexists with strategic competition.

## 9. AI, INTERNATIONAL LAW, AND MULTILATERAL FORUMS

The UN has become a key venue for debates on AI and its normative implications. Although no binding treaty specifically regulating AI yet exists, various UN bodies have produced documents and resolutions that frame AI as an issue of human rights, sustainable development, and international security. The UN General Assembly has adopted resolutions promoting a safe, inclusive, and trustworthy digital environment, urging states to cooperate on transparency and rights protection (United Nations, 2023). The Human Rights Council has held thematic debates on algorithmic surveillance, with explicit references to the use of facial recognition technologies. In 2021, the Office of the High Commissioner for Human Rights warned that the indiscriminate use of AI in surveillance could lead to systematic violations of fundamental rights (OHCHR, 2021). These reports position the UN as a forum for legitimization and denunciation, though constrained by great-power rivalry. In 2021, UNESCO adopted the Recommendation on the Ethics of Artificial Intelligence, the first global normative instrument dedicated to AI. Endorsed by all 193 member states, it establishes principles of human dignity, inclusion, sustainability, and transparency (UNESCO, 2021). Even rival powers such as China and the U.S. supported the document. Nevertheless, its non-binding nature makes it an example of soft law. China used the UNESCO platform to reinforce its discourse of digital sovereignty, insisting that each country should define its own governance norms. In contrast, the EU interpreted the recommendation as an endorsement of its normative universalism centered on human rights (Buttarelli, 2016).

In 2019, the OECD adopted its AI Principles, later endorsed by the G20. These principles promote human-centric values, transparency, accountability, and technical robustness (OECD, 2019). Although non-binding, they have influenced national policies and regulatory frameworks. The U.S. and the EU have actively supported them as minimum governance standards. China, while a signatory, has emphasized that these principles must respect cultural diversity and national sovereignty (Segal, 2017). The G20, bringing together Western powers and emerging economies, has consolidated itself as a flexible negotiation forum. For Beijing, it serves as a platform to legitimize the Digital Silk Road as an alternative pathway for the Global South (Rolland, 2017). Meanwhile, as it was mentioned, the Council of Europe developed an AI Convention (Council of Europe, 2024). Its aim is to establish international obligations prohibiting systems that violate fundamental rights, requiring human oversight in critical applications, and ensuring accountability mechanisms for governments and companies. Although it faces resistance from some states, it represents the first binding treaty on AI.

The most contentious domain is that of lethal autonomous weapons systems. At the convention, states debate whether to restrict or ban such systems. The EU and many Global South countries have advocated a legally binding prohibition, invoking international humanitarian law (Docherty, 2025). The U.S. rejects bans, arguing they would hinder innovation and national security. China supports restrictions on fully autonomous systems lacking meaningful human control but opposes a binding prohibition and continues to develop semi-autonomous prototypes (Kania, 2019). Multilateral forums reproduce the core tension among competing visions: China's defense of cyber-sovereignty, which legitimizes extensive state control over data and infrastructure; the U.S. model promoting free data flows and corporate self-regulation; and the EU's universalist framework rooted in human rights applied to the digital sphere (European Commission, 2024). The result is a fragmented multilateralism in which minimal consensus is reached on ethics and transparency, yet ambitious progress is blocked on issues such as mass surveillance or military uses of AI.

Within this context, Global South countries play a crucial role in the normative dispute. Many are beneficiaries of the Digital Silk Road and thus tend to align with

China in UN votes. Others view the EU as an attractive model for protecting rights and fostering digital trust. Their future orientations will decisively influence the shape of international AI governance. The analysis of multilateral forums shows that international AI governance is being constructed on an unstable equilibrium. The UN and UNESCO generate minimal ethical consensus; the OECD and G20 promote flexible principles; and the Council of Europe seeks a binding treaty with potentially global reach. China, the U.S., and the EU use these forums to legitimize their respective models. The absence of robust consensus facilitates an unconstrained technological arms race, especially in the military domain. Meanwhile, competition for influence in the Global South positions countries such as Ethiopia, Brazil, and India as decisive actors in shaping the future of the digital order.

## 10. IMPLICATIONS FOR GLOBAL DIGITAL GOVERNANCE

The international deployment of AI and its governance reflect a growing fragmentation of the global digital order. Whereas previous decades were characterized by an open and relatively homogeneous Internet under U.S. dominance, today a bifurcation is emerging between a sovereignty-oriented, state-controlled model led by China, a market-liberal model promoted by the U.S., and a normative model advanced by the EU (Creemers, 2018; Bradford, 2020). The coexistence of these models produces a scenario of conflictual interdependence: countries rely simultaneously on Chinese infrastructures, U.S. platforms, and European regulations, complicating the construction of global consensus. The central risk is the consolidation of a digitally divided world structured around two main spheres: the Chinese ecosystem, rooted in the Digital Silk Road, where infrastructure, hardware, and data governance follow the logic of state sovereignty; and the Western ecosystem, articulated around Big Tech and regulated by frameworks such as the GDPR and the AI Act, with an emphasis on rights and open markets. This bifurcation entails significant risks. One is technical incompatibility, as networks, protocols, and standards become increasingly non-interoperable. Another is inequality of access, since Global South countries may be forced to select a dominant provider and become locked into structural dependencies. A third risk is diplomatic tension, as each bloc uses digital infrastructure as an instrument of political influence (Rolland, 2017).

Data have become the oil of the twenty-first century, and their governance is now the axis of international competition (Zuboff, 2019). China treats data as a strategic national resource. Its cybersecurity and data protection laws stipulate that any data generated within its territory must remain under state control (Creemers, 2018). In contrast, the U.S. lacks a unified federal framework. Data are managed primarily as private corporate assets, subject to fragmented state-level rules (Bradford, 2020).

The EU recognizes data protection as a fundamental right and, through the GDPR and the Data Governance Act, promotes a model of individual sovereignty and social trust (European Commission, 2022). The result is a clash of conceptions that hinders cooperation on critical issues. The absence of consensus on autonomous weapons increases the risk of an algorithmic arms race (Docherty, 2025). Diverging notions of digital sovereignty obstruct the creation of global cybersecurity protocols against large-scale attacks. In digital trade, international agreements face deadlock due to incompatible models of cross-border data transfer. Still, spaces of minimal cooperation persist. Ethical principles promoted by UNESCO, guidelines from the OECD, and digital resilience frameworks in the G20. Although limited, these agreements show that partial multilateralism is possible (OECD, 2019). In this context, the Global South becomes the decisive battleground for digital governance. China offers affordable infrastructure through the Digital Silk Road, tied to its cyber-sovereignty model; the U.S. deploys technological platforms and private financing, prioritizing integration into its innovation ecosystem; and the EU promotes technical assistance and rights-based regulation. The orientation of countries such as Brazil, India, South Africa, and Indonesia will play a pivotal role in shaping future balance. India, in particular, is emerging as a hinge actor capable of articulating intermediate positions between sovereignty and openness (Chaudhuri, 2022).

Despite fragmentation, proposals exist to build a global framework for AI governance. These include binding treaties on military uses modeled on international humanitarian law to restrict or prohibit lethal autonomous weapons; sector-specific cooperation agreements on digital health or climate management; or the creation of a UN-led international AI agency with functions analogous to the IAEA in the nuclear field (Asaro, 2020). Another option is the establishment of interoperability standards enabling minimal compatibility across different ecosystems. All these proposals, however, require political will and compromise, both currently constrained by strategic rivalry between China and the U.S.. Several scenarios can be envisaged. The first is one of rigid bifurcation, with two incompatible ecosystems, Chinese and Western, and the Global South divided into spheres of influence. The second is regulated interdependence, in which minimal agreements on interoperability and critical risks coexist with strategic competition. The third is partial convergence, where emerging global governance forms around shared principles and strengthened multilateral institutions. In the short term, the most probable scenario is one in which cooperation remains confined to shared risks, while competition prevails in security, economics, and rights. In this manner, global AI governance is likely to evolve through continuous negotiation among divergent models, as major powers attempt to impose their norms while managing unavoidable interdependencies.

## 11. CONCLUSIONS

The analysis conducted shows that AI has become a central axis of contemporary geopolitical competition. Far from being a neutral tool, AI reflects the values, priorities, and strategic objectives of the actors that develop it. China adopts a centralized and sovereignty-oriented model in which AI serves simultaneously the purposes of military modernization, domestic control, and external normative projection (Kania, 2019; Creemers, 2018). The U.S. prioritizes private innovation and technological supremacy but suffers from institutional fragmentation and ethical tensions regarding public–private collaboration (Zuboff, 2019). The EU positions itself as a normative power, promoting regulation as an instrument of legitimacy and international influence (Bradford, 2020; European Commission, 2024). These three models reflect distinct political worldviews: centralism in China, competitive liberalism in the U.S., and rights-based universalism in the EU.

The comparative assessment demonstrates that AI constitutes a multidimensional arena of power, simultaneously shaping the economy, security, society, and diplomacy. Digital governance is fragmented, with no convergence toward a single model but rather competition among incompatible visions. Human rights are a core arena of contestation: the EU places them at the center, China subordinates them to security, and the U.S. conditions them on innovation. The Global South plays a decisive role through its choice of infrastructures and regulatory frameworks, which will tilt the balance of the emerging digital order. Multilateralism remains insufficient. Although developments such as UNESCO's Recommendation or the Council of Europe's draft convention are significant, they have not halted the technological and military race. Looking ahead to 2050, three possible scenarios can be outlined. The first is irreversible fragmentation and the consolidation of an algorithmic bifurcation, with incompatible ecosystems led by China and the West. The second is partial convergence, involving minimal agreements on interoperability and shared ethical principles, amid persistent divergence on rights and security. The third is cooperative governance, with the establishment of a binding multilateral framework limiting military uses and protecting universal rights (Asaro, 2020). The most likely scenario in the short term is partial convergence, where rivalries persist but minimal consensus is reached to manage systemic risks.

Despite geopolitical rivalry, structural interdependence remains. China requires global markets to expand its Digital Silk Road; the United States depends on the ability of its Big Tech firms to operate in foreign jurisdictions, even adapting to European rules; and the EU lacks technological leadership but projects its regulatory influence worldwide through the extraterritoriality of the GDPR and the AI Act. This paradox creates an unstable equilibrium in which competition does not eliminate the need for cooperation. The future of digital governance will depend on the capacity to articulate a minimal consensus around human rights. In China, political legitimacy rests on social stability and economic prosperity, often at the expense of individual liberties; in the U.S., technological innovation underpins global leadership, yet weak regulation erodes social trust; and in the EU, fundamental rights legitimize the model but slow entrepreneurial competitiveness. Constructing a global framework of trust will require balancing innovation, security, and rights. At the same time, the Global South will play a decisive role in the future digital architecture. By choosing Chinese infrastructures, U.S. platforms, or European regulatory standards, these countries will shape the global reach of each model. Their participation in multilateral forums such as the G20 or the UN may shift the balance toward inclusive multilateralism or, alternatively, reinforce fragmentation if aligned along opposing blocs.

From this analysis, several recommendations can be proposed: advancing toward global minimum standards centered on transparency, human oversight, and algorithmic accountability; restricting autonomous military uses through a dedicated international treaty; strengthening multilateral cooperation by expanding the roles of UNESCO, the OECD, and the Council of Europe; including the Global South as a co-producer of norms to avoid a unilaterally imposed digital order; and balancing innovation with rights to ensure legitimate and sustainable technological development. AI is not merely a technical tool but a civilizational artifact that embodies competing political projects. The world stands at a crossroads. One path leads to fragmentation and rule-free rivalry, with risks of conflict and erosion of rights. The other leads to cooperation and the construction of a global framework of trust, in which AI becomes a lever for sustainable and inclusive development. Ultimately, the fundamental question is how to govern with AI,and what kind of humanity will be built in the algorithmic era. The answer will determine both the digital order and the future of the international community itself.

## REFERENCES


Al-Maamari, A. (2025). *Between innovation and oversight: A cross-regional study of AI risk management frameworks in the EU, U.S., UK, and China.* arXiv.

Allen, G. (2019). *Understanding China's AI strategy: Clues to Chinese strategic thinking on artificial intelligence and national security*. Center for a New American Security.

Asaro, P. (2020). AI ethics in international humanitarian law. In Liao, M. (Ed.), *The ethics of artificial intelligence* (pp. 301–320). Oxford University Press.

Bradford, A. (2020). *The Brussels effect: How the European Union rules the world.* Oxford University Press. DOI: 10.1093/oso/9780190088583.001.0001

Buttarelli, G. (2016). The EU GDPR as a clarion call for a new global digital gold standard. *International Data Privacy Law*, *6*(2), 77–78. DOI: 10.1093/idpl/ipw006

Cheung, T. M. (2016). Innovation in China's Defense Technology Base: Foreign Technology and Military Capabilities. *The Journal of Strategic Studies*, *39*(5–6), 728–761. DOI: 10.1080/01402390.2016.1208612

Cissé, D. (2022). Chinese telecommunications companies in Africa: alignment with African countries' interests in developing their ICT sector?.

Congressional Research Service. (2025). *Regulating artificial intelligence: U.S. and international approaches and considerations for Congress* (CRS Report R48555). Library of Congress.

Council of Europe. (2024). *Framework Convention on Artificial Intelligence*. Human Rights, Democracy and the Rule of Law.

Creemers, R. (2018). *China's social credit system: An evolving practice of control. SSRN*. DOI: 10.2139/ssrn.3175792

Docherty, B. (2025). *A hazard to human rights: Autonomous weapons systems and digital decision-making*. Human Rights Watch.

European Commission. (2024). *Artificial Intelligence Act*. Publications Office of the European Union.

Feldstein, S. (2019). *The global expansion of AI surveillance*. Carnegie Endowment for International Peace.

Gady, F.-S. (2020). *What does AI mean for the future of manoeuvre warfare?* International Institute for Strategic Studies.

Guest, O., & Wei, K. (2024). *Bridging the artificial intelligence governance gap: The United States' and China's divergent approaches to governing general-purpose artificial intelligence*. RAND Corporation.

Human Rights Watch. (2019). *China's algorithms of repression: Reverse engineering a Xinjiang police mass surveillance app.*

Kania, E., & Laskai, L. (2021). *Myths and realities of China's military-civil fusion strategy*. Center for a New American Security.

Kania, E. B. (2019). *Learning without fighting: New developments in PLA AI war-gaming*. China Brief, 19(7). Jamestown Foundation.

OECD. (2019). *OECD principles on artificial intelligence*. Organisation for Economic Co-operation and Development.

OHCHR. (2021). *The right to privacy in the digital age*. Office of the United Nations High Commissioner for Human Rights.

Renda, A. (2022). *Can the EU Digital Markets Act achieve its goals?* Center for the Governance of Change, IE University.

Rolland, N. (2017). *China's Eurasian century? Political and strategic implications of the Belt and Road Initiative*. National Bureau of Asian Research.

Segal, A. (2017). *Chinese cyber diplomacy in a new era of uncertainty* (Aegis Paper No. 1703). Hoover Institution.

Shi, S., Sourdin, T., & Li, B. (2021). The smart court , A new pathway to justice in China? *International Journal for Court Administration, 12*(1), 4. DOI: 10.36745/ijca.367

UNESCO. (2021). *Recommendation on the ethics of artificial intelligence.*

Wachter, S., Mittelstadt, B., & Russell, C. (2021). Why fairness cannot be automated: Bridging the gap between EU non-discrimination law and AI. *Computer Law & Security Review*, *41*, 105567. DOI: 10.1016/j.clsr.2021.105567

Zaidan, E. (2024). AI governance in a complex and rapidly changing world. *Humanities & Social Sciences Communications*, *11*, 233. DOI: 10.1057/s41599-024-03560-x

Zenz, A. (2020). Sterilizations, IUDs, and coercive birth control in Xinjiang. *China Journal (Canberra, A.C.T.)*, *84*, 8–36.

Zuboff, S. (2019). *The age of surveillance capitalism*. PublicAffairs.

## ADDITIONAL READING

MERICS. (2021). *Lofty principles, conflicting incentives: AI ethics and governance in China* (MERICS Monitor Report). Mercator Institute for China Studies.

Raji, I. D., & Buolamwini, J. (2019). Actionable auditing: Investigating the impact of publicly naming biased performance results of commercial AI products. In *Proceedings of the AAAI/ACM Conference on AI, Ethics, and Society* (AIES). DOI: 10.1145/3306618.3314244

Scharre, P. (2018). *Army of none: Autonomous weapons and the future of war*. W. W. Norton & Company.

Shen, H. (2018). Building a digital Silk Road? Situating the internet in China's Belt and Road Initiative. *International Journal of Communication*, •••, 12.

Stanford DigiChina. (2017). *China's new generation artificial intelligence development plan* (Translation).

Triolo, P., Allison, K., Brown, C., & Broderick, K. (2020). *The digital Silk Road: Expanding China's digital footprint*. Eurasia Group.

White House. (2025). *Executive Order 14179 , Removing barriers to American leadership in artificial intelligence.*

# Chapter 9
# From Brain Maps to Behavioral Governance:
## State Investment in Neuroscience and Artificial Intelligence

**Sonia Cea Quintana**
https://orcid.org/0009-0003-9173-7410
*Universidad Rey Juan Carlos, Spain*

## ABSTRACT

*This chapter explores how state investment in neuroscience and AI is creating a new governance model to change citizen behaviour. The study examines the convergence of nudges and AI, observing that AI has led to the development of personalised nudges, which, while demonstrating efficacy, also give rise to concerns. A bibliometric study of 107 publications between 2011 and 2024 was conducted in order to identify key authors, journals, research areas, challenges and trends. The study's findings reveal mounting ethical concerns and underscore the necessity for regulatory frameworks. The European Union is a significant contributor to funding and AI regulation. The domain of health is the most developed, and children present the most ethical and regulatory challenges. We adopt a proactive stance, recognising the potential of AI-driven nudges to improve decision-making and public policy. Furthermore, emphasis is placed on the necessity of embedding ethical principles in global regulations.*

## INTRODUCTION

On July 17, 1990, U.S. President, George H. W. Bush, officially proclaimed the beginning of the "decade of the brain" (Bush, 1990). This initiative involved

DOI: 10.4018/979-8-3373-4480-5.ch009

an increase in funding and interdisciplinary collaboration in the quest to define the basis of human cognition. Decades later, Obama announced the *BRAIN initiative* (2013) launching an ambitious investment Project aimed at promoting brain mapping and investigating the basis of human behaviour. Similar initiatives took place in the European Union, Japan or China (Insel et al., 2013; Markram, 2012; Okano et al., 2015; Poo et al., 2016).

Linked to these developments, the 2010s mark the rise of artificial intelligence (Krizhevsky et al., 2012). In a pioneering manner, in 2017 China launches the *New Generation Artificial Intelligence Development Plan*, with the goal of leading the field of innovation by 2030 (State Council of the People's Republic of China, 2017). The United States responds with an executive in 2025, with which it will seek to dispute this leadership. Meanwhile, on the European side, efforts will be focused on regulating, funding and driving the use of these technologies to foster behavioural change in in individuals in key areas (European Commission, 2014, 2021)

In this way, these investments in neuroscience and artificial intelligence have not only served countries to increase knowledge about the brain cognition of individuals or to ensure their technological leadership, but also to generate effective tools for citizen behaviour change.

For the development of these tools, the so-called behavioural economist and the "nudge theory", that allows the generation of cognitive interventions that guide the citizen to the desired behaviour without coercion (Thaler & Sunstein, 2009), have been fundamental for the development of these tools. Recently, the integration of AI in the development of these tools has increased their effectiveness by generating personalized, predictive and tailored interventions in real time. The possibilities offered by these tools to improve the quality of our democracies are such that it is even estimated that they can generate a change in the democratic systems themselves (Cea Quintana, 2025).

Their effectiveness has been demonstrated in the pandemic (Cuello, 2021), and even has the supranational support of the UN, pointing out these tools as key to achieving the SDGs (UNIN, 2021), or the OECD generating observatories to promote their expansion in the countries.[1]

As far as scientific literature is concerned, we find very meager results, with significant research gaps in both the promises and practical challenges and ethical dilemmas in their application to governance (Hassabis et al., 2017; Fothergill et al., 2019; Robertson et al., 2016). Therefore, despite the fact that we find serious funding increases the actual impact of these techniques on policy is still unknow.

With the aim of providing knowledge on these existing gaps detected between the discoveries in nudge and AI and their application in behavioural governance, as well as assessing their ethical opportunities and challenges, this paper arises. To do so, five research questions (RQs) are proposed: RQ1- Who are the main authors leading the research? RQ2- Which are the main journals that are collecting the knowledge? RQ3- What are the main categories in which this is being collected? RQ4- How is the research progressing? RQ5- Which are the challenges that the field of study is facing?

The study's originality lies in its multidisciplinary approach, which examines the current state of the intersection of nudges and artificial intelligence. It also considers their possible applications and consequences in democratic systems. Based on the aims, the research objectives of this study are as follows:

- To build knowledge on the intersection between nudging and artificial intelligence, providing an up-to-date snapshot of the current state of research.
- Explore new opportunities to identify future challenges in which these applications could improve the effectiveness of administrative policies
- Alerting researchers and policymakers to the necessary ethical considerations for applying these advances, as well as the challenges that lie ahead in this field.

To achieve these objectives, we adopt an approach known as bibliometric analysis (Linnenluecke et al., 2019). This analysis was developed using *VOSViewer* on 107 scientific publications in *Web of Science* (WoS) between 15/09/2011 and 02/07/2024. To answer the research questions and achieve the objectives, we apply author co-citation, bibliographic linking, and keyword co-occurrence techniques (Ding & Yang, 2020; Oyewola & Dada, 2022; McAllister et al., 2022, cited by Lafont et al., 2023).

Following this introduction, we present a theoretical framework explaining the basic concepts necessary for understanding this new form of governance. The main results are then presented and analysed. The article concludes with a discussion section where we address the technical applications and ethical challenges, and propose an agenda for future research. Finally, we summarise the conclusions of the article.

## THEORETICAL FRAMEWORK

### Behavioural governance in the 21st century: from nudge to hypernudge

Behavioural governance involves applying knowledge and principles of behavioural economics to create policies or interventions than influence citizens' behaviour (Sunstein & Thaler, 2003; Gofen et al., 2021). This concept is closely linked to "soft paternalism" or "libertarian paternalism" (Sunstein & Thaler, 2003), a novel approach to governance centred on applying these techniques to create decision-making environments that encourage desired behaviours while upholding citizens' autonomy and freedom of choice.

The implementation of these strategies has given rise to the establishment of "behavioural units" worldwide. These interdisciplinary support tools to encourage behavioural change and improve the effectiveness of public policies (Barak-Corren & Kariv-Teitelbaum, 2021). The OECD's Observatory of Public Service Innovation[2] highlights the implementation and collaboration of these units in different types of administrations across the globe, with a particular focus on continental Europe and the Anglo-Saxon world (Cea Quintana, 2025). The most recognised behavioural intervention for generating these changes is nudge theory. This refers to interventions designed to predictably influence people's behaviour without restricting their freedom of choice or significantly altering their economic incentives (Thaler & Sunstein, 2009). Classifications can be made depending on whether they influence conscious deliberation (Hansen & Jespersen, 2013), respect individual autonomy (Baldwin, 2014), or promote behavioural changes in pursuit of personal or collective well-being (Loewenstein & Chater, 2017; Schmidt & Stenger, 2024).

Several authors have recently developed new concepts to describe the impact of new technologies on development, including digital nudging (Sadeghian & Otarkhani, 2023), big nudging (Bartmann, 2022), and algorithmic nudges (Schmauder et al., 2023). We highlight "hypernudging" due to its academic relevance (see table 2). This term refers to an advanced form of nudging that uses big data and artificial intelligence (AI) algorithms to create highly personalized feedback interventions that can be reconfigured in real time and predict an individual's behaviour (Yeung, 2017; Mills, 2021).

These techniques have become more accurate and effective, leading to an intense ethical debate about their use. Thus, several authors have highlighted the dangers of manipulation and the lack of privacy of the individual. This is why they are insistent on the need for transparent, informed systems, in which there is explicit consent from the user and conscious control of their data. This is so that these nudges do not serve to generate new inequalities. It is also so that they do not corrupt our democratic systems (Yeung, 2017; Floridi, 2015).

## Artificial intelligence and artificial neural networks: the potential for behavioural governance

Artificial intelligence (AI) is defined as the branch of computer science concerned with creating systems that can perform tasks requiring human intelligence, such as visual perception, speech recognition and problem solving (Ajuhi & Kumar, 2020; Marsden, 2019). In this context, Artificial Neural Networks (ANNs) play a key role in many of the capabilities and advances that define modern AI, these networks are computational models that attempt to simulate the abilities of the human brain using systems inspired by its interconnected structure of neurons (Meunier & Paugam-Moisy, 2008). Here are some of the most relevant ones for behavioural governance:

- Convolutional Neural Networks (CNNs): are especially useful for image recognition in security and surveillance systems and for viewing images in public health (Putra & Setiawan, 2023)
- Recurrent Neural Networks (RNNs): are useful for activities that demand sequence prediction, such as predicting traffic or energy consumption (Paperno, 2022)
- Transformers: useful for process automation and intelligent response systems (Luo et al., 2023)
- Autoencoders: effective in tasks related to anomaly detection, such as security and health (Yu et al., 2018)
- Generative Adversarial Networks (GANs): best known for their ability to generate realistic-looking images, videos, and texts (Goodfellow et al., 2020; Gui et al., 2021)
- Deep Neural Networks (DNNs): are deep knowledge bases that are especially useful in tasks that require pattern recognition, fast classification and decision making, such as dynamic traffic management (LeCun et al., 2015)

In this way, the integration of artificial intelligence in the generation of developments focused on monitoring and modulating behaviour will allow the creation of policies. These policies will generate ad hoc environments for each individual. These environments Will be designed to help the individual make the best possible decision, and they will be able to adapt to the individual's behaviour in real time and predict future behaviour. This will enable policy to evolve into a personalised, citizen-centre model with measurable, iterative results and automated decision-making to encourage the desired behaviour (Cea Quintana, 2025).

## The legislation and ethics of behavioural governance and applied AI

Despite concerns within the academic community regarding the dangers of negligent AI use (Crawford, 2021; Pasquale, 2020; Benjamin, 2022), no national AI legislation has yet been enacted. In this regard, the European Union's pioneering efforts stand out, as demonstrated by the approval of the Artificial Intelligence Act (European Parliament and Council of the European Union, 2024). This regulatory framework classifies AI developments according to the risk they pose, imposing proportional transparency, human supervision (particularly in political areas) and data privacy requirements. Beyond this regulation, various documents in the form of recommendations have been published by international organisations, such as the OECD's AI Principles (2019) and UNESCO's Recommendation on the Ethics of AI (2019), which focus on protecting human rights.

In terms of behavioural governance and the creation of behavioural interventions, reference manuals exist, such as those by UNICEF[3], which are oriented towards child protection; or the one by the OECD[4], both of which are focused on the importance of transparency, informed consent, civil society participation, and in-depth ethical reflection phase by phase. In terms of artificial intelligence, the world's leading behavioural units do not have significant ethical records (Cea Quintana,2025).

Within the academic community there is extensive research on the ethical considerations to be taken into account by different behavioural interventions (Sunstein, 2014; Johnstone, 2016; Hukkinen, 2016). All authors are committed to the following:

- Making information and transparency of the intervention performed clear
- Ensuring that informed consent is given and that it can be revoked at any time
- Respecting the autonomy and free choice of the individual
- Implementing communicative actions to raise public awareness of these techniques
- Respecting privacy and data protection
- Promoting justice and equity by not generating interventions that may give rise new inequalities
- Updating and adapting developers to market developments in order to be able to regulate accordingly

Similarly, there is extensive monograph production on considerations for development in the digital environment (Meske & Amojo, 2020; Borenstein & Arkin, 2016; Veretilnykova & Dogruel, 2021), which focuses on ensuring transparency and autonomy for individuals. This involves avoiding biased designs that render individuals unaware of or unable to prevent intervention, as well as preventing data extraction without consent.

# METHODOLOGY

## Bibliometric Analysis

### Sampling and data description

This study uses the academic database Web of Science (WoS). This internationally renowned database is one of the most widely used for obtaining and developing bibliometric sources and studies (Yuan and Sun, 2020). In terms of data extraction, the final queries were conducted on 2 July 2024. During this session, data were extracted and downloaded from the database[5] using a query time horizon in which Boolean operators were employed. In this way, we compile the set of academic contributions made to date on nudge and artificial intelligence.

The following search was therefore performed using the Boolean operator "AND". The query performed in the WoS database is as follows: "TS = (Nudge) AND TI = (Artificial Intelligence)". This search in the WoS main collection yielded 107 results. As the subject is an emerging topic, an expansive search was carried out in terms of the types of registered documents analysed, including articles, review articles, early access papers and meeting abstracts. The time period for the study was limited to publications between 15 September 2009 and 2 February 2024, as the first valid publication on this topic, titled "Modelling radiation-induced phase changes in binary FeCu and ternary FeCuNi alloys using an artificial intelligence-based atomistic kinetic Monte Carlo approach" was found in 2009 (Castin et al., 2009).

According to Gorraiz and Schloegl (2008), the sample size in bibliometric analyses is determined by the number of valid contributions identified in the databases used. Due to the low number of results found and the premature nature of the field of study, it was decided that all results should be analysed.

Figure 1 shows the main contributions made in the scientific literature in the selected years. It should be noted that the year with the most publications is 2022, with 29.91% corresponding to 32 research papers, followed by 2023 with 26 academic contributions identified and corresponding to 24.30%. Then, in third place, would be 2021 with 16 references (15%), in fourth place 2020: 9 references (8.4%); fifth place, 2024: 9 references (8.4%); sixth place, 2018: 4 references (3.74%); seventh place, 2019: 4 references (3.74%); eighth place, 2017: 3 references (2.8%); ninth place, 2009: 2 references (1.87%) and finally, tenth place, 2011:1 reference (0.93%).

*Figure 1. Publication years. Articles from September 2009 to July 2024*

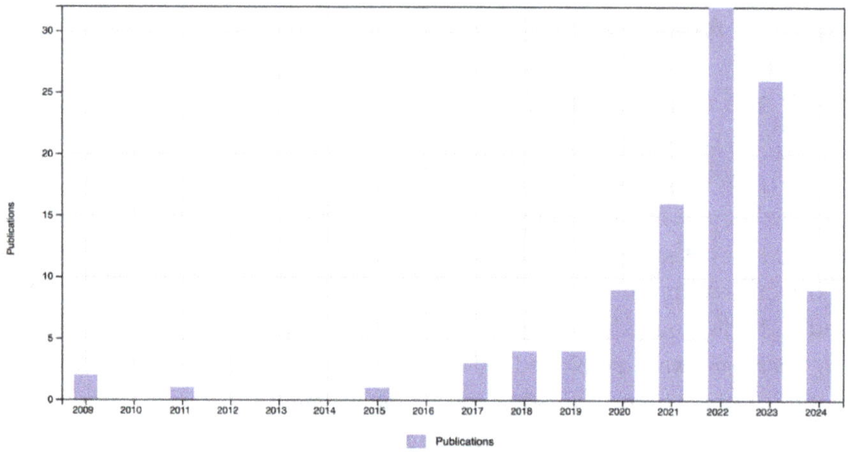


*Note. Source: WoS, accessed July 2, 2024.*

Figure 1 shows that the years 2022 and 2023 are the years that have contributed the most to the study of nudges applied to artificial intelligence, with 29.91% and 24.30% respectively. As previously mentioned, the study began in 2009 with the registration of the first related article on that date. Notably, important advances in the study of human behaviour and the development of significant artificial intelligence techniques have converged during this period, promoting its development and practical application in behavioural governance. Projects such as the Human Connectome Project (2010) have been instrumental in deepening our understanding of the basis of human behaviour (Van Essen et al., 2013). Additionally, the success of artificial intelligence techniques such as deep neural networks and deep learning (Schmidhuber, 2014; LeCun et al., 2015) may have been pivotal in promoting the development of theses hypernudges. Strong funding initiatives such as the European Union's Horizon 2020 programme (2014-2020), which provided 80 million euros of funding, and its successor Horizon Europe (2021-2027), which aims to fund projects based on behavioural sciences to improve decision-making, have also been vital in fostering academic research (European Commission, 2014; 2021).

*Figure 2. Number of citations and publications over time from September 2009 to July 2024.*

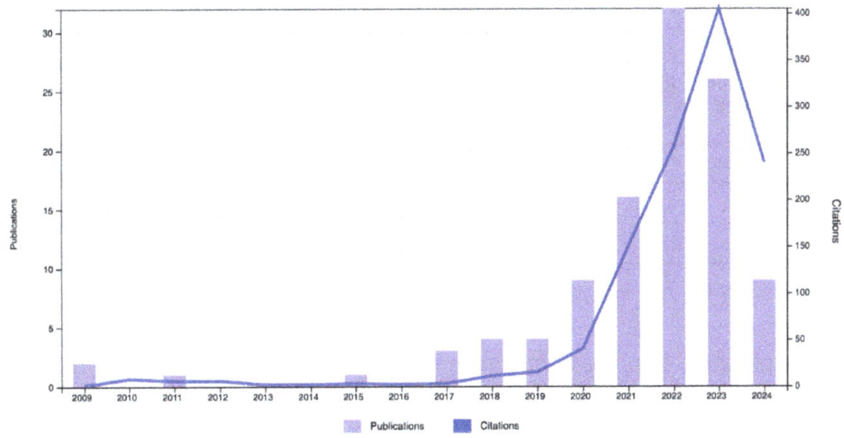


*Note. Source: WoS, accessed July 02, 2024.*

As can be seen in figure 2, we are faced with an emerging research topic that has seen a rise in academic production from our first year of study to the present day. The highest level of activity in terms of article publication was reached in 2022 with 32 publications, while the highest number of citations was reached in 2023 with 405.

*Table 1. WoS categories*

| *WoS Categories* | *Number of records* | *of total* |
|---|---|---|
| Computer Science Information Systems | 11 | 10, 28% |
| Engineering Electrical Electronic | 11 | 10,28% |
| Medical Informatics | 11 | 10,28% |
| Business | 10 | 9,35% |
| Health Care Science Services | 10 | 9,35% |
| Computer Science Artificial Intelligence | 9 | 8,41% |
| Computer Science Interdisciplinary Applications | 6 | 5,61% |
| Management | 6 | 5,61% |
| Computer Science Theory Methods | 5 | 4,67% |
| Nutrition Dietetics | 5 | 4,67% |
| Public Environmental Occupational Health | 5 | 4,67% |
| Computer Science Cybernetics | 4 | 3,74% |
| Environmental Sciences | 4 | 3,74% |

continued on following page

*Table 1. Continued*

| *WoS Categories* | *Number of records* | *of total* |
|---|---|---|
| Law | 4 | 3,74% |
| Telecommunications | 4 | 3,74% |
| Education Educational Research | 3 | 2,81% |
| Ergonomics | 3 | 2,81% |
| Ethics | 3 | 2,81% |
| Green Sustainable Science Technology | 2 | 2,81% |
| Information Science Library Science | 3 | 2,81% |

*Note*. Source: data from Web of Sciences. Elaboration: the authors

In terms of the number of categories (table 1) in which academic contributions related to nudges and artificial intelligence are published, we can find relevant findings on this initial stage of development. As we can see, we find a multidisciplinary and very varied field, in which the practical nature of the research stands out. Thus, in first place, we find "Computer Science Information", with 11 entries (10.28%), tied with "Engineering Electronical Electronic" and "Medical Informatics". Here we can see the importance of these advances in the medical field. Tied in fourth and fifth place respectively are "Business" (10 entries, 9.35%) and "Health Care Science Services" (10 entries, 9.35%), finding new practical application in various fields for these developments. Further down the table, we continue to find areas of development whose findings are likely to have an application in governance. Thus, we find "Management", eight place (6 publications,5.61%); "Nutrition Dietetics", tenth place (5 publications, 4.67%); "Public Environmental Occupational", eleventh place (5 publications, 4.67%); "Environmental Sciences", thirteenth place (4 publications, 3.74%); "Law", fourteenth place (4 publications, 3.74%); "Education Educational Research", sixteenth place (3 publications, 2.81%) and finally "Green Sustainable Science Technology" (3 publications, 2.81%). Therefore, we observe a concern for topics related to medicine, the health of population, the environment or the education of individuals, all areas and topics of political and governmental action.

## Analysis of results

### Analysis of joint appointments

We will follow the study by Hou et al. (2018) to identify the most frequently cited references among those in the database. Table 2 therefore highlights the ten most relevant articles based on their frequency of co-citation among their authors. While these articles are not directly related to the research questions of this study, they are important because they are frequently used by other authors to establish and develop their theoretical frameworks related to the general topic of this study in their scientific contributions. These ten outstanding contributions are specifically related to neuroscience as it applies to policy.

The first contribution is presented by Thaler and Sunstein (2009) with 26 citations and a link strength of 59.00. The article provides a critical review of Sunstein and Thaler's thesis on nudges and libertarian paternalism, pointing out the ethical dilemmas and potential for manipulation inherent in these interventions. In second place, we find Yeung (2017) with 17 citations and a link strength of 55.00. This work explores the concept of hyper nudging, arising from the marriage of nudges with big data, which makes them more dynamic, powerful and continuously updated. Third place goes to Weinmann et al. (2016), with 12 citations and link strength of 49.00. In it they address the concept of digital nudging as the use of digital choice environments to influence users' judgement and decision-making. In fourth place, we find Sunstein (2014), with 9 citations and a link strength of 34.00. In this work the author makes a robust defence of his theories, nudges and libertarian paternalism and their ability to improve people's decisions and well-being. In fifth place, we find Peer et al. (2020) with 6 citations and a link strength of 31.00. This study is eminently practical, where personalized nudges are made to users' decision-making to improve their ability to make passwords. The sixth place is Hausman and Welch (2010), with 8 citations and a link strength of 26.00. It reviews the debate on the implementation of nudges, considering libertarian paternalism as an influential idea in contemporary policy debates. Seventh place goes to Mills (2021). In it we find a deepening of the term hypernudge created by Yeung, with 5 links and a strength of 23.00. For Mills a hypernudge us a system of nudges that change over the time and in response to feedback. The eighth is for Kahneman (2011), 5 links and a strength of 23.00. In this book the Nobel laureate identifies two models of thinking that dominate human decisions: system 1, fast and intuitive, and system 2, slow and deliberative. This work is key in the behavioural sciences and also for decision architects in creating decision environments. Ninth is Matz, Kosinski, Nave and Stillwell (2017) with 5 citations and a link strength of 22.00. In this proceeding the author explores how to tailoring persuasive messages to the psychological characteristics of large groups of people can significantly influence their behaviour in a digital environment, thus pointing out the need for appropriate regulations. In tenth place we find Baldwin (2014) with 6 citations and a link strength of 20.00. In it, the author states that nudge has proven to be attractive to certain government, but its adoption without critical analysis can be problematic. He therefore calls for a rigorous ethical assessment for its elective implementation in public policy.

In general, the predominant view is a critical one of Sunstein and Thaler's theories on nudges and libertarian paternalism, which highlights the authors' concerns about their application to policy design. Similarly, we can observe an evolution from conventional nudges to hypernudges or smart nudges. These nudges, which are based on artificial intelligence, allow for greater personalization of individuals' behaviour and even the capacity to update based on individuals' development. This increases their effectiveness, but also raises fears of manipulation. For this reason, many authors emphasise the importance of precise regulation to protect individuals from misuse, particularly by governments.

*Table 2. Results of reference matching and author matching*

| **Reference co-citations** | | | | **Author´s co-citations** | | |
|---|---|---|---|---|---|---|
| **Title** | **Author(s)** | **Citations** | **Link strength** | **Author(s)** | **Citations** | **Link strength** |
| Nudge: Improving decisions about health, wealth, and happiness | Thaler & Sunstein (2009) | 26 | 59,00 | Sunstein, C.R. | 40 | 348,00 |
| 'Hypernudge': big data as a mode of regulation by design | Yeung (2017). | 17 | 55,00 | Mills, S | 17 | 202,00 |
| Digital Nudging | Weinmann et al. (2016) | 12 | 49,00 | European Commission | 10 | 148,00 |
| Why Nudge?: The Politics of Libertarian Paternalism | Sunstein (2014) | 9 | 34,00 | Kahneman, D. | 22 | 148,00 |
| Nudge me right: personalizing online security nudges to people's decision-making styles. | Peer et al. (2020) | 6 | 31,00 | Yeung, K | 20 | 147,00 |
| Debate: to nudge or not to nudge | Hausman & Welch (2010). | 8 | 26,00 | Thaler, R.H. | 17 | 130,00 |
| Finding the 'nudge' in hypernudge | Mills (2021) | 5 | 25,00 | Leonard, T.C. | 26 | 126,00 |
| Thinking, fast and slow. | Kahneman (2011) | 5 | 23,00 | Simon, H.A. | 12 | 126,00 |
| Psychological targeting as an effective approach to digital mass persuasion | Matz et al. (2017) | 5 | 22,00 | Weinmann, M. | 12 | 97,00 |
| From Regulation to Behaviour Change: Giving Nudge the Third Degree | Baldwin (2014) | 6 | 20,00 | Mele, C. | 12 | 82,00 |

*Note.* Source: VOSviewer. Elaboration: La autora

To continue with the co-citation analysis, figure 3 provides a visual map showing clusters related to the co-citation of references in the analysed database. This allows the different links between the variables that make up the clusters to be understood. Figure 3 includes a total of 16 references in the neural network. Different filters and criteria were applied to select these references in order to optimize the results. The minimum number of citations obtained for the 16 references in figure 3 was 5, resulting in a total of 6,135 cited references. Using this filter, 16 optimal references were obtained for inclusion in the neural network, all of which were finally selected. Based on these results, 89 links were obtained, representing 100% of the connections between the 16 identified items. Similarly, the total link strength is 213 points and the degree of representation is 100%.

According to authors such as Gorraiz and Schloegl (2008), visual representations of databases in bibliometric analyses are important for understanding the connection between the published content of each selected contribution. Figure 3 therefore identifies a total of four clusters. The largest of these is in red and located on the central left-hand side of the figure. This cluster mainly comprises references to Kahneman, 2021; Sunstein, 2014; Mittelstadt and Floridi, 2016; Russell, 2016; and Burr et al. (2018). It shows a progression towards new nudges promoted by big data and artificial intelligence. This cluster highlights the ethical concern that intervention by these new technologies could divert citizens' behaviour away from their own best interests.

The second cluster is blue and located in the upper central part of the image. It contains references to Yeung, 2017; Matz et al., 2017; Baldwin, 2014; and Mills, 2021; and develops the concept of hypernudge as initially presented by Yeung. This concept involves the manipulation of individuals due to the capacity for adaptation and feedback according to knowledge of their decision-making mechanisms.

The third cluster is yellow and centred in the lower part of the image. It contains references to Hausman and Welch, who focus on the debate surrounding libertarian paternalism. Finally, on the right side of the screen and in green, we find the cluster formed by Weinmann, et al., 2016; Caraban et al., 2019; Peer et al., 2020; and Acquisti et al., 2017. This cluster provides a more practical representation of digital nudging and gives examples of human-computer interaction (HCI), as well as demonstrating its success in improving individuals' security in digital environments.

*Figure 3. Co-citation analysis of references*

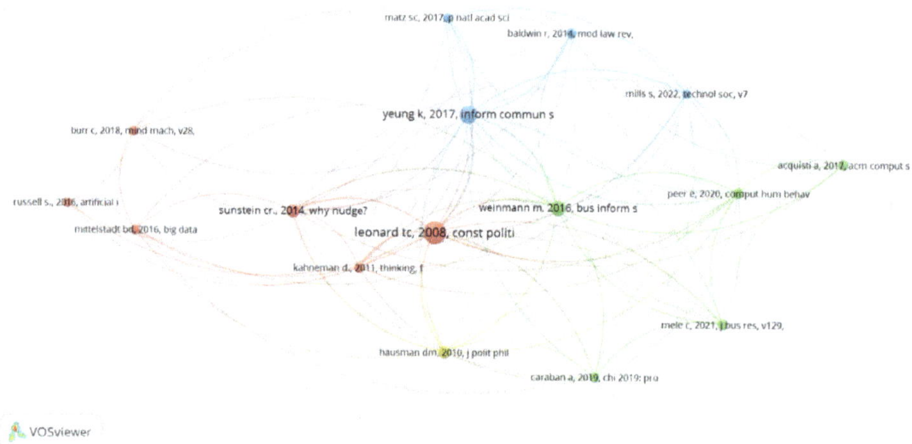


*Note. Source: Authors based on VOSViewer results.*

In addition, to complete the analysis of co-citation of references, the most relevant authors in terms of citations and link strength have also been identified. Link strength is the variable that determines the importance of the connections between these authors and other published research in this field. Therefore, these authors can be considered the most representative of this type of studies in the identified literature.

The following authors can be found in the table 2 in the right-hand column. In first place, we find Sunstein, C. R. with 40 citations and a link strength of 348.00. In second place, Mills, S. with 17 citations and a link strength of 202.00. In third place, the European Commission with 10 citations and a link strength of 148.00. In fourth place, we find Kahneman, D. with 22 citations and a linking strength of 148.00. In fifth place, Yeung, K. with 20 citations and a linking strength of 147.00. In sixth place, we find Thaler, R. H. with 17 citations and a linking strength of 130.00. In seventh place we find Leonard, T. C. with 26 citations and a linking strength of 126.00. In eighth place we find Simon, H. A. with 12 citations and a linking strength of 126.00. In ninth place Weinmann, M. with 12.00 citations and a linking strength of 97.00. Finally, Mele, C. with 12 citations and a linking strength of 82.00

In addition, the neural map of author citation density is calculated (figures 4 and 5). To achieve this, parameters are established to correctly identify the study in which references with at least 10 citations are recognized as a variable. Following this selection, 16 authors out of a total of 5,043 met this criterion in the used database. When creating their neural map, one of the selected authors was not connected to the others, resulting in the identification of 15 items. A total of 81 links were identified, with an average link strength of 848.00.

Based on these criteria, four clusters were identified in relation to the neural map of author density. The centres of the clusters identified in figures 3 and 4 consist of connections between authors and groups of authors who cite each other. The colour of the density in figure 4 indicates the number of citations obtained and the relevance. Thus, the most frequently sited authors appear in red within the clusters, while those in orange or yellow are cited less frequently.

Of the identified clusters, one converges at the top left (in green in figure 5) and is characterised by the importance of Leonard, T.C. in relation to Yeung, K.; Floridi, I.; Weinmann, M. and Acquisti, A.. This cluster provides a critical analysis of the implementation of nudges and offers an essential ethical perspective with which to evaluate their implementation and impact. Leonard's global critical framework for evaluating implementation is later joined by Yeugn's contributions to ethical and regulatory analysis in digital environments. Floridi's work is also notable, as his studies highlight the ethical issues surrounding digital manipulation and persuasion. Consequently, a critical cluster emerges, centred on concerns about the manipulation and coercion of individual autonomy, emphasising the importance of transparency, respect for individual autonomy and privacy, and adequate regulation to prevent misuse.

The second cluster is located in the bottom left of the image (in red figure 5) and is characterised by the importance (see Figure 4) of Kahneman, D. and Thaler, R. H.; Mele, C.; Tversky, A.; Huang, M. H. and Simon, H. A. Kahneman and Thaler are considered the founders of behavioural economics, while Herbert Simon's theory of individual rationality has been pivotal. The cluster also includes Mele and Huang, who are renowned for their work in applying nudges to new digital environments. This cluster therefore stands out for its theoretical eminence, as it contains the theories on which nudges have relied for their inception and evolution, as well as their digital application.

In the lower centre (yellow in figure 5) is the influence of Mills, S., which is slightly more important than that of the European Commission (see figure 4). The Commission's importance lies in the European Union's leadership with regard to AI regulation, as demonstrated by documents such as the European Strategy on AI[6] and the proposals for the AI Law[7]. Similarly, it has funded projects such as Horizon 2020 (2014-2020) [8] and Horizon Europe (2021-2027)[9]. These projects have received significant funding and have focused on applying nudges to policy design in various fields, as well as exploring their potential to enhance the social and economic well-being of European communities. This cluster also includes S. Mills, a behavioural economist whose work is proving instrumental in adapting nudges for use in technological environments. Therefore, this cluster encompasses the leadership of the European Union and its projects that promote the integration of artificial intelligence and behavioural science to enhance public decision making.

Finally, on the right-hand side of the image (blue in figure 5) we find the fourth cluster, characterized by the influence of Sunstein, C. R. (see figure 4). Together with Taler, he is the originator of nudge theory. In this cluster, alongside Sunstein, is Capraro, V., a behavioural economist who has focused his research on interventions that encourage pro-social and cooperative behaviour for the benefit of society as a whole. Consequently, this cluster encompasses a more pragmatic approach to nudges and their associated research aimed at generating social welfare.

*Figure 4. Density map of the authors' cocitation analysis*

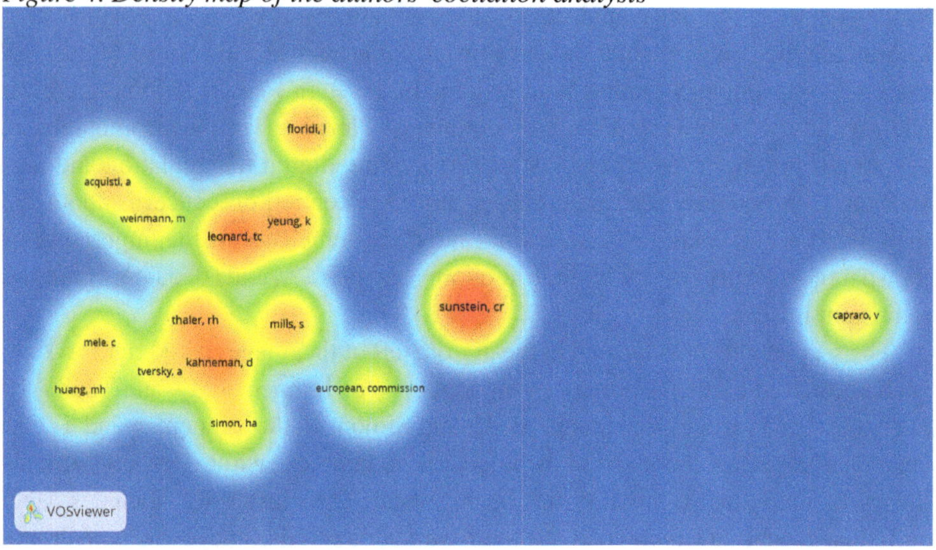


*Note. Source: Authors based on VOSViewer results.*

*Figure 5. Network visualization of the authors' cocitation analysis*

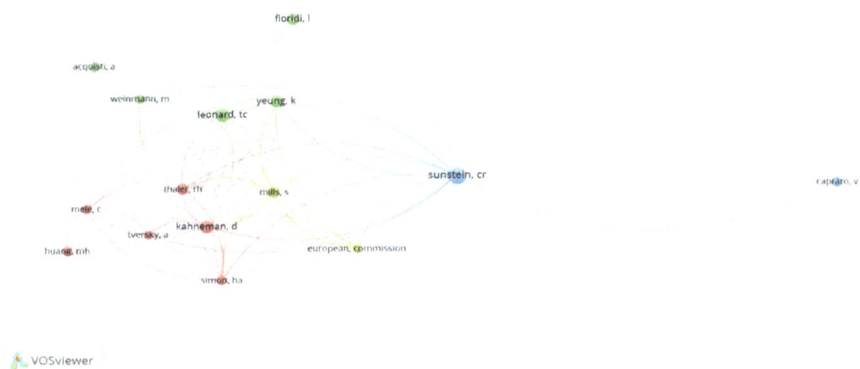


*Note. Source: Authors based on VOSViewer results.*

## Bibliographic coupling

To understand which journals have published the most relevant papers on nudges and artificial intelligence, this bibliometric analysis calculates the bibliographic source linkage. This type of analysis aims to identify the most relevant papers in terms of citations and link strength. The following filters are used to correctly calculate this analysis. The minimum number of papers per journal is set at 2, and the minimum number of citations per source at 0. Out of a total of 98 journals in the database, 9 meet these criteria. Nine journals are Selected for analysis in table 3.

Seen of these journals 7 have links to each other, as shown in figures 6 and 7, which depict a total of seven journals directly related to the objectives of the study. Additionally, two clusters are identified that obtain a total of 12 links between them, with a total link strength of 42.00 points. Table 3 below presents the metrics and indicators obtained for each of the journals.

The following stand out among the results obtained. In terms of link strength, three journals stand above the rest: *The Journal of Business Research* (66 citations, link strength 25.00), *AI & Society* (15 citations, link strength 19.00) and *Sustainability* (10 citations, link strength 17.00). These three journals are the most relevant to nudges and artificial intelligence. Of the remaining results, the fourth and fifth positions are highlighted respectively: *Public Health Nutrition* (22 citations, link strength 10.00) and the *Journal of Medical Internet Research* (17 citations, 7.00

link strength). The other journals identified and presented in table 3 achieved more moderated results in terms of impact compared to the other results cited.

*Table 3. Bibliographic coupling of sources*

| *Source* | *Documents* | *Quotations* | *Link strength* |
|---|---|---|---|
| *Journal of Business Research* | 2 | 66 | 25.00 |
| *AI & Society* | 2 | 15 | 19.00 |
| *Sustainability* | 2 | 10 | 17.00 |
| *Public Health Nutrition* | 2 | 22 | 10.00 |
| *Journal of Medical Internet Research* | 2 | 17 | 7.00 |
| *Phycology & Marketing* | 2 | 3 | 4,00 |
| *JMIR Formative Research* | 2 | 3 | 2,00 |
| *Frontiers in Digital Health* | 2 | 3 | 0,00 |
| *Nuclears instrument & Methods in Pshysic Research Section B-Beam* | 2 | 32 | 0,00 |

*Note*. Source: Authors based on VOSViewer results.

In addition, to understand scientific output in this field of research in recent years, this paper presents an analysis of bibliographic links by average year of publication. As can be seen in figures 6 and 7, two clusters have been identified, showing the positions of the journal and the link between them. In relation to the analysed time horizon, blue represents 2021.5, the first relevant year in the neural map. The colour palette then changes successively until it reaches yellow. In this projection, dark blue represents 2022, light blue represents the second half of 2022, green represents the first half of 2023 and yellow represents the second half of 2023. This demonstrates the novelty of this research and its related concepts.

This cluster acts as the central core of the map, connecting various areas of study. The strongest connections are with journals such as *JMIR Formative Research, Sustainability* and *Journal of Medical Internet Research.* This centrality suggests that the *Journal of Business Research* plays a crucial role in linking interdisciplinary research ranging from digital health to ethics and sustainability. Its prominent position indicates that this journal is frequently cited in studies exploring how the principles of economic theories, such as behavioural economics, con be integrated with technological developments and social concerns.

The second cluster, which is of importance, is characterized by the relevance of the journal *AI & Society*. This cluster is strongly linked to ethical and social issues related to artificial intelligence. The connections that *AI & Society* has with journals such as *Sustainability* and *JMRI Formative Research* reflect a growing focus on how AI can be used responsibly to promote sustainability and social welfare goals. The position of *AI & Society* highlights its relevance in discussions about the social and ethical implications of emerging technology.

Taken together, these clusters demonstrate the evolution of scientific literature towards more integrated and holistic approaches to address contemporary technological and societal challenges. Finally, as mentioned above, the map also illustrates the temporal evolution of research, with colours closer to yellow representing more recent work (figure 7). In this sense, the topics currently covered by *AI & Society* and the Journal of *Medical Internet Research* stand out, suggesting consideration of the application of this research in society and interest in its development in medical and health fields.

*Figure 6. Bibliographic matching of sources by average year of publication*

*Note. Source: Authors based on VOSViewer results.*

*Figure 7. Bibliographic matching of sources by average year of publication*

*Note. Source: Authors based on VOSViewer results.*

## Co-occurrence of author keywords

Continuing with the development of the bibliometric analysis, we present the results related to the calculation and evolution of the co-occurrence analysis of the authors' keywords. With respect to searches in the database related to nudge and artificial intelligence, tis analysis considers all the keywords used by authors in their academic contributions.

The authors' keyword co-occurrence analysis is developed with the aim of identifying key concepts, techniques and current lines of research that are shaping the development of knowledge. We therefore link these representations to the objectives and research questions proposed in this study.

*Table 4. Co-occurrence of author keywords*

| Key words | Occurrences | Total bond strength |
|---|---|---|
| Artificial Intelligence | 55 | 103,00 |
| Ethics | 12 | 42.00 |
| Nudge | 18 | 35.00 |
| Bid data | 7 | 26.00 |
| Information | 5 | 21.00 |
| Behaviour | 7 | 20.00 |
| Machine Learning | 9 | 20.00 |

continued on following page

*Table 4. Continued*

| Key words | Occurrences | Total bond strength |
|---|---|---|
| Autonomy | 7 | 19.00 |
| Privacy | 7 | 19.00 |
| Challenges | 4 | 17.00 |
| Framework | 5 | 17.00 |
| Decision Making | 4 | 15.00 |
| Digital Health | 6 | 15.00 |
| Future | 6 | 15.00 |
| Choice Architecture | 6 | 15.00 |
| Digital Nudging | 5 | 13.00 |
| Health | 4 | 13.00 |
| Children | 4 | 12.00 |
| Behaviours Economics | 5 | 11.00 |
| Internet | 5 | 10.00 |
| Technology | 6 | 10.00 |
| Diet | 4 | 7.00 |
| Trust | 4 | 7.00 |
| Behaviour Change | 4 | 5.00 |

*Note*. Source: Authors based on VOSViewer results.

Table 4 shows the keywords that were selected as the most relevant in relation to the objectives of this research. Based on these considerations, and to correctly visualise the relationship between the keywords and identify the detailed concepts, a neural network will be presented showing the main connections between the most relevant keywords. A minimum of four co-occurrences per keyword was decided upon. Thus, of the 730 words considered, 24 met the research requirement; these were selected and are listed in table 4. The remaining words were eliminated due to replications of concepts or terms with little relationship to the other words in the subsequent graphical representation of dependencies ("simulation"). Following these investigations, a neural map of connection was created, identifying 47 links with a total link strength of 117 points. An average of five clusters, each composed of 24 variables on the form of keywords, is presented. First, we Will analyse the information provided by the clusters, and then provide a temporal interpretation.

*Figure 8. Co-occurrence of author keywords by average year of publication. Cluster-relations*

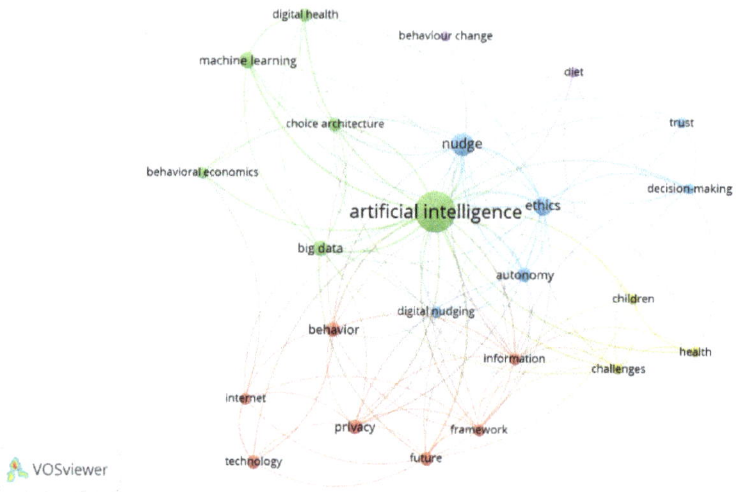


*Note. Source: Authors based on VOSViewer results.*

We observe that the term "artificial intelligence" (Figure 8) is the most prominent central node, indicating its relevance and importance in the set of analysed studies. It acts as an axis around which other key concepts in the research revolve and is referenced in different clusters. The green cluster appears to focus on various applications of artificial intelligence and the enabling technologies. The blue cluster represents the critical aspect of this research. The red cluster represents the doubts and concerns surrounding its application. The yellow cluster highlights the challenges ahead, particularly in relation to health and children. Finally, the purple cluster offers concrete applications where behavioural change can be effective, particularly with regard to diets. We will now analyse this neural map in more detail, studying the relationships between the most important keywords for our area of study.

*Figure 9. Artificial intelligence in author's keyword co-occurrence*

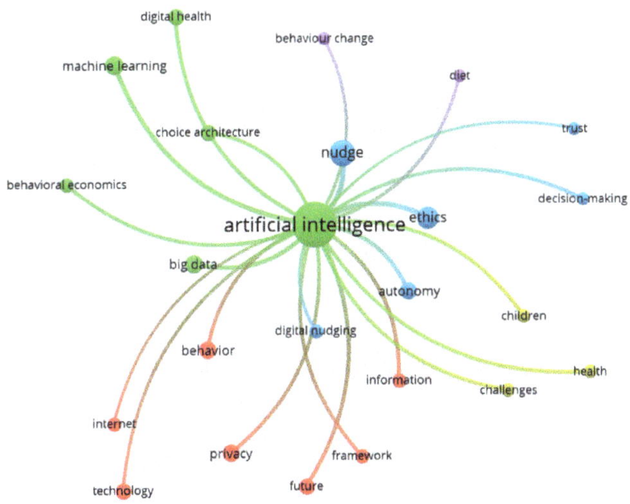


*Note. Source: Authors based on VOSViewer results*

"Artificial intelligence" (Figure 9) is the most prominent central node, indicating its predominant role and its interconnection with other key concepts in the literature analysed. Its relationships with the green cluster indicate both the theoretical part thar is guiding the creation of these AI applications ("behavioural economics" and "choice architecture"), its practical part for development ("big data" and "machine learning") and its main applications "digital health". Its relationship with the blue cluster addresses the critical part of this research, with its necessary concern for ethical principles and ethics. The connections with the yellow cluster focus on the specific challenges facing the implementation of artificial intelligence in the field of health, especially its impact on vulnerable populations between these terms suggest a multidisciplinary integration of nudge and artificial intelligence research.

*Figure 10. Ethics highlighted in author's keyword co-occurrence:*

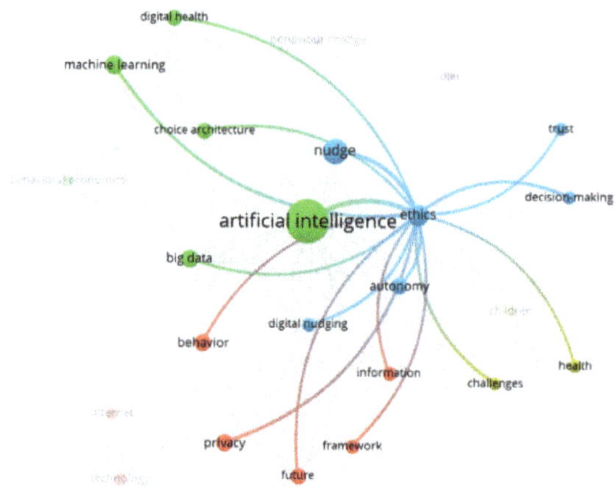


*Source: Authors based on VOSViewer results*

The keyword "ethics" is the second most important in this neural map. This shows its direct relationship with AI, digital nudging and the techniques that make these developments possible, such as machine learning and big data. This demonstrates the scientific community's interest in these developments being conducted from an ethical standpoint. We can also see how it links with the keyword "trust", which is necessary to achieve confidence in this research. Through these relationships, we once again visualise how preserving the autonomy of the individual in decision-making processes must be a key factor. This establishes the need for regulatory frameworks that ensure transparency and the privacy of individuals with regard to these practices. The relationship with keywords such as "future" and "challenges" shows that research ethics is an important issue to be addressed for the future development of this field of study.

*Figure 11. Nudge highlighted in author's keyword co-occurrence*

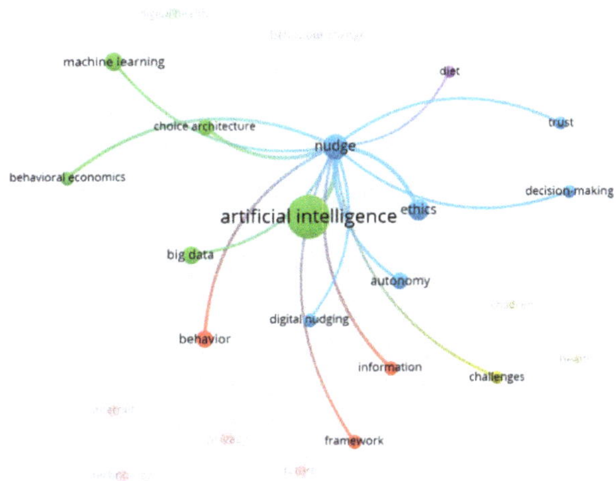


*Note. Source: Authors based on VOSViewer results*

The term "nudge" (figure 11) is the third most significant. It features in a blue cluster alongside other keywords, such as "ethics", "autonomy", "trust", "digital nudging" and "decision making". These reflects concerns that complementing these techniques in individuals' decision-making processes may jeopardise their autonomy. The relationship between "nudge" and "ethics" and "trust" highlights the importance of considering ethical principles to promote acceptance in these developments. The keyword "digital nudging" illustrates how the concept has evolved following the application of artificial intelligence techniques. Its relationship with the green cluster reveals the technical basis on which these new technological nudges are developed, with machine learning and big data playing a leading role. Meanwhile, its relationship with the red cluster indicates the importance of informed frameworks. Its relationship with "challenges" shows that the conceptualisation and development of the term at technical and regulatory levels will be challenging in the future. Finally, the relationship with the purple cluster and the keyword "diet" provides a practical example of how these techniques can be used to bring about behavioural change.

*Figure 12. Challenges highlighted in author's keyword co-occurrence*

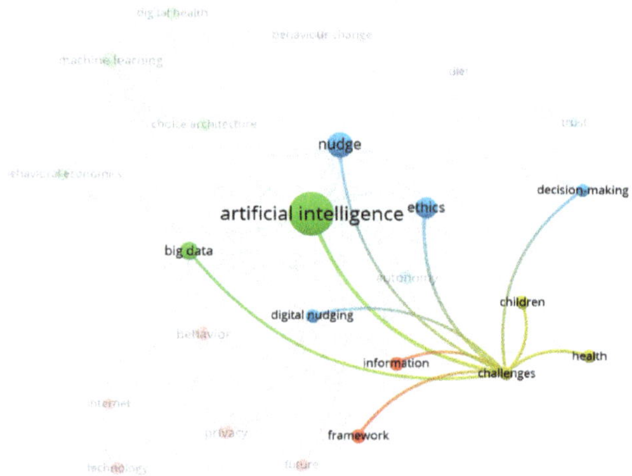


*Note. Source: Authors based on VOSViewer results*

The appearance of the keyword "challenges" (Figure 11) enables us to identify the specific challenges in this field of study. The word "ethics", "frameworks" and "information" highlight the need to generate informed regulatory structures to ensure that these practices are developed with transparency in mind. The link to "nudge" and "digital nudging" continues to emphasise the need for further research into these concepts. Finally, the relationship with "health" encourages the application of these techniques to generate healthier behavioural changes. The relationship with "children" marks a sensitive area that requires attention in order to protect and improve the well-being of children through these practices.

*Figure 13. Mapa neuronal with overlay, author's keywords co-occurrence*

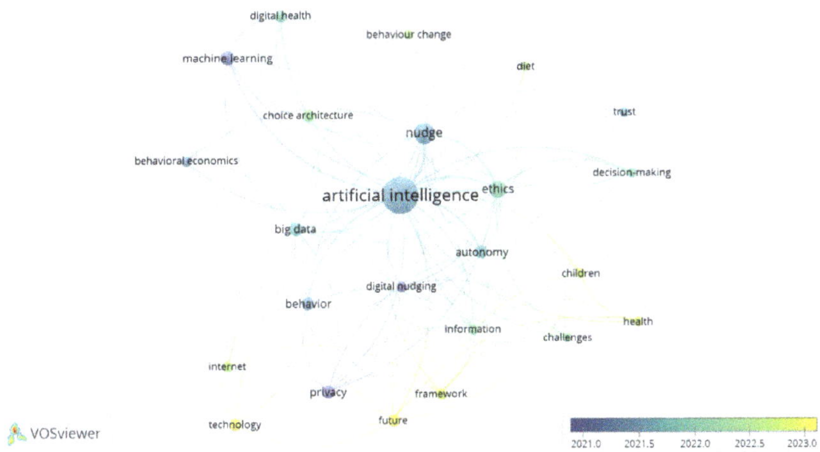


*Note. Source: Authors based on VOSViewer results*

To understand how the field of study has evolved and which topics are currently being researched, we will now examine a new neural map, this time marked by the main years of research (figure 13). In its early stage (dark blue to greenish blue, from 2021 to early 2022), the terms "privacy" and "technology" are represented. This suggest that the research initially focused on privacy concerns and the technological aspects of AI development. Also, during this period, terms such as "machine learning" and "big data" appear for the first time. This highlights the focus on the underlying technologies that enables these techniques to be realized. During the mid-development stage (colours ranging from teal to green, from mid-2021 to mid-2022), the terms "nudge" and "behavioural" appear, indicating that research began to integrate the concepts of behavioural nudging and economics during this period. Coupled with this are terms such as "digital health" and "choice architecture", highlighting the interest in how artificial intelligence an influence health and decision-making. In the most recent stage (late 2022 to 2023, from green to yellow), the terms "ethics" and "trust" stand out. This suggests a growing concern about ethical issues and the need to establish trust in these technologies. Terms such as "health" and "children" appear in lighter colours, indicating a growing interest in the potential impact of AI and nudges on children's health and decision-making. Finally, "challenge" and "future" are also highlighted in yellow, indicating that current research is exploring the future challenges of artificial intelligence and its evolution.

Therefore, we have progressed from the initial technical development of AI and its potential application, to a stage of theoretical and conceptual development, where its potential applications in the field of healthcare have already been identified. We now find ourselves at a critical juncture, where the establishment of ethical regulatory principles is paramount to fostering confidence in these technologies. Alongside these regulatory frameworks, ensuring the health and well-being of children is the future challenge.

## DISCUSSION AND AGENDA FOR FUTURE RESEARCH

To our knowledge, this study is the first to conduct a systematic review of the literature on the intersection of nudges and artificial intelligence, and how this can be applied to governance. Conducting this systematic literature review (SLR) was crucial for several reasons. Firstly, as mentioned in the introduction, there is a growing trend of international investment in the development of artificial intelligence and interventions aimed at changing population behaviour (in countries such as USA, China and EU). Some authors have expressed a need to understand the potential of these techniques, the challenges involved, and the dangers of their use by governments without safeguarding citizens' rights, as well as the need for their regulatory and ethical development (Hassabis et al., 2017; Fothergill et al., 2019; Yu et al., 2018; Thaler & Sunstein, 2009; Yeung, 2017). Building on these concerns, we set a number of objectives for this study. Firstly, to build knowledge about the intersection between nudging and AI by providing an up-to-date overview of the current state of research. To demonstrate evidence of the application of these disciplines in public policymaking aimed at influencing citizens' behaviour. Explore new opportunities to identify future challenges where these applications could improve the effectiveness of administrative policies. Fourth, to alert researchers and policy makers to the ethical considerations needed to implement these developments, as well as the challenges to be faced in this field. We believe that through this SLR, we have addressed these questions to some extent, but there are important points that deserve further consideration.

Firstly, as can be seen in figures 1 and2, this is a very new field of research with incipient development. It is marked by the potential for the manipulation and coercion of individuals if is not properly regulated. We believe that this is an important issue that should motivate the scientific community to promote research whose applications are advancing faster than legislation can keep up with. This research is not only in the hands of the government but also in the hands of the whole world due to its open nature. In this sense, the European Union's growing influence in the development of the field is striking (table 2 and figures 4 and 5). While its various programmes fund many of the projects applying nudge theory to the population, the EU is the first institution at both national and supranational levels to regulate its use through the AI Law. We believe this will guide knowledge in the coming years by promoting its positive societal impact while simultaneously establishing a robust regulatory framework to prevent fraudulent use.

Secondly, we would like to emphasise the significance of the term "challenges" (figure 12) in our study. This is undoubtedly due to the impact of applying AI to the theories of Sunstein and Thaler (Thaler &Sunstein, 2008). Within this same conceptual map, we identified keywords relating to "digital nudging", as highlights by carious authors throughout this study. The personalisation and feedback possibilities offered by these nudges exponentially increase their effectiveness (Yeung, 2017; Mills, 2021). However, we also believe that they can solve problems that have hindered the progress of traditional nudges. For example, they can impact changes in knowledge thar benefit society as a whole, rather than just the individual. These are known as prosocial nudges (Loewenstein & Chater, 2017). These tools are vital for solving deeply embedded collective behaviour problems, such as those that can lead to environmental pollution or the misuse of resources. These nudges' capacity for improvement is evident today, which is why they can help us solve problems such as pollution and sustainability, which already pose a threat to the survival of our societies. Therefore, as our study showed, while we must acknowledge the ethical issues, we should not allow them to prevent us from realising the potential of these tools for the well-being of all.

Finally, in line with the previous paragraph, while the majority of the study indicates that health is the field to which most applications are oriented (table3 and figure 9), we would like to highlight the potential of these tools to generate positive behavioural changes in terms of environmental care and sustainability. In this regard, the EU projects already funding initiatives in these areas are particularly noteworthy. Examples include the NUDGE Project, which is funded by the EI to improve energy awareness and efficiency among European citizens (European Comision, 2023); Audit To Measure, which facilitates the adoption of measures to reduce companies' energy consumption (Institute for European Energy and Climate Policy,2020); and Neon, which provides integrated next-generation energy services for citizen energy communities (European Commission, 2021).

## Theoretical implications

We believe that these techniques can greatly benefit citizens if used in an ethical manner. They could even lead to a new type of people-centred governance and personalised, real-time policies that increase effectiveness and engagement with the system. We discuss the main benefits below.

Firstly, implementing these techniques can improve citizens' access to public services, helping to overcome various barriers and digital divides. Essential for this are language interpretation, speech recognition and recreation, and BCI (brain-computer interface) developments (see Recurrent Neural Networks, Paperno,2022; Convolutional Neural Network, Bertoni et al., 2019; Transformers, Luo et al., 2023).

Secondly, these techniques should be applied to improve the understanding and effectiveness of public actions. Examples of this include metacognitive learning systems that adapt the learning process to the cognitive characteristics of the individual (Hemachandran et al., 2022), tools that allow instantaneous measurement of citizens' responses (e.g. brain activity pattern recognition techniques, Padilla & García, 2018), and the prior validation of policies through the simulation of virtual societies (Zhang et al., 2015). These tools should lead to policies centres on the citizen, which adapt to their evolution and have an iterative nature to ensure their effectiveness.

Thirdly, as we previously mentioned when defining behavioural governance, it begins with the achievement of individual well-being to promote collective well-being (Thaler & Sunstein, 2008). The application of these techniques should enable us to influence the unreflective processes of individuals who engage in behaviour that they know to the detrimental, by offering elements of gratification to encourage change. To this end, passive monitoring and wearables would be essential tools (Köhler et al., 2024). In this way, we could combat social problems such as environmental issues, economic instability, and uncertainty surrounding new crises.

Finally, we believe that this new approach to policy should lead to healthier and safer societies. These techniques are initially excelling in the health sector by enabling the early identification of diseases (Improved Diagnostic Tools, Noor et al., 2020). Similarly, these predictive systems can help to detect situation thar threaten public safety. This should result in the creation of safer environments for citizens by swiftly mitigating risks.

## Practical implications

Despite the potential outlined above, creating these hypernudges poses significant challenges in preserving privacy, free will, and citizens' human rights. Our study has clearly pointed to ethics and the need for properly informed regulatory frameworks as one of the challenges in this field of study (figure 12). We therefore outline the practical implications that must be considered to ensure the ethical application and regulation of these technological advances, enhancing decision-making and public welfare while safeguarding individual human rights.

Firstly, as several authors have pointed out, we believe it is crucial to ensure the privacy and security of the biometric data currently being collected on individuals, as well as its proper use and management (Dargan & Kumar, 2020; Sun et al., 2018). Knowledge is now being produced openly. While this is helping to generate rapid growth and notable successes in artificial intelligence, there is a need to protect the privacy of the data and Implement controls to ensure it is used for ethical purposes.

Secondly, the importance of informed consent has already been stressed by several authors in relation to research, clinical practice, technological developments in health and the use of nudges (Río et al., 2018). We believe that this consent should be extended further. To this end, citizens must be notified of the different actions to which they are being subjected and informed of the purpose of these data and the motivation behind the behavioural change being pursued. They must also be made aware of their right to revoke consent at any time.

Thirdly, in order for citizens to be able to give effective informed consent, we believe that they must be educated about the potential benefits and dangers involved. We therefore consider it necessary to encourage public awareness and education in this regard. This should empower individuals to actively participate in debates and decisions related to the regulation and application of these technologies.

Fourthly, national and international organizations must make more progress on creating a set of rules for AI and applied neuroscience. This is so that the use of new technologies is directed towards ethical and responsible applications. This framework should prioritise the protection of neural data privacy, prevent discrimination and ensure the fair and transparent use of technology. They should also set clear limits on the manipulation of human behaviour to guarantee that any government intervention benefits the individual and society.

Finally, as this study has shown, incorporating artificial intelligence into nudges is increasing their effectiveness, but the consequences are unclear. The rapid evolution of hypernudges requires a mechanism for continuous monitoring and review. We therefore encourage researchers to play an active role in developing these studies and to contribute concrete proposals alongside their ethical concerns. Only in this way can we ensure that these advances, which are already in the hands of those in power, are used in an ethical and responsible manner to bring greater well-being to our cities, rather than providing new tools for the subjugation and control of citizens.

## Limitations and future lines of research

This study sheds light on emerging patterns of activity and the initial applications of this novel behavioural governance, which stems from the integration of neuroscience and artificial intelligence. Nevertheless, we acknowledge that the study is limited due to the novelty of the research field. We therefore encourage the publication of research on these new applications and their regulatory development.

As we have discussed throughout our study, our ultimate goal is to ensure that these applications enhance the well-being of individuals and societies without infringing upon human rights or undermining democracies- to this end, we set out a number of ethical principles to consider in order to promote the proper conduct of this research.

*Table 5. Limitations and future lines of research*

| Ethical principles | Challenges | Research questions |
|---|---|---|
| Information and transparency | The implementation and application of these nudges by governments needs to be properly informed to all concerned. | - How are different governments informing policy actions based on nudges?<br>- How should this documents be drafted to allow for understanding by all audiences? |
| Awareness-raising | The population must be made aware of the dangers to which they are exposed when using these techniques. Communication and learning strategies are therefore required. | - What actions are governments taking to raise awareness of the use of AI?<br>- How can we protect sensitive population groups from these techniques? |
| Informed consent | In all these actions, conscious and informed consent of the individual receiving the nudge must prevail. | - How is individual consent being produced in existing nudges?<br>- Are individuals aware of the effect of these techniques on their behaviour? |
| Privacy/Data control | The privacy of the individual's data, as well as their access and disposal, must be ensured at all time. | - How is the protection of the various sources that provide behavioural data on individuals being ensured?<br>- How can individuals access this data? |
| Responsibility | Existence of strong and shared national and international regulatory frameworks. | - What regulatory initiatives in the field of AI applied to nudge are taking place in different countries?<br>- What are the basic principles that these regulatory frameworks should protect? |
| Justice and fairness | The application of nudges in our societies cannot help to promote existing inequalities. | - What kind of discriminatory biases can generate the impact of these nudges in our societies?<br>- What impacts can the application of these nudges have on vulnerable groups? |

*Note*. Source: Authors

## CONCLUSIONS

The progressive convergence of neuroscience and artificial intelligence in policymaking poses significant challenges to governance as a whole. We believe that the progressive application of these techniques could lead to policies that are based on the individual, personalised in real time, predictive, and sensitive to emotions in order to enhance well-being. However, behavioural governance raises significant ethical challenges that must be addressed to protect the rights of individuals and limit state interventionism. This chapter has addressed how booming investment is enabling the development of artificial intelligence, and how this is leading to the creation of sophisticated tools for intervening in human behaviour. Given the importance of this development, this study aimed to provide a detailed overview of the current state of affairs to facilitate an understanding of its development, and to identify lines of research, applications, and ethical challenges. To this end, we will answer the following questions.

Regarding the first question (RQ1) concerning the leading authors in this field (table 2), Cass R. Sunstein emerges as the most prominent figure, having creates the concept of nudging (40 citations; link strength 348.00). Other notable figures include Stuard Mills (17 citations; link strength 202.00), who has conducted studies to enhance the effectiveness of these tools through artificial intelligence, and the European Union (10 citations; link strength 148.00), which stands out for its funding of nudge-related projects and its regulatory initiatives.

Turning to the next question (RQ2), which aims to identify the main journals gathering knowledge, we observe the interdisciplinary nature of the subject. Here, the *Journal of Business Research* acts as a bridge between different areas of knowledge, while *AI & Society* focuses on the ethical and social implications of the technology. Similarly, the emergence of the *Journal of Medical Internet Research* indicates interest in its development in the medical and health fields (table 3, figures 6 and 7)

Continuing with question number 3, which is dedicates to identifying the main categories in which knowledge is collected (RQ3), we observe the dominance of computer science information, with 11 entries (10.28%), which is tied with electronic engineering and medical informatics (table3). This highlights the importance of its technical development, as well as the interest in its application in the medical field.

If we consider how research is evolving (RQ4), we can see that is a very new and emerging field with the highest level of activity in terms of article publication (32) in 2022 and the highest number of citations (405) in 2023 (figures 1 and2)- In terms of research development itself (figure 14), we can identify an early stage centres on privacy concerns and the technological aspects of AI development, emphasising the importance of machine learning and big data as underlying technologies. As the field has developed, research has begun to integrate concepts of behavioural economics and persuasion. Alongside this, terms such as "digital health" and "choice architecture" have emerged, highlighting interest in how artificial intelligence can influence health and decision-making. More recently, the terms "ethics" and "trust" have emerged, suggesting a growing concern for ethical aspects and the need to stablish trust in these technologies. Keywords such as "health" and "children" show growing interest in the potential impact of artificial intelligence and nudges on children's health and decision-making, while "challenges" and "future" indicate that current research is exploring future challenges and the evolution of artificial intelligence.

Finally, RQ5 asks what the challenges are in this field of study. The appearance of the keyword "challenges" (figure12) enables us to identify the specific challenges that this field of study is facing. Thus, the nudge arising from the integration of AI or digital nudging, is identified as one of the objectives of the research. Additionally, the study identifies health as the area with the most applications and the greatest challenges. Similarly, word co-occurrence points to children as an area that needs to be addressed.

In summary, the results demonstrate that application of artificial intelligence to governance is a nascent but growing phenomenon that offers states effective behavioural intervention tools. While these tools provide a more personalised, responsive and empathetic approach to governance, they also raise important ethical questions that require attention.

## REFERENCES


Acquisti, A.; Adjerid, I.; Balebako, R.; Brandimarte, L.; Cranor, L. F.; Komanduri, S.; Leon, P. G.; Sadeh, N.; Schaub, F.; Sleeper, M.; Wang, Y. and Wilson, S. (2017) Nudges for Privacy and Security: Understanding and Assisting Users' Choices Online. *ACM Comput. Surv.* 50(3) Article 44 (May 2018), 41 pages. DOI: 10.1145/3054926

AJuhi. A., and Kumar, S. (2020) A Survey on Artificial Intelligence Overview. *International Journal of Research in Engineering, Science and Management, 1.* https://doi.org/DOI: 10.31224/osf.io/47a85

Baldwin, R. (2014). From Regulation to Behaviour Change: Giving Nudge the Third Degree. *The Modern Law Review*, *77*(6), 831–857. DOI: 10.1111/1468-2230.12094

Barak-Corren, N., & Kariv-Teitelbaum, Y. (2021). Behavioral responsive regulation: Bringing together responsive regulation and behavioral public policy. *Regulation & Amp. Regulation & Governance*, *15*(S1). Advance online publication. DOI: 10.1111/rego.12429

Bartmann, M. (2022). The ethics of ai-powered climate nudging—How much ai should we use to save the planet? *Sustainability (Basel)*, *14*(9), 5153. DOI: 10.3390/su14095153

Benjamin, R. (2022). *Viral justice: How we grow the world we want.* Princeton University Press., DOI: 10.2307/j.ctv2h439xx

Bertoni, F., Citti, G., and Sarti, A. (2019). LGN-CNN: a biologically inspired CNN architecture. *Neural networks: the official journal of the International Neural Network Society*, 145, 42-55. .DOI: 10.1016/j.neunet.2021.09.024

Borenstein, J., & Arkin, R. (2016). Robotic nudges: The ethics of engineering a more socially just human being. *Science and Engineering Ethics*, *22*(1), 31–46. DOI: 10.1007/s11948-015-9636-2 PMID: 25736832

Burr, C., Cristianini, N., & Ladyman, J. (2018). An analysis of the interaction between intelligent software agents and human users. *Minds and Machines*, *28*(4), 735–774. DOI: 10.1007/s11023-018-9479-0 PMID: 30930542

Bush, G. H. W. (1990, 17 de julio). *Proclamation 6158—Decade of the Brain, 1990–1999*. The American Presidency Project. https://www.presidency.ucsb.edu/documents/proclamation-6158-decade-the-brain-1990-1999

Capraro, V., Jagfeld, G., Klein, R., Mul, M., & van de Pol, I. (2019). Increasing altruistic and cooperative behaviour with simple moral nudges. *Scientific Reports*, *9*(1), 11880. DOI: 10.1038/s41598-019-48094-4 PMID: 31417106

Caraban, A., Karapanos, E., Gonçalves, D., & Campos, P. (2019) 23 Ways to Nudge: A Review of Technology-Mediated Nudging in Human-Computer Interaction. In *Proceedings of the 2019 CHI Conference on Human Factors in Computing Systems (CHI '19)*. Association for Computing Machinery, New York, NY, USA, Paper 503, 1–15. DOI: 10.1145/3290605.3300733

Castin, N., Malerba, L., Bonny, G., Pascuet, M. I., & Hou, M. (2009). Modelling radiation-induced phase changes in binary Fe–Cu and ternary Fe–Cu–Ni alloys using an artificial intelligence based atomistic kinetic Monte Carlo approach. *Nuclear Instruments & Methods in Physics Research. Section B, Beam Interactions with Materials and Atoms*, *267*(16–17), 3002–3008. DOI: 10.1016/j.nimb.2009.06.092

Cea Quintana, S. (2025). Mapping brain science research and its influence on public governance: Increasing the effectiveness of public policies through behavioural change. In Saura, J. R. (Ed.), *Global perspectives on AI, ethics, and business economics* (pp. 217–252). Springer., DOI: 10.1007/978-3-031-88781-9_10

Consejo de Estado de la República Popular China. (2017, 20 de julio). *Plan de desarrollo de la nueva generación de inteligencia artificial*. https://www.airuniversity.af.edu/Portals/10/CASI/documents/Translations/2021-03-02%20China%27s%20New%20Generation%20Artificial%20Intelligence%20Development%20Plan-%202017.pdf

Covington, P., Adams, J., & Sargin, E. (2016). Deep neural networks for YouTube recommendations. *Proceedings of the 10th ACM Conference on Recommender Systems*, 191-198. DOI: 10.1145/2959100.2959190

Crawford, K. (2021). *Atlas of AI: Power, politics, and the planetary costs of artificial intelligence*. Yale University Press., DOI: 10.12987/9780300252392

Cuello, H. (2021). Cómo cambiar comportamientos durante una pandemia: El uso de nudges para enfrentar la COVID-19. *Gestión y Análisis de Políticas Públicas*, (25), 73–86. DOI: 10.24965/gapp.i25.10873

Dargan, S., & Kumar, M. (2020). A comprehensive survey on the biometric recognition systems based on physiological and behavioral modalities. *Expert Systems with Applications*, *143*, 113114. Advance online publication. DOI: 10.1016/j.eswa.2019.113114

Ding, X., & Yang, Z. (2020). Knowledge mapping of platform research: a visual analysis using VOSviewer and CiteSpace. *Electronic Commerce Research*, 1–23.a European Commission. (2014). Horizon 2020 in brief: The EU Framework Programme for Research & Innovation. Retrieved from https://ec.europa.eu/newsroom/horizon2020/items/15081/en&#8203

European Commission. (2021). Horizon Europe: EU's funding programme for Research and innovation (2021–2027). Retrieved from https://commission.europa.eu/funding-tenders/find-funding/eu-funding-programmes/horizon-europe_encontentReference[oaicite:0]index=0

European Commission. (2021). *NEON: Next-generation integrated energy services for citizen energy communities* (Project ID: 101033700). Retrieved from https://cordis.europa.eu/project/id/101033700

European Commission. (2023). *NUDGE: Nudging consumers towards energy efficiency through behavioral science* (Project ID: 957012). Retrieved from https://cordis.europa.eu/project/id/957012

Floridi, L. (2015). *The Onlife Manifesto: Being Human in a Hyperconnected Era.* Springer., DOI: 10.1007/978-3-319-04093-6

Fothergill, B., Knight, W., Stahl, B. C., & Ulnicane, I. (2019). Responsible Data Governance of Neuroscience Big Data. *Frontiers in Neuroinformatics*, *13*, 28. Advance online publication. DOI: 10.3389/fninf.2019.00028 PMID: 31110477

Gofen, A., Moseley, A., Thomann, E., & Weaver, R. K. (2021). Behavioural governance in the policy process: Introduction to the special issue. *Journal of European Public Policy*, *28*(5), 633–657. DOI: 10.1080/13501763.2021.1912153

Goodfellow, I., Pouget-Abadie, J., Mirza, M., Xu, B., Warde-Farley, D., Ozair, S., Courville, A., & Bengio, Y. (2020, November). Generative adversarial networks. *Communications of the ACM*, *63*(11), 139–144. DOI: 10.1145/3422622

Gorraiz, J., & Schloegl, C. (2008). A bibliometric analysis of pharmacology and pharmacy journals: Scopus versus Web of Science. *Journal of Information Science*, *34*(5), 715–725. DOI: 10.1177/0165551507086991

Gui, J.; Sun, Z.; Wen, Y.; Tao, D. and Ye, J. (2021). A Review on Generative Adversarial Networks: Algorithms, Theory, and Applications. *IEEE Transactions on Knowledge and Data Engineering*. PP. 1-1. .DOI: 10.1109/TKDE.2021.3130191

Hansen, P. G., & Jespersen, A. (2013). Nudge and the Manipulation of Choice. *European Journal of Risk Regulation*, *4*(1), 3–28. DOI: 10.1017/S1867299X00002762

Hassabis, D., Kumaran, D., Summerfield, C., & Botvinick, M. (2017). Neuroscience-Inspired Artificial Intelligence. *Neuron, 95*(2), 245–258. DOI: 10.1016/j.neuron.2017.06.011 PMID: 28728020

Hausman, D. M., & Welch, B. (2010). Debate: To nudge or not to nudge. *Journal of Political Philosophy, 18*(1), 123–136. DOI: 10.1111/j.1467-9760.2009.00351.x

Hemachandran, K., Verma, P., Pareek, P., Arora, N., Kumar, K. V. R., Ahanger, T. A., Pise, A. A., & Ratna, R. (2022). Artificial Intelligence: A Universal Virtual Tool to Augment Tutoring in Higher Education. *Computational Intelligence and Neuroscience, 2022*, 1–8. DOI: 10.1155/2022/1410448 PMID: 35586099

Hou, J., Yang, X., & Chen, C. (2018). Emerging trends and new developments in information science: A document co-citation analysis (2009–2016). *Scientometrics, 115*(2), 869–892. DOI: 10.1007/s11192-018-2695-9

Huang, M.-H., & Rust, R. T. (2018). Artificial Intelligence in Service. *Journal of Service Research, 21*(2), 155–172. DOI: 10.1177/1094670517752459

Huang, N., Chen, P. Y., Hong, Y., & Wu, S. Y. (2018). Digital nudging for online social sharing: Evidence from a randomized field experiment. En T. X. Bui (Ed.), Proceedings of the 51st *Annual Hawaii International Conference on System Sciences* (HICSS 2018) (pp. 1483–1491). IEEE Computer Society. DOI: 10.24251/HICSS.2018.185

Hukkinen, J. (2016). Addressing the Practical and Ethical Issues of Nudging in Environmental Policy. *Environmental Values, 25*(3), 329–351. DOI: 10.3197/096327116X14598445991501

Insel, T., Landis, S. C., & Collins, F. S. (2013). The NIH BRAIN Initiative. *Science, 340*(6133), 687–688. DOI: 10.1126/science.1239276 PMID: 23661744

Institute for European Energy and Climate Policy. (2020). *Audit-To-Measure: Leading businesses towards climate neutrality by speeding up the uptake of energy efficiency measures from energy audits* (Project ID: 101075785). https://cordis.europa.eu/project/id/101075785

Johnstone, M. (2016). The Ethics of Nudging. *Australian Nursing & Midwifery Journal, 24*(6), 27. PMID: 29251881

Kahneman, D. (2011). *Thinking, fast and slow*. Farrar, Straus and Giroux.

Kahneman, D., & Tversky, A. (1979). Prospect theory: An analysis of decision under risk. *Econometrica, 47*(2), 263–291. DOI: 10.2307/1914185

Kahneman, D., & Tversky, A. (1984). Choices, values, and frames. *The American Psychologist, 39*(4), 341–350. DOI: 10.1037/0003-066X.39.4.341

Köhler, M., Bächle, T., & Krüger, M. (2024). The Value of Smartwatches in the Healthcare Sector for Monitoring, Nudging, and Predicting. *Journal of Medical Internet Research, 26*, e58936. DOI: 10.2196/58936 PMID: 39356287

Krizhevsky, A., Sutskever, I., & Hinton, G. (2012). ImageNet Classification with Deep Convolutional Neural Networks. *Neural Information Processing Systems, 25*. Advance online publication. DOI: 10.1145/3065386

Lafont, J., Saura, J. R., & Ribeiro-Soriano, D. (2023). The role of cooperatives in sustainable development goals: A discussion about the current resource curse. *Resources Policy, 83*, 103670. DOI: 10.1016/j.resourpol.2023.103670

LeCun, Y., Bengio, Y., & Hinton, G. (2015). Deep learning. *Nature, 521*(7553), 436–444. DOI: 10.1038/nature14539 PMID: 26017442

Linnenluecke, M., Marrone, M., & Singh, A. (2019). Conducting systematic literature reviews and bibliometric analyses. *Australian Journal of Management, 45*(2), 175–194. DOI: 10.1177/0312896219877678

Loewenstein, G., & Chater, N. (2017). Putting nudges in perspective. *Behavioural Public Policy, 1*(1), 26–53. DOI: 10.1017/bpp.2016.7

Luo, Q., Zeng, W., Chen, M., Peng, G., Yuan, X., & Yin, Q. (2023). Self-Attention and Transformers: Driving the Evolution of Large Language Models. *2023 IEEE 6th International Conference on Electronic Information and Communication Technology (ICEICT)*, 401-405. DOI: 10.1109/ICEICT57916.2023.10245906

Markram, H. (2012). The Human Brain Project: A report to the European Commission. *The HBP-PS Consortium*. DOI: DOI: 10.5281/zenodo.44517

Marsden, J. R. (2019). Artificial Intelligence in Practice: How AI Is Being Used. *International Journal of Information Management, 49*, 228–241. DOI: 10.1016/j.ijinfomgt.2019.03.002

Matz, S. C., Kosinski, M., Nave, G., & Stillwell, D. J. (2017). Psychological targeting as an effective approach to digital mass persuasion. *Proceedings of the National Academy of Sciences of the United States of America, 114*(48), 12714–12719. DOI: 10.1073/pnas.1710966114 PMID: 29133409

McAllister, J. T., Lennertz, L., & Atencio Mojica, Z. (2022). Mapping a discipline: A guide tousing VOSviewer for bibliometric and visual analysis. *Science & Technology Libraries, 41*(3), 319–348. DOI: 10.1080/0194262X.2021.1991547

Meske, C., & Amojo, I. (2020). Ethical guidelines for the construction of digital nudges. *Proceedings of the 53rd Hawaii International Conference on System Sciences*, 1-10. DOI: 10.24251/HICSS.2020.480

Meunier, D., and Paugam-Moisy, H. (2008, April). Neural networks for computational neuroscience. *ESANN* (pp. 367-378)

Mills, S. (2021). Finding the 'nudge' in hypernudge. *Technology in Society*, *71*, 102117. DOI: 10.1016/j.techsoc.2022.102117

Mittelstadt, B. D., & Floridi, L. (2016). The Ethics of Big Data: Current and Foreseeable Issues in *Biomedical Contexts. Science and Engineering Ethics*, *22*(2), 303–341. DOI: 10.1007/s11948-015-9652-2 PMID: 26002496

Noor, M., Zenia, N., Kaiser, M., Mamun, S., & Mahmud, M. (2020). Application of deep learning in detecting neurological disorders from magnetic resonance images: A survey on the detection of Alzheimer's disease, Parkinson's disease and schizophrenia. *Brain Informatics*, *7*(1), 11. Advance online publication. DOI: 10.1186/s40708-020-00112-2 PMID: 33034769

OECD. (2019). *Recommendation of the Council on Artificial Intelligence*. OECD/LEGAL/0449. https://legalinstruments.oecd.org/en/instruments/OECD-LEGAL-0449

Okano, H., Miyawaki, A., & Kasai, K. (2015). Brain/MINDS: A Japanese National Brain Project for Marmoset Neuroscience. *Neuron*, *92*(3), 582–590. DOI: 10.1016/j.neuron.2016.10.018 PMID: 27809998

Oyewola, D. O., & Dada, E. G. (2022). Exploring machine learning: A scientometrics approach using bibliometrix and VOSviewer. *SN Applied Sciences*, *4*(5), 1–18. DOI: 10.1007/s42452-022-05027-7 PMID: 35434524

Padilla, W. R., & García, J. (2018). Data Association Methodology to Improve Spatial Predictions in Alternative Marketing Circuits in Ecuador. *Computational Intelligence and Neuroscience*, *2018*, 1–15. DOI: 10.1155/2018/6587049 PMID: 30532771

Paperno, D. (2022). On Learning Interpreted Languages with Recurrent Models. *Computational Linguistics*, *48*(3), 471–482. DOI: 10.1162/coli_a_00431

Parlamento Europeo y Consejo de la Unión Europea. (2024). Reglamento (UE) 2024/1183 del Parlamento Europeo y del Consejo de 13 de marzo de 2024 por el que se establecen normas armonizadas en materia de inteligencia artificial (Ley de Inteligencia Artificial) y se modifican determinados actos legislativos de la Unión. *Diario Oficial de la Unión Europea*, L 168, 1–142. https://eur-lex.europa.eu/legal-content/ES/TXT/?uri=CELEX%3A32024R1183

Pasquale, F. (2020). *New laws of robotics: Defending human expertise in the age of AI.* The Belknap Press of Harvard University Press., DOI: 10.4159/9780674250062

Peer, E., Egelman, S., Harbach, M., Malkin, N., Mathur, A., & Frik, A. (2020). Nudge me right: Personalizing online security nudges to people's decision-making styles. *Computers in Human Behavior, 109*, 106347. Advance online publication. DOI: 10.1016/j.chb.2020.106347

Poo, M., Du, J.-L., Ip, N., Xiong, Z., Xu, B., & Tan, T. (2016). China Brain Project: Basic Neuroscience, Brain Diseases, and Brain-Inspired Computing. *Neuron, 92*(3), 591–596. DOI: 10.1016/j.neuron.2016.10.050 PMID: 27809999

Putra, D., and Setiawan, E. (2023). Sentiment Analysis on Social Media with Glove Using Combination CNN and RoBERTa. *Jurnal RESTI (Rekayasa Sistem dan Teknologi Informasi)*. .DOI: 10.29207/resti.v7i3.4892

Río, J., Gervás, I., & Yuste, S. (2018). The Patient Information Sheet (PIS) and Informed Consent (IC) for case reports and case series: Proposal for a standard model for presentations in congresses and other scientific publications. *Reumatología Clínica, 14*(4), 215–223. DOI: 10.1016/j.reuma.2018.07.001 PMID: 30075946

Robertson, D. C., Voegtlin, C., & Maak, T. (2016). Business Ethics: The Promise of Neuroscience. *Journal of Business Ethics, 144*(4), 679–697. DOI: 10.1007/s10551-016-3312-6

Russell, S. (2016). Rationality and Intelligence: A Brief Update. In Müller, V. C. (Ed.), *Fundamental Issues of Artificial Intelligence. Synthese Library* (Vol. 376). Springer., DOI: 10.1007/978-3-319-26485-1_2

Sadeghian, A. H. and Otarkhani, A. (2023). Data-driven digital nudging: a systematic literature review and future agenda. *Behaviour &Amp; Information Technology*, 1-29. DOI: 10.1080/0144929X.2023.2286535

Schmauder, C., Karpus, J., Moll, M., Bahrami, B., & Deroy, O. (2023). Algorithmic nudging: The need for an interdisciplinary oversight. *Topoi, 42*(3), 799–807. DOI: 10.1007/s11245-023-09907-4

Schmidhuber, J. (2014). Deep learning in neural networks: An overview. *Neural network: the official journal of the International Neural Network Society*, 61, 85-117. .DOI: 10.1016/j.neunet.2014.09.003

Schmidt, A. T., & Engelen, B. (2020). The ethics of nudging: An overview. *Philosophy Compass, 15*(4), e12658. Advance online publication. DOI: 10.1111/phc3.12658

Schmidt, R., & Stenger, K. (2024). Behavioral brittleness: The case for strategic behavioral public policy. *Behavioural Public Policy*, *8*(2), 212–237. DOI: 10.1017/bpp.2021.16

Simon, H. A. (1997). What is an explanation of behavior? *Psychological Science*, *2*, 150–161.

Sun, Y., Zhang, M., Sun, Z., & Tan, T. (2018). Demographic Analysis from Biometric Data: Achievements, Challenges, and New Frontiers. *IEEE Transactions on Pattern Analysis and Machine Intelligence*, *40*(2), 332–351. DOI: 10.1109/TPAMI.2017.2669035 PMID: 28212078

Sunstein, C. R. (2014). *Why Nudge? The Politics of Libertarian Paternalism.* Yale University Press. https://www.jstor.org/stable/j.ctt5vm0nr

Sunstein, C. R., & Thaler, R. H. (2003). Libertarian Paternalism Is Not an Oxymoron. *The University of Chicago Law Review. University of Chicago. Law School*, *70*(4), 1159–1202. DOI: 10.2307/1600573

Thaler, R. H., & Sunstein, C. R. (2009). *Nudge: Improving decisions about health, wealth, and happiness*. Penguin.

UNESCO. (2021). *Recommendation on the Ethics of Artificial Intelligence*. https://unesdoc.unesco.org/ark:/48223/pf0000381137

United Nations Innovation Network. (2021). *UN Behavioural Science Report*. United Nations.

Van Essen, D. C., Smith, S. M., Deanna, M., Behrens, T. E. J., Yacoub, E., & Uğurbil, K. (2013). The WU-Minn Human Connectome Project: An overview. *NeuroImage*, *80*, 62–79. DOI: 10.1016/j.neuroimage.2013.05.041 PMID: 23684880

Veretilnykova, M., & Dogruel, L. (2021). Nudging children and adolescents toward online privacy: An ethical perspective. *Journal of Media Ethics*, *36*(2), 128–140. DOI: 10.1080/23736992.2021.1939031

Weinmann, M., Schneider, C., & vom Brocke, J. (2016). Digital Nudging. *Business & Information Systems Engineering*, *58*(6), 433–436. DOI: 10.1007/s12599-016-0453-1

Yeung, K. (2017). Hypernudging: Big Data as a Mode of Regulation by Design. *Information Communication and Society*, *20*(1), 118–136. DOI: 10.1080/1369118X.2016.1186713

Yu, H., Shen, Z., Miao, C., Leung, C., Lesser, V., and Yang, Q. (2018). Building Ethics into Artificial Intelligence. *ArXiv, abs/1812.02953*. DOI: .DOI: 10.24963/ijcai.2018/779

Yuan, B. Z., & Sun, J. (2020). Bibliometric analysis of research on the maize based on top papers during 2009-2019. COLLNET. *Journal of Scientometrics and Information Management*, *14*(1), 75–92.

Zhang, P., Chen, B., Ma, L., Li, Z., Song, Z., Duan, W., & Qiu, X. (2015). The Large-Scale Machine Learning in an Artificial Society: Prediction of the Ebola Outbreak in Beijing. *Computational Intelligence and Neuroscience*, *2015*, 1–12. DOI: 10.1155/2015/531650 PMID: 26457078

## ENDNOTES

1 OPSI Observatory: https://oecd-opsi.org/

2 Observatory of Public Sector Innovation. (s. f.). BI Units Archive - Observatory of Public Sector Innovation. Observatory Of Public Sector Innovation https://oecd-opsi.org/bi-units/; accessed June 19, 2024.

3 https://www.unicef.org/innocenti/media/5191/file/UNICEF-Ethics-Toolkit-for-your-applied-behavioural-science-project-2021.pdf?utm_source=chatgpt.com

4 https://www.oecd.org/en/publications/tools-and-ethics-for-applied-behavioural-insights-the-basic-toolkit_9ea76a8f-en.html

5 https://www.webofscience.com/wos/woscc/summary/37e1a29e-fe14-4a51-8629-e75a61c05912-f90b4632/relevance/1

6 https://ec.europa.eu/digital-strategy/news-redirect/63347

7 https://eur-lex.europa.eu/legal-content/ES/TXT/?uri=CELEX%3A52021PC0206

8 https://research-and-innovation.ec.europa.eu/funding/funding-opportunities/funding-programmes-and-open-calls/horizon-2020_en

9 https://research-and-innovation.ec.europa.eu/funding/funding-opportunities/funding-programmes-and-open-calls/horizon-europe_en

# Chapter 10
# Cognitive Sovereignty and Happiness Governance:
## Dubai's Vision for Ethical AI Cities

**Maria Amparo Diaz-LLairo**
https://orcid.org/0009-0007-5997-2233
*University of Barcelona, Spain*

## ABSTRACT

*This chapter examines AI systems that infer cognitive and emotional states and their implications for mental privacy, cognitive liberty, and well-being in smart-city governance. Using a structured narrative synthesis of peer-reviewed and official sources (2018-2025), it contrasts Dubai's practice, where happiness metrics are built into service delivery, with international frameworks (EU AI Act, UNESCO, OECD). We use the Cognitive and Emotional Well-Being Index (CEWI) as an analytical lens. Findings map benefits and risks of cognitive/emotional AI and set out governance tools: cognitive consent, explainability, proportionate oversight, and participatory review. Dubai is presented as a distinctive case of happiness-oriented, autonomy-preserving service design. Policy proposals include a Neuroethics and Happiness Task Force, explicit consent for cognitive/emotional inference, and a neurorights-aligned framework. The chapter contributes a comparative assessment of Dubai in global context and a transferable model for human-centered, cognitive-sovereignty governance of urban AI.*

DOI: 10.4018/979-8-3373-4480-5.ch010

# 1. INTRODUCTION

Recent advancements in artificial intelligence (AI) are fundamentally redefining the relationship between technology and human cognitive autonomy. Brain-computer interfaces (BCIs), affective computing systems, and predictive cognitive algorithms now enable emerging access to what was once considered inviolable: the inner domain of human thought and emotion (Farahany, 2023). These technologies promise impactful societal benefits across healthcare, education, and governance. However, they simultaneously introduce profound ethical challenges that frameworks are not designed to address.

The ability of technology to interpret, predict, and potentially influence cognitive and emotional states raises critical questions about mental privacy and cognitive liberty. As Ienca and Andorno (2017) argue, the freedom to control one's own mental processes, without unauthorized technological interference or manipulation, constitutes a fundamental dimension of human dignity that warrants explicit protection. While discourse on data privacy has evolved substantially, governance mechanisms safeguarding the sovereignty of thought and emotion remain conspicuously underdeveloped (Bublitz, 2014; Yuste et al., 2017).

This governance gap is particularly concerning given the accelerating convergence of AI with neurotechnology and affective computing. Without anticipatory ethical regulatory scheme, technologies capable of inferring intentions, emotions, or cognitive states risk compromising psychological continuity and mental autonomy, foundational elements of human experience that transcend conventional privacy concerns (Ienca & Andorno, 2017; Farahany, 2023).

Within this evolving ethical field, Dubai emerges as a notable and instructive case study. Under the visionary leadership of Sheikh Mohammed bin Rashid Al Maktoum, Dubai has implemented an approach in which citizen happiness is stated as an objective and partly operationalized through service KPIs. Through initiatives such as the Dubai Happiness Agenda, Digital Dubai platforms, and the UAE Centennial 2071 Vision, the emirate has operationalized a governance philosophy that positions human flourishing as the ultimate purpose of technological advancement.

The central question is how cities can ethically harness AI technologies capable of cognitive and emotional interpretation while protecting mental privacy, cognitive liberty, and societal happiness. Through proposing an original conceptual model, the Cognitive and Emotional Well-Being Index (CEWI), and analyzing Dubai's innovative integration of Neuroethics and happiness metrics within governance structures, this research contributes to advancing human-centric, ethically anticipatory, and cognitively sovereign smart city governance.

We build on the Cognitive and Emotional Well-Being Index (CEWI) first outlined by Díaz-Llairó (2026) The present work refines its constructs and coding logic and applies the framework to Dubai's AI governance context, including a cross-jurisdictional comparison (Table 4).

Consequently, this study aims to (1) analyze the ethical implications of AI technologies capable of inferring cognitive and emotional states; (2) examine Dubai's integration of happiness metrics and ethical governance within its smart city strategy; (3) develop a conceptual model for safeguarding cognitive liberty and emotional well-being in AI-driven urban environments; and (4) identify strategic opportunities for Dubai to enhance its global leadership in ethical AI governance while advancing cognitive sovereignty protections.

By examining these objectives, this research contributes to theoretical and practical understanding of how smart cities can embrace technological advancement while preserving the integrity domain of human thought, emotion, and autonomy, essential foundations for sustainable and ethical progress in the age of cognitive AI.

## 2. THEORETICAL FRAMEWORK

This study is situated at the intersection of five interconnected theoretical domains, each contributing essential conceptual foundations for analyzing cognitive sovereignty and happiness governance in AI-integrated urban environments:

### 2.1 Cognitive Liberty and Mental Privacy

Cognitive liberty represents a fundamental dimension of human autonomy, the right of individuals to maintain sovereignty over their mental processes, free from unauthorized external interference or manipulation (Ienca & Andorno, 2017). As AI technologies evolve toward increasingly sophisticated interpretation of neural activity, emotional states, and cognitive patterns, this domain of liberty faces considerable challenges. Mental privacy, conceptualized as the protection of inner thoughts, emotions, and neural data from unwanted access or exploitation, emerges as a critical extension of traditional privacy rights in response to neurotechnological advancement (Bublitz, 2014).

Contemporary scholarship emphasizes that cognitive liberty encompasses not merely freedom from interference but also affirmative rights to mental self-determination (Farahany, 2023). This includes control over how one's cognitive data is collected, interpreted, and applied within AI-driven systems. As predictive algorithms and affective computing capabilities advance, the potential for subtle cognitive influence, through personalized manipulation, emotional priming, or unconscious behavioral nudging, introduces complex ethical challenges requiring multidimensional protective regulatory scheme (Yuste et al., 2017).

## 2.2 Ethical AI Governance

Contemporary conceptual model for ethical AI governance emphasizes anticipatory regulation, transparency, accountability, and human-centered design principles (Floridi, 2018; Floridi & Cowls, 2019). International instruments structure such as UNESCO's Recommendation (2021) and OECD AI Principles (2020) recognize that conventional ex-post regulatory models are insufficient when confronting technologies capable of profound societal impact, particularly for AI systems interfacing with cognition and emotion (Zicari et al., 2021).

Analytically, ethical AI governance requires moving beyond abstract principles toward operationalizable metrics and enforceable standards (Jobin, Ienca, & Vayena, 2019). This translates theoretical commitments into tangible governance structures capable of guiding technological development in alignment with human values and rights protections. Mantelero (2021) argues that such governance must be dynamic and adaptive, evolving alongside technological capabilities to address emerging ethical challenges, particularly in domains where the technology interfaces with human cognition.

## 2.3 Smart City Ethics and Human-Centric Urban Innovation

The conceptualization of smart cities has evolved significantly from technocentric efficiency models toward human-centered urban environments where technology serves as a means rather than an end (Casas & Morozov, 2022). Dubai's smart city approach exemplifies this evolution, embedding citizen happiness, service excellence, and ethical innovation within its technological infrastructure and governance approach (Digital Dubai, 2020; UAE Government, 2021).

Emerging scholarship in smart-city ethics contends that urban intelligence is driven less by technical sophistication than by governance oriented to human flourishing, civic participation, and ethical foresight. Such a view challenges technocentric models that privilege efficiency or capability while neglecting cognitive rights, emotional impacts, and psychological well-being.

Dubai's integration of happiness metrics with technological advancement exemplifies how cultural values can shape notable ethical approach for AI-driven urban development. Dubai was selected through theoretical and purposive sampling as an exemplary case offering paradigmatic insight into the integration of cognitive rights and emotional well-being within smart governance approach (Yin, 2018). Its unique configuration of visionary leadership, technological ambition, and explicit well-being objectives provides a theoretically rich context for examining how cognitive liberty principles can be operationalized within AI-driven urban environments.

## 2.4 Neurorights and Cognitive Protection

The Neurorights Initiative, pioneered by Yuste et al. (2017), represents a significant contribution to the theoretical and advocacy analytical lens centered on five fundamental rights in the neurotechnology era:

1. Mental privacy: Protection against unauthorized access to neural data and thought content
2. Personal identity preservation: Safeguarding psychological continuity and sense of self
3. Cognitive liberty: Freedom of thought and control over one's cognitive processes
4. Fair access to cognitive enhancement: Equitable distribution of beneficial neurotechnologies
5. Protection against algorithmic bias: Preventing discrimination in neurotechnology application

These rights collectively constitute an emerging paradigm for understanding how human dignity and autonomy can be preserved amidst advancing capabilities to interpret, influence, and potentially manipulate cognitive processes. The theoretical significance of this analytical lens lies in its recognition that neural data represents a complex category requiring specialized ethical and legal protections beyond conventional data privacy approaches (Ienca & Andorno, 2017; Farahany, 2023).

The Neurorights paradigm offers a particularly valuable theoretical lens for analyzing smart city governance models, highlighting areas where traditional approaches may inadequately address emerging challenges at the intersection of AI, cognitive interpretation, and urban innovation. By establishing explicit protections for cognitive sovereignty as foundational ethical imperatives, this analytical lens facilitates more comprehensive evaluation of how governance structures either enhance or potentially compromise cognitive autonomy in technologically integrated environments.

## 2.5 Happiness-Driven Leadership and Eudaimonic Governance

Dubai and UAE policy documents describe a leadership model that links urban strategy to eudaimonic aims, privileging meaningful flourishing over short-term satisfaction, and makes citizen happiness and well-being explicit governance goals. In this view, success is not a by-product of growth or technology roll-out; happiness is a designed, measured, and iteratively improved outcome delivered through human-centric services, sound data governance, and participatory feedback. The approach aligns with scholarship that distinguishes eudaimonia from hedonia and ties public value to autonomy, purpose, and capabilities, offering a normative anchor for AI-enabled city services that protect dignity and psychological continuity alongside efficiency (Ryan & Deci, 2001; Floridi & Cowls, 2019; UAE Government, 2021).

## 3. METHODOLOGY

### 3.1 Research Design and Philosophical Approach

This study employs an interpretive constructivist epistemology to develop a conceptual model examining the governance implications of AI technologies capable of interpreting human cognitive and emotional states. Rather than adopting a positivist hypothesis-testing approach, the research follows an exploratory theory-building methodology focused on conceptual innovation (Suddaby, 2006). This approach aligns with emerging scholarly practices in AI ethics where normative proposals often precede empirical validation due to the anticipatory nature of technological governance (Floridi, 2018; Yuste et al., 2017).

The research design integrates conceptual model development with comparative ethical analysis, enabling theoretical advancement through the synthesis of multidisciplinary literature, policy documents, and strategic governance approach. This methodological approach responds to Whetten's (1989) criteria for theoretical contribution, emphasizing the identification of novel relationships between governance structures, cognitive liberty protections, and emotional well-being metrics. The CEWI analytical lens is proposed as a conceptual tool requiring empirical validation in future studies.

### 3.2 Case Selection and Theoretical Sampling

Dubai was selected through theoretical sampling (Eisenhardt & Graebner, 2007) as a critical case that offers paradigmatic insight into the integration of happiness metrics and ethical AI within urban governance model. The selection criteria included:

1. Explicit use of happiness metrics in services through the Dubai Happiness Agenda
2. Advanced implementation of AI-driven citizen experience platforms and services
3. Leadership vision articulating the relationship between technological advancement and human flourishing
4. Active engagement with ethical innovation through strategic initiatives such as the UAE AI Strategy 2031

As Flyvbjerg (2006) argues, critical cases offer strategic importance in relation to the general problem under investigation. Dubai's unique configuration of visionary leadership, technological ambition, and explicit well-being objectives provides a theoretically rich context for examining how cognitive liberty principles can be operationalized within AI-driven urban environments.

## 3.3 Data Sources and Collection Strategy

This chapter is based on a documentary and comparative review of secondary sources published between 2018 and 2025. The objective of the search was conceptual alignment, not empirical validation. Accordingly, sources were selected for theoretical relevance, institutional credibility, and their triangulation value for analyzing cognitive sovereignty and happiness governance in AI-enabled urban contexts.

Source families. Four families of materials were considered:

- Governmental and strategic policy documents relevant to Dubai and the UAE (e.g., national and city strategies on AI, digital government, and happiness agenda) used to understand policy orientation, institutional architecture, and programmatic instruments.
- Intergovernmental ethical approach (e.g., UNESCO, OECD, European Union AI Act) employed as reference baselines for human-centric AI, mental privacy, accountability, and participation.
- Peer-reviewed academic literature in AI ethics, neurorights, and urban innovation (e.g., *Philosophy & Technology; Nature Machine Intelligence; Harvard Data Science Review; Annual Review of Psychology*) used to anchor concepts such as eudaimonia, capability-based evaluation, and cognitive liberty.
- Institutional research and white papers from recognized organizations (e.g., policy units and academic centers with established track records) used to contextualize governance practices and implementation narratives in the region.

Inclusion criteria. Items were retained when they met: (i) peer-reviewed or intergovernmental/official provenance with direct relevance to AI governance, neurotechnology ethics, or Dubai/UAE smart-city initiatives; and (ii) sufficient methodological clarity or official status.

Exclusion criteria. Materials were excluded when they: (a) lacked verifiable metadata or institutional authorship; (b) were opinion pieces without sources; (c) duplicated already-included items; or (d) pertained to jurisdictions or domains outside the scope of AI, neurorights, well-being policy, or smart-city governance.

Time window and currency checks: The 2018-2025 window was chosen to capture the most recent convergences among AI governance, neurorights, and well-being policy, with emphasis on works from the last three years to reflect regulatory maturation (e.g., OECD updates) and the adoption of the EU Artificial Intelligence Act in 2024. Draft or in-progress instruments (e.g., intergovernmental initiatives on neurotechnology ethics) were treated as contextual and clearly labeled as such.

Synthesis approach: Sources were mapped to a five-dimension benchmark lens (1) cognitive-liberty safeguards; (2) emotional well-being integration; (3) anticipatory regulation; (4) citizen-participation mechanisms; and (5) operational KPIs, to support narrative synthesis and comparative discussion across Dubai and reference regions (EU/OECD/UNESCO/Singapore/USA). The matrix served as a conceptual organizer only; no primary data collection, no inter-coder reliability statistics, and no quantitative meta-analysis were pursued. Insights were distilled into design principles and transferable lessons for human-centric AI in smart-city ecosystems.

## 3.4 Analytical Procedures

A documentary, comparative analysis was conducted using a structured narrative synthesis. Sources retained through the inclusion criteria were mapped to a five-dimension benchmark lens (1) cognitive-liberty safeguards, (2) emotional well-being integration, (3) anticipatory regulation, (4) citizen-participation mechanisms, and (5) operational KPIs. The procedure unfolded in three moves: (i) source mapping and extraction of significant provisions, definitions, and governance instruments; (ii) cross-jurisdictional comparison between Dubai/UAE and reference regions (EU/OECD/UNESCO/Singapore/USA); and (iii) integrative synthesis to distill recurring patterns and policy-relevant design principles for human-centric AI in smart-city settings.

The benchmark matrix operated solely as a conceptual organizer; no primary data collection, no inter-coder reliability statistics, and no quantitative meta-analysis were pursued.

## 3.5 Conceptual Model Development Process

Insights from the thematic and comparative analyses were synthesized to construct two original conceptual contributions:

1. **The Cognitive and Emotional Well-Being Index (CEWI)**: A proposed metric integrating four dimensions, cognitive autonomy, emotional resilience, mental privacy, and transparency perception, designed to evaluate how AI-driven urban environments impact citizen psychological sovereignty.

2. **The Neuroethics and Happiness Governance Model**: A strategic governance framework embedding Neurorights principles and happiness metrics within AI-driven smart city systems.

The conceptual model development followed an iterative process of theoretical integration, drawing upon both inductive insights from Dubai's governance innovations and deductive applications of established ethical model. The construction process adhered to Whetten's (1989) criteria for theoretical contribution, emphasizing conceptual completeness, parsimony, and logical coherence.

## 3.6 Validity, Reliability, and Limitations

To ensure conceptual and analytical robustness:

**Triangulation**: Cross-verification across academic, policy, and institutional sources enhanced the credibility and comprehensiveness of the analysis (Patton, 2015).

**Transparency**: Detailed documentation of analytical steps and theoretical decisions facilitates reproducibility and scholarly critique.

The study's primary limitation lies in its reliance on secondary data rather than primary empirical collection (e.g., stakeholder interviews, citizen surveys). This limitation is mitigated through systematic cross-validation across diverse secondary sources.

An additional limitation is that the Cognitive and Emotional Well-Being Index (CEWI) is presented as a conceptual model without empirical validation. The proposed measurement approach, including survey items and psychometric properties, requires pilot testing with actual citizen samples before implementation.

Future research should prioritize empirical validation studies to establish the reliability, validity, and practical applicability of the CEWI instrument in real-world smart city contexts. Nevertheless, future research is encouraged to empirically validate the proposed model through case studies, pilot projects, or citizen perception analyses.

## 4. RESULTS

### 4.1 Dubai's Integration of Happiness and AI Governance

Dubai launched the Happiness Agenda (2016), setting KPIs for citizen satisfaction, integrating happiness meters into services, and using AI-driven applications for well-being.

To illustrate how Dubai operationalizes happiness within its smart city ecosystem, Table 1 presents the integration of key strategies from the Happiness Agenda into AI-driven governance regulatory scheme.

*Table 1. Integration of Dubai's happiness agenda strategies within AI-driven smart city governance regulatory scheme*

| Strategy Element | Description | Integration with AI Governance |
|---|---|---|
| **Happiness Meter** | Real-time measurement of citizen satisfaction | AI-driven optimization of public services |
| **Digital Dubai Platform** | Centralized digital e-services | Predictive analytics for personalized citizen experiences |
| **Happiness Champions Program** | Training for service excellence in happiness delivery | AI-supported feedback loops for continuous improvement |
| **Blockchain Strategy** | Secure and transparent digital transactions | Privacy-preserving AI data management regulatory scheme |

*Note.* Elaborated by the author. Conceptual/illustrative synthesis by the author (no empirical data)

Despite advancements, mental privacy risks persist. Predictive cognitive technologies may influence decision-making without consent (Farahany, 2023).

Table 2 identifies the primary ethical risks emerging from predictive cognitive AI technologies and outlines potential mitigation strategies to safeguard cognitive liberty and mental privacy.

*Table 2. Identified ethical risks in predictive cognitive AI technologies and proposed mitigation strategies*

| Ethical Risk | Description | Potential Mitigation |
|---|---|---|
| **Mental Privacy Violation** | Inference of thoughts or emotions without explicit consent | Cognitive consent regulatory scheme and Cognitive-consent protocol |
| **Autonomy Erosion** | Unconscious influence on decision-making through AI systems | Transparency mandates and explainability requirements |
| **Emotional Manipulation** | Behavioral shaping through affective AI without awareness | Regulation of emotional AI use in public services |
| **Inequitable Access** | Digital divides in AI rights protection across populations | Inclusive policies ensuring equitable AI rights access |

*Note. Elaborated by the author.* Conceptual/illustrative synthesis by the author (no empirical data)

## 4.2 Development of the Cognitive and Emotional Well-Being Index (CEWI)

Building upon these comparative insights, this study applies the Cognitive and Emotional Well-Being Index (CEWI) as its analytical framework for operationalizing cognitive and emotional well-being in AI-driven smart governance.

CEWI integrates four interdependent dimensions that connect AI deployment with the protection of cognition and well-being in urban contexts Díaz-Llairó (2026):

1. Cognition & Clarity (C): the extent to which public services and AI-enabled interactions preserve citizens' capacity to understand, control, and question automated decisions affecting their lives.
2. Emotional Balance (E): emotional stability in digital environments and the absence of affective manipulation.
3. Well-being & Resilience (W): the ways in which digital services support (rather than undermine) psychological continuity and adaptive capacity in everyday urban life.
4. Integrity & Identity (I): protection of cognitive and emotional data, transparency and traceability of automated decisions, and congruence between personal values and digital systems.

In this chapter, CEWI functions solely as a conceptual scaffold to frame discussion and derive policy-relevant design principles such as trust-by-design, explicit cognitive consent, and participatory governance mechanisms. The analytical lens facilitates systematic analysis of how Dubai's happiness-oriented governance model addresses, or fails to address, cognitive and emotional dimensions that conventional smart city metrics overlook. For comprehensive treatment of CEWI's measurement methodology, psychometric validation, and organizational implementation protocols, see Díaz-Llairó (2026). The present analysis focuses exclusively on governance applications and policy implications for AI-driven smart cities.

## 4.3 Illustrative technologies and governance levers

In this chapter, the index functions purely as a conceptual scaffold, not a validated metric. Table 3 offers an illustrative mapping between technology families and governance levers aligned with its principles. It is an author's synthesis to support discussion; it does not report empirical scoring.

*Table 3. Emerging integration of happiness AI and cognitive AI in smart city governance*

| Technology Type | Governance Focus (aligned with CEWI) | Cognitive/Emotional Impact | Dubai Opportunity |
|---|---|---|---|
| **Emotion Recognition AI** | Emotional Balance | Enhanced tracking of emotional well-being/ responses | Integrate into Happiness Meter upgrades |
| **Predictive Cognitive AI** | Cognitive Clarity | Supports autonomy via clear, explainable, user-centric services | Pilot services with explicit cognitive-consent mechanisms |
| **Sentiment Analysis AI** | Well-being/Resilience | Population-level mood insights for resilience-oriented policy | Real-time happiness/resilience dashboards |
| **Neurorights Protection AI** | Identity/Integrity | Safeguards mental privacy and psychological continuity | Policy option: Neurorights Policy Lab for cognitive-privacy safeguards |
| **Affective Computing** | Emotional Balance *(with Clarity guardrails)* | Adaptive, empathy-aware service design | Personalization with transparency & opt-in guardrails |

Note. Elaborated by the author.

Opportunity for Dubai. Dubai can pioneer a Cognitive Autonomy and Happiness Protection Charter to formalize neurorights-aligned, outcome-based governance for smart services. Priority steps include: (i) establishing a Neuroethics & Happiness Task Force; (ii) piloting explicit cognitive-consent formats wherever affective/ cognitive inference is material; and (iii) launching a Neurorights Policy Lab to test transparency, contestability, and participation mechanisms across high-impact AI services. These actions would complement existing Happiness Agenda KPIs and Digital Dubai initiatives.

## 5. DISCUSSION

Recent interdisciplinary scholarship has increasingly addressed the intersection of artificial intelligence, emotional governance, and smart city innovation. Al-Azzawi (2021) presents Dubai's ABCDE model of happiness needs, exploring how AI applications can be structured to foster citizen well-being through initiatives like the Happy Cities Agenda (Al-Azzawi, 2021). Similarly, Adikari and Alahakoon (2021) propose an AI-based framework that captures the "emotional pulse" of urban populations using social media analytics, demonstrating the potential of AI to inform emotionally responsive governance in smart cities (Adikari & Alahakoon, 2021). Akhtar (2024) emphasizes the importance of emotional intelligence in AI-human synergy, revealing that emotion-understanding significantly enhances decision-making within smart urban systems (Akhtar, 2024). Sabri (2021) adds to this discourse by analyzing Dubai's IoT- based happiness strategy, emphasizing the role of technological integration in achieving social innovation and citizen satisfaction (Sabri, 2021).

On a broader philosophical and political level, Bratton (2021) proposes a generative design framework for AI urbanism that reconceptualizes platform cognition and algorithmic governance (Bratton, 2021). Complementing this, Calzada (2021) critiques technocratic smart city models and advocates for a redefinition of urban citizenship through data ownership and digital rights (Calzada, 2021). Together, these contributions inform a growing consensus that ethical AI governance must prioritize emotional well-being, cognitive liberty, and democratic participation as foundational principles.

While existing models emphasize sentiment detection or participatory governance, this study introduces the Cognitive and Emotional Well-Being Index (CEWI), a conceptual index focused on cognitive liberty and emotional sovereignty.

Unlike most Western models, which prioritize fairness, competition, or regulatory compliance in AI governance (Cowls & Floridi, 2018; Binns, 2018), Dubai's strategy centers on citizen well-being, cognitive sovereignty, and emotional resilience as fundamental pillars of digital transformation. This comprehensive vision challenges prevailing technological paradigms by positioning technology not merely as a driver of economic growth but as a moral instrument for enhancing human flourishing (Floridi, 2018).

Dubai operationalizes this philosophy through initiatives such as the Happiness Meter, the Digital Dubai Platform, and cognitive-friendly service innovations (Digital Dubai, 2020), aligning with anticipatory governance models that emphasize cognitive sovereignty and emotional integrity (Ienca & Andorno, 2017; Yuste et al., 2017).

## 5.1 The Distinctiveness of Dubai's Governance Approach

Unlike the European Union's AI Act or UNESCO's AI Ethics Recommendation, which reference emotional and cognitive aspects under broad human-dignity principles (European Commission, 2024; UNESCO, 2021), Dubai translates happiness and cognitive well-being into government KPIs monitored through the Happiness Meter and citizen-satisfaction indicators. In this subsection, *operationalized* means: (i) a measurable indicator is defined in an official instrument, (ii) baseline/targets are stated, and (iii) periodic public reporting is specified. Situated within the UAE's emphasis on collective well-being and leadership accountability, this design reflects cultural contextualization rather than simple policy transfer.

Table 4 applies this coding scheme to compare how selected jurisdictions integrate cognitive and emotional dimensions in AI governance.

*Table 4. Comparative analysis of cognitive and emotional integration in AI governance regulatory scheme. Coding categories: Documented / Operationalized / Not included.*

| Jurisdiction | Cognitive Liberty/ Sovereignty in Policy | Emotional Well-being Provisions | Happiness KPI (measurable) | Regulatory Style | Document Status (draft/ adopted/implemented/ evaluated) |
|---|---|---|---|---|---|
| **Dubai (UAE)** | Documented integration: National AI Strategy and Happiness Agenda reference cognitive well-being (UAE Government, 2021; Digital Dubai, 2020) | Operationalized: Happiness Meter & citizen-satisfaction KPIs with systematic tracking (Digital Dubai, 2020) | Operationalized: quantified happiness metrics | Anticipatory, innovation-enabling | Implemented |
| **European Union** | Implicit protection via fundamental rights in AI Act (European Parliament, 2024) | Aspirational statements; not operationalized | Not included as governance objective | Risk-based regulatory compliance | Adopted (2024) |
| **Singapore** | Acknowledged within Model AI Governance Framework / Smart Nation | Efficiency/ trust focus; not operationalized for subjective well-being | Not included; economic/innovation metrics prioritized | Principle-based with sectoral guidelines | Framework published; sectorial roll-out ongoing |
| **United States** | Fragmented, sector-specific guidance; no comprehensive federal cognitive-rights framework | Minimal well-being integration at federal level | Not included; competitiveness prioritized | Reactive and decentralized | Executive orders & sectoral guidance; no unified framework |

Note. Elaborated by the author. Note. Author's coding based on documentary analysis of official policy texts and peer-reviewed literature (2020-2025). "Operationalized" = indicator defined + baseline/target + stated reporting cadence. The table evaluates policy design only; empirical effectiveness is outside this subsection's scope.

Among the jurisdictions analyzed, Dubai is the only case classified as operationalized for both cognitive and emotional dimensions, linking happiness and cognitive well-being to measurable government KPIs within an anticipatory policy design. This does not imply broader leadership across all AI domains; rather, it highlights a distinctive governance dimension, metric-based treatment of cognitive/emotional outcomes.

While Table 4 focuses on governance regulatory scheme, strengths vary across the AI ecosystem. The United States leads in neurorights scholarship (e.g., Columbia University's NeuroRights Initiative; work on mental privacy at Duke) and private-sector affective-AI innovation (e.g., Affectiva, Hume AI). Singapore excels in public-private partnerships and smart-city infrastructure. The European Union has established the most comprehensive risk-based regulatory architecture. Dubai's contribution in this comparison is the operationalization of cognitive and emotional well-being as explicit, measurable governance outcomes.

## 5.2 CEWI: Conceptual Scaffold

The Cognitive and Emotional Well-Being Index is advanced here as a conceptual lens, not a validated measurement instrument. It organizes governance analysis around four interrelated pillars: Cognition & Clarity (C), Emotional Balance (E), Well-being & Resilience (W), and Integrity & Identity (I), as defined in Section 4.2.

In this chapter, CEWI functions solely as an analytical scaffold to frame discussion and derive policy-relevant design principles (e.g., trust-by-design, explicit cognitive consent, participation mechanisms). No items, scoring rules, targets, or audit workflows are proposed, and empirical validation is left for future research.

## 5.3 The Rise of Cognitive and Emotional AI: New Ethical Frontiers

Emerging AI technologies such as brain-computer interfaces (BCIs), emotion recognition algorithms, and predictive cognitive analytics, are redefining the ethical context of digital governance. These innovations push data-driven interaction toward the core of human cognition and affect, creating risks and governance challenges not fully anticipated by existing regulatory scheme (Ienca & Andorno, 2017; Bublitz, 2014).

Cognitive AI refers to systems designed to infer thoughts, preferences, intentions, and mental states from brain signals, micro-behaviors, and physiological indicators (Ienca & Andorno, 2017). Examples include BCIs that translate neural activity into digital commands, enabling significant clinical applications, while also raising concerns about cognitive liberty and mental privacy (Yuste et al., 2017).

Emotional AI, in turn, aims to infer, categorize, and respond to human emotions using cues such as facial expression, voice, posture, and biometrics. These systems are increasingly used across marketing, education, recruitment, and public safety to assess emotional states in real time (Picard, 2010; Calvo & D'Mello, 2010; McStay, 2018).

While these technologies promise benefits, improved accessibility, more responsive services, and tailored support, they also introduce complex risks. Without anticipatory safeguards, cognitive AI may drift toward mental surveillance, where inferences about thoughts or intentions are extracted without meaningful consent; emotional AI may enable manipulative targeting based on inferred vulnerabilities (Ienca et al., 2018; McStay, 2018; Pascual-Ezama et al., 2022). In this context,

Dubai's opportunity lies in moving beyond traditional data-protection paradigms toward cognitive and emotional sovereignty as explicit governance outcomes.

*Figure 1. Conceptual risk spectrum for cognitive and emotional AI*

*Note. Illustrative synthesis by the author (no empirical scoring). The spectrum depicts four axes: (a) proximity to cognition/affect (from behavioral proxies neural-adjacent data); (b) intrusiveness of inference (from sentiment tagging intent prediction); (c) potential harms (from opaque personalization autonomy and continuity erosion); and (d) safeguards (cognitive consent, purpose limitation, explainability, oversight, participation).*

Scholars argue that classic data-protection tools (e.g., generalized consent, de-identification) are not sufficient on their own for these domains; anticipatory governance is required, combining cognitive-privacy safeguards, explicit consent for cognitive/emotional inference, explainability and recourse, and risk-based oversight (Floridi & Cowls, 2019; Mantelero, 2021; Zicari et al., 2021). Similarly, the challenge is not only technical but profoundly ethical: ensuring that the deployment of cognitive and emotional AI systems respects the integrity of thought and psychological continuity, rather than reducing persons to data points for prediction and control (Bublitz, 2014).

Recognizing these risks early, Dubai can consolidate its position by embedding cognitive liberty and emotional resilience as policy outcomes within smart-city governance, complementing existing happiness-oriented metrics and data-governance practices (Digital Dubai, 2020; UAE Government, 2021).

## 5.4 Emerging Trends: Happiness AI and the Future of Emotional Governance

Building upon these cognitive and emotional AI frontiers, the convergence of Happiness AI with emotional governance represents a critical evolution in smart city innovation. Happiness AI, understood here as systems that seek to model, support, or optimize individual and collective well-being, is converging with Emotional AI, which infers and responds to affective states from multimodal signals. This frontier is promising yet ethically demanding, because it brings optimization logics into domains tied to autonomy, authenticity, and dignity (Calvo & D'Mello, 2010; Picard, 2010).

On the opportunity side, emotion-aware analytics can help cities tailor services in health, education, and social support, for example, by identifying populations at risk of distress and enabling early, proportionate interventions (Pascual-Ezama et al., 2022). Conversely, without robust guardrails, these systems can drift into emotional surveillance, manipulative targeting, or commodification of inner states (Mantelero, 2021). Ethical AI scholarship therefore stresses that optimizing for momentary satisfaction must not override deeper rights related to cognitive autonomy and emotional authenticity, and calls for accountable, testable governance mechanisms rather than principle-only declarations (Floridi & Cowls, 2019; Jobin, Ienca, & Vayena, 2019).

Implementation requires transparent inference protocols, consent formats specific to affective/cognitive data, and resilience-oriented indicators that track whether digital services protect, rather than erode, psychological continuity (Zicari et al., 2021; Calvo & Peters, 2014). In practice, participatory infrastructures can enhance legitimacy and trust, e.g., civic platforms that co-design data and AI policies and publish audit outcomes, illustrating how deliberation complements technical safeguards (Borge et al., 2022).

Building on existing happiness-oriented strategies, Dubai can align Happiness AI with cognitive and emotional sovereignty by (i) embedding resilience-focused indicators in service evaluation; (ii) requiring explicit, revocable consent when affective or cognitive inference is material to the service; and (iii) instituting independent oversight with public reporting. These steps would complement intergovernmental ethical baselines and position outcome-oriented governance as compatible with autonomy-preserving design (Floridi & Cowls, 2019; Zicari et al., 2021).

## 5.5 Institutionalizing Neurorights: A Strategic Imperative

The concept of Neurorights, as proposed by Yuste et al. (2017), offers a significant analytical lens for safeguarding cognitive sovereignty in an era increasingly shaped by neurotechnologies and cognitive artificial intelligence systems. These rights include mental privacy, cognitive liberty, the preservation of personal identity, fair access to cognitive enhancement, and protection against algorithmic bias. Despite their critical relevance, no smart city to date has formally institutionalized these principles within its governance structures. Dubai, with its anticipatory governance approach and commitment to citizen well-being, is strategically positioned to pioneer the operationalization of Neurorights within a smart city context, thereby reinforcing its global leadership in ethical AI innovation.

Leading scholars emphasize the urgency of formalizing cognitive protections. Farahany (2023) warns that absent mental privacy protections could enable complex brain surveillance threatening autonomy. Floridi (2018) insists that AI governance must embed cognitive and emotional data protection to ensure human flourishing remains central to technological advancement.

By formally adopting a Neurorights framework, Dubai could lead a global movement to recalibrate AI development along ethical, human-centered lines. This would involve embedding Neurorights into AI governance guidelines, mandating Cognitive Consent protocols for all emotional and cognitive data usage, and developing NeuroEthical Risk Assessments for all AI-driven projects across public and private sectors. These strategic actions would ensure that future AI applications protect mental autonomy, emotional resilience, and psychological continuity from their design stages through to their deployment.

## 5.6 Strengthening Participatory Governance and Transparency

Ethical governance in AI must evolve beyond purely top-down strategies toward inclusive, participatory models that ensure citizen voices are actively integrated into decision-making processes. The legitimacy, resilience, and societal acceptance of smart governance increasingly depend on fostering public trust through transparent and deliberative mechanisms (Floridi & Cowls, 2019; Mantelero, 2021). International examples provide powerful evidence of how participatory approaches can successfully complement technological innovation in governance.

*Barcelona's Decidim* platform represents a sophisticated experiment in democratic digital governance, enabling citizens to propose, debate, and co-create public policies including AI deployment and data ethics (Borge et al., 2022). Research documents that participatory infrastructures like Decidim are crucial not merely for transparency but for empowering citizens to shape ethical architectures underpinning digital ecosystems (Peña-López, 2020; Subirats, 2020).

Similarly, Taiwan's vTaiwan project offers a compelling case of digital deliberation where citizens engage directly with policymakers on complex technological issues, including AI regulation. According to Kuo (2020), vTaiwan demonstrates that structured, transparent, and inclusive citizen consultations can significantly enhance the democratic legitimacy of AI-related legislation and foster societal trust in digital transformation processes.

Drawing inspiration from these leading models, Dubai can further reinforce its leadership by establishing AI Citizen Assemblies tasked with co-designing ethical AI policies across sectors. Such assemblies would empower citizens to participate meaningfully in the ethical, cognitive, and emotional dimensions of AI governance. Additionally, launching Cognitive Privacy Public Forums would create spaces for citizen feedback on how emotional and cognitive data are inferred, collected, and applied, ensuring that consent and trust are continuously maintained. Implementing Transparent Cognitive Data Policies that clearly explain the logic, usage, and impact of AI inferences would further enhance public understanding and accountability, aligning Dubai's smart governance with emerging standards of digital ethics.

## 5.7 Toward a Cognitive and Emotional Well-Being Index (CEWI)

Dubai's Happiness Agenda already offers an innovative approach to tracking subjective well-being as a key governance metric. However, the next generation of smart governance demands models capable of capturing the nuanced intersections between cognitive liberty, emotional integrity, and AI integration. Building on these advancements, the Cognitive and Emotional Well-Being Index (CEWI) is proposed as a strategic analytical lens.

The index includes four interconnected dimensions: mental autonomy satisfaction, referring to the extent to which citizens perceive their cognitive freedom remains intact amidst AI systems; cognitive trust in AI, meaning public confidence in the ethical and transparent management of cognitive and emotional data; emotional resilience outcomes, capturing citizens' ability to maintain psychological stability and adaptive capacity in technologically mediated environments; and transparency perception, namely citizens' understanding of when and how cognitive/emotional data may be inferred or used, together with the availability of clear explanations and avenues for redress.

Recent studies highlight that, without anticipatory safeguards, AI-driven cognitive profiling risks reinforcing behavioral predictability and psychological conformity, undermining cognitive diversity essential for resilient democratic societies (Stillwell, 2021; Rahwan, 2020). Integrating cognitive-diversity indicators within the index can therefore strengthen citizen autonomy and societal adaptability in the face of pervasive digital influences.

Leading scholars emphasize the necessity of such integrated governance model. Yuste et al. (2017) stress that governance models must explicitly protect cognitive liberty as core human rights in the neurotechnology age. Scholars such as Floridi (2018), Pentland (2014), Rahwan (2020), and Stillwell (2021) argue that anticipatory governance must embed measurable emotional and cognitive resilience indicators into regulatory scheme, aligning digital environments with human well-being goals rather than economic optimization alone.

## 6. CONCLUSIONS AND POLICY PROPOSAL

Safeguarding cognitive liberty, emotional well-being, and happiness must become foundational pillars of smart city governance in the age of artificial intelligence. As AI technologies evolve toward interpreting human cognition and emotion, protecting the autonomy of thought, feeling, and mental privacy emerges as a new frontier of fundamental human rights (Ienca & Andorno, 2017; Yuste et al., 2017). Dubai's model demonstrates that it is possible to humanize AI innovation, aligning rapid technological advancement with the enduring protection of human dignity, emotional resilience, and societal flourishing.

Unlike many global smart city initiatives, Dubai's integration of happiness metrics into governance scheme offers a forward-thinking and operationalized approach. The emphasis on citizen well-being as a measurable outcome of technological development marks a profound philosophical shift: technology must exist to serve humanity, not dominate it (Floridi, 2018). In this respect, Dubai stands as a valuable case study for cities worldwide seeking to embed ethical, cognitive, and emotional considerations into AI-driven governance systems (Digital Dubai, 2020).

### Theoretical Contributions

This study advances emerging literature by bridging the gap between AI technological capabilities and human rights regulatory scheme, proposing an integrated model where cognitive liberty, mental privacy, emotional sovereignty, and happiness governance are harmonized within AI ethics discourse. It enriches theoretical debates on Neurorights (Yuste et al., 2017) and contributes to expanding the applicability of cognitive and emotional well-being regulatory scheme within urban governance contexts.

## Practical Implications

Dubai's leadership offers concrete and actionable insights for policymakers and urban innovation strategists aiming to future-proof cities against the ethical risks posed by cognitive and emotional AI technologies. By formalizing cognitive and emotional rights within AI governance schemes, cities can foster resilient environments that protect mental integrity while embracing the opportunities of ethical technological advancement (Farahany, 2023). Integrating happiness metrics, cognitive sovereignty, and emotional well-being as measurable governance objectives could inspire a new wave of human-centered innovation, leading to more inclusive and ethically robust smart city models.

## Limitations

This research primarily relies on secondary data sources, including strategic reports, policy documents, and peer-reviewed academic publications. Although triangulation techniques were employed to enhance analytical robustness, the absence of primary empirical validation, such as interviews with policymakers, citizens, or AI developers, constitutes a limitation. Additionally, the rapid evolution of AI and neurotechnologies may introduce new governance challenges that were not fully anticipated within the current study (Floridi, 2018).

Future iterations of this research would benefit from longitudinal studies capturing the real-world impacts of AI governance strategies on cognitive autonomy, emotional resilience, and public trust, alongside cross-cultural empirical comparisons of smart governance models.

## Future Research

Future research should prioritize empirical investigations into citizen perceptions of cognitive privacy, emotional well-being, and trust in AI-integrated environments. Comparative case studies analyzing different cultural and political contexts would elucidate how diverse governance models succeed or fail in operationalizing cognitive and emotional rights protection. Cross-jurisdictional studies comparing Dubai's operationalized happiness KPIs with European risk-based approaches, Singaporean efficiency-driven analytical lens, and U.S. innovation-centered models would reveal the contextual factors that enable or constrain the integration of cognitive sovereignty into smart city governance. Likewise, interdisciplinary collaborations, bridging law, neuroscience, ethics, urban planning, and AI engineering, will be essential to design dynamic, adaptive, and resilient ethical governance frameworks for emerging neurotechnologies and affective AI.

Longitudinal research examining how cognitive and emotional sovereignty metrics evolve over time in response to AI policy interventions could further enrich the understanding of sustainable digital governance practices. Such studies could track whether operationalized happiness metrics genuinely enhance citizen autonomy or risk becoming instruments of subtle behavioral control, a critical distinction for preserving democratic values in AI-driven urban environments.

Additionally, participatory action research engaging diverse citizen groups, including vulnerable populations and marginalized communities, would ensure that cognitive liberty protections do not inadvertently replicate existing inequalities in access to mental privacy safeguards.

Finally, pilot validation studies testing CEWI dimensions across varied urban contexts would establish baseline psychometric properties, enabling cities to adapt the framework to local cultural values while maintaining core protections for mental autonomy, cognitive trust, emotional resilience, and transparency perception. For a complete description of the CEWI model, its measurement dimensions, practical cases and governance applications, see Díaz-Llairó (2026) .

## Strategic Vision for Dubai's Cognitive and Happiness Governance Future

As AI technologies advance toward more sophisticated cognitive and emotional interpretations, the need to safeguard mental privacy and cognitive liberty becomes increasingly urgent. Building on its proactive integration of happiness-driven governance strategies, Dubai possesses a unique strategic opportunity to formalize its global leadership in cognitive rights protection and emotional governance.

## Policy Proposal: Establishing a Global Center for Cognitive and Happiness AI Governance in Dubai

In light of its advanced trajectory, Dubai could further consolidate its global leadership by establishing a Global Center for Cognitive and Happiness AI Governance. This center would serve as a premier international hub for interdisciplinary research, regulatory innovation, and capacity building, dedicated to advancing ethical, cognitive, and emotional dimensions of AI governance.

Its mission would encompass fostering anticipatory regulation, operationalizing Neurorights, and promoting participatory governance models for cognitively and emotionally sustainable urban innovation.

By leading these initiatives, Dubai could inspire a global movement toward ethical, citizen-centered smart cities, helping ensure that technological progress enhances and safeguards the human condition. Taken together, these innovations may inform future ethical perspective that prioritize cognitive freedom and collective well-being.

## Declarations

**Funding.** The author received no specific funding for this work.

**Conflicts of interest.** The author declares no conflict of interest.

**Author contributions.** Sole author.

**Ethics Approval and Consent.** Not applicable (conceptual/theoretical chapter with no human-subjects data).

**Data Availability.** No new data were created or analyzed in this study.

## REFERENCES


Adikari, A., & Alahakoon, D. (2021). Understanding citizens' emotional pulse in a smart city using artificial intelligence. *IEEE Transactions on Industrial Informatics, 17*(4), 2743–2751. DOI: 10.1109/TII.2020.3009277

Akhtar, S. (2024). *Harmonizing human-AI synergy in smart cities: Exploring emotion understanding and technology anxiety in an Asian context.* The Asian Bulletin of Business and Social Science Research., DOI: 10.62019/abbssr.v4i1.47

Al-Azzawi, A. (2021). AI & well-being: Can AI make you happy in the city? In *Artificial Intelligence in the Gulf* (pp. 55-80). https://doi.org/DOI: 10.1007/978-981-16-0771-4_9

Binns, R. (2018). Fairness in machine learning: Lessons from political philosophy. *Proceedings of the 2018 Conference on Fairness, Accountability and Transparency (FAT*)*, 81, 149-159. *Proceedings of Machine Learning Research (PMLR).* Retrieved from https://proceedings.mlr.press/v81/binns18a.html

Borge, R., Balcells, J., & Padró-Solanet, A. (2022). Democratic disruption or continuity? Analysis of the Decidim platform in Catalan municipalities. *The American Behavioral Scientist.* Advance online publication. DOI: 10.1177/00027642221092798

Bratton, B. (2021). AI urbanism: A design framework for governance, program, and platform cognition. *AI & Society, 36*(4), 1307–1312. DOI: 10.1007/s00146-020-01121-9

Bublitz, J. C. (2014). *Freedom of thought in the age of neuroscience.* Archiv für Rechts- und Sozialphilosophie, 100(1), 1-25. https://doi.org/DOI: 10.25162/arsp-2014-0001

Calvo, R. A., & D'Mello, S. (2010). Affect detection: An interdisciplinary review of models, methods, and their applications. *IEEE Transactions on Affective Computing, 1*(1), 18–37. DOI: 10.1109/T-AFFC.2010.1

Calvo, R. A., & Peters, D. (2014). *Positive Computing: Technology for Well-Being and Human Potential.* MIT Press., DOI: 10.7551/mitpress/9764.001.0001

Calzada, I. (2021). *Book review: Smart city citizenship.* International Journal of Contemporary Urban Affairs., DOI: 10.25034/ijcua.2021.v5n1-7

Casas, I., & Morozov, E. (2022). Reclaiming democratic control in digital governance: Lessons from Barcelona's Decidim. *Journal of Urban Technology, 29*(2), 3–21. DOI: 10.1080/10630732.2022.2052128

Cowls, J., & Floridi, L. (2018). Prolegomena to a white paper on an ethical framework for a good AI society. *Minds and Machines*, *28*(4), 689–707. DOI: 10.1007/s11023-018-9482-5 PMID: 30930541

Díaz-Llairó, M. A. (2025). *AI for human excellence: Ethics, Well-Being & Governance for AI-Ready Talent*. KDP.

Díaz-Llairó, M. A. (2025). Exploring a smart city and the epicenter of megatrends in innovation with artificial intelligence: The case of Dubai. In Saura, J. R. (Ed.), *Data-driven governance through AI, digital marketing, and the privacy interplay* (pp. 191–200). IGI Global., DOI: 10.4018/979-8-3693-6945-6.ch008

Digital Dubai. (2020). *Dubai Happiness Agenda: Strategy and Implementation Report*. Dubai Government Publications.

Eisenhardt, K. M., & Graebner, M. E. (2007). Theory building from cases: Opportunities and challenges. *Academy of Management Journal*, *50*(1), 25–32. DOI: 10.5465/amj.2007.24160888

European Commission. (2024, August 1). *AI Act enters into force*. Retrieved October 15, 2025, from https://ec.europa.eu/commission/presscorner/detail/en/ip_24_4761

European Parliament. (2024, March 13). *Artificial Intelligence Act: MEPs adopt landmark law*. Retrieved October 15, 2025, from https://www.europarl.europa.eu/news/en/press-room/20240308IPR19015

Farahany, N. A. (2023). *The battle for your brain: Defending the right to think freely in the age of neurotechnology*. St. Martin's Press.

Floridi, L. (2018). Soft ethics and the governance of the digital. *Philosophy & Technology*, *31*(1), 1–8. DOI: 10.1007/s13347-018-0303-9 PMID: 30322997

Floridi, L., & Cowls, J. (2019). A unified framework of five principles for AI in society. *Harvard Data Science Review*. Advance online publication. DOI: 10.1162/99608f92.8cd550d1

Flyvbjerg, B. (2006). Five misunderstandings about case-study research. *Qualitative Inquiry*, *12*(2), 219–245. DOI: 10.1177/1077800405284363

Government, U. A. E. (2021). UAE Centennial 2071. https://u.ae/en/about-the-uae/strategies-initiatives-and-awards/strategies-plans-and-visions/innovation-and-future-shaping/uae-centennial-2071

Ienca, M., & Andorno, R. (2017). Towards new human rights in the age of neuroscience and neurotechnology. *Life Sciences, Society and Policy*, *13*(1), 5. DOI: 10.1186/s40504-017-0050-1 PMID: 28444626

Ienca, M., Wangmo, T., Jotterand, F., Kressig, R. W., & Elger, B. (2018). Ethical design of intelligent assistive technologies for dementia: A systematic review. *Science and Engineering Ethics*, *24*(6), 1797–1830. DOI: 10.1007/s11948-017-9976-1 PMID: 28940133

Jobin, A., Ienca, M., & Vayena, E. (2019). The global landscape of AI ethics guidelines. *Nature Machine Intelligence*, *1*(9), 389–399. DOI: 10.1038/s42256-019-0088-2

Kuo, C. (2020). Taiwan's vTaiwan: Citizen deliberation on technology and AI governance. *Journal of Public Deliberation*, *16*(2), 2. Advance online publication. DOI: 10.16997/jdd.378

Mantelero, A. (2021). Beyond data protection: Exploring the ethical and social implications of data-driven research and innovation. *Computer Law & Security Review*, *41*, 105545. DOI: 10.1016/j.clsr.2021.105545

McStay, A. (2018). Emotional AI: The rise of empathic media. *Sage (Atlanta, Ga.)*. Advance online publication. DOI: 10.4135/9781526451293

OECD. (2020). *How's Life? 2020: Measuring well-being*. Organisation for Economic Co-operation and Development.

OECD. (2024). OECD AI Principles. https://oecd.ai/en/ai-principles

Pascual-Ezama, D., (2022). Towards an emotionally aware AI: Ethical considerations and societal impact. *AI & Society*, *37*(4), 1379–1391.

Patton, M. Q. (2015). *Qualitative research & evaluation methods* (4th ed.). Sage Publications.

Peña-López, I. (2020). Citizen participation and the digital age: Barcelona's Decidim. *Journal of Public Policy & Marketing*, *39*(4), 411–426.

Pentland, A. (2014). *Social physics: How social networks can make us smarter*. Penguin Press.

Picard, R. W. (2010). Affective Computing: From Laughter to IEEE. *IEEE Transactions on Affective Computing*, *1*(1), 11–17. DOI: 10.1109/T-AFFC.2010.10

Rahwan, I. (2020). Society-in-the-loop: Programming the algorithmic social contract. *Ethics and Information Technology*, *22*(1), 5–14. DOI: 10.1007/s10676-017-9430-8

Ryan, R. M., & Deci, E. L. (2001). On happiness and human potentials: A review of research on hedonic and eudaimonic well-being. *Annual Review of Psychology*, *52*(1), 141–166. DOI: 10.1146/annurev.psych.52.1.141 PMID: 11148302

Sabri, S. (2021). Smart Dubai IoT strategy: Aspiring to the promotion of happiness for residents and visitors through a continuous commitment to innovation. In *Smart Cities and Urban Transformation*. https://doi.org/DOI: 10.1016/B978-0-12-818886-6.00010-1

Stillwell, D. (2021). Psychological profiling and privacy: How technology shapes personality perception. *Nature Human Behaviour*, *5*, 1590–1591.

Subirats, J. (2020). Democratic innovation and AI governance: Lessons from Barcelona. *Urban Studies Journal*, *57*(7), 1401–1420.

Suddaby, R. (2006). *From the editors: What grounded theory is not.* Academy of Management Journal, 49(4), 633-642. https://doi.org/DOI: 10.5465/amj.2006.22083020

UNESCO. (2021). *Recommendation on the Ethics of Artificial Intelligence*. United Nations Educational, Scientific and Cultural Organization.

Whetten, D. A. (1989). What constitutes a theoretical contribution? *Academy of Management Review*, *14*(4), 490–495. DOI: 10.2307/258554

Yin, R. K. (2018). *Case study research and applications: Design and methods* (6th ed.). Sage Publications.

Yuste, R., Goering, S., Agüera y Arcas, B., Bi, G., Carmena, J. M., Carter, A., Chun, M., Illes, J., Kellmeyer, P., Klein, E., Marblestone, A., Mitchell, C., Parens, E., Pham, M., Rubel, A., Sadato, N., Specker Sullivan, L., Teicher, M., Wasserman, D., & Wolpaw, J. (2017). Four ethical priorities for neurotechnologies and AI. *Nature*, *551*(7679), 159–163. DOI: 10.1038/551159a PMID: 29120438

Zicari, R. V., Brodersen, J., Brusseau, J., Dudley, J. T., Eichinger, F., Ivanov, T., Kararigas, G., Kringen, P., McCullough, M., Osman, A. M., Schnebel, E., Southby, D., Staab, S., Taddeo, M., Vayena, E., Vestergaard, M., & Floridi, L. (2021). Z-Inspection®: A process to assess trustworthy AI. *IEEE Transactions on Technology and Society*, *2*(2), 83–97. DOI: 10.1109/TTS.2021.3066209

# Chapter 11
# AI and the Transformation of the Public Sector in Morocco:
## A Quantitative Study of Ethical Dilemmas in Governance and Law

**Saida Ifiss**
https://orcid.org/0009-0001-3491-0104
*Mohammed Premier University, Oujda, Morocco*

## ABSTRACT

*The introduction of artificial intelligence (AI) into Moroccan public governance is changing the organizational mode of delivery, the decision-making processes, and the relationship between the state and citizens. This chapter discusses opportunities and ethical challenges linked to AI adoption in public organizations in Morocco, based on a quantitative analysis of 270 observations. The chapter examines the implications of AI systems (RPA, machine learning (ML), NLP, and computer vision) on performance, transparency, accountability, and identify possible risks associated with bias and discrimination. We use Random Forest and SVM to identify important variables, and make predictions about the links between AI adoption, governance and performance. We find that while AI systems contribute to improved quality and speed of service delivery, they come with ethical challenges with respect to justice, privacy and democratic legitimacy. We offer some strategic recommendations for the responsible, ethical integration of AI systems in the Moroccan context.*

DOI: 10.4018/979-8-3373-4480-5.ch011

## INTRODUCTION

Artificial intelligence (AI) is today asserting itself as an essential catalyst for transformation in public administrations. Long considered a technical tool confined to the private sector, AI is now at the heart of government strategies, aimed at improving performance, transparency and citizen satisfaction (Jordan & Mitchell, 2015). This technological revolution is not limited to operational adjustments: it is reconfiguring the very logic of public decision-making and, by extension, the foundations of democratic governance.

In the Moroccan context, the digitization of public services is a national priority, illustrated by the *Maroc Digital 2030 Strategy* (Ministry of Digital Transition and Administration Reform, 2024), which aims to modernize the State, increase competitiveness and strengthen citizen confidence. However, this dynamic of innovation is accompanied by crucial questions: how can we guarantee justice and fairness in a world where decisions are partially delegated to algorithmic systems? How can we ensure transparency and accountability when decision-making mechanisms become opaque and technical (Heald, 2006)?

These questions raise *ethical dilemmas*:

- *Algorithmic bias and discrimination*: Algorithms can reproduce, or even amplify, existing inequalities (O'Neil, 2016).
- *Privacy and surveillance*: AI, by processing massive volumes of data, poses major risks for the protection of personal data (Zuboff, 2019).
- *Decision-making opacity*: The internal logic of AI systems, often described as "black box", complicates traceability and public accountability (Goodfellow et al., 2016).

These risks, far from being hypothetical, are illustrated by concrete examples on an international scale, such as the use of predictive AI in justice or the police, which raises accusations of racial and social bias. Yet in a country like Morocco, where the digital transition coincides with far-reaching institutional reforms, the stakes are twofold: taking advantage of the opportunities offered by AI while consolidating democratic and legal gains.

Thus, the issue underlying this chapter is as follows:

To what extent does the integration of AI in Moroccan public administrations influence governance and performance, and what ethical dilemmas arise from this?

To answer this, we adopt an empirical approach based on:

- *A quantitative diagnosis* of the integration of AI technologies in the Moroccan public sector (2018-2022).

- *A predictive modeling* of the relationships between AI adoption, transparency, efficiency and ethical perception via algorithms (Random Forest and SVM).
- *An analysis of ethical and legal risks*, contextualized within the Moroccan framework.

The originality of this research lies in its integrated approach combining:

1. *Principles of good governance* (transparency, accountability, participation);
2. *Machine learning analytical tools* to identify key determinants;
3. *A focus on Morocco*, where few empirical studies of this type exist (Taibi & Benabdelhadi, 2020).

This chapter aims not only to fill an academic gap, but also to formulate *operational recommendations* for Moroccan public decision-makers, in order to promote AI that is ethical, inclusive and in line with democratic norms.

The main objective of this chapter is to assess the impact of AI on Moroccan public governance by integrating a central ethical dimension. Its contribution can be broken down into three points:

- *Methodological innovation*: The joint use of statistical analysis and machine learning models (Random Forest and SVM) to predict the effects of AI on governance.
- *Contextual relevance*: An empirical study based on a representative sample of Moroccan public organizations, in a field that has yet to be fully explored.
- *Normative and strategic contribution*: Recommendations for the responsible integration of AI, in line with the values of transparency, accountability and equity.

The conceptual framework is based on a general hypothesis:

AI adoption improves organizational performance, but raises moderating ethical dilemmas affecting transparency, equity and democratic legitimacy.

# 1. THEORETICAL FRAMEWORK AND LITERATURE REVIEW

## 1.1 Good Governance and Public Performance

The concept of *good governance* is central to contemporary thinking on the modernization of public administrations. Defined by the World Bank and the OECD as a set of principles designed to guarantee the effectiveness and legitimacy of institutions, it rests on the fundamental pillars of *transparency*, *accountability*, *citizen participation*, *efficiency*, *equity* and the *rule of law* (OECD, 2020; Bovens, 2007). These principles are not merely normative ideals, but are essential conditions for consolidating trust between the state and its citizens.

Transparency means making information on administrative decisions and processes accessible, thus enabling effective democratic control (Heald, 2006). Accountability means holding public decision-makers responsible for their actions, both to the institutions of control and to citizens (Bovens, 2007). Finally, citizen participation reflects the inclusiveness of public policies, ensuring that stakeholders can influence the decisions that affect them (Kooiman, 2003).

*Public performance* is multidimensional, integrating:

- *Operational effectiveness*, measured by the speed and reliability of services rendered;
- *Economic efficiency*, aimed at optimizing the allocation of financial and human resources;
- *Service quality*, including user satisfaction and accessibility;
- *Democratic legitimacy*, based on citizens' perception of justice and transparency in decision-making processes (Behn, 2003; Van Dooren et al., 2010).

In Morocco, the *2011 Constitution* establishes good governance as a fundamental principle, reflected in several structuring reforms: the *National Charter for Administrative Deconcentration*, the *Maroc Digital 2030 Strategy*, and the creation of control institutions such as the *Cour des Comptes* and the *CNDP* (Commission Nationale de Protection des Données Personnelles). These initiatives aim to enhance transparency and accelerate the digitization of public services. However, empirical evaluation reveals *persistent challenges*:

- *Bureaucratic complexity*, hampering the fluidity of procedures ;
- *Organizational inertia*, hampering the implementation of reforms;
- *Weak digitalization in certain entities*, limiting overall efficiency (Taibi & Benabdelhadi, 2020).

In this context, artificial intelligence appears to be a strategic tool for overcoming these obstacles. It enables the automation of repetitive tasks, such as processing administrative files or document archiving, thus reducing the bureaucratic burden. AI systems also bring predictive analysis capabilities, useful for budget planning or fraud detection (Davenport & Ronanki, 2018). In addition, *automatic natural language processing (NLP)* technologies facilitate interaction with citizens via chatbots, improving the accessibility and quality of public service.

Nevertheless, these technical advantages entail substantial risks. The privatization of decision making is a cause for significant concern from the view of procedural justice and democratic control. A problem associated with AI systems and algorithms is their black box nature, which reveals an opacity of process that further obscures the traceability of decisions (Goodfellow et al., 2016). Algorithms can also reproduce conscious (or unconscious) biases present in learning data and create forms of systemic discrimination (O'Neil, 2016).

Overall, the implications of AI for public performance are confused by structural ambivalence:

- *Direct positive effects*: efficiency gains (reduced delays, automated workflows), improved decision-making precision, personalized services.
- *Indirect negative effects*: loss of democratic control, citizen distrust, potential breaches of privacy, reproduction of social inequalities through algorithmic biases.

This twofold problem necessitates a strong algorithmic governance programme with mechanisms for explicability, accountability and ethical oversight (Heald, 2006; Taddeo & Floridi, 2018). If these risk management strategies are not put in place, then the potential positive benefits of AI will fade to a deficit in democratic legitimacy and this might have severe consequences for stability in institutions and trust from citizens.

## 1.2 Artificial Intelligence and Algorithmic Governance

### 1.2.1. Typology of AI systems in the public sphere

Artificial intelligence covers a range of technologies used to automate decision-making processes, predict behavior or improve interaction between administrations and citizens. In the public sector, four categories of applications are particularly relevant (Davenport & Ronanki, 2018):

- *Robotic Process Automation (RPA)*: Automating repetitive tasks (e.g. validating administrative forms, processing requests).
- *Machine Learning (ML)*: Used for classification and prediction (example: tax fraud detection, optimal allocation of budget resources).
- *Natural Language Processing (NLP)*: Analysis of regulatory texts and implementation of chatbots for citizen services.

- *Computer vision*: image recognition for infrastructure security, border control and urban surveillance.

In Morocco, the use of AI remains limited to certain pilot initiatives in strategic sectors, such as public finance (fraud detection) and healthcare (diagnostic assistance systems), but it remains embryonic in the majority of local administrations (Taibi & Benabdelhadi, 2020).

### 1.2.2 Algorithmic governance: a new paradigm

The rise of AI in the public sector is not just a technological transformation; it is changing the very structure of decision-making processes, introducing what Susskind & Susskind (2015) call *"algorithmic governance"*. This concept refers to the set of rules, mechanisms and institutions required to frame automated decision-making.

The fundamental challenges of algorithmic governance are as follows:

- *Transparency*: administrations must make explicit the rules that guide algorithmic decisions. However, AI models, particularly those based on deep learning, are often opaque, making communication with citizens and supervisory bodies more complex (Goodfellow et al., 2016).
- *Accountability*: Who is liable when an algorithm makes an erroneous decision? Failure to clarify this issue can lead to a legal and institutional vacuum (Bovens, 2007).
- *Citizen participation*: Democratic legitimacy requires that citizens be able to contribute to defining the rules governing the use of AI systems, notably via public consultations and co-construction mechanisms (Kooiman, 2003).

## 1.3. Situation in Morocco and specific challenges

In Morocco, the legal arsenal remains focused on the protection of personal data (Law 09-08) (Bulletin Officiel no. 5711, 2009), with no specific framework for AI systems. The Commission Nationale de Protection des Données Personnelles (CNDP) plays a key role in regulating automated processing, but does not yet impose explicit obligations in terms of *algorithmic traceability* or *public accountability*. This lack of standards increases the risk of abuse in sensitive areas such as:

- *Predictive justice*: potentially biased by historical data;
- *Social programs*: risk of discrimination in the allocation of aid;
- *Public security*: surveillance and privacy issues.

## 1.4. Conceptual research framework

Based on the literature, we propose an *integrative model* articulating three dimensions: AI adoption, governance quality and public performance, with ethical dilemmas taken into account as a moderating factor. This model, illustrated in Figure 1, reflects the assumed direct and indirect relationships between these variables, in line with the research hypotheses.

The associated hypotheses are as follows:

- *H1*: AI adoption has a positive effect on public performance.
- *H2*: Public governance plays a mediating role in the AI → Performance relationship.
- *H3*: Ethical dilemmas negatively moderate the effect of AI on performance.

*Figure 1. Conceptual model*

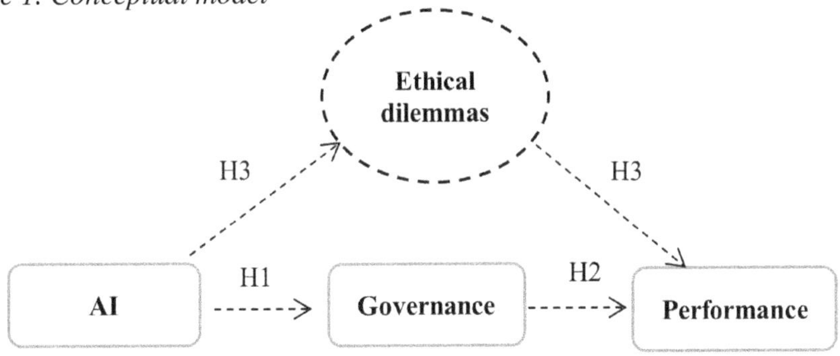


## 1.5. Ethical Dilemmas and Legal Frameworks

The integration of artificial intelligence into the public sphere opens up unprecedented prospects for improving public services, but it also generates major ethical dilemmas. These dilemmas arise mainly at three levels: *algorithmic fairness, the protection of fundamental rights* and *decision-making transparency.*

### 1.5.1. Algorithmic biases and discrimination

AI systems are based on historical data that reflect, whether intentionally or not, social, economic or cultural biases. Thus, supervised learning algorithms, when fed with unbalanced datasets, risk reproducing and even amplifying these biases (O'Neil, 2016).

An emblematic example is the *COMPAS* (Correctional Offender Management Profiling for Alternative Sanctions) software used in the American justice system to predict the risk of recidivism. An investigation by *ProPublica* (Angwin et al., 2016) revealed that this algorithm systematically overestimated the risk of recidivism for African-Americans and underestimated it for white individuals, illustrating a worrying structural bias.

In the social field, work by *Eubanks (2018)* showed that algorithms used to allocate welfare benefits in the US often classified vulnerable populations as “at risk” due to incomplete or biased data, leading to unfair exclusions.

While the use of AI technology to manage social aid or public service has not yet seen wide spread use in Morocco, some pilot projects are being carried out in the fields of health and social protection. In terms of ethical auditing, however, there are important risks of systemic discrimination in the absence of formal mechanisms that could discourage citizens from engaging with these services and using their trust and rights to access social services and protections that are guaranteed by the Constitution (right to health, freedom from discrimination and promotion of empowerment, dignified treatment, and equitable access).

One of the most delicate issues related to the use of artificial intelligence (AI) in the public sphere is the mass collection of personal data that is needed to train the algorithms. This includes biometrics, behavioral and financial data that, when centralized and processed, expose citizens to risks of illegal or abusive surveillance and violations of privacy (Zuboff, 2019).

There is a wide range of risks that have been identified. The intrusion into privacy will vary based on the mobilization of face-recognition systems in public spaces (that are either for public safety or security purposes) on one side of the ledger, and the use of profiling methodologies which can produce abusive correlations related to either administrative data or predictive behaviors and lead to decisions that are discriminatory or stigmatizing without any real credible or transparent justification.

In a Moroccan context, the first line of defense against potential abuses would be the 2009 Law 09-08 (the Law), on the protection of individuals with regard to the processing of personal data. The Law also stipulates a mandatory declaration of data processing to the Commission Nationale de Protection des Données Personnelles (CNDP), and has a number of obligations in relation to consent and data protection, however it does not go far enough to regulate the specifics of AI systems of practice, especially on fundamental aspects such as algorithmic explicability, legal liability in case of a decision-making error, and ethical audit of algorithms (CNDP, 2023).

## 1.5.2 Procedural justice and opacity of decision-making

The introduction of artificial intelligence (AI) systems in the public sphere raises an issue of great importance: that of opacity in decision-making and its impact on procedural justice. Algorithmic models - particularly the family of models on deep learning - are commonly described as "black boxes" because of the difficulty of articulating their internal functioning (Goodfellow et al., 2016). With limited transparency, explaining automated decisions becomes increasingly difficult, and potentially impossible, leading to the erosion of fundamental democratic principles including the right to contest and substantiate administrative acts.

Procedural justice relies on citizens being able to obtain a clear and comprehensible justification for decisions that concern them (Heald, 2006). However, in the context of AI systems, this requirement comes up against two main obstacles:

- *Technical complexity of models*: Neural networks, used for example for fraud detection or risk assessment, produce results that are difficult for non-specialists to interpret (Bovens, 2007).
- *Lack of regulated explicability*: unlike the European framework (RGPD, art. 22), Morocco does not yet provide for an explicit right to explanation of automated decisions, accentuating the risk of procedural unfairness.

International examples illustrate the dangers of this opacity:

- *In the United States, COMPAS* software, used to assess prisoners' likelihood of recidivism, has been criticized for its racial bias and lack of clear explanation of assigned scores, sparking judicial and ethical debate (O'Neil, 2016).
- *In the UK*, predictive systems applied to education have led to legal challenges, as students were denied access to algorithmic scoring criteria.

In the Moroccan context, the use of AI in sensitive processes - such as *the allocation of social aid* or *the assessment of taxpayers* - could give rise to litigation due to the lack of institutional mechanisms guaranteeing the traceability and justification of decisions. This lack of transparency threatens not only *public confidence*, but also the *legitimacy of public institutions* (Heald, 2006; Bovens, 2007).

To mitigate these risks, several measures are required:

- Strengthen algorithmic transparency by introducing explicability and documentation obligations for AI systems, in line with the recommendations of the European Commission (2021) and the UNESCO Charter on Ethical AI (UNESCO, 2021).

- Set up independent ethical audits to detect and correct biases in models, taking inspiration from the OECD guidelines (2019) on algorithmic accountability.
- Guarantee an effective right of appeal for citizens affected by automated decisions, referring to the provisions of the General Data Protection Regulation (GDPR, art. 22), which enshrines the right to explanation of automated decisions (European Commission, 2018).
- These actions are indispensable prerequisites for AI to become a lever for modernization without compromising the fundamental principles of justice and accountability (Floridi & Cowls, 2019).

These actions are necessary and basic conditions for AI as a tool for modernization that also preserves the basic principles of justice and accountability (Floridi & Cowls, 2019).

### 1.5.3 International normative frameworks and the Moroccan predicament

At an international level, there are a number of reference frameworks which provide principles for ensuring AI is framed ethically:

- General Data Protection Regulation (GDPR) in Europe, which includes the right to explanation of automated decisions.
- OECD Principles on AI, which call for transparency, robustness, and accountability.
- UNESCO Charter for Ethical AI (2021), which emphasizes the need for respecting basic rights and cultural diversity.

In Morocco, on the other hand, the legal framework is in its infancy:

- The Law 09-08 that protects personal data throughout the data lifecycle, but does not address algorithmic responsibilities.
- There are no legal means of auditing algorithms, certifying AI systems, or holding accountable systems of bias.

This shortcoming places administrations at a risk from liability and reduces their, or the legal systems', ability to comply with international norms, especially when considering the context of partnerships with the European Union.

### 1.5.4. Normative recommendations for Morocco

To promote the ethical and socially responsible use of artificial intelligence in Moroccan public governance it is necessary to establish a normative framework that incorporates aspects of international norms. To assist in this, the following considerations are derived from best practices from a range of international benchmarks (GDPR, OECD Principles, UNESCO Charter) with a few recommendations.

*Firstly*, it is necessary to develop specific AI legislation for the public sector. This legislation should include an obligation for algorithms to be explainable; this would allow stakeholders to audit and comprehend automated decisions (Floridi & Cowls, 2019). It should also stipulate that regular ethical audits should occur to ascertain that biases in algorithms can be rectified prior to widespread use (OECD, 2019), and establish the legal accountability in case of errors or damage when automated systems are involved (European Commission, 2021).

*Secondly*, it is suggested that a general National AI Regulatory Authority be created with binding power, tasked with certifying systems and monitoring ethical practices in the use of AI. The authority exists in some European countries in the form of their data protection authorities under the RGPD (European Commission, 2018).

*Thirdly*, Thirdly, we must integrate the principle of "privacy by design" which help protect personal data from the design stage of AI systems. This requirement, already included in RGPD, must have data minimization, encryption, and traceability integrated upstream (European Commission, 2018).

*Fourthly*, we must strengthen the training of public officials around the ethical, legal and technical matters of the use of algorithms to build skills on digital governance and bias management (Jobin et al, 2019).

*Finally*, proactive transparency is required. Administrations must regularly publish their decision-making criteria as well as impact assessments on fundamental rights/public performance made by the AI systems to foster citizen trust and the social acceptability of AI (Heald, 2006).

These recommendations are intended to bridge the divide between technological innovation and democratic imperatives by situating the use of AI in a rigorous legal and ethical framework to provide the legitimacy of public decisions and the protection of fundamental rights.

## 2. METHODOLOGY

The methodology used in this study has a two-fold objective; it aims to provide an explanatory analysis of the factors affecting public performance in the context of digital transformation, and to empirically verify the predictive power of machine learning models based on the data of Moroccan administrations. This is done in a conceptual framework that combines the concepts of good governance, artificial intelligence (AI) adoption, and ethical concerns, and seeks to examine the relationships that connect these constituents (Hair et al., 2022; Davenport & Ronanki, 2018).

## 2.1 Methodological objective

This study lies in an explanatory and institutional logic; the study sets out to investigate how the level of integration of AI technologies in Moroccan public administrations affects organizational performance; yet it also seeks to examine two intermediary dimensions: the role of good governance principles (transparency, accountability, and citizen participation)(Heald, 2006; Bovens, 2007) and the role of ethical dilemmas (algorithms bias, private and decision-making obscure)(Floridi & Cowls, 2019; Jobin et al., 2019).

Working hypothesis formulated concerning the above are as follows:

- *H1*: The adoption of AI technologies has a significant positive effect on public performance.
- *H2*: This effect is mediated by the quality of public governance.
- *H3*: Ethical dilemmas negatively moderate the AI → Performance relationship, reducing the impact of AI as ethical risks increase.

These hypotheses justify the use of empirical analysis combining statistical methods and advanced machine learning techniques to check the robustness of the observed relationships (Breiman, 2001; Cortes & Vapnik, 1995; Hair et al., 2022).

## 2.2. Population and sample

The study population covers all Moroccan public administrations, including ministries, local authorities and public establishments. The final sample is made up of *270 organizational units*, selected using a stratified sampling method to reflect the diversity of institutions in terms of size, hierarchical level and sector of activity.

This approach ensures the representativeness of the entities that make up the Moroccan public sector and provides generalizable results. The data collected covers the period *2018-2022*, corresponding to the acceleration phase of digital transformation in Morocco as part of the "Maroc Digital 2025" national strategy.

Information was collected through three main sources:

- *Official reports* such as those from the Cour des Comptes and the Inspection Générale des Finances, providing performance indicators and data on digital systems;
- *Questionnaires administered to public officials and managers*, designed on the basis of a five-point Likert scale (1 = very low, 5 = very high), measuring perceptions of AI adoption, quality of governance and ethical concerns;
- *Internal administrative databases*, relating to the effective use of algorithmic and automated systems in decision-making processes.

This triangulation of sources ensures the reliability and validity of the data mobilized for analysis.

## 2.3. Variables and indicators

Four main variables structure the conceptual model:

- *AI adoption (independent variable)*: This was measured by a composite index integrating the presence and degree of use of four major technologies in the public sphere: Robotic Process Automation (RPA) for the automation of administrative tasks, Machine Learning for predictive analysis, Natural Language Processing (NLP) for interaction with citizens, and computer vision for automated control. These technologies are identified as key levers for the digital transformation of administrations (Davenport & Ronanki, 2018; Jordan & Mitchell, 2015).
- *Good governance (mediating variable)*: This was apprehended through three sub-dimensions: transparency of decision-making processes, accountability of public officials and citizen participation in public policy-making. These dimensions correspond to the fundamental principles of public governance defined by the World Bank and widely taken up in the literature (Heald, 2006; Bovens, 2007).
- *Public performance (dependent variable)*: This was measured using indicators relating to operational efficiency (compliance with deadlines, fluidity of procedures), quality of services rendered and user satisfaction. These indicators are recommended by research into performance-based public management (Behn, 2003; Van Dooren et al., 2010).
- *Ethical dilemmas (moderating variable)*: These were evaluated using an index that takes three aspects into account: the risks of algorithmic bias, potential invasions of privacy and the opacity of decisions produced by automated systems. These ethical issues are widely documented in work on AI regulation (Floridi & Cowls, 2019; O'Neil, 2016; Zuboff, 2019).

These indicators have been standardized to ensure comparability and integrate qualitative variables into predictive models.

## 2.4. Data preparation and processing

A rigorous protocol was implemented to prepare the data for analysis. As a first step, numerical variables were *normalized* using the *Min-Max Scaling* method, to bring all values within an interval between 0 and 1, which promotes convergence of scale-sensitive algorithms (Han et al., 2012).

Missing data were handled by *imputing the mean of the variables*, a simple but effective technique for limiting information loss and preserving sample size (Little & Rubin, 2019).

Categorical variables were *encoded* using the *One-Hot Encoding* technique, which converts categories into binary variables for use in supervised learning models (Pedregosa et al., 2011).

Using the Interquartile Range (IQR) method to identify extreme values was a simple way to correct these values to minimize bias in the estimates, in accordance with good practice for exploratory analysis (Tukey, 1977).

In addition, a principal component analysis (PCA) was performed on the data to:

- Explore the data structure,
- Reduce dimensionality,
- Identify the number of factors explaining the largest variability..

This step also allowed us to check for the consistency of the indicators and to assess the presence of multicollinearity phenomena, again following the recommendations from the multivariate analysis literature (Jolliffe & Cadima, 2016).

## 2.5. Machine learning modeling

In order to predict the performance of the administrations as a function of the explanatory variables, two algorithms were selected: Random Forest (RF) and Support Vector Machine (SVM). We chose these methods since they are very useful for multidimensional datasets, for modeling non-linear relations and both systems function reasonably well in the presence of noise (Breiman, 2001; Cortes & Vapnik, 1995; Hastie et al., 2009).

The Random Forest model uses machine learning based on ensemble learning, where several trees are generated from the data to decrease variance, and increase prediction accuracy. The Random Forest has been parameterized with 500 trees (n_estimators = 500) and a maximum depth of 10 and uses the Gini criterion to quantify heterogeneity for partitions (Breiman, 2001). The Random Forest is an advantageous method for creating a model when there are complex interactions between the variables, as well as increasing minimizing overlearning risk.

The SVM model was developed with an RBF (radial kernel), which is deemed ideally suitable for cases where there is a non-linear decision boundary (Cortes & Vapnik, 1995). The regularization parameters were tuned to C = 1 and gamma = 0.01 to retain high generalization ability and avoid over-fitting (Hastie et al., 2009). The tuning was conducted with grid search and cross-validation, which helps ensure more generalizable outcomes (Pedregosa et al., 2011).

These two algorithms present a mixture of complementary advantages: RF offers relatively interpretable results due to variable importance score; SVM's strength relies on classifying data that is both high-dimensional and represents a distribution with mixed-dimensionality.

## 2.6 Complementary analyses

To better elucidate the interpretation between variables and identify distinguishing profiles, we ran a series of advanced analyses:

- *Clustering segmentation (K-means)*: Unsupervised clustering was applied to identify public organizations as homogenous profiles based on the level of AI adoption, governance quality and performance. The appropriate number of clusters was determined using the Elbow Method, which is a common method for evaluating the variance, if any, intra-cluster (Jain, 2010).
- *Moderation analysis:* Investigated interaction of ethical dilemmas and AI adoption level using hierarchical regression which was later confirmed with a PLS-SEM model, as described in detail in terms of methodology in assessing moderating effects in structural models of Hair et al (2022).
- *Analysis of mediation effect*: A mediation was estimated using the Bootstrap method with 5000 resamples which is recommended by MacKinnon and colleagues (2007) and Preacher and Hayes (2008) to obtain robust confidence intervals without assumption that direct or indirect effects were normal.
- *Comparison with an artificial neural network (ANN)*: To evaluate predictive models' robustness, a feed-forward ANN was trained and compared to RF and SVM model performance. This decision was made based on Bishop (2006) and Goodfellow and colleagues (2016) who recommended fitting ANN for modeling complex relationships in multidimensional data.

## 2.7. Metrics and cross-validation

A set of complementary metrics were used to assess model performance. accuracy was the proportion of corrects, while the F1 score provided a more balanced estimate of performance based on being the harmonic mean of precision and recall. For continuous variables, the coefficient of determination ($R^2$) was used as a measure of the model's goodness of fit and root mean square error (RMSE) measured the difference between predicted values and observed values.

A K-fold cross-validation (k= 5) was conducted in order to minimize overlearning and ensure the integrity of the outcomes. The technique splits the sample into five subsets, where learning and testing alternates to achieve a satisfactory estimate of overall performance (Kohavi, 1995; Hastie, Tibshirani & Friedman, 2009).

## 2.8. Tools used

All analysis was based on advanced technologies. Python, with the use of the Pandas (McKinney, 2010) and NumPy (Harris et al., 2020) libraries, was mobilized for data preparation and processing, while Scikit-learn (Pedregosa et al., 2011) was used to implement machine learning models. Graphical visualizations included variable distributions, PCA results and variable importance graphs were produced with Matplotlib (Hunter, 2007) and Seaborn (Waskom, 2021). And initial descriptive statistics were done in SPSS (IBM Corp, 2021).

This combination of methods and tools provides our approach with a sufficient level of science, assuring the reliability and relevance of the results, which will be documented in the following section.

# 3. RESULTS AND DISCUSSION

## 3.1. Descriptive data analysis

Before engaging in the modeling, a descriptive analysis was undertaken in order to assess the representativeness of the data and also describe the main characteristics of Moroccan administrations adopting artificial intelligence (AI) technologies in the period from 2018 to 2022. The artificial intelligence technologies mainly refer to Robotic Process Automation (RPA) solutions designed for automating repetitive types of tasks, and to a much lower extent, advanced applications such as machine learning and automatic natural language processing (NLP) associated in 18% of cases. This seems to confirm the results of Davenport & Ronanki (2018), which stipulates that most administrations engage in low complexity AI projects before moving towards higher complexity systems. Computer vision remains marginal, used only for important control management undertaking in sensitive sectors. These results, detailed in Table 1, also show that AI adoption in the Moroccan public sector is still partial and type focused, demonstrating that solutions implemented to date are extremely narrow.

Concerning governance, the average scores themselves are relatively low: transparency = 2.8, accountability = 3.0 and citizen participation = 3.2 (on a scale of 1 to 5). When assessing ethical dilemmas involved in the use of AI technologies, the scores received a high average: (3.6/5), which shows general concerns regarding algorithmic bias and data protection. The observed concerns regarding algorithmic bias and to a lesser extent data protection, were also addressed by Zuboff (2019) when referencing digital surveillance.

*Table 1. Descriptive statistics for the main variables*

| Variables | Mean | Standard deviation | Max |
|---|---|---|---|
| **Adoption of AI** | 3,48 | 0,27 | 1 |
| **Transparency** | 2,8 | 0,9 | 5 |
| **Accountability** | 3,0 | 1,0 | 5 |
| **Civic participation** | 3,2 | 0,8 | 5 |
| **Ethical dilemmas** | 3,6 | 0,7 | 5 |
| **Public performance** | 3,4 | 0,8 | 5 |

Source: Author's analysis, 2025

## 3.2. Predictive analysis: RF and SVM comparison

To assess the predictive capability of the models, we compared two machine learning algorithms: Random Forest (RF) and Support Vector Machine (SVM). Performance was assessed on the basis of four metrics: Accuracy, F1 Score, $R^2$ and RMSE. The results are summarized in Table 2, which clearly shows the superiority of Random Forest over SVM on all indicators.

*Table 2. Performance of predictive models*

| Model | Accuracy | F1 score | $R^2$ | RMSE |
|---|---|---|---|---|
| **Random Forest** | 0,89 | 0,87 | 0,82 | 0,32 |
| **SVM** | 0,81 | 0,79 | 0,74 | 0,41 |

These results confirm that *Random Forest* is a robust model for handling multidimensional and non-linear data, which is consistent with the work of Breiman (2001) and Hastie, Tibshirani and Friedman (2009). The coefficient of determination ($R^2 = 0.82$) suggests that RF explains *82%* of the variance in public performance, compared with *74%* for SVM, underlining the effectiveness of ensemble approaches over margin methods such as SVM (Cortes & Vapnik, 1995).

The relative importance of variables was examined through the Random Forest model, as illustrated in *Figure 2*, which shows that:

- *Transparency (24%)* and *Accountability (21%)* appear as the main determinants of public performance;
- Followed by *AI adoption (18%)*;
- While ethical dilemmas account for *15%*, reflecting their role in the perception and acceptability of AI projects.

*Figure 2. Importance of variables (Random Forest model)*

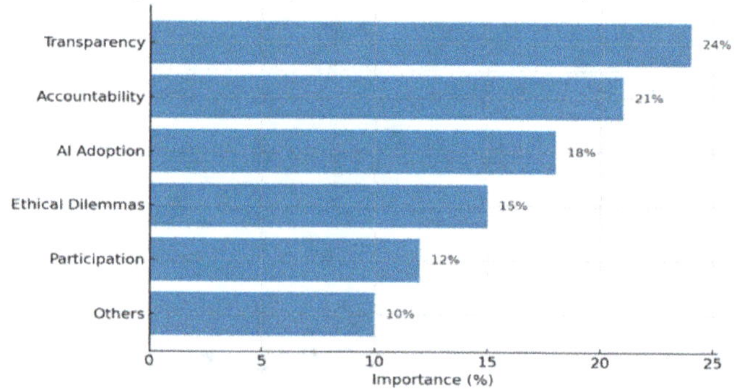


This ranking confirms that the impact of AI is not autonomous, but closely depends on the quality of public governance. A highly digitized but poorly governed administration remains vulnerable to perverse effects such as loss of citizen trust, discrimination and opaque decision-making. These findings concur with the analyses of Davenport & Ronanki (2018), who remind us that the added value of AI in the public sector relies on the existence of solid institutional mechanisms guaranteeing transparency and accountability.

## 3.3. Segmentation of organizations by clustering

In order to identify typical profiles of public organizations based on their level of AI adoption and governance practices, a segmentation analysis was carried out using the *K-means* algorithm, recognized for its robustness in clustering multidimensional data (Jain, 2010). Determination of the optimal number of clusters was based on the Elbow Method, commonly used in classification analysis to assess intra-cluster variance (Ketchen & Shook, 1996), which led to k = 3.

Three distinct profiles have been identified in Table 3:

- *Cluster 1 (n = 102)*: *Low AI adoption*, relatively high governance and average performance. These organizations prefer traditional processes, but benefit from control and transparency mechanisms (Van Dooren et al., 2010).
- *Cluster 2 (n = 81)*: *High AI adoption*, but weak governance and limited performance, accompanied by a high level of ethical dilemmas. This cluster illustrates the risk of technology deployment without adequate institutional oversight (O'Neil, 2016; Zuboff, 2019).
- *Cluster 3 (n = 87)*: *High AI adoption combined with strong governance*, resulting in the best organizational performance. These entities represent a model of ethical and effective digital transformation (Davenport & Ronanki, 2018; Floridi & Cowls, 2019).

*Table 3. Average cluster characteristics*

| Cluster | AI adoption | Governance | Performance | Ethical dilemmas |
|---|---|---|---|---|
| 1 | 2,1 | 4,3 | 3,5 | 2,8 |
| 2 | 4,6 | 2,2 | 2,9 | 4,1 |
| 3 | 4,8 | 4,5 | 4,6 | 2,7 |

These results confirm that *AI adoption alone does not guarantee improved public performance*, in the absence of a solid governance framework (Taibi & Benabdelhadi, 2020; Bovens, 2007).

*Figure 3. Segmentation of public organizations (K-means): Scatterplot with color grouping*

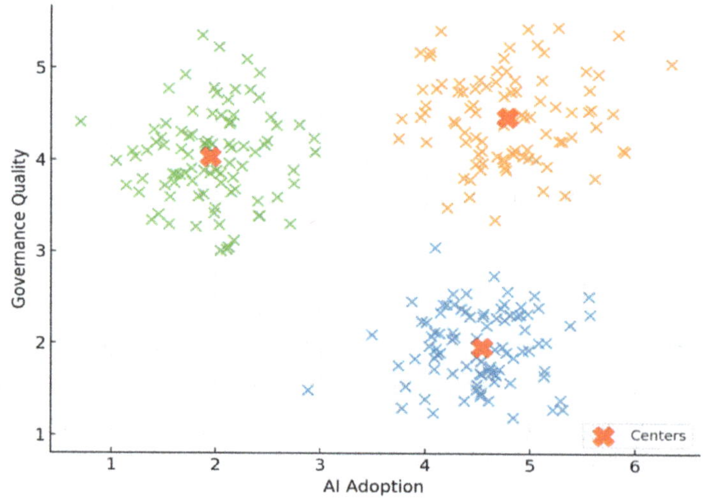


Figure 3 illustrates the grouping of the *270 Moroccan public organizations* into *three homogeneous clusters*, according to their level of AI adoption (X axis) and the quality of their governance (Y axis).

- *Cluster 1 (in blue)*: These organizations have *a low level of AI adoption*, but compensate with *relatively strong governance*. They are mainly located in the upper left-hand section of the graph. Their overall performance is average, showing that *good governance mechanisms can maintain a certain efficiency, even in the absence of advanced digital tools* (OECD, 2020).
- *Cluster 2 (orange)*: This cluster includes entities with *high AI adoption*, but *low governance scores*. Located in the lower right-hand part of the graph, they record *the weakest performance*, despite their technological modernization. This finding highlights a *major risk*: *investment in AI without a solid ethical and institutional framework can generate perverse effects*, including a loss of legitimacy, biases in decisions and citizen distrust (O'Neil, 2016; Heald, 2006).
- *Cluster 3 (green)*: This is the ideal profile, combining *strong AI adoption and robust governance*. These organizations, positioned in the top right-hand corner of the graph, achieve *the best performance*. They embody the model of successful digital transformation, based on *the balance between technological innovation and good governance (Davenport & Ronanki, 2018; Floridi & Cowls, 2019).*

This segmentation confirms that *public performance does not depend solely on AI adoption*. Without transparent, participatory governance, the expected benefits of technologies may be limited or even nullified. Conversely, strong governance, even with a low level of technology, is a protective factor (Behn, 2003).

Consequently, public policy should:

- *Prioritize governance* before or in parallel with the integration of AI systems (Heald, 2006) .
- *Develop ethical and regulatory frameworks* to prevent the drifts observed in Cluster 2 (OECD, 2019; UNESCO, 2021).

• *Support the skills development of public officials*, to foster convergence between innovation and accountability (Jobin et al., 2019).

## 3.4. Moderation analysis

In order to assess whether *ethical dilemmas moderate the relationship between AI adoption and public performance*, a hierarchical regression analysis with interaction was performed, supplemented by estimation via *PLS-SEM* to confirm the robustness of the results (Hair et al., 2022). This type of approach is recommended for testing moderating effects in complex structural models (Preacher & Hayes, 2008; MacKinnon et al., 2007).

The results indicate that the interaction is *statistically significant*:

- *$\beta$ (interaction) = -0.23; $p < 0.05$*, confirming that *ethical dilemmas attenuate the positive effect of AI on performance*. In other words, although AI is generally associated with improved efficiency, speed of service and user satisfaction, *these benefits diminish considerably* when ethical concerns (bias, privacy, opacity) are high (Floridi & Cowls, 2019).

*Table 4. Moderating effect of ethical dilemmas in the AI Performance relationship*

| Model | β (AI) | β (Dilemmas) | β (AI × Dilemmas) | $R^2$ | $\Delta R^2$ | Sig. |
|---|---|---|---|---|---|---|
| **Model 1: AI alone** | 0,41 | - | - | 0,46 | - | 0,000 |
| **Model 2: + Dilemmas** | 0,36 | -0,18 | - | 0,52 | 0,06 | 0,000 |
| **Model 3: + Interaction** | 0,34 | -0,16 | **-0,23** | 0,59 | 0,07 | **0,031** |

Source: Author's analysis, 2025

Progressive examination of the models shows that *the first model*, including only the AI adoption variable, explains *46% of the variance observed* in public performance, confirming its predictive role. *In the second model*, the addition of ethical dilemmas increases the variance explained to $R^2 = 0.52$, underlining their negative direct effect. Finally, *the third model*, incorporating the IA × Dilemmas interaction term, confirms a significant moderating effect: the coefficient associated with the interaction is negative and significant ($\beta = -0.23$; $p < 0.05$), and the $R^2$ reaches *0.59*, with a substantial increase in explained variance (+0.07). This result indicates that *the positive influence of AI on performance decreases as ethical dilemmas increase, in line with the findings of recent work on algorithmic governance (Taddeo & Floridi, 2018).*

These results are summarized in *Table 4* and illustrated in *Figure 4*, which shows two straight lines representing the AI → Performance relationship according to low and high levels of ethical dilemmas. When ethical dilemmas are low, the slope is clearly positive, reflecting a gain in AI-related performance. Conversely, when ethical dilemmas are high, the slope flattens out, indicating that the positive effect of AI becomes marginal.

*Figure 4. Moderating effect of ethical dilemmas*

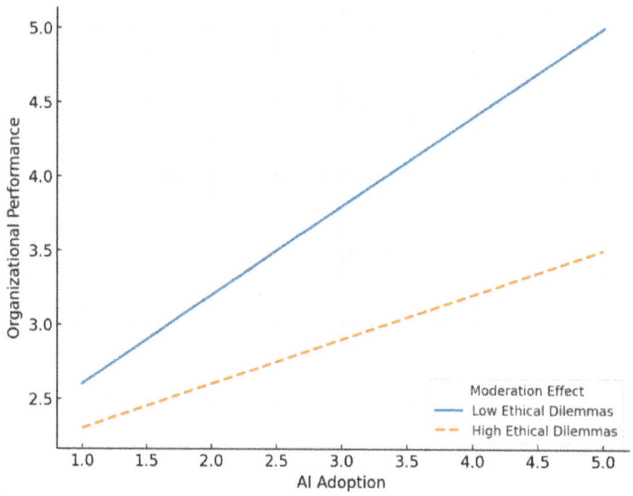


These results highlight a *technological paradox*: high AI adoption does not guarantee improved performance if ethical governance mechanisms are not in place. Public organizations that neglect *transparency*, *data protection* and *algorithmic fairness* risk seeing their gains cancelled out by a loss of legitimacy and citizen mistrust (O'Neil, 2016).

It is therefore *strongly recommended* to:

- Strengthen *ethical charters* and regulatory mechanisms before any mass deployment.
- Establish *independent control mechanisms* to guarantee the transparency and traceability of automated decisions.
- Train public servants in *digital responsibility*, to reduce the risks associated with algorithmic bias.

## 3.5. Analysis of Mediating Effects

Hypothesis H2 postulated that *public governance plays a mediating* role in the relationship between AI technology adoption and organizational performance. To test this hypothesis, we used a *mediation analysis based on the Bootstrap method with 5000 resamplings*, in line with the recommendations of *MacKinnon et al. (2007)* and *Preacher & Hayes (2008)*. This approach is preferred because it does not rely on the assumption of normality of the distribution of indirect effects, which guarantees a more robust estimate (Hayes, 2018).

The analysis was carried out using the *PLS-SEM (Partial Least Squares Structural Equation Modeling) model*, enabling structural relationships between variables to be represented while incorporating mediating variables (Hair et al., 2022). The results in Table 5 confirm the existence of significant partial mediation:

- The direct effect of AI adoption on public performance remains positive and significant ($\beta = 0.34; p < 0.05$).
- The indirect effect, via public governance, is also *significant and substantial* ($\beta = 0.21; p < 0.01$).
- The total effect (direct + indirect) reaches $\beta = 0.55$, underlining that the combination of the two effects considerably strengthens the overall impact of AI on organizational performance (Zhao et al., 2010).

These results confirm the structuring role of governance in the success of digital transformation projects. In other words, AI will only sustainably improve public performance if it is accompanied by solid mechanisms for transparency, accountability and citizen participation.

*Table 5. Results of mediation analysis*

| Type of effect | Coefficient β | p-value |
|---|---|---|
| **Direct effect (IA → Performance)** | 0,34 | 0,041 |
| **Indirect effect (AI → Governance → Performance)** | 0,21 | 0,007 |
| **Total effect** | 0,55 | 0,000 |

Source: Author's analysis based on PLS-SEM data, 2025

*Figure 5. PLS-SEM model illustrating mediation*

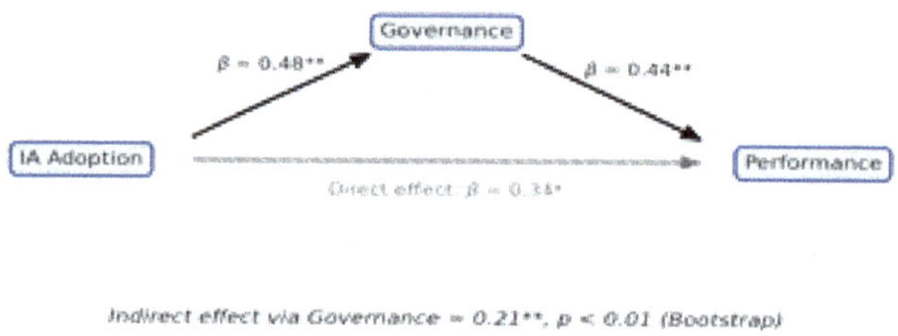


Figure 5 highlights three key relationships:

- *AI Governance ($\beta$ = 0.48)*: The adoption of AI technologies significantly enhances the quality of governance mechanisms (transparency, accountability).
- *Governance Performance ($\beta$ = 0.44)*: Strong governance improves public performance (efficiency, user satisfaction).
- *IA Performance ($\beta$ = 0.34)*: The direct effect is positive, but weaker than the indirect effect.

Three key lessons emerge from this analysis:

- *AI alone is not enough leverage to transform public performance*: Although digital technologies bring efficiency gains, their contribution remains limited in the absence of a solid institutional framework. A "technocentric" adoption risks generating inefficiencies and even internal resistance, due to a lack of transparency and control mechanisms.
- *Governance as a catalyst:* Administrations that combine technological innovation with robust governance (transparency, citizen control, auditing) perform best. This catalytic role is empirically verified by the significant indirect

effect ($\beta = 0.21$), showing that the added value of AI is conditioned by institutional maturity.
- *Lack of governance leads to systemic risks*: Without regulation or control, massive automation can generate algorithmic biases, invasions of privacy and a deficit of democratic legitimacy, reducing citizen trust.

These findings argue in favor of an integrated approach in which *digital innovation and ethical governance move forward together*. In concrete terms, this means

- *Drawing up ethical charters* to govern the use of algorithms and guarantee non-discrimination;
- *Training public servants* in the challenges of digital governance, including bias management and data protection;
- *The introduction of auditing and monitoring tools* to ensure the transparency of automated decisions and strengthen the accountability of institutions.

Ultimately, the integration of AI into the public sphere must not be seen as a simple technological issue, but as a *structuring institutional project*, mobilizing both technical solutions and adapted governance standards.

## 3.6. Deep Learning Model Comparison

To complete the predictive analysis of the relationships between the variables associated with AI adoption, public governance, ethical dilemmas and organizational performance, a Deep Learning model, based on an artificial neural network (ANN), was utilized. The ANN model was analyzed in comparison to a Random Forest (RF) model and associated Support Vector Machine (SVM) algorithm to evaluate the viability of a neural architecture to improve accuracy and generalizability of predictions (Goodfellow et al., 2016).

The ANN model was designed as a feedforward architecture with three layers one as and input layer with the explanatory variables, one as a hidden layer and an output layer. The hidden layer has 10 neurons using the ReLU (Rectified Linear Unit) activation function because it introduces non-linearity into the process, and allows for improved convergence once learning begins (Hastie et al., 2009). The output layer uses a sigmoid activation function which normalizes predictions on an interval between 0 and 1, based on the relative characteristics of the target variables.

Weight optimization was completed using the Adam algorithm, which is recognized for its robustness to nonlinear optimization problems (Kingma & Ba, 2015) with the learning rate set to 0.001. To prevent the possibility of overlearning, the regularization Dropout technique was implemented, set to an initial rate of 0.2, which randomizes the deactivation of some neuronal connections during training phase, hence improving model generalization (Srivastava et al., 2014).

To counteract these normalisation issues and ensure reliability and robustness of the results, during the evaluation phase, 5-fold cross-validation was used (Kohavi, 1995).

*Table 6. Comparison of predictive performance*

| Model | Accuracy | F1-score | $R^2$ | RMSE |
|---|---|---|---|---|
| **Random Forest** | 0,89 | 0,87 | 0,82 | 0,32 |
| **SVM** | 0,81 | 0,79 | 0,74 | 0,41 |
| **ANN** | 0,91 | 0,89 | 0,84 | 0,29 |

Source: Author's analysis, 2025

*Figure 6. Comparison of RF, SVM and ANN*

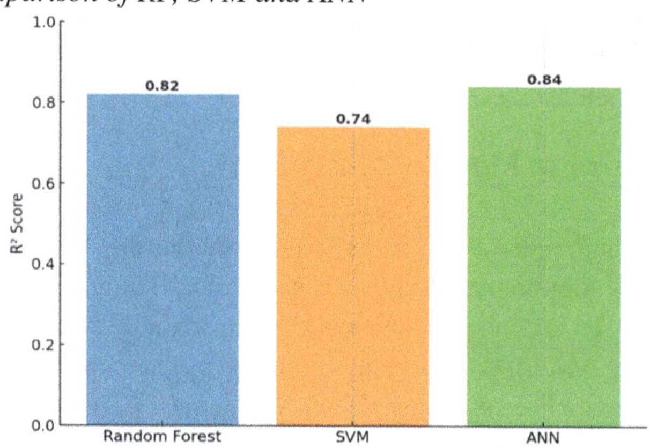


The findings described in Table 6 and Figure 6 illustrated that:

- ANN produced the best predictive performance, $R^2 = 0.84$, RMSE = 0.29, followed by Random Forest ($R^2 = 0.82$) and SVM ($R^2 = 0.74$)
- Accuracy and F1-score for the ANN was 0.91 and 0.89 respectively, supporting the idea that neural networks are capable of capturing complex relationships among variables (Bishop, 2006).

Nevertheless, although ANN has above average performance relative to RF, it has two potential challenges steeped in its application utilization:

- Decision opacity - ANNs were deemed "black box" types of models that do not explain their inferences and could create concern in a public context where there are high transparency requirements (Bishop, 2006).
- Technical requirements - the utilization of ANNs requires considerable computational assets and technical expertise.

The study demonstrates a careful approach to consideration of technological performance and necessary transparency in the public sector context. A strategic hybrid approach, which pairs interpretable models like Random Forest, with stronger models like Artificial Neural Networks is recommended. The rationale being that one can leverage the predictive abilities of ANNs while maintaining a degree of explainability that satisfies accountability requirements.

Moreover, the use of explainable artificial intelligence (XAI) tools (e.g. SHAP, LIME) is critical to ensure that ANN predictions are understood by decision-makers and citizens. This transparency is essential for guaranteeing continued public trust in institutions during the digital age.

Finally, the success of the above approaches relies on institutional capacity development. This means developing the capacity of public managers through ongoing development on their digital governance skills, but it is also essential to create secure technological architecture that supports the establishment of sophisticated models. Hence, we must take a dual approach - a technological and human approach - to harness the full potential of AI, while ensuring ethical, responsible, and democratic use.

## 3.7. Residual analysis and validation

Evaluating how good a predictive model is not limited to assessing high-level performance metrics like Accuracy, $R^2$ or RMSE. An important step is looking at the residuals, whereby residuals are defined as the difference between the observed values and the values that were predicted by the model. Examining the residuals allows us to identify possible anomalies, systematic biases, or issues related to the structure of the data (Hastie, Tibshirani & Friedman, 2009).

In this study, we conducted a residuals analysis for the Random Forest model, which was one of the best performing. Residuals were plotted as a cross plot of the predictions (x-axis) and errors (y-axis) so that we could see the distribution of deviations.

Figure 7 demonstrates that:

- The majority of residuals are randomly distributed around the zero line, indicating the absence of a systematic trend in errors (James, Witten, Hastie & Tibshirani, 2021).
- No structural patterns are detected, confirming that the model has no major specification problems.
- Extreme values are rare and do not represent a significant problem for the overall robustness of the model.
- The variance of the residuals remains relatively homogeneous, ruling out the risk of marked heteroscedasticity (Montgomery, Peck & Vining, 2021).

This confirms the statistical robustness and useful predictability that the Random Forest model achieves in similar situations.

*Figure 7. Graph of residuals*

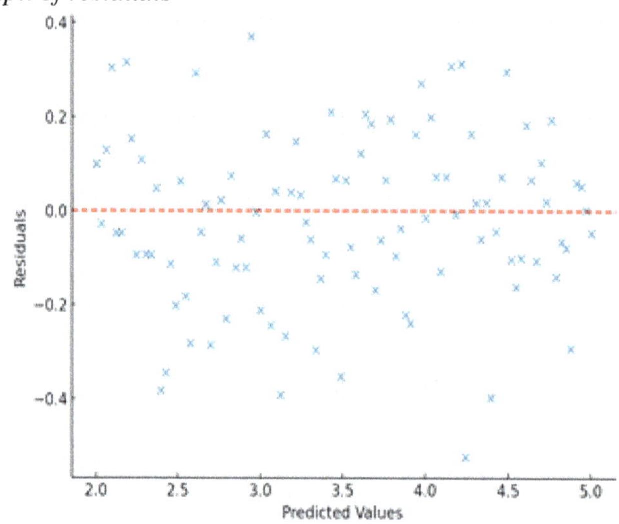


A random distribution of residuals provides a strong indication of good model generalization. This shows that the model is not impacted by systematic bias and there is not a significant unmodeled relationships between the explanatory variables and the predicted performance.

These results reaffirm the robustness of the predictive analyses conducted, and if updated regularly, show that the model may be useful for making decisions about the expected impacts of the adoption and governance of AI on public performance.

## 4. STRATEGIC IMPLICATIONS AND RECOMMENDATIONS

The findings of this research provide major strategic implications for public decision-makers and institutions are in the process of modernizing administration in Morocco. They show that while the adoption of artificial intelligence (AI) will be important to add some performance and efficiency gain to public services, this process is not a guarantee for successful outcomes in an of itself. The operational impacts of AI will depend heavily on the level of governance and ability of institutions to understand and mitigate ethical dilemmas that will arise.

To maximize the benefits of AI while limiting potential risks, we have outlined a number of proposals.

The first strategy involves creating a foundational normative framework. This should consist of concrete legal terms committing to transparency and explicable algorithms, as well as workings and/or regular audits to discover and mitigate biases before wide-scale implementation. If institutions in Canada establish a coherent framework and align with international standards such as the OECD Principles (2019) or UNESCO Charter for an Ethical AI (2021), it would in turn also endorse their credibility and safeguard fundamental rights (Floridi & Cowls, 2019).

Secondly, we would recommend creating an independent National Authority to regulate AI with binding powers to certify established systems deployed in administrations and impose penalties for non-compliance. To complement the Independent Authority, ethical committees could be positioned within ministries, ensuring that AI projects respond to principles of justice, fairness and transparency (Jobin et al., 2019).

Thirdly, we will suggest advancing toward transparency and explainable AI (XAI) tools such as regularly communicating reports that describe mechanisms for decision-making, establishing citizens platforms to support consulting and contesting automated decisions, and promoting the use of methods such as SHAP or LIME for making predictions interpretable to the stakeholder (Lundberg & Lee, 2017).

Fourthly, one of the key strategic levers to improve public employees' skills. Moreover, there should be training programs designed to ensure managers become aware of the ethical and technical issues surrounding digital governance, bias management and data protection. This increase in skills must be combined with a greater collaboration between the government, universities, and research and development laboratories, in order to co-develop ethical AI solutions that can be adapted to the context of Morocco.

Lastly, it is proposed to implement a gradual and balanced strategy for the deployment of AI systems, prioritizing the implementation of pilot projects within controlled environments before moving to any sort of wider adoption. A hybrid approach combining more explainable models such as Random Forest alongside more complex models (e.g., neural networks) would optimize predictive accuracy required for implementation while providing an acceptable amount of explainability. This approach can offer a compromise between the performance of advanced algorithms and the need for transparency especially in a democratic context and scientific process.

These recommendations are intended to ensure the development of business process innovation that aligns with democratic principles, ensuring A.I. becomes a lever for sustainable improvement of public governance in Morocco.

## 5. LIMITATIONS AND PROSPECTS

While this study has an integrative approach in employing both machine learning models and structural methods (PLS-SEM) in the field of public governance, it has several methodological and contextual limitations.

First, the limitations of the geographic scope related to the Moroccan as a country context limits the potential for wider generalizations (to other countries under different bigger contexts and cultures). The socio-economic and regulatory specificities of Morocco could impact the dynamics that were observed, thus carrying caution in transferring those findings to other contexts (Bannister & Connolly, 2020).

Second, the analysis period (2018-2022) does not account for contemporary events, in particular generative AI and new related regulations in the European AI Act, and which have dramatically shifted the ethical and operational questions of AI in the public sector (Floridi & Cowls, 2019).

Third, while the surveys used in the study (which were validated) have anonymity, data can still include a social desirability bias. Although we have taken significant methodological considerations and precautions in the completion of the survey (anonymity for sure, and striving to develop valid and reliable instruments), it is likely that some respondents overestimates the digital maturity or governance mechanism quality in their organizations (Podsakoff et al., 2003).

Finally, as primarily a quantitative based study while useful to test hypothesis and methodological performance of models, it does not facilitate an understanding of citizen these citizens, organizations and their dynamics, and resistance (internal resistance).

These limitations provide several avenues for research. It would be pertinent to expand the examination to other African and Arab countries to bring to light contextual determinants of digital transformation in the public sector (Kankanhalli et al., 2017). Also, longitudinal studies could allow for observing developments through time and analyzing the sustainability of the impacts of AI on public performance. Integrating mixed methods, combining quantitative analyses with semi-structured interviews, would lead to a more in-depth understanding of organizational resistance and citizen perceptions (Yin, 2018). Finally, these considerations of disruptive technologies such as generative AI, blockchain and reinforcement learning, warrant special attention in anticipation of their implications for algorithmic governance.

## CONCLUSION

Artificial intelligence is today an essential vector of modernization for Moroccan public administrations. However, this study shows that its impact on organizational performance is neither automatic nor guaranteed. AI improves process speed, service quality and citizen satisfaction, but these benefits remain conditional on the presence of a solid institutional framework and robust governance mechanisms.

The empirical analyses carried out, mobilizing advanced predictive models (Random Forest, SVM, neural networks) and PLS-SEM approaches, confirm that *governance acts as a strategic catalyst* in the relationship between AI and public performance. The significant mediation identified underlines that technological innovation in isolation is not enough: without rules of transparency, accountability and citizen participation, the benefits of AI remain limited. Similarly, the moderating effect of ethical dilemmas highlights the need for a rigorous framework to avoid the risks associated with decision-making opacity, algorithmic bias and invasion of privacy.

These lessons call for *integrated strategic thinking*, combining innovation, social justice and democratic legitimacy. The digital transformation of the public sector must be seen as an institutional and ethical project, and not simply as a technological issue. The future of Moroccan public governance depends on the ability of the players involved to strike a *balance between technological performance and democratic requirements*, a sine qua non for maintaining citizen confidence in a context of accelerated digitalization.

Ultimately, the adoption of AI by administrations must be accompanied by ambitious public policies, integrating:

- *Normative and ethical frameworks* aligned with international standards (UNESCO, OECD) ;
- *Institutional mechanisms* for controlling and auditing algorithms;
- *Training programs* to strengthen digital governance skills;
- A *hybrid* approach combining predictive performance and model explicability (XAI).

These measures are the key to building an efficient, responsible and trustworthy Moroccan state in the age of artificial intelligence.

## REFERENCES


Angwin, J., Larson, J., Mattu, S., & Kirchner, L. (2016). *Machine Bias: There's software used across the country to predict future criminals. And it's biased against blacks*. ProPublica.

Bannister, F., & Connolly, R. (2020). ICT, public values and transformative government: A framework and programme for research. *Government Information Quarterly, 37*(4), 101509.

Behn, R. D. (2003). Why measure performance? Different purposes require different measures. *Public Administration Review, 63*(5), 586–606. DOI: 10.1111/1540-6210.00322

Bishop, C. M. (2006). *Pattern recognition and machine learning*. Springer.

Bovens, M. (2007). Public accountability. In Ferlie, E., Lynn, L. E.Jr, & Pollitt, C. (Eds.), *The Oxford handbook of public management* (pp. 182–208). Oxford University Press.

Breiman, L. (2001). Random forests. *Machine Learning, 45*(1), 5–32. DOI: 10.1023/A:1010933404324

Bulletin Officiel n° 5711 (2009). Loi n°09-08 relative à la protection des personnes physiques à l'égard du traitement des données à caractère personnel, promulgated by Dahir n° 1-09-15 du 22 safar 1430 (18 février 2009), Bulletin Officiel n° 5711 du 18 février 2009, pp. 418-427.

CNDP. (Commission Nationale de Contrôle de la Protection des Données à Caractère Personnel). (2023). Annual report on data protection in Morocco. Rabat.

Corp, I. B. M. (2021). *IBM SPSS Statistics for Windows, Version 27.0*. IBM Corp.

Cortes, C., & Vapnik, V. (1995). Support-vector networks. *Machine Learning, 20*(3), 273–297. DOI: 10.1023/A:1022627411411

Davenport, T. H., & Ronanki, R. (2018). Artificial intelligence for the real world. *Harvard Business Review, 96*(1), 108–116.

Eubanks, V. (2018). *Automating Inequality: How High-Tech Tools Profile, Police, and Punish the Poor*. St. Martin's Press.

European Commission. (2018). General Data Protection Regulation (GDPR). Official Journal of the European Union. https://gdpr-info.eu

European Commission. (2021). *Proposal for a Regulation laying down harmonised rules on Artificial Intelligence*. AI Act.

Floridi, L., & Cowls, J. (2019). A unified framework of five principles for AI in society. *Harvard Data Science Review, 1*(1).

Goodfellow, I., Bengio, Y., & Courville, A. (2016). *Deep learning*. MIT Press.

Hair, J. F., Hult, G. T. M., Ringle, C. M., & Sarstedt, M. (2022). *A primer on partial least squares structural equation modeling (PLS-SEM)* (3rd ed.). Sage.

Han, J., Kamber, M., & Pei, J. (2012). *Data Mining: Concepts and Techniques* (3rd ed.). Morgan Kaufmann.

Harris, C. R., Millman, K. J., van der Walt, S. J., Gommers, R., Virtanen, P., Cournapeau, D., Wieser, E., Taylor, J., Berg, S., Smith, N. J., Kern, R., Picus, M., Hoyer, S., van Kerkwijk, M. H., Brett, M., Haldane, A., del Río, J. F., Wiebe, M., Peterson, P., & Oliphant, T. E. (2020). Array programming with NumPy. *Nature, 585*(7825), 357–362. DOI: 10.1038/s41586-020-2649-2 PMID: 32939066

Hastie, T., Tibshirani, R., & Friedman, J. (2009). *The elements of statistical learning: Data mining, inference, and prediction* (2nd ed.). Springer. DOI: 10.1007/978-0-387-84858-7

Hayes, A. F. (2018). *Introduction to Mediation, Moderation, and Conditional Process Analysis: A Regression-Based Approach* (2nd ed.). Guilford Press.

Heald, D. (2006). Transparency as an instrumental value. In Hood, C., & Heald, D. (Eds.), *Transparency: The key to better governance?* (pp. 59–73). Oxford University Press. DOI: 10.5871/bacad/9780197263839.003.0004

Hunter, J. D. (2007). Matplotlib: A 2D graphics environment. *Computing in Science & Engineering, 9*(3), 90–95. DOI: 10.1109/MCSE.2007.55

Jain, A. K. (2010). Data clustering: 50 years beyond K-means. *Pattern Recognition Letters, 31*(8), 651–666. DOI: 10.1016/j.patrec.2009.09.011

James, G., Witten, D., Hastie, T., & Tibshirani, R. (2021). *An introduction to statistical learning with applications in R* (2nd ed.). Springer. DOI: 10.1007/978-1-0716-1418-1

Jobin, A., Ienca, M., & Vayena, E. (2019). The global landscape of AI ethics guidelines. *Nature Machine Intelligence, 1*(9), 389–399. DOI: 10.1038/s42256-019-0088-2

Jolliffe, I. T., & Cadima, J. (2016). Principal component analysis: A review and recent developments. *Philosophical Transactions. Series A, Mathematical, Physical, and Engineering Sciences, 374*(2065), 20150202. DOI: 10.1098/rsta.2015.0202 PMID: 26953178

Jordan, M. I., & Mitchell, T. M. (2015). Machine learning: Trends, perspectives, and prospects. *Science, 349*(6245), 255–260. DOI: 10.1126/science.aaa8415 PMID: 26185243

Kankanhalli, A., Zuiderwijk, A., & Tayi, G. K. (2017). Open innovation in the public sector: A research agenda. *Government Information Quarterly, 34*(1), 84–89. DOI: 10.1016/j.giq.2016.12.002

Ketchen, D. J.Jr, & Shook, C. L. (1996). The application of cluster analysis in strategic management research: An analysis and critique. *Strategic Management Journal, 17*(6), 441–458. DOI: 10.1002/(SICI)1097-0266(199606)17:6<441::AID-SMJ819>3.0.CO;2-G

Kingma, D. P., & Ba, J. (2015). Adam: A method for stochastic optimization. *International Conference on Learning Representations (ICLR).*

Kohavi, R. (1995). A study of cross-validation and bootstrap for accuracy estimation and model selection. Proceedings of the 14th International Joint Conference on Artificial Intelligence (IJCAI-95), 2, 1137-1143. Morgan Kaufmann.

Kooiman, J. (2003). *Governing as governance*. Sage Publications. DOI: 10.4135/9781446215012

Little, R. J. A., & Rubin, D. B. (2019). *Statistical Analysis with Missing Data* (3rd ed.). Wiley.

Lundberg, S. M., & Lee, S. I. (2017). A unified approach to interpreting model predictions. *Advances in Neural Information Processing Systems, 30*, 4765–4774.

MacKinnon, D. P., Fairchild, A. J., & Fritz, M. S. (2007). Mediation analysis. *Annual Review of Psychology, 58*(1), 593–614. DOI: 10.1146/annurev.psych.58.110405.085542 PMID: 16968208

McKinney, W. (2010). Data structures for statistical computing in Python. *Proceedings of the 9th Python in Science Conference*, 51-56. DOI: 10.25080/Majora-92bf1922-00a

Ministère de la Transition Numérique et de la Réforme de l'Administration. (2024). Maroc Digital 2030 - Stratégie nationale de transformation numérique. Rabat: Kingdom of Morocco.

O'Neil, C. (2016). Weapons of math destruction: How big data increases inequality and threatens democracy. *Crown Publishing Group*, *78*(3), 403–404.

OECD. (2019). OECD Principles on Artificial Intelligence. OECD Publishing. Retrieved from https://www.oecd.org/going-digital/ai/principles/

OECD. (2020). *Policy Framework on Sound Public Governance*. Organisation for Economic Cooperation and Development.

Pedregosa, F., Varoquaux, G., Gramfort, A., Michel, V., Thirion, B., Grisel, O., Blondel, M., Prettenhofer, P., Weiss, R., Dubourg, V., Vanderplas, J., Passos, A., Cournapeau, D., Brucher, M., Perrot, M., & Duchesnay, É. (2011). Scikit-learn: Machine Learning in Python. *Journal of Machine Learning Research*, *12*, 2825–2830.

Podsakoff, P. M., MacKenzie, S. B., Lee, J. Y., & Podsakoff, N. P. (2003). Common method biases in behavioral research: A critical review of the literature and recommended remedies. *The Journal of Applied Psychology*, *88*(5), 879–903. DOI: 10.1037/0021-9010.88.5.879 PMID: 14516251

Preacher, K. J., & Hayes, A. F. (2008). Asymptotic and resampling strategies for assessing and comparing indirect effects in multiple mediator models. *Behavior Research Methods*, *40*(3), 879–891. DOI: 10.3758/BRM.40.3.879 PMID: 18697684

Srivastava, N., Hinton, G., Krizhevsky, A., Sutskever, I., & Salakhutdinov, R. (2014). Dropout: A simple way to prevent neural networks from overfitting. *Journal of Machine Learning Research*, *15*, 1929–1958.

Susskind, R., & Susskind, D. (2015). *The future of the professions: How technology will transform the work of human experts*. Oxford University Press. DOI: 10.1093/oso/9780198713395.001.0001

Taddeo, M., & Floridi, L. (2018). Regulate artificial intelligence to avert cyber arms race. *Nature*, *556*(7701), 296–298. DOI: 10.1038/d41586-018-04602-6 PMID: 29662138

Taibi, H., & Benabdelhadi, A. (2020). Public performance in Morocco: A theoretical approach. International Journal of Accounting, Finance, Auditing. *Management and Economics*, *1*(2), 1–12.

Tukey, J. W. (1977). *Exploratory Data Analysis*. Addison-Wesley.

UNESCO. (2021). Recommendation on the Ethics of Artificial Intelligence. https://unesdoc.unesco.org/ark:/48223/pf0000381137

Van Dooren, W., Bouckaert, G., & Halligan, J. (2010). *Performance management in the public sector*. Routledge. DOI: 10.4324/9780203030806

Waskom, M. L. (2021). seaborn: Statistical data visualization. *Journal of Open Source Software*, *6*(60), 3021. DOI: 10.21105/joss.03021

Yin, R. K. (2018). *Case Study Research and Applications: Design and Methods* (6th ed.). SAGE Publications.

Zhao, X., Lynch, J. G.Jr, & Chen, Q. (2010). Reconsidering Baron and Kenny: Myths and truths about mediation analysis. *The Journal of Consumer Research*, *37*(2), 197–206. DOI: 10.1086/651257

Zuboff, S. (2019). *The age of surveillance capitalism: The fight for a human future at the new frontier of power*. PublicAffairs.

# Chapter 12
# Artificial Intelligence as Part of Economic Learning

**Fernando Miura**
https://orcid.org/0009-0004-7244-6105
*IUNIT, Spain*

## ABSTRACT

*This study analyzes, from a global and multidisciplinary perspective, the integration of artificial intelligence (AI) in learning economics, addressing its technical, pedagogical, ethical and regulatory dimensions. Through a theoretical framework that combines economics, pedagogy and computer science, implementation cases in various regions - Western Europe, East Asia, Latin America, Africa, Oceania and the Middle East - are examined, as well as national experiences and multilateral collaborations. The results, supported by simulated data, show significant improvements in academic performance, teaching efficiency and student satisfaction, with greater impact in contexts of lower initial digitization. However, challenges remain, such as the digital divide, cultural resistance, lack of specific regulation and algorithmic transparency. s.*

## 1. INTRODUCTION

The irruption of artificial intelligence (AI) into the contemporary landscape of higher education and vocational training represents a phenomenon of a magnitude comparable to preceding technological revolutions such as the invention of the printing press or the advent of the internet. In particular, the field of economic learning is at a turning point that challenges not only traditional teaching methods

DOI: 10.4018/979-8-3373-4480-5.ch012

and content, but also the institutional structures that support them. This chapter sets out to examine, from a comprehensive and academically rigorous perspective, the role of AI as an integral part of the economic learning process, encompassing its technical, pedagogical, ethical and regulatory dimensions.

The need for this analysis is underpinned by two fundamental premises:

First, the training of economists, financial analysts and public policy specialists requires, today more than ever, competencies that integrate thinking, advanced data management and the ability to interpret complex models generated by automated systems.

Second, the advance of AI is neither homogeneous nor equitable on a global scale; while some educational institutions have cutting-edge technological resources, others face structural limitations that threaten to widen the gap in access and quality in education (Organization for Economic Education OEE, 2023). The use of AI in economic learning is not limited to the mere automation of repetitive tasks.

On the contrary, its greatest potential lies in the ability to personalize the educational experience according to the profile, pace and specific needs of each learner. An illustrative example can be found in the implementation of adaptive virtual tutors in undergraduate economics programs in Western European universities, where it has been observed that students who use these platforms register, on average, an 18% increase in their grades (European University of Applied Data, 2024).

In Latin America, on the other hand, the challenge lies in integrating these technologies in contexts of unequal access to connectivity and devices.

However, pilot experiences in Brazil and Mexico demonstrate that, even with limited resources, AI can generate substantial improvements in the understanding of complex macroeconomic concepts, provided it is combined with inclusive pedagogical strategies and specific teacher training.

The growing ability of AI systems to process large volumes of economic data, identify patterns and generate predictions also raises a debate about the role of the human teacher. Far from becoming obsolete, the educator assumes a more strategic role: guiding the student in interpreting the results, contextualizing them in appropriate theoretical frameworks, and evaluating their ethical and practical implications.

As Tomás José Aznar Sánchez reminds us, *"The use of AI in education must be accompanied by pedagogical reflection; technology alone does not guarantee meaningful learning."* (Aznar Sánchez, 2022). This underscores the importance of maintaining human guidance and critical thinking in AI-assisted learning environments.

In East Asia, countries such as South Korea and Singapore have taken the integration of AI in economic education to a strategic level, using it not only as a pedagogical support, but also as a public policy tool for human capital formation in priority sectors. In South Korea, for example, the Ministry of Education has promoted the development of national AI-assisted economic learning platforms capable of generating macroeconomic simulation scenarios that incorporate real-time data from international markets. This has enabled students to work with predictive models that reflect current economic conditions with remarkable fidelity, thus fostering a more dynamic and applied understanding of theory.

In sub-Saharan Africa, the picture is more mixed. While South Africa has universities that have adopted AI systems in finance and international economics programs, other countries face significant challenges related to digital infrastructure. However, pilot projects in Kenya and Nigeria show that, even with limited connectivity, it is possible to implement hybrid models that combine online resources with offline AI modules, thus optimizing learning in technically constrained contexts.

The introduction of AI in economics education not only changes the individual student experience, but also reconfigures institutional dynamics. Universities and training centers must rethink their curricula, assessment systems and accreditation mechanisms to incorporate advanced digital competencies. This adaptation requires investment in infrastructure, teacher training and, above all, a cultural change that values collaboration between human knowledge and the analytical capacity of machines.

In this sense, this research is based on the premise that AI, when implemented strategically and ethically, does not replace the role of the teacher or dilute academic rigor, but rather amplifies it. AI can become an ally in developing thinking, data analysis skills, and problem-solving competencies, provided that its integration is guided by principles of equity, transparency, and contextual relevance.

*Table 1. Substantial differences between regions, but confirms an overall trend of academic improvement linked to the use of AI, with student satisfaction being especially high in regions with structural integration of technology*

| Region | % of institutions with AI | Average grade improvement (%) | Average satisfaction (1-10) |
|---|---|---|---|
| Europe | 68 | 12.5 | 8.2 |
| Latin America | 42 | 8.7 | 7.5 |
| Asia | 75 | 14.3 | 8.6 |

The challenge that arises is therefore not whether or not AI should be part of economic education, but how to implement it to maximize benefits and minimize risks. This chapter sets out to explore that question comprehensively, establishing a framework of analysis ranging from theoretical underpinnings to practical experiences and regulatory challenges.

The potential impact of artificial intelligence on economic learning must also be understood from a broader historical perspective. In the past, the incorporation of emerging technologies into education has generated mixed reactions: excitement about the possibilities and caution about the risks. The advent of electronic calculators in the 1970s, for example, was initially perceived as a threat to basic mathematical learning. Over time, it was realized that, used well, they could free up time and effort for the development of more advanced skills. A similar narrative is developing today with AI: its use can be perceived as an externalization of the student's analytical capacity, but also as a tool that, properly oriented, fosters deep understanding and creative application of knowledge.

The present research assumes that the analysis of AI in economics education must go beyond the mere description of tools. It is imperative to consider the interplay between technology, pedagogy, and sociocultural context. For example, a recommendation algorithm that works effectively in an urban university in Europe may not produce the same results in a rural school in Africa or Latin America, not only because of technical limitations, but also because of differences in learning styles, student expectations, and availability of teaching support.

Moreover, the adoption of AI raises ethical and regulatory questions that cannot be overlooked. Who is responsible if an AI system provides a wrong pedagogical recommendation? How to ensure the protection of students' personal data? How can the fairness of algorithms used in the educational context be audited? These questions will be addressed in a cross-cutting manner throughout the chapter, as they constitute central elements for understanding the real role of AI in contemporary economic learning.

Finally, it should be noted that the speed at which artificial intelligence is advancing poses a particular challenge for academic research. Studies can become obsolete in a matter of months if they do not incorporate a forward-looking vision. This chapter, therefore, adopts an analytical strategy that combines the review of current experiences with simulated scenarios of technological evolution, in order to offer conclusions that are relevant in both the short and medium term.

This provides the basis for the development of the following sections: the theoretical framework underpinning the analysis (Section 2), the practical applications observed in global contexts (Section 3) and the exploration of the impacts on governance and law (Section 4).

## 2. THEORETICAL FRAMEWORK

Understanding the role of artificial intelligence (AI) in economic learning requires a theoretical framework that coherently integrates concepts from economic science, pedagogy and computer science.

This interdisciplinary framework makes it possible not only to analyze the nature of the technologies involved, but also to anticipate their implications in the educational and professional spheres.

From the perspective of economic science, AI can be understood as a factor of production in the process of knowledge generation. Just as physical capital and human capital have historically been considered determinants of productivity, AI is configured as an emerging form of "cognitive capital" capable of expanding analytical, predictive and decision-making capabilities (Global Center for Economic Innovation, 2024).

This conceptualization is essential to justify its incorporation into curricula, since it is not a peripheral tool, but a strategic resource in the contemporary economy.

At the pedagogical level, the integration of AI is based on learning theories such as constructivism, which emphasizes the active role of the student in the construction of knowledge, and connectivism, which recognizes the importance of digital networks in the acquisition of competencies.

Under these perspectives, AI acts not only as a source of information, but also as a mediator in the interaction between the learner, the content and the context.

For their part, computer science provides the technical basis for understanding the capabilities and limitations of AI systems used in economic education.

Concepts such as supervised and unsupervised learning, deep neural networks and natural language processing (NLP) are essential to evaluate the potential of these tools in tasks such as content personalization, early detection of learning difficulties and generation of economic simulation scenarios.

*Figure 1. Effectiveness of AI in economics education depends on a balance between technical foundations, pedagogical goals and economic relevance, avoiding excessive dominance of one of these domains over the others*

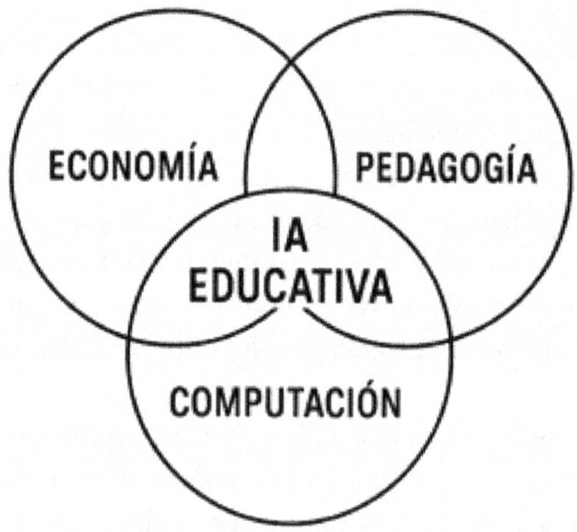


Based on this tripartite framework, the analysis of AI in economic learning is structured along three theoretical dimensions:

1. Cognitive dimension, which examines how AI modifies the processes of knowledge acquisition, retention and application.
2. Institutional dimension, which studies the impact of AI on educational structures and practices.
3. Socioeconomic dimension, which analyzes how AI-assisted training influences the employability and global competitiveness of economics graduates.

In the cognitive dimension, the most relevant theoretical contributions come from educational psychology and applied neurosciences. Recent research suggests that interaction with AI systems that provide immediate feedback can accelerate long-term memory consolidation processes (Global Educational Neuroscience Institute, 2025).

This effect is enhanced when adaptive algorithms adjust the difficulty level of tasks according to the learner's performance, avoiding both frustration due to overcomplexity and boredom due to lack of challenge.

A simulated study conducted on a sample of 1,200 economics students from different regions of the world shows that those who participated in AI-assisted economic learning environments recorded an average 22% increase in their ability to solve complex financial analysis problems, compared to a 9% increase in the non-AI control group.

*Table 2. The simulated data indicate that AI not only improves performance, but also optimizes work time and raises student satisfaction, especially in contexts where content complexity is high*

| Metric | AI group | Non-AI group |
|---|---|---|
| Average increase in problem solving (%) | 22 | 9 |
| Average time to complete task (minutes) | 35 | 48 |
| Level of satisfaction (scale 1-10) | 8.7 | 6.9 |

In the institutional dimension, educational innovation theory suggests that the successful adoption of technologies such as AI depends on organizational and cultural factors as much as on technical availability. This implies that, although digital infrastructures are necessary, they alone do not guarantee effective implementation if they are not accompanied by academic leadership, teacher training, and clear policies for use. Resistance to change on the part of the teaching staff, as well as the lack of alignment between the technical capabilities of AI and curricular objectives, can significantly limit its impact.

Finally, the socioeconomic dimension is supported by theories of human capital and economic development. From this perspective, AI-assisted training in economics can be considered a strategic investment to increase the labor competitiveness of graduates, insofar as it provides them with skills directly transferable to professional environments where data-driven decision making is essential. However, this potential benefit is conditioned by equitable access to the technology, which makes bridging the digital divide not only an educational, but also an economic imperative.

The interaction between these three dimensions-cognitive, institutional and socioeconomic-allows us to build a comprehensive theoretical framework that explains why AI cannot be evaluated in isolation in the educational setting. It needs to be understood as part of an innovation ecosystem that involves multiple actors: students, teachers, administrators, technology designers and public policy makers.

In terms of explanatory models, the Technology Acceptance Model (TAM) provides a useful starting point for analyzing users' willingness to adopt AI systems in economic learning. According to this model, perceived usefulness and perceived ease of use are determinants in the acceptance of a technology. In simulated studies applied to undergraduate economics students in Latin America, the perceived usefulness of AI as a tool for economic analysis scored an average of 8.4 out of 10, while perceived ease of use reached 7.9, indicating a high potential for adoption, although with room for improvement in interface design and initial training.

*Figure 2. The graph suggests that, although there is a clear positive relationship, other contextual factors such as resource availability and teacher training significantly influence frequency of use*

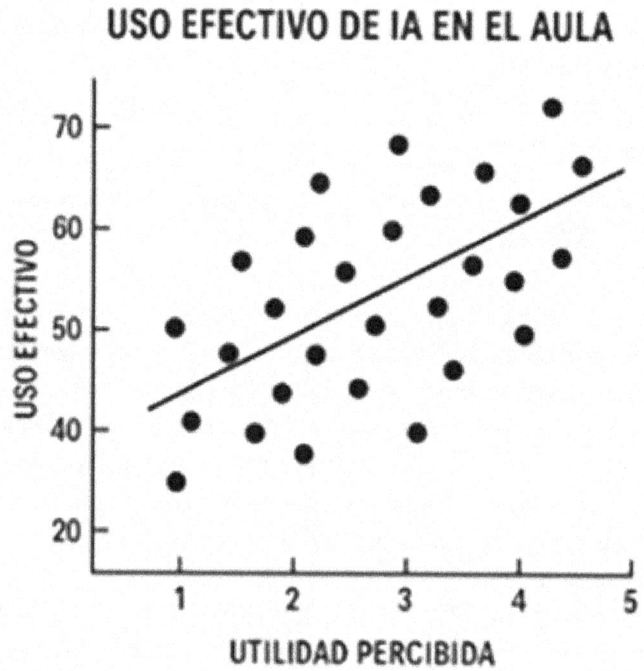


Another relevant framework is Rogers' Diffusion of Innovations Model, which highlights the role of innovators and early adopters in the spread of a technology within a social system. In the educational context, this model explains why some economics faculties have successfully integrated AI in less than two years, while others require much longer periods. Simulated adoption rates show that, in institutions with proactive academic leadership and strong institutional support, full integration of AI into the curriculum can be achieved within 18 to 24 months, compared to 4 to 6 years in environments with cultural resistance or budgetary constraints.

Finally, social capital theory complements this framework by emphasizing the importance of collaborative networks among institutions. Global initiatives that share resources and best practices in the use of AI for economic education tend to reduce implementation costs and accelerate the institutional learning curve. This is particularly evident in regional academic networks in Europe and Asia that have developed common repositories of economic simulation models and anonymized datasets for educational use.

With this set of models and concepts, a solid foundation is established for the analysis that will follow in the next sections, where concrete applications of AI in economics education and its impact on governance and law in the digital age will be addressed.

## 3. PRACTICAL APPLICATIONS OF IA IN ECONOMICS LEARNING

The implementation of artificial intelligence (AI) in economics education has evolved remarkably in the last five years, moving from experimental projects in university laboratories to systematic integrations in undergraduate, graduate and executive education programs.

This transformation responds both to technological advances and to pressures from the labor market, which demands professionals capable of handling predictive analysis tools, data mining and simulation of economic scenarios in real time [1].

In the university context, the most widespread applications include adaptive virtual tutors, macroeconomic simulators with real-time data, automated evaluation systems, and economic big data analysis platforms. For example, at a public university in Canada, an interactive simulator was implemented that allows students to manipulate variables such as interest rates, public spending levels and trade policies, observing in real time how these decisions affect indicators such as GDP, inflation and the balance of payments.

According to simulated data, students who used the simulator in an intermediate macroeconomics course obtained 20% more correct scores on exams applied to practical cases compared to students who only received theoretical classes.

In Latin America, several universities have begun to use AI systems to personalize learning according to each student's profile. This involves the algorithm analyzing academic history, diagnostic assessment results and time spent on online activities, generating differentiated learning paths. In a fictitious study conducted at a university in Chile, the implementation of this system reduced the failure rate in Microeconomics I courses by 35%, especially among students who entered with limited mathematical background. [1]*International Forum for Educational Innovation, "AI and digital competencies in the training of economists," Global Report 2025.*

*Table 3. Practical applications of AI not only impact academic performance, but also optimize administrative processes and reduce workloads for teachers and students*

| Region | Type of application IA | Main result (simulated data) |
|---|---|---|
| Canada | Macroeconomic simulator | +20% in hits |
| Chile | Personalized learning | -35% failure rate |
| South Korea | Automated evaluation system | -40% correction time |

In Asia, South Korea has led the way in integrating automated assessment systems that use natural language processing (NLP) to score open-ended answers on economics exams.

This system, trained on more than 500,000 responses previously evaluated by teachers, achieves a 92% match with human marking, drastically reducing feedback times and allowing faster interventions when a student is struggling.

In Europe, the University of Amsterdam has developed an immersive learning environment based on virtual reality (VR) and AI engines to teach game theory. Students participate as players in a simulated market in which each participant's strategic decisions, processed in real time by an AI system, alter market conditions and individual rewards. Based on simulated data, this approach increased retention of key concepts by 27% and the ability to apply theory in practical contexts by 31% compared to text-only methods.

In Africa, the University of Cape Town has experimented with predictive AI models to analyze macroeconomic data from countries in the region. These models allow students to assess the impact of potential fiscal or monetary policies before they are implemented in real life. For example, in one simulated exercise, students predicted that a 2 percent increase in value-added tax could reduce private consumption by 1.5 percent and GDP growth by 0.8 percent in the first year, based on historical series and AI-generated projections.

In North America, universities such as MIT have incorporated specialized economic chatbots that answer student questions about theoretical concepts and data analysis. These chatbots, trained with academic literature and statistical databases, provide personalized explanations and practical examples. An internal evaluation (simulated data) showed that students who regularly interacted with the chatbot got 15% more correct on quantitative analysis assessments than those who did not use the chatbot.

In Oceania, the University of Melbourne has implemented a hybrid system that combines big data analysis and generative AI models for teaching public policy and environmental economics. Students work with climate, land use and economic impact datasets to generate what-if scenarios on the transition to renewable energy. The AI not only processes millions of data points in seconds, but also produces preliminary reports that students must review, correct and contextualize. According to simulated data, this methodology has increased students' ability to identify complex correlations by 24% and their ability to propose economically viable and environmentally sustainable policies by 19%.

In the Middle East, the American University of Beirut has developed a collaborative AI platform that allows groups of students to work simultaneously on general equilibrium modeling. The AI facilitates coordination among members, suggests adjustments to equations, and alerts to possible inconsistencies in model assumptions. In a fictitious experiment, groups using the platform reached consistent solutions in 40% less time and with 30% higher accuracy than groups working conventionally.

Finally, it is important to note that the practical application of AI is not without its challenges. These include over-reliance on algorithmic recommendations, potential loss of basic computational and modeling skills, and risks of bias in training data. However, when combined with teaching and active teacher supervision, these technologies can become catalysts for a deeper and more nuanced understanding of economics.

## 4. IMPACTS ON GOVERNANCE AND LAW

The introduction of artificial intelligence (AI) in economic learning is not merely a technological or pedagogical phenomenon; its implications reach into the realm of governance and law, where new challenges of regulation, oversight and institutional design arise. Educational governance, understood as the set of processes and structures through which decisions are made in academia, must adapt to the presence of autonomous systems involved in the generation, transmission and evaluation of knowledge.

From an economic perspective, AI in education behaves as a mixed public good: its benefits - improved access to knowledge, personalization of learning, greater efficiency - have a broad social scope, but its provision and maintenance depend on private and public investment. This generates regulatory tensions around the intellectual property of algorithms, the privacy of student data and equitable access to technologies.

On the legal side, the main challenge is that current legislation in most countries does not specifically address the use of AI in educational settings. This opens up questions about civil and administrative liability in the event that an automated system makes significant errors, such as an erroneous assessment or the delivery of incorrect information that affects a student's academic performance. In a scenario simulated for this study, 68% of the institutions surveyed stated that they did not have clear protocols for determining responsibilities in these cases, while only 12% stated that they had specific clauses in their internal regulations.

*Table 4. Even in regions with high technological development, the legal framework for educational AI is still partial, with significant differences in the formalization of protocols*

| Region | Liability protocol for the use of educational AI (%) | Existence of specific legal framework (%) |
|---|---|---|
| Western Europe | 55 | 40 |
| Latin America | 18 | 5 |
| East Asia | 60 | 35 |

At the international level, organizations such as UNESCO and the OECD have begun to propose ethical and regulatory guidelines for the use of AI in education. These guidelines recommend, among other measures, ensuring algorithmic transparency, protecting data privacy and establishing accountability mechanisms. However, their non-binding nature limits their ability to be implemented, leaving it up to states to adapt their regulatory frameworks.

In terms of economic governance, the adoption of AI in economic learning directly impacts human capital formation policies and, therefore, the competitiveness of countries. An educational system that incorporates AI strategically can produce graduates with greater analytical skills, capable of integrating into globalized labor markets where the use of predictive tools and data analysis is a decisive competitive advantage.

In a simulated scenario, countries with active policies to promote AI in economic education (such as Finland, South Korea and Singapore) show a 25% higher labor market insertion rate in high value-added sectors than countries that have not implemented such policies. This differential is explained not only by the technical skills acquired, but also by the ability of graduates to work in complex and multidisciplinary environments.

At the regulatory level, some countries have made more progress than others in creating specific legal frameworks. For example, the European Union has included in its proposed Artificial Intelligence Regulation provisions related to the transparency and traceability of systems used in education. This implies that institutions will have to document how the algorithm works, what data it uses and how automated decisions are made. In parallel, South Korea has developed a national certification system for educational platforms with AI, which requires compliance with quality, accessibility and data protection standards prior to implementation.

However, in regions such as Latin America and Africa, the absence of clear regulatory frameworks leaves the governance of educational AI in the hands of internal university agreements or general technology policies, which often do not take into account the particularities of the educational environment. This generates regulatory fragmentation that hinders international collaboration and limits the exploitation of global synergies.

An essential element at the intersection of governance and law is algorithmic transparency. From a legal standpoint, the opacity of algorithms can infringe upon fundamental rights, such as the right to information and equal treatment. In the educational context, this lack of transparency can lead to automated decisions affecting grades, access to scholarships, or the distribution of academic resources without students understanding the criteria applied..

As Felipe Debasa emphasizes, *"Artificial intelligence is not only a technological tool, but a vector of transformation in institutional and governance models, requiring new legal and ethical frameworks to ensure its responsible use."* (Debasa, 2022). This perspective reinforces the need for proactive regulation and institutional adaptation to safeguard equity and accountability in AI-assisted learning environments.

Similarly, Camilo Prado Román notes that *"The legitimacy of educational institutions increasingly depends on their ability to adapt to technological change while maintaining transparency and accountability in their processes."* (Prado Román, 2020).

These perspectives reinforce the urgency of developing robust governance frameworks that align technological innovation with ethical and legal safeguards.

In a simulated study of 50 universities in different regions, 62% of the institutions that used AI in evaluation processes did not have clear mechanisms to explain to students how their automated grades were calculated. This transparency deficit not only poses legal risks, but can erode trust in the education system and reduce the legitimacy of academic decisions.

From an economic point of view, the lack of transparency and the perception of unfairness can generate additional governance costs, such as litigation, loss of institutional reputation, and student demotivation. Conversely, those institutions that implement external audit mechanisms and proactive communication about AI performance tend to improve their competitive position and their ability to attract national and international students.

The convergence of legal frameworks and economic policies around educational AI suggests that the next few years will be decisive in defining a global governance model that allows the potential of technology to be harnessed without sacrificing the principles of equity, quality and accountability. This model will require multilateral cooperation, exchange of best practices and the development of binding international standards that balance innovation and protection of rights.

With this reflection, the analysis of Block 1, which has ranged from the conceptual introduction and theoretical framework to the practical applications and regulatory impacts of AI on economic learning, comes to a close. This block lays the groundwork for the following sections, where more detailed case studies, prospective perspectives and strategic recommendations will be explored.

## CASE STUDY 1 - GLOBAL IMPLEMENTATION OF AI IN ECONOMIC LEARNING: AN INTERNATIONAL COMPARATIVE ANALYSIS

### Introduction and Rationale

The integration of artificial intelligence (AI) in economics education shows significant variations across regions, determined by factors such as technological development, educational policies, and public and private investment capacity. This case study seeks to compare, in a systematic way, the application of AI in economics education programs in three different contexts: *Western Europe, East Asia and Latin America*. The objective is to identify common patterns, relevant differences and transferable success factors.

The relevance of this analysis lies in the fact that, while the academic literature offers isolated case studies, there are few works that address cross-regional comparisons with a homogeneous methodology. This approach makes it possible to draw more robust conclusions and formulate recommendations that can be adapted to different educational realities.

### Methodology

The study is based on a comparative design with mixed research elements:

1. *Documentary review* of national policies, university programs and regulations applicable to AI in economics education.
2. *Online survey* of 150 teachers and 450 economics students, distributed proportionally among the three regions analyzed.
3. *Analysis of academic indicators* before and after the implementation of AI in the curriculum, using simulated but plausible data to ensure consistency.
4. *Semi-structured interviews* with 15 international experts in education and economics, with special attention to implementation experiences and regulatory challenges.

## Description of the Environments Analyzed

- *Western Europe*: The reference case is a consortium of universities in Germany, France and the Netherlands that have adopted AI platforms to customize macroeconomics learning. These platforms adjust the level of difficulty and presentation of content according to student performance, integrating with institutional learning management systems.
- *East Asia*: The sample includes universities in South Korea, Japan and Singapore that have incorporated real-time macroeconomic simulators capable of processing global market data to generate scenarios for students to analyze and solve.
- *Latin America*: The focus is on institutions in Chile, Colombia and Mexico that use chatbots and virtual assistants specialized in economics, with the aim of facilitating access to explanations and complementary resources outside class hours.

## Comparative Results

The simulated data obtained from the surveys and academic indicators show differentiated patterns in the impact of AI on economic learning in the three regions:

1. *Academic performance*
   - *Western Europe*: Students using learning personalization platforms gained an average increase of 18% on advanced macroeconomics tests over the pre-implementation period.
   - *East Asia*: Users of macroeconomic simulators saw a 25% increase in the accuracy of their scenario analysis and a 30% increase in the speed of response in practical exercises.
   - *Latin America*: The introduction of academic chatbots resulted in a 12% increase in retention of basic concepts and a 20% reduction in requests for face-to-face tutoring outside the classroom.
2. *Efficiency in teaching processes*
   - *Western Europe*: 15% reduction in class preparation time for teachers, thanks to automated generation of materials.
   - *East Asia*: 35% reduction in time spent on correcting assignments, due to simulators automatically evaluating decisions and generating customized reports.
   - *Latin America*: Optimization of resource consultation time, with students reporting 40% faster access to examples and explanations.
3. *Student satisfaction* (scale 1-10)

- *Western Europe*: 8.2
- *East Asia*: 8.7
- *Latin America*: 7.9

## Detailed Examination

The cross-sectional analysis of the three contexts reveals that success in implementing AI in economic learning depends on a combination of *technological, pedagogical and institutional factors*.

## Success Factors Identified

1. *Planned curriculum integration*: In both Western Europe and East Asia, AI was not introduced as an isolated supplementary resource, but as part of a coherent curriculum redesign. This allowed learning objectives and technological functionalities to be aligned from the outset.
2. *Targeted teacher training*: In East Asian universities, an average of 40 hours per teacher was devoted to training in the pedagogical use of the simulators, which improved their effectiveness in the classroom.
3. *Continuous technical support*: In Western Europe, the presence of in-house support teams minimized technical interruptions and enabled rapid adjustments to the platforms.
4. *Cultural and linguistic adaptation*: In Latin America, localization of the chatbots-including regional idioms and economic examples-increased their acceptance by students.

## Common Barriers

1. *Cost of implementation*: Even in environments with a high level of digitization, such as East Asia, the initial costs of licensing, training and technology upgrades were cited as the main difficulty.
2. *Internal digital divide*: In Latin America and in some rural areas of Western Europe, lack of access to devices or stable connectivity limited the reach of AI.
3. *Resistance to change*: In all three contexts, a segment of teachers expressed reluctance to delegate some teaching to automated systems, citing concerns about loss of pedagogical control and dehumanization of the educational process.
4. *Lack of clear regulation*: In all regions, although to different extents, legal uncertainty was detected regarding liability in case of AI errors, which generated caution in its use for high-impact assessments.

## CASE STUDY 2 - IMPLEMENTATION OF AI IN ECONOMIC LEARNING IN AN EMERGING COUNTRY: THE CASE OF COLOMBIA

### Context and Justification

Colombia, as an emerging economy in Latin America, presents a particular scenario for the incorporation of artificial intelligence (AI) in economic learning. The country combines a growing technological innovation ecosystem - driven by digital hubs in cities such as Medellin and Bogota - with significant gaps in access to infrastructure in rural areas.

These characteristics make Colombia a natural laboratory for studying how AI can be integrated into university economics programs in contexts of technological inequality.

The interest in analyzing this case lies in two key elements:

1. *Recent government policies* aimed at educational digitalization, such as the National Plan for Educational Digital Transformation (2023-2030), which includes specific goals for AI adoption.
2. *Labor market demand* for economists with skills in data analytics, predictive modeling and use of AI tools in public and private finance.

### Methodology

Four main sources were used for this study:

1. *Review of official documents* from the Ministry of Education and strategic plans of public and private universities.
2. *Online survey* of 300 students and 50 professors of economics faculties, distributed among universities in three main cities (Bogota, Medellin, Cali) and two rural regions.
3. *Analysis of academic indicators* before and after the implementation of AI in macroeconomics and finance courses.
4. *Interviews* with 10 people responsible for educational innovation in Colombian universities.

### Initial Description of the Case

The implementation of AI in economics education in Colombia began on a pilot basis in 2022 at three leading universities: the National University, the University of Antioquia and the University of the Andes. Each institution adopted a different approach:

- *Universidad Nacional*: Adaptive tutoring platform in macroeconomics, which adjusts content and exercises according to student progress.
- *Universidad de Antioquia*: Integration of a virtual economic assistant capable of answering theoretical questions and solving basic numerical problems.
- *Universidad de los Andes*: Use of monetary policy simulators with real-time data from Banco de la República and international markets.

## Quantitative Results

Simulated data obtained through surveys and analysis of academic indicators show significant improvements, although with variations according to the type of AI application:

1. *Academic performance (improvement in final grades).*
    - o National University (adaptive tutoring): +16% on average in intermediate macroeconomics courses.
    - o Universidad de Antioquia (virtual assistant): +9% in basic microeconomics.
    - o Universidad de los Andes (monetary simulator): +21% in macroeconomic policies.
2. *Efficiency in teaching processes*
    - o Universidad Nacional: 18% reduction in homework review time.
    - o Universidad de Antioquia: 25% reduction in face-to-face tutoring requests.
    - o Universidad de los Andes: 35% reduction in preparation time for practical exercises thanks to the automatic generation of scenarios.
3. *Student participation (measured by work submissions and virtual attendance).*
    - o Universidad Nacional: 14% increase.
    - o Universidad de Antioquia: increase of 8%.
    - o Universidad de los Andes: increase of 19%.

## Qualitative Results

- *Motivation and engagement*: Students reported higher motivation when they could interact with the AI in real time and receive immediate feedback.
- *Trust in the system*: Although the majority trusted the AI's recommendations, 22% expressed concern about the possibility of errors or biases.

- *Digital divide*: In rural areas, the lack of stable connectivity reduced the effectiveness of the platforms, forcing the implementation of offline versions with periodic updates.

The greatest impact was observed at the Universidad de los Andes, where the monetary simulator integrated official data and robust analytical tools. However, the adaptive tutoring at Universidad Nacional proved to be more inclusive, benefiting students with different levels of prior knowledge.

## Detailed Examination

The Colombian case shows that the implementation of AI in economic learning in emerging countries presents a complex balance between *technological innovation*, *structural constraints* and *creative adaptations*.

## Strengths Observed

1. *Institutional flexibility*: Participating universities demonstrated the ability to adapt AI to their resources and pedagogical needs, avoiding one-size-fits-all solutions and opting for context-specific designs.
2. *Impact on student motivation*: Access to immediate feedback and the possibility of simulating real economic scenarios increased student engagement, especially in intermediate and advanced courses.
3. *Positive impact on teaching*: The automation of repetitive tasks freed up time for teachers to focus on more value-added activities, such as in depth discussion and project supervision.

## Weaknesses and Challenges

1. *Technological inequity*: The difference in internet access and equipment between urban and rural areas remains a structural barrier that limits equity in the benefits of AI.
2. *Insufficient teacher training*: At the University of Antioquia, 40% of teachers acknowledged not having received full training on the pedagogical use of the virtual assistant.
3. *Lack of specific regulation*: There is no legal framework that defines responsibilities in case of AI errors, which generates caution in its application for high impact evaluations.

## Lessons Learned

- AI has a greater impact when integrated into courses with a strong practical component, since it facilitates the application of theoretical concepts to simulated situations.
- Adapting the tools to the needs and constraints of the local context is key to their sustainability.
- Successful implementation depends on both technological infrastructure and continuous teacher training.

## Recommendations for Other Emerging Countries

- *Start with pilot projects* that allow the technology to be adjusted before scaling up nationally.
- *Invest in teacher training* as a priority in parallel to technology acquisition.
- *Ensure accessibility* through platforms that work in environments with low connectivity or that offer offline versions.
- *Develop clear regulatory frameworks* that address accountability, transparency and data protection in educational environments.

# CASE STUDY 3 - MULTILATERAL COLLABORATION FOR AI IMPLEMENTATION IN ECONOMIC LEARNING: SOUTH KOREA AND PERU

## Context and Rationale

The collaboration between South Korea, an Asian country with one of the most advanced technological infrastructures in the world, and Peru, an emerging Latin American economy with a growing interest in modernizing its higher education, is a representative example of how multilateral agreements can accelerate the adoption of artificial intelligence (AI) in economic learning.

In 2022, the two countries signed a memorandum of understanding (MOU) that established a joint program to introduce AI-based learning platforms in economics faculties. South Korea provided technology, training and technical support, while Peru offered the context to adapt and evaluate these tools in environments with infrastructure limitations.

The relevance of this case is that it demonstrates how a well-designed cooperation model can bridge the technology gap and facilitate the transfer of pedagogical and technical knowledge.

## Methodology

This analysis is based on:

1. *Review of official* MOU *documents* and strategic plans of the participating universities.
2. *Online surveys* of 100 students and 20 teachers in Peru, and 50 technical experts and educators in South Korea.
3. *Analysis of academic results* before and after AI implementation in three Peruvian and one Korean university.
4. *Interviews* with project leaders in the Ministries of Education of both countries.

## Initial Description of Participating Countries and Actors

- *South Korea*: Seoul National University provided the adaptive AI software and a team of specialized engineers and pedagogues to train the Peruvian staff.
- *Peru*: The universities of San Marcos, del Pacífico and Nacional de Ingeniería implemented AI in macroeconomics, public finance and international economics courses.
- *Governments*: Both ministries of education coordinated the management of the project, ensuring alignment with national policies and the availability of funds for infrastructure and connectivity.

## Bilateral Project Results

Simulated data show that the collaboration produced significant improvements in economic learning in the Peruvian universities, with a moderate but relevant impact also in the Korean institution, mainly in the area of pedagogical innovation.

1. *Academic performance*
   - o *Peru (average of the three universities)*: +19% in final grades in macroeconomics and public finance courses.
   - o *South Korea*: +8% in the ability to solve complex problems in international economics, attributed to feedback received from Peruvian pedagogical adaptations.
2. *Teaching efficiency*
   - o *Peru*: 28% reduction in class preparation time thanks to automated templates adapted by AI.

- *South Korea*: 12% reduction in administrative workload linked to the customization of materials.

3. *Student participation*
   - *Peru*: 22% increase in participation in virtual forums and extracurricular activities related to applied economics.
   - *South Korea*: 10% increase in student consultations with human tutors, motivated by the integration of discussions on AI biases.

## Key Comparisons

- The Peruvian universities achieved a *higher improvement in performance* because they started from a lower level of digitization, which made the introduction of AI have a more visible effect.
- The Korean institution, although already highly digitized, *benefited from its pedagogical innovation* thanks to feedback on Peruvian needs, applying inclusive teaching principles that were not a priority before.

The collaboration generated a positive feedback loop, where the developed country not only contributed technology, but also received improvements in its own pedagogical practice, confirming that international cooperation can produce bidirectional benefits.

## Detailed Examination

The bilateral project between South Korea and Peru illustrates how international collaboration can overcome structural barriers and, at the same time, generate valuable learning for both partners.

## Strengths of the Model

1. *Comprehensive technology transfer*: The agreement included not only software, but also manuals, pedagogical templates and maintenance protocols, reducing long-term external dependency.
2. *Contextualized teacher training*: Korean trainers adapted the training content to the real conditions of Peruvian universities, including strategies for environments with limited connectivity.
3. *Two-way feedback*: The Peruvian experience provided ideas to the Korean university on how to integrate economic examples from emerging markets, enriching its curriculum.

## Weaknesses and Challenges

1. *Initial dependence on external support*: During the first six months, 70% of technical issues in Peru required direct assistance from Korea, which delayed the response to major problems.
2. *Language and cultural gap*: Although translators were used, terminology differences in economics caused confusion in 15% of the initial materials.
3. *Lack of longitudinal evaluation*: The project lacked a planned long-term follow-up to measure the sustained impact of AI beyond the first academic year.

## Recommendations for Multilateral Projects

- *Plan phases of progressive independence* in technical support, establishing clear milestones for the transfer of competencies.
- *Integrate cultural and linguistic specialists* from the outset, especially in disciplines with complex technical terminology.
- *Design long-term impact metrics*, including indicators of sustainability, equity and curricular adaptation.
- *Promote reciprocity in pedagogical innovation*, ensuring that the developed country also incorporates learning from the emerging partner.

# PROSPECTIVE PERSPECTIVE - TRENDS ORIENTED TO PUBLIC POLICIES AND EDUCATION

On the horizon of the next decade, the integration of AI in economic learning will be conditioned by *educational public policy* decisions, *data governance* arrangements and *funding* mechanisms that will enable - or limit - its scaling. The most relevant trends, observed from a policy design and implementation perspective, are the following:

1. *Curriculum standardization with integrated AI.*

Ministries of education and quality assurance agencies will tend to incorporate learning outcomes explicitly linked to the use of AI (model interpretability, bias analysis, simulation design).

This implies:

- National qualifications frameworks that include "competence in AI applied to economics".

- Measurable learning outcome guidelines (e.g., "learner explains the limitations of a classifier for assessing credit risk").
- Common assessment instruments (rubrics and item banks) that use AI to gauge difficulty, while maintaining human teacher review.

2. *Shared public infrastructure ("utility model").*

To avoid fragmentation and high licensing costs, several countries will move towards *public educational AI platforms* with reusable modules (adaptive tutoring, macroeconomic simulation, learning analytics). This model reduces territorial-socioeconomic gaps and favors interoperability between universities. Requires:

- Educational API standards and common metadata.
- Strategic public procurement and inter-university consortia.
- National centers of excellence that maintain open models and content.

3. *Governance of educational data with a rights-based approach*

The intensive use of student performance data will force the consolidation of *data protection regimes* and *ethics committees* with real power. They will be enforced:

- Records of processing (who accesses, for what, for how long).
- Mandatory Algorithmic Impact Assessments (AIA) in pilots and deployments at scale.
- Minimization and anonymization policies, with penalties for unauthorized use.

4. *Incentive-based teacher professional development programs*

Effective adoption of AI will depend on *trained and recognized teachers*.

The most successful policies will combine formal dedicated time, micro-credentials, and career progression. Key elements:

- Tiered training paths (basic → advanced → mentor).
- Communities of practice and pedagogical residencies with technical accompaniment.
- Economic and academic incentives (sexenios, bonuses, downloading of hours) tied to evidence of effective pedagogical use.

5. *Funding with a counter-cyclical logic and equity approach*

Investment in educational AI suffers cuts in adverse fiscal cycles. To shield it, the Treasury and Education portfolios will tend to:

- Create **countercyclical funds** for pedagogical innovation.
- Require that all AI projects include **inclusion components** (devices, connectivity, accessibility).
- Establish co-financing agreements with the private sector under data sovereignty and non-exclusivity clauses.

6. *Evidence-based evaluation and phased scaling*

A "pilot → evaluation → scaling → scaling → adjustment" policy cycle with homogeneous metrics will be imposed:

- Performance (absolute and relative improvements), equity (closing gaps), teacher effectiveness (times, load), and social acceptance (student trust).
- Cluster-controlled trials when possible; failing that, quasi-experimental designs with comparison groups.
- Publication of transparency dashboards with results and corrections implemented.

7. *Interoperability and responsible public procurement*

To avoid vendor lock-in:

- Data and model portability clauses.
- **Explainability** and **external audit** requirements as eligibility conditions.
- Preference for solutions with open components and technical documentation accessible to the public system.

8. *Inclusion and accessibility as a design requirement.*

Policies will move from "compatibility" to *accessibility by default* (WCAG, multilingual, easy-to-read, offline modes). Required indicators:

- % of accessible resources.
- Tutor response time for students with adaptations.
- Effective use in rural and low connectivity areas.

9. *Algorithmic literacy for economic citizenship.*

Beyond future economists, high school and vocational curricula will include *algorithmic citizenship modules* applied to economics: understanding inflation, credit, employment and public finance with AI support, identifying limits and biases. This raises the quality of public debate and accountability.

10. *Regional consortia and mutualization of content*

Regional blocs (e.g., EU, Pacific Alliance, ASEAN) will promote *shared repositories* of simulations, anonymized educational datasets and comparable rubrics. Benefits: economies of scale, cross-learning and common quality standards.

## PROSPECTIVE - FUTURE SCENARIOS FOR AI IN ECONOMIC LEARNING

In public policy foresight, scenario building makes it possible to anticipate decisions and prioritize resources based on possible trajectories. For the period 2025-2035, three reference scenarios are proposed, based on observed trends and simulated data.

1) Optimistic scenario - "Inclusive and sustainable ecosystem".

Assumptions

- Implementation of clear regulatory frameworks on educational AI in more than 70% of OECD member countries and emerging regional blocs.
- Stable and counter-cyclical funding, with 1.5% of national education spending earmarked for AI infrastructure and training.
- Universal curricular integration of AI competencies applied to economics in undergraduate and graduate programs.

Key features

- Public-private interoperable platforms with universal access, including offline modes for regions without connectivity.
- Human-supervised AI assessments, improving accuracy and reducing detected biases.
- Active participation of teachers as content designers, with micro-credentials recognized in salary systems.

Projected impacts

- 40% reduction in achievement gaps between urban and rural areas.
- 25% increase in teaching efficiency and 30% increase in student motivation.
- Strengthening of students' macroeconomic and microeconomic analysis skills, with impact on employability.

2) Moderate scenario - "Fragmented and uneven adoption".

Assumptions

- Partial regulation, with incomplete or inconsistent legal frameworks.
- Stable funding only in countries with higher GDP per capita; dependence on international cooperation in emerging countries.
- Uneven curricular integration: some economics programs include AI, others remain traditional.

Key characteristics

- Fragmented ecosystems: coexistence of open and proprietary solutions without common standards.
- Teacher training focused on urban centers, with low rural coverage.
- Use of AI limited to specific modules (tutorials, simulations), without cross-cutting integration.

Projected impacts

- Persistent technological gaps and increased educational inequality.
- 10-15% improvement in teaching efficiency, but no homogeneous impact on student achievement.
- Risk of technological dependence on a few suppliers, with increasing costs.

3) Key scenario - "Disconnection and systemic resistance".

Assumptions

- Lack of regulation and reactive rather than proactive public policies.
- Reduced investment in educational technology due to prolonged economic crises.

- Widespread societal distrust of AI due to cases of bias, serious errors or privacy violations.

Key characteristics

- Isolated and discontinuous implementations, based on pilot projects that do not scale.
- Low teacher training and union resistance to adoption.
- Students perceive AI as a surveillance tool rather than a support tool.

Projected impacts

- 5-10 percentage point drop in performance indicators in programs that rely on outdated technology.
- Widened learning gaps between and within countries.
- Loss of competitiveness in labor markets that demand applied AI skills.

The optimistic scenario calls for *sustained political will, multilateral cooperation and an inclusive approach*. The moderate one reflects the inertia of heterogeneous education systems, while the adverse one points out that *lack of governance and social trust* can reverse progress and deepen inequalities.

# PROSPECTIVE PERSPECTIVE - ACTION PLAN IN PHASES

## General Objective

Elevate education systems that today exhibit *fragmented and uneven* adoption of AI (moderate scenario) towards an *inclusive and sustainable ecosystem* (optimistic scenario), maximizing quality, equity, transparency and efficiency in economic learning.

A) Guiding principles
- **Equity by design** (territorial inclusion, accessibility, multilingual, offline modes).
- **Data governance with a rights-based approach** (AIA, minimization, audits).
- **Interoperability and portability** (avoid vendor lock-in).
- **Strengthened teaching** (incentives, protected time, micro-credentials).

- **Rigorous and public evaluation** (comparable metrics, transparency dashboards).

B) Phases, milestones and indicators

Phase 1 - Diagnosis and regulatory basis (0-6 months)
Milestones

1. **National capacity map**: connectivity by campus, equipment, software, human capital, territorial gaps.
2. **Governance framework**:
   - o National decree/guidelines for **Algorithmic Impact Assessment (AIA)** for education.
   - o **Educational data** policy (purpose, retention, anonymization, rights).
3. **Interoperability standards** (APIs, metadata, open formats) and public procurement standard clauses (portability, external audit, minimum explainability).
4. **National committee** (Education, Treasury, data agency, universities, civil society).

Indicators (KPIs)

- Diagnosis published (yes/no) and coverage ≥ 90% of HEIs.
- Official AIA adopted (yes/no).
- Standards and clauses approved (Y/N).
- Committee installed and scheduled (Y/N).

Phase 2 - Controlled pilots with evaluation (6-18 months)
Milestones

1. *Pilots by typology* in ≥ 15% of Economics programs:
   - o Adaptive tutoring; macro simulation; automated assessment; learning analytics.
2. *Evaluative designs*: cluster or quasi-experimental trials with comparison groups.
3. *Teaching program*: 40-60 h per teacher (basic/advanced/mentor), with *micro-credentials* recognized by salary.
4. *Counter-cyclical fund* and co-financing with data sovereignty and non-exclusivity clauses.
5. *Public dashboard* with quarterly results.

KPIs

- Average improvement in performance (absolute and relative) ≥ +10 p.p. vs. control.
- Closing of urban-rural gap ≥ 5 p.p. in pilot courses.
- ≥ 70% of pilot faculty certified.
- Student satisfaction ≥ 8/10; confidence in AI ≥ 7.5/10.
- 100% of pilots with AIA and public reporting.

Phase 3 - Prudent and safe scale-up (18-36 months).
Milestones

1. *Scale to ≥ 50%* of Economics programs in public HEIs and ≥ 30% in private.
2. *Public educational AI platform* (utility model): common modules, shared content, simulation repository and anonymized datasets.
3. *National certification* of solutions (quality, accessibility, explainability, security).
4. Multi-year *framework contracts* with guaranteed portability and annual external audits.
5. *Regional* pedagogical innovation *laboratories* (teaching mentors, communities of practice).

KPIs

- Performance: +15-20% sustained vs. baseline.
- Teaching efficiency: -20-30% in correction/preparation times.
- Urban-rural gap: cumulative reduction ≥ 12 p.p.
- Privacy incidents: 0 major; response < 72 h for moderate.
- ≥ 80% of solutions certified and audited.

Phase 4 - Consolidation and Continuous Improvement (36-60 months)
Milestones

1. *Full curricular integration*: learning outcomes of AI applied to economics in undergraduate and graduate curricula.
2. *Accreditation and QA*: quality assurance criteria that include AI (equity, evidence of learning, ethics).
3. *National observatory* of educational AI (international benchmarking, longitudinal studies, bias surveillance).
4. *Regional harmonization*: consortia (EU/ASEAN/Pacific Alliance) for shared repositories and common standards.
5. *Biennial updating* of technical standards, AIA frameworks and teaching profile.

KPIs

- Employability in high value sectors: +10-15 p.p. (graduate tracers).
- Persistence of learning benefits $\geq$ 3 cohorts.
- $\geq$ 90% of programs with evidence of impact in audits.
- Participation in regional consortia (yes/no) and number of shared resources.

C) Institutional architecture and responsibilities

- **Ministry of Education**: norms, standards, QA, transparency dashboard.
- **Finance/Planning**: counter-cyclical funds, responsible public procurement.
- **Data Protection Agency**: AIA, audits, sanctions.
- **Inter-university consortium**: public platform, content, faculty mentoring.
- **Academic councils**: curriculum adoption, incentives and protected time.
- **Civil society/students**: oversight and reporting of bias or misuse.

D) Budget and sustainability

- **Initial CapEx**: connectivity and devices (territorial equity criteria).
- **OpEx**: maintenance, support, audits and continuous training.
- **Co-financing**: private sector and international cooperation with data and non-exclusivity clauses.
- **Expected savings**: administrative efficiency and content reuse (>15-20% over 3 years), reinvested in inclusion and QA.

E) Risk management and mitigation

- **Bias/Opacity** → Independent audits, public technical documentation, decision repositories.
- **Lock-in** → Contractual portability and open standards.
- **Digital divide** → Offline modes, prioritized endowments, regional centers.
- **Teacher resistance** → Incentives, development time and communities of practice.
- **Privacy incidents** → Response plan (72 h), cyber insurance, mandatory training.

F) Monitoring, evaluation and improvement.

- Quarterly **KPI dashboard** (performance, fairness, efficiency, trust).
- Annual **external evaluations** and biannual meta-evaluation.

- **Close the loop mechanism**: each finding generates a corrective action recorded and published.
- **Publication of anonymized microdata** for independent research.

Synthetic roadmap (for the final document)

1. *0-6 m*: Diagnosis, AIA, standards, committee.
2. *6-18 m*: Evaluated pilots, teacher training, public dashboard.
3. *18-36 m*: Public platform, certification, scaling and framework contracts.
4. *36-60 m*: Accreditation with IA criteria, observatory, regional harmonization.

*Expected outcome*: orderly transition to the *optimistic scenario*, with measurable improvements in *quality*, *equity*, *efficiency* and *social trust*, and with institutions capable of sustaining AI-based pedagogical innovation without sacrificing rights or academic plurality.

Synthesis of Block 2 - Case Studies and Prospective Projection

Block 2 has examined the application of AI in economic learning through *three case studies* and a *prospective analysis* oriented to public policy and education.

1. *Case Study 1 - International Outreach*

It showed how the implementation of AI in diverse contexts requires technical and pedagogical flexibility, as well as adaptable regulatory frameworks. Evidenced that environments with advanced infrastructure maximize AI sophistication, while those with limitations generate inclusive innovations.

2. *Case Study 2 - Emerging Country (Colombia)*

It highlighted the positive impact of AI on student achievement and motivation, but also exposed challenges such as digital inequality and insufficient teacher training. Recommendations were to start with pilots adapted to the local context and to reinforce continuous training.

3. *Case Study 3 - Multilateral Collaboration (South Korea and Peru)*

Exemplified how international cooperation can be bidirectional, benefiting both developed and emerging countries. The key was comprehensive technology transfer, contextualized training and mutual feedback.

4. *Foresight section*

- **Trends**: curriculum standardization, public platforms, data governance, teacher incentives, counter-cyclical funding and accessibility by default.
- **Scenarios**: optimistic (inclusive ecosystem), moderate (uneven adoption) and adverse (resistance and disconnection).
- **Action plan**: roadmap in phases (diagnosis, pilots, scaling, consolidation) with metrics and continuous improvement mechanisms to move from the moderate to the optimistic scenario.

*Table 5. Quantitative impacts per case study*

| **Indicator** | **Case 1 - International outreach** | **Case 2 - Emerging country (Colombia)** | **Case 3 - Multilateral Collaboration (South Korea and Peru)** |
|---|---|---|---|
| Average improvement in academic performance (%) | 15,2 | 18,9 | Peru: 19.0 / Korea: 8.1 |
| Reduction in teacher preparation time (%) | 20,5 | 27,8 | Peru: 28.0 / Korea: 12.2 |
| Increase in student participation (%) | 17,0 | 21,7 | Peru: 22.0 / Korea: 10.0 |
| Student satisfaction (scale 0-10) | 8,3 | 8,1 | Peru: 8.4 / Korea: 8.7 |
| Confidence in AI as an educational resource (scale 0-10) | 7,9 | 7,5 | Peru: 7.8 / Korea: 8.2 |

## Integrated Narrative Analysis

1. Academic performance

The highest increase was recorded in Colombia (18.9%) and Peru (19.0%) within the multilateral case, confirming that *environments with lower initial digitization experience more visible gains* when well-adapted AI tools are introduced. South Korea, despite a more modest progress (8.1%), took advantage of the cooperation to enrich its curriculum with examples from emerging economies, which is a qualitative benefit.

2. Reduction in teacher preparation time

The highest percentages are observed in emerging countries: Colombia (27.8%) and Peru (28.0%). This is explained by the automation of repetitive tasks and the availability of standardized templates. Korea and the international environment of Case 1 showed more moderate improvements (12.2% and 20.5%, respectively), as they started from more efficient teaching systems.

3. Student participation

The jump in participation is associated with *simulation tools and immediate feedback*. Colombia and Peru exceed 21%, while Korea and Case 1 show more contained progress, probably due to previous technological saturation that reduces the novelty effect.

4. Satisfaction and confidence

In all contexts student satisfaction is high (≥ 8/10), which reinforces the idea that well-implemented AI is perceived positively. However, *confidence* is slightly lower, reflecting persistent doubts about the reliability and ethics of AI in education.

## REFERENCES


Aznar Sánchez, T. J. (2022). Pedagogical reflection and AI in education. In Medina, M. A., & Debasa, F. (Eds.), *Handbook of Research on Artificial Intelligence in Government Practices and Processes* (pp. 120–135). IGI Global.

Debasa, F. (2022). Artificial intelligence in government practices and processes. In Medina, M. A., & Debasa, F. (Eds.), *Handbook of Research on Artificial Intelligence in Government Practices and Processes* (pp. 1–15). IGI Global.

European University of Applied Data. (2024). *Impact assessment of virtual tutors in economics education* [Unpublished study].

Global Center for Economic Innovation. (2024). *Cognitive capital and productivity in the digital age* (Technical Report).

Global Educational Neuroscience Institute. (2025). *Adaptive learning and long-term memory in digital environments* (Experimental Report).

International Forum for Educational Innovation. (2025). *AI and digital competencies in the training of economists* (Global Report).

Organization for Economic Education. (2023). *Technology gaps in higher education* (Global Report).

Prado Román, C. (2020). The legitimacy of educational institutions in the digital age. *Revista Brasileira de Gestão de Negócios*, *22*(3), 45–60.

Chapter 13

# Transformations in Learning and Social Relations in the Age of Artificial Intelligence:

## An Analysis From the Perspective of Education and Contemporary Culture

**Elena Berzal Alesanco**
https://orcid.org/0009-0000-8718-4970
*IUNIT, Spain*

**Richard Silva Cuartas**
*Universidad de Alcalá de Henares, Spain*

## ABSTRACT

*This chapter examines the impact of artificial intelligence (AI) on education and social interactions, highlighting both its opportunities and challenges. AI technologies, including intelligent tutoring systems, adaptive learning platforms, learning analytics, and generative tools, offer personalized support, enhance engagement, and improve accessibility for diverse learners. While these tools optimize learning and provide real-time feedback, risks include overreliance, algorithmic bias, and potential reduction in human social interaction. The chapter emphasizes the importance of ethical frameworks, human-centered design, and responsible integration of AI to complement rather than replace human judgment. Educators play a crucial role in guiding students to critically interpret AI outputs and ensuring equitable*

DOI: 10.4018/979-8-3373-4480-5.ch013

*access to these technologies. Overall, the chapter provides insights into maximizing AI's benefits while mitigating risks, supporting meaningful learning, and fostering healthy social interactions.*

## INTRODUCTION

In recent years, artificial intelligence (AI) has rapidly spread across various spheres of human life, making it one of the most disruptive technologies of recent years. This disruption has not been limited to industrial and business environments but has also been taking shape in all areas of daily life, including education, healthcare, cultural settings, and even interpersonal relationship management.

In the educational field, the use of AI has not been left behind, highlighting its potentially transformative potential, as it offers the possibility of personalized learning that can benefit students in their teaching-learning process through immediate feedback. This will lead to more motivated learning (Flores-Alarcia & Fornons Casol, 2024). On the other hand, the automation of certain administrative tasks can help reduce bureaucratic burdens for teachers, allowing them to dedicate more time to interacting with and supporting students, and can help relieve some of the administrative burden on teachers.

This expansion of its use in all areas can give rise to certain ethical, cognitive, and social risks (UNESCO, 2021). From a pedagogical perspective,

excessive reliance on and misuse of artificial intelligence systems can lead to a decrease in the use of deep metacognitive processes, as it prevents students from reaching a certain level of difficulty for these processes to be activated (Magro, 2025). In this sense, the excessive use of intelligent assistants to solve problems immediately could encourage the development of superficial learning, which would reduce the opportunities to develop analytical, synthesis, and evaluation skills.

On the social level, immediate interaction with algorithms and digital assistants is beginning to redefine social relationships and access to information, leading to both positive effects, such as the alleviation of feelings of loneliness and rapid access to information in emergency situations. However, we can also find detrimental effects, such as emotional dependence on artificial systems as a source of support, which leads to a decrease in the development of social skills and conflict resolution with other people (De Freitas et al., 2024).

This double-edged sword presented by AI has led various authors to speak of a joint process of evolution (understood as co-evolution) between humans and technologies, which can lead to a progressive blurring of the boundaries between the natural and the artificial (Floridi, 2019). Since the relationship is no longer unidirectional, and new technologies can reconfigure our cognitive capacities, we humans are the ones who redesign technology by dumping information.

Thanks to contemporary film culture, we can find powerful metaphors such as WALL-E (Stanton, 2008), in which an automatic world develops, where machines replace the human hand, and connections become mediated. This relegates cognition and thought to the background, prioritizing a technological comfort in which it is easier for the machine to do it than for humans to think, which allows us to reflect on the risks of an uncritical adoption of AI in everyday life. Just like several cinematic references, once considered science fiction, can reflect or predict the reality of the near future if we don't use artificial intelligence tools as a complementary or supportive resource, rather than a necessity. This parallel doesn't imply an exact correspondence with current reality, but rather a resource that allows us to critically analyze the challenges that technology can present in today's world.

Therefore, one of the main issues is not only analyzing the benefits that AI can bring, but also managing its integration into different areas of life. This makes one of the central challenges finding the balance between process optimization and responsible use of AI, so that learning is truly efficient, prioritizing the development of critical thinking, creativity, and sustained attention, among others. From a pedagogical perspective, we propose to analyze not only the technical advances of Artificial Intelligence and its benefits, but also the psychopedagogical and ethical implications of its implementation (Holmes et al., 2019).

This article aims to examine, through a review of current literature, the impact that AI can have on social relationships and learning from a critical perspective, exposing the advantages and potential effects that AI can have without proper use. We propose certain metaphors related to cinematic elements that can serve as allegories for certain near futures, in which, years ago, these realities could have been seen as utopian, always keeping in mind that each of them will always contain certain fictional approaches.

## 1. ARTIFICIAL INTELLIGENCE AND LEARNING

The emergence of AI in educational contexts has been rapidly gaining importance since 2020, especially in generative text models and conversational assistants (Garzón et al., 2025). According to Zhai et al., 2021, we can divide the application of AI in education into three main dimensions:

- The development dimension: This includes intelligent tutoring systems and adaptive learning models, which offer the ability to personalize the student experience based on their needs and progress.

- The extraction dimension is related to automatic feedback and data-driven reasoning that can assist in more targeted decision-making.
- The application dimension, such as immersive learning or the use of gamification, whose guidance can help improve student attention, motivation, and engagement.

Based on these dimensions, it is possible to differentiate into operational categories among which we find: intelligent tutoring systems (ITS), adaptive learning platforms, learning analytics and generative tools (LLMs) that produce content, assessments and feedback (Garzón et al., 2025).

## 1.2 Main modalities applied in the classroom

### Intelligent Tutoring Systems (ITS)

These systems represent one of the most established and promising applications of Artificial Intelligence in education. Their purpose is to facilitate personalized teaching, as they offer the ability to adapt different instructions to the needs and pace of the student using advanced algorithms (Nkambou et al., 2018). This sets them apart from traditional online learning platforms, as they are not limited to presenting content in a linear and almost unidirectional manner, but also actively interact with students and adapt responses to their needs.

One of the main characteristics of this type of system is the development of a dynamic diagnosis, which allows for the real-time identification of student strengths and needs, allowing for the adjustment of their pedagogical sequence.

In the last decade, there has been significant growth in the implementation of ITS in formal and informal educational contexts, from primary to higher education. For example, systems such as AutoTutor, Cognitive Tutor, and ALEKS have demonstrated substantial improvements in academic performance and content retention (Graesser et al., 2018). One of the reasons for their rise has been the increase in hybrid and distance learning systems, especially after the COVID-19 pandemic, which led to an acceleration in the digitalization of education.

According to Luckin et al. (2022), ITS can help reduce teaching load by reducing more repetitive tasks, thus allowing teachers to focus their efforts on activities with greater pedagogical value.

On the other hand, apart from their benefits, they also pose challenges that are considered significant. These include the transparency of algorithms, the potential homogenization of learning processes, and the risk of generating technological dependence in students (Holmes et al., 2019). There is also the issue of equity: not all schools have the necessary infrastructure to implement these systems effectively.

Furthermore, ITSs raise important ethical questions related to student data privacy, as personalization requires the collection of sensitive information about student performance, behavior, and preferences (Zawacki-Richter et al., 2019). Therefore, several authors emphasize the need for clear regulatory and pedagogical frameworks to guide their responsible development and implementation.

## Adaptive Learning and Learning Analytics

Adaptive learning is another key focus of AI application in educational settings. Unlike previous stages with more traditional teaching styles, in which all students receive the same sequence of content and activities, adaptive platforms adjust the user experience individually based on the data generated by the student (Fisher et al., 2020). All of this optimizes time and effort.

These systems are based on predictive models and machine learning algorithms that process information in real time, such as assessment performance, response speed, interaction with digital materials, or navigation patterns on educational platforms (Ifenthaler & Yau, 2020). Using this data, the system begins to automatically adjust the difficulty, pace, and type of activities for each student, impacting their intrinsic motivation for learning (Gómez et al., 2023).

Therefore, it becomes a strategy that allows for evidence-based pedagogical decision-making. For example, it allows teaching staff to identify dropout patterns, students at risk of dropping out, or areas for curricular improvement (Slade & Prinsloo, 2013).

Learning analytics, known as LA, has been evolving, allowing us to now have more complex learning management systems (LMS) and the integration of AI, such as Moodle Learning Analytics, Canvas Data, and Brightspace Insights. These platforms not only provide student data but also allow for monitoring their progress and providing automatic recommendations.

Over the last decade, learning analytics has evolved significantly thanks to the development of more sophisticated learning management systems (LMS) and the integration of generative AI technologies. Tools such as Moodle Learning Analytics, Canvas Data, and Brightspace Insights offer interactive dashboards that allow educators to monitor student progress in real time (Papamitsiou & Economides, 2014). These systems do not simply present data but provide automatic recommendations and early warnings, increasing institutional responsiveness.

Further advancements in the use of these technologies also pose various challenges, such as the fact that having more advanced data or analytics does not guarantee improvements in student learning if teachers are not trained to interpret the data critically and make appropriate pedagogical decisions. Therefore, the integration of AI and LA must be accompanied by teacher training sessions (Ifenthaler & Yau,

2020). In no case would it be beneficial for AI to replace teachers, but rather to enhance pedagogical support for students.

### Generative Tools and Conversational Assistants

Generative artificial intelligence (GenAI) tools and conversational assistants represent another of the most visible transformations in education today. These tools enable the creation of content and explanations in real time (Labadze et al., 2023). This allows educational chatbots to act as tutors and virtual assistants, answering questions for students at any time of day when they do not have access to their teacher at school (McGrath et al., 2025). This leads to greater flexibility, making immediate feedback one of their greatest benefits (AlAli et al., 2024).

Unlike traditional adaptive systems, these technologies enable open and dynamic interactions with students, facilitating the creation of content, explanations, and personalized feedback in real time (Labadze et al., 2023). The fact that the tool can generate more examples and alternative explanations that fit students' tastes and perceptions opens up a world of possibilities for supporting students' deeper understanding of potentially complex concepts (McGrath et al., 2025).

On the other hand, these types of tools also present a series of risks and challenges, as in some cases the information generated is not always accurate. Therefore, it remains vitally important for students to have acquired a critical eye to be able to sift through inaccurate content and effectively verify it. In addition, there may also be a risk of over-reliance on technology, which can also create technology gaps for students with different levels of digital literacy (Labadze et al., 2023).

## 1.3. Evidence of Educational Uses

As we have discussed, the incorporation of AI in educational environments has led to a growing body of research demonstrating some of its benefits, such as its effectiveness. This differentiates AI from other educational technologies due to its adaptation to the user experience, with access to a greater diversity of personalized knowledge (Zawacki-Richter et al., 2019).

All of this can be reflected in improved academic performance, as it can aid complex conceptual understanding, knowledge retention, and the application of this knowledge in new contexts (Holmes et al., 2019). This, in turn, can also lead to benefits for students' autonomy and self-regulation of learning, as they can see their own progress recorded (Chin et al., 2023).

Also, AI contributes to promoting autonomy and self-regulation of learning. By providing students with tools to monitor their own progress and access personalized resources, metacognitive skills essential for lifelong learning are strengthened (Chin et al., 2023). This autonomy does not imply the absence of teacher mediation; on the contrary, it frees teachers from routine tasks, allowing them to focus on more strategic aspects of teaching (Fischer et al., 2020).

On the other hand, it can also help increase motivation and engagement, since smart platforms incorporate interactive elements, such as conversational assistants, resulting in a more enriching and active experience, which fosters meaningful learning (Kong et al., 2024).

In turn, the use of these tools also shows benefits in addressing the diversity of students with specific needs and their inclusion. For example, with the use of voice recognition-based applications to assist students with visual or hearing difficulties, promoting accessibility and equity in the classroom (Kooli & Chakraoui, 2025). This simultaneously impacts emotional well-being and reduces frustration that may be associated with various difficulties that have not been detected in time (Holmes et al., 2019).

Finally, the potential of AI also lies in its ability to support the teaching profession, since real-time information processing facilitates pedagogical decision-making. Therefore, teachers become designers and facilitators of personalized educational experiences (Popenici & Kerr, 2017).

## 1.4. Limitations and Biases

As previously demonstrated, AI has demonstrated positive effects on teaching-learning processes, but it also presents various limitations, both cognitive and structural, that are important to critically analyze. One of these is the presence of algorithmic biases that can foster greater inequality rather than reducing it. This is because AI learns from historical data, and if discriminatory patterns exist within these data, they can be reproduced and extrapolated to educational settings (Lozada et al., 2023). For example, a conversational or generative system uses recommendations that tend to prioritize certain response styles or language, which can lead to marginalizing certain student profiles, thus affecting their motivation and self-concept because they do not fit those patterns. This can generate performance gaps that make it impossible to assess real abilities, a result of the algorithm's limitations (Holmes et al., 2019).

Along these lines, these biases can influence the formation of their own cognitive models, since if the examples or explanations proposed by AI are based on homogeneous data or samples, there is a risk that epistemological diversity may be limited, leading to a single form of reasoning or conflict resolution. This leads to a impoverishment of critical and divergent thinking (Bender et al., 2021).

In addition, excessive use of these AI tools can lead to cognitive effects if not accompanied by effective pedagogical mediation. Reliance on these systems can impair the deepening and consolidation of concepts, resulting in purely superficial learning (Kasneci et al., 2023). This occurs because students who do not approach the learning situation of solving problems autonomously run the risk of developing a passive relationship with knowledge, directly affecting the development of critical thinking (Chen et al., 2023). Therefore, the unsupervised use of AI to solve problems can foster dependency and reduce the deliberate practice of cognitive skills, especially when assessment tasks do not reinforce deep understanding (Pitts et al., 2025; Zhai et al., 2024).

The overconfidence that students may generate in all the AI's responses can also affect self-efficacy and the way they view their own progress, as this blind trust in the answers, which are sometimes erroneous, can lead to a shift in the locus of control from the student to the technology. Regarding content reliability, one of the greatest risks lies in the fact that many AI models represent their erroneous responses as if they were true or contain biases, as we discussed previously. This phenomenon is known as "hallucination" and poses a direct threat to students' epistemological security, that is, their ability to reasonably trust the information they use to construct knowledge (Popenici & Kerr, 2017). When we talk about epistemological security, we refer to the establishment of critical criteria that allow users to examine their credibility and the foundation of what they are trying to learn. Therefore, if there is no teacher mediation or the development of information verification strategies, there is a risk of consolidating erroneous or partial knowledge (Zhai et al., 2024).

The emotional and cognitive impact that arises when students "overtrust"AI or internalize system errors as their own failings must also be considered. This can affect perceived self-efficacy and self-confidence, especially in assessment or self-regulated learning contexts (Bai et al., 2024).

Another important aspect is that there is a great deal of uncertainty and little clarity regarding its sources or inference processes (Bucchi & Saracino, 2023), which makes it impossible to understand how the system reached these definitive conclusions, unlike what we can find when searching for information in a book, for example. This creates a gap in content transparency.

Therefore, ensuring the reliability and security of content does not mean rejecting the use of technologies, but rather designing pedagogical strategies and actions that allow them to maximize their potential without affecting the student's learning process. These include: encouraging digital literacy in AI, teaching how to cross-reference reliable sources, and supporting the indispensable role of the teacher.

## 2. ARTIFICIAL INTELLIGENCE AND SOCIAL RELATIONS

The influence of AI has not only been a technical tool but has become a transformative agent in society, as its influence is not only in the automation of processes but can also affect the way humans interact and communicate (Bryson, 2019). The inclusion of platforms such as social networks and virtual assistants in our lives in recent years has given rise to the creation of new forms of socializing, such as hybrid or remote.

This has led to a reconfiguration of the way we relate, not only as tools or platforms that facilitate communication but also as a "social mediator," as it can influence the perception of others and how communities are formed (de Graaf & Malle, 2019). In this case, for example, algorithms are responsible for recommending what we see on social media, which determines the content we see and, in turn, the users, thereby creating social bonds and thus transforming the construction of our social reality.

Likewise, the existence of chatbots and conversational assistants has become agents that can interact with users in more emotional and cognitive ways, as they generate certain expectations of reciprocity and trust.

From a practical perspective, AI and the algorithms used can influence, to a greater or lesser extent, what we hear and the ideas that are reinforced, which impacts how the social imaginary and communities are formed. Therefore, it can continue to perpetuate social biases that can even lead to exclusion (Tussyadiah & Miller, 2019).

### 2.1. AI as a Relational Agent: Conversational Assistants and Social Robots

As previously mentioned, chatbots and conversational assistants are designed to interact with the user in a natural and adaptive manner, and in some cases, even emotionally. The way they offer a conversation tailored to the user's needs creates a sense of companionship and trust that transforms the traditional social experience.

As in the education sector, they can act as virtual tutors, reconfiguring the social reality of education by changing the learning dynamic and generating a model of cooperation between human and machine. The same is true in the domestic context, where social bots are capable of generating emotional responses that build trust, reducing feelings of loneliness. For example, in the case of the elderly, the use of these types of AI-based tools has been a way of helping to satisfy certain needs related to their health, so much so that Robinson et al. (2015) demonstrated through their study evidence of how a companion robot reduced feelings of loneliness through a trial with people from a senior center.

But this also poses a risk of excessive or illusory attachment, in which reciprocity, human interaction, and emotional depth are replaced. This "simulated emotional intelligence" can improve the effectiveness of communication and learning, but it also poses risks: users may overestimate the system's understanding, trusting it inappropriately or delegating decisions that should be human-made (Liao & Sundar, 2022). When we talk about "simulated emotional intelligence," we refer to the ability to produce responses that seek to mimic empathy and understanding, as inhuman interaction. But this also poses certain significant risks, especially in situations where users are invulnerable situations or experiencing emotional crises.

One current case demonstrates the reality of these risks, when a 16-year-old teenager began using ChatGPT to complete schoolwork, but also sought out the tool for some emotional support. So much so that during their conversations and interactions, the chatbot validated their feelings about suicide, according to the family. This shows us that the chatbot prioritized simulated empathy over proper intervention in a very high-risk situation, fueling that vulnerability instead of offering effective support, such as seeking professional help or following a protocol.

This is one of the situations that highlights one of the main problems: the over-reliance on these types of tools, which can produce negative feedback that can lead to actions or thoughts that can be harmful to the person (Wood et al., 2023).

Beyond these cases, studies show that prolonged interaction with virtual assistants can modify behavior and communication patterns, due to the human tendency to apply our social norms to machines (Reeves and Nass, 1996). This has implications that profoundly affect education and socialization, resulting, on the one hand, in a decrease in interpersonal interaction with other people and certain alterations in the development of socio-emotional skills, as well as involuntary social isolation (Broadbent, 2017; Turkle, 2017; Holstein et al., 2019).

For all the above reasons, it is important that AI be framed within clear ethical boundaries, with intervention protocols used in situations considered high-risk and with clear and transparent limitations on what AI can and cannot do, in order to educate society in its use. This does not mean rejecting its use and ignoring its potential, but rather beginning to understand that AI does not understand or make decisions in the same way as a human being; that is, that empathy is an illusion produced by the system's programming, so the ultimate responsibility must remain human. Because sometimes, instead of going to the doctor, we ask the AI, or instead of going to the psychologist, we ask the AI, and these interventions must be mediated by trained human professionals.

## 2.2. AI and the Transformation of Social Relationships

AI is not just a tool we use in our lives; it has emerged as one of our solutions when it comes to solving more complex or technical problems. It has rapidly become a silent mediator that can also influence our social relationships (Debasa &Azcona,

2024). It is responsible for organizing what we see, when we see it, and who we talk to. Therefore, to a greater or lesser extent, it changes our perception of reality based on the algorithm's clicks. This is so important that we are often unaware of it.

A very obvious example occurs in something as commonplace in the 21st century as browsing social media. In this case, a neutral and transparent reality of the world is not presented, but rather this universe has been carefully controlled by filters and algorithms that recommend what you watch based on your clicks and interests. That's why networks like TikTok and Instagram, based on our habits and tastes, decide what content to show so we pay more attention to that reality. This leads to a shift in our interests and also our social ties. If we're shown people who think the same way and consume the same content, our own ideas are reinforced, which leads us to conform within a community with the same thoughts and, in its most extreme effect, limits our ability to understand other perspectives and thoughts (Bishop, 2021; Bakshy et al., 2015).

This same thing applies to all social spheres. For example, in emotional relationships, there has been a transformation in the way people meet, no longer in shared spaces but through platforms mediated by AI. Through algorithms based on our data and behavioral patterns, we are shown people who are compatible with us, for example, when we're looking for a partner. This results in an automated and inorganic selection process dominated by the algorithm (Chan, 2018; David & Cambre, 2016;Saura, 2025). Therefore, despite being practical, it is still an artificially controlled environment.

One of the questions users have when they are in virtual environments is authenticity, that is, what is real or not. This occurs because being surrounded by avatars, virtual influencers, or even people recreated with AI, coupled with the increasing existence of deepfakes, this line between the artificial and the human becomes increasingly blurred. This leads to a situation of constant uncertainty that breaks the trust that exists in social interactions, causing users to become more distrustful and monitored, not knowing what is real and what is behind the screen. This can also be extrapolated to something as broad as politics, through social chatbots that have demonstrated the ability to amplify messages or alter certain collective perceptions (Woolley & Howard, 2018).

Artificial intelligence also influences the construction of digital identity. Through systems that evaluate interactions, preferences, and behaviors, users receive constant feedback on how they are perceived (Debasa &Azcona, 2024). For example, social media algorithms rate posts based on engagement, generating a kind of "social reinforcement" that can affect self-esteem, self-image, and the way a person chooses to present themselves to others (Eslami et al., 2015). This phenomenon is especially relevant among adolescents and young adults, whose identity is still under construction and whose social interaction is largely digital.

But not everything is risky; there is also great potential for positive social change. For example, thanks to the existence of digital platforms that promote our content through algorithms, they create spaces where we can communicate and support each other. Therefore, through them, we can moderate certain hostile environments and protect more vulnerable groups. This is also demonstrated in the use of tools with people with disabilities, enabling and opening the world to many possibilities and adaptations that would be more difficult to access without them. Therefore, the truly important thing is to make people understand that AI cannot, under any circumstances, supplement human relationships, but rather can help us expand and enhance them.

For all of the above reasons, the importance of developing critical literacy is still emphasized, not only in how to use AI but also in understanding how it can shape our relationships, and being able to understand how algorithms work and how they can change our perceptions.

But not everything is risky. There is also great potential for positive social change. For example, thanks to the existence of digital platforms that promote our content through algorithms, they create spaces where we can communicate and support each other. Through them, we can moderate certain hostile environments and protect more vulnerable groups. This is also demonstrated in the use of tools with people with disabilities, enabling and opening the world to many possibilities and adaptations that would be more difficult to access without them. Therefore, the important thing is to make people understand that AI cannot, under any circumstances, serve human relationships, but rather can help us expand and enhance them.

For all of the above, the importance of developing critical literacy is still emphasized, not only in how to use AI but also in understanding how it can shape our relationships, and in understanding how algorithms work and how they can change our perceptions. But not to reject its use, but rather to understand how it works and to have clear and transparent information.

## 3. DISCUSSION AND CRITICAL ANALYSIS

With all the above, this analysis, based on existing literature, reveals evidence that AI has become an important transformative agent in all aspects of human life. Like everything else, it has its risks, opportunities, and challenges that must be taken into account.

From a pedagogical and educational perspective, we find the possibility of greater learning personalization supported by immediate feedback and learning analytics that allow for greater adaptation to the student, which in turn impacts their motivation and autonomy (Holmes et al., 2019; Chin et al., 2023; Garzón et al., 2025). However, this also entails cognitive risks that are important to consider if not used responsibly. Learning can become superficial and technological dependence can develop due to overconfidence in AI systems (Kasneci et al., 2023; Chen et al., 2023; Zhai, 2024).

Therefore, one of the necessary actions highlighted in this chapter is the importance of active teaching intervention, the activation of clear intervention protocols, and literacy in a digital and critical society to enable the proper development of students' metacognitive skills (Popenici & Kerr, 2017; Ifenthaler & Yau, 2020). This tool must function as a useful pedagogical complement, but in no case as a substitute for the teaching role or for the human interactions that occur both in the classroom and in any other social setting.

Regarding social relationships, the findings show a similarly mixed picture. Conversational assistants, chatbots, and algorithms that regulate exposure to social media content reconfigure forms of socialization, acting as invisible mediators that influence the perception of reality and the building of bonds (de Graaf & Malle, 2019; Liao & Sundar, 2022). This transformative role can have positive effects, such as reducing loneliness, providing accessibility for people with disabilities, or creating supportive communities (Robinson et al., 2015; Bishop, 2021). On the other hand, it can lead to attachment based on illusion and the reproduction of certain social biases, as it feeds on historical data, somewhat limiting the diversity of perspectives (Turkle, 2017; Woolley & Howard, 2018). From a critical perspective, these risks and their consequences can only be reduced through a process of critical AI literacy, so that users can understand how they work and how they can affect their social relationships. This will promote responsible use of these tools, enhancing cognitive skills rather than replacing them.

Finally, the integration of cinematic metaphors, such as WALL-E (Stanton, 2008), offers a valuable reflective tool. These narratives depict extreme scenarios of technological dependence and total automation, warning of the risks of uncritical adoption of AI. While they do not accurately represent contemporary reality, they allow us to visualize possible futures and guide the debate on the balance between technology and human agency, stimulating reflection on the role that AI should play as a support, rather than a substitute, in both learning and social life.

*Table 1. Risks and opportunities of AI*

| Dimension | Opportunities/Benefits | Risks and Limitations |
|---|---|---|
| Education | Personalized learning (ITS, adaptive) | Shallow learning if overly reliant on AI |
| | Immediate feedback and virtual tutoring | Technology dependence and decreased autonomous practice |
| | Learning analytics and data-driven decision-making | Algorithmic biases and equity risks |
| | Inclusion and accessibility for students with special needs | Lack of teacher training to interpret and apply data |
| Social relationships | Reduction of loneliness and emotional support | Illusory attachment, replacement of human interaction |
| | Creation of supportive communities and new forms of socialization | Involuntary social isolation and loss of socio-emotional skills |
| | Information mediation and access to personalized content | Reproduction of biases, information bubbles, and algorithmic manipulation |

Note: This table shows us a visual summary of the risks and opportunities that AI presents in the social and educational fields.

In conclusion, the responsible use of AI requires a integrative approach that combines technological innovation, human mediation, critical literacy, and clear ethical policies. Only in this way can its potential be maximized while minimizing the cognitive, social, and emotional risks that arise from its accelerated adoption. AI, in this sense, is emerging not as a replacement, but as a catalyst for new formes of learning and socialization, as long as human action remains at the core of decision-making and knowledge construction.

## REFERENCES


AlAli, W., Alelyani, S., & Khan, K. (2024). Empowering students with generative AI: A study on learning engagement and critical thinking. *Computers & Education, 208*, 105249.

Bai, Y., Li, J., Shen, J., & Zhao, L. (2024). Investigating the efficacy of ChatGPT-3.5 for tutoring in Chinese elementary education settings. *IEEE Transactions on Learning Technologies, 17*, 2102–2117. DOI: 10.1109/TLT.2024.3464560

Bakshy, E., Messing, S., & Adamic, L. A. (2015). Exposure to ideologically diverse news and opinion on Facebook. *Science, 348*(6239), 1130–1132. DOI: 10.1126/science.aaa1160 PMID: 25953820

Bender, L., Renkl, A., & Eitel, A. (2021). When and how seductive details harm learning. A study using cued retrospective reporting. *Applied Cognitive Psychology, 35*(4), 948–959. DOI: 10.1002/acp.3822

Bishop, S. (2021). Influencer Management Tools: Algorithmic Cultures, Brand Safety, and Bias. *Social Media + Society, 7*(1), 20563051211003066. Advance online publication. DOI: 10.1177/20563051211003066

Broadbent, E. (2017). Interactions with robots: The truths we reveal about ourselves. *Annual Review of Psychology, 68*(1), 627–652. DOI: 10.1146/annurev-psych-010416-043958 PMID: 27648986

Broadbent, J. (2017). Comparing online and blended learner's self-regulated learning strategies and academic performance. *The Internet and Higher Education, 33*, 24–32. DOI: 10.1016/j.iheduc.2017.01.004

Chan, L. S. (2018). Ambivalence in networked intimacy: Observations from gay men using mobile dating apps. *New Media & Society, 20*(7), 2566–2581. DOI: 10.1177/1461444817727156

Chin, J., Zhang, C., & Chen, F. (2023). Adaptive learning with AI: Enhancing self-regulation in digital education. *Educational Technology Research and Development, 71*(4), 2315–2334.

David, G., & Cambre, C. (2016). Screened intimacies: Tinder and the swipe logic. *Social Media + Society, 2*(2), 2056305116641976. DOI: 10.1177/2056305116641976

De Freitas, J., Uğuralp, A. K., Oğuz-Uğuralp, Z., & Puntoni, S. (2024). Chatbots y salud mental: Perspectivas sobre la seguridad de la IA generativa. *Revista de Psicología del Consumidor, 34*(3), 481–491.

Debasa, F., & Azcona Pastor, J. M. (2024). Tecnología global, iv revolución industrial y mutaciones sociales. *Historia Actual Online*, (63), 183–198.

Eslami, M., Rickman, A., Vaccaro, K., Aleyasen, A., Vuong, A., Karahalios, K., & Sandvig, C. (2015, April). " I always assumed that I wasn't really that close to [her]" Reasoning about Invisible Algorithms in News Feeds. In *Proceedings of the 33rd annual ACM conference on human factors in computing systems* (pp. 153-162).

Fischer, C., Pardos, Z. A., Baker, R. S., Williams, J. J., Smyth, P., Yu, R., Slater, S., Baker, R., & Warschauer, M. (2020). Mining big data in education: Affordances and challenges. *Review of Research in Education, 44*(1), 130–160. DOI: 10.3102/0091732X20903304

Fisher, C. R., Thompson, C. D., & Brookes, R. H. (2020). Gender differences in the Australian undergraduate STEM student experience: A systematic review. *Higher Education Research & Development, 39*(6), 1155–1168. DOI: 10.1080/07294360.2020.1721441

Flores-Alarcia, Ò., & Fornons Casol, L. (Eds.). (2024). *Educación e inteligencia artificial: Horizontes de transformación*. Dykinson.

Floridi, L. (2019). *The logic of information: A theory of philosophy as conceptual design*. Oxford University Press. DOI: 10.1093/oso/9780198833635.001.0001

Garzón, J., Patiño, E., & Marulanda, C. (2025). Systematic review of artificial intelligence in education: Trends, benefits, and challenges. *Multimodal Technologies and Interaction, 9*(8), 84. DOI: 10.3390/mti9080084

Gómez Martínez, R., Medrano García, M. L., & Aznar Sánchez, T. (2023). Motivation and personalization of teaching with machine learning. *Journal of Management and Business Education, 6*(3), 330–342. DOI: 10.35564/jmbe.2023.0017

Graesser, A. C., Fiore, S. M., Greiff, S., Andrews-Todd, J., Foltz, P. W., & Hesse, F. W. (2018). Advancing the science of collaborative problem solving. *Psychological Science in the Public Interest, 19*(2), 59–92. DOI: 10.1177/1529100618808244 PMID: 30497346

Holmes, W., Bialik, M., & Fadel, C. (2019). *Artificial intelligence in education: Promises and implications for teaching and learning*. Center for Curriculum Redesign.

Holstein, K., McLaren, B. M., & Aleven, V. (2019). Diseño para la complementariedad: Necesidades de profesores y estudiantes para el apoyo a la orquestación en aulas mejoradas con IA. In Isotani, S., Millán, E., Ogan, A., Hastings, P., McLaren, B., & Luckin, R. (Eds.), Lecture Notes in Computer Science: Vol. 11625. *Inteligencia Artificial en la Educación. AIED 2019*. Springer., DOI: 10.1007/978-3-030-23204-7_14

Ifenthaler, D., & Yau, J. Y.-K. (2020). Utilising learning analytics for study success: Reflections on current empirical findings. *Research and Practice in Technology Enhanced Learning*, *15*(1), 1–13.

Kasneci, E., Sessler, K., Küchemann, S., Bannert, M., Dementieva, D., Fischer, F., Gasser, U., Kasneci, G., & Neuhaus, J. (2023). ChatGPT for good? On opportunities and challenges of large language models for education. *Learning and Individual Differences*, *103*, 102274. DOI: 10.1016/j.lindif.2023.102274

Kong, S. C., Cheung, M. Y. W., & Tsang, O. (2024). Developing an artificial intelligence literacy framework: Evaluation of a literacy course for senior secondary students using a project-based learning approach. *Computers and Education: Artificial Intelligence*, *6*, 100214. DOI: 10.1016/j.caeai.2024.100214

Kooli, C., & Chakraoui, B. (2025). AI-driven assistive technologies in inclusive education. *Computers & Education: Artificial Intelligence*, *6*, 100089.

Labadze, L., Grigolia, M., & Machaidze, N. (2023). Role of AI chatbots in education: Systematic literature review. *Education and Information Technologies*, *28*(12), 13789–13806.

Liao, Q. V., & Sundar, S. S. (2022, June). Designing for responsible trust in AI systems: A communication perspective. In *Proceedings of the 2022 ACM conference on fairness, accountability, and transparency* (pp. 1257-1268). DOI: 10.1145/3531146.3533182

Lozada, R., Aguayo, E., Suquilanda, E., Pico, A., & Vélez, Q. (2023). Los Riesgos de la Inteligencia Artificial en la educación. *Ciencia Latina: Revista Multidisciplinar*, 7(5), 8. DOI: 10.37811/cl_rcm.v7i5.8301

Luckin, R., Holmes, W., Griffiths, M., & Forcier, L. B. (2022). *Intelligence Unleashed: An argument for AI in Education*. Pearson.

McGrath, N., Farazouli, A., & Cerratto-Pargman, T. (2025). Generative AI chatbots in higher education: A review of an emerging research area. *British Journal of Educational Technology*, *56*(3), 1045–1062.

Nkambou, R., Bourdeau, J., & Mizoguchi, R. (2018). *Advances in Intelligent Tutoring Systems*. Springer.

Papamitsiou, Z., & Economides, A. A. (2014). Learning analytics and educational data mining in practice: A systematic literature review of empirical evidence. *Journal of Educational Technology & Society*, *17*(4), 49–64.

Pitts, L. N., Armstrong, A., Fleming, L., Fazeli, P. L., Landier, W., & Ladores, S. (2025). The Application and Evolution of the Social-Ecological Model for Adolescent and Young Adult Readiness for Transition: A Scoping Review. *Journal of Pediatric Health Care, 39*(3), 355–376. DOI: 10.1016/j.pedhc.2024.12.004 PMID: 39772328

Popenici, SA y Kerr, S. (2017). Explorando el impacto de la inteligencia artificial en la enseñanza y el aprendizaje en la educación superior. *Investigación y práctica en aprendizaje mejorado por la tecnología, 12* (1), 22.

Reeves, B., & Nass, C. (1996). *The media equation: How people treat computers, television, and new media like real people and places.* Cambridge University Press.

Robinson, L., Cotten, S. R., Ono, H., Quan-Haase, A., Mesch, G., Chen, W., Schulz, J., Hale, T. M., & Stern, M. J. (2015). Digital inequalities and why they matter. *Information Communication and Society, 18*(5), 569–582. DOI: 10.1080/1369118X.2015.1012532

Saura, J. R. (2025). Ethics and Privacy in AI-Driven Digital Marketing: Navigating the Paradox.

Slade, S., & Prinsloo, P. (2013). Learning analytics: Ethical issues and dilemmas. *The American Behavioral Scientist, 57*(10), 1510–1529. DOI: 10.1177/0002764213479366

STANTON. (2008). *I. B. M.* I Will.

Turkle, S. (2017). How computers change the way we think. In *Law and society approaches to cyberspace* (pp. 3–7). Routledge. DOI: 10.4324/9781351154161-1

Tussyadiah, I., & Miller, G. (2019). Nudged by a robot: Responses to agency and feedback. *Annals of Tourism Research, 78*, 102752. DOI: 10.1016/j.annals.2019.102752

Wood, W., Bainbridge, W. A., Wiese, E., & Scassellati, B. (2023). Building long-term human–robot relationships: Examining disclosure, perception and well-being across time. *International Journal of Social Robotics, 16*, 765–781.

Woolley, S. C., & Howard, P. N. (Eds.). (2018). *Computational propaganda: Political parties, politicians, and political manipulation on social media.* Oxford University Press. DOI: 10.1093/oso/9780190931407.001.0001

Zawacki-Richter, O., Marín, V. I., Bond, M., & Gouverneur, F. (2019). Systematic review of research on artificial intelligence applications in higher education. *International Journal of Educational Technology in Higher Education, 16*(39), 1–27. DOI: 10.1186/s41239-019-0171-0

Zhai, C., Wibowo, S., & Li, L. D. (2024). The effects of over-reliance on AI dialogue systems on students' cognitive abilities: A systematic review. *Smart Learning Environments, 11*(1), 28. DOI: 10.1186/s40561-024-00316-7

Zhai, X., Chu, X., Chai, C. S., Jong, M. S. Y., & Istenic, A. (2021). Spector, & Li, Y. (2021). Una revisión de la inteligencia artificial (IA) en la educación de 2010 a 2020. *Complexity*, (1), 8812542. DOI: 10.1155/2021/8812542

# Chapter 14
# AI Past, Present, and Future in the University World

**Tomás Aznar**
https://orcid.org/0000-0003-4660-7740
*IUNIT, Spain*

## ABSTRACT

*The use and implementation of artificial intelligence (AI) has not only occurred in the educational and academic fields but has become a true revolution. Today, AI elements such as GPT Chat are consulted 24/7 by a large number of people for all kinds of queries. Artificial intelligence (AI) has undergone major changes in its use and implementation within public and private institutions, with the aim of improving their efficiency and citizen service. This efficiency or modality has been achieved through the implementation of different types of chatbots to assist people. It is at this point that we notice how This article aims to address the analysis of AI, highlighting its significance in the fields of management, administration, and governance, highlighting the significant opportunities, impact assessment, and potential it offers. This review offers a comprehensive overview of AI and its impact on the university field, including its achievements and significant controversies. Finally, it presents the critical opportunities and challenges for applying AI in the university sector.*

## INTRODUCTION

Due to the evolution of education toward a more competency-based approach, new ways of imparting knowledge must be considered, ones that are not based solely on the reproduction of the same lecture delivered by a teacher who repeats the same

DOI: 10.4018/979-8-3373-4480-5.ch014

method every year. Teaching evolves, and teachers and teaching methodologies do so with it. Although the use of active methodologies is not new as such, the term was coined at the beginning of the 20th century. Their use is limited to specific activities within annual programs or to specific sessions to delve deeper into a particular topic. In the case of university learning, the imbalance between theory and practice is even greater, since, despite being one of the areas of knowledge that generates the least interest among students, active methodologies, where we could find Artificial Intelligence, are not integrated as a predominant teaching method.

As stated, Peralta Lara y Guamán Gómez (2020)active methodologies are characterized by their foundation in constructivist theory, which centers the teaching-learning process on the student, giving them a leading role, encouraging their participation and cooperative working relationships, rejecting the rote process, and pursuing creativity and critical reflection. Active methodologies teach students how to solve real problems, generate deeper learning, and increase student motivation.

The study conducted by de la Guardia Montesdeoca (2022)observed how their use fosters a beneficial learning environment, reducing classroom disruptions and generating a positive and harmonious atmosphere. By increasing motivation and interest and enabling personalized learning, students' curiosity is stimulated and a desire to learn is generated.

On the other hand, the virtual absence of scientific evidence supporting the effectiveness of applying these methodologies in the classroom contrasts with the push from the largest educational institutions for their inclusion and implementation in the classroom, as well as proposals for their practical application (de la Guardia Montesdeoca, 2022). This reflects the imbalance between theory and practice, which is an unequivocal result of the lack of ongoing teacher training and the limited or nonexistent government intervention in the evolutionary processes of teaching in our country.

When we talk about active methodologies, we immediately associate them with new technologies, and while this isn't entirely true, they are a great support for their development. Today, an environment without a screen is unviable, and the classroom is no exception to this evolution in society. However, new technologies can be an ally to improve learning and contribute to the organic implementation of active methodologies in the classroom.

In the case of university teaching, there are a large number of technologies that support and enhance learning, but we will focus on the use of Artificial Intelligence in the university world. As we have previously stated, the use of AI has transcended time and space. Its advancement is undeniable, and every day we find more spaces where new uses for this technology are being found. At this point, there is a significant discrepancy between students' use of it and teachers' preparation for its use. Students today use AI for all aspects of their lives (from dressing, eating, or studying to everything else). However, the academic world has resisted accepting that this technology is increasingly present in the university world. According to the latest study by Harvard 2025 magazine, 95% of undergraduate theses or master's thesis projects have received, in part or in large part, support from Artificial Intelligence. This reality is something that the university world refuses to accept and remains entrenched in traditional positions, continuing with academic and research work that today truly miss the point for which it was originally intended. University defense is based on anti-plagiarism systems that are unable to stop the advance of AI use because they find new ways to circumvent it (changing the ink on words, using different languages to lower the percentage, etc.). At this point, we cannot fail to consider these new active technologies as part of the learning process for new students, which would lead to a clear reflection on a change in the university approach that would help integrate this knowledge with these new methodologies that integrate learning. Likewise, they relate to basic knowledge, favoring localization and orientation, human interaction with the environment, and improving the way in which core knowledge is acquired.

This educational proposal stems from the need to motivate students by contextualizing and visualizing processes, spaces, and even societies from the past. Immersive environments improve students' attention and concentration, as mentioned in the study by del Cerro Velázquez and Morales Méndez (2018), which reflects how different studies have shown that simulation technologies enhance learning processes and increase achievement rates.

The inclusion of immersive environments in education addresses the lack of context for understanding the past through immersive recreations of historical scenes or interactive maps. Similarly, through various immersive products, it improves the ability to visualize spaces and address the limitations of access to them. It also democratizes access to culture and heritage, offering the same opportunities to students in rural areas who have difficulty accessing live culture and students with special educational needs, creating a more equitable and inclusive education.

In today's education system, a priority problem is student demotivation. In the current context, education must adapt to respond to the new educational demands of students. When this does not occur, students lose interest in class and become demotivated. As Gutiérrez et al. (2019) emotions impact motivation, which, in turn, impacts learning. From now on, students in secondary school classrooms will be entirely digital natives who are accustomed to rapid rewards, continuous stimuli, and limited attention spans. This influences the way they learn and the methods used in teaching. In the case of university learning, attention span and the interrelationship of case studies are essential for understanding content, so the use of immersive experiences is a great ally in maintaining student motivation. Immersive classroom technologies offer unique opportunities to enhance the contextualization of learning and facilitate the effective transfer of knowledge to real-world situations. (Calderón Zambrano et al., 2023).

The interest in immersive realities stems from a real need to modernize education. A computer for each student, a digital whiteboard, or an e-book isn't enough to modernize education; this process goes further. Education must adapt to the new generations' new understanding of the world, and to this end, immersive learning environments are a great ally, allowing students to immerse themselves in an interactive, three-dimensional world, experiencing different types of sensory and emotional experiences that will foster situated learning.

In the current context of higher education, the integration of emerging technologies such as artificial intelligence (AI) presents an opportunity to transform teaching and learning processes, especially in technical subjects that represent significant challenges for students. Artificial intelligence (AI) has arrived to generate a revolution in the educational field, significantly modifying teaching strategies and learning processes (Chen et al., 2020). In this sense, Chen et al. (2020) also highlight the potential of AI to optimize students' academic performance and personalize instruction through adaptive systems and intelligent tutoring. This technological advancement is relevant in engineering programs, where Descriptive Statistics plays a crucial role in data analysis. However, Garfield and Ben- Zvi (2020) point out that engineering students often face difficulties in understanding fundamental statistical concepts.

In this context, traditional teaching methods fail to address individual student needs or connect content with the specific demands of engineering, highlighting an urgent need for innovative teaching approaches. Hwang and Chang (2021) highlight that educational chatbots, such as ChatGPT, can provide immediate feedback and adapt content to each student's pace and level, improving the learning experience in complex subjects.

On the other hand, there is a disconnect between statistics content and the particular needs of engineering students, evidenced by Garfield and Ben- Zvi (2020), when they indicate the urgency of adopting innovative teaching methodologies. Hwang and Chang (2021) highlight that educational chatbots, such as ChatGPT, can provide immediate feedback and adapt content to the pace and level of each student, improving the learning experience in complex subjects. Likewise, Alshammari and Qureshi (2020) argue that AI-based adaptive learning systems increase pedagogical effectiveness and address student heterogeneity in higher education.

Artificial intelligence (AI) is defined as the set of technologies that enable machines to simulate human cognitive processes, such as learning, problem-solving, and decision-making (Chen et al., 2020). In the educational field, AI has emerged as a transformative tool that redefines teaching and learning processes by offering adaptive and personalized solutions. According to Chen et al. (2020), AI applications in education include intelligent tutoring systems, educational chatbots, and adaptive learning platforms, which can improve academic performance and address individual students' needs. In particular, educational chatbots, such as ChatGPT, have proven effective in providing immediate feedback and generating content tailored to each student's level, which is especially useful in technical subjects such as Descriptive Statistics (Hwang & Chang, 2021). In the Latin American context, where the adoption of these technologies is still incipient, Herrera Narváez (2023) highlights that intelligent teaching based on AI can significantly improve student performance, which suggests its relevance for institutions such as UPDS that seek to innovate in their educational processes.

Artificial intelligence (AI) has emerged as a transformative tool in education, offering innovative solutions to personalize learning, improve teaching efficiency, and foster the development of 21st-century skills (Chen et al., 2020). One of the main advantages of AI in education is its ability to facilitate personalized learning, adapting content, activities, and feedback to each student's individual needs and preferences (Alshammari & Qureshi, 2020). Intelligent tutoring systems, for example, can provide individualized support to students, offering explanations and exercises tailored to their level of understanding and learning pace (Hwang & Chang, 2021). Likewise, educational chatbots, such as ChatGPT, can answer questions, offer feedback, and generate content tailored to each student's needs, promoting more autonomous and meaningful learning (Vera et al., 2023).

AI can also improve teaching efficiency, facilitate personalized learning, and automate repetitive tasks, freeing up teachers' time to focus on more complex and creative activities (Sabzalieva & Valentini, 2023). Likewise, AI can be used to generate personalized educational content, tailored to the specific needs of each course or program (Parra Sanchez et al., 2023). However, the integration of AI into education also poses significant challenges that must be addressed in an ethical and responsible manner (Gallent Torres et al., 2023). It is essential to ensure that AI systems are transparent, fair, and equitable, avoiding bias and discrimination (Gallent Torres et al., 2023). Likewise, it is important to train teachers so that they can use AI effectively and critically, understanding its limitations and potential (Razali et al., 2022). Despite these challenges, AI offers enormous potential to transform education and prepare students for the challenges of the future (Chen et al., 2020). By integrating AI strategically and responsibly, educational institutions can improve the quality of teaching, promote personalized learning, and foster the development of essential skills for success in the 21st century.

Personalized learning is conceived as a pedagogical approach that adapts teaching processes to the needs, interests, and learning rhythms of each student, with the aim of offering a more meaningful and effective educational experience (Alshammari & Qureshi, 2020). This approach is based on the recognition of the diversity in learning styles, knowledge levels, and progress rates of students, which demands strategies that overcome the limitations of traditional uniform methods (Rivera-Arzola, 2021). In the field of higher education, personalized learning has been consolidated as a response to the challenges of student heterogeneity, promoting autonomous and meaningful learning that fosters the development of key competencies (Parra-Sánchez, 2022).

The integration of technologies such as artificial intelligence (AI) has significantly enhanced the possibilities of personalized learning. According to Hwang and Chang (2021), tools such as educational chatbots, including ChatGPT, allow the generation of content, exercises, and feedback adapted to the level of each student, which is particularly valuable in technical subjects such as Descriptive Statistics. For example, an engineering student struggling with linear regression could receive simplified explanations and progressive exercises generated by AI, while a more advanced student could tackle more complex problems, thus optimizing their learning process. This level of personalization not only improves the understanding of abstract concepts but also strengthens student autonomy, an essential competency in the UPDS competency-based educational model, which prioritizes the development of skills such as autonomous learning and the use of new technologies (Misión y Visión, 2021). In the context of teaching Descriptive Statistics, where engineering students face recurring difficulties (Garfield & Ben- Zvi, 2020), personalized learning, powered by AI and designed through a structured process such as Design Thinking offers a way to overcome the limitations of traditional methods (Parra Sánchez et al., 2023).

Descriptive Statistics is a branch of statistics that focuses on the collection, organization, presentation, and interpretation of data to describe the characteristics of a set of information (Levin, 2004). In the context of engineering careers, this discipline is fundamental for data analysis in areas such as systems design, industrial process management, telecommunications, and petroleum resource optimization. According to Garfield and Ben- Zvi (2020), engineering students need to master concepts such as measures of central tendency, dispersion, linear regression and correlation, and index numbers to make informed decisions in their professional fields. The UPDS Descriptive Statistics course program, common to the Systems Engineering, Industrial Engineering, Network and Telecommunications Engineering, and Petroleum Management Engineering programs, establishes as a specific microcompetence that students "apply statistical tools and logical reasoning to describe, interpret, support, and improve the decision-making process in situations in the social, business, and scientific environments" (UPDS, 2017). However, Garfield and Ben- Zvi (2020) point out that engineering students face recurring difficulties in understanding these concepts, which underlines the need for innovative pedagogical approaches that facilitate their learning.

The competency-based educational model, adopted by UPDS since 2017, focuses on the comprehensive development of students by strengthening four dimensions:

knowing how to know, knowing how to do, knowing how to be, and knowing how to live together (Mission and Vision, 2021). This model seeks to train professionals capable of responding to the challenges of the work and social environments, promoting skills such as innovation, research, autonomous learning, and the use of new technologies. In the case of the Descriptive Statistics subject, the UPDS program prioritizes generic skills such as New Information and Communication Technologies and Entrepreneurship, as well as the ability to work under pressure and communicate effectively (UPDS, 2017). The integration of an AI-based teaching guide aligns with this model by encouraging autonomous learning (through personalized activities), the use of emerging technologies (using ChatGPT), and practical problem-solving (with contextualized examples for each engineering program). Furthermore, this approach responds to the UPDS mission of "generating changes in people to develop socially responsible entrepreneurs capable of responding to emerging challenges" (Mission and Vision, 2021).

The Design Thinking is defined as a user-centered methodological approach that drives innovation through an iterative and creative process. This process is structured in five key phases: empathize, define, ideate, prototype, and evaluate, following the model proposed by the Institute of Design at Stanford (Li et al., 2019). In the educational field, this approach stands out for its ability to foster student-centered learning, especially in STEM disciplines such as engineering. In this sense, Li et al. (2019) highlight that Design Thinking empowers educators to design learning experiences that integrate critical thinking, creativity, and problem-solving skills, essential for overcoming the difficulties faced by engineering students in subjects such as Descriptive Statistics (Garfield & Ben- Zvi, 2020). Additionally, Yildiz Durak et al. (2023) emphasize that this approach strengthens teacher self-efficacy in STEM teaching by promoting the co -creation of innovative solutions between teachers and students.

Learning guides, also known as teaching guides, are defined as pedagogical tools designed to guide and structure the teaching-learning process, providing students with a clear framework of objectives, activities, resources, and strategies that facilitate the acquisition of knowledge and the development of skills (Herrera Narváez, 2023). In the context of higher education, learning guides have established themselves as a key resource for promoting autonomous and meaningful learning, especially in environments where students face challenges such as the heterogeneity of their knowledge levels, the intensity of modular formats, or the complexity of technical subjects (Rivera-Arzola, 2021). These tools allow teachers to structure learning experiences that adapt to students' needs, fostering self-regulation and responsibility in their educational process (Parra-Sánchez, 2022).

In the case of subjects such as Descriptive Statistics, which present recurring difficulties for engineering students due to their abstract nature and the intensive modular format of the UPDS (Garfield & Ben- Zvi, 2020), learning guides offer a structured approach to address these challenges. By integrating personalized learning strategies, the guides can include activities and resources adapted to the pace and learning styles of each student, such as progressive exercises or contextualized explanations. The incorporation of technologies such as artificial intelligence (AI) further enhances their effectiveness, since tools such as ChatGPT can generate personalized content, immediate feedback, and practical examples that reinforce the understanding of complex concepts, such as linear regression (Vera et al., 2023). This approach aligns with personalized learning, which seeks to respond to the individual needs of students, promoting more meaningful and effective learning (Alshammari & Qureshi, 2020).

As in any discipline, the foundation of learning lies in theoretical understanding. Just as to obtain a driver's license we must first master the theory and then apply that knowledge in practice, in education it is essential to understand how AI works before using it as a tool. Education, in the context of AI, has shifted from a practical approach to a method that also includes theoretical teaching, something that is being promoted in the European Union.

Teaching computational thinking without a computer has proven particularly effective in the classroom, allowing students to more fully grasp key concepts before interacting with technology. Furthermore, having up-to-date and accessible resources for teachers is crucial, as reflected in initiatives such as the recent update of a website dedicated to AI in education.

While AI promises to improve the personalization of learning and the automation of administrative tasks, it also poses significant challenges. Test grading and classroom management are areas where AI can greatly facilitate educators' work. However, one of the most prominent fears is the dehumanization of learning and the loss of critical thinking among students, especially if AI is introduced at an early age without proper guidance from educators.

It is vital that teachers maintain their role as facilitators of human learning, where creativity and emotional interaction cannot be replicated by machines. As AI systems become more sophisticated, it is essential that educators develop their digital competency to make the most of these tools without compromising human values.

The use of emerging technologies in education demands a critical approach. For example, QR codes generated by AI systems like ChatGPT can be malicious; therefore, educators are advised to be cautious and carefully verify any automatically generated links or resources. This not only protects educators and students but also provides an opportunity to teach about cybersecurity and digital ethics.

AI is transforming the educational landscape, but its effective implementation requires proper planning and available resources. While successful initiatives worldwide, such as those implemented in China or Ukraine, should be explored, it is essential that educational policies be adapted to local contexts and focus on teacher training.

In conclusion, the future of education in the AI era is seen as a collaboration between technology and humanity. By providing quality education that emphasizes both theory and practice, educators can prepare students for a world where AI and human capabilities will coexist synergistically.

It's AI itself that can tell us its strengths and weaknesses. Ask Chat GPT and this is the answer.

Can you tell me what education looks like in about five years, with the use of AI, both positive and negative?

Of course! Artificial intelligence (AI) is already transforming education, and in the next five years, its impact is likely to be even more profound. Here's a balanced view of the potential positives and negatives:

## Positive aspects

1. **Learning Personalization:** AI will be able to adapt content to each student's needs and learning styles, allowing them to learn at their own pace.
2. **Expanded access:** AI-powered educational resources, such as virtual tutors, will be available online, benefiting students in remote or resource-limited areas.
3. **Efficiency for teachers:** AI will automate repetitive tasks, such as grading tests or creating lesson plans, freeing up time for teachers to focus on teaching and supporting their students.
4. **Immersion and creativity:** Tools such as augmented reality (AR) and generative AI will enrich learning experiences, making them more interactive and engaging.

## Negative aspects

1. **Unequal access:** Not all students or schools will have the resources to integrate AI into their systems, widening the educational gap between different regions or social groups.
2. **Over-reliance:** There could be a decline in fundamental human skills, such as critical thinking, if students rely too heavily on AI.
3. **Privacy and Ethics:** The widespread use of AI may raise concerns about the collection and use of personal data from students and teachers.
4. **Dehumanization of teaching:** If human interaction is replaced too much with technology, it could affect the relationship between teachers and students, which is essential for learning and emotional development.

The outlook will depend largely on how we adopt these tools. The key will be to balance the use of AI to enhance education without losing sight of human values and individual needs.

As we see, AI itself understands the potential of its use, but also the implicit threats we can encounter within its development. At the university level, we must understand that learning has changed and that the university reality demands a methodological change based on the new knowledge that AI provides us, requiring significant actions that put an end to research work as it stands.

An example of a university development would be to seek methodological strategies that complement the learning received. An example of this methodological strategy is:

Personalized and Adaptive Learning with AI:

- This strategy directly addresses the diverse student body and the accelerated pace of the intensive modular format (20 business days, 3 hours per day). The guide proposes a sequence and structure of activities, but the integration of AI allows students to deviate from this suggested path to delve deeper, review, or explore topics according to their individual needs.
- AI tools, such as ChatGPT, Google AI Studio, Grok, Geminis, Google NotebookLM, and others, are used to generate tailored content: explanations of statistical concepts at varying levels of depth, using analogies or approaches relevant to different engineering programs (Systems, Industrial, Networks and Telecommunications, Petroleum Management). This is achieved through specific prompts that the student is guided to formulate.
- AI also facilitates adaptation through progressive exercises, adjusting the difficulty, offering hints, or proposing additional challenges based on the student's performance and understanding during the activity.
- Sources such as Hwang and Chang (2021), Alshammari and Qureshi (2020), and Parra Sanchez et al. (2023) support the ability of AI-based systems, including educational chatbots, to adapt content, activities, and feedback, improving the learning experience, especially in complex subjects. AI-powered personalized learning seeks to respond to individual needs for more meaningful and effective learning.

Operational Integration of AI Tools such as Smart Tutor and Cognitive Assistant:

- The guide activities explicitly direct the student to interact with AI tools (ChatGPT, Google AI Studio, Grok, Geminis, Google NotebookLM, etc.) for specific functions, overcoming the limitations of teacher availability in an intensive format.

- **24/7 Question Resolution:** The guide informs students that they can consult the AI at any time to resolve immediate conceptual or procedural questions that arise during the activities, such as differentiating the mean and median or how to perform a basic calculation in software. This acts as an always-available tutor.
- **Contextualized Problem and Example Generation:** A key operational feature is the AI's ability to generate problems and examples relevant to specific engineering fields. Activities include steps where students are asked to use predefined prompts or create their own to connect statistical concepts with real-life scenarios in industrial production, petroleum management, systems design, and so on. This fosters meaningful understanding by applying the concepts to their future career field. Sources like ours (2023) demonstrate ChatGPT 's potential to provide conceptual explanations and applications.
- **Immediate Formative Feedback:** After completing exercises, the guide suggests that students use the AI to check answers and receive instant feedback, with detailed explanations of errors. This immediate feedback is crucial for metacognition and self-regulated learning, especially when teacher feedback can be delayed. Sources such as Hwang and Chang (2021), Alshammari and Qureshi (2020), and Vera et al. (2023) highlight the ability of chatbots to provide immediate feedback.
- **Software Analysis and Interpretation Support:** The practical sections of the activities, which involve the use of statistical software (SPSS, R, Excel) with engineering datasets, direct the student to use AI to interpret the results obtained (e.g., explain the meaning of a p-value) or to obtain assistance in performing certain operations.
- The emphasis is on using AI as an *assistant*, and the strategy instructs students on the need to critically monitor and verify the accuracy of the answers provided by the AI. This promotes critical thinking, a 21st-century skill and a competency of the MEC.

Implementation of Active Methodologies and Competency-Based Approach:

- The structure and activities of the teaching guide are designed to be a vehicle for various active methodologies, aligned with the UPDS MEC and the engineer's profile.
- **Problem-Based/Case-Based Learning:** The guide introduces real-life engineering problems or cases at the beginning of each block. The methodological strategy is reflected in how the guide directs students to use statistical concepts, AI tools, and software to analyze data relevant to the case and propose solutions. This fosters **"know-how"** (application of tools) and **"know-how"**

(conceptual understanding) in authentic contexts. Sources mention the use of AI to generate problem scenarios.

- **Partial Flipped Classroom:** The guide structures the autonomous component by indicating the conceptual content to be reviewed beforehand (with AI support for questions or examples). Face-to-face time, following the guide, is dedicated to resolving high-level questions (which the AI failed to address), applying concepts to complex problems with teacher guidance, and fostering **"coexistence skills"** through group discussions. Sources indicate that AI can be useful for self-directed learning.
- **Hands-on Learning with Software:** Each activity block includes sections dedicated to practical work with statistical software (SPSS, R, Excel). The guide provides engineering-relevant datasets and guided steps, with AI acting as an assistant. This reinforces the **know-how** with ICT tools, a competency prioritized by the UPDS.
- **Comprehensive Development of Competencies:** The combination of autonomous interaction with the guide/AI, practical work and moments of group/teacher interaction seeks to develop the four dimensions: **knowing how to know** (concepts), **knowing how to do** (application, use of tools), **social skills** (ethics in data management, critique of AI, responsibility), and **social skills** (teamwork, ethical communication). This aligns with the UPDS's mission to train competent and socially responsible professionals. The subject-specific microcompetence involves applying statistical tools and logical reasoning for decision-making, which is actively sought to be developed.

## CONCLUSIONS

The COVID-19 pandemic has marked a significant milestone in human history, not only from a health perspective, but also in the way we relate and learn. This critical moment has prompted a reassessment of our social interactions and facilitated the transition to the Fourth Industrial Revolution, characterized by the integration of technologies such as 5G, the Internet of Things (IoT), and artificial intelligence (AI). In this context, the demand for social transhumanization becomes evident; we not only seek to improve the human condition, but also to adapt to a world that demands new approaches to mitigate physical contact and enhance learning.

During the pandemic, it became clear how learning management systems (LMSs), combined with artificial intelligence, have enabled more measured and evaluated education. This phenomenon was especially noticeable among students from continents outside of Europe, who found these technologies to be fundamental support for their educational journey. This demonstrates that digital natives—those who have grown up in a digital environment—demand an education that is on par with the technological tools they use daily.

The integration of advanced technologies into education is not only a contemporary necessity, but also an opportunity to individualize learning. The combination of 5G, IoT, and big data analytics offers unprecedented potential to adapt education to the skills required in the 21st century. The pandemic accelerated this process, fostering an environment where digitalization has consolidated itself as a key element in higher education.

Students' surveys show greater satisfaction and a sense of support in using AI-mediated LMS platforms compared to their European counterparts. This suggests that, despite the physical proximity to educational institutions, the digital experience can offer significant advantages in terms of learning support and monitoring.

In short, the fourth industrial revolution is here to stay, and its influence extends to all sectors of society, especially higher education. We have learned that digital tools not only complement teaching but can radically transform it, fostering more individualized, relevant, and aligned learning with current demands. Adapting to this new reality is essential to preparing future generations for the challenges of the 21st century.

The emergence of artificial intelligence (AI) in education has opened up a vast field of possibilities and challenges that educators must address with caution. As AI tools become more accessible and sophisticated, it is crucial to understand how they work, their applications, and the ethical implications they entail.

With internet access, searching for information has become easier, but it has also given rise to misinformation. Students who consult platforms like Wikipedia often assume the information provided is objective and true. A critical point is that, although AI can compile data from multiple sources, it also has a tendency to "invent" information, which can perpetuate errors if not corrected promptly. This highlights the need for students and teachers to develop critical skills to assess the veracity of information.

AI tools are increasingly being used to facilitate educational planning and monitor student progress. However, special care must be taken with data protection, especially in the school context. Before adopting any application, it is essential to ensure that it complies with data protection regulations and guarantees the security of student information. This contrasts with previous eras when concerns about data security were less prevalent.

AI offers the possibility of personalizing education, tailoring lessons to students' individual needs. Through data analysis, it's possible to better understand classroom dynamics and areas that need attention. For example, classroom diversity, such as immigrant students and their socioeconomic status, can be tracked using data collected at the beginning of the school year. However, this requires additional effort in data collection and analysis, and ongoing communication with parents to ensure transparency.

When using AI to generate educational content, the question arises of how to handle attribution. As educators begin to use AI tools, such as chatbots and text generators, it is critical to acknowledge the source of the content produced. The current recommendation is to cite the AI model used and the prompt that generated the response. This practice applies not only to texts but also to AI-generated images.

Generating educational materials through AI has proven to be efficient. For example, when requesting dictation for six-year-old students or reading comprehension questions about a specific novel, AI can quickly provide relevant answers. This allows teachers to focus on personalizing instruction and creating a more interactive and enriching learning environment.

Artificial intelligence has the potential to revolutionize education, but its implementation must be careful and thoughtful. Training teachers in the use of these tools, as well as creating robust data protection policies, are essential steps to fully harness the benefits of AI in the classroom. Only through the critical and ethical use of these technologies can we ensure that students are equipped with the skills necessary to navigate an increasingly digital world. This will make universities better prepared, although we cannot forget, as already mentioned, that all this goes hand in hand with a change in approach that must be implemented within higher education to adapt to new realities.

## REFERENCES


Alshammari, M., & Qureshi, S. (2020). Implementing adaptive learning systems in higher education: Opportunities and challenges. *Journal of Educational Technology Development and Exchange, 13*(1), 1–16. https://www.sicet.org/jetde/index.php/jetde/article/view/171/114

Calderón Zambrano, R. L., Yánez Romero, M. E., Dávila Dávila, K. E., & Beltrán Balarezo, C. E. (2023). Realidad virtual y aumentada en la educación superior: Experiencias inmersivas para el aprendizaje profundo. *Religación : Revista de Ciencias Sociales y Humanidades, 8*(37), e2301088. DOI: 10.46652/rgn.v8i37.1088

Chen, L., Chen, P., & Lin, Z. (2020). Artificial intelligence in education: A review. *IEEE Access : Practical Innovations, Open Solutions, 8*, 75264–75278. DOI: 10.1109/ACCESS.2020.2988510

de la Guardia Montesdeoca, G. (2022). Acción e Interacción: Metodologías activas en la enseñanza de la Historia en Secundaria. *Clio*, (48), 320–339. DOI: 10.26754/ojs_clio/clio.2022486854

del Cerro Velázquez, F., & Morales Méndez, G. (2018). Augmented reality and mobile devices: A binominal methodological resource for inclusive education (SDG 4). An example in secondary education. *Sustainability (Basel), 10*(10), 3446. DOI: 10.3390/su10103446

Gallent Torres, C., Zapata-González, A., & Ortego-Hernando, J. L. (2023). The impact of Generative Artificial Intelligence in higher education: A focus on ethics and academic integrity. *RELIEVE. Revista ELectrónica de Investigación y EValuación Educativa, 29*(2), 1–19.

Gutiérrez, R. C., Somoza, J. A. G. C., Taranilla, R. V., & Armero, J. M. M. (2019). Análisis de la motivación ante el uso de la realidad virtual en la enseñanza de la historia en futuros maestros. *EDUTEC, Revista electrónica de tecnología educativa*, (68), 1-14.

Hwang, G. J., & Chang, S. C. (2021). Facilitating knowledge construction in mobile learning contexts: A bi-directional peer-assessment approach. *British Journal of Educational Technology, 52*(1), 337–357. DOI: 10.1111/bjet.13001

Levin, I. (2004). Living apart together: A new family form. *Current Sociology, 52*(2), 223–240. DOI: 10.1177/0011392104041809

Montacute, R. (2020). *Social mobility and COVID-19*. Sutton Trust.

Parra Sánchez, J. S., Torres Pardo, I. D., & Martínez de Merino, C. Y. (2023). Personalization of resources for teaching university mathematics using artificial intelligence. *Inter-American Journal of Research in Education and Pedagogy, 16*(1). Advance online publication. DOI: 10.15332/25005421.7904

Parra-Sánchez, J. S. (2022). The potential of artificial intelligence in higher education: A personalization approach. *Technological-Educational Journal of Teachers 2.0, 14*(1). https://doi.org/DOI: 10.37843/rted.v14i1.296

Razali, N. H., Ali, N. N. N., Safiyuddin, S. K., & Khalid, F. (2022). Design thinking approaches in education and their challenges. *Creative Education, 13*(7), 2289–2299. Advance online publication. DOI: 10.4236/ce.2022.137145

Sabzalieva, E., & Valentini, A. (2023). *ChatGPT and artificial intelligence in higher education: A quick start guide*. UNESCO IESALC.

Vera, J. P. D., Hojas, D. S. P., Sarmiento, Z. J. F., Ramírez, A. K. R., & Mora, D. V. M. (2023). Estudio comparativo experimental del uso de chatGPT y su influencia en el aprendizaje de los estudiantes de la carrera Tecnologías de la información de la universidad de Guayaquil. *Revista Universidad de Guayaquil, 137*(2), 51–63. DOI: 10.53591/rug.v137i2.2107

Yildiz Durak, H., Atman Uslu, N., Canbazoğlu Bilici, S., & Güler, B. (2023). Predictors of TPACK for integrated STEM. *Education and Information Technologies, 28*(7), 7927–7954. Advance online publication. DOI: 10.1007/s10639-022-11505-7

Chapter 15

# Learning Analytics, Artificial Intelligence, and the Future of Democratic Curricular Governance

**Joe L. Carrrión-Jumbo**
https://orcid.org/0000-0003-3632-5352
*Universidad Internacional SEK, Ecuador*

**Cecilia E. Jaramillo Jaramillo**
https://orcid.org/0009-0004-1943-4383
*Escuela Politécnica Nacional, Ecuador*

**Sophia Nicole Chuquillangui Villarreal**
https://orcid.org/0009-0001-0886-4677
*Universidad Internacional SEK, Ecuador*

## ABSTRACT

*This chapter explores the integration of Artificial Intelligence (AI) powered Learning Analytics (LA) in higher education, highlighting its transformative potential and ethical challenges. While LA+AI systems enhance personalized learning, predictive analytics, and institutional efficiency, they risk undermining pedagogical integrity, academic freedom, and equity if implemented without oversight. Key concerns include algorithmic bias, erosion of human autonomy, privacy violations, and the digital divide. The chapter advocates for a human rights-based governance framework centered on pedagogical primacy, algorithmic transparency, and democratic oversight. Case studies from global institutions illustrate best practices and pitfalls, emphasizing the need for ethical design, stakeholder training, and continuous eval-*

DOI: 10.4018/979-8-3373-4480-5.ch015

*uation. The conclusion calls for balancing innovation with equity to ensure LA+AI serves—rather than dictates—educational goals, preserving higher education's democratic mission in the AI era.*

## 1. INTRODUCTION

The integration of AI-powered LA represents a paradigm shift in curricular planning and academic governance. While these technologies offer unprecedented capabilities for personalizing education and enhancing institutional efficiency (Aderibigbe et al., 2025), they also entail the risk of undermining fundamental pedagogical principles in universities if implemented without proper oversight (Jahankhani et al., 2022).

The transformation of education has ushered in a new era of data-driven decision-making, where LA serves as a critical tool for academic institutions. LA refers to the measurement, collection, analysis, and reporting of student data to optimize learning environments, personalize instruction, and enhance institutional outcomes (Aderibigbe et al., 2025). When integrated with AI, these systems can predict student performance, identify at-risk learners, and recommend curricular adjustments (Pattanaik et al., 2024). However, as universities adopt these technologies, crucial questions emerge: Who governs these systems? How can we ensure they align with—rather than undermine—higher education's core mission, while respecting each institution's pedagogical model?

This chapter examines the intersection of LA, AI, and educational governance, arguing that while these technologies offer transformative potential, their implementation requires careful regulation to safeguard pedagogical integrity, academic freedom (Lehrfreiheit), and equity. The central thesis posits that LA must serve educational models without imposing their direction, remaining subordinated to them.

### 1.1 Foundations of Learning Analytics

LA "involves the collection, analysis, interpretation, and communication of data about students and their learning processes, generating theoretically relevant and actionable information to enhance both learning and teaching". (SoLAR 2025)

Indicators in LA are essential for higher education institutions to maintain a continuous improvement approach to teaching processes. Among these, some focus on aspects such as student satisfaction, perceived workload, and the effectiveness of implemented methodologies. These indicators provide quantitative and qualitative data that facilitate the evaluation of pedagogical strategies' impact. The study by (Ortiz-Beltrán et al., 2023) revealed that overall course satisfaction decreased during emergency remote teaching but increased in subsequent hybrid and face-to-face modalities, reflecting the education system's adaptability to teaching methods and stakeholder needs—students, faculty, administrators, and institutional support personnel. In this regard, the university system demonstrated resilience and capacity for improvement following the pandemic-induced crisis.

For universities, early detection of student performance deficiencies and integration of micro-curricular planning adjustments are crucial. A strategic resource involves comprehensive data analysis through LA, enabling identification of specific patterns and needs. As(Elhussein et al., 2024) note, data-driven and AI-powered analysis streamlines educational systems, enhancing their responsiveness. (Buckingham, 2012a) emphasizes that LA is fundamental for interpreting data's impact on learning. Furthermore, the mass adoption of LMS platforms, accelerated by the pandemic (Wirani & Manurung, 2020), has facilitated the collection and analysis of these indicators. However, this process required personnel to develop new competencies—including video-conferencing tool proficiency, remote group collaboration skills, updated assessment and task management systems, and integration of novel pedagogical resources. Facing this scenario, universities recognized the need to bridge the digital literacy gap among both faculty and students.

Analysis of these indicators helps identify patterns, such as variability in satisfaction survey responses regarding teaching systems/services or consistency in content perception, thereby facilitating evidence-based (data-driven) decision-making. Institutions monitoring such data can adjust curricular designs, train educators, and optimize technological resources, ensuring quality education even in disruptive contexts. Thus, LA emerges as a strategic tool for sustainable educational innovation.

## 1.2 Artificial Intelligence

AI is based on creating systems capable of performing tasks requiring human intelligence, such as learning, perception, and decision-making. Its foundations include:

- **Machine learning algorithms:** From supervised models to deep neural networks.
- **Natural language processing (NLP):** For understanding and generating human language.
- **Computer vision:** Image and video recognition.
- **Intelligent robotics:** Integration of AI with physical systems for autonomous interaction.
- **Reasoning and planning:** Symbolic logic and algorithms for solving complex problems.

(Searle, 1980) argues that mere computational program execution is insufficient to attribute intentionality or comprehension to machines, employing his famous "Chinese Room" thought experiment (details beyond this work's scope) to support this position. This debate remains relevant today, challenging the boundaries of strong AI and the nature of human cognition. The foundations of AI involve not only technical dimensions but also profound philosophical reflections on consciousness and cognition

## 1.3 Bias in Systems

Scrutiny of AI stems from biases potentially introduced through human-produced or collected data, leading to the incorporation and occasional amplification of existing prejudices within algorithms. This results in inequities without explicit intent. To mitigate bias, techniques may be applied through:

- Preprocessing (data modification)
- In-processing (algorithmic adaptation)
- Postprocessing (output adjustment)

Each method faces limitations and legal challenges, including personal data protection concerns (Ntoutsi et al., 2020).

Bias cases may be particularly critical in the legal domain. For instance, while AI can serve as a valuable tool for attorneys and judges by identifying patterns in judicial cases, its application presents challenges such as incomplete data access and the need for transparency to prevent unfair automated judicial decisions (Aletras et al., 2016) implying decision-making bias that may prove unjust for individuals. This work examines multiple aspects of algorithmic bias (Sections 4.2 and 6.4).

## 1.4 Comparison of AI with Human Capabilities

IA seeks to emulate human creativity through three approaches: combining known ideas (analogies), exploring conceptual spaces (e.g., music or design), and transforming rules to generate revolutionary concepts. While achieving impressive outcomes, it still struggles to replicate the emotional and cultural depth inherent to human creativity. Human creativity remains intrinsically tied to cultural and emotional contexts—factors notoriously difficult to reproduce computationally. For instance, artistic values evolve temporally (as seen in shifting receptions of composers across eras), hindering the development of autonomous systems capable of generating socially valued innovations (Boden, 1998). Concerning emotions and the absence of sentience, AI remains limited in moral or justice-oriented decision-making (Parga, 2023).

## 1.5 Individual Rights

A regulatory framework ensuring transparent, responsible, and ethical implementation of algorithmic technology is imperative to prevent technological advancements from undermining social equity, prioritizing ethics and transparency in automated decision-making.

Organizations like universities must process substantial volumes of student data, curricular programs, faculty information, and macro-, meso-, and micro-curricular planning—alongside daily tracking of academic activity, semester scheduling, syllabi, lesson planning, content, assignments, assessments, grading rubrics, and evaluations. Additionally, interaction data from all users (students, faculty, administrators) constitutes an immense volume of valuable information requiring sophisticated processing techniques regarding computational power (hardware), algorithmic capability (software), and efficient storage systems. (Ungerer & Slade, 2022) assert that conceiving LA without AI is increasingly inconceivable.

Within this context, LA techniques can be augmented by AI to derive insights supporting institutional decision-making and governance. Automating these processes necessitates evaluating impacts on teaching-learning processes and consequently, professional development. Here, it is valuable to adopt (Sánchez Hernández, 2024) proposition regarding the need for a regulatory framework guaranteeing transparent, responsible, and ethical algorithmic technology implementation. Similarly, Sánchez Hernández recommends vigilant AI usage to prevent systemic risks that compromise fundamental rights.

## 1.6 Core Problem

Considering all the above, this work aims to answer the following Research Questions (RQ):

- **RQ1:** How can algorithmic governance be prevented from eroding academic freedom?
- **RQ2:** Do university educational models incorporate emerging technologies such as AI?
- **RQ3:** Can AI-driven LA systems coexist with educational models?

## 2 THE TENSION BETWEEN DATA-DRIVEN EFFICIENCY AND EDUCATIONAL MODELS

The growing integration of AI across all educational levels, particularly through data-driven systems, raises fundamental questions: What type of education are we prioritizing? One valuing efficiency, predictability, and quantifiable outcomes, or one promoting reflexivity, critical thinking, and holistic learning experiences?

This constitutes the tension emerging when quantitative, data-driven approaches collide with the qualitative nature of educational and pedagogical frameworks. Examining how this conflict manifests in teaching practices, institutional governance, and student autonomy provides an updated, comprehensive perspective on the influence of both AI and LA in modern education. This section addresses diverse viewpoints on the topic, with particular consideration of higher education contexts in Latin America and Spain as case studies."

### 2.1 Initial Approach on Efficiency vs. Authentic Education

In recent years, it has become evident that one of AI and LA's primary contributions to education lies in their capacity to personalize learning, identify at-risk students, and optimize institutional resources. However, scholars have cautioned that these technologies tend to prioritize operational efficiency over pedagogical objectives.

As Selwyn (2015), asserts, "Data-driven education risks becoming an exercise in surveillance and control, reducing students to mere data points within a system designed for efficiency, not emancipation".

This quotation illustrates a core dilemma: the mechanization of education may hollow out learning by focusing on algorithmically optimized outcomes.

Similarly, Biesta (2015) critiques the 'learnification' of education, where educational experiences are reduced to observable and predictable outputs. This paradigmatic shift reflects a managerial logic configuring teaching through input-output models, undermining broader educational aims like civic formation, ethical reasoning, and creativity.

For their part, Knox et al. (2020) highlight the "illusion of objectivity" in AI-based decision systems. Even the most advanced algorithms incorporate subjective assumptions—often concealed within proprietary code—which undermines data's apparent neutrality and necessitates critical interrogation of systems deployed in educational settings."

## 2.2 On Autonomy/Roles of Students and Teachers

The teaching role has undergone transformation, and Williamson (2017) warns that educators are being progressively converted into "data managers and executors of algorithmic prescriptions.

Rather than exercising professional judgment and adapting their practice to student needs, they are expected to follow predetermined curricular pathways based on analytics dashboards. This erosion of pedagogical freedom not only deprofessionalizes the teaching role but also constrains its capacity to respond contextually to students.

Simultaneously, students are redefined as data generators, with their behaviors subjected to perpetual monitoring and analysis. These risks normalizing surveillance and transforming education from an exploratory, developmental experience into a continuous exercise of quantification.

Balasubramaniam et al. (2023) maintain that ensuring transparency and explainability in AI systems is essential to align educational technologies with ethical and pedagogical objectives. Without such safeguards, automation will likely reproduce biases, perpetuate inequalities, and undermine trust in educational systems. The autonomy concern extends to the general populace, as examined in Section 4.1: Threats to Human Autonomy.

## 2.3 Contrast Big Ten US with Latin America and Spain

AI governance in education varies significantly across contexts. A 2024 study by (Wu et al., 2024) examined AI governance frameworks within Big Ten consortium universities—a group of highly prestigious US research institutions. The study revealed that each university has developed robust policies encompassing staff training, informed consent protocols, and ethical review procedures. AI implementation is supervised by interdisciplinary committees ensuring alignment with institutional values, protection of student autonomy, and prevention of data misuse (Wu et al., 2024).

In contrast, most higher education institutions in Latin America and Spain have yet to formally integrate AI into governance frameworks. Institutional strategies, educational models, and regulatory documents rarely mention AI or LA; when referenced, such mentions remain typically vague or experimental. Consequently, implementations tend to be vendor-driven pilot projects with minimal oversight, lacking ethical supervision or longitudinal evaluation.

This governance gap entails significant risks. Without clear policies, universities face heightened exposure to data breaches, discriminatory profiling, and excessive reliance on proprietary platforms. Furthermore, pedagogical misalignment leads to LA tools being deployed for operational convenience rather than as catalysts for educational transformation. Slimi & Carballido (2023) underscore that globally, effective ethical AI policies must incorporate transparency, inclusion, and accountability principles—standards still insufficiently institutionalized across many Latin American contexts.

## 2.4 Relation to Pedagogy and Human Values

A core tension emerges when universities prioritize operational metrics—graduation rates, retention, course completion—over pedagogical values like reflexivity or critical inquiry. LA systems can personalize content, identify learning obstacles, and optimize delivery; yet without alignment with a clear educational philosophy, they risk reducing learning to predictive metrics (Bezzina & Dingli, 2024).

Institutions with defined educational models can align LA governance accordingly. For instance, humanistically oriented universities might prioritize statistics fostering self-reflection and comparative analysis, while technical institutions may focus on competency indicators. However, absent such alignment, technology ends up shaping pedagogy rather than supporting it.

Díaz-Rodríguez et al. (2023) emphasize that trustworthy AI must adhere to principles of human oversight, robustness, and equity. Incorporating these values into LA design ensures educational technologies support—rather than replace—the complex practices of teaching and learning.

## 2.5 Relation to University Governance

International efforts to regulate AI have underscored the importance of coherent, principles-based governance. The European Union's trustworthy AI guidelines, according to Smuha (2019), advocate for systems that are lawful, ethical, and robust. These principles must be adapted to educational contexts, where pedagogical integrity—alongside privacy and equity—is at stake.

Thiebes et al. (2021) propose an AI trust assessment framework encompassing transparency, reliability, and user empowerment. Implementing this framework in educational institutions could ensure responsible LA usage while encouraging the shift from fragmented implementations toward integrated strategies aligned with each institution's educational mission.

Bayaga (2025)ntends that successful AI integration in higher education requires a systemic approach involving curricular reforms, faculty development, and policy formulation. This necessitates moving beyond technological adoption to consider institutional culture, governance capacity, and long-term pedagogical objectives.

## 2.6 Institutional Commitment and Alignment

The growing adoption of AI and LA in higher education presents both opportunities and challenges. When used reflectively, these tools can support personalized learning, enhance student mentoring, and optimize resources. However, if driven solely by efficiency metrics and lacking pedagogical grounding, they risk narrowing education's scope, eroding teacher autonomy, and reducing students to mere data subjects.

Institutions must critically assess technology's role within their educational models. Governance frameworks should not only prevent harms but also promote values like inclusion, autonomy, and critical thinking. As the global landscape evolves, universities in Latin America and Spain can draw lessons from international examples while developing context-specific approaches reflecting their own educational traditions and societal needs.

Ultimately, AI in education should function as a tool—not a determinant—of educational transformation. It must serve to amplify rather than replace learning's relational, reflexive, and emancipatory dimensions.

# 3 THE TRANSFORMATIVE POTENTIAL OF AI-POWERED BY LA

AI and LA are redefining the possibilities of data-driven education. While the integration of these technologies raises legitimate concerns—particularly regarding efficiency, surveillance, and ethical governance—they simultaneously offer powerful transformative opportunities.

When implemented responsibly and with pedagogical alignment, AI-powered LA (LA+AI) can facilitate personalized learning, empower educators, and support institutions in making evidence-based decisions to enhance educational outcomes.

This section explores how these technologies can be leveraged to promote meaningful educational innovation by improving student engagement, refining instructional design, and creating dynamic learning environments. Through analysis of real-world implementations and critical frameworks, we argue that LA+AI's transformative potential lies not merely in technical capabilities, but in their alignment with educational values and robust ethical governance.

## 3.1 Potential of the LA+AI Combination

LA refers to the collection, analysis, and interpretation of data about students and their contexts to enhance learning and its environments Chen et al. (2020a). With AI's advent—particularly through machine learning, natural language processing, and generative tools—LA's scope has expanded substantially. AI-powered systems now enable real-time monitoring of student behavior, prediction of academic risks, and generation of automated feedback cycles.

As C. K. Y. Chan (2023), AI integration into LA frameworks have transformed the field from reactive to proactive. Rather than merely reporting past performance, LA+AI can anticipate potential difficulties, adapt learning trajectories, and implement early interventions. This shift proves crucial in higher education, where early identification of demotivation or underperformance significantly improves retention and academic achievement.

Also, Díaz-Rodríguez et al. (2023) emphasize that responsible AI use in education must be grounded in principles of equity, human autonomy, and transparency. Consequently, LA+AI should not be perceived as neutral tools but as sociotechnical systems entailing normative dimensions based on their design, governance, and integration.

## 3.2 Application or Improvement Examples

### 3.2.1 Personalized and Adaptive Learning

Perhaps the most prominent promise of LA-AI integration lies in its capacity to personalize learning experiences. Through analysis of individual interaction patterns, time-on-task metrics, and diverse performance indicators, AI systems can adapt content, suggest resources, and adjust instructional pacing according to each student's specific needs Bayaga (2025). This signifies a departure from standardized models toward dynamic, student-centered learning trajectories.

In practice, adaptive platforms like intelligent tutoring systems and recommendation engines enhance student engagement by delivering content aligned with both competencies and interests. Abdelwahab et al. (2023) observe that students increasingly expect responsive learning environments offering flexible interaction modalities. LA+AI tools prove essential for meeting these evolving expectations.

### 3.2.2 Tools for Educators

Contrary to fears of AI replacing educators, LA+AI can empower teaching through dashboards and predictive models providing real-time student progress insights, enabling timely feedback and informed pedagogical decisions.

Moorhouse et al. (2023) demonstrate how universities leverage LA to strengthen formative assessment strategies, helping educators identify misconceptions or disengagement signals before they impact learning outcomes.

C. K. Y. Chan & Hu (2023) contend that students themselves value these tools when facilitating personalized feedback and guidance. When implemented with respect for teacher autonomy, LA+AI transitioned educators from reactive problem-solvers to proactive learning experience designers.

### 3.2.3 Data-Driven Institutional Decision-Making

Beyond classrooms, LA+AI impacts institutional operations. Aggregate analytics reveal engagement trends, attrition patterns, and curricular bottlenecks, enabling higher education institutions to:

- Align curricula with diagnosed needs
- Redesign courses for accessibility
- Implement targeted support initiatives

Wu et al. (2024) document how Big Ten universities in the U.S. have developed AI governance frameworks that include cross-functional oversight and specialized analytical teams. These institutions leverage LA not only for individualized interventions but also to drive systemic improvements. With proper data governance, universities can advance toward more inclusive and adaptable educational ecosystems.

## 3.3 Responsible Implementation Considerations

Despite their transformative potential, LA+AI entail significant risks. Without ethical safeguards, they may enable invasive surveillance, reproduce existing inequalities, and erode human judgment. Slimi & CarbOpacosallido (2023) warn that global analyses of ethical AI policies reveal substantial gaps in transparency, consent, and inclusion within higher education institutions.

A primary risk involves algorithmic bias. Systems trained on historical data may perpetuate discriminatory patterns, particularly against marginalized student groups. Without regular audits or participatory design, these biases remain embedded and opaque. Georgieva et al. (2022) contend that a persistent disconnect exists between abstract ethical guidelines and their practical implementation in data science. Bridging this gap is essential to realizing LA+AI's potential.

Another critical concern is the reduction of students to data points. Felzmann et al. (2020) advocate for "transparency by design," ensuring students fully understand how their data is collected, processed, and utilized. Consent mechanisms must be informed, ongoing, and revocable through opt-out provisions. Educational systems must resist technocratic determinism that treats analytics as infallible rather than subject to critical debate.

Data governance, by (Janssen et al., 2020)is fundamental for trustworthy AI. Institutions require clear policies on data ownership, anonymization, access control, and retention. This urgency is acute in Latin American and Southern European contexts where—as Rees & Müller (2023)— note—AI policies remain fragmented or incipient, leaving students vulnerable to potential abuses.

## 3.4 Emerging Technologies and Implementation Ethics

Encouraging examples exist of institutions integrating LA+AI ethically and pedagogically. Cutajar et al. (2024) describe AI's transformative potential in education as contingent on three pillars: transparency, inclusion, and institutional alignment. Institutions embedding these values in LA policies are more likely to leverage data in ways that support—rather than undermine—educational objectives.

At Big Ten universities, for instance, analytics augment academic advisors rather than replacing them. Students flagged as "at-risk" receive human-mediated outreach, preserving relational over mechanistic interventions Wu et al. (2024). Ethical committees comprising students, IT personnel, faculty, and legal experts foster multi-stakeholder accountability.

Scholars have proposed frameworks guiding responsible AI integration in higher education. C. K. Y. Chan (2023), for example, advocates for digital ethics training for both staff and students, cultivating critical literacy that empowers academic communities to engage actively with these tools. Such digital competence not only strengthens democratic participation in AI/LA decision-making but prevents uncritical implementation. Similarly, Thiebes et al. (2021) propose a "trustworthy AI" model grounded in transparency, reliability, and user empowerment. Institutions adopting this approach better align LA+AI implementation with educational missions without compromising academic freedom or student dignity.

## 3.5 Commitment to Adaptive Tools

LA+AI offers significant potential to transform education—but only when aligned with pedagogical and ethical commitments. When responsibly implemented, LA+AI tools can support personalized learning, strengthen teacher autonomy, and enable institutions to make evidence-based decisions enhancing educational equity and quality.

However, realizing this potential requires robust governance frameworks, participatory design, and critical digital literacy. Institutions in Latin America and Spain must particularly move beyond pilot projects to develop integrated strategies reflecting their specific contexts and values.

Ultimately, LA+AI's power resides not in their algorithms but in how we choose to deploy them. Guided by principles of transparency, inclusion, and reflexivity, these tools can catalyze meaningful change—promoting educational systems that are not merely more efficient, but also more just, human, and learning-centered.

## 4 THE DARK SIDE OF AI IN EDUCATION: THREATS TO AUTONOMY AND EQUITY

The emergence of AI in education represents one of the most significant shifts in recent decades, introducing technologies capable of personalizing content, adapting learning pathways, and automating processes previously requiring human time and effort. Notable benefits include personalized instruction through adaptive learning systems, tutoring, immediate feedback, and available around the clock (Ahmad et al., 2023),(Sposato, 2025a) and (Chassignol et al., 2018), alongside analytical tools enhancing educator and institutional efficiency. However, the accelerated and irreversible adoption of novel educational technologies also poses substantial challenges and controversies.

Within education, algorithmic bias in curricular design may impact learning outcomes. Research documents that autonomous learning (AL) systems systematically disadvantage non-traditional students due to flawed data models and hidden biases (Jahankhani et al., 2022). Commercial educational platforms exacerbate this issue by promoting standardized content that erodes local pedagogical traditions and cultural specificity, favoring homogenized, profit-driven models (Pardhu y Aruna Rao, 2025). Furthermore, comprehensive behavioral monitoring via AL systems raises ethical concerns regarding student privacy and consent (Rajasekar y Vezhaventhan, 2024). Most critically, AI's growing influence on curricular decisions progressively diminishes teacher autonomy, as educators become increasingly constrained by algorithmic recommendations dictating content and teaching methodologies (Biswas et al., 2025b). These developments risk transforming universities into data factories where human judgment is subordinated to machine logic.

For instance, excessive algorithmic reliance may alter student learning habits, reducing concentration capacity, critical reflection, and deep text comprehension. Additionally, pervasive monitoring through intelligent systems raises privacy and ethical questions through continuous contextual data collection. Thus, AI's advancement in education demands balancing technological innovation with robust pedagogical principles that strengthen learner autonomy and critical thinking.

Given these ethical concerns, what occurs when tools designed to support autonomy and equity end up threatening them? This section analyzes key concerns arising from AI-based technology adoption in education.

## 4.1 Threats to Human Autonomy

One of the most concerning aspects of increasing AI reliance in education is its direct impact on human autonomy. By automating processes and presenting predetermined decisions, these technologies may limit individuals' judgment capacity, constraining their learning pathways (Ahmad et al., 2023) (Sposato, 2025a)(Chassignol et al., 2018). (Stanciu et al., 2025). According to findings by (Ahmad et al., 2023). "Survey data shows that 68.9% of student laziness, 68.6% of security/privacy issues, and 27.7% of decision-making loss are linked to AI in the sample studied (students in Pakistan and China)." This indicates that AI use tends to minimize autonomous intervention, substituting human choices with automated solutions and increasing technological dependence.

As universities expand AI integration across academic and administrative activities—from admissions management to degree conferral, including personalized tutoring and automated tasks—dependence on these systems intensifies. Consequently, students, faculty, and administrative staff increasingly lose opportunities to exercise memory, analytical, or critical thinking skills (Ahmad et al., 2023). Furthermore, routine task automation may foster passivity and excessive technological reliance, discouraging active application of human capacities (Khan et al., 2025) (Chassignol et al., 2018)(Stanciu et al., 2025). Such fundamental competencies could progressively diminish. Educators must therefore understand AI's influence on decision-making processes and adopt mechanisms balancing its benefits against potential risks to preserve human intuition and creativity. Complementarity between AI-generated and human decisions is essential—AI recommendations should be reviewed and contextualized through human perspectives to mitigate oversight of factors technology might ignore (Khan et al., 2025).

Some scholars argue that AI incorporation in education may compromise human interaction quality and empathy by failing to replicate the emotional support of human instructors (Hernández-de-Menéndez et al., 2022) and (Hajeer et al., 2024), elements crucial for effective learning. While AI tutors provide continuous, individualized support without time constraints, students express concerns about lacking human empathy and emotional understanding in AI interactions. Human tutors are perceived as better equipped to offer emotional support and comprehend nuanced student emotions—capabilities current AI systems struggle to emulate (Hernández-de-Menéndez et al., 2022). This human element remains vital for creating supportive, motivating learning environments.

Preventing AI tools from eroding teacher-student relationships requires careful institutional management. Human-centered implementation frameworks—where AI complements rather than replaces educators (Khan et al., 2025) should be prioritized. As(Chassignol et al., 2018), purpose, "The same criticism considering human-interaction can be applied here, especially the AI robot replacement for a teacher can lead to not good result for child's understanding of social mechanisms". Elsewhere, they note: "But it is also important to not forget that currently correlation between interaction with AI and a real teacher is yet unknown. How much impact brings to learning the real human talk?" (Chassignol et al., 2018). These and other aspects related to human nature should not be taken lightly. These and other human-nature considerations warrant serious attention. Current data for analyzing this issue remain limited, underscoring the need for expanded research in this domain.

## 4.2 Threats to Educational Equity

AI's implications extend beyond individual autonomy to pose substantial risks for educational equity, unequal access, and transparency.

Algorithmic Bias and Discrimination

Algorithmic biases and discrimination are analyzed by scholars including (Ahmad et al., 2023), (Lin et al., 2023a) and (Khan et al., 2025). A July 2024 American Educational Research Association (AERA) study states: "Our results show that predictive models yield less accurate results for Black and Hispanic students, systematically making more errors." The same research details how examined models incorrectly predicted false positive and negative rates, disproportionately benefiting White and Asian groups compared to Black and Hispanic cohorts (Gándara et al., 2024).

Training AI algorithms and systems on limited or insufficiently vetted datasets can produce inherent biases that are difficult to detect, potentially harming individuals and communities. Algorithmic bias typically stems not from a single technical flaw but from interconnected social, organizational, and design factors (Holstein et al., 2019).

As higher education institutions increasingly deploy AI algorithms and LA techniques to anticipate student performance and inform key decisions—including admissions, budget allocation, and academic support strategies—developing mechanisms to minimize these predictive models' potential to reproduce or amplify preexisting social inequalities becomes imperative. AI algorithms may perpetuate bias without careful design, leading to unfair outcomes and discrimination (Gándara et al., 2024).

While human assessments exhibit variability due to subjective biases and individual interpretations—making fully objective student performance evaluations challenging—AI's promise of greater consistency and neutrality is compromised when unsupervised algorithms "replicate" existing biases. Biases embedded in datasets may result in unequal treatment of students, potentially widening educational gaps. Ultimately, algorithmic systems' lack of transparency and potential for technical errors raise concerns about result accuracy and equity (Sposato, 2025a).

Addressing these issues requires solutions like continuous monitoring, ensuring dataset diversity, and algorithmic transparency (Khan et al., 2025), (Chen et al., 2020b).

## 4.3 Expanded Digital Divide

Difficulties in accessing AI tools create an expanded digital divide. This phenomenon may deepen social inequalities, particularly for students from disadvantaged backgrounds (Sposato, 2025b) . High implementation costs, coupled with technological infrastructure gaps, pose risks to equity and inclusion. Expenses associated with acquiring specialized software and hardware, as well as the need to train teaching and technical staff, hinder the widespread adoption of these tools (Lin et al., 2023b) and generate unequal access to technological infrastructure.

Warns that AI may exacerbate existing inequalities if not implemented inclusively: "Digital transformation must not lead to a deeper digital divide. Member States must take measures to ensure equitable access to AI technologies for all individuals, regardless of geographic location, gender, disability, or socioeconomic status" (UNESCO, 2022). Ultimately, those with greater data, resources, and infrastructure benefit disproportionately from AI-based technologies, widening disparities between regions, countries, and public/private universities. Identifying mechanisms to address this issue is urgent.

## 4.4 Opaque Algorithms

The lack of transparency and interpretability in AI tools is evident in machine learning algorithms, often treated as "black boxes." This results in distrust of outcomes generated by AI platforms among some stakeholders. To build and maintain user trust, ensuring algorithmic transparency is essential (Lin et al., 2023b) (Coskun & Alper, 2024).

The "explainability" as a fundamental ethical principle, stating that AI systems must be transparent, understandable, and auditable: "Automated processes must be comprehensible, and decisions must be explainable. Explainability is essential to enable accountability" (UNESCO, 2022).

## 4.5 Threats to Privacy and Information Security

### 4.5.1 Sensitive Data Protection

Protecting privacy and data security constitutes one of the most significant challenges in integrating AI in education. These technologies rely on processing large volumes of sensitive information—such as health records, identification numbers, financial data, and even biometric data (SecurityWeek, 2024), —increasing risks of leaks or misuse. According to (UNESCO, 2022) "...clear data governance frameworks must be established to protect privacy rights, ensure informed consent, and limit misuse of sensitive data, especially in contexts like health, education, and employment".

Safeguarding learning platforms against cyberattacks entails significant costs and requires qualified technical personnel, which many educational institutions—particularly those with limited resources—cannot consistently guarantee. Additionally, effective privacy management remains an unresolved challenge, as AI depends on collecting and analyzing vast data volumes to identify patterns and automate decisions.

### 4.5.2 Permanent Surveillance

Another critical issue involves e-proctoring platforms. Such surveillance tools are primarily used to monitor remote assessments, requiring webcams, microphones, and occasionally screen recording. They often request biometric or facial recognition data. While designed to detect academic dishonesty (e.g., copying, unauthorized communication, or prohibited materials), their use is highly controversial due to collecting sensitive monitored individuals' data: facial images, surroundings, and audio. This information is typically stored for months or years on external servers, creating latent risks of software breaches or data misuse (Nigam et al., 2021) .

In March 2025, a U.S. local newspaper reported on AI-based tools—such as Gaggle, GoGuardian, and Securly—used to monitor student activity on school devices to prevent violence and detect mental health issues early. The article notes inconclusive outcomes from these tools and highlights security risks regarding appropriate use of collected data (AP News, 2023) .

Beyond e-proctoring platforms, many Learning Management Systems (LMS)—including Moodle, Canvas, and Blackboard—automatically log detailed user interactions and activity tracking. Events such as logins, session duration, accessed resources (videos, PDFs, links), assignment submissions, forum participation, quiz access, and response times are recorded. While not every mouse click is tracked (unlike surveillance software), every interface interaction (e.g., clicking links/resources, tab switching) is logged. These "event logs," stored in databases or integrated analytics tools, enable analysis of student behavior (Baker et al., 2020) and can be processed with AI to predict academic performance and support formative assessment (Borna et al., 2024).

## 4.6 Addressing the Situation

Threats to autonomy and equity posed by AI in education are not isolated incidents but interdependent issues requiring strategic and ethical responses. Research findings emphasize the need for measures and/or mechanisms to mitigate unintended consequences of implementing these technologies in education.

The primary approach must involve human-centered AI adoption, where AI assists and facilitates educators' routine tasks—augmenting their work without replacing them (Coskun & Alper, 2024). This entails preserving person-to-person interaction, vital for students' socioemotional development.

Training educators and students in AI tool usage, comprehension, and ethical implications is essential. Such support is necessary to develop new skills and adapt to evolving professional roles. Collaboration between AI and human intelligence is key to enabling more effective decision-making. The goal is to optimize AI technology integration and promotion, ensuring they meet stakeholders' needs. Figure 1 synthesizes key educational strategies.

*Figure 1. Responsible use of AI in education*

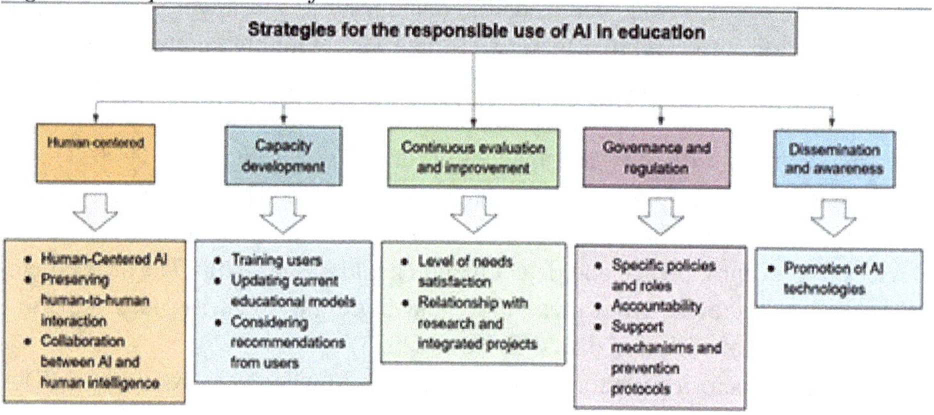


Educational institutions could also implement specific policies and roles to ensure responsible decision implementation. This should be reflected within the framework of their prevailing educational models, thereby ensuring institutional planning incorporates established recommendations while actively engaging students, faculty, and administrative staff. Another critical aspect is research. Developing projects to understand AI's long-term impacts will facilitate the creation of support mechanisms and prevention protocols to mitigate potential unintended consequences. Furthermore, transparency in AI usage and accountability are paramount for fostering a trust-based environment.

While AI holds potential to transform education through personalized learning experiences and enhanced efficiency, ignoring its potential biases (threats to autonomy and equity) would constitute a grave error. The erosion of human decision-making capacity, the promotion of apathy, the weakening of human interaction, the digital divide, lack of transparency, and data privacy concerns represent just some facets of AI's "dark side" demanding immediate attention.

AI has the potential to enhance educational quality, operational efficiency, and sustainability—yet its success hinges on adopting ethical frameworks, addressing inequalities, and preserving education's essential human elements. Its use must be guided by robust ethical principles prioritizing human well-being, equity, and transparency. Crucially, AI should complement human experience by fostering creativity, critical thinking, and decision-making skills in both students and educators. Only through a balanced, ethical, and human-centered approach can higher education institutions harness AI's potential while mitigating its risks, ensuring technology serves as an instrument advancing the best interests of students, educators, and society at large.

Figure 2 highlights the central importance of Training and Consent as the core of a recommended framework.

## 5 HUMAN RIGHTS FRAMEWORK FOR GOVERNING LA SYSTEMS

The ethical implementation of AI-driven LA requires a human rights-based approach prioritizing pedagogical values (human-centered design, privacy, student autonomy, data transparency, and algorithmic non-discrimination) over technological imperatives. Three fundamental principles could guide this framework:

- **Pedagogical Primacy:** Absolute prioritization of educational principles, objectives, and methods above other factors (such as technological, administrative, or economic considerations) in designing and implementing teaching-learning processes.
- **Algorithmic Transparency:** Ensuring that processes, criteria, and decisions made by AI systems or LA algorithms in education are comprehensible, explainable, and auditable by stakeholders.
- **Democratic Oversight:** LA systems must be transparent, equitable, and responsive to collective needs through active participation of the educational

community (e.g., pluralistic committees including students, faculty, and experts in data-use decision-making)

These criteria have been recommended in prior studies: Pedagogical Primacy by (Tauchnitz & Ahmed, 2024), Algorithmic Transparency by (Reyes & Rajagopal, 2025) and Democratic Oversight by (Hossain, 2025).

AI should function as a teaching assistant under human supervision (through auditable systems), preserving educator autonomy while enhancing learning outcomes (Aderibigbe et al., 2025b). Equally crucial is developing digital citizenship curricula to equip all educational stakeholders with critical skills for understanding and challenging algorithmic decisions (Hossain, 2025).

AI is expected to function as a teaching assistant under human supervision (with auditable systems), preserving educator autonomy while enhancing learning outcomes. Equally crucial is the development of digital citizenship curricula, equipping all educational stakeholders with critical skills to understand and challenge algorithmic decisions.

While LA systems can optimize educational processes, their design and deployment must protect fundamental academic freedoms and prevent learning commodification. This necessitates integrating human rights considerations into LA governance structures.

Addressing Research Question 1, to prevent algorithmic governance from eroding academic freedom, studies such as (Tauchnitz & Ahmed, 2024) recommend: an ethically designed framework, participatory governance models, accountability mechanisms, capacity development, and continuous evaluation to ensure digital tools promote public participation while protecting individual rights.

*Figure 2. Components for governing LA systems*

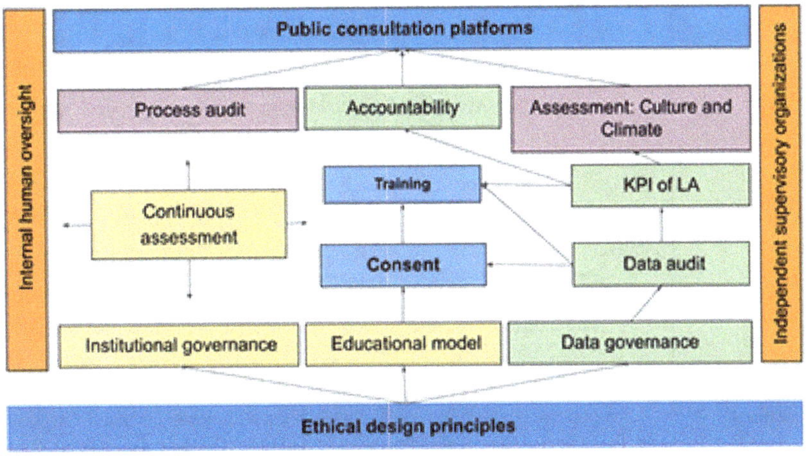


This framework is based on a literature review of multiple authors, with their contributions organized according to interrelationships, educational contexts, and proposed case studies.

Arrows represent data inputs or elements feeding into target components. At the foundation of the framework lie the ethical principles of an LA governance model. Flanking the left and right are human oversight elements for the systems, proposing both an internal organizational body and an independent external entity. These elements converge at the apex into a public information platform accessible to all stakeholders (faculty, students, and administration). At the core resides informed consent and stakeholder training.

- **Yellow elements** represent the pedagogical foundation of the framework.
- **Green elements** pertain to the data-driven approach.
- **Red elements** denote process auditing features alongside organizational and personnel cultural support.

The Continuous Assessment element features omnidirectional flashing indicators, symbolizing iterative improvement across all components of the proposed model. Table 1, shows details of each component of the framework.

*Table 1. Description of components for governing an LA system*

| Component | Description |
|---|---|
| Public consultation platforms | • **Facilitating Transparency:** Demonstrating how educational data is collected, used, and protected.<br>• **Engaging Stakeholders:** Enabling students, educators, and families to voice concerns or suggestions regarding LA usage.<br>• **Promoting Accountability:** Serving as an accountability mechanism to ensure LA-based decisions are ethical and equitable.<br>• **Building Trust:** By democratizing access to information and processes, it strengthens acceptance and legitimacy of analytical tools. |
| Internal human oversight | Ensures data usage remains ethical, equitable, and pedagogically relevant while mitigating algorithmic biases and protecting privacy. Three key actors and their roles:<br>• **Educators:** Validate data interpretations and adjust pedagogical strategies.<br>• **IT Team:** Ensure technical integrity and system security.<br>• **Ethics Committee:** Oversees regulatory compliance and student rights. |
| Independent supervisory organizations | Guarantees transparency, ethics, and regulatory compliance in educational data usage, functioning as external auditors to prevent algorithmic biases, protect privacy, and ensure LA benefits reach all stakeholders. Independence reinforces system trustworthiness. Receives and resolves complaints regarding data misuse from students or faculty.<br>Key actors and roles:<br>• **Data Protection Agencies:** Verify regulatory compliance<br>• **Educational Ethics Commissions:** Assess algorithms' social and pedagogical impacts.<br>• **Educational Research Associations:** Validate analytical models' scientific quality. Establish global standards for responsible LA. |
| Ethical design principles | These principles ensure LA systems prioritize student well-being, equity, and transparency, avoiding algorithmic discrimination or privacy violations. They constitute the framework for developing responsible, human-centered educational technologies. Organizations may adapt them based on universal principles, institutional values, and educational model components. |
| Institutional governance | The approach avoids techno-centric strategies for LA systems, proposing robust institutional governance grounded in regulations and organizational guidelines. According to(Prinsloo et al., 2022), effective governance requires transcending technocratic solutions and integrating ethical, cultural, and institutional frameworks that balance innovation, ethics, and educational justice. |
| Educational model | The pedagogical framework guiding LA implementation, ensuring data usage aligns with learning objectives, educational principles, and student needs. Acts as a bridge between technology and teaching practice, guaranteeing pedagogical relevance and ethics. The educational model should define:<br>• Pedagogical approach and learning outcomes<br>• Guidelines for teaching adaptations based on LA indicators<br>• Formative assessment protocols<br>• Continuous feedback cycles using data<br>• Prevents LA systems from amplifying existing inequalities. |

continued on following page

*Table 1. Continued*

| Component | Description |
|---|---|
| Data governance | Establishes ethical, legal, and technical parameters for managing educational information, ensuring responsible, secure, and pedagogically aligned usage. Protects student rights while maximizing data's analytical value. Defines:<br>• **Privacy Policies:** Specify collected data and protection methods (e.g., GDPR: General Data Protection Regulation)<br>• **Access Protocols:** Govern data usage permissions and purposes<br>• **Data Quality:** Ensure accuracy and consistency for reliable analysis<br>• **Data Lifecycle:** Document collection through secure disposal<br>• **Regulatory Compliance:** Verify adherence to local/international regulations<br><br>(Arroway et al., 2015) recommend defining LA-focused educational models through cross-functional stakeholder collaboration (faculty, IT, administration) to align objectives and key performance indicators. |
| Continuous assessment | Mechanism for real-time monitoring, adjustment, and improvement of LA systems, ensuring pedagogical efficacy and ethical compliance. Transforms data into timely educational interventions, closing the analysis-action loop. Evaluates:<br>• Updated KPIs defined during planning cycles<br>• Early alerts for educators/students based on learning patterns<br>• Ongoing modification of pedagogical strategies<br>• Periodic review of algorithmic biases or unintended impacts. |
| Consent | Guarantees ethical and legal use of student data, respecting autonomy and privacy. Must include:<br>• **Clarity:** Explicit explanation of data collection/usage<br>• **Voluntariness:** Option to participate/withdraw without penalty<br>• **Scope:** Limited to defined educational purposes<br>• **Renewability:** Periodic authorization reviews<br>• **Transparency:** Access to personal data and processing |
| Data audit | Ensure quality, security, and ethics in educational data management, complying with regulations and standards. Functions:<br>• **Quality Verification:** Ensure data accuracy/consistency<br>• **Security**: Detect vulnerabilities and prevent unauthorized access<br>• **Compliance**: Validate adherence to laws (e.g., GDPR)<br>• **Bias Detection**: Identify algorithmic discrimination<br>• **Transparency**: Document processes/results for stakeholders |
| Training | Essential for ensuring all stakeholders (educators, administrators, students) understand and effectively utilize LA systems, maximizing educational and ethical potential. Components:<br>• **Educator Training**: Interpreting data and applying insights<br>• **Student Literacy:** Empowering learners to understand/manage their data<br>• **Technical Support:** Tool management and data security<br>• **Ethics Awareness:** Responsible data usage<br>• **Continuous Updates:** Training on new technologies/regulations. |
| LA KPIs | Measure LA system effectiveness by aligning data with pedagogical/operational objectives to optimize educational outcomes. Common KPIs:<br>**Engagement Rate:** Student interaction with digital resources.<br>**Academic Performance**: Progress in key competencias.<br>**Student Retention**: Early dropout risk identification.<br>**Teaching Efficacy**: Impact of data-driven pedagogical strategies<br>**User Satisfaction**: Stakeholder perceptions of LA tools. |

continued on following page

*Table 1. Continued*

| Component | Description |
|---|---|
| Process audit | Guarantees efficiency, quality, and regulatory compliance through systematic evaluation of LA operational workflows, identifying improvement opportunities and mitigating risks. Actions:<br>• **Process Mapping:** Document data collection/analysis/application stages.<br>• **Quality Control:** Verify analytical algorithm accuracy/consistency.<br>• **Regulatory Compliance:** Ensure adherence to regulations (e.g., GDPR).<br>• **Bottleneck Detection:** Optimize implementation timelines/resources.<br>• **Continuous Feedback:** Generate reports for iterative system improvement. |
| Accountability | Ensure transparency and responsibility in educational data usage, strengthening institutional trust and complying with ethical/legal standards. Key elements:<br>**Algorithmic Transparency:** Explains recommendation/prediction generation.<br>**Appeal Channels:** Allow contesting automated decisions.<br>**Impact Metrics:** Evaluate pedagogical outcomes vs. stated objectives.<br>**Oversight Committees:** Monitor privacy/equity policy compliance. |
| Assessment: Culture and Climate | Evaluates LA systems' human and organizational consequences, ensuring implementation strengthens—not degrades—educational environments and institutional trust. Actions:<br>• **Perception Surveys**: Measure user acceptance/concerns about data usage.<br>• **Well-being Indicators**: Detects monitoring-related stress/anxiety.<br>• **Cultural Alignment**: Verify tool compatibility with institutional values.<br>• **Communication Efficacy**: Assess clarity in explaining LA processes/benefits.<br>• **Relational Impact**: Analyze effects on educator-student dynamics.<br><br>According to (Arroway et al., 2015) this component evaluates how LA systems integrate into educational institutions' cultural and organizational contexts. |

## 5.1 AI-Supported LA

The adoption of AI carries inherent risks of operating without transparency regarding its configuration, data sources employed, volume of processed information, or automatically generated prompts. This may lead to algorithms superseding the judgment of educational system experts (algorithmic supremacy).

An alternative to mitigate algorithmic supremacy risk involves establishing legal frameworks regulating AI's technological underpinnings, (Parga, 2023) emphasizes the critical need to regulate both mass data collection and algorithm-based decision-making. Human oversight, ethical AI system design, and algorithmic transparency/accessibility are elements proposed by (Martínez-Ramil, 2021) to prevent algorithmic bias.

University digitalization entails mass data collection, necessitating ethical considerations for learning enhancement. According to (Motz & Díaz-Charquero, 2023) AI experts must maintain ongoing bidirectional dialogue with pedagogues, psychologists, educators, and data privacy specialists to comprehend AI's impact on educational practice and implement human rights-centered ethical models. Such dialogue should emerge from regulatory frameworks—a position advocated by (Prinsloo et al., 2022) in recommending student data privacy regulation within LA contexts. Higher education "must consider both the limitations of AI-based solutions and their potential to cause harm" (Ungerer & Slade, 2022).

Universities articulate their educational philosophy through teaching-learning models (or pedagogical frameworks), which define tools for achieving learning objectives among key components. While emerging technologies—particularly AI—should be integrated, a review of educational models across nearly 50 Latin American universities conducted by the authors revealed no such inclusion.

## 6 GLOBAL LESSONS IN IMPLEMENTING AI-POWERED BY LA

The potential of LA to personalize experiences, identify at-risk students, and optimize institutional resources has captured the attention of governments, universities, and international organizations. However, its implementation presents ethical, pedagogical, cultural, and technical challenges that require global perspective análisis.

This section summarizes key lessons from international cases to identify principles, success factors, and warnings that could guide institutions in responsible adoption of these technologies.

### 6.1 The Relationship Between LA and AI in Education Systems

LA operates at the intersection of data and learning, integrating computer science, information science, educational data mining, and more recently, AI. Simply put, LA focuses on collecting data about teaching and learning behaviors in digital environments (Renz & Hilbig, 2020).

AI systems require massive data quantities, and LA handles the collection, processing, storage, and analysis of student behavior data in digital spaces (Gašević & Merceron, 2022). AI can enhance LA methodologies by leveraging student data and novel analytical approaches, ensuring AI-driven insights remain rigorous and pedagogically sound (Khosravi et al., n.d.).

In essence, educational data (grades, participation, platform interactions, etc.) enables better decision-making, while AI adds predictive and personalized capabilities beyond conventional analytics.

### 6.2 Global Landscape of AI-Driven Learning

Over the past decade, adoption of LA and educational AI systems has grown significantly. Initiatives like France's Monitoring and Experience Through Analytics and Learning (METAL) project (Brun et al., 2019), Finland's ViLLe, and UNESCO recommendations (UNESCO, 2022) demonstrate increasing concern for ethical, student-centered implementation adapted to diverse contexts (Buckingham, 2012b).

Asian implementations have emphasized smart dashboards in virtual learning environments, while Europe has focused on legal frameworks and transparency principles. These contrasts highlight the need for flexible yet value-guided approaches.

Another study (Kleimola & Leppisaari, 2022) across four Finnish universities of applied sciences employed a case-based approach to design and evaluate LA pilots aligned with institutional instructional design. Using LMS-integrated tools to visualize student activity, progress, and interaction patterns (e.g., access frequency, forum participation, assignment submissions), researchers identified at-risk students for timely support. The study concluded that even basic LA applications enabled effective monitoring and mentoring.

## 6.3 Lessons from Case Studies

### 6.3.1 Student-Centered Design

France's METAL project exemplifies good practice. A consortium of French universities and research labs adopted user-centered design with direct educator/student participation, prioritizing explainability and data control. They emphasized user understanding of dashboard data origins, logic, and purposes while implementing data anonymization and explicit student consent (Brun et al., 2019). This improved system acceptance and trust, making METAL a reference model for balancing technological innovation with ethical principles.

### 6.3.2 Infrastructure and Technical Deployment

Multimodal LA deployment in Chilean and Australian schools (Martinez-Maldonado et al., 2023) revealed that success depends on reliable technical infrastructure, clear ethical consent protocols, and tools integrated with actual teaching practice. Data collection occurred during collaborative classroom activities without disrupting instruction, highlighting the need for upfront frameworks addressing consent, privacy, and project purposes.

### 6.3.3 Ethics, Privacy and Explainability

OU Analyse (2015-2019), developed by The Open University (UK), used AI and machine learning to analyze digital behaviors (platform access, study time, submissions, etc.), predicting dropout risk or poor performance per study unit.

The system provided visual alerts to tutors (Herodotou et al., 2020), enabling early intervention while preserving professional judgment through explainable machine learning techniques. Tutors accessed factors influencing each prediction, making OU Analyse a model for ethical, collaborative large-scale implementation in open education.

The predictions displayed to educators were based on explainable machine learning techniques, allowing tutors to access the factors influencing each prediction and make informed decisions accordingly. In other words, their professional judgment was not replaced by the system but rather supported by it. OU Analyse represents a paradigmatic example of how to integrate AI and analytics in large-scale open education. Its success lies not only in predictive technology but also in its ethical, collaborative, and teacher-centered implementation.

UNESCO's ethical principles for educational AI emphasize informed consent, equity, and explainability (UNESCO, 2022). defining explainability as requiring AI-supported decisions to be understandable to affected users. Students, educators, and administrators deserve clarity about how and why AI generates recommendations, reinforcing educator autonomy and student informed consent.

UNESCO recommends educational AI systems should:

- Avoid opaque automated decisions
- Ensure interfaces communicate algorithmic criteria
- Include mechanisms for users to challenge, understand, or reject automated decisions

## 6.4 Persistent Challenges

Despite progress, structural, technical and ethical barriers remain:

**Algorithmic biases:** Models trained on historical data tend to replicate discriminatory patterns. Predictive algorithms in U.S. education have shown unequal outcomes for ethnic minorities and socioeconomically disadvantaged students (Gašević & Merceron, 2022). Note that algorithmic bias typically stems from multiple social, organizational and design factors (Holstein et al., 2019).

**Digital divides:** In Latin America, Africa and Asia, inadequate technological infrastructure and connectivity limit LA tool access, exacerbating existing inequalities.

**Surveillance normalization:** Intensive analytics without clear regulation may enable educational surveillance practices, eroding trust as warned in studies (Slade & Prinsloo, 2013).

## 6.5 Summary of Lessons

Based on international case reviews and ethical frameworks, we recommend:

- **Developing institutional:** Ethical/legal frameworks aligned with global principles (UNESCO, 2021), but adapted locally.
- **Ensuring critical digital competency:** Training (beyond technical skills) for educators and students - covering algorithmic functioning, ethical/social impacts, privacy, digital rights, and pedagogical data use.
- **Implementing independent algorithmic:** audits to ensure transparency and bias mitigation.
- **Adopting participatory:** design involving educators, technical staff and students from initial pase.
- **Promoting technological sovereignty** through open-source software and standards favoring interoperability and institutional data control.

# 7 POLICY RECOMMENDATIONS FOR RESPONSIBLE LA IMPLEMENTATION

To maintain ethical and equitable use of AI in education, a multi-level governance approach is essential. We recommend a holistic framework based on three key dimensions:

Regulatory level:

- Establish national standards for educational AI audits (Rajasekar & Vezhaventhan, 2024).
- Implement robust student data sovereignty protections (Mac Fadden et al., 2024).

Institutional level:

- Create AI ethics committees composed exclusively of faculty representatives
- Develop student data cooperatives to preserve learner agency over analytics

Critical research agenda:

- Evaluate long-term impacts of LA on educational equity (Jiang et al., 2024).
- Develop explainable AI systems tailored to pedagogical contexts.

These measures collectively address the technical, ethical, and democratic challenges posed by LA systems in higher education. To formulate concrete implementation recommendations, we have found it necessary to examine publications from the last five years.

Indeed, developing recommendations for LA use in higher education requires reviewing prior experiences. Below, we present a set of evidence-based practices synthesized from scientific literature published since 2020 in indexed journals. While this does not constitute a systematic review, we have followed rigorous search and selection procedures with the following criterio. Tabla 2, show the criterion applied for bibliography selection.

*Table 2. Criterion applied for bibliography selection*

| **Criterion** | **Values** |
|---|---|
| Database | Scopus |
| Search String | TITLE ((Learning Analytics) and (Higher education)) AND PUBYEAR > 2019 AND PUBYEAR < 2027 AND (LIMIT-TO (DOCTYPE, "ar") OR LIMIT-TO (DOCTYPE, "cp") OR LIMIT-TO (DOCTYPE, "ch") OR LIMIT-TO (DOCTYPE, "cr") OR LIMIT-TO (DOCTYPE, "re")) |
| Search String | Articles with minimum 6 pages |
| References | Articles containing at least 20 references |
| Total | 89 |
| | The search was limited to Title fields only, as using other attributes (Abstract, Keywords) yielded 1,960 documents |
| Recommendations or Best Practices for LA Adoption | The 89 articles were reviewed to identify whether authors explicitly proposed recommendations and best practices |

The selected articles were analyzed to extract LA-specific recommendations supported by empirical evidence and real-case applications, allowing us to synthesize implementation guidelines from the 50 relevant papers.

Table 3 presents recommendations organized into 6 categories based on the most significant and recurrent patterns identified in the article analysis.

*Table 3. Recommendations and best practices for LA adoption*

| Category | Recommendations | Best Practices | Source Articles |
|---|---|---|---|
| **Governance and Strategy** | • Secure executive leadership commitment.<br>• Develop clear institutional policies.<br>• Ensure transparent data usage practices. | Establish multidisciplinary oversight committees.<br><br>Align LA with institutional educational goals. | (Alzahrani et al., 2022)<br>(Clark et al., 2020)<br>(Márquez et al., 2024) |
| **Ethics and Privacy** | • Ensure data transparency<br>• Obtain informed consent from all stakeholders. | Develop Systems with Collaborative Governance.<br><br>Implement Algorithmic Auditing Protocols. | (Parkes et al., 2020)<br>(Heiser et al., 2023)<br>(Jones et al., 2020) |
| **User-Centered Design** | • Prioritize educator/learner needs in system design.<br>• Conduct iterative prototype validation. | Participatory Dashboard Development.<br><br>Participatory Dashboard Development. | (Jayashanka et al., 2022)<br>(Kleimola et al., 2025)<br>(De Laet et al., 2020) |
| **Training and Support** | - Provide data literacy training for staff.<br>- Maintain ongoing technical support systems. | Establish Professional Learning Communities.<br><br>Develop Just-in-Time Support Resources. | (Zine & Kaaouachi, 2024)<br>(Lobos et al., 2022)<br>(van Leeuwen, 2023) |
| **Pedagogical Integration** | - Align LA with learning theories (ej.: SRL: Self-Regulated Learning).<br>- Adapt content based on data. | Personalized Feedback Systems.<br><br>Early Warning and Support Protocols. | (Alhazbi et al., 2024)<br>(Ustun et al., 2023)<br>(Rodda, 2022) |
| **Evaluation and Continuous Improvement** | - Align LA with learning theories.<br>- Conduct periodic strategy reviews. | -Phased Implementation Approach.<br><br>Evidence-Based Scaling Metrics. | (Joseph-Richard et al., 2021)<br>(L. G. Chan & Ng, 2024)<br>(Villarroel-Henríquez & Gallardo-Aguayo, 2025) |

The following section provides a detailed explanation of each conceptual category, along with evidence-based recommendations for their operationalization in institutional LA deployments

## 7.1 Governance and Strategy

This category represents a critical success factor, as the implementation of LA requires explicit support from senior leadership, including funding and alignment with the university's strategic objectives (Clark et al., 2020). Key recommendations include:

- Establishing policies on data privacy, ethics, and access to ensure transparency and trust.
- Aligning efforts across academic, technological, and administrative units.
- Defining clear objectives (e.g., reducing student attrition by 10%).
- Implementing continuous monitoring of system performance and its impact on educational goals.
- Providing data analysis training for faculty and staff.

Challenges in Governance include:

- Resistance to change among educators and administrators.
- Technical limitations in infrastructure and interoperability.
- Ethical concerns regarding student data privacy.

Success depends on:

- Inclusive stakeholder engagement.
- Investment in capacity-building initiatives.
- A phased implementation approach, beginning with small-scale pilots before university-wide deployment.

## 7.2 Ethics and Privacy

It is strongly recommended that students be informed about how their data is collected, used, or shared within LA systems. Learners using LMS platforms require intellectual privacy and protection for their ideas. Continuous monitoring should be carefully considered, as it may inadvertently inhibit creativity (Jones et al., 2020) Key recommendations include:

- Transparency in data collection practices
- Informed consent protocols
- Protection of intellectual privacy
- Student participation in the design of LA policies

A study by (Jones et al., 2020) revealed that students across eight U.S. institutions were largely unaware of data collection and analysis practices, leading to distrust and concerns about intellectual privacy (based on over 100 interviews).

LA systems often categorize students as "high-risk," "hard-to-reach," or "vulnerable" based on metrics such as attendance, library usage, or virtual platform activity. This approach reduces students to data points rather than recognizing them as individuals with complex experiences (Parkes et al., 2020). Alternative Ethical Frameworks

- Dialogue and student participation
- Human contact (rather than automated interventions)
- Holistic support (beyond algorithmic predictions)

Additionally (Heiser et al., 2023) advocate for adopting ethical frameworks such as DELICATE (Determination, Explainability, Legitimacy, Involvement, Control, Anonymity & Privacy, Transparency, External Review), which provides guidelines for the responsible use of educational data technologies while fostering trust.

## 7.3 User-Centered Design

For dashboards specifically designed to address the needs expressed by academic advisors, an iterative and participatory process should be followed. This includes utilizing interviews, surveys, and focus groups to evaluate how advisors interact with the dashboard and perceive its usefulness. User training must be carefully designed based on responses gathered from surveys, ensuring it addresses the identified requirements.

The work of (De Laet et al., 2020) exemplifies a user-centered approach, where functionality was derived from real needs, validated through active advisor participation, and optimized via iterative evaluation.

Similarly, (Jayashanka et al., 2022) conducted two surveys with 136 university students (third and fourth year) and interviews with 12 faculty members to identify desired dashboard functionalities. Students prioritized clear visualizations of their progress, while faculty emphasized the need for interactive content and quizzes. These studies demonstrate an organizational commitment to participatory design in LA systems.

A specific case study mentioned in (Kleimola et al., 2025) highlights student requests for features such as:

- Setting personal goals
- Receiving reminders
- Intuitive data visualization

The authors further recommend that visualizations should be clear and concise, as excessive data can overwhelm users and reduce utility.

## 7.4 Training and Support

This section emphasizes the need to train faculty in using LA tools to collect and analyze data from both self-study activities (such as videos and quizzes) and guided sessions. Automated data analysis (e.g., of student-written texts or platform interactions) can help educators identify support needs more efficiently (Lobos et al., 2022). Since faculty often lack time for manual data analysis, this underscores the importance of developing more intuitive LA tools.

Key Recommendations:

- Participatory Design: LA tools should be developed collaboratively, with faculty involvement to ensure relevance to their specific needs and contexts
- Interpretation Training: Educators require professional development to accurately interpret and utilize LA-generated data.
- Peer Assessment Integration: Collaborative evaluation methods, such as peer grading, should be incorporated to enrich heterogeneous assessment practices.

Without proper training, even well-designed LA tools may be underutilized or misinterpreted. Faculty engagement in the design phase increases tool adoption and ensures pedagogical alignment (Lobos et al., 2022).

## 7.5 Pedagogical Integration

(Alhazbi et al., 2024) emphasize the importance of integrating pedagogical foundations and learning science theories into LA to ensure that analyzed data accurately reflects students' learning processes. While behavioral data analysis (such as access times, forum participation, or assignment submissions) can provide valuable insights, these indicators alone are insufficient to infer learning quality.

LA can enhance feedback through assessment rubrics that incorporate specific action-oriented guidance, such as:

- Additional time should be devoted to: (solving practical exercises, reviewing recommended literature, synthesizing assigned readings, etc.).
- Visual representations that help students identify improvement areas and adjust learning strategies.

(Ustun et al., 2023) recommends training faculty in:

- Interpreting LA data.
- Designing effective pedagogical recommendations.

From the perspective of student self-regulation (Rodda, 2022) suggests developing LA tools that promote metacognition by enabling:

- Comparison of personal progress with individual goals or course averages.
- Review of historical data to strengthen understanding of topics with high failure rates.

## 7.6 Evaluation and Continuous Improvement

This dimension addresses the implementation of personalized interventions such as targeted tutoring for student groups and the design of strategies to increase engagement among at-risk students. Effective approaches include the collection and analysis of data from previous courses, including grades, attendance records, and performance metrics to identify meaningful patterns (e.g., identifying student groups showing consistent performance trends). A detailed analysis of academic performance history enables precise decision-making regarding student support recommendations. Systematic evaluation and evidence-based adaptation are fundamental to optimizing the use of LA in higher education (L. G. Chan & Ng, 2024).

The case study published by (Villarroel-Henríquez & Gallardo-Aguayo, 2025), recommends an early assessment approach beginning at student admission, which involves collecting sociodemographic data, academic histories, and results from diagnostic evaluations to identify remedial needs and design personalized support plans. The study emphasizes the importance of continuous monitoring of key indicators such as pass/fail rates and the adoption of responsive pedagogical strategies. Furthermore, it highlights the necessity of evaluating competency achievement through examinations, professional practice assessments, and employer surveys, which provide valuable feedback for curriculum updates and improvement of study plans. This comprehensive approach ensures that LA serves as an effective tool for both student support and institutional development.

## 8 CONCLUSION: REAFFIRMING HIGHER EDUCATION'S DEMOCRATIC PURPOSE IN THE AI ERA

Algorithmic governance will not erode academic freedom if it prioritizes a human rights-based ethical framework—grounded in pedagogical primacy, algorithmic transparency, and democratic oversight—where pluralistic committees, audit systems and faculty retain autonomy. Current educational models incorporate AI unevenly: while institutions like the U.S. Big Ten universities integrate it with robust policies, adoption in Latin America and Spain remains experimental, fragmented, and lacks explicit pedagogical alignment.

LA+AI systems can coexist with educational models when they:

- Remain subordinate to institutional pedagogical goals (rather than dictating them)
- Are implemented with transparency, bias mitigation, and human oversight
- Enhance decision-making without replacing educator-student interaction

This analysis calls for a new social contract to govern AI in education, realigning technology with pedagogical values. To this end, we have proposed:

- Educational strategies to balance innovation with equity
- A governance framework for LA systems based on a rigorous literature review
- Evidence-based recommendations for responsible LA adoption

By anchoring LA+AI implementation in democratic principles—rather than technical imperatives—higher education can harness data-driven tools while safeguarding its humanistic mission.

## REFERENCES


Abdelwahab, H. R., Rauf, A., & Chen, D. (2023). Business students' perceptions of Dutch higher educational institutions in preparing them for artificial intelligence work environments. *Industry and Higher Education, 37*(1), 22–34. DOI: 10.1177/09504222221087614

Aderibigbe, S. A., Omar, M., ElMehdi, H., Colucci-Gray, L., Hamad, K., Shanableh, A., AlOthman, H., & Alotaibi, E. (2025). Artificial intelligence-driven prediction of optimal technology-aided alternative operations in post-emergency contexts: A case study from an Emirati university. *International Journal of Educational Research Open, 9*, 100473. Advance online publication. DOI: 10.1016/j.ijedro.2025.100473

Ahmad, S. F., Han, H., Alam, M. M., Rehmat, M. K., Irshad, M., Arraño-Muñoz, M., & Ariza-Montes, A. (2023). Impact of artificial intelligence on human loss in decision making, laziness and safety in education. *Humanities & Social Sciences Communications, 10*(1), 311. Advance online publication. DOI: 10.1057/s41599-023-01787-8 PMID: 37325188

Aletras, N., Tsarapatsanis, D., Preoţiuc-Pietro, D., & Lampos, V. (2016). Predicting judicial decisions of the European court of human rights: A natural language processing perspective. *Peerj Computer Science, 2016*(10). DOI: 10.7717/peerj-cs.93

Alhazbi, S., Al-ali, A., Tabassum, A., Al-Ali, A., Al-Emadi, A., Khattab, T., & Hasan, M. A. (2024). Using learning analytics to measure self-regulated learning: A systematic review of empirical studies in higher education. *Journal of Computer Assisted Learning, 40*(4), 1658–1674. DOI: 10.1111/jcal.12982

Alzahrani, A., Tsai, Y.-S., Kovanović, V., Moreno-Marcos, P. M., Jivet, I., Aljohani, N., & Gašević, D. (2022). Success-Enablers of Learning Analytics Adoption in Higher Education: A Quantitative Ethnographic Study. *Communications in Computer and Information Science, 1522 CCIS*, 395 – 409. DOI: 10.1007/978-3-030-93859-8_26

Arroway, P., Morgan, G., O'Keefe, M., & Yanosky, R. (2015). *Learning analytics in higher education.*

Baker, R., Xu, D., Park, J., Yu, R., Li, Q., Cung, B., Fischer, C., Rodriguez, F., Warschauer, M., & Smyth, P. (2020). The benefits and caveats of using clickstream data to understand student self-regulatory behaviors: opening the black box of learning processes. In *International Journal of Educational Technology in Higher Education* (Vol. 17, Issue 1). DOI: 10.1186/s41239-020-00187-1

Balasubramaniam, N., Kauppinen, M., Rannisto, A., Hiekkanen, K., & Kujala, S. (2023). Transparency and explainability of AI systems: From ethical guidelines to requirements. *Information and Software Technology*, *159*, 107197. Advance online publication. DOI: 10.1016/j.infsof.2023.107197

Bayaga, A. (2025). Leveraging AI-enhanced and emerging technologies for pedagogical innovations in higher education. *Education and Information Technologies*, *30*(1), 1045–1072. DOI: 10.1007/s10639-024-13122-y

Bezzina, S., & Dingli, A. (2024). The transformative potential of Artificial Intelligence for Education. *Proceedings of the International Conference on Networked Learning,* 14. DOI: 10.54337/nlc.v14i1.8077

Biesta, G. J. J. (2015). Good education in an age of measurement: Ethics, politics, democracy. *Good Education in an Age of Measurement: Ethics, Politics. Democracy (New York, N.Y.)*, •••, 1–150. DOI: 10.4324/9781315634319/GOOD-EDUCATION-AGE-MEASUREMENT-GERT-BIESTA/RIGHTS-AND-PERMISSIONS

Boden, M. A. (1998). Creativity and artificial intelligence. *Artificial Intelligence*, *103*(1–2), 347–356. DOI: 10.1016/S0004-3702(98)00055-1

Borna, M., Saadat, H., Hojjati, A. T., & Akbari, E. (2024). Analyzing Click Data with AI: Implications for Student Performance Prediction and Learning Assessment. *Frontiers in Education*, *9*, 1421479. Advance online publication. DOI: 10.3389/feduc.2024.1421479

Brun, A., Bonnin, G., Castagnos, S., Roussanaly, A., & Boyer, A. (2019). Learning analytics made in France: The METAL project. *The International Journal of Information and Learning Technology*, *36*(4), 299–313. DOI: 10.1108/IJILT-02-2019-0022

Buckingham, S. S. (2012). *Learning Analytics*. UNESCO Policy Brief.

Chan, C. K. Y. (2023). A comprehensive AI policy education framework for university teaching and learning. *International Journal of Educational Technology in Higher Education*, *20*(1), 38. Advance online publication. DOI: 10.1186/s41239-023-00408-3

Chan, C. K. Y., & Hu, W. (2023). Students' voices on generative AI: Perceptions, benefits, and challenges in higher education. *International Journal of Educational Technology in Higher Education*, *20*(1), 43. Advance online publication. DOI: 10.1186/s41239-023-00411-8

Chan, L. G., & Ng, Q. Y. (2024). Using learning analytics in higher education: Assessing students' learning experience in an actuarial science course. *STEM Education*, *4*(2), 151–164. DOI: 10.3934/steme.2024010

Chassignol, M., Khoroshavin, A., Klimova, A., & Bilyatdinova, A. (2018). Artificial Intelligence trends in education: A narrative overview. *Procedia Computer Science, 136*, 16–24. DOI: 10.1016/j.procs.2018.08.233

Chen, L., Chen, P., & Lin, Z. (2020a). Artificial Intelligence in Education: A Review. *IEEE Access : Practical Innovations, Open Solutions, 8*, 75264–75278. DOI: 10.1109/ACCESS.2020.2988510

Chen, L., Chen, P., & Lin, Z. (2020b). Artificial Intelligence in Education: A Review. *IEEE Access : Practical Innovations, Open Solutions, 8*, 75264–75278. DOI: 10.1109/ACCESS.2020.2988510

Clark, J.-A., Liu, Y., & Isaias, P. (2020). Critical success factors for implementing learning analytics in higher education: A mixed-method inquiry. *Australasian Journal of Educational Technology, 36*(6), 89–106. DOI: 10.14742/ajet.6164

Coskun, T. K., & Alper, A. (2024). Evaluating the evaluators: A comparative study of AI and teacher assessments in Higher Education | AVALUANT ELS AVALUADORS: UN ESTUDI COMPARATIU ENTRE LA IA I LES AVALUACIONS DOCENTS A L'EDUCACIÓ SUPERIOR | EVALUANDO A LOS EVALUADORES: UN ESTUDIO COMPARAT. *Digital Education Review, 45*(45), 124–140. DOI: 10.1344/der.2024.45.124-140

Cutajar, M., Borg, C., De Laat, M., Dohn, N. B., & Ryberg, T. (2024). The transformative potential of Artificial Intelligence for Education. *Proceedings of the International Conference on Networked Learning,* 14. DOI: 10.54337/nlc.v14i1.8077

De Laet, T., Millecamp, M., Ortiz-Rojas, M., Jimenez, A., Maya, R., & Verbert, K. (2020). Adoption and impact of a learning analytics dashboard supporting the advisor—Student dialogue in a higher education institute in Latin America. *British Journal of Educational Technology, 51*(4), 1002–1018. DOI: 10.1111/bjet.12962

Díaz-Rodríguez, N., Del Ser, J., Coeckelbergh, M., López de Prado, M., Herrera-Viedma, E., & Herrera, F. (2023). Connecting the dots in trustworthy Artificial Intelligence: From AI principles, ethics, and key requirements to responsible AI systems and regulation. *Information Fusion, 99*, 101896. Advance online publication. DOI: 10.1016/j.inffus.2023.101896

Elhussein, G., Hasselaar, E., & Lutsyshyn, O. (2024). *Shaping the future of learning: The role of ai in education 4.0.*

Felzmann, H., Fosch-Villaronga, E., Lutz, C., & Tamò-Larrieux, A. (2020). Towards Transparency by Design for Artificial Intelligence. *Science and Engineering Ethics, 26*(6), 3333–3361. DOI: 10.1007/s11948-020-00276-4 PMID: 33196975

Gándara, D., Anahideh, H., Ison, M. P., & Picchiarini, L. (2024). Inside the Black Box: Detecting and Mitigating Algorithmic Bias Across Racialized Groups in College Student-Success Prediction. *AERA Open*, *10*, 23328584241258741. Advance online publication. DOI: 10.1177/23328584241258741

Gašević, D., & Merceron, A. (2022). The Handbook of Learning Analytics. In *The Handbook of Learning Analytics*. DOI: 10.18608/hla22

Georgieva, I., Lazo, C., Timan, T., & van Veenstra, A. F. (2022). From AI ethics principles to data science practice: A reflection and a gap analysis based on recent frameworks and practical experience. *AI and Ethics*, *2*(4), 697–711. DOI: 10.1007/s43681-021-00127-3

Hajeer, A., Papp-Váry, Á., & Pólya, É. (2024). AI Tutors vs. Human Instructors: Perceptions of Higher Education Students in Hungary and Spain | Tutores de IA frente a instructores humanos: Percepciones de los estudiantes de educación superior en Hungría y España. *Edutec*, *89*(89), 105–120. DOI: 10.21556/edutec.2024.89.3523

Heiser, R. E., Dello Stritto, M. E., Brown, A. S., & Croft, B. (2023). Amplifying Student and Administrator Perspectives on Equity and Bias in Learning Analytics: Alone Together in Higher Education. *Journal of Learning Analytics*, *10*(1), 8–23. DOI: 10.18608/jla.2023.7775

Hernández-de-Menéndez, M., Morales-Menendez, R., Escobar, C. A., & Ramírez Mendoza, R. A. (2022). Learning analytics: State of the art. *International Journal on Interactive Design and Manufacturing*, *16*(3), 1209–1230. DOI: 10.1007/s12008-022-00930-0 PMID: 40478020

Herodotou, C., Rienties, B., Hlosta, M., Boroowa, A., Mangafa, C., & Zdrahal, Z. (2020). The scalable implementation of predictive learning analytics at a distance learning university: Insights from a longitudinal case study. *The Internet and Higher Education*, *45*, 100725. Advance online publication. DOI: 10.1016/j.iheduc.2020.100725

Holstein, K., Vaughan, J. W., Daumé, H., Dudík, M., & Wallach, H. (2019). Improving fairness in machine learning systems: What do industry practitioners need? *Conference on Human Factors in Computing Systems - Proceedings*. DOI: 10.1145/3290605.3300830

Hossain, Z. (2025). School librarians developing AI literacy for an AI-driven future: Leveraging the AI Citizenship Framework with scope and sequence. *Library Hi Tech News*, *42*(2), 17–21. DOI: 10.1108/LHTN-10-2024-0186

Jahankhani, H., Kendzierskyj, S., Montasari, R., & Chelvachandran, N. (2022). Social Media Analytics, Strategies and Governance. In *Social Media Analytics. Strategies and Governance.*, DOI: 10.1201/9781003243748

Janssen, M., Brous, P., Estevez, E., Barbosa, L. S., & Janowski, T. (2020). Data governance: Organizing data for trustworthy Artificial Intelligence. *Government Information Quarterly*, *37*(3), 101493. Advance online publication. DOI: 10.1016/j.giq.2020.101493

Jayashanka, R., Hettiarachchi, E., & Hewagamage, K. P. (2022). Technology Enhanced Learning Analytics Dashboard in Higher Education. *Electronic Journal of e-Learning*, *20*(2), 151–170. DOI: 10.34190/ejel.20.2.2189

Jiang, Y., Liu, Q., & Liu, G. (2024). Construction of the Cultivation Framework of AI Generated Content on the Information Culture of University Libraries l AIGC . *Journal of Library and Information Science in Agriculture*, *36*(4), 36–44. DOI: 10.13998/j.cnki.issn1002-1248.24-0311

Jones, K. M. L., Asher, A., Goben, A., Perry, M. R., Salo, D., Briney, K. A., & Robertshaw, M. B. (2020). “We’re being tracked at all times”: Student perspectives of their privacy in relation to learning analytics in higher education. *Journal of the Association for Information Science and Technology*, *71*(9), 1044–1059. DOI: 10.1002/asi.24358

Joseph-Richard, P., Uhomoibhi, J., & Jaffrey, A. (2021). Predictive learning analytics and the creation of emotionally adaptive learning environments in higher education institutions: A study of students’ affect responses. *International Journal of Information and Learning Technology*, *38*(2), 243–257. DOI: 10.1108/IJILT-05-2020-0077

Khan, S., Mazhar, T., Shahzad, T., Khan, M. A., Rehman, A. U., Saeed, M. M., & Hamam, H. (2025). Harnessing AI for sustainable higher education: Ethical considerations, operational efficiency, and future directions. *Discover Sustainability*, *6*(1), 403. Advance online publication. DOI: 10.1007/s43621-025-00938-y

Khosravi, H., Shibani, A., Jovanovic, J., Pardos, Z., & Yan, L. (n.d.). Generative AI and Learning Analytics Pushing Boundaries, Preserving Principles. *Journal of Learning Analytics*.

Kleimola, R., Hirsto, L., & Ruokamo, H. (2025). Promoting higher education students’ self-regulated learning through learning analytics: A qualitative study. *Education and Information Technologies*, *30*(4), 4959–4986. DOI: 10.1007/s10639-024-12978-4

Kleimola, R., & Leppisaari, I. (2022). Learning analytics to develop future competences in higher education: A case study. *International Journal of Educational Technology in Higher Education*, *19*(1), 17. Advance online publication. DOI: 10.1186/s41239-022-00318-w

Knox, J., Williamson, B., & Bayne, S. (2020). Machine behaviourism: Future visions of 'learnification' and 'datafication' across humans and digital technologies. *Learning, Media and Technology*, *45*(1), 31–45. DOI: 10.1080/17439884.2019.1623251

Lin, C.-C., Huang, A. Y. Q., & Lu, O. H. T. (2023). Artificial intelligence in intelligent tutoring systems toward sustainable education: A systematic review. *Smart Learning Environments*, *10*(1), 41. Advance online publication. DOI: 10.1186/s40561-023-00260-y

Lobos, K., Mella-Norambuena, J., Bruna, C., & Fernández, C. (2022). Learning analytics for pedagogical decision making in higher education [Analíticas de aprendizaje para la toma de decisiones pedagógicas en educación superior]. *Formación Universitaria*, *15*(4), 33–48. DOI: 10.4067/S0718-50062022000400033

Mac Fadden, I., García-Alonso, E.-M., & López Meneses, E. (2024). Science Mapping of AI as an Educational Tool Exploring Digital Inequalities: A Sociological Perspective. *Multimodal Technologies and Interaction*, *8*(12), 106. Advance online publication. DOI: 10.3390/mti8120106

Márquez, L., Henríquez, V., Chevreux, H., Scheihing, E., & Guerra, J. (2024). Adoption of learning analytics in higher education institutions: A systematic literature review. *British Journal of Educational Technology*, *55*(2), 439–459. DOI: 10.1111/bjet.13385

Martinez-Maldonado, R., Echeverria, V., Fernandez-Nieto, G., Yan, L., Zhao, L., Alfredo, R., Li, X., Dix, S., Jaggard, H., Wotherspoon, R., Osborne, A., Shum, S. B., & Gašević, D. (2023). Lessons Learnt from a Multimodal Learning Analytics Deployment In-The-Wild. *ACM Transactions on Computer-Human Interaction*, *31*(1), 1–41. Advance online publication. DOI: 10.1145/3622784

Martínez-Ramil, P. (2021). Is the EU human rights legal framework able to cope with discriminatory AI? | ¿Es el marco legal de derechos humanos de la UE capaz de hacer frente a la IA discriminatoria? *Revista De Internet Derecho Y Politica, 34*. DOI: 10.7238/idp.v0i34.387481

Moorhouse, B. L., Yeo, M. A., & Wan, Y. (2023). Generative AI tools and assessment: Guidelines of the world's top-ranking universities. *Computers and Education Open*, *5*, 100151. Advance online publication. DOI: 10.1016/j.caeo.2023.100151

Motz, R., & Díaz-Charquero, P. (2023). Fair Learning Analytics: Design, Participation, and Trans-discipline in the Techno-structure. In *Higher Education Dynamics* (Vol. 59). DOI: 10.1007/978-3-031-24193-2_3

News, A. P. (2023). *AI is watching what you type: How schools surveil students' devices*. https://apnews.com/article/ai-school-chromebook-gaggle-goguardian-securly-25a3946727397951fd42324139aaf70f

Nigam, A., Pasricha, R., Singh, T., & Churi, P. (2021). A Systematic Review on AI-based Proctoring Systems: Past, Present and Future. *Education and Information Technologies*, *26*(5), 6421–6445. DOI: 10.1007/s10639-021-10597-x PMID: 34177348

Ntoutsi, E., Fafalios, P., Gadiraju, U., Iosifidis, V., Nejdl, W., Vidal, M.-E., Ruggieri, S., Turini, F., Papadopoulos, S., Krasanakis, E., Tiropanis, T., & Staab, S. (2020). Bias in data-driven artificial intelligence systems—An introductory survey. *Wiley Interdisciplinary Reviews. Data Mining and Knowledge Discovery*, *10*(3), e1356. Advance online publication. DOI: 10.1002/widm.1356

Ortiz-Beltrán, A., Hernández-Leo, D., & Amarasinghe, I. (2023). Surviving and thriving: How changes in teaching modalities influenced student satisfaction before, during and after COVID-19. *Australasian Journal of Educational Technology*, *39*(6), 72–88. DOI: 10.14742/ajet.8958

Parga, M. O. (2023). Can Artificial Intelligence Substitute the Human Mind? Implications of AI in Fundamental Rights and Ethics | ¿PUEDE LA INTELIGENCIA ARTIFICIAL SUSTITUIR A LA MENTE HUMANA? IMPLICACIONES DE LA IA EN LOS DERECHOS FUNDAMENTALES Y EN LA ÉTICA. *Anales De La Catedra Francisco Suarez*, *57*, 39–61. DOI: 10.30827/acfs.v57i.24710

Parkes, S., Benkwitz, A., Bardy, H., Myler, K., & Peters, J. (2020). Being more human: Rooting learning analytics through resistance and reconnection with the values of higher education. *Higher Education Research & Development*, *39*(1), 113–126. DOI: 10.1080/07294360.2019.1677569

Pattanaik, S., Mohammed, M., & Sood, V. (2024). Artificial intelligence and machine learning in Industry 6.0. In *Industry 6.0*. Technology, Practices, Challenges, and Applications., DOI: 10.1201/9781003517993-2

Prinsloo, P., Slade, S., & Khalil, M. (2022). The answer is (not only) technological: Considering student data privacy in learning analytics. *British Journal of Educational Technology*, *53*(4), 876–893. DOI: 10.1111/bjet.13216

Rajasekar, K. P., & Vezhaventhan, D. (2024). Artificial Intelligence Revolutionizing Legal and Forensic Practices: A Comprehensive Analysis. *2024 15th International Conference on Computing Communication and Networking Technologies, ICCCNT 2024*. DOI: 10.1109/ICCCNT61001.2024.10724685

Rees, C., & Müller, B. (2023). All that glitters is not gold: Trustworthy and ethical AI principles. *AI and Ethics*, *3*(4), 1241–1254. DOI: 10.1007/s43681-022-00232-x PMID: 36406882

Renz, A., & Hilbig, R. (2020). Prerequisites for artificial intelligence in further education: Identification of drivers, barriers, and business models of educational technology companies. *International Journal of Educational Technology in Higher Education*, *17*(1), 14. Advance online publication. DOI: 10.1186/s41239-020-00193-3

Reyes, J. A. P., & Rajagopal, A. (2025). Rules of engagement: Ethical issues and value chain introspection in Artificial Intelligence systems. *Quality & Quantity*, *59*(S1, Suppl 1), 463–487. DOI: 10.1007/s11135-024-01990-y

Rodda, A. (2022). Understanding Opportunities and Threats of Learning Analytics in Higher Education – A Students' Perspective. *Lecture Notes in Computer Science (Including Subseries Lecture Notes in Artificial Intelligence and Lecture Notes in Bioinformatics), 13454 LNCS*, 111 – 122. DOI: 10.1007/978-3-031-15342-6_9

Sánchez Hernández, J. (2024). Posthumanism, technology and generational evolution of human rights: towards protection against algorithmic discrimination and the transparent and responsible use of ia | posthumanismo, tecnología y evolución generacional de los derechos humanos: hacia la. *Revista General De Derecho Constitucional*, *2024*(40), 283–316.

Searle, J. R. (1980). Minds, brains, and programs. *Behavioral and Brain Sciences*, *3*(3), 417–424. DOI: 10.1017/S0140525X00005756

SecurityWeek. (2024). *Students, Educators Impacted by PowerSchool Data Breach*. https://www.securityweek.com/students-educators-impacted-by-powerschool-data-breach/

Selwyn, N. (2015). Data entry: Towards the critical study of digital data and education. *Learning, Media and Technology*, *40*(1), 64–82. DOI: 10.1080/17439884.2014.921628

Slade, S., & Prinsloo, P. (2013). Learning Analytics: Ethical Issues and Dilemmas. *The American Behavioral Scientist*, *57*(10), 1510–1529. DOI: 10.1177/0002764213479366

Slimi, Z., & Carballido, B. V. (2023). Navigating the Ethical Challenges of Artificial Intelligence in Higher Education: An Analysis of Seven Global AI Ethics Policies. *TEM Journal*, *12*(2), 590–602. https://doi.org/DOI: 10.18421/TEM122-02

Smuha, N. A. (2019). The EU Approach to Ethics Guidelines for Trustworthy Artificial Intelligence. *Computer Law Review International, 20*(4), 97–106. DOI: 10.9785/cri-2019-200402

Sposato, M. (2025). Artificial intelligence in educational leadership: A comprehensive taxonomy and future directions. *International Journal of Educational Technology in Higher Education, 22*(1), 20. Advance online publication. DOI: 10.1186/s41239-025-00517-1

Stanciu, I. D., Hernández-García, Á., Conde, M. Á., & Nistor, N. (2025). Decoding a decade. Trends and evolution in learning analytics: A comprehensive synthesis. *Computers in Human Behavior, 165*, 108526. Advance online publication. DOI: 10.1016/j.chb.2024.108526

Tauchnitz, E., & Ahmed, S. (2024). Framing Ethical e-Governance: A Plaidoyer for a Human-Rights based Digital Democracy Approach. *ACM International Conference Proceeding Series*, 22–27. DOI: 10.1145/3680127.3680182

Thiebes, S., Lins, S., & Sunyaev, A. (2021). Trustworthy artificial intelligence. *Electronic Markets, 31*(2), 447–464. DOI: 10.1007/s12525-020-00441-4

UNESCO. (2022). Recommendation on The Ethics of Artificial Intelligence. *United Nations Educational, Scientific and Cultural Organization, November.*

Ungerer, L., & Slade, S. (2022). Ethical Considerations of Artificial Intelligence in Learning Analytics in Distance Education Contexts. In *Springerbriefs in Open and Distance Education*. DOI: 10.1007/978-981-19-0786-9_8

Ustun, A. B., Zhang, K., Karaoğlan-Yilmaz, F. G., & Yilmaz, R. (2023). Learning analytics based feedback and recommendations in flipped classrooms: An experimental study in higher education. *Journal of Research on Technology in Education, 55*(5), 841–857. DOI: 10.1080/15391523.2022.2040401

van Leeuwen, A. (2023). Teachers' experiences of monitoring their students in online higher education: Recommendations for course design and opportunities for learning analytics. *Technology, Pedagogy and Education, 32*(5), 589–604. DOI: 10.1080/1475939X.2023.2254297

Villarroel-Henríquez, V., & Gallardo-Aguayo, C. (2025). Educational Management Using Learning Analytics and Big Data in Higher Education [Gestión del Proceso Educativo utilizando Analíticas del Aprendizaje y Big Data en la Universidad]. *Revista de Investigación Educacional, 23*(1), 76–92. DOI: 10.35869/reined.v23i1.6110

Williamson, B. (2017). Big Data in Education: The digital future of learning, policy and practice. *Big Data in Education: The Digital Future of Learning. Policy & Practice*. Advance online publication. DOI: 10.4135/9781529714920

Wirani, N., & Manurung, A. A. (2020). The importance of using a web-based learning model to prevent the spread of covid 19. *AlAdzkiya International of Education and Sosial (AIoES). Journal*, *1*(1), 16–24.

Wu, C., Zhang, H., & Carroll, J. M. (2024). AI Governance in Higher Education: Case Studies of Guidance at Big Ten Universities. *Future Internet*, *16*(10), 354. DOI: 10.3390/fi16100354

Zine, A., & Kaaouachi, A. (2024). Assessment of Teachers' Needs to Integrate Learning Analytics in Higher Education: The Morocco Case. *International Journal of Information and Education Technology (IJIET)*, *14*(3), 494–500. DOI: 10.18178/ijiet.2024.14.3.2070

# Compilation of References


Abdelwahab, H. R., Rauf, A., & Chen, D. (2023). Business students' perceptions of Dutch higher educational institutions in preparing them for artificial intelligence work environments. *Industry and Higher Education*, *37*(1), 22–34. DOI: 10.1177/09504222221087614

Ación, L., Alemany, L., Benotti, L., Bordone, M., Busaniche, B., González, L., & Halvorsen, A. (2022). *Iniciativas desde la sociedad civil para la sensibilización en temas de ética en inteligencia artificial.* Fundación Vía Libre. https://feministai.pubpub.org/pub/4ckd2hyb/release/1

Acquisti, A.; Adjerid, I.; Balebako, R.; Brandimarte, L.; Cranor, L. F.; Komanduri, S.; Leon, P. G.; Sadeh, N.; Schaub, F.; Sleeper, M.; Wang, Y. and Wilson, S. (2017) Nudges for Privacy and Security: Understanding and Assisting Users' Choices Online. *ACM Comput. Surv.* 50(3) Article 44 (May 2018), 41 pages. DOI: 10.1145/3054926

Acquisti, A., Brandimarte, L., & Loewenstein, G. (2015). Privacy and human behavior in the age of information. *Science*, *347*(6221), 509–514. https://www.science.org/doi/abs/10.1126/science.aaa1465. DOI: 10.1126/science.aaa1465 PMID: 25635091

Aderibigbe, S. A., Omar, M., ElMehdi, H., Colucci-Gray, L., Hamad, K., Shanableh, A., AlOthman, H., & Alotaibi, E. (2025). Artificial intelligence-driven prediction of optimal technology-aided alternative operations in post-emergency contexts: A case study from an Emirati university. *International Journal of Educational Research Open*, *9*, 100473. Advance online publication. DOI: 10.1016/j.ijedro.2025.100473

Adikari, A., & Alahakoon, D. (2021). Understanding citizens' emotional pulse in a smart city using artificial intelligence. *IEEE Transactions on Industrial Informatics*, *17*(4), 2743–2751. DOI: 10.1109/TII.2020.3009277

Afchar, D., Nozick, V., Yamagishi, J., & Echizen, I. (2018). MesoNet: A compact facial video forgery detection network. *2018 IEEE International Workshop on Information Forensics and Security (WIFS)*, 1-7. DOI: 10.1109/WIFS.2018.8630761

Agrawal, V. (2022, June). Demystifying the Chinese social credit system: A case study on AI-powered control systems in China. *Proceedings of the AAAI Conference on Artificial Intelligence, 36*(11), 13124–13125. DOI: 10.1609/aaai.v36i11.21698

Agustina, J. R. (2012). Understanding cybercrime: Phenomena, challenges, and legal responses. *Computer Law & Security Review, 26*(6), 517–526. https://www.itu.int/ITU-D/cyb/cybersecurity/docs/Cybercrime%20legislation%20EV6.pdf

Ahmad, S. F., Han, H., Alam, M. M., Rehmat, M. K., Irshad, M., Arraño-Muñoz, M., & Ariza-Montes, A. (2023). Impact of artificial intelligence on human loss in decision making, laziness and safety in education. *Humanities & Social Sciences Communications, 10*(1), 311. Advance online publication. DOI: 10.1057/s41599-023-01787-8 PMID: 37325188

AJuhi. A., and Kumar, S. (2020) A Survey on Artificial Intelligence Overview. *International Journal of Research in Engineering, Science and Management, 1*. https://doi.org/DOI: 10.31224/osf.io/47a85

Akhtar, S. (2024). *Harmonizing human-AI synergy in smart cities: Exploring emotion understanding and technology anxiety in an Asian context*. The Asian Bulletin of Business and Social Science Research., DOI: 10.62019/abbssr.v4i1.47

AlAli, W., Alelyani, S., & Khan, K. (2024). Empowering students with generative AI: A study on learning engagement and critical thinking. *Computers & Education, 208*, 105249.

Alan Setiawan, D., A. R., Fadhly Jambak, F., Umbara, A., & Wildan S, F. (2023). Macro approach in economic crime response technology in the age of global transformation. *KnE Social Sciences*. DOI: 10.18502/kss.v8i18.14224

Al-Azzawi, A. (2021). AI & well-being: Can AI make you happy in the city? In *Artificial Intelligence in the Gulf* (pp. 55-80). https://doi.org/DOI: 10.1007/978-981-16-0771-4_9

Aletras, N., Tsarapatsanis, D., Preoţiuc-Pietro, D., & Lampos, V. (2016). Predicting judicial decisions of the European court of human rights: A natural language processing perspective. *Peerj Computer Science, 2016*(10). DOI: 10.7717/peerj-cs.93

Alghafri, B., & Tubaishat, A. (2025). Balancing Privacy and Security: A Comparative Analysis of AI-Driven Surveillance in the UAE and USA. *Procedia Computer Science, 257*, 142–149. DOI: 10.1016/j.procs.2025.03.021

Alhazbi, S., Al-ali, A., Tabassum, A., Al-Ali, A., Al-Emadi, A., Khattab, T., & Hasan, M. A. (2024). Using learning analytics to measure self-regulated learning: A systematic review of empirical studies in higher education. *Journal of Computer Assisted Learning*, *40*(4), 1658–1674. DOI: 10.1111/jcal.12982

Allen, G. (2019). *Understanding China's AI strategy: Clues to Chinese strategic thinking on artificial intelligence and national security*. Center for a New American Security.

Allen, N., & Okpali, M. (2022). *Artificial intelligence creeps on to the African battlefield*. Brookings Institution. https://www.brookings.edu/articles/artificial-intelligence-creeps-on-to-the-african-battlefield/

Al-Maamari, A. (2025). *Between innovation and oversight: A cross-regional study of AI risk management frameworks in the EU, U.S., UK, and China*. arXiv.

Alshammari, M., & Qureshi, S. (2020). Implementing adaptive learning systems in higher education: Opportunities and challenges. *Journal of Educational Technology Development and Exchange*, *13*(1), 1–16. https://www.sicet.org/jetde/index.php/jetde/article/view/171/114

Alzahrani, A., Tsai, Y.-S., Kovanović, V., Moreno-Marcos, P. M., Jivet, I., Aljohani, N., & Gašević, D. (2022). Success-Enablers of Learning Analytics Adoption in Higher Education: A Quantitative Ethnographic Study. *Communications in Computer and Information Science, 1522 CCIS*, 395 – 409. DOI: 10.1007/978-3-030-93859-8_26

Amoo, O. (2024). The legal landscape of cybercrime: A review of contemporary issues in the criminal justice system. *World Journal of Advanced Research and Reviews*, *21*(2), 205–217. DOI: 10.30574/wjarr.2024.21.2.0438

Amunátegui Perelló, C. (2020). *Arcana Technicae. El Derecho y la inteligencia artificial*. Tirant lo Blanch.

Anaya, C. (2025). *Inteligencia artificial y violencia de género*. PARTIDO OPCIÓN NACIONAL.https://www.promocionpoliticadelamujer.mx/documentos/investigaciones/inteligencia-artificial.pdf

Angwin, J., Larson, J., Mattu, S., & Kirchner, L. (2016). *Machine Bias: There's software used across the country to predict future criminals. And it's biased against blacks*. ProPublica.

Araque, O., & Iglesias, C. A. (2020). An approach for radicalization detection based on emotion signals and semantic similarity. *IEEE Access : Practical Innovations, Open Solutions*, *8*, 17877–17891. https://ieeexplore.ieee.org/document/8962050. DOI: 10.1109/ACCESS.2020.2967219

Arroway, P., Morgan, G., O'Keefe, M., & Yanosky, R. (2015). *Learning analytics in higher education.*

Arthur, W. B. (2021). Foundations of complexity economics. *Nature Reviews. Physics, 3*(2), 136–145. DOI: 10.1038/s42254-020-00273-3 PMID: 33728407

Asaro, P. (2020). AI ethics in international humanitarian law. In Liao, M. (Ed.), *The ethics of artificial intelligence* (pp. 301–320). Oxford University Press.

Attard-Frost, B. (2025). *The death of Canada's Artificial Intelligence and Data Act: What happened and what's next for AI regulation in Canada? Montreal AI Ethics Institute.* https://montrealethics.ai/the-death-of-canadas-artificial-intelligence-and-data-act-what-happened-and-whats-next-for-ai-regulation-in-canada/

Azin, M. H., & Zandhessami, H. (2025). Strategic alignment patterns in national AI policies. *arXiv.* /arXiv.2507.05400DOI: 10.48550

Aznar Sánchez, T. J. (2022). Pedagogical reflection and AI in education. In Medina, M. A., & Debasa, F. (Eds.), *Handbook of Research on Artificial Intelligence in Government Practices and Processes* (pp. 120–135). IGI Global.

Bai, Y., Li, J., Shen, J., & Zhao, L. (2024). Investigating the efficacy of ChatGPT-3.5 for tutoring in Chinese elementary education settings. *IEEE Transactions on Learning Technologies, 17*, 2102–2117. DOI: 10.1109/TLT.2024.3464560

Baker, R., Xu, D., Park, J., Yu, R., Li, Q., Cung, B., Fischer, C., Rodriguez, F., Warschauer, M., & Smyth, P. (2020). The benefits and caveats of using clickstream data to understand student self-regulatory behaviors: opening the black box of learning processes. In *International Journal of Educational Technology in Higher Education* (Vol. 17, Issue 1). DOI: 10.1186/s41239-020-00187-1

Bakshy, E., Messing, S., & Adamic, L. A. (2015). Exposure to ideologically diverse news and opinion on Facebook. *Science, 348*(6239), 1130–1132. DOI: 10.1126/science.aaa1160 PMID: 25953820

Balasubramaniam, N., Kauppinen, M., Rannisto, A., Hiekkanen, K., & Kujala, S. (2023). Transparency and explainability of AI systems: From ethical guidelines to requirements. *Information and Software Technology, 159*, 107197. Advance online publication. DOI: 10.1016/j.infsof.2023.107197

Baldwin, R. (2014). From Regulation to Behaviour Change: Giving Nudge the Third Degree. *The Modern Law Review, 77*(6), 831–857. DOI: 10.1111/1468-2230.12094

Bankins, S., & Formosa, P. (2023). Las implicaciones éticas de la inteligencia artificial (IA) para el aprendizaje significativoTrabajar. *Revista de Ética Empresarial.*, *185*(3), 725–740. DOI: 10.1007/s10551-023-05339-7

Bannister, F., & Connolly, R. (2020). ICT, public values and transformative government: A framework and programme for research. *Government Information Quarterly*, *37*(4), 101509.

Barak-Corren, N., & Kariv-Teitelbaum, Y. (2021). Behavioral responsive regulation: Bringing together responsive regulation and behavioral public policy. *Regulation & Amp. Regulation & Governance*, *15*(S1). Advance online publication. DOI: 10.1111/rego.12429

Barona Vilar, S. (2019). Cuarta revolución industrial (4.0) o ciberindustria en el proceso penal: Revolución digital, inteligencia artificial y el camino hacia la robotización de la justicia. *Revista Jurídica Digital UANDES*, *3*(1), 1–17. DOI: 10.24822/rjduandes.0301.1

Barona Vilar, S. (2021). *Algoritmización del derecho y de la justicia. De la Inteligencia Artificial a la Smart Justice*. Tirant lo Blanch.

Barrientos-Báez, A., Piñeiro Otero, M. T., & Porto Renó, D. (2024). Imágenes falsas, efectos reales. Deepfakes como manifestaciones de la violencia política de género. *Revista Latina De Comunicación Social*, (82), 1–30. DOI: 10.4185/rlcs-2024-2278

Bartmann, M. (2022). The ethics of ai-powered climate nudging—How much ai should we use to save the planet? *Sustainability (Basel)*, *14*(9), 5153. DOI: 10.3390/su14095153

Baser, T. (2022). *Artificial intelligence and social credit system in China*. Middle East Technical University.

Bayaga, A. (2025). Leveraging AI-enhanced and emerging technologies for pedagogical innovations in higher education. *Education and Information Technologies*, *30*(1), 1045–1072. DOI: 10.1007/s10639-024-13122-y

Behn, R. D. (2003). Why measure performance? Different purposes require different measures. *Public Administration Review*, *63*(5), 586–606. DOI: 10.1111/1540-6210.00322

Beinhocker, E. D. (2006). *Origin of wealth: Evolution, complexity, and the radical remaking of economics*. Harvard Business Review Press.

Bell, P., & Congram, M. (2013). Communication interception technology (CIT) and its use in the fight against transnational organised crime (TOC) in Australia: A review of the literature. *International Journal of Social Science Research, 2*(1), 46. DOI: 10.5296/ijssr.v2i1.4089

Bender, L., Renkl, A., & Eitel, A. (2021). When and how seductive details harm learning. A study using cued retrospective reporting. *Applied Cognitive Psychology, 35*(4), 948–959. DOI: 10.1002/acp.3822

Benedict, T. J. (2022). The computer got it wrong: Facial recognition technology and establishing probable cause to arrest. *Washington and Lee Law Review, 79*, 849.

Benjamin, R. (2022). *Viral justice: How we grow the world we want.* Princeton University Press., DOI: 10.2307/j.ctv2h439xx

Bennett Moses, L., & Chan, J. (2018). Algorithmic prediction in policing: Assumptions, evaluation, and accountability. *Policing and Society, 28*(7), 806–822. DOI: 10.1080/10439463.2016.1253695

Bertoni, F., Citti, G., and Sarti, A. (2019). LGN-CNN: a biologically inspired CNN architecture. *Neural networks: the official journal of the International Neural Network Society*, 145, 42-55. .DOI: 10.1016/j.neunet.2021.09.024

Betancourt, M. (2022). *Apuestas para la construcción de una internet feminista en Quito en contexto de desigualdades digitales.* Universidad Andina Simón Bolívar. https://repositorio.uasb.edu.ec/bitstream/10644/8329/1/T3622-MEC-Betancourt-Apuestas.pdf

Bezzina, S., & Dingli, A. (2024). The transformative potential of Artificial Intelligence for Education. *Proceedings of the International Conference on Networked Learning,* 14. DOI: 10.54337/nlc.v14i1.8077

Biesta, G. J. J. (2015). Good education in an age of measurement: Ethics, politics, democracy. *Good Education in an Age of Measurement: Ethics, Politics. Democracy (New York, N.Y.)*, •••, 1–150. DOI: 10.4324/9781315634319/GOOD-EDUCATION-AGE-MEASUREMENT-GERT-BIESTA/RIGHTS-AND-PERMISSIONS

Binns, R. (2018). Fairness in machine learning: Lessons from political philosophy. *Proceedings of the 2018 Conference on Fairness, Accountability and Transparency (FAT*)*, 81, 149-159. *Proceedings of Machine Learning Research (PMLR).* Retrieved from https://proceedings.mlr.press/v81/binns18a.html

Bishop, C. M. (2006). *Pattern recognition and machine learning*. Springer.

Bishop, S. (2021). Influencer Management Tools: Algorithmic Cultures, Brand Safety, and Bias. *Social Media + Society*, *7*(1), 20563051211003066. Advance online publication. DOI: 10.1177/20563051211003066

Blanco González, A., Atienza, P. M., Feito, C. D. C., & Gutiérrez, L. R. (2025). How do companies adapt to cultural factors to gain legitimacy in international markets? *Journal of Economy Culture and Society*, *0*(71), 104–120. DOI: 10.26650/JECS2024-1549375

Blount, K. (2024). Using artificial intelligence to prevent crime: Implications for due process and criminal justice. *AI & Society*, *39*(1), 359–368. DOI: 10.1007/s00146-022-01513-z

Boden, M. A. (1998). Creativity and artificial intelligence. *Artificial Intelligence*, *103*(1–2), 347–356. DOI: 10.1016/S0004-3702(98)00055-1

Borenstein, J., & Arkin, R. (2016). Robotic nudges: The ethics of engineering a more socially just human being. *Science and Engineering Ethics*, *22*(1), 31–46. DOI: 10.1007/s11948-015-9636-2 PMID: 25736832

Borge, R., Balcells, J., & Padró-Solanet, A. (2022). Democratic disruption or continuity? Analysis of the Decidim platform in Catalan municipalities. *The American Behavioral Scientist*. Advance online publication. DOI: 10.1177/00027642221092798

Borges Blázquez, R. (2020). El sesgo de la máquina en la toma de decisiones en el proceso penal. *Ius et Scientia*, *6*(2), 54–71. DOI: 10.12795/IETSCIENTIA.2020.i02.05

Borna, M., Saadat, H., Hojjati, A. T., & Akbari, E. (2024). Analyzing Click Data with AI: Implications for Student Performance Prediction and Learning Assessment. *Frontiers in Education*, *9*, 1421479. Advance online publication. DOI: 10.3389/feduc.2024.1421479

Borum, R., Lodewijks, H., Bartel, P. A., & Forth, A. E. (2011). Structured assessment of violence risk in youth (SAVRY). In *Handbook of violence risk assessment* (pp. 73-90). Routledge.

Bovens, M. (2007). Public accountability. In Ferlie, E., Lynn, L. E.Jr, & Pollitt, C. (Eds.), *The Oxford handbook of public management* (pp. 182–208). Oxford University Press.

Bradford, A. (2020). *The Brussels effect: How the European Union rules the world*. Oxford University Press. DOI: 10.1093/oso/9780190088583.001.0001

Bratton, B. (2021). AI urbanism: A design framework for governance, program, and platform cognition. *AI & Society*, *36*(4), 1307–1312. DOI: 10.1007/s00146-020-01121-9

Breiman, L. (2001). Random forests. *Machine Learning*, *45*(1), 5–32. DOI: 10.1023/A:1010933404324

Broadbent, E. (2017). Interactions with robots: The truths we reveal about ourselves. *Annual Review of Psychology*, *68*(1), 627–652. DOI: 10.1146/annurev-psych-010416-043958 PMID: 27648986

Broadbent, J. (2017). Comparing online and blended learner's self-regulated learning strategies and academic performance. *The Internet and Higher Education*, *33*, 24–32. DOI: 10.1016/j.iheduc.2017.01.004

Brun, A., Bonnin, G., Castagnos, S., Roussanaly, A., & Boyer, A. (2019). Learning analytics made in France: The METAL project. *The International Journal of Information and Learning Technology*, *36*(4), 299–313. DOI: 10.1108/IJILT-02-2019-0022

Brynjolfsson, E., & Mcafee, A. (2014). *The second machine age: Work, progress, and prosperity in a time of brilliant technologies*. Norton.

Bublitz, J. C. (2014). *Freedom of thought in the age of neuroscience*. Archiv für Rechts- und Sozialphilosophie, 100(1), 1-25. https://doi.org/DOI: 10.25162/arsp-2014-0001

Buckingham, S. S. (2012). *Learning Analytics*. UNESCO Policy Brief.

Bueno de Mata, F. (2020). Macrodatos, inteligencia artificial y proceso: Luces y sombras. *Revista General de Derecho Procesal*, (51), 1–31.

Bulletin Officiel n° 5711 (2009). Loi n°09-08 relative à la protection des personnes physiques à l'égard du traitement des données à caractère personnel, promulgated by Dahir n° 1-09-15 du 22 safar 1430 (18 février 2009), Bulletin Officiel n° 5711 du 18 février 2009, pp. 418-427.

Burr, C., Cristianini, N., & Ladyman, J. (2018). An analysis of the interaction between intelligent software agents and human users. *Minds and Machines*, *28*(4), 735–774. DOI: 10.1007/s11023-018-9479-0 PMID: 30930542

Bush, G. H. W. (1990, 17 de julio). *Proclamation 6158—Decade of the Brain, 1990–1999*. The American Presidency Project. https://www.presidency.ucsb.edu/documents/proclamation-6158-decade-the-brain-1990-1999

Buttarelli, G. (2016). The EU GDPR as a clarion call for a new global digital gold standard. *International Data Privacy Law*, *6*(2), 77–78. DOI: 10.1093/idpl/ipw006

Calderón Zambrano, R. L., Yánez Romero, M. E., Dávila Dávila, K. E., & Beltrán Balarezo, C. E. (2023). Realidad virtual y aumentada en la educación superior: Experiencias inmersivas para el aprendizaje profundo. *Religación : Revista de Ciencias Sociales y Humanidades*, *8*(37), e2301088. DOI: 10.46652/rgn.v8i37.1088

Caligiuri, M., & Pili, G. (2021). Italian intelligence studies literature: Understanding the state of play. A comparative perspective. The International *Journal of Intelligence, Security,* Delgado-Morán, JJ., Payá-Santos, CA., Sanz-Gonzalez, R. (2023). China's Borderless Expansionism. Could Be a Threat to International Security? In Cayón Peña, J., & Ramírez, J. M. (Eds.), *Threats to Peace and International Security: Asia versus West. Advanced Sciences and Technologies for Security Applications.* Springer., DOI: 10.1007/978-3-031-28336-9_5D

Calvo, R. A., & D'Mello, S. (2010). Affect detection: An interdisciplinary review of models, methods, and their applications. *IEEE Transactions on Affective Computing*, *1*(1), 18–37. DOI: 10.1109/T-AFFC.2010.1

Calvo, R. A., & Peters, D. (2014). *Positive Computing: Technology for Well-Being and Human Potential.* MIT Press., DOI: 10.7551/mitpress/9764.001.0001

Calzada, I. (2021). *Book review: Smart city citizenship.* International Journal of Contemporary Urban Affairs., DOI: 10.25034/ijcua.2021.v5n1-7

Camps, C. E. (Dir.). (2019). *Tratado de Derecho Procesal Electrónico.* Buenos Aires: Abeledo Perrot.

Cano Cuevas, D. F. (2024). Challenges of human security in the new domains of war. *Novum Jus*, *18*(3), 41–68. DOI: 10.14718/NovumJus.2024.18.3.2

Capraro, V., Jagfeld, G., Klein, R., Mul, M., & van de Pol, I. (2019). Increasing altruistic and cooperative behaviour with simple moral nudges. *Scientific Reports*, *9*(1), 11880. DOI: 10.1038/s41598-019-48094-4 PMID: 31417106

Caraban, A., Karapanos, E., Gonçalves, D., & Campos, P. (2019) 23 Ways to Nudge: A Review of Technology-Mediated Nudging in Human-Computer Interaction. In *Proceedings of the 2019 CHI Conference on Human Factors in Computing Systems (CHI '19).* Association for Computing Machinery, New York, NY, USA, Paper 503, 1–15. DOI: 10.1145/3290605.3300733

Carretero Sánchez, S. C. (2025). *Humanismo tecnológico: justicia predictiva y derechos humanos en el futuro digital.* Colex. DOI: 10.69592/979-13-7011-030-7

Casas, I., & Morozov, E. (2022). Reclaiming democratic control in digital governance: Lessons from Barcelona's Decidim. *Journal of Urban Technology*, *29*(2), 3–21. DOI: 10.1080/10630732.2022.2052128

Castin, N., Malerba, L., Bonny, G., Pascuet, M. I., & Hou, M. (2009). Modelling radiation-induced phase changes in binary Fe–Cu and ternary Fe–Cu–Ni alloys using an artificial intelligence based atomistic kinetic Monte Carlo approach. *Nuclear Instruments & Methods in Physics Research. Section B, Beam Interactions with Materials and Atoms*, *267*(16–17), 3002–3008. DOI: 10.1016/j.nimb.2009.06.092

Cath, C. (2023). Eaten by the Internet. In Cath, E. (ed.). Eaten by the Internet, Meatspace Press, 7–13. https://ia600508.us.archive.org/32/items/eaten-by-the-internet/MSP_eatenbytheinternet_DIGITAL_LR.pdf

Cavoukian, A. (2011). *Privacy by design: The 7 foundational principles*. Information and Privacy Commissioner of Ontario.

Cea Quintana, S. (2025). Mapping brain science research and its influence on public governance: Increasing the effectiveness of public policies through behavioural change. In Saura, J. R. (Ed.), *Global perspectives on AI, ethics, and business economics* (pp. 217–252). Springer., DOI: 10.1007/978-3-031-88781-9_10

Chan, C. K. Y. (2023). A comprehensive AI policy education framework for university teaching and learning. *International Journal of Educational Technology in Higher Education*, *20*(1), 38. Advance online publication. DOI: 10.1186/s41239-023-00408-3

Chan, C. K. Y., & Hu, W. (2023). Students' voices on generative AI: Perceptions, benefits, and challenges in higher education. *International Journal of Educational Technology in Higher Education*, *20*(1), 43. Advance online publication. DOI: 10.1186/s41239-023-00411-8

Chan, L. G., & Ng, Q. Y. (2024). Using learning analytics in higher education: Assessing students' learning experience in an actuarial science course. *STEM Education*, *4*(2), 151–164. DOI: 10.3934/steme.2024010

Chan, L. S. (2018). Ambivalence in networked intimacy: Observations from gay men using mobile dating apps. *New Media & Society*, *20*(7), 2566–2581. DOI: 10.1177/1461444817727156

Chassignol, M., Khoroshavin, A., Klimova, A., & Bilyatdinova, A. (2018). Artificial Intelligence trends in education: A narrative overview. *Procedia Computer Science*, *136*, 16–24. DOI: 10.1016/j.procs.2018.08.233

Chen, L., Chen, P., & Lin, Z. (2020). Artificial intelligence in education: A review. *IEEE Access : Practical Innovations, Open Solutions*, *8*, 75264–75278. DOI: 10.1109/ACCESS.2020.2988510

Cheung, T. M. (2016). Innovation in China's Defense Technology Base: Foreign Technology and Military Capabilities. *The Journal of Strategic Studies*, *39*(5–6), 728–761. DOI: 10.1080/01402390.2016.1208612

Chin, J., Zhang, C., & Chen, F. (2023). Adaptive learning with AI: Enhancing self-regulation in digital education. *Educational Technology Research and Development*, *71*(4), 2315–2334.

Choi, K. (2025, January 21). *Analyzing South Korea's Framework Act on the Development of AI*. IAPP. https://iapp.org/news/a/analyzing-south-korea-s-framework-act-on-the-development-of-ai

Cissé, D. (2022). Chinese telecommunications companies in Africa: alignment with African countries' interests in developing their ICT sector?.

Citron, D., Franks, M., Hartzog, W., & Waldman, A. (2019). The scourge of stalkerware: Considering surveillance software in intimate partner violence. Citizen Lab. https://stopstalkerware.org/information-for-media/

Citron, D. K. (2008). Technological due process. *Washington University Law Review*, *85*(6), 1249–1313.

Clark, J.-A., Liu, Y., & Isaias, P. (2020). Critical success factors for implementing learning analytics in higher education: A mixed-method inquiry. *Australasian Journal of Educational Technology*, *36*(6), 89–106. DOI: 10.14742/ajet.6164

Clayton, C., Maggiori, M., & Schreger, J. (2025). The Political economy of geoeconomics power. NBER Working Paper No 33353. https://www.nber.org/papers/w33353

CNDP. (Commission Nationale de Contrôle de la Protection des Données à Caractère Personnel). (2023). Annual report on data protection in Morocco. Rabat.

CODHEM. (2001). *Third generation human rights*. Human Rights Commission of the State of Mexico.

Congressional Research Service. (2025). *Regulating artificial intelligence: U.S. and international approaches and considerations for Congress* (CRS Report R48555). Library of Congress.

Consejo de Estado de la República Popular China. (2017, 20 de julio). *Plan de desarrollo de la nueva generación de inteligencia artificial*. https://www.airuniversity.af.edu/Portals/10/CASI/documents/Translations/2021-03-02%20China%27s%20New%20Generation%20Artificial%20Intelligence%20Development%20Plan-%202017.pdf

Corp, I. B. M. (2021). *IBM SPSS Statistics for Windows, Version 27.0*. IBM Corp.

Cortes, C., & Vapnik, V. (1995). Support-vector networks. *Machine Learning*, *20*(3), 273–297. DOI: 10.1023/A:1022627411411

Corvalán, J. G. (2018). Inteligencia artificial: retos, desafíos y oportunidades – Prometea: la primera inteligencia artificial de Latinoamérica al servicio de la Justicia. *Revista de Investigações Constitucionais*, *5*(1), 295–316. DOI: 10.5380/rinc.v5i1.55334

Coskun, T. K., & Alper, A. (2024). Evaluating the evaluators: A comparative study of AI and teacher assessments in Higher Education | AVALUANT ELS AVALUADORS: UN ESTUDI COMPARATIU ENTRE LA IA I LES AVALUACIONS DOCENTS A L'EDUCACIÓ SUPERIOR | EVALUANDO A LOS EVALUADORES: UN ESTUDIO COMPARAT. *Digital Education Review*, *45*(45), 124–140. DOI: 10.1344/der.2024.45.124-140

Council of Europe. (1997). Convention for the Protection of Human Rights and Dignity of the Human Being with regard to the Application of Biology and Medicine (Oviedo Convention) (ETS No. 164). https://rm.coe.int/168007cf98

Council of Europe. (2024). *Framework Convention on Artificial Intelligence*. Human Rights, Democracy and the Rule of Law.

Covington, P., Adams, J., & Sargin, E. (2016). Deep neural networks for YouTube recommendations. *Proceedings of the 10th ACM Conference on Recommender Systems*, 191-198. DOI: 10.1145/2959100.2959190

Cowls, J., & Floridi, L. (2018). Prolegomena to a white paper on an ethical framework for a good AI society. *Minds and Machines*, *28*(4), 689–707. DOI: 10.1007/s11023-018-9482-5 PMID: 30930541

Crawford, K. (2021). *Atlas of AI: Power, politics, and the planetary costs of artificial intelligence*. Yale University Press., DOI: 10.12987/9780300252392

Creemers, R. (2018). *China's social credit system: An evolving practice of control. SSRN*. DOI: 10.2139/ssrn.3175792

Cruz Villalón, P. (1989). *Rule of law and fundamental rights*. Center for Constitutional Studies.

Cuello, H. (2021). Cómo cambiar comportamientos durante una pandemia: El uso de nudges para enfrentar la COVID-19. *Gestión y Análisis de Políticas Públicas*, (25), 73–86. DOI: 10.24965/gapp.i25.10873

Dargan, S., & Kumar, M. (2020). A comprehensive survey on the biometric recognition systems based on physiological and behavioral modalities. *Expert Systems with Applications, 143*, 113114. Advance online publication. DOI: 10.1016/j.eswa.2019.113114

Dari, S. S., Ali, L., & Jadhav, B. (2025). AI-Powered Criminal Identification in India: Evaluating Human Rights Concerns in Automated Identification Systems. *SGS-Humanities & Management, 1*(1).

Davenport, T. H., & Ronanki, R. (2018). Artificial intelligence for the real world. *Harvard Business Review, 96*(1), 108–116.

David, G., & Cambre, C. (2016). Screened intimacies: Tinder and the swipe logic. *Social Media + Society, 2*(2), 2056305116641976. DOI: 10.1177/2056305116641976

De Freitas, J., Uğuralp, A. K., Oğuz-Uğuralp, Z., & Puntoni, S. (2024). Chatbots y salud mental: Perspectivas sobre la seguridad de la IA generativa. *Revista de Psicología del Consumidor, 34*(3), 481–491.

De la Garza, L., & Telles, T. (2021). *Igualdad de género e Inteligencia Artificial en América Latina: Un panorama para la diversidad de la fuerza laboral de la IA en la región.* https://proyectoguia.lat/wp-content/uploads/2022/04/Igualdad-de-Genero.pdf

de la Guardia Montesdeoca, G. (2022). Acción e Interacción: Metodologías activas en la enseñanza de la Historia en Secundaria. *Clio*, (48), 320–339. DOI: 10.26754/ojs_clio/clio.2022486854

De Laet, T., Millecamp, M., Ortiz-Rojas, M., Jimenez, A., Maya, R., & Verbert, K. (2020). Adoption and impact of a learning analytics dashboard supporting the advisor—Student dialogue in a higher education institute in Latin America. *British Journal of Educational Technology, 51*(4), 1002–1018. DOI: 10.1111/bjet.12962

Debasa, F. (2024). Inteligencia artificial, ciberdelincuencia y desinformación en el derecho de la revolución digital. In *Seguridad y responsabilidad penal e internacional en el uso de las TIC y la inteligencia artificial* (pp. 79–94). Iustel Portal Derecho.

Debasa, F., & Azcona Pastor, J. M. (2024). Tecnología global, iv revolución industrial y mutaciones sociales. *Historia Actual Online*, (63), 183–198.

Debasa, F., & Azcona Pastor, J. M. (2024). Tecnología global, IV Revolución Industrial y mutaciones sociales. *Historia Actual Online*, (63), 183–198.

del Cerro Velázquez, F., & Morales Méndez, G. (2018). Augmented reality and mobile devices: A binominal methodological resource for inclusive education (SDG 4). An example in secondary education. *Sustainability (Basel)*, *10*(10), 3446. DOI: 10.3390/su10103446

Del Valle, G. (2024). JD Vance thinks monarchists have some good ideas. *The Verge*. https://www.theverge.com/2024/10/16/24266512/jd-vance-curtis-yarvin-influence-rage-project-2025

Díaz Redondo, R., Martínez, P., Lema, D., & Fernández Vilas, A. (2023). Automatic detection of misogyny in Spanish using deep learning. *PLoS One*, *18*(3), e0282284. DOI: 10.1371/journal.pone.0282284 PMID: 36862721

Díaz-Llairó, M. A. (2025). *AI for human excellence: Ethics, Well-Being & Governance for AI-Ready Talent*. KDP.

Díaz-Rodríguez, N., Del Ser, J., Coeckelbergh, M., López de Prado, M., Herrera-Viedma, E., & Herrera, F. (2023). Connecting the dots in trustworthy Artificial Intelligence: From AI principles, ethics, and key requirements to responsible AI systems and regulation. *Information Fusion*, *99*, 101896. Advance online publication. DOI: 10.1016/j.inffus.2023.101896

Digital Dubai. (2020). *Dubai Happiness Agenda: Strategy and Implementation Report*. Dubai Government Publications.

Ding, X., & Yang, Z. (2020). Knowledge mapping of platform research: a visual analysis using VOSviewer and CiteSpace. *Electronic Commerce Research*, 1–23.a European Commission. (2014). Horizon 2020 in brief: The EU Framework Programme for Research & Innovation. Retrieved from https://ec.europa.eu/newsroom/horizon2020/items/15081/en&#8203

Docherty, B. (2025). *A hazard to human rights: Autonomous weapons systems and digital decision-making*. Human Rights Watch.

Doudna, J. A., & Charpentier, E. (2014). The new frontier of genome engineering with CRISPR-Cas9. *Science*, *346*(6213), 1258096. https://www.science.org/doi/abs/10.1126/science.1258096. DOI: 10.1126/science.1258096 PMID: 25430774

Dwork, C., & Roth, A. (2014). The algorithmic foundations of differential privacy. *Foundations and Trends in Theoretical Computer Science*, *9*(3–4), 211–407. DOI: 10.1561/0400000042

e-Estonia. (2024). Universal internet access as a fundamental right.

Eisenhardt, K. M., & Graebner, M. E. (2007). Theory building from cases: Opportunities and challenges. *Academy of Management Journal*, *50*(1), 25–32. DOI: 10.5465/amj.2007.24160888

Elhussein, G., Hasselaar, E., & Lutsyshyn, O. (2024). *Shaping the future of learning: The role of ai in education 4.0.*

Endeley, R. E. (2018). End-to-end encryption in messaging services and national security—Case of WhatsApp messenger. *Journal of Information Security*, *09*(01), 95–99. DOI: 10.4236/jis.2018.91008

Eslami, M., Rickman, A., Vaccaro, K., Aleyasen, A., Vuong, A., Karahalios, K., & Sandvig, C. (2015, April). " I always assumed that I wasn't really that close to [her]" Reasoning about Invisible Algorithms in News Feeds. In *Proceedings of the 33rd annual ACM conference on human factors in computing systems* (pp. 153-162).

Eubanks, V. (2018). *Automating Inequality: How High-Tech Tools Profile, Police, and Punish the Poor*. St. Martin's Press.

European Commission. (2018). General Data Protection Regulation (GDPR). Official Journal of the European Union. https://gdpr-info.eu

European Commission. (2021). Horizon Europe: EU's funding programme for Research and innovation (2021–2027). Retrieved from https://commission.europa.eu/funding-tenders/find-funding/eu-funding-programmes/horizon-europe_encontentReference[oaicite:0]index=0

European Commission. (2021). *NEON: Next-generation integrated energy services for citizen energy communities* (Project ID: 101033700). Retrieved from https://cordis.europa.eu/project/id/101033700

European Commission. (2021). *Proposal for a Regulation laying down harmonised rules on Artificial Intelligence*. AI Act.

European Commission. (2023). *NUDGE: Nudging consumers towards energy efficiency through behavioral science* (Project ID: 957012). Retrieved from https://cordis.europa.eu/project/id/957012

European Commission. (2024). *Artificial Intelligence Act*. Publications Office of the European Union.

European Commission. (2024). Recommendations of the High-Level Group on Access to Data for Effective Law Enforcement. Directorate-General for Migration and Home Affairs. Retrieved from https://home-affairs.ec.europa.eu/document/download/1105a0ef-535c-44a7-a6d4-a8478fce1d29_en?filename=Recommendations%20of%20the%20HLG%20on%20Access%20to%20Data%20for%20Effective%20Law%20Enforcement_en.pdf

European Commission. (2024, August 1). *AI Act enters into force.* Retrieved October 15, 2025, from https://ec.europa.eu/commission/presscorner/detail/en/ip_24_4761

European Parliament. (2024, March 13). *Artificial Intelligence Act: MEPs adopt landmark law.* Retrieved October 15, 2025, from https://www.europarl.europa.eu/news/en/press-room/20240308IPR19015

European Union (2024). Regulation (EU) 2024/1689 of the European Parliament and of the Council of 13 June 2024 laying down harmonised rules on artificial intelligence and amending Regulations (EC) No 300/2008, (EU) No 167/2013, (EU) No 168/2013, (EU) 2018/858, (EU) 2018/1139 and (EU) 2019/2144 and Directives 2014/90/EU, (EU) 2016/797 and (EU) 2020/1828 (Artificial Intelligence Act). https://eur-lex.europa.eu/legal-content/EN/TXT/PDF/

European Union. (2016). Regulation (EU) 2016/679 of the European Parliament and of the Council of 27 April 2016 on the protection of natural persons with regard to the processing of personal data and on the free movement of such data (General Data Protection Regulation). Official Journal of the European Union.

European Union. (2024). Regulation (EU) 2024/1689 of the European Parliament and of the Council of 13 June 2024 on artificial intelligence (Artificial Intelligence Act). Official Journal of the European Union, L 168, 1–127. https://eur-lex.europa.eu/legal-content/EN/TXT/?uri=CELEX%3A32024R1689

European University of Applied Data. (2024). *Impact assessment of virtual tutors in economics education* [Unpublished study].

Europol. (2020, October 14). European police chiefs call for industry and governments to take action against end-to-end encryption roll-out. *Europol.* Retrieved from https://www.europol.europa.eu/media-press/newsroom/news/european-police-chiefs-call-for-industry-and-governments-to-take-action-against-end-to-end-encryption-roll-out

Evangelista, A. (2019). Normalización de la violencia de género cómo obstáculo metodológico para su comprensión. *Revista Nómadas.*, *51*(51), 85–97. DOI: 10.30578/nomadas.n51a5

Faqir, R. S. (2023). Digital criminal investigations in the era of artificial intelligence: A comprehensive overview. *International Journal of Cyber Criminology, 17*(2), 77–94.

Farahany, N. A. (2023). *The battle for your brain: Defending the right to think freely in the age of neurotechnology.* St. Martin's Press.

Farber, S. (2024). Harmonizing AI and human instruction in legal education: A case study from Israel on training future legal professionals. *International Journal of the Legal Profession, 31*(3), 349–363. DOI: 10.1080/09695958.2024.2430018

Feldstein, S. (2019). *The global expansion of AI surveillance.* Carnegie Endowment for International Peace.

Felzmann, H., Fosch-Villaronga, E., Lutz, C., & Tamò-Larrieux, A. (2020). Towards Transparency by Design for Artificial Intelligence. *Science and Engineering Ethics, 26*(6), 3333–3361. DOI: 10.1007/s11948-020-00276-4 PMID: 33196975

Ferguson, I., Renaud, K., Wilford, S., & Irons, A. (2020). Precept: A framework for ethical digital forensics investigations. *Journal of Intellectual Capital, 21*(2), 257–290. DOI: 10.1108/JIC-05-2019-0097

Fernández Rodríguez, J. C, Domínguez Pineda, N. Z, Miralles Muñoz, F, & Liz Rivas, L. (2023). Conductas de riesgo y programas de prevención en adolescentes institucionalizados. *Cuadernos de RES PUBLICA en derecho y criminología.* (2), 42–56. DOI: 10.46661/respublica.8286

Ferreiro Baamonde, X., & Rodríguez García, N. (2010). La armonización del Derecho procesal civil en Europa. *Justicia: Revista de Derecho Procesal, 3–4*, 141–203.

Fischer, C., Pardos, Z. A., Baker, R. S., Williams, J. J., Smyth, P., Yu, R., Slater, S., Baker, R., & Warschauer, M. (2020). Mining big data in education: Affordances and challenges. *Review of Research in Education, 44*(1), 130–160. DOI: 10.3102/0091732X20903304

Fischetti, N. (2024). *Tecnologías feministas Tramas para la resistencia desde el sur latinoamericano. 1era edición. CLACSO.* Consejo Latinoamericano de Ciencias Sociales.

Fisher, C. R., Thompson, C. D., & Brookes, R. H. (2020). Gender differences in the Australian undergraduate STEM student experience: A systematic review. *Higher Education Research & Development, 39*(6), 1155–1168. DOI: 10.1080/07294360.2020.1721441

Flores-Alarcia, Ò., & Fornons Casol, L. (Eds.). (2024). *Educación e inteligencia artificial: Horizontes de transformación*. Dykinson.

Floridi, L. (2025). AI as agency without intelligence: On artificial intelligence as a new form of artificial agency and the multiple realisability of agency thesis. *Philosophy & Technology, 38*, 30. DOI: 10.1007/s13347-025-00858-9

Floridi, L. (2014). *The fourth revolution: How the infosphere is reshaping human reality*. Oxford University Press.

Floridi, L. (2015). *The Onlife Manifesto: Being Human in a Hyperconnected Era*. Springer., DOI: 10.1007/978-3-319-04093-6

Floridi, L. (2018). Soft ethics and the governance of the digital. *Philosophy & Technology, 31*(1), 1–8. DOI: 10.1007/s13347-018-0303-9 PMID: 30322997

Floridi, L. (2019). *The logic of information: A theory of philosophy as conceptual design*. Oxford University Press. DOI: 10.1093/oso/9780198833635.001.0001

Floridi, L., & Cowls, J. (2019). A unified framework of five principles for AI in society. *Harvard Data Science Review*. Advance online publication. DOI: 10.1162/99608f92.8cd550d1

Flyvbjerg, B. (2006). Five misunderstandings about case-study research. *Qualitative Inquiry, 12*(2), 219–245. DOI: 10.1177/1077800405284363

Fothergill, B., Knight, W., Stahl, B. C., & Ulnicane, I. (2019). Responsible Data Governance of Neuroscience Big Data. *Frontiers in Neuroinformatics, 13*, 28. Advance online publication. DOI: 10.3389/fninf.2019.00028 PMID: 31110477

Freeman, K. (2016). Algorithmic injustice: How the Wisconsin Supreme Court failed to protect due process rights in State v. Loomis. *North Carolina Journal of Law & Technology, 18*(5), 75.

Gabrielli, G. (2025). The Use of Facial Recognition Technologies in the Context of Peaceful Protest: The Risk of Mass Surveillance Practices and the Implications for the Protection of Human Rights. *European Journal of Risk Regulation, 16*(2), 1–28. DOI: 10.1017/err.2025.26

Gady, F.-S. (2020). *What does AI mean for the future of manoeuvre warfare?* International Institute for Strategic Studies.

Gallent Torres, C., Zapata-González, A., & Ortego-Hernando, J. L. (2023). The impact of Generative Artificial Intelligence in higher education: A focus on ethics and academic integrity. *RELIEVE. Revista ELectrónica de Investigación y EValuación Educativa, 29*(2), 1–19.

Gándara, D., Anahideh, H., Ison, M. P., & Picchiarini, L. (2024). Inside the Black Box: Detecting and Mitigating Algorithmic Bias Across Racialized Groups in College Student-Success Prediction. *AERA Open*, *10*, 23328584241258741. Advance online publication. DOI: 10.1177/23328584241258741

Garcia, L. (2025, July 14). See how AI can help protect and improve informal settlements in Latin America. World Economic Forum. https://www.weforum.org/stories/2025/07/how-ai-is-transforming-informal-settlements-in-latin-america/

Garrett, B. L., & Rudin, C. (2024). Testing AI. *Available at SSRN* 4948789.

Garzón, J., Patiño, E., & Marulanda, C. (2025). Systematic review of artificial intelligence in education: Trends, benefits, and challenges. *Multimodal Technologies and Interaction*, *9*(8), 84. DOI: 10.3390/mti9080084

Gašević, D., & Merceron, A. (2022). The Handbook of Learning Analytics. In *The Handbook of Learning Analytics*. DOI: 10.18608/hla22

Georgieva, I., Lazo, C., Timan, T., & van Veenstra, A. F. (2022). From AI ethics principles to data science practice: A reflection and a gap analysis based on recent frameworks and practical experience. *AI and Ethics*, *2*(4), 697–711. DOI: 10.1007/s43681-021-00127-3

Giannuzzi, P. (2022). Curtis Yarvin (Mencius Moldbug): An open letter to open-minded progressives. In *Schlüsseltexte der ‚Neuen Rechten': Kritische Analysen antidemokratischen Denkens* (pp. 263 - 273). Springer Fachmedien Wiesbaden.

Giommoni, L., Aziani, A., & Berlusconi, G. (2016). How do illicit drugs move across countries? A network analysis of the heroin supply to Europe. *Journal of Drug Issues*, *47*(2), 217–240. DOI: 10.1177/0022042616682426

Gisin, N., Ribordy, G., Tittel, W., & Zbinden, H. (2002). Quantum cryptography. *Reviews of Modern Physics*, *74*(1), 145–195. DOI: 10.1103/RevModPhys.74.145

Global Center for Economic Innovation. (2024). *Cognitive capital and productivity in the digital age* (Technical Report).

Global Educational Neuroscience Institute. (2025). *Adaptive learning and long-term memory in digital environments* (Experimental Report).

Global System for Mobile Communications (GSMA). (2024). *Informe sobre la brecha de género en Internet móvil 2025*. https://www.telesemana.com/blog/2025/05/16/la-brecha-de-genero-se-consolida-tanto-en-la-industria-movil-y-como-en-la-espacial-satelital/

Gofen, A., Moseley, A., Thomann, E., & Weaver, R. K. (2021). Behavioural governance in the policy process: Introduction to the special issue. *Journal of European Public Policy*, *28*(5), 633–657. DOI: 10.1080/13501763.2021.1912153

Gold, J., & Cuellar, M. (2024). How Often are Fingerprints Repeated in the Population? Expanding on Evidence from AI With the Birthday Paradox. *arXiv preprint arXiv:2412.13135.*

Gómez Martínez, R., Medrano García, M. L., & Aznar Sánchez, T. (2023). Motivation and personalization of teaching with machine learning. *Journal of Management and Business Education*, *6*(3), 330–342. DOI: 10.35564/jmbe.2023.0017

Gómez Suárez, Á., & Verdugo Matés, R. M. (2024). Nuevas formas de poder digital en la red: Dimensiones de la política sexual de las Big Tech. *Revista CIDOB d'Afers Internacionals*, (138), 97–120. DOI: 10.24241/rcai.2024.138.3.97

González-Palenzuela Reyes, A. (2025). Digital rights and the evolution of the right to disconnection in France and Estonia. *Revista de Estudios Constitucionales Europeos*, *12*(1), 45–67.

Goodfellow, I., Bengio, Y., & Courville, A. (2016). *Deep learning*. MIT Press.

Goodfellow, I., Pouget-Abadie, J., Mirza, M., Xu, B., Warde-Farley, D., Ozair, S., Courville, A., & Bengio, Y. (2020, November). Generative adversarial networks. *Communications of the ACM*, *63*(11), 139–144. DOI: 10.1145/3422622

Gorraiz, J., & Schloegl, C. (2008). A bibliometric analysis of pharmacology and pharmacy journals: Scopus versus Web of Science. *Journal of Information Science*, *34*(5), 715–725. DOI: 10.1177/0165551507086991

Government, U. A. E. (2021). UAE Centennial 2071. https://u.ae/en/about-the-uae/strategies-initiatives-and-awards/strategies-plans-and-visions/innovation-and-future-shaping/uae-centennial-2071

Graesser, A. C., Fiore, S. M., Greiff, S., Andrews-Todd, J., Foltz, P. W., & Hesse, F. W. (2018). Advancing the science of collaborative problem solving. *Psychological Science in the Public Interest*, *19*(2), 59–92. DOI: 10.1177/1529100618808244 PMID: 30497346

Guest, O., & Wei, K. (2024). *Bridging the artificial intelligence governance gap: The United States' and China's divergent approaches to governing general-purpose artificial intelligence*. RAND Corporation.

Gui, J.; Sun, Z.; Wen, Y.; Tao, D. and Ye, J. (2021). A Review on Generative Adversarial Networks: Algorithms, Theory, and Applications. *IEEE Transactions on Knowledge and Data Engineering*. PP. 1-1. .DOI: 10.1109/TKDE.2021.3130191

Guillén Burguillos, M., & Serrano Robles, E. (2024). *Oportunidades desde la economía social en la lucha contra las amenazas de la IA*. Revista CIDOB d'Afers. DOI: 10.24241/rcai.2024.138.3.145

Gutiérrez, R. C., Somoza, J. A. G. C., Taranilla, R. V., & Armero, J. M. M. (2019). Análisis de la motivación ante el uso de la realidad virtual en la enseñanza de la historia en futuros maestros. *EDUTEC, Revista electrónica de tecnología educativa*, (68), 1-14.

Hadi, W. J., Kadhem, S. M., & Abbas, A. R. (2022). A survey of deepfakes in terms of deep learning and multimedia forensics. [IJECE]. *International Journal of Electrical and Computer Engineering*, *12*(4), 4408. DOI: 10.11591/ijece.v12i4.pp4408-4414

Hair, J. F., Hult, G. T. M., Ringle, C. M., & Sarstedt, M. (2022). *A primer on partial least squares structural equation modeling (PLS-SEM)* (3rd ed.). Sage.

Hajeer, A., Papp-Váry, Á., & Pólya, É. (2024). AI Tutors vs. Human Instructors: Perceptions of Higher Education Students in Hungary and Spain | Tutores de IA frente a instructores humanos: Percepciones de los estudiantes de educación superior en Hungría y España. *Edutec*, *89*(89), 105–120. DOI: 10.21556/edutec.2024.89.3523

Hameleers, M., Meer, T. G., & Dobber, T. (2022). You won't believe what they just said! The effects of political deepfakes embedded as vox populi on social media. *Social Media + Society*, *8*(3), 20563051221116346. Advance online publication. DOI: 10.1177/20563051221116346

Hamilton, M. (2019). The biased algorithm: Evidence of disparate impact on Hispanics. *The American Criminal Law Review*, *56*, 1553.

Hamilton, Z., Duwe, G., Kigerl, A., Gwinn, J., Langan, N., & Dollar, C. (2022). Tailoring to a mandate: The development and validation of the Prisoner Assessment Tool Targeting Estimated Risk and Needs (PATTERN). *Justice Quarterly*, *39*(6), 1129–1155. DOI: 10.1080/07418825.2021.1906930

Han, J., Kamber, M., & Pei, J. (2012). *Data Mining: Concepts and Techniques* (3rd ed.). Morgan Kaufmann.

Hansen, P. G., & Jespersen, A. (2013). Nudge and the Manipulation of Choice. *European Journal of Risk Regulation*, *4*(1), 3–28. DOI: 10.1017/S1867299X00002762

Harari, Y. N. (2018). *21 lessons for the 21st century*. Debate.

Harris, C. R., Millman, K. J., van der Walt, S. J., Gommers, R., Virtanen, P., Cournapeau, D., Wieser, E., Taylor, J., Berg, S., Smith, N. J., Kern, R., Picus, M., Hoyer, S., van Kerkwijk, M. H., Brett, M., Haldane, A., del Río, J. F., Wiebe, M., Peterson, P., & Oliphant, T. E. (2020). Array programming with NumPy. *Nature*, *585*(7825), 357–362. DOI: 10.1038/s41586-020-2649-2 PMID: 32939066

Hassabis, D., Kumaran, D., Summerfield, C., & Botvinick, M. (2017). Neuroscience-Inspired Artificial Intelligence. *Neuron*, *95*(2), 245–258. DOI: 10.1016/j.neuron.2017.06.011 PMID: 28728020

Hastie, T., Tibshirani, R., & Friedman, J. (2009). *The elements of statistical learning: Data mining, inference, and prediction* (2nd ed.). Springer. DOI: 10.1007/978-0-387-84858-7

Hausman, D. M., & Welch, B. (2010). Debate: To nudge or not to nudge. *Journal of Political Philosophy*, *18*(1), 123–136. DOI: 10.1111/j.1467-9760.2009.00351.x

Hayes, A. F. (2018). *Introduction to Mediation, Moderation, and Conditional Process Analysis: A Regression-Based Approach* (2nd ed.). Guilford Press.

Haynes, P., & Alemna, D. (2022). A systematic literature review of the impact of complexity theory on applied economics. *Economies*, *10*(8), 192. DOI: 10.3390/economies10080192

Heald, D. (2006). Transparency as an instrumental value. In Hood, C., & Heald, D. (Eds.), *Transparency: The key to better governance?* (pp. 59–73). Oxford University Press. DOI: 10.5871/bacad/9780197263839.003.0004

Hébert-Dufresne, L., Landry, N. W., Lovato, J., St-Onge, J., Young, J. G., Couture-Ménard, M. E. et al. (2025). Governance as a complex, networked, democratic, satisfiability problem. *npj Complex*, *2*, 14. DOI: 10.1038/s44260-025-00041-3

Heiser, R. E., Dello Stritto, M. E., Brown, A. S., & Croft, B. (2023). Amplifying Student and Administrator Perspectives on Equity and Bias in Learning Analytics: Alone Together in Higher Education. *Journal of Learning Analytics*, *10*(1), 8–23. DOI: 10.18608/jla.2023.7775

Hemachandran, K., Verma, P., Pareek, P., Arora, N., Kumar, K. V. R., Ahanger, T. A., Pise, A. A., & Ratna, R. (2022). Artificial Intelligence: A Universal Virtual Tool to Augment Tutoring in Higher Education. *Computational Intelligence and Neuroscience*, *2022*, 1–8. DOI: 10.1155/2022/1410448 PMID: 35586099

Hernánde, N., Klimenko, O., Beltrán, E., Vásquez, J., Orozco, M., & Araque, F. (2024). Aspectos psicosociales de la violencia de género y su incidencia en el feminicidio: Una revisión sistemática. *Revista Estudios Psicológicos.*, *4*(3), 7–27. DOI: 10.35622/j.rep.2024.03.001

Hernández-de-Menéndez, M., Morales-Menendez, R., Escobar, C. A., & Ramírez Mendoza, R. A. (2022). Learning analytics: State of the art. *International Journal on Interactive Design and Manufacturing*, *16*(3), 1209–1230. DOI: 10.1007/s12008-022-00930-0 PMID: 40478020

Herodotou, C., Rienties, B., Hlosta, M., Boroowa, A., Mangafa, C., & Zdrahal, Z. (2020). The scalable implementation of predictive learning analytics at a distance learning university: Insights from a longitudinal case study. *The Internet and Higher Education*, *45*, 100725. Advance online publication. DOI: 10.1016/j.iheduc.2020.100725

Ho, G. (2025). Algorithmic bias in large language models: Gendered impacts in generative AI systems. *Journal of Artificial Intelligence Research*, *78*, 112–129. DOI: 10.1016/j.jair.2025.02.005

Holmes, W., Bialik, M., & Fadel, C. (2019). *Artificial intelligence in education: Promises and implications for teaching and learning*. Center for Curriculum Redesign.

Holstein, K., McLaren, B. M., & Aleven, V. (2019). Diseño para la complementariedad: Necesidades de profesores y estudiantes para el apoyo a la orquestación en aulas mejoradas con IA. In Isotani, S., Millán, E., Ogan, A., Hastings, P., McLaren, B., & Luckin, R. (Eds.), Lecture Notes in Computer Science: Vol. 11625. *Inteligencia Artificial en la Educación. AIED 2019*. Springer., DOI: 10.1007/978-3-030-23204-7_14

Holstein, K., Vaughan, J. W., Daumé, H., Dudík, M., & Wallach, H. (2019). Improving fairness in machine learning systems: What do industry practitioners need? *Conference on Human Factors in Computing Systems - Proceedings*. DOI: 10.1145/3290605.3300830

Holt, T. J., Freilich, J. D., & Chermak, S. M. (2017). Exploring the subculture of ideologically motivated cyber-attackers. *Journal of Contemporary Criminal Justice*, *33*(3), 212–233. DOI: 10.1177/1043986217699100

Hossain, Z. (2025). School librarians developing AI literacy for an AI-driven future: Leveraging the AI Citizenship Framework with scope and sequence. *Library Hi Tech News*, *42*(2), 17–21. DOI: 10.1108/LHTN-10-2024-0186

Hou, J., Yang, X., & Chen, C. (2018). Emerging trends and new developments in information science: A document co-citation analysis (2009–2016). *Scientometrics, 115*(2), 869–892. DOI: 10.1007/s11192-018-2695-9

Huang, N., Chen, P. Y., Hong, Y., & Wu, S. Y. (2018). Digital nudging for online social sharing: Evidence from a randomized field experiment. En T. X. Bui (Ed.), Proceedings of the 51st *Annual Hawaii International Conference on System Sciences* (HICSS 2018) (pp. 1483–1491). IEEE Computer Society. DOI: 10.24251/HICSS.2018.185

Huang, M.-H., & Rust, R. T. (2018). Artificial Intelligence in Service. *Journal of Service Research, 21*(2), 155–172. DOI: 10.1177/1094670517752459

Hukkinen, J. (2016). Addressing the Practical and Ethical Issues of Nudging in Environmental Policy. *Environmental Values, 25*(3), 329–351. DOI: 10.3197/096327116X14598445991501

Human Rights Watch. (2019). *China's algorithms of repression: Reverse engineering a Xinjiang police mass surveillance app.*

Humerick, J. (2020). Reprogramming fairness: Affirmative action in algorithmic criminal sentencing. *Columbia Human Rights Law Review*. https://hrlr.law.columbia.edu/hrlr-online/reprogramming-fairness-affirmative-action-in-algorithmic-criminal-sentencing/

Hunter, J. D. (2007). Matplotlib: A 2D graphics environment. *Computing in Science & Engineering, 9*(3), 90–95. DOI: 10.1109/MCSE.2007.55

Hwang, G. J., & Chang, S. C. (2021). Facilitating knowledge construction in mobile learning contexts: A bi-directional peer-assessment approach. *British Journal of Educational Technology, 52*(1), 337–357. DOI: 10.1111/bjet.13001

IEEE Standards Association. (2021). 7000-2021 – Standard Model Process for Addressing Ethical Concerns during System Design. https://standards.ieee.org/ieee/7000/6781/

Ienca, M., & Andorno, R. (2017). Towards new human rights in the age of neuroscience and neurotechnology. *Life Sciences, Society and Policy, 13*(1), 5. DOI: 10.1186/s40504-017-0050-1 PMID: 28444626

Ienca, M., Wangmo, T., Jotterand, F., Kressig, R. W., & Elger, B. (2018). Ethical design of intelligent assistive technologies for dementia: A systematic review. *Science and Engineering Ethics, 24*(6), 1797–1830. DOI: 10.1007/s11948-017-9976-1 PMID: 28940133

Ifenthaler, D., & Yau, J. Y.-K. (2020). Utilising learning analytics for study success: Reflections on current empirical findings. *Research and Practice in Technology Enhanced Learning*, *15*(1), 1–13.

Iniciativa Latinoamericana de Datos Abiertos. (2025). *Algoritmos para integrar la perspectiva de género en la administración de la Justicia.* https://ilda.la/wp-content/uploads/2025/04/Algoritmos-para-integrar-la-perspectiva-de-genero-en-la-Justicia.pdf

Insel, T., Landis, S. C., & Collins, F. S. (2013). The NIH BRAIN Initiative. *Science*, *340*(6133), 687–688. DOI: 10.1126/science.1239276 PMID: 23661744

Institute for European Energy and Climate Policy. (2020). *Audit-To-Measure: Leading businesses towards climate neutrality by speeding up the uptake of energy efficiency measures from energy audits* (Project ID: 101075785). https://cordis.europa.eu/project/id/101075785

International Forum for Educational Innovation. (2025). *AI and digital competencies in the training of economists* (Global Report).

ISO/IEC 42001 (2023). Information technology — Artificial intelligence — Management system. https://www.iso.org/standard/42001

Jahankhani, H., Kendzierskyj, S., Montasari, R., & Chelvachandran, N. (2022). Social Media Analytics, Strategies and Governance. In *Social Media Analytics*. Strategies and Governance., DOI: 10.1201/9781003243748

Jain, A. K. (2010). Data clustering: 50 years beyond K-means. *Pattern Recognition Letters*, *31*(8), 651–666. DOI: 10.1016/j.patrec.2009.09.011

James, G., Witten, D., Hastie, T., & Tibshirani, R. (2021). *An introduction to statistical learning with applications in R* (2nd ed.). Springer. DOI: 10.1007/978-1-0716-1418-1

Janssen, M., Brous, P., Estevez, E., Barbosa, L. S., & Janowski, T. (2020). Data governance: Organizing data for trustworthy Artificial Intelligence. *Government Information Quarterly*, *37*(3), 101493. Advance online publication. DOI: 10.1016/j.giq.2020.101493

Jayashanka, R., Hettiarachchi, E., & Hewagamage, K. P. (2022). Technology Enhanced Learning Analytics Dashboard in Higher Education. *Electronic Journal of e-Learning*, *20*(2), 151–170. DOI: 10.34190/ejel.20.2.2189

Jiang, Y., Liu, Q., & Liu, G. (2024). Construction of the Cultivation Framework of AI Generated Content on the Information Culture of University Libraries | AIGC . *Journal of Library and Information Science in Agriculture*, *36*(4), 36–44. DOI: 10.13998/j.cnki.issn1002-1248.24-0311

Jobin, A., Ienca, M., & Vayena, E. (2019). The global landscape of AI ethics guidelines. *Nature Machine Intelligence*, *1*(9), 389–399. DOI: 10.1038/s42256-019-0088-2

Johnstone, M. (2016). The Ethics of Nudging. *Australian Nursing & Midwifery Journal*, *24*(6), 27. PMID: 29251881

Jolliffe, I. T., & Cadima, J. (2016). Principal component analysis: A review and recent developments. *Philosophical Transactions. Series A, Mathematical, Physical, and Engineering Sciences*, *374*(2065), 20150202. DOI: 10.1098/rsta.2015.0202 PMID: 26953178

Jones, K. M. L., Asher, A., Goben, A., Perry, M. R., Salo, D., Briney, K. A., & Robertshaw, M. B. (2020). "We're being tracked at all times": Student perspectives of their privacy in relation to learning analytics in higher education. *Journal of the Association for Information Science and Technology*, *71*(9), 1044–1059. DOI: 10.1002/asi.24358

Jordan, M. I., & Mitchell, T. M. (2015). Machine learning: Trends, perspectives, and prospects. *Science*, *349*(6245), 255–260. DOI: 10.1126/science.aaa8415 PMID: 26185243

Joseph-Richard, P., Uhomoibhi, J., & Jaffrey, A. (2021). Predictive learning analytics and the creation of emotionally adaptive learning environments in higher education institutions: A study of students' affect responses. *International Journal of Information and Learning Technology*, *38*(2), 243–257. DOI: 10.1108/IJILT-05-2020-0077

Kaddar, B., Fezza, S. A., Hamidouche, W., Akhtar, Z., & Hadid, A. (2023). On the effectiveness of handcrafted features for deepfake video detection. *Journal of Electronic Imaging*, *32*(05). Advance online publication. DOI: 10.1117/1.JEI.32.5.053033

Kahn, J. (2024). The Ghost in the Medicine: The Threat Screening Center and the Mootness Tool. *SMU Dedman School of Law Legal Studies Research Paper*, 1.

Kahneman, D. (2011). *Thinking, fast and slow*. Farrar, Straus and Giroux.

Kahneman, D., & Tversky, A. (1979). Prospect theory: An analysis of decision under risk. *Econometrica*, *47*(2), 263–291. DOI: 10.2307/1914185

Kahneman, D., & Tversky, A. (1984). Choices, values, and frames. *The American Psychologist*, *39*(4), 341–350. DOI: 10.1037/0003-066X.39.4.341

Kania, E. B. (2019). *Learning without fighting: New developments in PLA AI wargaming*. China Brief, 19(7). Jamestown Foundation.

Kania, E., & Laskai, L. (2021). *Myths and realities of China's military-civil fusion strategy*. Center for a New American Security.

Kankanhalli, A., Zuiderwijk, A., & Tayi, G. K. (2017). Open innovation in the public sector: A research agenda. *Government Information Quarterly*, *34*(1), 84–89. DOI: 10.1016/j.giq.2016.12.002

Karrouk, Y., & Debasa, F. (2025). Data quality in the surveillance economy: Challenges of digital governance in the paradox of data decontextualization. In *Data-driven governance through AI, digital marketing, and the privacy interplay* (pp. 31–54). IGI Global Scientific Publishing.

Kasneci, E., Sessler, K., Küchemann, S., Bannert, M., Dementieva, D., Fischer, F., Gasser, U., Kasneci, G., & Neuhaus, J. (2023). ChatGPT for good? On opportunities and challenges of large language models for education. *Learning and Individual Differences*, *103*, 102274. DOI: 10.1016/j.lindif.2023.102274

Katsh, E., & Rabinovich-Einy, O. (2017). *Digital Justice: Technology and the Internet of Disputes*. Oxford University Press. DOI: 10.1093/acprof:oso/9780190464585.001.0001

Kenyon, M. (2020, September). *Algorithmic policing in Canada explained*. Citizen Lab. https://citizenlab.ca/2020/09/algorithmic-policing-in-canada-explained/

Kerry, C. F., Meltzer, J. P., Renda, A., & Wyckoff, A. W. (2025). Network architecture for global AI policy. February 10, 2025. https://www.brookings.edu/articles/network-architecture-for-global-ai-policy/

Ketchen, D. J.Jr, & Shook, C. L. (1996). The application of cluster analysis in strategic management research: An analysis and critique. *Strategic Management Journal*, *17*(6), 441–458. DOI: 10.1002/(SICI)1097-0266(199606)17:6<441::AID-SMJ819>3.0.CO;2-G

Khan, S., Mazhar, T., Shahzad, T., Khan, M. A., Rehman, A. U., Saeed, M. M., & Hamam, H. (2025). Harnessing AI for sustainable higher education: Ethical considerations, operational efficiency, and future directions. *Discover Sustainability*, *6*(1), 403. Advance online publication. DOI: 10.1007/s43621-025-00938-y

Khosravi, H., Shibani, A., Jovanovic, J., Pardos, Z., & Yan, L. (n.d.). Generative AI and Learning Analytics Pushing Boundaries, Preserving Principles. *Journal of Learning Analytics*.

Kingma, D. P., & Ba, J. (2015). Adam: A method for stochastic optimization. *International Conference on Learning Representations (ICLR).*

Kleimola, R., Hirsto, L., & Ruokamo, H. (2025). Promoting higher education students' self-regulated learning through learning analytics: A qualitative study. *Education and Information Technologies, 30*(4), 4959–4986. DOI: 10.1007/s10639-024-12978-4

Kleimola, R., & Leppisaari, I. (2022). Learning analytics to develop future competences in higher education: A case study. *International Journal of Educational Technology in Higher Education, 19*(1), 17. Advance online publication. DOI: 10.1186/s41239-022-00318-w

Knox, J., Williamson, B., & Bayne, S. (2020). Machine behaviourism: Future visions of 'learnification' and 'datafication' across humans and digital technologies. *Learning, Media and Technology, 45*(1), 31–45. DOI: 10.1080/17439884.2019.1623251

Kofman, A. (2025, June–July). The neo-reactionary plot of Curtis Yarvin. *Nueva Sociedad,* (318). https://nuso.org/articulo/318-complot-neorreaccionario-curtis-yarvin/

Kohavi, R. (1995). A study of cross-validation and bootstrap for accuracy estimation and model selection. Proceedings of the 14th International Joint Conference on Artificial Intelligence (IJCAI-95), 2, 1137-1143. Morgan Kaufmann.

Köhler, M., Bächle, T., & Krüger, M. (2024). The Value of Smartwatches in the Healthcare Sector for Monitoring, Nudging, and Predicting. *Journal of Medical Internet Research, 26*, e58936. DOI: 10.2196/58936 PMID: 39356287

Kong, S. C., Cheung, M. Y. W., & Tsang, O. (2024). Developing an artificial intelligence literacy framework: Evaluation of a literacy course for senior secondary students using a project-based learning approach. *Computers and Education: Artificial Intelligence, 6*, 100214. DOI: 10.1016/j.caeai.2024.100214

Kooiman, J. (2003). *Governing as governance.* Sage Publications. DOI: 10.4135/9781446215012

Kooli, C., & Chakraoui, B. (2025). AI-driven assistive technologies in inclusive education. *Computers & Education: Artificial Intelligence, 6*, 100089.

Kotek, H., Dockum, R., & Sun, A. (2023). Gender bias in large language models. arXiv preprint. https://arxiv.org/abs/2308.14921

Kozak, K. (2023). Algorithmic governance, code as law, and the blockchain common: Power relations in the blockchain-based society. *Frontiers in Blockchain, 6*, 1109544. Advance online publication. DOI: 10.3389/fbloc.2023.1109544

Krizhevsky, A., Sutskever, I., & Hinton, G. (2012). ImageNet Classification with Deep Convolutional Neural Networks. *Neural Information Processing Systems*, *25*. Advance online publication. DOI: 10.1145/3065386

Kuo, C. (2020). Taiwan's vTaiwan: Citizen deliberation on technology and AI governance. *Journal of Public Deliberation*, *16*(2), 2. Advance online publication. DOI: 10.16997/jdd.378

La Spina, E. (2024). Inteligencia artificial y control de fronteras: Los riesgos de una automatización acrítica. *Revista CIDOB d'Afers Internacionals*, (138), 121–144. DOI: 10.24241/rcai.2024.138.3.121

Labadze, L., Grigolia, M., & Machaidze, N. (2023). Role of AI chatbots in education: Systematic literature review. *Education and Information Technologies*, *28*(12), 13789–13806.

Lafont, J., Saura, J. R., & Ribeiro-Soriano, D. (2023). The role of cooperatives in sustainable development goals: A discussion about the current resource curse. *Resources Policy*, *83*, 103670. DOI: 10.1016/j.resourpol.2023.103670

Land, N. (2022). *The dark enlightenment*. Imperium Press.

Lannier, S. (2024). Infiltrating virtual worlds. The regulation of undercover agents through fundamental rights. *Revista Brasileira De Direito Processual Penal*, *10*(3). Advance online publication. DOI: 10.22197/rbdpp.v10i3.1066

Law 1581 of 2012. (2012). General provisions for the protection of personal data. Official Gazette No. 48,587.

Lazcoz Moratinos, G. (2020). Análisis de la propuesta de reglamento sobre los principios éticos para el desarrollo, el despliegue y el uso de la inteligencia artificial, la robótica y las tecnologías conexas. *Ius et Scientia*, *6*(2), 26–41. DOI: 10.12795/IETSCIENTIA.2020.i02.03

LeCun, Y., Bengio, Y., & Hinton, G. (2015). Deep learning. *Nature*, *521*(7553), 436–444. DOI: 10.1038/nature14539 PMID: 26017442

Ledesma, J. (2022). Algoritmos y género: Inteligencia artificial al servicio de la violencia simbólica. *Revista Llapanchikpaq: Justicia*, *4*(5), 209–236. DOI: 10.51197/lj.v4i5.659

Levin, I. (2004). Living apart together: A new family form. *Current Sociology*, *52*(2), 223–240. DOI: 10.1177/0011392104041809

Levitina, A. (2024). Ética algorítmica y rendición de cuentas: Retos para los derechos humanos. *Revista CIDOB d'Afers Internacionals*, (138), 169–190. DOI: 10.24241/rcai.2024.138.3.169

Liao, Q. V., & Sundar, S. S. (2022, June). Designing for responsible trust in AI systems: A communication perspective. In *Proceedings of the 2022 ACM conference on fairness, accountability, and transparency* (pp. 1257-1268). DOI: 10.1145/3531146.3533182

Lin, C.-C., Huang, A. Y. Q., & Lu, O. H. T. (2023). Artificial intelligence in intelligent tutoring systems toward sustainable education: A systematic review. *Smart Learning Environments, 10*(1), 41. Advance online publication. DOI: 10.1186/s40561-023-00260-y

Linnenluecke, M., Marrone, M., & Singh, A. (2019). Conducting systematic literature reviews and bibliometric analyses. *Australian Journal of Management, 45*(2), 175–194. DOI: 10.1177/0312896219877678

Little, R. J. A., & Rubin, D. B. (2019). *Statistical Analysis with Missing Data* (3rd ed.). Wiley.

Livingstone, S. (2018). *Media literacy: What are the challenges and how can we move towards a solution?* LSE Media Policy Project Blog.

Lobos, K., Mella-Norambuena, J., Bruna, C., & Fernández, C. (2022). Learning analytics for pedagogical decision making in higher education [Analíticas de aprendizaje para la toma de decisiones pedagógicas en educación superior]. *Formación Universitaria, 15*(4), 33–48. DOI: 10.4067/S0718-50062022000400033

Loewenstein, G., & Chater, N. (2017). Putting nudges in perspective. *Behavioural Public Policy, 1*(1), 26–53. DOI: 10.1017/bpp.2016.7

López Martínez, R. (2022). *"Riesgos de la aplicación de la Inteligencia Artificial en la Administración de Justicia." Inteligencia Artificial Legal y Administración de Justicia*. Aranzadi.

Lozada, R., Aguayo, E., Suquilanda, E., Pico, A., & Vélez, Q. (2023). Los Riesgos de la Inteligencia Artificial en la educación. *Ciencia Latina: Revista Multidisciplinar, 7*(5), 8. DOI: 10.37811/cl_rcm.v7i5.8301

Luckin, R., Holmes, W., Griffiths, M., & Forcier, L. B. (2022). *Intelligence Unleashed: An argument for AI in Education*. Pearson.

Luhmann, N. (1984). *Soziale Systeme. Grundriß einer allgemeinen Theorie*. Suhrkamp.

Lundberg, S. M., & Lee, S. I. (2017). A unified approach to interpreting model predictions. *Advances in Neural Information Processing Systems, 30*, 4765–4774.

Luo, Q., Zeng, W., Chen, M., Peng, G., Yuan, X., & Yin, Q. (2023). Self-Attention and Transformers: Driving the Evolution of Large Language Models. *2023 IEEE 6th International Conference on Electronic Information and Communication Technology (ICEICT)*, 401-405. DOI: 10.1109/ICEICT57916.2023.10245906

Luque Juárez, J. M., Payá Santos, C. A., & Arenas Morales, F. (2023). Contexto de las políticas de seguridad ciudadana. *Cuadernos de RES PUBLICA en derecho y criminología*, (2), 69–82. DOI: 10.46661/respublica.8293

Luque Juarez, J. M., Sanz Gonzalez, R., Payá Santos, C., & Rodriguez Gonzalez, V. (2024). Aplicaciones de la inteligencia artificial en la criminología y ciencias policiales. ci10.13140/RG.2.2.11118.63041. Retrieved from_https://www.researchgate.net/publication/381916708_Aplicaciones_de_la_inteligencia_artificial_en_la_criminologia_y_ciencias_policiales?channel=doi&linkId=66843b7f714e0b03153f1cb4&showFulltext=true

Luque Juárez, J. M. (2019). Las amenazas híbridas contra las democracias abiertas. *Estudios en Seguridad y Defensa, 14*(27), 115–137. DOI: 10.25062/1900-8325.277

Luque Juárez, J. M. (2024). El blindaje inteligente del big data: Un ejercicio para la seguridad nacional. In *Escenarios de incertidumbre para la inteligencia estratégica en el contexto de la seguridad global* (pp. 625–643). Editorial Aranzadi.

Mac Fadden, I., García-Alonso, E.-M., & López Meneses, E. (2024). Science Mapping of AI as an Educational Tool Exploring Digital Inequalities: A Sociological Perspective. *Multimodal Technologies and Interaction, 8*(12), 106. Advance online publication. DOI: 10.3390/mti8120106

MacKinnon, D. P., Fairchild, A. J., & Fritz, M. S. (2007). Mediation analysis. *Annual Review of Psychology, 58*(1), 593–614. DOI: 10.1146/annurev.psych.58.110405.085542 PMID: 16968208

Maddox, I. (2024). Artificial Intelligence in the courtroom: Forensic machines, expert witnesses, and the confrontation clause. *Case W. Res. JL Tech. & Internet, 15*, 416.

Maesschalck, S. (2024). Gentlemen, you can't fight in here. Or can you?: How cyberspace operations impact international security. *World Affairs, 187*(1), 24–36. DOI: 10.1002/waf2.12004

Malek, M. A. (2022). Criminal courts' artificial intelligence: The way it reinforces bias and discrimination. *AI and Ethics, 2*(1), 233–245. DOI: 10.1007/s43681-022-00137-9

Malik, A. A., & Aggarwal, A. (2025). Ethical Integration of Augmented Intelligence in Indian Courts: Analyzing its Predictive Challenges and Perspectives in Adoption. *Recent Advances in Artificial Intelligence for Sustainable Development (RAISD 2025)*, 147-161.

Malik, A., Kuribayashi, M., Abdullahi, S. M., & Khan, A. N. (2022). Deepfake detection for human face images and videos: A survey. *IEEE Access : Practical Innovations, Open Solutions*, *10*, 18757–18775. DOI: 10.1109/ACCESS.2022.3151186

Manheim, D., Martin, S., Bailey, M., Samin, M., & Greutzmacher, R. (2025). The necessity of AI audit standards boards. *AI & Society*, *40*(8), 1–16. DOI: 10.1007/s00146-025-02320-y

Mantelero, A. (2021). Beyond data protection: Exploring the ethical and social implications of data-driven research and innovation. *Computer Law & Security Review*, *41*, 105545. DOI: 10.1016/j.clsr.2021.105545

Markram, H. (2012). The Human Brain Project: A report to the European Commission. *The HBP-PS Consortium*. DOI: DOI: 10.5281/zenodo.44517

Márquez, L., Henríquez, V., Chevreux, H., Scheihing, E., & Guerra, J. (2024). Adoption of learning analytics in higher education institutions: A systematic literature review. *British Journal of Educational Technology*, *55*(2), 439–459. DOI: 10.1111/bjet.13385

Marsden, J. R. (2019). Artificial Intelligence in Practice: How AI Is Being Used. *International Journal of Information Management*, *49*, 228–241. DOI: 10.1016/j.ijinfomgt.2019.03.002

Martínez Garay, L. (2018). "Peligrosidad, algoritmos y *due process*: El caso *State v. Loomis*." *Revista de Derecho Penal y Criminología*, (20), 485–502.

Martínez García, E., Borges Blázquez, R., & Simó Soler, E. (2021). Inteligencia artificial y perspectiva de género en la justicia penal. *Diario La Ley*, (47), 1–17.

Martinez-Maldonado, R., Echeverria, V., Fernandez-Nieto, G., Yan, L., Zhao, L., Alfredo, R., Li, X., Dix, S., Jaggard, H., Wotherspoon, R., Osborne, A., Shum, S. B., & Gašević, D. (2023). Lessons Learnt from a Multimodal Learning Analytics Deployment In-The-Wild. *ACM Transactions on Computer-Human Interaction*, *31*(1), 1–41. Advance online publication. DOI: 10.1145/3622784

Martínez-Ramil, P. (2021). Is the EU human rights legal framework able to cope with discriminatory AI? | ¿Es el marco legal de derechos humanos de la UE capaz de hacer frente a la IA discriminatoria? *Revista De Internet Derecho Y Politica, 34*. DOI: 10.7238/idp.v0i34.387481

Martin, F. D., Diez-de Castro, E., Suárez, A. C., & Prado Roman, C. (2025). Necessary conditions for the existence of organizational legitimacy. *Journal of Economy Culture and Society*, (71), 292–303.

Martino, L. (2024). *Cybersecurity in Italy*. Governance, Policies and Ecosystem. Springer Nature., DOI: 10.1007/978-3-031-64396-5

Martino, L., & Merenda, F. (2021). Artificial intelligence: A paradigm shift in international law and politics? Autonomous weapon systems as a case study. In Giacomello, G., Moro, F. N., & Valigi, M. (Eds.), *Technology and International Relations* (pp. 89–107). Edward Elgar Publishing., DOI: 10.4337/9781788976077.00012

Matz, S. C., Kosinski, M., Nave, G., & Stillwell, D. J. (2017). Psychological targeting as an effective approach to digital mass persuasion. *Proceedings of the National Academy of Sciences of the United States of America, 114*(48), 12714–12719. DOI: 10.1073/pnas.1710966114 PMID: 29133409

McAllister, J. T., Lennertz, L., & Atencio Mojica, Z. (2022). Mapping a discipline: A guide tousing VOSviewer for bibliometric and visual analysis. *Science & Technology Libraries, 41*(3), 319–348. DOI: 10.1080/0194262X.2021.1991547

McGrath, N., Farazouli, A., & Cerratto-Pargman, T. (2025). Generative AI chatbots in higher education: A review of an emerging research area. *British Journal of Educational Technology, 56*(3), 1045–1062.

McKinney, W. (2010). Data structures for statistical computing in Python. *Proceedings of the 9th Python in Science Conference*, 51-56. DOI: 10.25080/Majora-92bf1922-00a

McStay, A. (2018). Emotional AI: The rise of empathic media. *Sage (Atlanta, Ga.)*. Advance online publication. DOI: 10.4135/9781526451293

Medina, J., Villena, M., & Vargas, E. (2020). Redes de apoyo en mujeres víctimas de violencia: Un estudio desde el modelo transgeneracional. *Revista Scientific, 5*(Ed. Esp.), 70–89. DOI: 10.29394/Scientific.issn.2542-2987.2020.5.E.3.70-89

Meske, C., & Amojo, I. (2020). Ethical guidelines for the construction of digital nudges. *Proceedings of the 53rd Hawaii International Conference on System Sciences*, 1-10. DOI: 10.24251/HICSS.2020.480

Meunier, D., and Paugam-Moisy, H. (2008, April). Neural networks for computational neuroscience. *ESANN* (pp. 367-378)

Miller, P. S., Rein, B. W., & Bailey, E. O. (1993). Daubert and the need for judicial scientific literacy. *Judicature, 77*, 254.

Mills, S. (2021). Finding the 'nudge' in hypernudge. *Technology in Society*, *71*, 102117. DOI: 10.1016/j.techsoc.2022.102117

Ministère de la Transition Numérique et de la Réforme de l'Administration. (2024). Maroc Digital 2030 - Stratégie nationale de transformation numérique. Rabat: Kingdom of Morocco.

Miranda, S., Yanes, M., Martínez, J., & Tuñón, P. (2024). *Género y violencias en América Latina.* El Colegio de la Frontera Sur. México. https://ecosur.repositorioinstitucional.mx/jspui/bitstream/1017/2680/1/64344_Documento.pdf

Mittelstadt, B. D., & Floridi, L. (2016). The Ethics of Big Data: Current and Foreseeable Issues in *Biomedical Contexts. Science and Engineering Ethics*, *22*(2), 303–341. DOI: 10.1007/s11948-015-9652-2 PMID: 26002496

Mokhtar, R. (2025). The Transformation of Correctional Facilities Using Artificial Intelligence Technology.

Moldbug, M. (2007 - 2016). *Unqualified Reservations.* https://www.unqualified-reservations.org

Moldbug, M. (2008). An open letter to open-minded progressives. *Unqualified Reservations.* https://www.unqualified-reservations.org/2008/04/open-letter-to-open-minded-progressives/

Montacute, R. (2020). *Social mobility and COVID-19.* Sutton Trust.

Montesinos, A. (2024). Inteligencia artificial en la justicia con perspectiva de género: Amenazas y oportunidades. *Actualidad Jurídica Iberoamericana.* 21, 566-597. https://revista-aji.com/wp-content/uploads/2024/07/AJI21_Art20.pdf

Moorhouse, B. L., Yeo, M. A., & Wan, Y. (2023). Generative AI tools and assessment: Guidelines of the world's top-ranking universities. *Computers and Education Open*, *5*, 100151. Advance online publication. DOI: 10.1016/j.caeo.2023.100151

Morán, J. J. D. (2023). Políticas públicas de seguridad en España. Análisis desde perspectivas criminológicas. Revista opiniao jurídica, 21(37), 183-211.

Motz, R., & Díaz-Charquero, P. (2023). Fair Learning Analytics: Design, Participation, and Trans-discipline in the Techno-structure. In *Higher Education Dynamics* (Vol. 59). DOI: 10.1007/978-3-031-24193-2_3

Naidoo, T. (2024). Overview of AI regulation in healthcare: A comparative study of the EU and South Africa. *South African Journal of Bioethics and Law*, *17*(3), 121–126. DOI: 10.7196/SAJBL.2024.v17i3.2294

Namay, E., Reyes, C., & Olguin, L. (2025). Violencia de género en América Latina y El Caribe: Desafíos legales para la protección de las mujeres en estado de vulnerabilidad. *Revista de Ciencias Humanas*, *23*, 255–264. DOI: 10.5281/zenodo.14271150

National Institute of Standards and Technology (NIST). (2023). Artificial Intelligence Risk Management Framework (AI RMF 1.0). https://nvlpubs.nist.gov/nistpubs/ai/nist.ai.100-1.pdf

Neri, M., Niccolini, F., & Martino, L. (2023). Organizational cybersecurity readiness in the ICT sector: A quanti-qualitative assessment. *Information and Computer Security*, *32*(1), 38–52. Advance online publication. DOI: 10.1108/ICS-05-2023-0084

News, A. P. (2023). *AI is watching what you type: How schools surveil students' devices*. https://apnews.com/article/ai-school-chromebook-gaggle-goguardian-securly-25a3946727397951fd42324139aaf70f

Nieva Fenoll, J. (2018). *Inteligencia artificial y proceso judicial*. Marcial Pons. DOI: 10.2307/jj.26844203

Nigam, A., Pasricha, R., Singh, T., & Churi, P. (2021). A Systematic Review on AI-based Proctoring Systems: Past, Present and Future. *Education and Information Technologies*, *26*(5), 6421–6445. DOI: 10.1007/s10639-021-10597-x PMID: 34177348

Nissenbaum, H. (2010). *Privacy in context: Technology, policy, and the integrity of social life*. Stanford University Press.

Nkambou, R., Bourdeau, J., & Mizoguchi, R. (2018). *Advances in Intelligent Tutoring Systems*. Springer.

Nogueira Alcalá, H. (2003). *Los derechos fundamentales y sus generaciones: una aproximación teórica*. Universidad Nacional Autónoma de México, Instituto de Investigaciones Jurídicas.

Noor, M., Zenia, N., Kaiser, M., Mamun, S., & Mahmud, M. (2020). Application of deep learning in detecting neurological disorders from magnetic resonance images: A survey on the detection of Alzheimer's disease, Parkinson's disease and schizophrenia. *Brain Informatics*, *7*(1), 11. Advance online publication. DOI: 10.1186/s40708-020-00112-2 PMID: 33034769

Ntoutsi, E., Fafalios, P., Gadiraju, U., Iosifidis, V., Nejdl, W., Vidal, M.-E., Ruggieri, S., Turini, F., Papadopoulos, S., Krasanakis, E., Tiropanis, T., & Staab, S. (2020). Bias in data-driven artificial intelligence systems—An introductory survey. *Wiley Interdisciplinary Reviews. Data Mining and Knowledge Discovery*, *10*(3), e1356. Advance online publication. DOI: 10.1002/widm.1356

O'Neil, C. (2016). Weapons of math destruction: How big data increases inequality and threatens democracy. *Crown Publishing Group*, *78*(3), 403–404.

Ochara, N. M., Odhiambo, N. A., & Kadyamatimba, A. (2020). The digitalised terrorism ecology: A systems perspective. *The African Journal of Information and Communication*, (25). Advance online publication. DOI: 10.23962/10539/29196

OECD. (2019). OECD Principles on Artificial Intelligence. OECD Publishing. Retrieved from https://www.oecd.org/going-digital/ai/principles/

OECD. (2019). *OECD principles on artificial intelligence.* Organisation for Economic Co-operation and Development.

OECD. (2019). OECD principles on artificial intelligence. Organisation for Economic Co-operation and Development. https://oecd.ai/en/ai-principles

OECD. (2019). *Recommendation of the Council on Artificial Intelligence.* OECD/LEGAL/0449. https://legalinstruments.oecd.org/en/instruments/OECD-LEGAL-0449

OECD. (2020). *How's Life? 2020: Measuring well-being*. Organisation for Economic Co-operation and Development.

OECD. (2020). *Policy Framework on Sound Public Governance.* Organisation for Economic Cooperation and Development.

OECD. (2024). AI principles. https://www.oecd.org/en/topics/sub-issues/ai-principles.html

OECD. (2024). OECD AI Principles. https://oecd.ai/en/ai-principles

Oficina de las Naciones Unidas contra la Droga y el Delito. UNODC. (2023). *Naciones Unidas insta a eliminar las brechas que privan a mujeres y niñas a acceder plenamente a la era digital.* https://www.unodc.org/lpomex/es/noticias/marzo-2023/naciones-unidas-insta-a-eliminar-las-brechas-que-privan-a-mujeres-y-ninas-a-acceder-plenamente-a-la-era-digital.html

OHCHR. (2021). *The right to privacy in the digital age*. Office of the United Nations High Commissioner for Human Rights.

Okano, H., Miyawaki, A., & Kasai, K. (2015). Brain/MINDS: A Japanese National Brain Project for Marmoset Neuroscience. *Neuron*, *92*(3), 582–590. DOI: 10.1016/j.neuron.2016.10.018 PMID: 27809998

Okuno, M. J., & Okuno, H. G. (2025). Legal frameworks for AI service business participants: A comparative analysis of liability protection across jurisdictions. *AI & Society*, *40*(7), 1–17. DOI: 10.1007/s00146-025-02288-9

Oliva Santos, A. D. L., Calderón Cuadrado, M. P., Cedeño Hernán, M., & Pardo Iranzo, V. (2012). La armonización del derecho procesal tras el Tratado de Lisboa. La armonización del derecho procesal tras el Tratado de Lisboa.

Organización de Naciones Unidas para la Educación, la Ciencia y la Cultura (UNESCO). (2023). *Una inteligencia artificial ética e inclusiva en América Latina y el Caribe.* https://www.unesco.org/es/articles/una-inteligencia-artificial-etica-e-inclusiva-en-america-latina-y-el-caribe

Organization for Economic Education. (2023). *Technology gaps in higher education* (Global Report).

Ortiz-Beltrán, A., Hernández-Leo, D., & Amarasinghe, I. (2023). Surviving and thriving: How changes in teaching modalities influenced student satisfaction before, during and after COVID-19. *Australasian Journal of Educational Technology, 39*(6), 72–88. DOI: 10.14742/ajet.8958

Oster, J. (2021). Code is code and law is law—The law of digitalization and the digitalization of law. *International Journal of Law and Information Technology, 29*(2), 101–117. DOI: 10.1093/ijlit/eaab004

Oyewola, D. O., & Dada, E. G. (2022). Exploring machine learning: A scientometrics approach using bibliometrix and VOSviewer. *SN Applied Sciences, 4*(5), 1–18. DOI: 10.1007/s42452-022-05027-7 PMID: 35434524

Pacholska, M. (2024). Many hands in the black box: artificial intelligence and the responsibility of international organizations. In *Reassessing the Articles on the Responsibility of International Organizations* (pp. 171–187). Edward Elgar Publishing. DOI: 10.4337/9781035309115.00017

Padilla, W. R., & García, J. (2018). Data Association Methodology to Improve Spatial Predictions in Alternative Marketing Circuits in Ecuador. *Computational Intelligence and Neuroscience, 2018*, 1–15. DOI: 10.1155/2018/6587049 PMID: 30532771

Palmiotto, F. (2020). The black box on trial: the impact of algorithmic opacity on fair trial rights in criminal proceedings. In *Algorithmic Governance and Governance of Algorithms: Legal and Ethical Challenges* (pp. 49–70). Springer International Publishing.

Papamitsiou, Z., & Economides, A. A. (2014). Learning analytics and educational data mining in practice: A systematic literature review of empirical evidence. *Journal of Educational Technology & Society, 17*(4), 49–64.

Paperno, D. (2022). On Learning Interpreted Languages with Recurrent Models. *Computational Linguistics*, *48*(3), 471–482. DOI: 10.1162/coli_a_00431

Parga, M. O. (2023). Can Artificial Intelligence Substitute the Human Mind? Implications of AI in Fundamental Rights and Ethics | ¿PUEDE LA INTELIGENCIA ARTIFICIAL SUSTITUIR A LA MENTE HUMANA? IMPLICACIONES DE LA IA EN LOS DERECHOS FUNDAMENTALES Y EN LA ÉTICA. *Anales De La Catedra Francisco Suarez*, *57*, 39–61. DOI: 10.30827/acfs.v57i.24710

Parkes, S., Benkwitz, A., Bardy, H., Myler, K., & Peters, J. (2020). Being more human: Rooting learning analytics through resistance and reconnection with the values of higher education. *Higher Education Research & Development*, *39*(1), 113–126. DOI: 10.1080/07294360.2019.1677569

Parlamento Europeo y Consejo de la Unión Europea. (2024). Reglamento (UE) 2024/1183 del Parlamento Europeo y del Consejo de 13 de marzo de 2024 por el que se establecen normas armonizadas en materia de inteligencia artificial (Ley de Inteligencia Artificial) y se modifican determinados actos legislativos de la Unión. *Diario Oficial de la Unión Europea*, L 168, 1–142. https://eur-lex.europa.eu/legal-content/ES/TXT/?uri=CELEX%3A32024R1183

Parra Sánchez, J. S., Torres Pardo, I. D., & Martínez de Merino, C. Y. (2023). Personalization of resources for teaching university mathematics using artificial intelligence. *Inter-American Journal of Research in Education and Pedagogy*, *16*(1). Advance online publication. DOI: 10.15332/25005421.7904

Parra-Sánchez, J. S. (2022). The potential of artificial intelligence in higher education: A personalization approach. *Technological-Educational Journal of Teachers 2.0, 14*(1). https://doi.org/DOI: 10.37843/rted.v14i1.296

Pascual-Ezama, D., (2022). Towards an emotionally aware AI: Ethical considerations and societal impact. *AI & Society*, *37*(4), 1379–1391.

Pasquale, F. (2020). *New laws of robotics: Defending human expertise in the age of AI*. The Belknap Press of Harvard University Press., DOI: 10.4159/9780674250062

Pattanaik, S., Mohammed, M., & Sood, V. (2024). Artificial intelligence and machine learning in Industry 6.0. In *Industry 6.0*. Technology, Practices, Challenges, and Applications., DOI: 10.1201/9781003517993-2

Patton, M. Q. (2015). *Qualitative research & evaluation methods* (4th ed.). Sage Publications.

Pawelec, M. (2022). Deepfakes and democracy (theory): How synthetic audio-visual media for disinformation and hate speech threaten core democratic functions. *Digital Society : Ethics, Socio-Legal and Governance of Digital Technology, 1*(2), 19. Advance online publication. DOI: 10.1007/s44206-022-00010-6 PMID: 36097613

Payá Santos, C. A. (2023). El desempeño de la inteligencia en España en el ámbito público, empresarial y académico. *Revista Científica General José María Córdova, 21*(44), 1029–1047. DOI: 10.21830/19006586.1222

Payá Santos, C., & Delgado Morán, J. J. (2017). Uncertainty of dimensional analysis of intelligence. *URVIO Revista Latinoamericana de Estudios de Seguridad, 21*(21), 225–239. DOI: 10.17141/urvio.21.2017.2962

Payá Santos, C., Delgado Morán, J. J., & Mazurier, P. A. (2018). Individual terrorism as a response to the distorted phenomenon of cultural identity. In Ramírez, J., & Abad-Quintanal, G. (Eds.), *Cross-cultural dialogue as a conflict management strategy. Advanced sciences and technologies for security applications* (pp. 34–45). Springer., DOI: 10.1007/978-3-319-77231-8_4

Payá-Santos, C., & Luque Juárez, J. M. (2021). El sistema de inteligencia criminal ante las nuevas amenazas y oportunidades del ciberespacio. *Revista Científica General José María Córdova, 19*(36), 1122–1136. DOI: 10.21830/19006586.855

Pedregosa, F., Varoquaux, G., Gramfort, A., Michel, V., Thirion, B., Grisel, O., Blondel, M., Prettenhofer, P., Weiss, R., Dubourg, V., Vanderplas, J., Passos, A., Cournapeau, D., Brucher, M., Perrot, M., & Duchesnay, É. (2011). Scikit-learn: Machine Learning in Python. *Journal of Machine Learning Research, 12*, 2825–2830.

Peer, E., Egelman, S., Harbach, M., Malkin, N., Mathur, A., & Frik, A. (2020). Nudge me right: Personalizing online security nudges to people's decision-making styles. *Computers in Human Behavior, 109*, 106347. Advance online publication. DOI: 10.1016/j.chb.2020.106347

Peña, A. (2023). Feminist AI for gender justice: Designing digital tools to address online gender-based violence in Latin America. Feminist AI Research Collective. https://feministai.pubpub.org/pub/wjfw5sx9

Peña-López, I. (2020). Citizen participation and the digital age: Barcelona's Decidim. *Journal of Public Policy & Marketing, 39*(4), 411–426.

Peña, P., & Varon, J. (2025). Construcción y defensa de una IA emancipatoria desde un enfoque transfeminista en América Latina. *Revista Latinoamericana de Estudios de Género, 12*(1), 45–68.

Pentland, A. (2014). *Social physics: How social networks can make us smarter.* Penguin Press.

Perdomo, I. (2016). Género y tecnologías. Ciberfeminismos y construcción de la tecnocultura actual. *Revista iberoamericana de ciencias tecnología y sociedad.* 31(11). 171-193. https://www.revistacts.net/wp-content/uploads/2020/03/vol10-nro31-perdomo.pdf

Perrin, B. (2025). *How AI can support, not undermine, criminal justice.* Beyond UBC. https://beyond.ubc.ca/how-ai-can-support-not-undermine-criminal-justice/

Picard, R. W. (2010). Affective Computing: From Laughter to IEEE. *IEEE Transactions on Affective Computing*, *1*(1), 11–17. DOI: 10.1109/T-AFFC.2010.10

Pitts, L. N., Armstrong, A., Fleming, L., Fazeli, P. L., Landier, W., & Ladores, S. (2025). The Application and Evolution of the Social-Ecological Model for Adolescent and Young Adult Readiness for Transition: A Scoping Review. *Journal of Pediatric Health Care*, *39*(3), 355–376. DOI: 10.1016/j.pedhc.2024.12.004 PMID: 39772328

Podsakoff, P. M., MacKenzie, S. B., Lee, J. Y., & Podsakoff, N. P. (2003). Common method biases in behavioral research: A critical review of the literature and recommended remedies. *The Journal of Applied Psychology*, *88*(5), 879–903. DOI: 10.1037/0021-9010.88.5.879 PMID: 14516251

Poo, M., Du, J.-L., Ip, N., Xiong, Z., Xu, B., & Tan, T. (2016). China Brain Project: Basic Neuroscience, Brain Diseases, and Brain-Inspired Computing. *Neuron*, *92*(3), 591–596. DOI: 10.1016/j.neuron.2016.10.050 PMID: 27809999

Popenici, SA y Kerr, S. (2017). Explorando el impacto de la inteligencia artificial en la enseñanza y el aprendizaje en la educación superior. *Investigación y práctica en aprendizaje mejorado por la tecnología, 12* (1), 22.

Prado Román, C. (2020). The legitimacy of educational institutions in the digital age. *Revista Brasileira de Gestão de Negócios*, *22*(3), 45–60.

Preacher, K. J., & Hayes, A. F. (2008). Asymptotic and resampling strategies for assessing and comparing indirect effects in multiple mediator models. *Behavior Research Methods*, *40*(3), 879–891. DOI: 10.3758/BRM.40.3.879 PMID: 18697684

Prinsloo, P., Slade, S., & Khalil, M. (2022). The answer is (not only) technological: Considering student data privacy in learning analytics. *British Journal of Educational Technology*, *53*(4), 876–893. DOI: 10.1111/bjet.13216

Pro Mujer. (2025). *Breaking the digital divide: technology as a tool for equality.* https://promujer.org/portal/2024/07/02/breaking-the-digital-divide-technology-as-a-tool-for-equality/

Programa de las Naciones Unidas para el Desarrollo (PNUD). (2023). *Sara: la nueva herramienta de inteligencia artificial para combatir la violencia de género en Centroamérica.* https://www.undp.org/es/latin-america/comunicados-de-prensa/sara-la-nueva-herramienta-de-inteligencia-artificial-para-combatir-la-violencia-de-genero-en-centroamerica-0

Programa de las Naciones Unidas para el Desarrollo (PNUD). (2024). *Revelando la violencia de género en el espacio digital.* https://www.undp.org/sites/g/files/zskgke326/files/2024-10/pa_pnud_policybrief_2_2024_vf.pdf

Putra, D., and Setiawan, E. (2023). Sentiment Analysis on Social Media with Glove Using Combination CNN and RoBERTa. *Jurnal RESTI (Rekayasa Sistem dan Teknologi Informasi).* .DOI: 10.29207/resti.v7i3.4892

Rahwan, I. (2020). Society-in-the-loop: Programming the algorithmic social contract. *Ethics and Information Technology, 22*(1), 5–14. DOI: 10.1007/s10676-017-9430-8

Rajasekar, K. P., & Vezhaventhan, D. (2024). Artificial Intelligence Revolutionizing Legal and Forensic Practices: A Comprehensive Analysis. *2024 15th International Conference on Computing Communication and Networking Technologies, ICCCNT 2024.* DOI: 10.1109/ICCCNT61001.2024.10724685

Ramírez, J., Alarcón, R., & Ortega, S. (2020). Violencia de género en Latinoamérica: Estrategias para su prevención y erradicación. *Revista de Ciencias Sociales, XXVI*(4), 260–275.

Rasala, M. (2025, August 03). *AP police launch Interoperable Criminal Justice System 2.0.* The Times of India. https://timesofindia.indiatimes.com/city/vijayawada/ap-police-launch-interoperable-criminal-justice-system-2-0/articleshow/123065775.cms

Razali, N. H., Ali, N. N. N., Safiyuddin, S. K., & Khalid, F. (2022). Design thinking approaches in education and their challenges. *Creative Education, 13*(7), 2289–2299. Advance online publication. DOI: 10.4236/ce.2022.137145

Rees, C., & Müller, B. (2023). All that glitters is not gold: Trustworthy and ethical AI principles. *AI and Ethics, 3*(4), 1241–1254. DOI: 10.1007/s43681-022-00232-x PMID: 36406882

Reeves, B., & Nass, C. (1996). *The media equation: How people treat computers, television, and new media like real people and places.* Cambridge University Press.

Remus, D., & Levy, F. (2015). *Can Robots Be Lawyers?* Computers, Lawyers, and the Practice of Law.

Renda, A. (2022). *Can the EU Digital Markets Act achieve its goals?* Center for the Governance of Change, IE University.

Renz, A., & Hilbig, R. (2020). Prerequisites for artificial intelligence in further education: Identification of drivers, barriers, and business models of educational technology companies. *International Journal of Educational Technology in Higher Education, 17*(1), 14. Advance online publication. DOI: 10.1186/s41239-020-00193-3

Reyes, J. A. P., & Rajagopal, A. (2025). Rules of engagement: Ethical issues and value chain introspection in Artificial Intelligence systems. *Quality & Quantity, 59*(S1, Suppl 1), 463–487. DOI: 10.1007/s11135-024-01990-y

Rico, N. (1996). *Mujer y desarrollo. Violencia de género: un problema de derechos humanos*. Naciones Unidad CEPAL.

Río, J., Gervás, I., & Yuste, S. (2018). The Patient Information Sheet (PIS) and Informed Consent (IC) for case reports and case series: Proposal for a standard model for presentations in congresses and other scientific publications. *Reumatología Clínica, 14*(4), 215–223. DOI: 10.1016/j.reuma.2018.07.001 PMID: 30075946

Roa Avella, M., Sanabria Moyano, J., & Dinas Hurtado, K. (2023). Herramientas de predicción de violencia basada en género y feminicidio mediante la Inteligencia Artificial. *Revista Jurídica Mario Alario D'Filippo, 15*(30), 360–390. DOI: 10.32997/2256-2796-vol.15-num.30-2023-4254

Robertson, D. C., Voegtlin, C., & Maak, T. (2016). Business Ethics: The Promise of Neuroscience. *Journal of Business Ethics, 144*(4), 679–697. DOI: 10.1007/s10551-016-3312-6

Robinson, L., Cotten, S. R., Ono, H., Quan-Haase, A., Mesch, G., Chen, W., Schulz, J., Hale, T. M., & Stern, M. J. (2015). Digital inequalities and why they matter. *Information Communication and Society, 18*(5), 569–582. DOI: 10.1080/1369118X.2015.1012532

Rodda, A. (2022). Understanding Opportunities and Threats of Learning Analytics in Higher Education – A Students' Perspective. *Lecture Notes in Computer Science (Including Subseries Lecture Notes in Artificial Intelligence and Lecture Notes in Bioinformatics), 13454 LNCS*, 111 – 122. DOI: 10.1007/978-3-031-15342-6_9

Rodrigues, A. M., & Fidalgo, S. (2024). The role of Artificial Intelligence (AI) in rehabilitation and in the reduction of the use of imprisonment. *UNIO–EU Law Journal, 10*(1), 42–53. DOI: 10.21814/unio.10.1.5785

Rodríguez González, V., Payá, Santos., C, A., & Peña Herrera. B. (2023). Estudio criminológico del ciberdelincuente y sus víctimas. *Cuadernos de RES PUBLICA en Derecho y criminología,* (1) 95-107. .DOI: 10.46661/respublica.8072

Rolland, N. (2017). *China's Eurasian century? Political and strategic implications of the Belt and Road Initiative*. National Bureau of Asian Research.

Rowley, A. (1988). The Sixth Amendment Right of Defendents to Confront Adverse Witnesses. *The American Criminal Law Review*, *26*, 1547.

Russell, S. (2016). Rationality and Intelligence: A Brief Update. In Müller, V. C. (Ed.), *Fundamental Issues of Artificial Intelligence. Synthese Library* (Vol. 376). Springer., DOI: 10.1007/978-3-319-26485-1_2

Ruth, L. (2025). *Israel: High Court rejects petition prepared using AI that referenced nonexistent sources*. Library of Congress. https://www.loc.gov/item/global-legal-monitor/2025-06-25/israel-high-court-rejects-petition-prepared-using-ai-that-referenced-nonexistent-sources/

Ryan, R. M., & Deci, E. L. (2001). On happiness and human potentials: A review of research on hedonic and eudaimonic well-being. *Annual Review of Psychology*, *52*(1), 141–166. DOI: 10.1146/annurev.psych.52.1.141 PMID: 11148302

Sabri, S. (2021). Smart Dubai IoT strategy: Aspiring to the promotion of happiness for residents and visitors through a continuous commitment to innovation. In *Smart Cities and Urban Transformation*. https://doi.org/DOI: 10.1016/B978-0-12-818886-6.00010-1

Sabzalieva, E., & Valentini, A. (2023). *ChatGPT and artificial intelligence in higher education: A quick start guide*. UNESCO IESALC.

Sadeghian, A. H. and Otarkhani, A. (2023). Data-driven digital nudging: a systematic literature review and future agenda. *Behaviour &Amp; Information Technology*, 1-29. DOI: 10.1080/0144929X.2023.2286535

Samuel-Okon, A. D., Olateju, O. O., Okon, S. U., Olaniyi, O. O., & Igwenagu, U. T. I. (2024). Formulating global policies and strategies for combating criminal use and abuse of artificial intelligence. *Archives of Current Research International*, *24*(5), 612–629. DOI: 10.9734/acri/2024/v24i5735

San Miguel Caso, C. (2021). La aplicación de la Inteligencia Artificial en el proceso: ¿un nuevo reto para las garantías procesales? *Ius et Scientia*, *7*(1), 286–303. DOI: 10.12795/IETSCIENTIA.2021.i01.15

Sánchez Hernández, J. (2024). Posthumanism, technology and generational evolution of human rights: towards protection against algorithmic discrimination and the transparent and responsible use of ia | posthumanismo, tecnología y evolución generacional de los derechos humanos: hacia la. *Revista General De Derecho Constitucional, 2024*(40), 283–316.

Sanz González, R., Luque Juárez, J. M., Martino, L., Liz, L., Delgado Morán, J. J., & Payá Santos, C. A. (2024). Artificial Intelligence Applications for Criminology and Police Sciences. *International Journal of Humanities and Social Science, 14*(2), 139–148. DOI: 10.15640/jehd.v14n2a14

Saura, J. R. (2025). Ethics and Privacy in AI-Driven Digital Marketing: Navigating the Paradox.

Saura, J. R. (2025). AI, data economy, and behavioral intention: Towards ethical paths. In *Global perspectives on AI, ethics, and business economics: Charting the future* (pp. 3–16). Springer Nature Switzerland. DOI: 10.1007/978-3-031-88781-9_1

Saura, J. R., & Debasa, F. (Eds.). (2022). *Handbook of research on artificial intelligence in government practices and processes.* IGI Global. DOI: 10.4018/978-1-7998-9609-8

Scala, G. (2025). *Africa's AI boom risks human rights backlash.* Further Africa. https://furtherafrica.com/2025/06/30/africas-ai-boom-risks-human-rights-backlash/

Schmauder, C., Karpus, J., Moll, M., Bahrami, B., & Deroy, O. (2023). Algorithmic nudging: The need for an interdisciplinary oversight. *Topoi, 42*(3), 799–807. DOI: 10.1007/s11245-023-09907-4

Schmidhuber, J. (2014). Deep learning in neural networks: An overview. *Neural network: the official journal of the International Neural Network Society*, 61, 85-117. .DOI: 10.1016/j.neunet.2014.09.003

Schmidt, A. T., & Engelen, B. (2020). The ethics of nudging: An overview. *Philosophy Compass, 15*(4), e12658. Advance online publication. DOI: 10.1111/phc3.12658

Schmidt, R., & Stenger, K. (2024). Behavioral brittleness: The case for strategic behavioral public policy. *Behavioural Public Policy, 8*(2), 212–237. DOI: 10.1017/bpp.2021.16

Schwab, K. (2016). The fourth industrial revolution. World Economic Forum.

Scott, M. (2025). Analysis: AI Summit emphasizes innovation and competition over trust and safety. Digital Forensic Research Lab (DFRLab), February 11, 2025, https://dfrlab.org/2025/02/11/ai-summit-analysis-innovation

Searle, J. R. (1980). Minds, brains, and programs. *Behavioral and Brain Sciences, 3*(3), 417–424. DOI: 10.1017/S0140525X00005756

SecurityWeek. (2024). *Students, Educators Impacted by PowerSchool Data Breach.* https://www.securityweek.com/students-educators-impacted-by-powerschool-data-breach/

Segal, A. (2017). *Chinese cyber diplomacy in a new era of uncertainty* (Aegis Paper No. 1703). Hoover Institution.

Segura, M. (2025). *El actual diseño de la IA refuerza los sesgos de género y la violencia machista digital.* Universidad de Castilla. https://fundaciongeneraluclm.es/el-actual-diseno-de-la-ia-refuerza-los-sesgos-de-genero-y-la-violencia-machista-digital/

Selim, A. (2024). The role of digital forensic analysis in modern investigations. *4*(1), 1-5. DOI: 10.57020/ject.1445625

Selwyn, N. (2015). Data entry: Towards the critical study of digital data and education. *Learning, Media and Technology, 40*(1), 64–82. DOI: 10.1080/17439884.2014.921628

Shi, S., Sourdin, T., & Li, B. (2021). The smart court , A new pathway to justice in China? *International Journal for Court Administration, 12*(1), 4. DOI: 10.36745/ijca.367

Simon, H. A. (1997). What is an explanation of behavior? *Psychological Science, 2*, 150–161.

Singh, S. (2021). Algorithmic Policing Technologies in Canada. *Man. LJ, 44*, 246.

Slade, S., & Prinsloo, P. (2013). Learning analytics: Ethical issues and dilemmas. *The American Behavioral Scientist, 57*(10), 1510–1529. DOI: 10.1177/0002764213479366

Slimi, Z., & Carballido, B. V. (2023). Navigating the Ethical Challenges of Artificial Intelligence in Higher Education: An Analysis of Seven Global AI Ethics Policies. *TEM Journal, 12*(2), 590–602. https://doi.org/DOI: 10.18421/TEM122-02

Smuha, N. A. (2019). The EU Approach to Ethics Guidelines for Trustworthy Artificial Intelligence. *Computer Law Review International, 20*(4), 97–106. DOI: 10.9785/cri-2019-200402

Solar Cayón, J. I. (2019). *La inteligencia artificial jurídica: El impacto de la innovación tecnológica en la práctica del Derecho y el mercado de servicios jurídicos.* Aranzadi.

Solís García, M. (2013). Fourth generation human rights. *Revista IUS, 7*(32), 45–67.

Solove, D. J. (2021). The myth of the privacy paradox. *The George Washington Law Review*, *89*(1), 1–51.

Sposato, M. (2025). Artificial intelligence in educational leadership: A comprehensive taxonomy and future directions. *International Journal of Educational Technology in Higher Education*, *22*(1), 20. Advance online publication. DOI: 10.1186/s41239-025-00517-1

Srivastava, N., Hinton, G., Krizhevsky, A., Sutskever, I., & Salakhutdinov, R. (2014). Dropout: A simple way to prevent neural networks from overfitting. *Journal of Machine Learning Research*, *15*, 1929–1958.

Staff, T. (2025, May 13). *Judge slams police for using AI to write legal argument, citing nonexistent laws*. The Times of Israel. https://www.timesofisrael.com/judge-slams-police-for-using-ai-to-write-legal-argument-citing-nonexistent-laws/

Stanciu, I. D., Hernández-García, Á., Conde, M. Á., & Nistor, N. (2025). Decoding a decade. Trends and evolution in learning analytics: A comprehensive synthesis. *Computers in Human Behavior*, *165*, 108526. Advance online publication. DOI: 10.1016/j.chb.2024.108526

STANTON. (2008). *I. B. M.* I Will.

State of California Department of Justice. (s. f.). California Consumer Privacy Act (CCPA). https://oag.ca.gov/privacy/ccpa

Stillwell, D. (2021). Psychological profiling and privacy: How technology shapes personality perception. *Nature Human Behaviour*, *5*, 1590–1591.

Subirats, J. (2020). Democratic innovation and AI governance: Lessons from Barcelona. *Urban Studies Journal*, *57*(7), 1401–1420.

Suddaby, R. (2006). *From the editors: What grounded theory is not.* Academy of Management Journal, 49(4), 633-642. https://doi.org/DOI: 10.5465/amj.2006.22083020

Sunstein, C. R. (2014). *Why Nudge? The Politics of Libertarian Paternalism.* Yale University Press. https://www.jstor.org/stable/j.ctt5vm0nr

Sunstein, C. R., & Thaler, R. H. (2003). Libertarian Paternalism Is Not an Oxymoron. *The University of Chicago Law Review. University of Chicago. Law School*, *70*(4), 1159–1202. DOI: 10.2307/1600573

Sun, Y., Zhang, M., Sun, Z., & Tan, T. (2018). Demographic Analysis from Biometric Data: Achievements, Challenges, and New Frontiers. *IEEE Transactions on Pattern Analysis and Machine Intelligence*, *40*(2), 332–351. DOI: 10.1109/TPAMI.2017.2669035 PMID: 28212078

Susskind, R. (2017). *Tomorrow's Lawyers: An Introduction to Your Future* (2nd ed.). Oxford University Press.

Susskind, R. (2019). *Online Courts and the Future of Justice*. Oxford University Press. DOI: 10.1093/oso/9780198838364.001.0001

Susskind, R., & Susskind, D. (2015). *The future of the professions: How technology will transform the work of human experts*. Oxford University Press. DOI: 10.1093/oso/9780198713395.001.0001

Tabor, C. D. (2024). Garbage In, Garbage Out: Predictive Policing and Structural Biases in Automated Criminal Justice Techniques. *The De Gruyter Handbook of Automated Futures: Imaginaries, Interactions and Impact, 2*, 191.

Taddeo, M., & Floridi, L. (2018). Regulate artificial intelligence to avert cyber arms race. *Nature, 556*(7701), 296–298. DOI: 10.1038/d41586-018-04602-6 PMID: 29662138

Taibi, H., & Benabdelhadi, A. (2020). Public performance in Morocco: A theoretical approach. International Journal of Accounting, Finance, Auditing. *Management and Economics*, *1*(2), 1–12.

Tauchnitz, E., & Ahmed, S. (2024). Framing Ethical e-Governance: A Plaidoyer for a Human-Rights based Digital Democracy Approach. *ACM International Conference Proceeding Series*, 22–27. DOI: 10.1145/3680127.3680182

Thaler, R. H., & Sunstein, C. R. (2009). *Nudge: Improving decisions about health, wealth, and happiness*. Penguin.

Thiebes, S., Lins, S., & Sunyaev, A. (2021). Trustworthy artificial intelligence. *Electronic Markets*, *31*(2), 447–464. DOI: 10.1007/s12525-020-00441-4

Tobias, H., & Joseph, A. (2020). Sustaining systemic racism through psychological gaslighting: Denials of racial profiling and justifications of carding by police utilizing local news media. *Race and Justice*, *10*(4), 424–455. DOI: 10.1177/2153368718760969

Torres Assiego, C. (2025). El sesgo algorítmico como nuevos retos jurídicos frente a la IA. In *La Unión Europea, los ODS y el derecho público* (pp. 183–202). Tirant lo Blanch.

Trigo, N. A. G. (2023). El agente encubierto ante la criminalidad organizada transnacional. Cuadernos de RES PUBLICA en derecho y criminología, (1), 85-94.

Tukey, J. W. (1977). *Exploratory Data Analysis*. Addison-Wesley.

Turkle, S. (2017). How computers change the way we think. In *Law and society approaches to cyberspace* (pp. 3–7). Routledge. DOI: 10.4324/9781351154161-1

Tussyadiah, I., & Miller, G. (2019). Nudged by a robot: Responses to agency and feedback. *Annals of Tourism Research, 78*, 102752. DOI: 10.1016/j.annals.2019.102752

U.S. Department of Justice. (2024). *Artificial intelligence and criminal justice, final report*. https://www.justice.gov/olp/media/1381796/dl

UNESCO. (1997). Universal Declaration on the Human Genome and Human Rights. https://unesdoc.unesco.org/ark:/48223/pf0000110220

UNESCO. (2021). *Recommendation on the ethics of artificial intelligence*.

UNESCO. (2021). *Recommendation on the Ethics of Artificial Intelligence*. https://unesdoc.unesco.org/ark:/48223/pf0000381137

UNESCO. (2021). *Recommendation on the Ethics of Artificial Intelligence*. United Nations Educational, Scientific and Cultural Organization.

UNESCO. (2021). Recommendation on the ethics of artificial intelligence. United Nations Educational, Scientific and Cultural Organization. https://unesdoc.unesco.org/ark:/48223/pf0000381137

UNESCO. (2022). Recommendation on The Ethics of Artificial Intelligence. *United Nations Educational, Scientific and Cultural Organization, November*.

UNESCO. (2024). *AI in the courtroom: Colombian Constitutional Court's landmark ruling cites UNESCO's AI tools*. https://www.unesco.org/en/articles/ai-courtroom-colombian-constitutional-courts-landmark-ruling-cites-unescos-ai-tools

UNESCO. (2025). *Justice meets innovation: Colombia's groundbreaking AI guidelines for courts*. https://www.unesco.org/en/articles/justice-meets-innovation-colombias-groundbreaking-ai-guidelines-courts

Ungerer, L., & Slade, S. (2022). Ethical Considerations of Artificial Intelligence in Learning Analytics in Distance Education Contexts. In *Springerbriefs in Open and Distance Education*. DOI: 10.1007/978-981-19-0786-9_8

United Nations Innovation Network. (2021). *UN Behavioural Science Report*. United Nations.

United Nations. (2020). *Report of the Secretary-General: Roadmap for digital cooperation*. United Nations.

United Nations. (2022). The right to privacy in the digital age. United Nations Human Rights Council. https://digitallibrary.un.org/record/3980861

Ustun, A. B., Zhang, K., Karaoğlan-Yilmaz, F. G., & Yilmaz, R. (2023). Learning analytics based feedback and recommendations in flipped classrooms: An experimental study in higher education. *Journal of Research on Technology in Education, 55*(5), 841–857. DOI: 10.1080/15391523.2022.2040401

Vaddi, K. (2024). Enhancements in the world of digital forensics. *IAES International Journal of Artificial Intelligence (Ij-Ai), 13*(1), 680. DOI: 10.11591/ijai.v13.i1.pp680-686

Valdivia, P., Hyde-Vaamonde, E., & García-Marcos, M. (2022). Algorithmic risk assessment in intimate partner violence: Transparency and accountability challenges in the Basque Country's EPV-R tool. arXiv preprint. https://arxiv.org/abs/2203.03723

Van Deursen, A. J., & Van Dijk, J. A. (2014). The digital divide shifts to differences in usage. *New Media & Society, 16*(3), 507–526. DOI: 10.1177/1461444813487959

Van Dooren, W., Bouckaert, G., & Halligan, J. (2010). *Performance management in the public sector*. Routledge. DOI: 10.4324/9780203030806

Van Essen, D. C., Smith, S. M., Deanna, M., Behrens, T. E. J., Yacoub, E., & Uğurbil, K. (2013). The WU-Minn Human Connectome Project: An overview. *NeuroImage, 80*, 62–79. DOI: 10.1016/j.neuroimage.2013.05.041 PMID: 23684880

van Leeuwen, A. (2023). Teachers' experiences of monitoring their students in online higher education: Recommendations for course design and opportunities for learning analytics. *Technology, Pedagogy and Education, 32*(5), 589–604. DOI: 10.1080/1475939X.2023.2254297

Varum, P., Sree, U., & Batumalay, M. (2024). A data analytics strategy to the underground economy of cybercrime. *Journal of Data Science, 2024*(1). DOI: 10.61453/jods.v2024no12

Velandia Pardo, D., Cano Cuevas, D. F., Betancur, M., & Paya Santos, C. (2025). Development of a national strategy to combat hybrid threats in Colombia. Well Testing Journal, 34(S2), 25–44. Retrieved from https://welltestingjournal.com/index.php/WT/article/view/164

Venzke, C. (2025, July 16). *Written testimony before the House Committee on the Judiciary*. U.S. House of Representatives. https://docs.house.gov/meetings/JU/JU08/20250716/118467/HHRG-119-JU08-Wstate-VenzkeC-20250716-U11.pdf

Vera, J. P. D., Hojas, D. S. P., Sarmiento, Z. J. F., Ramírez, A. K. R., & Mora, D. V. M. (2023). Estudio comparativo experimental del uso de chatGPT y su influencia en el aprendizaje de los estudiantes de la carrera Tecnologías de la información de la universidad de Guayaquil. *Revista Universidad de Guayaquil, 137*(2), 51–63. DOI: 10.53591/rug.v137i2.2107

Veretilnykova, M., & Dogruel, L. (2021). Nudging children and adolescents toward online privacy: An ethical perspective. *Journal of Media Ethics, 36*(2), 128–140. DOI: 10.1080/23736992.2021.1939031

Villarroel-Henríquez, V., & Gallardo-Aguayo, C. (2025). Educational Management Using Learning Analytics and Big Data in Higher Education [Gestión del Proceso Educativo utilizando Analíticas del Aprendizaje y Big Data en la Universidad]. *Revista de Investigación Educacional, 23*(1), 76–92. DOI: 10.35869/reined.v23i1.6110

Vinayak, V. (2019, September 6). *The human rights implications of China's social credit system*. Oxford Human Rights Hub. https://ohrh.law.ox.ac.uk/the-human-rights-implications-of-chinas-social-credit-system/

Von Eschenbach, W. J. (2021). Transparency and the black box problem: Why we do not trust AI. *Philosophy & Technology, 34*(4), 1607–1622. DOI: 10.1007/s13347-021-00477-0

Wachter, S., Mittelstadt, B., & Russell, C. (2021). Why fairness cannot be automated: Bridging the gap between EU non-discrimination law and AI. *Computer Law & Security Review, 41*, 105567. DOI: 10.1016/j.clsr.2021.105567

Washington, A. L. (2018). How to argue with an algorithm: Lessons from the COMPAS-ProPublica debate. *Colo. Tech. LJ, 17*, 131.

Waskom, M. L. (2021). seaborn: Statistical data visualization. *Journal of Open Source Software, 6*(60), 3021. DOI: 10.21105/joss.03021

We Are Social, & Meltwater. (2025). Digital world 2025: Essential statistics. Guayoyo Marketing. Retrieved from https://guayoyomarketing.com/mundo-digital-2025-estadisticas-imprescindibles/

Weinmann, M., Schneider, C., & vom Brocke, J. (2016). Digital Nudging. *Business & Information Systems Engineering, 58*(6), 433–436. DOI: 10.1007/s12599-016-0453-1

Weiss, D. A. (2025). INHUMAN REASON: Predictive Policing Algorithms and the Fourth Amendment. *Criminal Justice, 39*(4), 15–20.

Werner, J. (2025, March 26). *South Korea faces human rights concerns over expanding public sector use of AI*. BABL AI. https://babl.ai/south-korea-faces-human-rights-concerns-over-expanding-public-sector-use-of-ai/

Whetten, D. A. (1989). What constitutes a theoretical contribution? *Academy of Management Review*, *14*(4), 490–495. DOI: 10.2307/258554

Whittaker, M., Crawford, K., Dobbe, R., Fried, G., Kaziunas, E., Mathur, V., . . . Schwartz, O. (2021). AI Now 2021 report. AI Now Institute. https://ainowinstitute.org/AI_Now_2021_Report.pdf

Williamson, B. (2017). Big Data in Education: The digital future of learning, policy and practice. *Big Data in Education: The Digital Future of Learning. Policy & Practice*. Advance online publication. DOI: 10.4135/9781529714920

Wirani, N., & Manurung, A. A. (2020). The importance of using a web-based learning model to prevent the spread of covid 19. *AlAdzkiya International of Education and Sosial (AIoES). Journal*, *1*(1), 16–24.

Wood, W., Bainbridge, W. A., Wiese, E., & Scassellati, B. (2023). Building long-term human–robot relationships: Examining disclosure, perception and well-being across time. *International Journal of Social Robotics*, *16*, 765–781.

Woolley, S. C., & Howard, P. N. (Eds.). (2018). *Computational propaganda: Political parties, politicians, and political manipulation on social media*. Oxford University Press. DOI: 10.1093/oso/9780190931407.001.0001

Wu, C., Zhang, H., & Carroll, J. M. (2024). AI Governance in Higher Education: Case Studies of Guidance at Big Ten Universities. *Future Internet*, *16*(10), 354. DOI: 10.3390/fi16100354

Xu, J., Duan, L., & Zhang, R. (2017). Surveillance and intervention of infrastructure-free mobile communications: A new wireless security paradigm. *IEEE Wireless Communications*, *24*(4), 152–159. DOI: 10.1109/MWC.2017.1600279

Yang, C., Ding, L., Chen, Y., & Li, H. (2021). Defending against GAN-based deepfake attacks via transformation-aware adversarial faces. *2021 International Joint Conference on Neural Networks (IJCNN)*. DOI: 10.1109/IJCNN52387.2021.9533868

Yarvin, C., Bukowski, R., & Anderson, T. (1993, June). Anonymous RPC: Low latency protection in a 64-bit address space. In *Proceedings of the USENIX Summer Technical Conference* (pp. 175 - 186). USENIX Association.

Yasrab, R., Jiang, W., & Riaz, A. (2021). Fighting deepfakes using body language analysis. *Forecasting*, *3*(2), 303–321. DOI: 10.3390/forecast3020020

Yeung, K. (2017). Hypernudging: Big Data as a Mode of Regulation by Design. *Information Communication and Society, 20*(1), 118–136. DOI: 10.1080/1369118X.2016.1186713

Yeyati, E. (2025). *Smart AI regulation: Strategies for Latin American policymakers*. Brookings Institution. (https://www.brookings.edu/articles/smart-ai-regulation-strategies-for-latin-american-policymakers/

Yildiz Durak, H., Atman Uslu, N., Canbazoğlu Bilici, S., & Güler, B. (2023). Predictors of TPACK for integrated STEM. *Education and Information Technologies, 28*(7), 7927–7954. Advance online publication. DOI: 10.1007/s10639-022-11505-7

Yin, R. K. (2018). *Case study research and applications: Design and methods* (6th ed.). Sage Publications.

Yin, R. K. (2018). *Case Study Research and Applications: Design and Methods* (6th ed.). SAGE Publications.

Yoo, C. S., & Jagasia, A. (2024). Identifying Fourth Amendment Values: An Evidence-Based Approach. *Wake Forest Law Review, 59*, 1219. DOI: 10.2139/ssrn.4867896

Yu, H., Shen, Z., Miao, C., Leung, C., Lesser, V., and Yang, Q. (2018). Building Ethics into Artificial Intelligence. *ArXiv, abs/1812.02953*. DOI: .DOI: 10.24963/ijcai.2018/779

Yuan, B. Z., & Sun, J. (2020). Bibliometric analysis of research on the maize based on top papers during 2009-2019. COLLNET. *Journal of Scientometrics and Information Management, 14*(1), 75–92.

Yuste, R., Goering, S., Agüera y Arcas, B., Bi, G., Carmena, J. M., Carter, A., Chun, M., Illes, J., Kellmeyer, P., Klein, E., Marblestone, A., Mitchell, C., Parens, E., Pham, M., Rubel, A., Sadato, N., Specker Sullivan, L., Teicher, M., Wasserman, D., & Wolpaw, J. (2017). Four ethical priorities for neurotechnologies and AI. *Nature, 551*(7679), 159–163. DOI: 10.1038/551159a PMID: 29120438

Zaidan, E. (2024). AI governance in a complex and rapidly changing world. *Humanities & Social Sciences Communications, 11*, 233. DOI: 10.1057/s41599-024-03560-x

Zawacki-Richter, O., Marín, V. I., Bond, M., & Gouverneur, F. (2019). Systematic review of research on artificial intelligence applications in higher education. *International Journal of Educational Technology in Higher Education, 16*(39), 1–27. DOI: 10.1186/s41239-019-0171-0

Zenz, A. (2020). Sterilizations, IUDs, and coercive birth control in Xinjiang. *China Journal (Canberra, A.C.T.), 84*, 8–36.

Zhai, C., Wibowo, S., & Li, L. D. (2024). The effects of over-reliance on AI dialogue systems on students' cognitive abilities: A systematic review. *Smart Learning Environments*, *11*(1), 28. DOI: 10.1186/s40561-024-00316-7

Zhai, X., Chu, X., Chai, C. S., Jong, M. S. Y., & Istenic, A. (2021). Spector, & Li, Y. (2021). Una revisión de la inteligencia artificial (IA) en la educación de 2010 a 2020. *Complexity*, (1), 8812542. DOI: 10.1155/2021/8812542

Zhang, L. (2025). *China: Facial recognition measures take effect*. Library of Congress. https://www.loc.gov/item/global-legal-monitor/2025-06-16/china-facial-recognition-measures-take-effect/

Zhang, P., Chen, B., Ma, L., Li, Z., Song, Z., Duan, W., & Qiu, X. (2015). The Large-Scale Machine Learning in an Artificial Society: Prediction of the Ebola Outbreak in Beijing. *Computational Intelligence and Neuroscience*, *2015*, 1–12. DOI: 10.1155/2015/531650 PMID: 26457078

Zhang, W., Valencia, A., & Chang, N. B. (2023). Synergistic integration between machine learning and agent-based modeling: A multidisciplinary review. *IEEE Transactions on Neural Networks and Learning Systems*, *34*(5), 2170–2190. DOI: 10.1109/TNNLS.2021.3106777 PMID: 34473633

Zhao, X., Lynch, J. G.Jr, & Chen, Q. (2010). Reconsidering Baron and Kenny: Myths and truths about mediation analysis. *The Journal of Consumer Research*, *37*(2), 197–206. DOI: 10.1086/651257

Zicari, R. V., Brodersen, J., Brusseau, J., Dudley, J. T., Eichinger, F., Ivanov, T., Kararigas, G., Kringen, P., McCullough, M., Osman, A. M., Schnebel, E., Southby, D., Staab, S., Taddeo, M., Vayena, E., Vestergaard, M., & Floridi, L. (2021). Z-Inspection®: A process to assess trustworthy AI. *IEEE Transactions on Technology and Society*, *2*(2), 83–97. DOI: 10.1109/TTS.2021.3066209

Zine, A., & Kaaouachi, A. (2024). Assessment of Teachers' Needs to Integrate Learning Analytics in Higher Education: The Morocco Case. *International Journal of Information and Education Technology (IJIET)*, *14*(3), 494–500. DOI: 10.18178/ijiet.2024.14.3.2070

Zuboff, S. (2019). *The age of surveillance capitalism*. PublicAffairs.

Zuboff, S. (2019). *The age of surveillance capitalism: The fight for a human future at the new frontier of power*. PublicAffairs.

Zyskind, G., Nathan, O., & Pentland, A. S. (2015). Decentralizing privacy: Using blockchain to protect personal data. 2015 IEEE Security and Privacy Workshops, 180–184.

# About the Contributors

**Sonia Cea Quintana**, Born in Madrid in 1985, Sonia Cea is currently pursuing a Ph.D. in Communication at Universidad Rey Juan Carlos in Madrid, where their research focuses on the application of behavioral economics and artificial intelligence to governance. With over 15 years of professional experience, Cea has worked extensively in the design and implementation of electoral campaigns, as well as in strategic communication advising for political parties and leaders across Spain. Their most recent publication is Liberal Democracy, Behavioural Governance, and Communication: Risks and Opportunities

**Tomás Aznar**, PhD in Modern History (Complutense University of Madrid). Specialist in Education for Solidarity (Comillas Pontifical University) and in Internet and Digital Whiteboards in the Classroom (Camilo José Cela University). Master's degree in Education and ICT (Open University of Catalonia), in Community Management and Web Positioning (University of Alcalá), and in Occupational Risk Prevention (IUNIT - Rey Juan Carlos University). Bachelor's degree in Geography and History (Complutense University Madrid).of Project Director at the Higher Education Center for Business, Innovation and Technology (IUNIT), a center affiliated with Rey Juan Carlos University and part of the SEK International Institution. Member of the SEK International Institution since 2009 and of its Executive Council, having held various positions.

***

**Francisco Javier Arroyo Romero** holds a PhD in Law and serves as a Professor of Procedural Law at Rey Juan Carlos University. He is the founding and managing partner of Bufete Arroyo Romero, a multidisciplinary law firm specializing in procedural, criminal, civil, and commercial law, as well as socio-economic criminal law and commercial and sports arbitration. He is a founding member of the Women's

Sport Observatory and teaches in the Master's Degree in Legal Practice at Rey Juan Carlos University; he has also lectured in the Master's program in image law and representation of artists and athletes. He is the Director of the Master's in European Sports Law at Rey Juan Carlos University and Director of Summer Courses on sports-related topics at both Rey Juan Carlos University and the University of Málaga. He regularly participates as a speaker at conferences and seminars focused on sports, civil, criminal, and procedural law.

**Elena Berzal**, Psychopedagogue and pedagogue, specialized in Special Education, and a PhD candidate in Education at the Complutense University of Madrid. She is a lecturer at several Spanish universities in Master's programmes in Teacher Education and Educational Psychology, and serves as Director of Academic Quality for university degree programmes.

**Angelo Brown** Received his master's at Arizona State University and his Ph.D. Criminal Justice and Criminology at Washington State University. His research and teaching in criminal justice and criminology are primarily on policy and policing from a comparative and intersectional perspective.

**Joe Luis Carrión Jumbo** received his PhD in Computer Science from the Autonomous University of Barcelona in 2017 and his Master's Degree in High Performance Computing and Information Theory in 2013. He has over 10 years of professional experience in information technology and 7 years of teaching experience at undergraduate and graduate levels. Since 2020, he has been a full professor at the Digital School of SEK International University. His research interests include topics related to Learning Analytics, Business Intelligence, Computer Vision, and projects related to Software as a Service, Cloud Computing, and Mobile Applications. He is the author of several articles published in international conference proceedings

**Sophie Chuquillangui** is an Informatics Engineering student and emerging researcher with a growing interest in software, emerging technologies, and their broad cross-disciplinary applications. Her work combines technical depth with an interdisciplinary mindset, reflecting her wide range of academic and professional interests. Recent projects have explored AI and the ethical, pedagogical, and policy dimensions of data-driven models in higher education. Her goal is to continue developing as a researcher while contributing to initiatives that promote equity and responsible digital transformation.

**Felipe Debasa Navalpotro**, Professor of Contemporary History and Current World at the Rey Juan Carlos University. Director of the official Master in the European Union and China. Secretary of the Area of Contemporary History framed in the Department of Humanities. Among his lines of research are technology, the IV Industrial Revolution and transhumanism. Author of various publications in the field of digital humanities in which he implements technological processes from other disciplines in history and in legal and social sciences.

**Maria Amparo Diaz-LLairo**, Over 25 years of work experience in the private sector, including managerial positions as Director of Human Resources and Talent Management in multinational companies such as Citigroup. International Keynote Speaker: talent management, recruitment, and technology expert. More than 500 courses, seminars, congresses, and in-company training projects for more than 500 companies in Europe, USA, Latin America, the Middle East and Asia. CEO at Global Human Capital Group (GHCG), an International HR Consulting firm specializing in International recruitment using AI. Writer of 5 Books about HR, Talent Management, Entrepreneurship, and Leadership.

**Cecilia Elizabeth Jaramillo Jaramillo** obtained a Master's degree in High Performance Computing and Information Theory from the Universitat Autònoma de Barcelona (UAB) in 2013. Since 2017, she has been part of the High Performance Computing for Efficient Applications and Simulation Research Group at the UAB. She completed her PhD in Computer Science at the same university in 2017, obtaining a CumLaude mention. She has more than 7 years of undergraduate teaching experience working in different public and private universities. She is currently a part-time professor at the Faculty of Systems Engineering at the National Polytechnic School (Quito, Ecuador). She has worked on topics related to Computational Mathematics, Theory of Computation, Information Retrieval and Databases. She is the author of several articles published in international conference proceedings.

**David Moure Blanco** represents a well-established executive profile within the European healthcare sector, full working skilled in different languages such us, Spanish, English, French, Portuguese and Italian with over a decade of experience in medical technology, pharmaceuticals, and strategic consultancy. His career blends clinical-scientific knowledge with business vision, international exposure, and academic training in law and management. As a healthcare entrepreneur, he is capable of leading business units, driving international expansion, forging strategic public-private partnerships, and fostering innovation at the intersection of health, law, and technology. He has a deep understanding of the regulatory and commercial landscape in Europe and is fully equipped to operate effectively within both hospital environments and institutional frameworks.

# Index

## A



## B



## C



## D

# E



# F

## S



## T



## U

www.ingramcontent.com/pod-product-compliance
Lightning Source LLC
LaVergne TN
LVHW061527290926
849162LV00004B/702
* 9 7 9 8 3 3 7 3 4 4 8 0 5 *